MASS MEDIA ISSUES

ANALYSIS AND DEBATE
second edition

GEORGE RODMAN
Brooklyn College
of the City University
of New York

Acquisition Editor	Michael Zamczyk
Project Editor	James C. Budd
Editor	Mary Alexander
Compositor	Interactive Composition Corp.
Text Designer	Barbara Ravizza
Cover Photo by	Phoenix Color Corporation

To Linda and Jennifer

Library of Congress Cataloging in Publication Data
Main entry under title:

Mass media issues.

Bibliography: p.
Includes index.
1. Mass media--United States--Addresses, essays, lectures. I. Rodman, George R., 1948-.
P92.U5M29 1984 302'.2'34'0973 83-27143
ISBN 0-574-22610-9

Printed in the United States of America.

10 9 8 7 6 5 4 3 2 1

Acknowledgments

We acknowledge with thanks these picture sources listed on the following pages:
3 Reprinted by permission from *The Progressive*, 409 East Main Street, Madison, Wisconsin 53703, Copyright © 1979, The Progressive, Inc.; 86, Courtesy Owen Ranken, Stock, Boston; 203, Courtesy Chris Morrow, Stock, Boston; 213, Reprinted by permission WTTW/Chicago; 313, Courtesy Vicki Lawrence, Stock, Boston; 366, Wide World Cable News Network; 369, Reprinted by permission of Warner Amex Cable Communications; 397, Wide World Cable News Network.

Contents

part five

THE NEW ELECTRONICS AND THE INFORMATION AGE 367

Alternate Table of Contents

selected articles arranged by medium

I. NEWSPAPERS

II. MAGAZINES

III. BOOKS

IV. RADIO AND POPULAR MUSIC

V. TELEVISION

VI. FILM

Preface

Although most of the articles in this second edition of *Mass Media Issues: Analysis and Debate* are new, the goal of the book remains unchanged: to expand on controversial media issues in such a way that students can debate them, either in class or on their own.

In this edition, several of the articles play devil's advocate for positions out of the mainstream. In such cases the mainstream positions, which are already well articulated in most texts (and are, in most cases, equally present in the student's consciousness), are not repeated. The other articles fall into several categories: some were originally published as direct debates between leading proponents on each side of an issue; other articles were published separately, but have been juxtaposed here to form a debate. Still other articles attempt to present a balanced analysis of two or more sides of an issue.

The materials presented here come from a wide range of sources: there are news clippings, editorials, interviews, advertisements, popular magazine articles, scholarly journal articles, and excerpts from books. Some of these items are short illustrative pieces; others are in-depth analyses.

An instructor's manual is available that includes a short summary of each article, as well as suggested test items.

The articles selected strike a balance between standard issues of importance in an introductory course on American media and issues that have received significant publicity and generated student interest over the last few years. New to this edition are several "classic" statements, some from historical figures. All the articles were selected for their validity vis-à-vis the state of mass media today as well as their relevance for at least the next few years.

Generally, the articles address issues that are important for all media. This is reflected in the organization of the main table of contents. However, an alternate table of contents, divided by media, is also provided.

Of the more than one hundred items in this edition, only fourteen reappear from the first edition. There is a new section on mass media and the political process, as well as several new chapters on various topics.

I would like to thank the following reviewers for their many helpful suggestions: Mary V. Crowley (Kingsborough Community College), Gilbert Len Fowler, Jr. (Arkansas State University), John B. Haney, (Queens College, CUNY), Russell Hulet (Fort Steilacoom Community College), Mark Kozaki (University of Maryland), Robert G. Main (California State University, Chico), James Mattimore (Suffolk Community College), J. Dennis Mercier (Glassboro State College), and Michael Torreano (University of Colorado).

PART ONE

SOME PERENNIAL ISSUES

The four chapters in Part One present the student with a representative sample of the issues that have been of ongoing concern to the mass media and their public. Some of these issues, such as pornography and censorship, were topics of social debate for centuries prior to the emergence of mass media as we know them. These concerns, as well as the more strictly modern concerns that are also discussed, go beyond themselves in bringing into debate some of the basic moral and philosophical questions of our society.

Chapter 1 covers censorship of pornography, obscenity, and art. Chapter 2 deals with press censorship. A discussion of mass media ethics from the Watergate victories of the mid-70s to the Pulitzer Prize scandal of 1981 is presented in Chapter 3, and Chapter 4 addresses the perennial issue of mass media violence.

CHAPTER 1

Pornography, Obscenity, and Censorship

The question of censorship has been debated for centuries, and has come to revolve around some now classic arguments. Pro-censorship arguments are presented in this chapter by Irving Kristol, a professor of urban values at New York University. Hollis Alpert, a film critic and contributing editor for *Saturday Review*, presents the opposing view.

Although some philosophical arguments are made, the debate is not abstract—the materials that provoke the discussion are all around us, as is censorship itself. Indeed, in recent years there has been a sharp rise in the censorship of public school reading materials. Author Jerzy Kosinski presents his view of this trend in the third reading.

Also in recent years, one of the hottest censorship controversies has brewed over the proposal to boycott products advertised on sexually explicit or violent television programs. The last two articles address this issue: first Donald Wildmon explains why he thinks it's the network executives, and not his Coalition for Better Television, who are the real TV censors. Finally, Gloria Steinem, an editor of *MS.* magazine, makes a short statement of her feelings about such a boycott.

PORNOGRAPHY, OBSCENITY, AND THE CASE FOR CENSORSHIP

Irving Kristol

Being frustrated is disagreeable, but the real disasters in life begin when you get what you want. For almost a century now, a great many intelligent, well-meaning, and articulate people—of a kind generally called liberal or intellectual, or both—have argued eloquently against any kind of censorship of art and/or entertainment. And within the past 10 years, the courts and the legislatures of most Western nations have found these arguments persuasive—so persuasive that hardly a man is now alive who clearly remembers what the answers to these arguments were. Today, in the United States and other democracies, censorship has to all intents and purposes ceased to exist.

Is there a sense of triumphant exhilaration in the land? Hardly. There is, on the contrary, a rapidly growing unease and disquiet. Somehow, things have not worked out as they were supposed to, and many notable civil libertarians have gone on record as saying this was not what they meant at all. They wanted a world in which

From *The New York Times Magazine* (March 28, 1971).

Desire under the Elms could be produced, or *Ulysses* published, without interference by philistine busybodies holding public office. They have got that, of course; but they have also got a world in which homosexual rape takes place on the stage, in which the public flocks during lunch hours to witness varieties of professional fornication, in which Times Square has become little more than a hideous market for the sale and distribution of printed filth that panders to all known (and some fanciful) sexual perversions.

But disagreeable as this may be, does it really matter? Might not our unease and disquiet be merely a cultural hangover—a "hangup," as they say? What reason is there to think that anyone was ever corrupted by a book?

Today, in the United States and other democracies, censorship has to all intents and purposes ceased to exist.

This last question, oddly enough, is asked by the very same people who seem convinced that advertisements in magazines or displays of violence on television do indeed have the power to corrupt. It is also asked, incredibly enough and in all sincerity, by people—e.g., university professors and school teachers—whose very lives provide all the answers one could want. After all, if you believe that no one was ever corrupted by a book, you have also to believe that no one was ever improved by a book (or a play or a movie). You have to believe, in other words, that all art is morally trivial and that, consequently, all education is morally irrelevant. No one, not even a university professor, really believes that.

To be sure, it is extremely difficult, as social scientists tell us, to trace the effects of any single book (or play or movie) on an individual reader or any class of readers. But we all know, and social scientists know it too, that the ways in which we use our minds and imaginations do shape our characters and help define us as persons. That those who certainly know this are nevertheless moved to deny it merely indicates how a dogmatic resistance to the idea of censorship can—like most dogmatism—result in a mindless insistence on the absurd.

I have used these harsh terms—"dogmatism" and "mindless"—advisedly. I might also have added "hypocritical." For the plain fact is that none of us is a complete civil libertarian. We all believe that there is some point at which the public authorities ought to step in to limit the "self-expression" of an individual or a group, even where this might be seriously intended as a form of artistic expression, and even where the artistic transaction is between consenting adults. A playwright or theatrical director might, in this crazy world of ours, find someone willing to commit suicide on the stage, as called for by the script. We would not allow that—any more than we would permit scenes of real physical torture on the stage, even if the victim were a willing masochist. And I know of no one, no matter how free in spirit, who argues that we ought to permit gladiatorial contests in Yankee Stadium, similar to those once performed in the Colosseum at Rome—even if only consenting adults were involved.

The basic point that emerges is one that Professor Walter Berns has powerfully argued: no society can be utterly indifferent to the ways its citizens publicly entertain themselves.[1] Bearbaiting and cockfighting are prohibited only in part out of compassion for the suffering animals; the main reason they were abolished was because it was felt that they debased and brutalized the citizenry who flocked to witness such spec-

1. This is as good a place as any to express my profound indebtedness to Walter Berns's superb essay, "Pornography vs. Democracy," in the winter 1971 issue of *The Public Interest*.

tacles. And the question we face with regard to pornography and obscenity is whether, now that they have such strong legal protection from the Supreme Court, they can or will brutalize and debase our citizenry. We are, after all, not dealing with one passing incident—one book, or one play, or one movie. We are dealing with a general tendency that is suffusing our entire culture.

I say pornography *and* obscenity because, though they have different dictionary definitions and are frequently distinguishable as "artistic" genres, they are nevertheless in the end identical in effect. Pornography is not objectionable simply because it arouses sexual desire or lust or prurience in the mind of the reader or spectator; this is a silly Victorian notion. A great many non-pornographic works—including some parts of the Bible—excite sexual desire very successfully. What is distinctive about pornography is that, in the words of D. H. Lawrence, it attempts "to do dirt on [sex]. . . . [It is an] insult to a vital human relationship."

In other words, pornography differs from erotic art in that its whole purpose is to treat human beings obscenely, to deprive human beings of their specifically human dimension. That is what obscenity is all about. It is light years removed from any kind of carefree sensuality—there is no continuum between Fielding's *Tom Jones* and the Marquis de Sade's *Justine*. These works have quite opposite intentions. To quote Susan Sontag: "What pornographic literature does is precisely to drive a wedge between one's existence as a full human being and one's existence as a sexual being—while in ordinary life a healthy person is one who prevents such a gap from opening up." This definition occurs in an essay *defending* pornography—Miss Sontag is a candid as well as gifted critic—so the definition, which I accept, is neither tendentious nor censorious.

Along these same lines, one can point out—as C. S. Lewis pointed out some years back—that it is no accident that in the history of all literatures obscene words—the so-called "four-letter words"—have always been the vocabulary of farce or vituperation. The reason is clear; they reduce men and women to some of their mere bodily functions—they reduce man to his animal component, and such a reduction is an essential purpose of farce or vituperation.

Similarly, Lewis also suggested that it is not an accident that we have no offhand, colloquial, neutral terms—not in any Western European language at any rate—for our most private parts. The words we do use are either (a) nursery terms, (b) archaisms, (c) scientific terms, or (d) a term from the gutter (i.e., a demeaning term). Here I think the genius of language is telling us something important about man. It is telling us that man is an animal with a difference: he has a unique sense of privacy, and a unique capacity for shame when this privacy is violated. Our "private parts" are indeed private, and not merely because convention prescribes it. This particular convention is indigenous to the human race. In practically all primitive tribes, men and women cover their private parts; and in practically all primitive tribes, men and women do not copulate in public.

No society can be utterly indifferent to the ways its citizens publicly entertain themselves.

It may well be that Western society, in the latter half of the twentieth century, is experiencing a drastic change in sexual mores and sexual relationships. We have had many such "sexual revolutions" in the past—and the bourgeois family and bourgeois ideas of sexual propriety were themselves established in the course of a revolution against eighteenth century "licentiousness"—and we shall doubtless have others in the future. It is, however, highly improbable (to put it mildly) that what we are witnessing is the Final Revolution which will make sexual relations utterly unproblematic, permit us to dispense with any kind of ordered relationships between the sexes, and allow us freely to redefine the human condition. And so long as humanity has not reached that utopia, obscenity will remain a problem.

One of the reasons it will remain a problem is that obscenity is not merely about sex, any more than science fiction is about science. Science fiction, as every student of the genre knows, is a peculiar vision of power: what it is really about is politics. And obscenity is a peculiar vision of humanity: what it is really about is ethics and metaphysics.

Imagine a man—a well-known man, much in the public eye—in a hospital ward, dying an agonizing death. He is not in control of his bodily functions, so that his bladder and his bowels empty themselves of their own accord. His consciousness is overwhelmed and extinguished by pain, so that he cannot communicate with us, nor we with him. Now, it would be, technically, the easiest thing in the world to put a television camera in his hospital room and let the whole world witness this spectacle. We don't do it—at least we don't do it as yet—because we regard this as an *obscene* invasion of privacy. And what would make the spectacle obscene is that we would be witnessing the extinguishing of humanity in a human animal.

Incidentally, in the past our humanitarian crusaders against capital punishment understood this point very well. The abolitionist literature goes into great physical detail about what happens to a man when he is hanged or electrocuted or gassed. And their argument was—and is—that what happens is shockingly obscene, and that no civilized society should be responsible for perpetrating such obscenities, particularly since in the nature of the case there must be spectators to ascertain that this horror was indeed being perpetrated in fulfillment of the law.

Sex—like death—is an activity that is both animal and human. There are human sentiments and human ideals involved in this animal activity. But when sex is public, the viewer does not see—cannot see—the sentiments and the ideals. He can only see the animal coupling. And that is why, when men and women make love, as we say, they prefer to be alone—because it is only when you are alone that you can make love, as distinct from merely copulating in an animal and casual way. And that, too, is why those who are voyeurs, if they are not irredeemably sick, also feel ashamed at what they are witnessing. When sex is a public spectacle, a human relationship has been debased into a mere animal connection.

It is also worth noting that this making of sex into an obscenity is not a mutual and equal transaction, but is rather an act of exploitation by one of the partners—the male partner. I do not wish to get into the complicated question as to what, if any, are the essential differences—as distinct from conventional and cultural differences—between male and female. I do not claim to know the answer to that. But I do know—and I take it as a sign which has meaning—that pornography is, and always has been, a man's work; that women rarely write pornography; and that women tend to be indifferent consumers of pornography.[2] My own guess, by way of explanation, is that a woman's sexual experience is ordinarily more suffused with human emotion than is man's, that men are more easily satisfied with autoerotic activities, and that men can therefore more easily take a more "technocratic" view of sex and its pleasures. Perhaps this is not correct. But whatever the explanation, there can be no question that pornography is a form of

2. There are, of course, a few exceptions—but of a kind that prove the rule. *L'Histoire d'O*, for instance, written by a woman, is unquestionably the most *melancholy* work of pornography ever written. And its theme is precisely the dehumanization accomplished by obscenity.

"sexism," as the Women's Liberation Movement calls it, and that the instinct of Women's Lib has been unerring in perceiving that, when pornography is perpetrated, it is perpetrated against them, as part of a conspiracy to deprive them of their full humanity.

But even if all this is granted, it might be said—and doubtless will be said—that I really ought not to be unduly concerned. Free competition in the cultural marketplace—it is argued by people who have never otherwise had a kind word to say for laissez-faire—will automatically dispose of the problem. The present fad for pornography and obscenity, it will be asserted, is just that, a fad. It will spend itself in the course of time; people will get bored with it, will be able to take it or leave it alone in a casual way, in a "mature way," and, in sum, I am being unnecessarily distressed about the whole business. The *New York Times,* in an editorial, concludes hopefully in this vein:

> In the end . . . the insensate pursuit of the urge to shock, carried from one excess to a more abysmal one, is bound to achieve its own antidote in total boredom. When there is no lower depth to descend to, ennui will erase the problem.

I would like to be able to go along with this line of reasoning, but I cannot. I think it is false, and for two reasons, the first psychological, the second political.

The basic psychological fact about pornography and obscenity is that it appeals to and provokes a kind of sexual regression. The sexual pleasure one gets from pornography and obscenity is autoerotic and infantile; put bluntly, it is a masturbatory exercise of the imagination, when it is not masturbation pure and simple. Now, people who masturbate do not get bored with masturbation, just as sadists don't get bored with sadism, and voyeurs don't get bored with voyeurism.

In other words, infantile sexuality is not only a permanent temptation for the adolescent or even the adult—it can quite easily become a permanent, self-reinforcing neurosis. It is because of an awareness of this possibility of regression toward the infantile condition, a regression which is always open to us, that all the codes of sexual conduct ever devised by the human race take such a dim view of autoerotic activities and try to discourage autoerotic fantasies. Masturbation is indeed a perfectly natural autoerotic activity, as so many sexologists blandly assure us today. And it is precisely because it is so perfectly natural that it can be so dangerous to the mature or maturing person, if it is not controlled or sublimated in some way. That is the true meaning of Portnoy's complaint. Portnoy, you will recall, grows up to be a man who is incapable of having an adult sexual relationship with a woman; his sexuality remains fixed in an infantile mode, the prison of his autoerotic fantasies. Inevitably, Portnoy comes to think, in a perfectly *infantile* way, that it was all his mother's fault.

The sexual pleasure one gets from pornography and obscenity is autoerotic and infantile; put bluntly, it is a masturbatory exercise of the imagination.

It is true that, in our time, some quite brilliant minds have come to the conclusion that a reversion to infantile sexuality is the ultimate mission and secret destiny of the human race. I am thinking in particular of Norman O. Brown, for whose writings I have the deepest respect. One of the reasons I respect them so deeply is that Mr. Brown is a serious thinker who is unafraid to face up to the radical consequences of his radical theories. Thus, Mr. Brown knows and says that for his kind of salvation to be achieved, humanity must annul the civilization it has created—not merely the civilization we have today, but all civilization—so as to be able to make the long descent backward into animal innocence.

What is at stake is civilization and humanity, nothing less. The idea that "everything is permitted," as Nietzsche put it, rests on the premise of nihilism and has nihilistic implications. I will not pretend that the case against nihilism and for civilization is an easy one to make. We are here confronting the most fundamental of philosophical questions, on the deepest levels. But that is precisely my point—that the matter of pornography and obscenity is not a trivial one, and that only superficial minds can take a bland and untroubled view of it.

In this connection I might also point out those who are primarily against censorship on liberal grounds tell us not to take pornography or obscenity seriously, while those who are for pornography and obscenity, on radical grounds, take it very seriously indeed. I believe the radicals—writers like Susan Sontag, Herbert Marcuse, Norman O. Brown, and even Jerry Rubin—are right, and the liberals are wrong. I also believe that those young radicals at Berkeley, some five years ago, who provoked a major confrontation over the public use of obscene words, showed a brilliant political instinct. Once the faculty and administration had capitulated on this issue—saying: "Oh, for God's sake, let's be adult: what difference does it make anyway?"—once they said that, they were bound to lose on every other issue. And once Mark Rudd could publicly ascribe to the president of Columbia a notoriously obscene relationship to his mother, without provoking any kind of reaction, the S.D.S. had already won the day. The occupation of Columbia's buildings merely ratified their victory. Men who show themselves unwilling to defend civilization against nihilism are not going to be either resolute or effective in defending the university against anything.

I am already touching upon a political aspect of pornography when I suggest that it is inherently and purposefully subversive of civilization and its institutions. But there is another and more specifically political aspect, which has to do with the relationship of pornography and/or obscenity to democracy, and especially to the quality of public life on which democratic government ultimately rests.

Though the phrase, "the quality of life," trips easily from so many lips these days, it tends to be one of those clichés with many trivial meanings and no large, serious one. Sometimes it merely refers to such externals as the enjoyment of cleaner air, cleaner water, cleaner streets. At other times it refers to the merely private enjoyment of music, painting, or literature. Rarely does it have anything to do with the way the citizen in a democracy views himself—his obligations, his intentions, his ultimate self-definition.

What is at stake is civilization and humanity, nothing less.

Instead, what I would call the "managerial" conception of democracy is the predominant opinion among political scientists, sociologists, and economists, and has, through the untiring efforts of these scholars, become the conventional journalistic opinion as well. The root idea behind this "managerial" conception is that democracy is a "political system" (as they say) which can be adequately defined in terms of—can be fully reduced to—its mechanical arrangements. Democracy is then seen as a set of rules and procedures, and *nothing but* a set of rules and procedures, whereby majority rule and minority rights are reconciled into a state of equilibrium. If everyone follows these rules and procedures, then a democracy is in working order. I think this is a fair description of the democratic idea that currently prevails in academia. One can also fairly say that it is now the liberal idea of democracy par excellence.

I cannot help but feel that there is something ridiculous about being this kind of a democrat, and I must further confess to having a sneaking sympathy for those of our young radicals who also find it ridiculous. The absurdity is the absurdity of idolatry—of taking the symbolic for the real, the means for the end. The purpose of democracy cannot possibly be the endless functioning of its own political machinery. The purpose of any political regime is to achieve some version of the good life and the good society. It is not at all difficult to imagine a perfectly functioning democracy which answers all questions except one—namely, why should anyone of intelligence and spirit care a fig for it?

There is, however, an older idea of democracy—one which was fairly common until about the beginning of this century—for which the conception of the quality of public life is absolutely crucial. This idea starts from the proposition that democracy is a form of self-government, and that if you want it to be a meritorious polity, you have to care about what kind of people govern it. Indeed, it puts the matter more strongly and declares that, if you want self-government, you are only entitled to it if that "self" is worthy of governing. There is no inherent right to self-government if it means that such government is vicious, mean, squalid, and debased. Only a dogmatist and a fanatic, an idolater of democratic machinery, could approve of self-government under such conditions.

And because the desirability of self-government depends on the character of the people who govern, the older idea of democracy was very solicitous of the condition of this character. It was solicitous of the individual self, and felt an obligation to educate it into what used to be called "republican virtue." And it was solicitous of that collective self which we call public opinion and which, in a democracy, governs us collectively. Perhaps in some respects it was nervously oversolicitous—that would not be surprising. But the main thing is that it cared, cared not merely about the machinery of democracy but about the quality of life that this machinery might generate.

And because it cared, this older idea of democracy had no problem in principle with pornography and/or obscenity. It censored them—and it did so with a perfect clarity of mind and a perfectly clear conscience. It was not about to permit people capriciously to corrupt themselves. Or, to put it more precisely: in this version of democracy, the people took some care not to let themselves be governed by the more infantile and irrational parts of themselves.

If you care for the quality of life in our American democracy, then you have to be for censorship.

I have, it may be noticed, uttered that dreadful word, "censorship." And I am not about to back away from it. If you think pornography and/or obscenity is a serious problem, you have to be for censorship. I'll go even further and say that if you want to prevent pornography and/or obscenity from becoming a problem, you have to be for censorship. And lest there be any misunderstanding as to what I am saying, I'll put it as bluntly as possible; if you care for the quality of life in our American democracy, then you have to be for censorship.

But can a liberal be for censorship? Unless one assumes that being a liberal *must* mean being indifferent to the quality of American life, then the answer has to be: yes, a liberal can be for censorship—but he ought to favor a liberal form of censorship.

Is that a contradiction in terms? I don't think

so. We have no problem in contrasting *repressive* laws governing alcohol and drugs and tobacco with laws *regulating* (i.e., discouraging the sale of) alcohol and drugs and tobacco. Laws encouraging temperance are not the same thing as laws that have as their goal prohibition or abolition. We have not made the smoking of cigarettes a criminal offense. We have, however, and with good liberal conscience, prohibited cigarette advertising on television, and may yet, again with good liberal conscience, prohibit it in newspapers and magazines. The idea of restricting individual freedom, in a liberal way, is not at all unfamiliar to us.

I therefore see no reason why we should not be able to distinguish repressive censorship from liberal censorship of the written and spoken word. In Britain, until a few years ago, you could perform almost any play you wished—but certain plays, judged to be obscene, had to be performed in private theatrical clubs which were deemed to have a "serious" interest in theater. In the United States, all of us who grew up using public libraries are familiar with the circumstances under which certain books could be circulated only to adults, while still other books had to be read in the library reading room, under the librarian's skeptical eye. In both cases, a small minority that was willing to make a serious effort to see an obscene play or read an obscene book could do so. But the impact of obscenity was circumscribed and the quality of public life was only marginally afffected.[3]

I am not saying it is easy in practice to sustain a distinction between liberal and repressive censorship, especially in the public realm of a democracy, where popular opinion is so vulnerable to demagoguery. Moreover, an acceptable system of liberal censorship is likely to be exceedingly difficult to devise in the United States today, because our educated classes, upon whose judgment a liberal censorship must rest, are so convinced that there is no such thing as a problem of obscenity, or even that there is no such thing as obscenity at all. But, to counterbalance this, there is the further, fortunate truth that the tolerable margin for error is quite large, and single mistakes or single injustices are not all that important.

This possibility, of course, occasions much distress among artists and academics. It is a fact, one that cannot and should not be denied, that any system of censorship is bound, upon occasion, to treat unjustly a particular work of art—to find pornography where there is only gentle eroticism, to find obscenity where none really exists, or to find both where its existence ought to be tolerated because it serves a larger moral purpose. Though most works of art are not obscene, and though most obscenity has nothing to do with art, there are some few works of art that are, at least in part, pornographic and/or obscene. There are also some few works of art that are in the special category of the comic-ironic "bawdy" (Boccaccio, Rabelais). It is such works of art that are likely to suffer at the hands of the censor. That is the price one has to be prepared to pay for censorship—even liberal censorship.

But just how high is this price? If you believe, as so many artists seem to believe today, that art is the only sacrosanct activity in our profane and vulgar world—that any man who designates himself an artist thereby acquires a sacred office—then obviously censorship is an intolerable form of sacrilege. But for those of us who do not subscribe to this religion of art, the costs of censorship do not seem so high at all.

If you look at the history of American or English literature, there is precious little damage you

3. It is fairly predictable that someone is going to object that this point of view is "elitist"—that, under a system of liberal censorship, the rich will have privileged access to pornography and obscenity. Yes, of course they will—just as, at present, the rich have privileged access to heroin if they want it. But one would have to be an egalitarian maniac to object to this state of affairs on the grounds of equality.

can point to as a consequence of the censorship that prevailed throughout most of that history. Very few works of literature—of real literary merit, I mean—ever were suppressed; and those that were, were not suppressed for long. Nor have I noticed, now that censorship of the written word has to all intents and purposes ceased in this country, that hitherto suppressed or repressed masterpieces are flooding the market. Yes, we can now read *Fanny Hill* and the Marquis de Sade. Or, to be more exact, we can now openly purchase them, since many people were able to read them even though they were publicly banned, which is as it should be under a liberal censorship. So how much have literature and the arts gained from the fact that we can all now buy them over the counter, that, indeed, we are all now encouraged to buy them over the counter? They have not gained much that I can see.

And one might also ask a question that is almost never raised: how much has literature lost from the fact that everything is now permitted? It has lost quite a bit, I should say. In a free market, Gresham's law can work for books or theater as efficiently as it does for coinage—driving out the good, establishing the debased. The cultural market in the United States today is being preempted by dirty books, dirty movies, dirty theater. A pornographic novel has a far better chance of being published today than a nonpornographic one, and quite a few pretty good novels are not being published at all simply because they are not pornographic, and are therefore less likely to sell. Our cultural condition has not improved as a result of the new freedom. American cultural life wasn't much to brag about 20 years ago; today one feels ashamed for it.

Just one last point which I dare not leave untouched. If we start censoring pornography or obscenity, shall we not inevitably end up censoring political opinion? A lot of people seem to think this would be the case—which only shows the power of doctrinaire thinking over reality. We had censorship of pornography and obscenity for 150 years, until almost yesterday, and I am not aware that freedom of opinion in this country was in any way diminished as a consequence of this fact. Fortunately for those of us who are liberal, freedom is not indivisible. If it were, the case for liberalism would be indistinguishable from the case for anarchy; and they are two very different things.

But I must repeat and emphasize: what kind of laws we pass governing pornography and obscenity, what kind of censorship—or, since we are still a Federal nation—what kinds of censorship we institute in our various localities may indeed be difficult matters to cope with; nevertheless the real issue is one of principle. I myself subscribe to a liberal view of the enforcement problem: I think that pornography should be illegal *and* available to anyone who wants it so badly as to make a pretty strenuous effort to get it. We have lived with under-the-counter pornography for centuries now, in a fairly comfortable way. But the issue of principle, of whether it should be over or under the counter, has to be settled before we can reflect on the advantages and disadvantages of alternative modes of censorship. I think the settlement we are living under now, in which obscenity and democracy are regarded as equals, is wrong; I believe it is inherently unstable; I think it will, in the long run, be incompatible with any authentic concern for the quality of life in our democracy.

THE CASE AGAINST CENSORSHIP

Hollis Alpert

The idea of censorship, particularly when it is aimed against pornography, has its attractions. What could be seemingly more wholesome than newsstands cleansed of those obnoxious little weekly sheets filled with gleeful celebrations of sexual acts, the more perverse the more gleeful? In what way would the community—any community—be harmed if stores purveying stacks of photographs, glossy magazines, and film strips devoted to illustrating what used to be known as private parts were closed down by police order? Or if cinema houses featuring acts of "love," natural and unnatural, were shuttered? Little would be lost, really.

Even so, I am against censorship.

Over the years, I have had occasion, for journalistic reasons, to examine the question of censorship. I have met and talked to censors; I have been called as an "expert" witness in court cases aimed at suppressing certain films. I have viewed a good part of the Kinsey Institute's collection of pornographic film material and talked to members of the staff. I have read a great many of the available works, legal, sociologic, and psychiatric, on the subject. Nothing I have encountered has changed the opinion stated above.

This is not to say that I, personally, have not been offended by some of what I have encountered. Pornography, according to the dictionary on my desk, is "writings, pictures, etc., intended to arouse sexual desire." It is nonsense to claim, as some do, that there is no such thing as pornography, and that the use of the word indicates something suspicious about the mental and emotional state of the accuser. (There *can* be something suspicious, of course.) Pornography, simply, does intend to arouse sexual desire, and it fails as pornography if it doesn't. The problem is, for the habitual fancier of the stuff, that it takes more and more to arouse; and as a result, the tendency is for pornography to go farther and farther beyond the pale. Unfortunately, there are limits; and eventually, pornography, even for the addict, becomes dull and stale. The problem for the non-addict is that it becomes increasingly offensive.

> I am not for pornography; I am merely against censoring it.

What I dislike most about pornography is not the fact of its existence, but the level of its taste which, for the most part, is abysmal. Pornography represents a market—literary, journalistic, and cinematic—for unimaginative clods, neurotics of many different persuasions, and the untalented everywhere. All such professional matters such as style, taste, craft, and artistry give way to the tasteless, the brainless, the mercenary, the scatological, the obscene. What is so annoying about obscenity, however it may be defined, is the mockery of human aspirations it

---

essentially represents. I do not admire those who so proudly flaunt the banner of their sexual liberalism, for they mock what has meaning for me.

Therefore, I am not for pornography; I am merely against censoring it.

I do not regard pornography as an evil, but some of it I do regard as an abomination of sorts. I do not know if exposure to pornography harms either the young, the middle-aged, or the old, but this is not to say that it does not have its effects. It obviously increases the incidence (to use a Kinsey Institute term) of masturbation; but since we hear that masturbation is not harmful and that it is difficult to masturbate to excess, this would not seem to be necessarily a harmful effect.

I don't share the zeal of those who claim for pornography certain benefits for the repressed, the frustrated, the bewildered, and the confused; but I can see where, in certain cases, it might help overcome inhibitions, unwanted modesty, lack of ardor. Yet talking or a modicum of alcoholic drinking can achieve pretty much the same results. As an antidote for boredom and loneliness, pornography may well have some positive value. And by its very frankness, pornography may actually represent an improvement, educationally speaking, for the young who pick up their sexual knowledge on the street or even in some of those earnest sex education courses in schools.

I see very little reason to forbid pornography, except that I don't happen to like it.

But, again, its therapeutic value needs establishing far more than has been done up to now. In no country where the question has been studied has it yet been found that pornography increases crime. Where rape has been found to be on the rise, it is almost invariably due to social and economic conditions, not to the presence of pornography. While it probably does lead to more sexuality—conjugal and private—for those exposed and attracted to it, pornography does not seem to lead to much in the way of sexual abuse, and here I am speaking primarily of violent forms of sexuality.

In prisons, however, where pornography clearly is not present, sexual abuse, particularly of the homosexual kind, has become a matter of shocking public knowledge.

So I see very little reason to forbid pornography, except that I don't happen to like it.

On the other hand, the mentality of those censors I have met, and of those who advocate censorship, has often filled me with foreboding. All too frequently they have a way of equating pornography with "Godless un-American Communists," and the like. They cite religious tracts, even the Bible (generally overlooking the Song of Solomon) as "scientific" reason for their opposition to pornography and for the straitjackets they would impose on publishing and film making. The zeal with which they have attempted to counterattack against the glut of smut is worrisome in itself, revealing, perhaps, of a secret attraction to what they publicly proclaim as "sinful." Beware he of the impassioned rhetoric. All too often his voice, his words, his tone, remind of the righteous Goebbels.

But it is hardly news that there exists a tremendous amount of cant and hypocrisy among those who assume that a battle against pornography is a battle for law and order. While researching material for "History of Sex in Cinema," a lengthy series published by *Playboy Magazine*, I found that the very pillars of our society—veterans' groups, patriotic organizations, policemen and firemen—were the principal supporters of that hoary American institution, the "stag party." During these evenings one or two hours of a collection of stag reels would be shown to an all-male audience, and where did the evening's entertainment come from? Often enough from the local police or fire chief—confiscated, of course.

While testifying for the release of *I Am Curious—Yellow* and other cinematic works confiscated by U.S. Customs, I was interested to find that in conversation afterward with U.S. attorneys, a good many of them were not at all in agreement, personally, with the views they presented to the jurors. "Of course the film should be shown," said one young assistant district attorney, "it's really all a kind of infighting." Those twelve good men and true didn't exactly convince me either that the jury system was the best way to achieve a fair verdict.

In one case the attorneys for Customs didn't even bother to make a case for their point of view. They merely exhibited the film in question to the jurors, most of whom seldom left their television sets at night. They had no way of knowing precisely what was commonly shown in theaters across the country and around the world. The attorneys counted on only one thing: that they would be shocked by what they saw. They were, and they declared the film guilty. Of what? Of offensiveness to them, naturally.

And just as naturally, an appeals court overturned their verdict.

But of judges, too, I happen to be suspicious. One U.S. District judge, while upholding a Customs seizure of a film, presumably saw more of a sexually nefarious nature in it than I did; and the horrified language he used to describe those "unspeakable acts" was remarkably similar to what I once heard thundered from a pulpit. Too little separation of church and state, in other words.

Thus, I am inclined to think that pornography and what to do about it should be taken out of the legal sphere entirely. Lawyers and judges use terms like "indecent" without bothering to define "decency." Is killing a stranger in a strange land "decent"? Our decent soldiers do it every day, are encouraged to do it, and are not termed indecent except when they rape one or more of the local women. "Does the film appeal to the prurient interest. . . ?" I have long given up attempting to discover what "prurient interest" means—not even the dictionary is of much help here. "The average member of the community." Who is he? And where is this community? Times Square? Scarsdale? Spanish Harlem? Birmingham, Alabama?

The legal battle continues to be fought over a terrain that is inadequately defined, and perhaps cannot be. It may not even exist any longer.

For look what we have: pornography shown in hundreds of theaters, openly; magazines of a crudity unimaginable just a few years ago; "revolutionary" newspapers filled with erotic junk.

In 1964, when my colleague (Arthur Knight) and I began to look into the erotic content of films, beginning with a clip of Fatima, who electrified Chicago's Columbian Exposition in 1893 with her "dance of the veils" and was subsequently immortalized on film in 1906, the stag film was very much underground, photographs showing male and female organs were still taboo, and movies were still obeying a set of restraints known as the Production Code. All that has changed in a mere half-dozen years.

Fatima, we discovered, was the first victim of movie censorship. Peep show patrons had been vouchsafed a glimpse of her belly as she undulated, and the authorities of that day quickly stenciled picket fences over the offending portion of her anatomy. It was not more than ten years before the question of movie censorship reached the august halls of Congress; we very nearly had a national censorship statute. And the agitation for such a statute has not died down to this day.

What agitated censors in 1906, 1916, 1926, and 1936, would strike us as silly and laughable today. A bit of revealed nudity, for instance, as in *Ecstasy*, brought out the Comstockery in thousands across the land. Remember how long it took for one of the literary masterpieces of our century, *Ulysses,* to be sold publicly? It was not hard to reach a conclusion that standards of morality have varied, not to say gyrated, from period to period. Yesterday's obscenity is not necessarily today's. Would that all pornography were as gracefully written as, say, *Fanny Hill.*

Yesterday's obscenity is not necessarily today's. Would that all pornography were as gracefully written as, say, Fanny Hill.

But one thing has always existed and presumably always will: the urge to create pornography. And even more widespread is the curiosity it evokes and has evoked in untold millions. All efforts to suppress pornography have failed. If made illegal, it springs up illegally. If made legal, it springs up legally. Presumably, we will always have it. And in a measure never envisioned at a time when Victorian gentlemen took up their pens to relate their erotic experiences, real or imagined.

For technology has made pornography the realm of everyman. When it was discovered that the home movie camera could be employed to record bedroom activities in private, processing plants, in self-protection, refused to develop such intimate and illegal (then) goings-on. But there was always that unscrupulous employee who knew how to turn a buck by channeling furtive prints into the furtive stag market. Thus, in the Kinsey Institute collection and many private ones, are 8 mm and 16 mm films made by amateurs and employing amateurs who were mortified to discover (when, on occasion, the police knocked on their doors) that their private activities were being viewed by thousands.

Surcease came in the form of the Polaroid camera. Stills could be taken and developed instantly without recourse to a lab, and one wonders how much effect this "development" had on the stock of the corporation. More realism came with the Polaroid color camera. One reason, perhaps, that Americans were so ready for public pornography was that they had become so adept at producing it privately.

Then came the home video outfit, an expensive toy, surely, but its uses at home immediately evident for those with the insatiable urge to view the sexual behavior of themselves and sometimes intimate friends and sometimes intimate strangers.

Now, upon us, is the cassette and cartridge recorder, much cheaper, much simpler. Just as television brought havoc to the film industry, the home visual recording devices may wreck the public pornography industry. Instantly erasable, a record need never be there for prying officials.

That is why I strongly suspect that the legal terrain has all but vanished. Within another few years, there may be only one way of quelling the production of pornography and the voyeuristic habits it entails. And that is to bring on "Big Brother," which would amount to electronic surveillance and eavesdropping in every suspected home, in corn fields and on boats, in barns, garages, and garrets.

And that is the main reason I am so strongly opposed to the censorship of pornography, for it would require, sooner or later, a vast national (even international) effort, and *1984* would be here long before its time.

Must we live with it then?

Probably so. But should an actual community wish to control its availability, it does have a certain amount of legal leeway. The Supreme Court has already ruled that a community, a legally defined entity such as a township or a county, can "protect" its young by prosecuting those who purvey it to those under a certain age.

If sexual debasement has been ruled out of court, so to speak, as it has been by many, many "sexologists," psychiatrists, and so-called experts on the subject, surely the debasement of taste has not. And there are ways to make clear to the community why pornography usually represents a nadir level of taste. This judgment can be made on the theater owner who prefers to show "X" films over the less gamier kind because "it sells better." No reason not to let him know, through editorials and in community meetings, that his profit motive does not necessarily make him an admirable member of the community.

But censor him not, please, for the dangers in such action are too great.

The current flood of pornography may well be a symptom, but not with any certainty, of a moral decline. What *has* declined is the hold of religious faith, doctrine, and institutions over human impulses and desires. Even among the more devout, a demarcation now is being made between sexual and spiritual morality. With an increasing degree of scientific inquiry into the nature of human sexuality, sex has been taken out of the realm of the morally harmful and has been given literally a clean bill of health when practiced, so the legal language tells us, among consenting adults. Pre-adult sex is on the rise, too, according to gynecologists. For proof they simply cite the prescriptions for pills and other contraceptive methods dispensed to girls 14 and 15 years old. "The change," said one veteran woman gynecologist, "has been particularly striking during the past five years."

One aspect of the generational gap is the difference between how young people and their elders view the sex act. Among the older generation, there is still evidence of guilt and anxiety over sexual behavior that varies from what they assume to be the norm—and that norm being the sexual act practiced primarily for the purpose of procreation between females over 18 and males over 21. Taboos, though seldom spoken, still exist. The newer generation has tossed aside most of these taboos. Many among them practice experimental and communal forms of cohabitation. Sex is taken for granted, is thought of as natural, healthy, and an expression of a loving nature. Not by all young people, certainly, but by larger percentages than in previous generations. Community standards—by which censorship has traditionally justified itself—vary widely and extremely and often within the same community. No code of censorship could possibly do justice to the liberalized attitudes toward sex that exist today.

The day may not be far off when the commonly accepted standards of today may totally reverse themselves. In fact, right now the most commonly approved sexual activity—marital copulation aimed at producing an offspring—is being viewed with alarm by many. For the population explosion, long due, is now imminent. The population projections for 10, 20, and 30 years from now are eerily frightening. Already, in several states abortion has been legalized. But the awful pity of it is that the most economically and educationally blighted groups reproduce the most and perpetuate the problems that create the most stress in this society and others. A new sexual ethic—already existing in many groupings—that substitutes pleasure and release of tensions as its primary goals certainly makes more practical sense if the human race is to survive with any degree of comfort. For there would now seem to be a real need to channel sexual instincts so that they do not result in a cancerous surplus of population.

Perhaps today's pornography can even be regarded as a primitive expression of society's as yet inchoate recognition that sex, divorced from its procreative aspect and even from romantic and sentimental notions of love, can have its positive values. And it can also be regarded as evidence of the widespread frustration that exists in the sexual area, for pornography gets its appeal from its fantasy portrayal of sex. Fantasies arise when instincts are frustrated. In pornography females of any age and racial or ethnic coloration are ever-willing. Males are ever-potent. Thus, whether in the printed word, in photographs, or moving film images, pornography presents to the reader and the viewer fantasy situations that have something to tell us about the human sexual condition.

The artist, viewing his fellows through his personal vision, has through the ages attempted to portray what he sees and to present his understanding of it. Censorship in his case has perpetrated heavy and sometimes reprehensible blunders. Such recognized literary artists as Joyce and Lawrence were for many years relegated to pirated editions that were sold from beneath the counter. What untold artistic riches still reside, barred from the gaze of civilized man, in the Vatican's rumored collection of erotic treasures? The censor, when presented with this kind of evidence of artistic repression, usually has as his answer that a few geniuses may be deprived of their potential publics, but the many will benefit. But how? The censor, by hoping to bar all that he deems reprehensible, commits errors of taste at least equal to those committed by the most foul of pornographers. For each rules out a vast spectrum of gradations and distinctions.

Of the two dangers, restrictive censorship on the one hand and unrestrained pornography on the other, the latter would seem to be the lesser, by far. For the former can create real harm. The unscrupulous politician can take advantage of the emotional, hysterical, and neurotic attitudes toward pornography to incite the multitude toward approval of repressive measures that go far beyond the control of the printed word and the photographed image. Even with a report from a presidential commission that concluded that no societal or individual harm has resulted from the existence of pornography, highly placed officials still took the warpath against its dissemination. Since there seems to be no substantive base for the officials' stand, one must suspect other motives, the simplest one being, perhaps, that of corralling the votes of conservative elements of the population. Implicitly asking for censorship, they overlook the question of who should do the censoring. Whom shall we trust? Whom can we trust? How shall we agree on standards and criteria? Perhaps they don't really care.

I rather suspect that, left alone, the various media tend to regulate themselves. The largest mass medium, television, presents no pornography at all that I know of, unless it be that of violence which some would translate into fantasy sexual sadism and masochism. Thus disguised, much pornography finds its way into the most respectable channels.

Movies are regulated by their markets, and major film companies now espouse four main grades of entertainment which tend to take into account existing types of theatrical exhibition and audiences.

Radio has only the disguised kind of pornography—actually, no more than mild erotic stimulation—that comes from certain kinds of music and suggestive lyrics.

Magazines run a vast gamut; but no one is prevented from reading *Commentary* or *Harper's* by the fact that girlie publications are sold at the same corner newsstand.

Actually, the human mind is so various in its interests that its concentration on pornography takes but a minute portion of its attention. It is at worst a flea that bites an elephant. It requires little effort to overlook it entirely. It does take enormous effort to try to do something about it; and in the long run, it is no more productive than flailing at windmills.

AGAINST BOOK CENSORSHIP

Jerzy Kosinski

The impetus for Jerzy Kosinski's article on book censorship in the schools was a report that the Woodbridge, N.J. School District, under pressure from a local citizens' group, had banned his novel, *Being There*.

Media & Methods contacted the Woodbridge School District, and obtained the following information:

The Kosinski book was being used as a supplementary title in a high school course on mass media. A group of parents, claiming that *Being There* contained "objectionable passages," prevailed on the school officials to have the work removed from the reading lists for the course. This was done, and *Being There* is no longer available in the Woodbridge schools.

While the Kosinski article obviously reflects the particulars of the Woodbridge action, its scope is much broader. At issue is the overall danger that school censorship of books poses and what educators can do when confronted by demands that a book be banned.

If properly learned, reading can prepare students to deal perceptively with the complexities of society. But it cannot be properly learned if self-appointed censors are permitted to force the exclusion from the schools of any literary work which they label as "objectionable." Such action, however lofty its stated motives, undermines one of the basic reasons for teaching contemporary literature: to present the students with hypothetical situations—emotional, moral, political, religious, sexual—which they are likely to face once they leave the protective structures of school, family, or community, or which they may be struggling to face already.

Zealots of the book-banning persuasion invariably confuse the literary work with the instructional manual, ascribing the same purpose to these two very different kinds of writing: to control the reader's behavior. Thus they see the reader reduced to a robot, destined to imitate the events portrayed in whatever book he or she happens to be reading.

Zealots of the book-banning persuasion invariably confuse the literary work with the instructional manual.

Furthermore, the typical anti-literary mind perceives the student as an ideal, isolated being removed from the myriad influences that mass media, violence, social unrest, and commercialism bring to bear in contemporary society. Yet students today are anything but uncontaminated mentally. These forces reach them despite all attempts to sanitize the classroom (or the living room) and quarantine its occupants. Still, the zealot, locked in a past of fictitious purity, tends to see the student as inviolable, a perpetual child, and will stress his or her "immaturity," remaining oblivious to the student's need to understand the wider world and to grow socially and emotionally.

One source of this growth can be the confrontation between a student and a book. Exposure to various forms of fiction usually teaches students that they can (and *must* if they are to enjoy reading) re-create the text's situations within their own mind's eye. This ability to visualize, to know that one can shape and control images triggered by the printed word, is invaluable. Its presence or absence will color every aspect of an individual's life—as a member of the community, as a spouse or parent, as a participant in professional activities.

In this act of imaginative projection, readers remain aware that, however involved they may be in the act of reading, they nevertheless stand outside the depicted events. Such forced separation between reading and imagining can act as a catalyst for a formative realization: that the reader is a mediator, able to distinguish between false and true images, between appropriate and inappropriate responses. This goes beyond mental or aesthetic ability; it implies the power to judge, to see a novel's people and events in moral terms. And such judgment demands that the reader develop—or have already developed—a working ethical code. This is the irony of censorship, that it thwarts the very ethical development that its proponents see threatened by access to diverse literary works.

Of course, the actual process by which students come to terms with their complex role as reader is a highly personal, internal one that cannot be taught. But students can be led to read correctly, to appreciate unfamiliar literary terrain, and to choose books which will challenge their minds and continually demand new responses, new ethical judgments. As their reading skills develop, so too does their imagination—not to conjure up deviant spectacles and behaviors, but to project themselves into complexities of life which are yet beyond their present experiential perimeters.

Banning fiction of a certain type from the classroom is one of the surest ways to keep students from exercising and expanding their imaginations. Denied the opportunity to learn how to respond to all literature imaginatively—instead of simply accepting it—a student can lose the ablity to handle real and potentially damaging events. The tragic outcome is that the myopia which characterizes the zealot's outlook may become reincarnated in the life of the student who is barred from a literary work because it contains an "objectionable passage."

Clearly, life in contemporary American society is not easy for most people, including the young. Suicide is the second most frequent cause of death among persons between the ages of 15 and 24. (The most frequent cause, accidental death, includes many drug-induced, de facto suicides.) A recent national survey of prosperous American business executives indicates that more than half of them feel too pressured to enjoy life; one third admit that the strain and tension of their jobs have hurt their health; over half say that their work is at best unrewarding; nearly half have changed or considered changing their professions; and about 70 percent admit they have been expected to compromise personal principles in order to conform to standards established by their superiors within the corporate structure.

One of the bulwarks against this increasing sense of personal frustration is a strengthening of the intellectual life. Yet Americans seem to be growing further and further away from such a life. And what is worse, they are abandoning the very tools upon which this life is built—a major one of which is reading. One-fifth of all Americans are known to be functionally illiterate. During the past few years the verbal aptitude of American high school graduates has consistently declined—hardly surprising since that same graduate has logged 18,000 hours of TV viewing, the equivalent of nine years of full-time employment. Only now are we recognizing the intellectual destruction that this unreflective pastime can produce. (See my comments in "A Nation of Videots," *Media & Methods,* April 1975.)

As this trend toward depression, passivity, and isolation becomes increasingly irreversible, schools are among the few remaining institutions that can help tomorrow's adults become thinking individuals, able to judge and function in a world of pressures, conflicting values, and moral ambiguities. The classroom experience in general, and the reading experience in particular, are two of the few demanding mental activities left in modern society. And both must be allowed to flourish freely—without arbitrary restrictions on what is taught and what is read—if we are to keep at least some small part of the student population from becoming emotionally and intellectually crippled.

Of course, ours is a free society and zealots are at liberty to suppress what they consider wrong and alien, just as teachers are at liberty to defend their authority and knowledge in the selection of material to be read. Yet there is a difference: professional training and the rights vested in teachers by the community should confer a special authority. But, at the hands of the small-minded traditionalists, teachers are often exposed to prejudice and attack. They are cast as scapegoats and forced to present time-consuming, humiliating defenses. They may be called upon to testify on behalf of a literary work they have selected for a course, or to justify such a choice as if *they* were the proponent of an outlandish vision of life, rather than being the victim of a handful of hysterical parents.

Since the specter of book censorship can emerge anywhere in America, a general plan for counterattack must be drawn up. When the book-banners gather together, the teacher—in addition to alerting the teachers' association, the school, the library, and (if he or she is involved as an individual) the Civil Liberties Union—should promptly notify the novel's author, publishers, and regional and local book distributors. Some or all of these parties will no doubt be interested in providing assistance by furnishing materials (reviews from mass media and religious publications, scholarly analyses, and other pertinent opinions) that can assist the teacher in making a stand.

Teachers constrained from discharging their responsibilities must notify the community at large, and the larger the better. This is a national as well as a local issue; the entire country should be kept aware of every student's right to have access to all forms of art. So the national media should be alerted, in addition to local TV and radio stations, magazines, and newspapers.

Embattled teachers might also consider occasional visits to local magazine and newspaper stands where they can find materials which make the "objectionable passages" in school texts seem ridiculous. The students, whose protection is so earnestly invoked, have free access to these sources. A cursory review of local theaters will turn up films which portray violence and human destruction on a much more impressive scale than the "objectionable" passages in some school readings. Many a local supermarket offers boudoir confessional accounts in publications of questionable character, lubriciously illustrated, and placed conveniently near the check-outs for casual perusal if not actual purchase.

It is argued that such materials, though available, do not have any official sanction, that the schools are the guardians of public morals and thus should be more selective about what is approved for student use. This opinion undermines the more vital function of education, which is to help students cope with life by exploring with them the realities and ambiguities expressed in recognized literary works. The school offers one of the few structured forums for analyzing such situations—an opportunity to critically evaluate the human condition within the guidelines of literary value and human interchange. If students are exposed to a situation which departs from their ethical sense, better that this occur within the school context than behind some magazine rack. But the question is not one of exposure—that will occur no matter how protective the local citizenry might be. The quesiton is rather one of analysis and evaluation—a function which the school is established to provide.

Finally, local boards of education as well as other community organizations would do well to recognize the importance of teachers who make their students aware of personal and world events, particularly at a time of political polarization, economic turmoil, and general unpredictability. These teachers, who want to prepare their students for various contingencies, deserve considerable respect. They are often attacked as "experimentalists," but they play a vital role in ensuring that schools will produce responsible individuals, men and women without fear of the world around them.

HERE'S WHO THE NETWORK TV CENSORS REALLY ARE

Rev. Donald E. Wildmon

Officials from the three commercial networks recently were on PBS-TV talking about the Coalition for Better Television. They made some very interesting statements. I would like to share some thoughts with you concerning the response of the networks to the coalition.

All three officials were asked if a boycott of the leading sponsors of sex, violence, profanity, etc., on television would work. Each of them, to a man, responded with an absolute "no". All three were in total agreement that a boycott would not work. These responses were shocking to me.

For the past year now the networks have been doing all they could possibly do to belittle the coalition by calling us names ranging from "Ayatollah" and "Hitler" to "McCarthy." Now, if a boycott of the leading sponsors of television trash will not work, why on earth do network officials find it necessary to condemn the coalition with all the adjectives they can muster? If a boycott will not work why not simply ignore those who propose it?

Reverend Wildmon is the founder of the National Federation for Decency.

From *Conservative Digest* (March, 1982). Reprinted by permission.

We are condemned for even suggesting a boycott. I think there are some things we need to clear up in this matter as we head into one. First, the networks are free to show anything they desire. No one is prohibiting them from exhibiting their wares. If they desire to fill our dens with a nightly dose of filth, they are free to do so—coalition or no coalition.

Next, advertisers are free to sponsor any program they wish. No one in the coalition is forcing any advertiser to get off or on any program. The advertiser is free to spend his money where he wishes. If an advertiser thinks it good business to help sponsor garbage and filth, he is free to do so.

WHO ARE THE REAL CENSORS?

Viewers are free to watch any program they wish. No one, except the networks and local stations, tells the viewer what they can or cannot watch. The only people practicing censorship are the networks. They are that small handful of people who decide for all the rest of us what we can and cannot watch, what is fit or unfit for all of us to see.

> The only people practicing censorship are the networks.

Finally, the consumer is free to spend his money where he wishes. No one is forcing any individual to refuse to spend his money with any advertiser or network. Any individual who wants to support the coalition in a boycott can do so freely and voluntarily, of his own free will.

What then is the real issue involved in all of this? Simply put, it is whether or not an individual is free to spend his money where he wants to. What the networks are really saying is that not only can they tell us what we can and cannot watch, but that we must also support whatever they decide to offer us with our money! They want to take away the right of every individual to spend his money where he wants.

The networks think they have the right to sell a shoddy product at a guaranteed profit. Fortunately, that situation does not exist in a capitalistic society—only in a communistic one.

The networks must respond like any other business does in a capitalistic society—to the consumer. They can continue to put forth cheap, exploitative trash. But if no one is interested in buying, they have no one to blame but themselves.

They cry "censorship" but they are the ones who are doing the censoring. They still have full and complete control over their programming. No one has ever suggested anything to the contrary.

Do you want the networks telling you where you can or cannot spend your money? Personally, I don't. If they have their way they will do exactly that. Gene Mater, a vice-president of CBS, told me that what I was doing (trying to promote constructive television) was immoral. Funny how things can get twisted sometimes. Fighting immorality on television is immoral, but promoting immorality on television is moral.

HOLLYWOOD'S REACTION

It has been interesting to watch how the networks and Hollywood have reacted to the coalition. When I made the statement that Christians would no longer accept the ugly discrimination against Christian characters, values and culture on television, that we would call for a boycott, the *Hollywood Reporter* ran these headlines on the front page: "Rev. Wildmon On The Rampage Again: New Boycott Threatened." However, when Benjamin Hooks said that the blacks would boycott if they didn't get better treatment from the film industry, the headlines *did not* read: "Benjamin Hooks On The Rampage Again: New Boycott Threatened." I guess only ministers concerned about trash on TV go on a rampage when calling for a boycott. Others who do so are sane.

There was no outcry from the same folks who condemned us for suggesting a boycott when the Directors Guild of America (the organization of Hollywood film directors) called for a boycott of the 15 states who have not ratified the ERA. Strange, isn't it? Where were Norman Lear and Lee Rich? Why weren't they condemning the directors for boycotting the states that have not passed the ERA? Is there a double standard here?

The networks attempt to deny viewers the right to organize. The only option they offer is to turn your TV set off. If we don't like crime in the streets, they would have us stay in our houses. They would give us the option to vote for a candidate, but not work to get others to vote for that candidate. If anyone is forcing their morality on anyone in this whole affair (which is what the networks have accused us of doing), it is the networks. Why are they afraid of taking their case to the people?

The networks consistently say that they have not lost any money, that they have made no changes, and that they will not make any change in their programming because of the coalition—in other words the coalition is totally and completely ineffective. If that is the case, and if I were in their position, I would not worry. I wouldn't go around the country calling the coalition all the ugly names one could think of. I would simply ignore the coalition. That would be the best thing to do. I would ignore it and continue to turn out the same cheap trash that has provided me with billions of dollars in the past.

Another thing the networks consistently say is that their programming does not cause people to act differently than they would if their programs were more positive. The odd thing here is that when they go to the advertisers to sell their time, they say exactly the opposite. "Put your money on our network, and we can sell your products," they say. And they are right about that. They have sold more products than any other advertising medium in history. But while selling products they have also been selling ideas, values, concepts, etc.

The networks have been selling the idea that adultery and homosexuality are normal, and that violence is a legitimate way to resolve conflict and achieve one's goals in life. They have been promoting the idea that profanity is the way intelligent people express themselves, and that the use of the term "God" is fine for profanity. They have been selling the idea that the only drink "respectable" people offer others is an alcoholic one. By their form of censoring they have been saying to the American public that Christian values and their culture aren't important and are irrelevant to today's society.

So some of us say enough is enough. We say to the networks: "Go on show your trash if you wish." We say to the advertisers: "Go on and help pay to ridicule and demean those values we consider important." We say to others in the public: "Go on watch trash if that fits your mentality." We don't get condemned for saying these things.

> Many of the programs on television are either morally offensive or mentally insulting.

When we tell them: "Our money is our money and we will no longer use it to help you promote those values that we feel are detrimental to our society," you would think the devil himself had spoken out. We are condemned, blasted, called ugly and vicious names, accused of wanting to ruin the networks, etc. Why? Simply because we decided to be good stewards with the money God has given us. Sin of all sins—the unforgivable sin!

A HUGE STOCKPILE

Of one thing in all this I am certain—that if I am as right as the networks think they are and if my opposition was as wrong as they think I am—then Lord knows I certainly wouldn't worry about taking my case to the people. Look at the imbalance of the battle lines. The networks are rich and powerful. They control the source of most of the news in this country. They own huge chunks in the publishing and printing industries. They have complete control over how a given situation is presented. They have millions of dollars to support their battle. They have astute people to formulate and implement their policy. In short, they have every conceivable weapon known to wage a successful fight.

What do those of us in the coalition have? Little money. No access to television except what is offered. No interest in the publishing or printing industries. No astute people to formulate and implement our policy. In short, there is no conceivable way we can succeed in bringing about a better, wholesome, and more constructive kind of television.

Then why do the networks and Hollywood worry? I would worry too if I was forced to defend the trash they have to defend. Many of the programs on television are either morally offensive or mentally insulting. All the loud rhetoric in the world won't change garbage into a choice T-bone.

Why are the networks so worried about this situation? Perhaps the networks think we are right? They are trying to defend the indefensible—not because it is right but because it is profitable. There's the rub. Why spend $2 million producing a program that brings in $3 million when you can produce a cheaper program (which appeals to the base instincts of man) for $1 million and still bring in the $3 million. Therein lies the answer. As long as the networks can make your money by selling the cheaper product, you can bet your bottom dollar they will do so.

This country has achieved what it has economically because it has operated on a form of capitalism which was nurtured by Christian ethics. There was a sense of corporate responsibility not only to make money but to be a good corporate citizen. The networks have exploited this situation. Now they are forced to defend their actions. This will be hard for them to do. It is hard to convince people that the sewer smells as sweet as perfume.

NIGHT THOUGHTS OF A MEDIA WATCHER

Gloria Steinem

Dear TV advertiser and executive:

If you read carefully the threats of the Moral Majority and the Coalition for Better Television to boycott sponsors of any show they find "antifamily" or "violent," how could you take them seriously?

In the first place, statements of the same groups make clear that only sex *outside* patriarchal marriage is either "indecent" or "antifamily." Within the bounds of male-dominated marriage, just about anything (including some violence) seems to be okay. Moral Majority leaders hope to cut off aid for battered women's centers, for instance, and to eliminate federal laws against child abuse. "Total Woman" courses are taught in fundamentalist church basements. From disciplining family members to having your wife meet you at the door in Saran Wrap, a man's house is his castle.

Second, these censoring groups are enthusiastic about war, military spending, and other forms of institutionalized violence. Vietnam, the military budget, and the neutron bomb have all benefited from Moral Majority support. So has capital punishment.

Finally, and most important, if you ask any movement groups who have run boycotts, you'll find that the Moral Majority threats are just hot air. Either they don't know how to run a boycott effectively, or they're counting on the fact that *you* don't.

Grapes, for instance. This simple, one-word boycott took two years to be felt at all. Ask the United Farm Workers. When the items to be boycotted are as various as 15 different states, as in the long-running boycott of states that haven't ratified the ERA, it takes even more time and work.

Frankly, I'm not sure the boycott threatened by these right-wing groups could be successful in *any* amount of time. There are hundreds of brand names involved, and that requires an almost impossible nationwide organizing effort. Furthermore, Moral Majority members themselves don't agree with their leadership. When polled, most said they *liked* the very shows whose sponsors they were supposed to boycott, and watched them in about the same proportion as other Americans.

No wonder the boycott was called off at the last minute. It was actually just a rhetorical con job.

The tragedy is that some TV decision-makers seem to have given in. I've been hearing that shows were turned down by advertisers because of this nonexistent threat; that more actors have been asked to sign morals clauses; that some scripts have been refused because they didn't offer enough "patriotism," "active male characters," or "traditional family life."

So here is my question: why allow hypocritical, even impossible threats to deliver what reality never could?

From *Ms.* (November, 1981). Reprinted by permission.

SUGGESTIONS FOR FURTHER READING

Those interested in the basic arguments presented in this chapter will want to read Harold H. Hart, ed., *Censorship: For and Against*, New York: Hart Publishing, 1971, which contains twelve essays from important thinkers on both sides of the issue. One of those essays, the article by Hollis Alpert, is included in this chapter.

Also of interest:

Angela Bonavoglia, "America, Apple Pie, and Pornography: Do Feminists Stand a Chance?" *USA Today* (May, 1981), pp. 28–31. The author examines the idea of pornography as violence against women versus the idea of pornography as liberated fun.

David Copp and Susan Wendell, eds., *Pornography and Censorship*. Buffalo, New York: Prometheus Books, 1982.

Edward DeGrazia and Roger K. Newman, *Banned Films: Movies, Censors, and the First Amendment*. New York: Bowker, 1982.

Neil Gallagher, *The Porno Plague*. Minneapolis: Bethany House, 1982.

M. M. Kambi, "Censorship vs. Selection—Choosing Books for Schools." *American Education* 18 (March 1982), 11–16.

Laura Lederer, ed., *Take Back the Night: Women on Pornography*. New York: Morrow, 1980.

Joseph Nocera, "The Big Book-Banning Brawl." *The New Republic*, September 13, 1982, p. 20. "In local school districts all across the country, book-banners are on the warpath—and librarians are fighting back. Mostly the librarians are right, but things aren't always as simple as they say."

CHAPTER 2

Press Censorship

The three readings in this chapter give an historical perspective on press censorship. The first reading is an excerpt from John Milton's 1644 pamphlet *Areopagitica.* Milton, the author of *Paradise Lost* and the foremost English poet of his time (some believe of all time), wrote *Areopagitica* to protest censorship of printers and publishers. His pamphlet reflects the Puritan belief that humanity was placed on the earth to be tested by, and to choose between, truth and falsehood. The founders of our country were also influenced by these beliefs, which became part of our cultural heritage. Milton's articulation of these beliefs is still quoted today.

The second reading, Benjamin Franklin's "An Apology for Printers," illustrates some changes that Puritan beliefs had undergone by the time they influenced the American founders. Franklin wrote this explanation of the benefits of press freedom sixty years before the First Amendment was adopted.

The third reading contains some of Thomas Jefferson's thoughts on press censorship. Taken from a letter to his friend Edward Carrington, the piece includes his much-quoted statement, ". . . were it left to me to decide whether we should have a government without newspapers or newspapers without a government, I should not hesitate to prefer the latter." These sentiments preceded his presidency, however, an experience that seems to have hardened Jefferson somewhat toward the press (See Chapter 6).

The final item is a newspaper trade ad that features a quotation by Nikolai (also known as Vladimir Ilyich) Lenin, that highlights some differences between Soviet Communist and western democratic beliefs about press censorship.

AREOPAGITICA

John Milton

. . . Truth indeed came once into the world with her divine master, and was a perfect shape most glorious to look on: but when he ascended, and his apostles after him were laid asleep, then straight arose a wicked race of deceivers, who . . . took the virgin Truth, hewed her lovely form into a thousand pieces, and scattered them to the four winds. From that time ever since, the sad friends of Truth, such as dare appear, imitating the careful search that Isis made for the mangled body of Osiris, went up and down gathering up limb by limb still as they could find them. We have not yet found them all, Lords and Commons, nor ever shall do, till her Master's second coming; he shall bring together every joint and member, and shall mold them into an immortal feature of loveliness and perfection. Suffer not these licensing prohibitions to stand at every place of opportunity forbidding and disturbing them that continue seeking, that continue to do our obsequies to the torn body of our martyred saint. . . .

By John Milton, 1644, in Henry Morley, ed., *English Prose Writings of John Milton* (London: George Routledge and Sons, 1889).

. . . Give me the liberty to know, to utter, and to argue freely according to conscience, above all liberties. . . .

Let truth and falsehood grapple; who ever knew truth put to the worse, in a free and open encounter?

And though all the winds of doctrine were let loose to play upon the earth, so truth be in the field, we do injuriously by licensing and prohibiting to misdoubt her strength. Let her and falsehood grapple; who ever knew truth put to the worse, in a free and open encounter?

AN APOLOGY FOR PRINTERS
Pennsylvania Gazette, June 10, 1731

Benjamin Franklin

Being frequently censur'd and condemn'd by different Persons for printing things they say ought not to be printed, I have sometimes thought it might be necessary to make a standing Apology for my self, and publish it once a Year, to be read upon all Occasions of that Nature. Much Business has hitherto hindered the execution of this Design; but having very lately given extraordinary Offence by printing an Advertisement with a certain N.B. at the End of it, I find an Apology more particularly requisite at this Juncture, tho' it happens when I have not yet Leisure to write such a Thing in the proper Form, and can only in a loose manner throw those Considerations together which should have been the Substance of it.

I request all who are angry with me on the Account of printing things they don't like, calmly to consider these following Particulars.

1. That the Opinions of Men are almost as various as their Faces; an Observation general enough to

From *Voices of the Past: Key Documents in the History of American Journalism*, Calder M. Pickett (Ed.) Columbus, Ohio: Grid, Inc., 1977.

become a common Proverb, *So many Men so many Minds.*

2. That the Business of Printing has chiefly to do with Mens Opinions; most things that are printed tending to promote some, or oppose others.
3. That hence arises the peculiar Unhappiness of that Business, which other Callings are no way liable to; they who follow Printing being scarce able to do any thing in their way of getting a Living, which shall not probably give Offence to some, and perhaps to many; whereas the Smith, the Shoemaker, the Carpenter, or the Man of any other Trade, may work indifferently for People of all Persuasions, without offending any of them: and the Merchant may buy and sell with Jews, Turks, Hereticks and Infidels of all sorts, and get Money by every one of them, without giving Offense to the most orthodox, of any sort; or suffering the least Censure or Ill will on the Account from any Man whatever.
4. That it is unreasonable in any one Man or Set of Men to expect to be pleas'd with every thing that is printed, as to think that nobody ought to be pleas'd but themselves.

The opinions of men are almost as various as their faces. If all printers were determin'd not to print anything till they were sure it would offend no body, there would be very little printed.

5. Printers are educated in the Belief, that when Men differ in Opinion, both Sides ought equally to have the Advantage of being heard by the Publick; and that when Truth and Error have fair Play, the former is always an overmatch for the latter: Hence they chearfully serve all contending Writers that pay them well, without regarding on which side they are of the Question in Dispute.
6. Being thus continually employ'd in serving both Parties, Printers naturally acquire a vast Unconcernedness as to the right or wrong Opinions contain'd in what they print; regarding it only as the Matter of their daily labour: They print things full of Spleen and Animosity, with the utmost Calmness and Indifference, and without the least Ill-will to the Persons reflected on; who nevertheless unjustly think the Printer as much their Enemy as the Author, and join both together in their Resentment.
7. That it is unreasonable to imagine Printers approve of every thing they print, and to censure them on any particular thing accordingly; since in the way of their Business they print such great variety of things opposite and contradictory. It is likewise as unreasonable what some assert, "That Printers ought not to print any Thing but what they approve," since if all of that Business should make such a Resolution, and abide by it, an End would thereby be put to Free Writing, and the World would afterwards have nothing to read but what happen'd to be the Opinions of Printers.
8. That if all Printers were determin'd not to print anything till they were sure it would offend no body, there would be very little printed.
9. That if they sometimes print vicious or silly things not worth reading, it may not be because they approve such things themselves, but because the People are so viciously and corruptly educated that good things are not encouraged. I have known a very numerous Impression of Robin Hood's Songs go off in this Province at 2s. per Book, in less than a Twelve-month; when a small Quantity of David's Psalms (an excellent Version) have lain upon my Hands above twice the time.
10. That notwithstanding what might be urg'd in behalf of a Man's being allow'd to do in the Way of his Business whatever he is paid for, Yet Printers do continually discourage the Printing of great Numbers of bad things, and stifle them in the Birth. I my self have constantly refused to print any thing that might countenance Vice, or promote Immorality; tho' by complying such Cases, with the corrupt Taste of the Majority, I might have got much Money. I have also always refus'd to print such things as might do real Injury to any Person, how much soever I have been solicited and tempted with Offers of Great Pay; and how much soever I have by refusing got the Ill-will of those who would have employ'd me. I have hith-

erto fallen under the Resentment of large Bodies of Men, for refusing absolutely to print any of their Party or Personal Reflections. In this Manner I have made my self many Enemies, and the constant Fatigue of denying is almost insupportable. But the Publick being unacquainted with all this, whenever the poor Printer happens either through Ignorance or much Persuasion, to do any thing that is generally thought worthy of Blame, he meets with no more Friendship or Favour on the above Account, than if there were no Merit in't at all. Thus, as Waller says,

Poets lose half the Praise they would have got
Were it but known what they discreetly blot;
Yet are censur'd for every bad Line found in their
Works with the utmost Severity.

I come now to the Particular Case of the N.B. above mention'd, about which there has been more Clamour against me, than ever before on any other Account.—In the Hurry of other Business an Advertisement was brought to me to be printed; it signified that such a Ship lying at such a Wharff, would sail for Barbadoes in such a Time, and that Freighters and Passengers might agree with the Captain at such a Place; so far is what's common: But at the Bottom this odd Thing was added, "N.B. No Sea Hens or Black Gowns will be admitted on any Terms." I printed it, and receiv'd my Money; and the Advertisement was stuck up round the Town as usual. I had not so much Curiosity at that time as to enquire the Meaning of it, nor did I in the least imagine it would give so much Offence. Several good Men are very angry with me on this Occasion; they are pleas'd to say I have too much Sense to do such things ignorantly; that if they were Printers they would not have done such a thing on any Consideration; that it could proceed from nothing but my abundant Malice against Religion and the Clergy. They therefore declare they will not take any more of my Papers, nor have any farther Dealings with me; but will hinder me of all the Custom they can. All this is very hard!

I believe it had been better if I had refused to print the said Advertisement. However, 'tis done, and cannot be revok'd. I have only the following few Particulars to offer, some of them in my behalf, by way of Mitigation, and some not much to the Purpose; but I desire none of them may be read when the Reader is not in a very good Humour.

1. That I really did it without the least Malice, and imagin'd the N.B. was plac'd there only to make the Advertisement star'd at, and more generally read.
2. That I never saw the Word Sea-Hens before in my Life; nor have I yet ask'd the meaning of it; and tho' I had certainly known that Black Gowns in that place signified the Clergy of the Church of England, yet I have that confidence in the generous good Temper of such of them as I know, as to be well satisfied such a trifling mention of their Habit gives them no Disturbance.
3. That most of the Clergy in this and the neighbouring Provinces, are my Customers, and some of them my very good Friends; and I must be very malicious indeed, or very stupid, to print this thing for a small Profit, if I had thought it would have given them just Cause of Offence.
4. That if I had much Malice against the Clergy, and withal much Sense; 'tis strange I never write or talk against the Clergy myself. Some have observed that 'tis a fruitful Topic, and the easiest to be witty upon of all others; yet I appeal to the Publick that I am never guilty this way, and to all my Acquaintances as to my Conversation.
5. That if a Man of Sense had Malice enough to desire to injure the Clergy, this is the foolishest Thing he could possibly contrive for that Purpose.
6. That I got Five Shillings by it.
7. That none who are angry with me would have given me so much to let it alone.
8. That if all the People of different Opinions in this Province would engage to give me as much for not printing things they don't like, as I can get by printing them, I should probably live a very easy

Life; and if all Printers were everywhere so dealt by, there would be very little printed.

9. That I am oblig'd to all who take my Paper, and am willing to think they do it out of meer Friendship. I only desire they would think the same when I deal with them. I thank those who leave off, that they have taken it so long. But I beg they would not endeavor to dissuade others, for that will look like Malice.
10. That 'tis impossible any Man should know what he would do if he was a Printer.
11. That notwithstanding the Rashness and Inexperience of Youth, which is most likely to be prevail'd with to do things that ought not to be done; yet I have avoided printing such Things as usually give Offence either to Church or State, more than any Printer that has followed the Business in this Province before.
12. And lastely, that I have printed above a Thousand Advertisements which made not the least mention of *Sea-Hens* or *Black Gowns;* and this being the first Offence, I have the more Reason to expect Foregiveness.

I take leave to conclude with an old Fable, which some of my Readers have heard before, and some have not.

A certain well-meaning Man and his Son, were travelling towards a Market Town, with an Ass which they had to sell. The Road was bad; and the old Man therefore rid, but the Son went a-foot. The first Passenger they met, asked the Father if he was not ashamed to ride by himself, and suffer the poor Lad to wade along thro' the Mire; This induced him to take up his Son behind him: He had not travelled far, when he met others, who said, they are two unmerciful Lubbers to get both on the Back of that poor Ass, in such a deep Road. Upon this the old Man gets off, and let his Son ride alone. The next they met called the Lad a graceless, rascally young Jackanapes, to ride in that Manner thro' the Dirt, while his aged Father trudged along on Foot; and they said the old Man was a Fool, for suffering it. He then bid his Son come down, and walk with him, and they travell'd on leading the Ass by the Halter; 'till they met another Company, who called them a Couple of senseless Blockheads, for going both on Foot in such a dirty way, when they had an empty Ass with them, which they might ride upon. The old Man could bear no longer; My Son, said he, it grieves me much that we cannot please all these People. Let me throw the Ass over the next bridge, and be no further troubled with him.

Had the old Man been seen acting this last Resolution, he would probably have been called a Fool for troubling himself about the different Opinions of all that were pleas'd to find Fault with him: Therefore, tho' I have a Temper almost as complying as his, I intend not to imitate him in this last Particular. I consider the Variety of Humors among Men, and despair of pleasing every Body; yet I shall not therefore leave off Printing. I shall continue my Business. I shall not burn my Press and melt my Letters.

ON PRESS CENSORSHIP

Thomas Jefferson

. . . The people are the only censors of their governors; and even their errors will tend to keep these to the true principles of their institution. To punish these errors too severely would be to suppress the only safe-guard of the public of the public liberty. The way to prevent these irregular interpositions of the people is to give them full information of their affairs thro' the channel of the public papers, & to contrive that those papers should penetrate the whole mass of the people. The basis of our governments being the opinion of the people, the first object should be to keep that right; and were it left to me to decide whether we should have a government without newspapers or newspapers without a government, I should not hesitate to prefer the latter. But I should mean that every man should receive those papers & be capable of reading them. I am convinced that those societies (as the Indians) which live without government enjoy in their general mass an infinitely greater degree of happiness than those who live under the European governments. Among the former, public opinion is in the place of law, & restrains morals as powerfully as laws ever did anywhere. Among the latter, under pretence of governing they have divided their nations into two classes, wolves & sheep. I do not exaggerate. This is a true picture of Europe. Cherish therefore the spirit of our people, and keep alive their attention. Do not be too severe upon their errors, but reclaim them by enlightening them.

Were it left to me to decide whether we should have a government without newspapers or newspapers without a government, I should not hesitate to prefer the latter.

Letter to Edward Carrington, Paris, January 16, 1787, in Adrienne Koch and William Peden, eds., *The Life and Standard Writings of Thomas Jefferson* (New York: Modern Library, 1944), pp. 411–12.

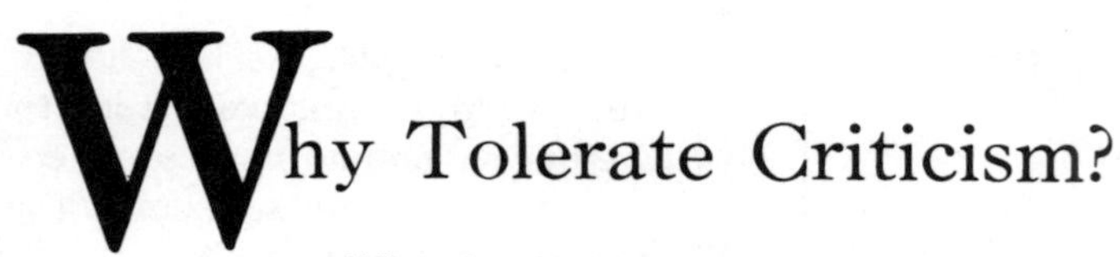

Why Tolerate Criticism?

"Why should freedom of speech and freedom of the press be allowed? Why should a government which is doing what it believes to be right allow itself to be criticized?
It would not allow opposition by lethal weapons.
Ideas are much more fatal things than guns.
Why should any man be allowed to buy a printing press and disseminate pernicious opinion calculated to embarrass the government?"

—*Nikolai Lenin*

THE CAPITAL CITY PRESS. PUBLISHERS

MORNING ADVOCATE **STATE TIMES** **SUNDAY ADVOCATE**

525 LAFAYETTE STREET BATON ROUGE, LOUISIANA 70821

SUGGESTIONS FOR FURTHER READING

Those interested in historical perspectives on press freedom might want to look at the following:

Leonard W. Levy, ed., *Freedom of the Press from Zenger to Jefferson*. New York: Bobbs-Merrill, 1966.

Harold L. Nelson, ed., *Freedom of the Press from Hamilton to the Warren Court*. New York: Bobbs-Merrill, 1966.

Calder M. Pickett, *Voices of the Past: Key Documents in the History of American Journalism*. Columbus, Ohio: Grid, 1977.

For an introductory analysis that stresses the current condition of the First Amendment, see Maurice R. Cullen, Jr., *Mass Media and the First Amendment*. Dubuque, Iowa: Wm. C.Brown, 1981.

CHAPTER 3

Ethics

The question of media ethics arises at various places in this book. The conflicts of government, public, and media rights discussed in Part Four, for example, can be interpreted as ethical issues.

But ethics deserves a chapter in its own right, especially in light of particular problems that have been publicized in the last few years.

The first reading in this chapter, an editorial by Horace Greeley, decries sensationalism, an ethical problem of long standing. Greeley became one of the giants of American journalism as editor of the *New York Tribune,* where this editorial appeared in 1849.

The second reading is an editorial that

appeared in the *Brooklyn Eagle* in 1901. The writer's attack on yellow journalism was aimed at William Randolph Hearst, who was engaged in a circulation battle with Joseph Pulitzer. The third reading is Joseph Pulitzer's statement of his "cardinal principles" of journalism.

In the fourth reading, David Shaw discusses some ethical problems that have recently come to light, as well as some attempted solutions. Shaw is a staff writer for the *Los Angeles Times,* where his article appeared in 1981.

In the fifth reading, Walker Lundy, the executive editor of the *Tallahassee* (Fla.) *Democrat,* relates ethics to credibility by outlining six reasons readers mistrust the press.

The sixth reading, by Janet Guyon of the *Wall Street Journal,* examines the ethical problem of advertiser control of media content. She gives several examples of how cigarette advertising affects the content of newspapers and magazines in which it appears.

Of course all media, not just newspapers and magazines, have their ethical problems. The final reading in this chapter brings up a problem that we haven't heard much about in recent years—payola. According to Steve Coll, this form of conflict of interest is not only alive, but thriving in the radio and recording industries. Mr. Coll, whose article appeared originally in *The Progressive* in 1982, is a Los Angeles free-lance writer.

ON "SATANIC" NEWSPAPERS

THE NEW YORK TRIBUNE
New York, February 17, 1849

Horace Greeley

The age we live in is remarkable for its multiplication and enlargement of all the agencies alike of good and evil. Life is more intense, more active, more eventful with us than it was with our grandfathers, and he who lives to see sixty years has really lived longer than the man who lived to eighty a century ago. Steamships, Railroads, Electric Telegraphs, Power-Presses, render communication so rapid that ideas circulate from mind to mind like the lightning, and are received in all the vivid energy of their fresh conception. . . .The moral world shares the new momentum of the intellectual and the physical, and transcendent virtues and revolting crimes are alike less rare than formerly. Philanthropy, Charity, Religion impel their votaries to unvented exertion; so do Lechery, Selfishness and Impiety. And foremost among the instrumentalities of these last stands THE SATANIC PRESS . . . .

[It] had its foreshadowings among the darkest days of atheistic butchery and terror in Revolu-

From *Voices of the Past: Key Documents in the History of American Journalism,* Calder M. Pickett (Ed.) Columbus, Ohio: Grid, Inc., 1977.

tionary France. . . . [It is the] perverted product of a diseased Civilization wherein debauched and prurient appetites gloat upon the unripe and poisonous fruit of the Tree of Knowledge. . . . It has one sole aspiration—to achieve notoriety and coin gold for its director by pandering to whatever is vile and bestial in a corrupted and sensual populace.

YELLOW JOURNALISM AND ANARCHY

THE BROOKLYN EAGLE
Brooklyn, September 11, 1901

The journalism of anarchy shares responsibility for the attack on President McKinley. It did not mean that he should be shot. It only wished to sell more papers by commenting on and car-

The journalism of anarchy shares responsibility for the attack on President McKinley.

tooning him as "a tyrant reddening his hands in the blood of the poor and filling his pockets and those of others with dollars coined out of the sweat and tears and hunger of helpless strikers, their wan wives, and their starving children." Today the journalism or the oratory which may have inspired Leon Czolgosz to his deed is the most tearful, sympathetic, and grief-stricken journalism or oratory in America. It editoralizes, interviews, and moralizes on the lovableness of

From *Voices of the Past: Key Documents in the History of American Journalism,* Calder M. Pickett (Ed.) Columbus, Ohio: Grid, Inc., 1977.

the man whom it lately and long and habitually portrayed as a monster, a despot, and a coward. It is very scared, very sorry—or very politic, or would like to seem to be so. Let us hope it is really sorry. Then let us hope that its sorrow will last long enough to persuade it that the selling of more papers or the getting of more votes is not the chief end of journalism or of oratory, when it leads one to defamation as a delight, to vilification as an industry, and to printed, pictorial, or platform blackguardism as a trade.

THE PLATFORM OF THE POST-DISPATCH

Joseph Pulitzer

I know that my retirement will make no difference in its cardinal principles, that it will always fight for progress and reform, never tolerate injustice or corruption, always fight demagogues of all parties, never belong to any party, always oppose privileged classes and public plunderers, never lack sympathy with the poor, always remain devoted to the public welfare, never be satisfied with merely printing news, always be drastically independent, never be afraid to attack wrong, whether by predatory plutocracy or predatory poverty.

This originally appeared on April 10, 1907. From *The Story of the St. Louis Post-Dispatch* (St. Louis: Post-Dispatch booklet, 1968, 9th ed.).

THE PRESS TAKES AN INWARD LOOK AT ITS ETHICS

David Shaw

She's Sally Field, movie star. In *Absence of Malice*, she's Megan Carter, newspaper reporter. Bright. Feisty. Tenacious. Unethical.

Megan Carter illegally wears a concealed tape recorder during an interview. She plunges into a sexual relationship with a man she's writing about. She betrays the confidence of at least one news source. She invades the privacy of another. She is so eager to rush into print with a story about a murder investigation that she blindly allows herself to be used by a ruthless prosecutor to blacken an innocent man's reputation—without making the slightest effort to investigate the prosecutor's story or to discover his motive (and without making more than a token effort to get the alleged suspect's side of what is actually a phony story).

When Carter is all through—well, almost all through—one innocent person is dead and several others are wretchedly unhappy.

'THERE MUST BE RULES'

"A lot of damage has been done, and I'm responsible for a lot of it," Carter says near the end of the movie. "I keep thinking there must be rules to tell me what I'm supposed to do now. Maybe not."

But there are rules—journalistic principles—and Carter has violated so many of them that even though Field often makes her seem sympathetic and vulnerable, most viewers will probably empathize with the man she first victimizes. . . . He is portrayed by Paul Newman.

Given the luster of these stars—and the essentially cynical view of the press embodied in this movie (written by a former newspaper editor)—*Absence of Malice* is almost certain to trigger anew both public discussion and private soul-searching about journalistic ethics.

> Are reporters ever justified in lying to get a story?

The film could not come at a more appropriate time.

Several well-publicized breaches of journalistic ethics have so besmirched the journalist's image this year that a *Times* reporter traveling around the country on a story recently was repeatedly greeted, by journalist and non-journalist alike, with the comment:

"Oh, you're writing about journalism ethics, huh? Tell me—have you found any?"

The question was asked only partially in jest.

No wonder:

—In April, a *Washington Post* reporter was forced to resign her job and surrender her Pulitzer Prize when it was discovered that her story about an 8-year-old heroin addict was a piece of fiction.

—In May, a *New York Daily* News columnist was forced to resign when he was accused of having fabricated a story about a clash between a British army patrol and a gang of youths in Belfast.

—In June, a *Toronto Sun* reporter was fired and another was forced to resign when it was revealed that they had no documentation for their story charging that a member of Prime Minister Pierre Elliott Trudeau's Cabinet had benefited from stock manipulations through inside government information.

SKEPTICAL PUBLIC VIEW

No wonder several polls in recent years have shown that most people don't rate journalists very high in terms of honesty and ethical standards. No wonder a *Washington Post* poll just last month showed that most people are "sharply critical of the national press"—in large part because of ethical considerations.

"I'm not too sanguine about our profession any more," says Michael J. O'Neill, editor of the *New York Daily News* and president of the American Society of Newspaper Editors.

Widespread evidence of such unethical behavior as bias, carelessness and sensationalism has left O'Neill discouraged, and his discouragement has been deepened, he says, by the refusal of many in journalism to adopt anything other than what he calls "a holier-than-thou attitude" toward their critics.

But most reporters and editors say recent press scandals are just isolated incidents—an unfortunate concatenation of unforgiveable *individual* acts that should not be used to indict an entire profession.

In one sense, they may be right.

By virtually any standard of measurement, the press today is more ethical—more responsible—than at any time in history. Most journalists are now well-educated and (at big-city papers) well-paid; they're respectable men and women working in a true "profession," and they generally demand far more of themselves and their peers in terms of ethical behavior than their predecessors ever did.

TOPIC FOR DISCUSSION

As syndicated columnist Nicholas Von Hoffman says, in an admitted oversimplification:

"In the old days in the newspaper business, almost everyone accepted free gifts and free trips and other freebies, and no one talked about ethics. Now, no reputable reporter takes anything free, and everyone's talking about ethics."

Indeed they are.

The press is more visible and more influential now, and that—combined with its often controversial coverage of the sociopolitical upheavals of the 1960s and early 1970s—has brought increasing public scrutiny and criticism.

The nightly network news shows—which made Vietnam "the living-room war"—now reach more than 40 million people every day. The major daily newspapers and weekly newsmagazines—almost all of them now divisions of massive communications conglomerates—help shape the national social, political and cultural agenda. Robert Redford and Dustin Hoffman (as *Washington Post* reporters Bob Woodward and Carl Bernstein) and Ed Asner (as television's Lou Grant) have helped turn journalists into celebrities, with all the glamour, prestige and potential for self-indulgence and public disenchantment that celebrityhood inevitably brings.

Thus, shocked by some journalists' recent betrayals of both professional obligation and public trust—and acutely aware of the damage this has done to the reputation of the press with an already skeptical public—many reporters and editors throughout the country are reexamining among themselves a whole range of ethical questions:

Are reporters relying too heavily on confidential or unnamed sources? Does the media unnecessarily invade the privacy of the people they write about? Is it fair for a reporter to reduce someone's thoughtful 30-minute speech to one colorful sentence for the evening news or the morning paper?

Are reporters ever justified in lying or misrepresenting themselves to get a story? Are reporters—and editors and publishers—compromised by certain personal relationships, business investments and social or political activities? Is the media ever justified in paying interviewees to cooperate on stories?

Does competition for readers, ratings, advertisers, fame and fortune induce some journalists to behave irresponsibly?

"You run into talk about journalistic ethics everywhere journalists get together these days," says Gene Goodwin, a journalism professor at the University of Pennsylvania. "You go to a bar now just to have a drink with some reporters, and you wind up talking about ethics."

But there is more than just talk going on.

Goodwin, for example, is writing a book on journalism ethics, and another new book on ethics—a 90-page book, *Playing It Straight*, by John Hulteng, a professor of communications at Stanford University—is already in widespread circulation in many newsrooms around the country.

Other academics are also assisting in the examination of ethical problems in journalism:

—Mark Pastin, a professor of philosophy at Arizona State University and a longtime teacher of business ethics, is planning a November ethics seminar for journalists, focusing in large part on the potential conflict between the social responsibility and the profit incentive of the press.

—Columbia University has taken over sponsorship of a series of Socratic seminars on the media and the law, confronting journalists, attorneys, judges and law enforcement officials with hypothetical ethical problems.

—Professors at Utah State University, Brigham Young University and the University of Kentucky are using psychological tests to study the relationship between an individual journalist's personal belief system and his response to ethical problems on the job.

There are other signs that journalists—long as resistant to self-examination as they are resentful of external criticism—are taking their ethical problems seriously.

PANEL DISCUSSIONS SET

There will be a two-day program in Chicago next month and a panel discussion in Los Angeles tomorrow night on ethics and investigative reporting.

Earlier this year, the Modern Media Institute in St. Petersburg, Fla. began trying to design an interdisciplinary program to guide publishers, editors and reporters in developing ethical standards

At the *Los Angeles Times*, six specially selected reporters who meet monthly with the paper's four top editors to discuss matters of policy and performance have raised such ethical questions in recent months as:

Was a *Times* story on a new drug-use trend irresponsible in giving a fairly explicit formula for the drug? Were several other *Times* stories insensitive and inflammatory in their depiction of black ghetto youths committing violent crimes in predominantly white suburbs? Are some of the paper's special advertising supplements misleading to readers? Was it appropriate for the publisher and editor of the *Times* to participate in a testimonial dinner given by the Times Mirror Co. for Sen. Howard Baker?

Elsewhere in the media:

—A National News Council in New York, a statewide news council in Minnesota and a community media council in Honolulu investigate public complaints of unethical (and other improper) activity by the media.

—Independent journalism reviews in New York, Washington, San Francisco and St. Louis criticize media performance.

—Ombudsmen at two dozen daily papers across the country now respond to readers' complaints and write both internal memos for their editors and periodic columns for their readers, criticizing their papers for unfair, inaccurate, irresponsible or unethical reporting.

—Several large newspapers (the *Seattle Times* and *Minneapolis Star* among them) regularly mail questionnaires to the subjects of stories in their papers, asking if the subjects think they were treated fairly and accurately.

—Hodding Carter III, former assistant secretary for public affairs in the State Department, is the host of a public television program called "Inside Story," a weekly critique of press performance that examined such ethical issues this year as bias, invasion of privacy, conflict of interest, sensationalism and irresponsibility.

Television journalism has also begun examining its own ethical standards:

—"Sixty Minutes" is scheduled to broadcast a program Sunday in which several prominent journalists criticize the show's interview and editing techniques.

—ABC last July broadcast "Viewpoint," the first of several programs providing critics of television news a public forum.

George Watson, whose duties as an ABC News vice president include supervision of "Viewpoint," says he is so concerned about ethics among journalists that he is trying to write a policy book for the network news division—"a code of conduct (to) define the principal areas of ethical concern."

CBS and NBC already have such codes. So do most major professional journalism organizations—the American Society of Newspaper Editors, the Associated Press Managing Editors, the Society of Professional Journalists (Sigma Delta Chi). An increasing number of individual newspapers, both large and small, also have written codes of ethics.

But there is no widespread agreement among editors that a code of ethics—or an ombudsman or a news council or an academic seminar or anything else—is the best way for the press to resolve ethical questions. These matters are now a subject of considerable, often heated debate in media circles.

DISAGREEMENT AMONG EDITORS

The top editors of the *New York Times* and the *Los Angeles Times* don't believe in written codes of ethics, for example, but the top editors of the *Washington Post* and the *Philadelphia Inquirer* do. The *Minneapolis Star* has a written code, the *Minneapolis Tribune* does not.

Of the 88 editors surveyed earlier this year by the Professional Standards Committee of the Associated Press Managing Editors, 58 said they had no written code of ethics.

Why not?

Many editors interviewed by the *Times* insist that a code is useless because it can't possibly cover every contingency a reporter or editor might actually encounter.

"We carry our code of ethics in our hip pocket," is the way one editor phrases his opposition to a formal, written code.

But pockets get frayed. They wear out. They develop holes. Some pants have very small pockets. Or no pockets at all.

"It's not so much the printed word (in a code of ethics) that has an effect as it is the wide participation of the people on the paper in discussing and drawing up the code," says Gene

Roberts, executive editor of the *Philadelphia Inquirer*.

Involving everyone in the process of developing a code has the effect of raising everybody's consciousness about the issues, and I think that's very healthy—and much more important than just getting a formal statement of policy or a written rationale that you can later use as a reason for firing someone who violates it."

PROBLEMS IN THE PAST

Roberts thought this heightened consciousness was essential at the *Inquirer* because in the 1960s, before he and the current ownership took over, unethical behaviour was pervasive at the paper; one *Inquirer* reporter was actually jailed for extorting money from his news sources.

But not all editors face such problems, and many editors are convinced that a code of ethics is neither necessary nor practicable.

Most codes are just "a bunch of platitudes" and self-evident prohibitions, says William F. Thomas, editor and executive vice president of the *Los Angeles Times*.

To Thomas, Roberts' argument that the development of a written code makes reporters more aware of ethical concerns is "nonsense . . . stupid."

"We all know we're supposed to be honest," Thomas says. "We all know we're not supposed to take free gifts from people who could be perceived as influencing what we do . . . . If you don't know . . . those things when you come here, then you don't deserve to be here.

"I don't like . . . codes of ethics . . . and other things like that which I think would look like we're denigrating the people we're handing them to," Thomas says. "I don't like to be treated like a child . . . and that's what those codes of ethics seem to say to me . . . . It's insulting.

"I've never seen a written code of ethics that wasn't so damned obvious that it was clear that you were doing it more for its outside PR (public relations) value than for any inward impact."

'BALONEY' OR NOT?

Although many editors say this view is naive and shortsighted—"a lot of baloney" in the words of *Milwaukee Journal* Editor Richard Leonard—many others agree with Thomas. Some of these editors also think an ombudsman is largely a public relations device—and they cite as evidence the 18,000-word report the *Washington Post* ombudsman wrote on the *Post's* Janet Cooke/Pulitzer Prize scandal in April.

In the report—published in the *Post* four days after the scandal broke—ombudsman Bill Green criticized *Post* editors for a number of errors, including their failure to demand that Cooke identify her sources for them.

For many readers, Green's report helped restore some of the credibility the *Post* lost when Cooke's charade was exposed. But many editors say—with considerable justification—that if the ombudsman system had worked properly, Green would have written about suspicions that Cooke's story was fictitious back when those suspicions were first voiced in the *Post* news room, shortly after her story was published, rather than waiting until the Pulitzer Prize announcement triggered public exposure of the sham.

Other editors have a more fundamental criticism.

"If they (the *Post* editors) had set up a system under which the first time Janet Cooke refused to divulge her sources to an editor, they would have fired her or stopped the story, that would have increased their credibility," says one editor. "But after the fact, if somebody comes along and says, 'I did it,' does that increase their credibility? That's false credibility."

"I do not believe in the ombudsman system," this editor says. "It's a red herring . . . a PR gimmick . . . a great way to get the editor off the hook."

When a *Times* reporter repeated these comments to Benjamin C. Bradlee, executive editor of the *Washington Post*, without naming the man who made them, Bradlee shook his head angrily, then laughed and said, "Terrific. Terrific . . . I'll just tell you, he's the editor of some paper that can't hold the *Post's* socks."

Wrong.

The man who made those statements about the *Post* is A.M. Rosenthal, executive editor of the *New York Times*. And Rosenthal is not alone in his criticism of the ombudsman as essentially public relations gimmickry.

Eugene Patterson, editor and president of the *St. Petersburg Times* and former president of the American Society of Newspaper Editors, is a longtime advocate of improved ethical standards for journalists. But after having had various ombudsmen over the past 10 years, Patterson fired his latest ombudsman last year and decided not to hire another.

'JUST WINDOW DRESSING'

"An ombudsman is just window dressing," Patterson says now. "Any editor who can't make value judgments on his own and make them correctly is in the wrong job."

Isn't that both self-serving and self-deluding, though? Isn't it possible that even an editor as excellent and as ethical as Patterson might make a mistake and not realize he'd made a mistake?

William Rusher, publisher of *National Review* and a charter member of the National News Council, says of Patterson's comments: "Anybody who thinks that about himself is halfway to the loony bin. That is exactly . . . the kind of pride that goes before a fall."

Bradlee also scoffs at Patterson's judgment on this issue.

"I just wish I were as wise as Gene," Bradlee says, grinning. Then he adds, "Every editor has got to be an ombudsman. You can't abdicate your responsibility for ethical judgments . . . but I tell you, I think he's just as wrong as he can be. . . .

"In monopoly situations (and more and more newspapers are in monopoly situations), an independent representative—some public embodiment of ethical judgment—is a useful tool for the public and a useful tool for the paper," Bradlee says.

"Most editors are scared of it (an ombudsman) because . . . as soon as you give somebody independence, you can get zapped."

ALL LINEN IN THE WASH

But newspapers "zap" other institutions; why shouldn't newspapers themselves be "zapped"? Why shouldn't the media wash its own dirty linen in public—just as they wash everyone else's dirty linen in public? Wouldn't that be both fair play *and* good public relations?

"Any editor who says he is his own ombudsman might succeed in fooling himself, but not the readers," says Barry Bingham Jr., editor and publisher of the *Louisville Courier-Journal*, the first paper in the nation to appoint an ombudsman (in 1967).

In fact, many critics say the attitude that Patterson, Rosenthal and most other editors have toward ombudsmen is typical of the arrogance of which the press is often accused.

"To Abe, the *New York Times* is a temple, and he is . . . its high priest and protector," says Lester Bernstein, editor of *Newsweek*. "Criticism of the *New York Times's* motivation . . . or performance . . . just shouldn't be done in Abe's view."

'POSTURE OF INFALLIBILITY'

Adds Robert Maynard, editor and publisher of the *Oakland Tribune* and a member of the National News Council:

"Our attitude . . . is appalling. . . . We have assumed a posture of infallibility, and we are afraid to let anybody ever look at what we're doing critically."

Quite so. And anyone who's written critically about the media knows that Bob Pisor, former press critic for television station WDIV in Detroit, is right when he says, "I doubt that anyone in the whole world is more sensitive to criticism than people in the media . . . especially newspapers."

But the refusal of most journalists to accept criticism gracefully or to acknowledge public accountability as an ethical principle can only intensify the resentment that many increasingly feel toward the press.

Is there a solution to this dilemma?

"We've tried to solve the problem . . . by having a reporter write about the media the way we write about other institutions—and that includes making critical judgments about what we do . . . and talking openly about our mistakes," says L.A. *Times* editor Thomas.

"But no other paper has done it that way . . . that comprehensively . . . on a regular basis."

Thomas insists that a story in the paper's news columns speaks with more authority than "one man's voice" in an ombudsman column on the editorial pages. Some critics say, however, that the L.A. *Times* approach is even more deceptive and cosmetic than the ombudsman concept, giving the illusion of accountability, without the substance of an ombudsman's independent editorial voice.

The most popular approach to editorial accountability these days seems to be in the establishment of new policies on correcting specific errors.

Until relatively recently, most newspapers tried to avoid publicly admitting any errors—or, if they did admit them, they did so in a sentence or two buried amid the advertisements for foot powder and trusses.

Now many newspapers have begun to publish regularly—indeed daily, in a prominent or consistent position in the paper—various corrections and clarifications of (and apologies for) their errors and oversights, whether of omission or commission.

QUESTION OF RECOURSE

But if an editor doesn't think his paper has made a mistake and he refuses to publish a correction—or if the correction he publishes is inadequate—people who feel they have been wronged by the paper still have no recourse.

Several months ago, for example, the *New York Times* published a financial column listing "some of the wealthiest individuals in the nation"—those who purportedly owned more than $100 million worth of stock in various American companies. The list included the name of William L. Cary, former chairman of the Securities and Exchange Commission.

"Mr. Cary, who now teaches at the Columbia University School of Law, has $130.5 million worth of United States Filter Corp. stock and earns $1.91 million in dividends annually," the story said.

Although the story described Cary's name as "perhaps the most surprising name on the list," the reporter who wrote the story apparently wasn't sufficiently surprised (or curious) to bother calling Cary to ask how he had managed to amass such a fortune.

Big mistake.

Cary never owned that stock. He was only the trustee for it, at a fee of about $25,000 a year, he says. When Cary complained, the *New York Times* published a correction, saying that Cary's stockholdings had been "incorrectly stated" and noting that he was only a trustee for the stock "and therefore does not share in the dividends."

But this brief correction, published amid other corrections resulting from the same story, did not really make clear that Cary had no equity interest in the stock, would not benefit from its sale and is not, in fact, a member of what that first *Times* story called "The $100 Million Club."

Because Cary has children, he says he was worried that the original *New York Times* story might make them seem lucrative kidnap/ransom targets. Because of his SEC service, he was worried that the story might lead some readers to assume that he had illegally enriched himself by using inside information he had gained while he had a sensitive government position.

There was nothing Cary could do about any of this, though.

The *Times'* Rosenthal says he did not know of this incident when it happened, but he concedes that if Cary's account is correct (which it is), the paper "should have had a corrective article."

'NOT DOING A JOB'

To Rosenthal, "poor handling" of a correction by the *New York Times* is "not a matter of ethics; it's a matter of somebody not doing a job very well . . . "

To Cary, however, the incident reflected what he sees as the all-too-common "high-handed" attitude the press takes toward those it covers, as well as toward those who criticize its performance or its ethics.

" . . . some kind of sanction beyond retraction may become more and more frequent unless the industry shows a willingness to discipline itself," Cary warns.

Those sanctions, most critics inside and outside the media agree, would probably take two forms—more punitive court rulings in libel cases (several of which have already been made) and more restrictive government regulation (which the press sees as the ultimate threat to its freedom).

Fred Friendly, formerly of CBS and now teaching journalism at Columbia University, says journalists who stubbornly resist self-regulation are behaving in much the same way that many businessmen behaved before passage of the Sherman Antitrust Act—and in so doing, they, too, risk inviting government intervention.

Are reporters ever justified in lying to get a story? Are reporters relying too heavily on confidential sources? Does the media invade privacy?

"I care a lot about the First Amendment," Friendly says, "but . . . because they (journalists) are not constitutionally Accountable (with a big 'A') to government, doesn't mean that they are not accountable (with a small 'a') to . . . their readers. . . .

"When newspapers get on their high horse and say, 'We're different from everybody else; we are accountable only to ourselves,' and that's somehow what the Constitution of the United States says, that's almost a blasphemy."

WHY DO READERS MISTRUST THE PRESS?

Walker Lundy

How do you feel about the phone company? Or the oil companies? Or politicians? Think about it. Chances are you don't trust those guys very much, and you're not alone.

Rightly or wrongly, lots of people see them as too big, too powerful and not answerable to anybody most of the time. They think the phone company's arrogant, the oil companies are greedy, and the politicians are lazy or incompetent or both.

Well, brace yourselves, brother and sister editors: *Lots of readers put newspapers right up there with those other guys*. And in lots of ways, we deserve it.

Newspapers *are* arrogant sometimes. "You ever try to talk to a newspaper?" Paul Newman asks rhetorically in *Absence of Malice*.

Many readers think complaining to a newspaper is pointless. We don't tell them whom to complain to, and if they do telephone us, they usually get a gruff, overworked news clerk who's making the minimum wage and doesn't give a hoot in hell about their beef. If they manage to get through to an editor, they often find that editor defensive and patronizing. Too often, it's like arguing with the umpire.

Sometimes it's a question of just plain good manners. For instance, when a newspaper takes a photo of someone and, for whatever reason, doesn't publish it, the person photographed—who perhaps went to some effort for the photo to be shot—is left wondering what happened. No one from the newspaper has time to call. That makes us look rude.

Newspapers are greedy sometimes, too. Most of us are the only unregulated monopoly in town, so we sure *look* greedy to lots of people. And we act greedy when we charge the highest advertising rates for such noncommercial items as death notices and political advertising. (And then editorialize sanctimoniously against the high cost of campaigning.)

Talk about greedy? Some papers even make a few bucks by charging to print wedding announcements. They aren't news, the editors claim. (It also has the unfortunate effect of eliminating poor people's nuptials from the paper.)

Even papers as prestigious as the *New York Times* and the *St. Petersburg Times* peddle part of their front page for ads.

Newspapers are lazy sometimes, too. Journalists can get pretty damned impressed with themselves. Why else do we have to wear black ties to the ASNE banquet? It is a fact that many journalists stop hustling at an early age. I know some who even have taken up *golf*.

Newspapers are incompetent sometimes, too. You ever listened to the complaints of people misquoted in your paper? You ever try to get Circulation to stop your paper when you go on vacation?

Perhaps we should all put aside our First Amendment speeches for a few moments and own up: We journalists will never see the newspaper business with anything but a warm, lifelong affection. That's our blind spot. Readers,

---

From the *Asne Bulletin* (March, 1982). Reprinted with permission.

however, don't have that handicap. To many of them, we're just another Big Business to be viewed with the same suspicions and mistrust. Some even think we're the worst of the bunch.

What reasons do we give readers to mistrust us? I can think of six. Some we can't avoid. But some we can:

1. We make too many errors.

Why don't newspapers have fact checkers? We have graphics editors and assistant managing editors for administration and ombudsmen for hearing about mistakes *after* they happen. But who's in charge of checking the facts *before* they're printed? Everyone, you say? We all know what happens when *everyone's* in charge of something.

Our concern for accuracy often amounts to writing that mother up and shoving it in the paper pronto. If it's wrong, we'll run a correction the next day on page 2. Give us "100" for honesty and "0" for accuracy. Average grade: "50."

If we expect to keep the readers believing us, we'd better develop a deeper commitment to getting things right the first time. We'd also better quit making up stories and using nameless sources, whose truthfulness is unknown to the readers.

Suggestion: Now that the writing revolution is old hat, why don't we adopt accuracy as the next Great Newsroom Cause?

2. We employ almost exclusively young reporters and editors who are liberal—politically and otherwise—and who don't reflect the range of our readership.

Mortgage rates are a big story for many of our readers, but how many members of your staff own homes? Education is an important issue, but how many members of your staff have children?

If I were a political conservative, I'd suspect the nation's press of bias. (How many anti-ERA columns have you read on editorial pages?) If I were a member of the Moral Majority, I'd be convinced we're biased. (How many pro-Moral Majority cartoons have you seen on editorial pages?)

If I were older than 50 and visited the average newsroom, I'd wonder how that paper possibly could relate to people my age. If I were black and attended the news meeting, I'd wonder why only white people were in charge. If your staff doesn't reflect the community, some readers will be less likely to believe what the staff has to say.

Suggestion: List balancing the staff as one of your recruiting goals and try to broaden the range of employees.

3. Most of us are monopolies.

Who doesn't love to hate a monopoly? For a newspaper, it's impossible sometimes not to rub people's noses in it. What do advertisers do when we make them so angry they want to take their business elsewhere? Where do readers go when they want to do the same thing? Some editors might say those people are free to quit us any time they want. But not in most communities, at least not if the advertiser wants to stay in business. And not if the reader wants to remain halfway informed about local news, or even what's playing at the movies or what supermarket has a special on toilet paper.

Suggestion: Have a system for making sure every complaint to the paper gets answered. Work hard at developing staff telephone manners. Demand that all employees be polite to everyone. Make it easy for complaining readers to get to the editors on the phone. When a reader phones, does your secretary ask, "Who's calling?" What difference does it make who's calling?

4. Most of us are large corporations.

Who doesn't love to hate Big Business?

Suggestion: Take time and space in the paper to explain yourself and your business decisions to your readers and customers. If you're having a subscription rate increase, make sure the story explains where the extra money's going and why.

5. We're our own sacred cow.

A newspaper is a pretty mysterious business for most people, and who trusts what he doesn't understand? Over the years, we've done a decent job of reporting on everyone's business but our own. Most people get their impressions of us from Hollywood.

Suggestion: The editor should write a regular column that tries to explain how the newspaper operates. Reporters should be assigned to cover the paper's news just like anyone else's.

6. A good, aggressive newspaper is often not a very likable institution.

Eventually, we get around to angering most people and organizations in town. We can't really avoid that, but we need to recognize that it also affects our credibility.

Suggestion: Insist that your staff be fair. Before you lambast somebody in an editorial, make sure you know in advance what that person's explanation is. Always get both sides. Check to make sure followup stories about the charges being dropped get the same play as the earlier arrest story. Do periodic spot checks to make sure your news report has balance. For example, pull the school beat reporter's byline file and see whether he's written any stories about what the school system's doing right.

We editors need to realize that many readers—perhaps a growing number—do not view our newspapers with the same warm trust that we do. They see us more as we see the other too-big, too-powerful monopolies in this country.

That's a problem we'd all better start trying to solve.

DO PUBLICATIONS AVOID ANTI-CIGARETTE STORIES TO PROTECT AD DOLLARS?

Janet Guyon

Paul Maccabee, an aggressive young reporter at the *Twin Cities Reader* in Minneapolis, was always alert to offbeat angles in his stories. So, when he covered a press conference announcing Brown & Williamson Tobacco Corp.'s annual Kool Jazz Festival last spring, he inserted an unexpected twist: a list of jazz greats who had died of lung cancer. The next day he was fired.

Carol Wheeler, a free-lance writer for *Savvy* magazine in New York, was listed on the magazine's masthead until last May, when *Savvy* published her review of a book titled *The Lady-killers: Why Smoking Is a Feminist Issue.* Miss Wheeler maintains that her name was subsequently striken from *Savvy's* masthead because its publisher feared offending tobacco-company advertisers.

Such incidents, while isolated, are cited by anti-smoking groups like the American Cancer Society as evidence of the tobacco industry's subtle yet powerful influence over what is—and is not—published about the hazards of smoking.

Although tobacco companies aren't accused of heavy-handed direct pressure on editors and publishers, critics contend that smaller and weaker publications especially may engage in self-censorship when it comes to the smoking issue. The sheer weight of the cigarette advertising budget, critics say, is enough to make some magazines and newspapers tread lightly when covering the negative effects of smoking, toning down stories or ignoring the issue.

CIGARETTES AND PRINT

Ever since cigarette commercials were taken off television in 1971, tobacco companies have bought a disproportionate amount of print-media advertising. The tobacco industry outspends all other national advertisers in newspapers, and cigarettes constitute the second-largest category of magazine advertising, behind transportation. According to the research firm Leading National Advertisers, eight cigarette companies spent $309 million last year on magazine advertising. The same companies bought $386 million of newspaper ads, according to the Newspaper Advertising Bureau.

Were it not for such outlays, anti-smoking activists suggest, the public would read far more bad news about smoking. John F. Banzhaf, the founder of the anti-smoking group Action on Smoking and Health, observes that although articles about teen-age drug use and drinking frequently appear, "I never see an article about where kids get cigarettes and what a parent group might do about it." He cites the fire hazard of smoking and new research on combating addiction as two areas that have been under-reported in the press. The American Council on Science and Health, a nonprofit group financed by various corporations and foundations, contends that magazines like the *Reader's Digest* and *Good Housekeeping* that refuse to accept cigarette advertising are much more aggressive in their coverage of the hazards of smoking.

THE LOCAL ADVERTISER

Cigarette makers pooh-pooh such charges. "Baloney," says William Kloepfer, senior vice president of the Tobacco Institute, the cigarette manufacturers' lobbying group in Washington. "The suggestion that buying an ad buys the judgment of reportorial people is a contemptible red herring." Adds Marty Orlowsky, the director of marketing services for R.J. Reynolds Tobacco Co., a Unit of R.J. Reynolds Industries Inc.: "We try very hard not to get involved in the editorial side of anything. We're very sensitized to that whole issue."

> Critics say the shakier ones at least soften the text.

The extent of advertiser influence on news has long been debated by journalists. It isn't unheard of, for example, for a newspaper to bury or kill a story detrimental to the local car dealer or grocery chain on whose advertising it depends. "The weaker a newspaper is, the more it's prone to influence," says Richard Gray, the dean of the journalism school at Indiana University. But he adds that such incidents are less frequent today than in the 1920s or 1930s, "when newspapers weren't as financially stable."

Because of the vast sums spent to promote cigarettes, because of the sophistication of the industry's media relations, and because smoking is highly controversial, cigarette makers are singled out for more criticism than most advertisers for their unspoken influence on the news. A look at how the industry places its ads, and how editors report on the smoking and health controversy, suggests that any big advertiser can, to a degree, blunt negative publicity about its product.

COSMOPOLITAN AND *Ms.*

The American Council on Science and Health periodically surveys magazines to compare their smoking coverage with the amount of tobacco advertising revenues they receive. The council's latest survey of 18 popular publications showed that those heavily reliant on cigarette advertising gave short shrift to the smoking issue.

The survey noted that *Cosmopolitan*, which derived 9.20% of its annual ad revenues from tobacco companies, published 155 articles on dieting between 1971 and 1981, but only eight on smoking. Among those taken to task for completely ignoring the issue were *Redbook* (where nearly 16% of ad revenues come from cigarettes) and *Ms.* (13.7%). Of *Ms.*, the study said: "The complete absence of articles on the hazards of smoking is particularly striking in this magazine which covers many other important issues in women's health."

Pat Carbine, editor and publisher of *Ms.*, says that the magazine has cited the hazards of smoking for women during pregnancy or when using the Pill. But its policy, she says, is to let its largely college-educated readers decide for themselves whether or not to smoke. Louis Porterfield, *Cosmopolitan's* publisher, says the magazine's stories about cancer do mention smoking. "We don't have a policy that we don't write about cancer and smoking because we take cigarette advertising. One isn't connected with the other," he says. Anne Mollenger Smith, editor of *Redbook*, calls the council's research "sloppy" and says she sent them copies of stories from *Redbook* that called smoking a health hazard. She says she demanded, but didn't get, an apology from the council. "Their attitude seemed to be if I wasn't campaigning against smoking, I had sold out to the tobacco industry," Mrs. Smith says.

A few years ago, Elizabeth Whelan, the American Council's executive director, wrote an article for *Harper's Bazaar* on the causes of cancer. The article led off with smoking. Jane Ogle, who was then the magazine's health and beauty editor, says that when Anthony Mazzola, the magazine's editor, saw the cancer story, he said, "Christ, Jane, I can't open this article with smoking." Mrs. Ogle says she moved the smoking segment to the end of the article, "so it wouldn't jump in the face of every cigarette advertiser."

Mr. Mazzola failed to return numerous telephone calls from this newspaper. But the magazine's current health editor, Denise Fortino, says the policy still stands. In a recent story about health hazards in the office, for example, three paragraphs devoted to smoking were condensed into one, she says. *Harper's Bazaar* last year received about $1 million, or 6.8%, of its ad revenues from cigarette companies, according to Publishers Information Bureau. Such spending represents "an unspoken pressure," Miss Fortino says, adding: "We do have to consider the advertisers, but we've still managed not to quench the story."

A publication that frequently crusaded against smoking could hardly hope to attract tobacco advertising. For cigarette makers—like liquor companies—are among the most persnickety about the editorial environment in which their ads appear. Says the advertising manager at a major Texas daily: "One is a poison and the other causes cancer, so they're very sensitive about it."

Most advertisers cancel ads when a news event reflects badly on their product. Airlines, for example, routinely instruct publications to drop their ads after a major airline crash. "It's a situation where you're in a very negative environment and you can better use your money later," a Delta Air Lines spokesman says.

Because cigarettes exist in a perpetually negative environment, tobacco companies take special pains to see that their ads don't call undue attention to that fact. They stipulate that cigarette ads can't run near obituaries, for example, or near news stories "antithetical" to smoking or tobacco. Should a publication fail to follow these guidelines, the tobacco company usually asks for—and gets—a "make-good," or free ad, as amends.

Until recently, Reynolds went even further: Outraging many editors, it asked to be notified in advance if a publication planned to run a negative story about smoking. Reynolds dropped its policy after it received critical scrutiny from the *Columbia Journalism Review* and after this newspaper inquired about it.

INFORMAL ALERTS

In practice, publishing and advertising executives say, big advertisers are often informally alerted in advance about stories that could be detrimental to their business. "Almost any publication that has a brain does it," says one adman.

Editors and publishers insist that this practice doesn't inhibit them from printing a negative story. Larry Martz, an assistant managing editor at *Newsweek*, says: "If the magazine is going to run a cover story on the newest advances in the surgeon general's attitude on cancer or alcoholism, the ad guys who have that account may call up the advertiser and say, 'Charlie, I don't think you want to run this week.'" However, Mr. Martz says, "It doesn't mean editors are under any pressure not to run articles on alcoholism or cancer. The editorial side doesn't even know that call was made."

Smaller publications aren't so well insulated from advertiser influence. Thus, when Mark Hopp, the publisher of the 100,000-circulation

Twin Cities Reader, saw Mr. Maccabee's devastating article on the Kool Jazz Festival, he was furious. Mr. Maccabee had quoted an American Cancer Society spokesman calling the festival "a PR ploy to give respectability to cigarettes." The 26-year-old reporter also wrote that cigarettes are linked to such ailments as Buerger's disease, "a degenerative nicotine-lined condition which leads doctors to amputate toes and feet one at a time, like snipping grapes off a vine. Definitely not sexy. Definitely unKool."

Mr. Hopp felt Mr. Maccabee had editorialized too much. And, he concedes, he feared losing the paper's cigarette ads. "We're not big enough to change an issue like this," Mr. Hopp says. "The paper is a local publication whose job is to cover local events. We will not cover national, international or social issues." The paper's national sales manager wrote to all its cigarette advertisers, apologizing for the story and informing them that Mr. Maccabee had been fired.

At *Savvy*, Wendy Crisp, the editor, says she neglected to read Miss Wheeler's review before it appeared in the May issue. When it ran, she says, the magazine worried that its tone might offend cigarette advertisers. Miss Wheeler's name was removed from the masthead.

Mrs. Crisp concedes that she told Miss Wheeler that her name was dropped because of the review, though she says other factors were involved—including prior disagreements between the writer and Alan Bennett, *Savvy's* publisher. (Mr. Bennett declines to be quoted on the matter.)

Mrs. Crisp says she worried that *Savvy's* competitors might show the review to cigarette companies as a way of grabbing their business. "*Savvy* isn't a primary buy," she says. "It took one guy a whole year to get the Reynolds account. We're a very young magazine, and I don't want to get hurt by one lousy book review." As in the case of the *Twin Cities Reader*, the publisher acted without any pressure from advertisers.

The controversy surrounding smoking has forced tobacco companies to become increasingly ingenious in promoting their products. Sometimes, they have enlisted the help of the nation's press. For over a year, for example, Reynolds has "sponsored" the daily sports results appearing in some 72 newspapers across the nation. Reynolds buys the space devoted to the scores—previously regarded as editorial matter—and surrounds them with a flashy border touting Camel cigarettes. These "Camel Scoreboards" contain the slogan: "Camel. Where a Man Belongs," as well as the surgeon general's warning about smoking's hazards.

The Lorillard unit of Loews Corp. currently is running ads in this newspaper called "Kent Sports Business," which contain stories about the business side of sports, and also feature pictures of Kent cigarette packages and the Surgeon General's warning.

Philip Morris Inc. has become a news source by conducting "The Merit Report," a public-opinion survey on a variety of issues. The results are distributed to newspapers and television stations in hopes of a mention. The object is to help Merit cigarettes gain greater public recognition.

Even though some editors are wary of anti-smoking stories, it's difficult to argue that the public is unaware of the hazards of cigarette smoking. A 1978 Roper poll showed that more than nine out of every 10 Americans believed smoking endangers a smoker's health. Editors argue that because the smoking-and-health story has changed little since the surgeon general's report in 1964, there has been a dearth of smoking news to cover. "I think you have to be pretty dense not to know there's some health risk associated with cigarette smoking," says *Newsweek's* Mr. Martz.

AGAIN, PAYOLA

Steve Coll

When Congress came to Hollywood last spring to sniff out rumors of widespread cocaine use and influence-peddling in the film and television industries, it was greeted with something less than a gala reception. Studio executives, directors, and actors joined in unusual solidarity to brand the House subcommittee hearings a "witch hunt." Tinsel Town withheld its star witnesses and sent the embarrassed Representatives back to Washington without a trace of the scandal they came looking for.

In another quarter of the entertainment industry, however, some insiders are calling for a Congressional investigation. They claim the recession-plagued record industry is resorting to the "payola" methods of the 1950s in an effort to boost album sales. In particular, the finger is being pointed at independent record promoters, who, some say, are using illegal payoffs to line up radio airplay in crucial markets for client record companies and performers. Large sums are going for bribes and special favors that win the hearts of radio programmers—and that ultimately shape our musical tastes, deciding for us what music we will hear and which records we will buy.

The specter of the middleman paying radio programmers to make a song a hit has haunted the record business from its birth. "The Government has tried over the years to investigate payola," one independent promoter with over two decades in the business says. "All they've come up with is a few Judases to put on pedestals to take the rap for an awful lot of people. I think they've given up hope, and by doing so they've given the radio and record business a license to steal."

In fact, the only effective investigation of payoffs in the record business took place more than twenty years ago, when Representative Oren Harris of Arkansas chaired a special House subcommittee during the 1959–1960 Congressional session. For months, revelations of payoffs and corruption in the television and recording industries were splashed on newspaper front pages across the country. The committee found that most of the day's popular television quiz shows were rigged, and that top disc jockeys in cities like New York, Boston, and Los Angeles were on the take, receiving regular "salaries" from record promoters in exchange for airplay for certain albums or songs.

Some indictments resulted. Peter Tripp, the most popular DJ in New York City at the time, was charged by the Justice Department with accepting bribes, as was Hunter Hancock, a renowned jock in Los Angeles. Alan Freed, who has since been immortalized in film as the "father" of rock 'n' roll, was fired from a prestige-laden job at WABC in New York because he refused to sign a statement saying he had never accepted money for putting a record on the air.

It was clear, though, that the revelations only scratched the surface of the payola problem. During the hearings, scores of record distributors and promoters confessed to handing out bribes to get music on the air. "We didn't think the

---

payoffs were illegal," says one promoter who was working in New York at the time. "They were routine. When I went out on the road I picked up an envelope from the distributor that was filled with hundred dollar bills. It was my job to hand them out as I saw fit."

Though grand juries handed down few indictments, the publicity generated by the Congressional investigation did force some reforms. Most important, radio stations began to give programming and music directors sole responsibility for deciding what would go on the air. The disc jockey became nothing more than an air "personality," with little or no control over what made it to the turntable. The number of potential bribe-takers was smaller; in-house accountability for radio stations increased.

The most sweeping change in the record business since the days of the Harris Committee, however, was unrelated to the industry's black eye; nor did it herald reform. From a handful of maverick outfits, the industry has swollen into a world-wide corporate network dominated by multinational entertainment companies. In the last two decades, annual U.S. record sales have shot up from hundreds of thousands to hundreds of millions. Conglomerates like Warner Brothers-Elektra-Atlantic gross tens of billions of dollars in yearly revenue. The pop music world of open request lines and obscure all-night disc jockeys is gone, replaced by a new order of formulaic, superstar programming and "multi-platinum" album sales.

The growth over the last fifteen years of album-oriented FM radio, programmed for the huge twenty-five-to-forty-year-old record-buying market, helped set off the record sales explosion of the 1970s. Sales are slumping now, but the big labels still regard radio as the best way to reach consumers; air time for new releases thus remains the single most important means of pitching a record. A relative pittance is spent on advertising on television or in other media.

But air time is not directly purchased like radio spots for other goods and services. It isn't for sale—that's illegal. Programming directors *supposedly* select music to play for the enjoyment of the listener and promoters are sent in to influence their choices.

As radio airplay became the keystone of record company marketing strategy, the importance of the independently contracted promoter grew by leaps and bounds. Successful independent promoters boast special access to station programming directors in particular regions or cities. Often, they align themselves with a certain label or contract themselves to promote the albums of several artists or groups.

'I know one programming director who was offered a night in L.A. with a vial of cocaine and a woman. And that was in the suburbs, not a big market.'

Record promoters work with radio programming directors in much the same way lobbyists stroke politicians: They treat them to expensive meals and supply them with services designed both to increase a station's audience and to ensure exposure for a new album. Often enough, the largesse includes giveaway albums and concert tickets as listener bait.

This kind of influence is expensive, even in the eyes of big-time labels with deep pockets. Retainers for independent promoters can run in the tens of thousands of dollars per record per week—a far cry from the cash-stuffed envelopes of yore. Once the fees are paid, record companies have no way of accounting for how the money is spent—and no responsibility if some of it goes for bribes. The only results they see are tallies in airplay charts published regularly by music trade papers such as *Billboard* and *Radio & Records*.

Since the companies rely solely on the trade sheets to find out what kind of airplay their singles and albums are getting nationally, promoters devote their efforts to the handful of major stations that report their playlists. This set-up places tremendous pressure on both the programming directors of these stations and on the promoters who must get results from them. Further, the trades do not monitor the reporting stations and have no way of knowing whether what is reported to them actually reflects the stations' choices. This gap in the reporting system allows independent promoters extra "flexibililty" when lobbying for airplay of their records; it is not the playlist but the trade report that counts in the end.

All this concentrates an enormous amount of money and power in the hands of a small number of independent promoters and radio programmers. Ostensibly, the large sums are the salaries the promoters command because of their access to the right people. But programmers and promoters alike acknowledge that the retainers record companies cough up for independent promotion often hide the costs of taking care of key programmers' "habits"—and outright cash bribes. And since the payoffs are made by independents—and not by staff promoters—it is difficult to implicate record companies in any illegal doings.

Says one independent promoter on the West Coast, "I know one programming director who was invited by a promoter to spend a night at the Bonaventure Hotel in L.A. with the promise that a vial of cocaine and a woman would be provided for his amusement. He turned [the offer] down because he knew it'd be a long time paying it back. But the amazing thing is that he's PD [programming director] at a secondary station in the *suburbs,* not in a big market."

This throwback to the payola days both coincides with and grows out of the record industry's current doldrums. Since 1977 and 1978, when sales of such albums as *Saturday Night Fever* and *Fleetwood Mac* surged to almost fifteen million and seemed to promise nothing but rosy futures, sales figures have declined steadily. Label staffs have been cut back across the board, and the industry's notorious expense accounts have been fitted with bottoms. Several big labels have gone under; others are on the way down.

As for radio promotion, the prolonged slump has created a mood of desperation. For some companies, the success of a single new release by a well-known artist may mean the difference between profit and loss. So despite their enormous fees, prominent independent promoters have become even more important to record companies. "No one trusts anyone," says one independent promoter. "People have become more desperate because of the sales slump. Some of the tactics have gotten almost obscene."

Said another promoter, "There is what I call a 'Gang of 12' out there who have a direct line into key programmers' offices. They are by far the most important promoters in their regions. They can *guarantee* airplay. But there are a lot of guys out there carrying around a lot of things besides records to get records on the air."

For their part, record company executives admit that promoter fees are high, but most see them as a necessary marketing cost. A few labels, including Columbia and Elektra Records, claim they are phasing the independents out of their promotion budgets altogether. "It has simply gotten to be too expensive to carry on," says Bill Smith, national singles promotion director for Elektra. Smith says that the decision to drop the independents was purely a business one.

That does not mean that such top-selling Elektra artists as the Eagles or Jackson Browne will release new albums without the benefit of high-powered independent promotion. Artists' managers often pay for promotion out of their own pockets—as do some artists themselves.

It is an odd characteristic of corporate capitalism that when a market begins to dry up or stiff competition looms, large businesses retrench rather than retool. That is exactly what the record business has done since its recession began. By pouring money desperately into radio promotion, the corporate labels have fostered corruption under their own roofs—and ensured that the trend of declining record sales will continue.

General economic circumstances probably triggered the decline. Since 1978, consumers have been spending less on entertainment in general; records are among the first discretionary items passed up. But the companies gave momentum to the downward slide by raising record prices as much as 60 per cent in the last two years. In part, the increase reflects the rise in the price of oil-based vinyl, but it can also be chalked up to bad planning: Record companies jumped to cash in on the mega-platinum sales of the mid-1970s with higher prices. Some believe that the price hikes alone have caused the recession. Says Bob Delanoy, a manager of several major retail outlets in California, "Record prices are fragile. I think they've reached a breaking point where they've priced the middle-income consumer out of the market."

Companies can spend tens of thousands of dollars pushing an album to key people in radio before the public has heard one cut.

If inflation made times hard, though, the companies have made them harder by emphasizing one-on-one promotion over advertising at the consumer level. Companies can spend tens of thousands of dollars pushing an album to key people in the radio industry before the public has ever heard one cut. If the record is a bomb, the outlays can be suicidal. And even if the music sells, these business practices drive the price up because they increase overhead but do nothing to stimulate new sales growth.

Still, the corporate labels continue to pour money into radio promotion because that is what brought them success in the first place. In Hollywood, where there is always hope for a redeeming blockbuster, old ways of doing things die hard. Why change anything, when somewhere around the corner there may lurk an idea or an artist who will rejuvenate consumer interest (a la *Star Wars* in the movie world) and set the snowball rolling once again? If only the Beatles could regroup . . . even just the three of them . . . And so the industry retrenches, waiting for the big one.

In the meantime, arguments for "retooling" present themselves in the operations of the hundreds of small record companies that have sprung up across the country during the last few years. These labels concentrate on artists whose music lacks the broad commercial appeal necessary to justify the enormous costs of old-style radio promotion. The new companies ignore corporate radio altogether because they cannot afford high-priced promoters. Instead, they identify narrow markets and invest in more direct approaches: television and print advertising, extensive touring and live performances, regional marketing, and grass-roots publicity campaigns. In general, these smaller companies are flourishing, though their profits are certainly not on the scale of the large corporate labels.

The majors can learn a great deal about alternative marketing strategies from the newcomers. In fact, several big, established labels have signed distribution agreements with some of the more prosperous small-timers, and others have formed "satellite" labels where new talent can be developed and tested, even with limited marketing resources. But when it comes to the bread-and-butter acts, the major labels are relying on schmoozy, big-dollar radio promotion more than ever.

The corruption and diversion of resources that

this strategy engenders distorts the kind of music we hear and shapes our preferences. It is virtually impossible for any small company to break the hold that independent promoters have on radio in the major cities. And the record companies will develop only those acts which fit easily into the constricted formats that evolved as radio programming itself became a profitable corporate endeavor. For consumers, the result is stale, utterly predictable repetition of popular musical styles. Innovation is rare, and never so radical as to upset the system of radio marketing.

Only in Hollywood, where all sins are atoned for by success in our media culture, could such corruption and inefficiency flourish. Undoubtedly, a renewed Government investigation of payoffs in the record industry would meet the same indignation and resistance that greeted the last Congressional touring party to visit the city of bright lights. But such an inquiry would at least shake the record business out of its rotting complacency, something music lovers everywhere deserve.

SUGGESTIONS FOR FURTHER READING

Since both publications and writers have a professional interest in media ethics, there are always good current articles dealing with the topic. A good example from a few years ago is Ken Auletta's "Bribe, Seduce, Lie, Steal: Anything to Get the Story?," *More: The Media Magazine* (March 1977), pp. 14–20. A good book on the topic is *Questioning Media Ethics*, Bernard Rubin, ed., New York: Praeger, 1978.

Also of interest:

Jessica Mitford, *Poison Penmanship: The Gentle Art of Muckraking*. New York: Random House, *1980*.

Lee Thayer, ed., *Ethics, Morality, and the Media: Reflections of American Culture*. New York: Hastings, 1980.

CHAPTER 4

Violence

Early in May 1982 the United States government released a report stating that "violence on television does lead to aggressive behavior by children and teenagers who watch the programs." The report was meant to update the well-known U.S. Surgeon General's report of 1972. Our first two readings are representative samples of the various editorial opinions on the 1982 study. They are followed by Dr. Thomas Elmendorf's 1976 speech before the House Subcommittee on Communications. Dr. Elmendorf was testifying as the California delegate to the American Medical Association, and his speech is still one of the clearest and most straightforward statements on the relationship between violence and TV.

In spite of the strong evidence against TV, its effect on societal violence remains a controversial issue. An article by psychologist Jerome J. Lopiparo, "Aggression on TV Could Be Helping Our Children," suggests that TV violence might actually be a beneficial "safety valve" that helps reduce societal aggression.

After television, movies have been closest to the center of the violence controversy. In the movie *The Deerhunter,* the intense, dream-like quality of the movie seems to have made one violent episode—the Russian roulette scene—especially powerful. Showings of the film—first in theaters and later on television—were followed by real incidents of Russian roulette and subsequent tragedies. Peter Koper, a New York-based writer, discusses the phenomenon in his article "Can Movies Kill?"

Nor is the violence controversy limited to TV and movies, as we are reminded in the chapter's final reading, "Is Rock the Music of Violence?" by John Rockwell. Rockwell is a music critic for the *New York Times.* His article appeared in that paper in December 1979, a few days after eleven young people were killed at a rock concert in Cincinnati.

ON THE UPDATE OF THE SURGEON GENERAL'S REPORT

EVENING EXPRESS
Portland, Maine, May 7, 1982

A newly issued federal report suggests that "overwhelming" scientific evidence now exists to link violence in television programs directly to aggressive and violent behavior among children.

In fact, evidence that has emerged from the report so far is decidedly unscientific. So is any suggestion that TV must do a job which rightfully belongs to parents.

There's nothing new about findings that blame popular diversions for everything that may be wrong with American kids. The line stretches back through time from video games to rock 'n' roll, comic books, chewing gum and Saturday afternoons at the movies. Over and over again, however, the blame stops short of where it belongs: on the inattention of parents.

So it is with the federal report, "Television and Behavior: 10 Years of Scientific Progress and Implications for the Eighties," based not upon new research, but upon 2,500 studies and publications of varying merit that have appeared since 1970.

Every television set comes with a channel selector, and an off-button as well.

The basic point which the report makes is obvious. And it just as obviously makes sense. Surely no one would argue that every program on television is suitable viewing for kids. Certainly television is open to criticism for excessive violence and attention to sex.

Just as surely, however, there's more needed in the lives of children who are allowed to become heavy, unselective television watchers than merely reprogramming an appliance. Television sets are not babysitters. They should not be misused that way.

Every television set comes with a channel selector, and an off-button as well. It's up to parents to use them—and to insist their children learn to use them well.

THE CINCINNATI POST
Cincinnati, Ohio, May 12, 1982

Violence has been a part of storytelling since cavemen sat around the fire describing the day's hunt. Where would Shakespeare be without it?

But many people have long felt that there is too much of it coming off the electronic fire we gather around today, the television set. Not only too much but the wrong kind—gratuitous violence that is not dramatically necessary but merely pads out flimsy plots.

It can't be good for kids.

Now a new report by the Department of Health and Human Services, reviewing 10 years of research into the subject, concludes that the "great majority" of studies show that there is, indeed, a causal relationship between televised violence and aggressive behavior by children and teenagers.

That's bad enough. But what may be even more alarming is the finding that too much of any kind of television can have an adverse effect on viewers.

The report cites one five-year study of 732 children in which aggressive behavior—conflict with parents, fighting, delinquency, etc.—was positively correlated with the total amount of television viewing, not just viewing violent programs.

Unfortunately, "parents do not seem to restrict the amount of time their children spend in front of the television set, nor do they usually prevent them from looking at certain programs," says the report.

On the optimistic side, research also shows that television has the potential to do a lot of good by teaching constructive social behavior in children.

The question is, how do you make the good as attractive as the bad? As long as junk "sells," the networks will continue to provide it, and television will continue to teach, not just children but adults as well, a distorted view of the world.

VIOLENCE ON TV

The Effect on Children

Dr. Thomas Elmendorf

Suppose you sent your child off to the movies for three hours next Sunday. And three hours on Monday and the same number of hours Tuesday, Wednesday, Thursday, Friday and Saturday. That is essentially what is happening to the average child in America today, except it is not the screen in the movie house down the street he sits in front of, it is instead the television set right in your own home.

According to the Nielsen Index figures for TV viewing, it is estimated that by the time a child graduates from high school he has had 11,000 hours of schooling, as opposed to 15,000 hours of television. I would like to repeat that. By the time a child is 18 years old, he has spent more hours in front of the television set than he has in school. Over TV he will have witnessed by that time some 18,000 murders and countless highly detailed incidents of robbery, arson, bombings, shooting, beatings, forgery, smuggling and torture—averaging approximately one per minute in the standard television cartoon for children

Speech before the House Subcommittee on Communications, Los Angeles, August 17, 1976. From *Vital Speeches of the Day* (October 1, 1976). Reprinted by permission.

under the age of ten. In general, seventy-five percent of all network dramatic programs contain violence with over seven violent episodes per program hour.

> Television has become a school of violence and a college for crime.

Concurrent with this massive daily dose of violence over our television screens has been a dramatic rise in violence in our society. In 1973, 18,000 young Americans from 15 to 24 years of age died in motor-vehicle accidents, with one of every six of these fatalities estimated to be due to suicide. In 1973, more than 5,000 were murdered, and an additional 4,000 committed suicide. The death rate for this age group was 19 percent higher in 1973 than in 1960, due entirely to deaths by violence.

The largest rise in deaths by homicide during the past two decades was at the ages of one to four. More than a million American children suffer physical abuse or neglect each year, and at least one in five dies from mistreatment. It is a social problem of epidemic proportions.

In fact, murder is the fastest growing cause of death in the United States. The annual rate of increase exceeded 100 percent between 1960 and 1974. Our homicide rate is 10 times greater than in the Scandinavian countries. More murders are committed yearly in Manhattan, with a population of one-and-a-half-million, than in the entire United Kingdom, with a population of 60-million.

The age group most involved, with the greatest number of both victims and arrests, is 20 to 24. In 1972, 17 percent of all homicide victims and 24 percent of all arrests were in this age group. Teenagers from 15 to 19 account for another nine percent of all murder victims and nearly 19 percent of the arrests. In commenting about such crimes by youths, one author said, "It is as though our society has bred a new genetic strain, the child-murderer, who feels no remorse and is scarcely conscious of his acts."

What is to blame for these heinous statistics? What are the chances that this trend of rising violence can be controlled and reversed? The probabilities are small unless something is done about the moral and socioeconomic environment in which our young people are growing up today in America. One thing is certain. For a considerable proportion of American children and youth, the "culture of violence" is now both a major health threat and a way of life.

We of the medical profession believe that one of the factors behind this violence is televised violence. Television has become a school of violence and a college for crime.

Let us take a look at some of the evidence. The Surgeon General of the United States has said, based on a six-volume study of the problem, that "there is a causative relationship between televised violence and subsequent antisocial behavior, and that the evidence is strong enough that it requires some action on the part of responsible authorities, the TV industry, the government, the citizens."

This report was a twin to the Surgeon General's report on smoking. This report on TV violence, in effect implied, "Warning: The Surgeon General Has Determined That Viewing of TV Violence is Dangerous to Your Health."

Much of the report has been clouded in dispute, so that its full impact has not reached society as effectively as it could. Let me point out just one of the disputes. The committee responsible for summing up the evidence gathered said that the 23 studies of the report, done by renowned scientists, provide "suggestive evidence in favor of the interpretation that viewing violence on television is conducive to an increase in aggressive behavior, although it must be emphasized that the causal sequence is very likely applicable only to some children who are predisposed in this direction." This has led critics to downgrade the report and say that violence on TV really only affects those already aggressive individuals, anyway. I would like to say to that, so what? If it makes aggression-prone people more aggressive, that is enough to make me say something should be done about violence on TV. But what is even more alarming is what the Surgeon General said about those predisposed to violence. He said that television can *cause* the predisposition. This point has been overlooked. So, televised violence can increase a child's aggressive behavior, especially if he has a predisposition for aggression. And, in addition to this, the predisposition itself can be caused by the viewing of TV.

Dr. Robert M. Liebert, associate professor of psychology at the State University of New York at Stony Brook, concluded in a overview of several studies of the report that "at least under some circumstances, exposure to television aggression can lead children to accept what they have seen as a partial guide for their own actions. As a result, the present entertainment offerings of the television medium may be contributing, in some measure, to the aggressive behavior of many normal children. Such an effect has been shown in a wide variety of situations."

And earlier in the report he said, "Experimental studies preponderantly support the hypothesis that there is a directional, causal link between exposure to television violence and an observer's subsequent aggressive behavior."

Let us go beyond the report to other findings. Dr. Albert Bandura of Stanford University set out to determine what happens to a child who watches as aggressive personalities on television slug, stomp, shoot and stab one another. His research team reached two conclusions about aggression on TV: 1, that it tends to reduce the child's inhibitions against acting in a violent, aggressive manner, and, 2, that children will copy what they see. Dr. Bandura points out that a child won't necessarily run out and attack the first person he sees after watching violence on the screen, but that, if provoked later on, evidence suggests that then he may very well put what he has learned into action. The reasons that children do not indiscriminately copy their TV characters is that parents suppress any such learning that they don't consider desirable—that is, the children get punished—and children rarely have access to weapons necessary for showing off what they have learned. "If," says Dr. Bandura, "they were provided with switchblade knives, blackjacks, explosives, six-shooters and nooses, it is safe to predict that the incidence of tragic imitative aggression connected with television viewing would rise sharply."

One of the lessons of television is that violence works. If you have a problem with someone, the school of TV says to slap him in the face, stab him in the back. By aggressive acts, the bad guy, for example, may gain control of grazing land, gold mines, nightclubs, and perhaps the whole town. Not until the very end is he usually punished. And, as in the case of *The Godfather*, parts one and two, punishment may never really occur. Because most of the program has shown how well violence has paid off, punishment at the end tends not to have much of an inhibitory effect.

"From these findings," Dr. Bandura says, "we can conclude that if children see the bad guy punished, they are *not* likely to imitate spontaneously his behavior. But they do acquire—and retain—concrete information about how to behave aggressively, and punishment of the bad guy does not make them forget what they have learned. They may put into practice this knowledge on future occasions if they are given adequate instigation, access to the necessary weapons and the prospect of sufficiently attractive rewards for the successful execution of the behavior."

Other studies have shown that viewing violence blunts a child's sensitivity to it. They become jaded to violence on the screen. They condition themselves to avoid being upset by the gougings, smashings and stompings they see on TV. If they *did* get involved, their emotions could be shattered.

What about the long-term effects of violence on TV? Researcher D. J. Hicks found that even eight months after viewing a violent episode only once, almost half of all the children could act out again what they had seen so long ago. In 1955, Dr. Leonard Eron, head of research for the Rip Van Winkle Foundation, looked into the long-range correlations between a child's favorite television program, the program's violence content and the aggressiveness of the child as reported by his classmates. The project, which covered a span of about 10 years, from age eight to 18, was later picked up by the Surgeon General's study on TV violence. The investigators found a strong correlation between the early viewing of television violence and aggressive behavior in the teenage years. In fact, according to the study, a child's television habits at age eight were more likely to be a predictor of his aggressiveness at eighteen than either his family's socioeconomic status, his relationships with his parents, his IQ or any other single factor in his environment. The report concluded that a preference for violent television at a young age leads to the building of aggressive habits.

As equally alarming as these studies are the findings of researcher George Gerbner, dean of the Annenberg School of Communications at the University of Pennsylvania. He said, "Anyone who watches evening network TV receives a heavy diet of violence. More than half of all characters on prime-time TV are involved in some violence, about one-tenth in killing." Because of this, TV breeds suspicion and fear. The report said, "People who watch a lot of TV see the real world as more dangerous and frightening than those who watch very little. Heavy viewers are less trustful of their fellow citizens."

To cope with this fear the heavy watcher also gets a thick skin. He becomes conditioned to being a victim. He becomes apathetic to violence. Gerbner concludes with the observation that "acceptance of violence and passivity in the face of injustice may be consequences of far greater social concern than occasional displays of individual aggression."

So, we have a two-edged sword. Television violence tends to make some people more violent, and others it makes more willing to accept violence as a way of life.

All in all, 146 articles in behavioral science journals and related reports, representing 50 studies involving 10,000 children and adolescents from every conceivable background, all showed that viewing violence produces increased aggressive behavior in the young.

The accumulation of evidence suggests, as you have heard, that children will copy TV violence, that they often do *not* do so because of parental control and lack of access to weapons, that TV teaches a child that often violence succeeds and that problems can be solved by violence, that viewing TV violence blunts sensitivity to violence in the real world, that children remember specific acts of TV violence, and that prefering violent television at an early age leads to more aggressive teenage behavior.

What happens when these children grow up? There should be further studies on this. In-depth studies. What happens when these children grow up and no longer are under parental control, when they are conditioned into thinking that violence works, and when they have a diminished sensitivity to violence? What happens to these children when they grow up and *do* have access to weapons? What happens when they grow up in a world apathetic to violence?

Is it any coincidence, then, that our real world is looking more and more like the violent world of television? Sadistic, ingenious murders, hijackings, kidnappings, ransoms—news reports are sounding like TV plots. Many of us are questioning whether this resemblance is more than coincidental. In fact, a surprising number of bizarre crimes have been committed by young people who admit they were influenced by television.

There is no doubting the power of TV. Possibly no other innovation of the twentieth century has so affected our daily lives. More than cars, planes, radios, movies, and appliances, TV is the most likely to alter our living patterns. Studies have shown that TV has reduced the amount of time we spend visiting and entertaining friends. We read fewer books and see fewer movies. Leisure time for such things as sports and hobbies has been reduced. We go to bed later because of TV, and we spend less time on household care, play and conversation. It has changed our meal time, and most of us use it as an "electronic babysitter."

The response of the television industry has been generally to uphold the need for violence because violence is what keeps the Nielson ratings up. They say themselves that the network is run by salesmen, and that violence sells.

The TV industry has just recently made some effort to control the content of violence by instituting the "family viewing hour," and for that we applaud the industry. But there are indications that violence is merely being diverted to other hours, not reduced. And the "family viewing hour" is in jeopardy: the concept is being challenged by a Writers Guild lawsuit as censorship and in violation of free speech.*

Violence may make money for television, but it should not be made at the expense of our children. And I am not so sure that only violence makes money. The National Citizens Committee For Broadcasting recently released a report saying that according to their ratings the 10 least violent programs are successful network offerings with high ratings.

Based on the evidence that has been developed, the American Medical Association recently authorized a remedial course of action. The AMA will publish a booklet that will emphasize parental responsibility for their children's viewing and will indicate what to look for in terms of suitable programming.

Is it any coincidence that our real world is looking more and more like the violent world of television?

AMA will explore with the National Association of Broadcasters the possibility of convening periodic joint conferences on the impact of TV on children. It will support full funding of research by the National Institute of Mental Health on the influence of television. AMA will urge television stations, in deciding on program content and scheduling, to use violence indexes, which are being prepared by various groups.

We of the medical profession agree with Dr. Liebert when he said that "the most potent, the smoothest way to change television is through even a small minority of citizens who give the impression that they are going to react negatively to content."

That is why the American Medical Association at its recent annual meeting, acting on a resolution introduced by the California delegation, has declared violence on TV an environmental health risk and has asked doctors, their families and their patients to actively oppose programs containing violence, as well as products and services of the sponsors of such programs.

In other words, if you, as a parent, see something on TV that you feel is too violent for your child to watch, turn the TV off or change the channel, and don't buy the products of the firms that support the program through their advertising.

*Editor's note: The "family viewing hour" *was* found unconstitutional, and it was abandoned.

AGGRESSION ON TV COULD BE HELPING OUR CHILDREN

Jerome J. Lopiparo

In this age where adults are constantly being told that most of the exotic foods we eat are bad for us, anything that intoxicates is harmful, and our government is not as gloriously above reproach as we once believed, it should not come as any surprise that a lot of people are saying that our children's favorite diversion is bad for them too. However, in view of the fact that a child born today will, by the time he or she is 18, have spent more of his or her life watching TV than in any other activity except sleep, the subject of TV aggression deserves a long, hard look.

What kind of TV program offers children the most fascination? Which ones do they sit looking at in excited wonder? It does not take a great deal of expertise to pick either the horror (or monster) movies or the "shoot-em-up" crime shows. This applies not only to television, since violent, aggressive plots are the favorites of children, whether they be in movies, cartoons, or comic books. It seems that, the more gore the program has, the more they like it.

Are these presentations of violence and aggression really hurting our youngsters? The National Commission on the Causes and Prevention of Violence stated in 1969 that:

> It is reasonable to conclude that a constant diet of violent behavior on television has an adverse effect on human character and attitudes. Violence on television encourages violent forms of behavior and fosters moral and social values about violence in daily life which are unacceptable in a civilized society.

This statement is but one example of the highly speculative and naive warnings we have all heard. To attribute to TV the sole responsibility for the unfortunate state our "moral and social values" are in smacks of closed-minded scapegoating.

THE ROOTS OF VIOLENCE

To begin with, let us all agree that we live in very violent times. The Vietnam conflict, the Arab-Israeli wars, and the disastrous murder of the Olympic athletes are only a few examples. Still, can we recall any period in recent history when we were without violence? In the 1960s, we experienced the tragic assassinations of the Kennedys, while, in the 1950s, we almost became involved in a war in Lebanon, in addition to the horrors of the Korean war. Few of us could foresee the terrible precedent that would be set by the abortive attempt on President Truman's life in that same decade. The 1940s saw us involved in a worldwide holocaust, while the 1920s and 1930s were the setting for Dillinger, the Capone gang, and the emergence of that weapon many foreigners still see as a symbol of mid-America—the machine gun. We could go on and on, but can we say with any degree of validity that one era was any more violent than another? Suffice it to say that everyone has been so busy getting on the bandwagon to ban violence on TV that perhaps, in the confusion, our understanding of children and the basic processes underlying their behavior has become muddled.

It seems that behavioral scientists have been wrestling with the causes and effects of violence forever. Freud believed that man is instinctually aggressive and that within all of us there is a drive leading us either to destroy ourselves or, if the aggression is directed outward, to destroy others. Konrad Lorenz, renowned for his studies of animal behavior, makes an even stronger point. He feels that human aggressiveness is biologically caused, becoming a destructive force through the shaping and molding of our society. He warns that this aggressive energy literally swells within us and, sooner or later, simply explodes in the form of destructive behavior. The frightening implication about Lorenz's theory is that this aggressive energy needs no special stimulus to set it off (although humans usually find no difficulty encountering triggering stimuli), and so its dangerous quality is further enhanced by its unpredictability. A consideration which is most important in terms of our television-viewing child is that *both* of these scientists agree that to fail to express this inborn aggression can have negative effects.

CHILDREN AND AGGRESSIVENESS

If aggression reposes within all of us, whether we choose to believe it to be instinctual or caused by the circumstances of living in our society (as the behaviorists would have us believe), how are we to manage it? To answer this, let us look at the confused way that most parents perceive aggression. A parent soon discovers that aggression is a chauvinistic phenomenon. Boys are allowed—if not openly encouraged—to show anger and to be assertive. Girls—women's liberation notwithstanding—are still being advised by their parents that aggressive behavior is not wholly appropriate for a female. Certainly, when aggression manifests itself in physical violence, it usually becomes an exclusively male prerogative.

Most psychologists working with school-age children will tell you that parents—fathers included—will be quite disturbed when they are told that their son has been exhibiting aggressive behavior. They will generally assure you that they will put a quick stop to it. How? Why they will spank the child, of course. It should not come as a surprise then that the child, in complete innocence and, when you think about it, with complete justification, later explains that his approving authority, his role model for his aggression, is none other than his parents! It becomes analogous to the satirical commentary of the "peaceniks" about our efforts in Vietnam:

"We'll teach them to be peaceful even if we have to fight and destroy every last one of them to do it."

> Many of the frustrations children feel can be worked out via the TV screen.

Can a child develop normally if he does not experience aggression? It is generally agreed that some aggression in a child is a desirable thing, since it is one of the most effective ways of expressing independence. When we stifle this behavior, we may be cheating the child out of opportunities to experience his potential as a developing human being.

Another beneficial aspect of a child's expressing aggression is the very fact that he is expressing it, and therefore is not holding his feelings in. A potential danger lies with the child who inhibits his outward displays of aggression in the sense that, if we are not careful, he may direct them inward. The consequences of this may be seen in excessive nail-biting, deliberate pulling out of hair, depression, or self-abasement.

POSITIVE ASPECTS OF AGGRESSION

Earlier, I cited the negative aspect of aggressive-behaving parents, but, if the aggression is toned down a bit and assertiveness is substituted, a very positive situation may take place. The child who perceives his parents as assertive may derive a feeling of security from it, related to a sense that his parents will obviously be well equipped to *protect him* should danger threaten their home. Thus, the hostile world may be a little less frightening for him.

Probably the most important reason aggression must be part of a child's life is that it helps him cope with his feelings of powerlessness. Children do not feel powerful! They do not feel that they can effect change either in their own lives or in the lives of others. If they want to do something, they must ask an adult; if they want something changed, they have to hope adults feel the same way, for that is the only way it is going to happen. It is for this reason that children are drawn to TV violence. Many of the frustrations they feel can be very effectively worked out via the TV screen. It is safe, the person you're attacking cannot retaliate, you can be a hero or a villain with just a flip of the dial, and, most important, you can experience that elusive feeling of *power!*

Closely tied in with the quest for power, aggression has also been linked with what Dr. Gregory Rochlin, a prominent psychiatrist and author of a recent text on aggression, terms our "narcissistic balance." He believes that, when something threatens our accomplishments, our relationships with others, or puts our system of rewards in jeopardy, our self-respect is in danger of being lowered. When self-respect is affected, our "narcissistic balance" may be impaired, and aggression usually is the result. Are any of the foregoing conditions probable in a child's life? There seems little disagreement that they are. We thus uncover another potential source of the aggression we are so ready to lay at the doorstep of violent television programs.

What has been said here is óbviously not the last word on the subject of media-depicted aggression. Most psychologists will tell you that there is a small minority of individuals who have a predisposition for violence, and, when they see it portrayed on a TV screen, it may well trigger overt aggressiveness. This is not an area of dispute. What is argued, however, is the fact that most critics have failed to advise the public of the positive aspects of media aggression for the vast majority of children *and* adults who are *not* on the brink of violent behavior, but who, nonetheless, need the vicarious release these programs provide. Perhaps the bulk of the difficulty lies in our unwillingness to accept the premise that within all of us—child and adult alike—there reposes a potential for violence, TV or no TV. Once this is accepted, we may then be more receptive to the notion that the *expression* of this aggression, whether via fantasy or outright overt behavior, is not only normal, but, in many respects, quite beneficial. What we are then left with is the possibility that the aggressiveness our children watch on TV may actually be *reducing* overt expressions of violence, rather than increasing them as the critics would have us believe.

CAN MOVIES KILL?

Peter Koper

On a cold Thursday night last November, Ted Tolwinski sat in the living room of his modest four-room apartment near Chicago and watched *The Deer Hunter* on television. Leaning forward on the couch, he stared intently as two American soldiers, played by Robert De Niro and Christopher Walken, were taken prisoner by the Vietcong, held in half-submerged cages infested by large, hungry water rats, and forced to risk their lives in a game of Russian roulette for the amusement of their captors. The two prisoners survived and escaped, but toward the end of the film, Tolwinski watched another scene, even more harrowing. De Niro returns to Saigon to rescue his buddy and finds Walken, now hooked on heroin, voluntarily playing Russian roulette in a sleazy gambling den. Ignoring De Niro's anguished protests, Walken points the large revolver at his head one last time, pulls the trigger, and blows his brains out.

On the following Saturday night, Tolwinski went out with an old pal he hadn't seen in a while and they got drunk. The friend had a gun, which they locked in the trunk of Ted's car while they barhopped. Returning home later that evening, Ted carried the gun into the apartment and woke his wife. He sat at the kitchen table, took some bullets out of the gun, and placed them on the Formica tabletop. Assuring his wife that there was nothing to fear, the twenty-six-year-old tool-and diemaker and father of two sons spun the cylinder, pointed the gun at his head, and pulled the trigger. Nothing happened. Then he did it again. His wife tried to take the gun away from him, but Ted kept insisting there was no danger. Looking into her eyes, he spun the cylinder, placed the muzzle against his head, and pulled the trigger a third time. The gun went off, shattering the quiet of the early morning hour with ear-splitting finality.

Russian roulette is a curious game. Reputedly invented by czarist soldiers to allay their boredom at cold, remote outposts, the game represents the final gamble. Only one person need play and the rules are simple—load a revolver with a single live round, spin the cylinder, put the muzzle to your head, and squeeze the trigger.

The Russian roulette player must bring to the game a peculiar attitude toward the basic question of existence. A person who commits suicide presumably wants death, and a person who does not destroy himself chooses life. The Russian roulette player, however, is uncommitted, tossing the decision to fate. In this sense, the game requires a sort of mad courage, or an awesome suspension of judgment that most people would call insane, absurd, or just plain stupid.

"I think those scenes [in *The Deer Hunter*] influenced him," says someone who knew Ted Tolwinski well. "Maybe he wanted to prove he could do it, that it was only a game. He liked fantasy, he thought he would be a hero, that he could win—just like it happened in the movie."

Michael Cimino's *Deer Hunter* was a critical and box-office success, winning five Academy Awards after its 1978 release. Everyone who has seen the film remembers the chilling Russian roulette scenes. But what is even more chilling is the contention that in real life at least thirty-one persons, purportedly influenced by the film, played the game themselves. Three of them sur-

From *American Film* (July/Aug., 1982). Reprinted by permission.

vived, but when Ted Tolwinski shot himself that Saturday night, he became one of an estimated twenty-eight men and boys who did not.

"In 1980 we started to notice that *The Deer Hunter* was being followed around by death," recalls Linda Talbott of Handgun Control, Inc., an antihandgun lobby in Washington, D.C. The organization uses a clipping service to collect information on gun-related deaths, and Talbott began to pull out reported incidents of Russian roulette that could be tied to *The Deer Hunter*. These incidents have raised questions about the influence of film and television on audience behavior, the availability of handguns, First Amendment rights . . . and the role of violence in the media.

Twenty-eight people died from playing Russian roulette—apparently after watching *The Deer Hunter*.

It is certainly not news that there are millions of "vidiots," whose eyes are glued to the cathode-ray tube. The pervasive, and largely uncharted, influence of television is obvious—it is an overwhelmingly powerful force in the acculturation of children. In the average American home the television set is on six and a half hours a day, and in many homes, it is kept on day and night—a murmuring, flickering presence that babysits children and keeps adults company. The result is that the images of television, and film, become a shared experience in the society. Small children reenact scenes in their play, young boys run around city streets punching the air with kung-fu chops . . . and soap operas are the currency of continual chit-chat.

Critics like Talbott argue that television and *The Deer Hunter* proved to be a lethal combination. The Universal film is syndicated by MCA-TV, and when it was offered to the networks in 1979, all three turned it down because of the graphic violence in the crucial Russian roulette scenes. MCA-TV sold the rights to Home Box Office, which ran it nationally in May and June of 1980. The film was also offered to independent broadcast stations, and was aired in Chicago, Los Angeles, Philadelphia, New York, Washington, D.C., and San Antonio, among other localities.

According to Talbott, Handgun Control alerted WOR-TV in New York to the controversy surrounding the film and worked with the station in preparing announcements to warn viewers about its violent content. The value of such announcements is dubious, however, since they may have the opposite effect of waving a red flag to attract the attention of the morbidly curious. "WOR still had two deaths following its airing of the film," says Talbott.

Freddy Saganowski was one of them. An eighth-grader at Holy Cross School in Trenton, New Jersey, Freddy was a typical thirteen-year-old, complete with braces on his teeth. The first signs of puberty were playing on his face—a little fuzz on the upper lip, a few pimples. Freddy enjoyed fishing, roller skating, riding trail bikes. He displayed a talented hand with draftsmanlike drawings of rock-group logos, such as those of Styx and Kiss. He was crazy about cops and cars, and, naturally enough, his favorite television shows were "Starsky and Hutch," "The Dukes of Hazzard," and "CHiPs." His favorite movie stars were Clint Eastwood and Burt Reynolds.

"That Halloween he dressed like a policeman; he wanted to be like the guys in 'CHiPs,'" recalls his mother, Lucia. She and her husband brought up their two boys as good Catholics; their First Communion pictures hang on the imitation wood-paneled walls. An aquarium gurgles peacefully next to the large console television set.

The Saganowskis live in a small, tidy frame house. The neighborhood brings to mind the fictional Pennsylvania factory town in *The Deer Hunter*. Hardworking families live on clean, modest streets; workingmen's bars are situated on many of the corners; and the smokestacks of the Home Rubber Company darken the end of the road, two blocks from the Saganowski's house.

On November 4, 1980, Freddy and his brother, Johnny, watched the first of two parts of *The Deer Hunter* being broadcast on WOR. "We talked about how bad they had it there, and about when they started playing the Russian roulette," remembers Johnny. Two weeks later, Johnny and Freddy were home alone after school in their upstairs bedroom. Freddy found his father's unloaded .38 Police Special in a closet. He picked up a bullet and loaded it into the cylinder. Putting it up to his head, he looked at Johnny, who was laying back on the bed watching, and pulled the trigger. The gun went off.

"I'm pretty sure he got the idea from the movie," speculated Freddy's father, Godfried. "And sometimes he wanted to show off a little bit. He probably said, 'Ah, I can do the same thing like in the movie.' He probably took the gun out and wanted to be a tough guy. He wanted to show Johnny how to do it."

Johnny, who is soft-spoken and reticent in front of strangers, believes that Freddy put the bullet in directly to the right of the chamber, thinking that the cylinder would revolve clockwise. But when the trigger is pulled on a .38 Smith & Wesson, it moves the cylinder counterclockwise. So when the hammer came down, it hit the live round.

After the tragic incident, Freddy's friends at school, under the direction of their social studies teacher, formed a group to protest violence and sex on television. They even took a bus to WTAF-TV in Philadelphia to protest its scheduled showing of *The Deer Hunter*. "They didn't want to talk to us. They locked themselves in and they didn't want to hear us," says Mrs. Saganowski.

Mr. Saganowski, a large man who at home wears a white T-shirt and slippers, says that he was offered a cable television service but turned it down. "Like things are nowadays, with these TV programs, especially now with cable TV, they are showing more violence and more sex. What can you do?"

In August 1980, Handgun Control began sharing its information with the National Coalition on Television Violence (NCTV), a group that monitors television and film, urges consumer boycotts of products advertised during violent shows, and lobbies for less violence in the media. Both organizations now keep a running list of persons they claim to be victims of Russian roulette incidents attributed to the influence of *The Deer Hunter*. They begin in February 1980, and the victims range in age from eight to thirty-one, and reside in fifteen different states. Many station managers, broadcast executives, and communications scholars are skeptical of the lobbyists' claims, and argue that to demonstrate a convincing correlation between *The Deer Hunter* and the deaths, each case must be looked at individually. An examination of a random sampling drawn from one list reveals circumstances as various as the individuals involved. Some incidents seem clearly related to the viewing of the film; others seem entirely unrelated.

Matt Cianciulli III, a Philadelphia teenager, shot himself last November 4 while playing Russian roulette at his kitchen table while a friend looked on—the same day *The Deer Hunter* aired on Channel 29. But his father points out that when the tuner was checked, it was on Channel 3. He blames sensation-mongering reporters for making the connection between the film and his son's death.

David Radnis's case is similarly inconclusive. The twenty-eight-year-old self-employed plumber watched the movie with his wife in their suburban Woodridge, Illinois, home. Two days later, the couple argued and the wife left the house.

Drunk, Radnis called some friends, who came over to talk; as they sat around the kitchen table, he abruptly walked into his bedroom and returned with a revolver. "He had one slug in the gun; then he put it up to his head one time and it clicked. The second time he did it, the bullet was in there," says a member of the Radnis family who denies that there was a connection between the viewing of *The Deer Hunter* and the fatal game. According to the same source, Radnis had a drinking problem.

But Brian Jackson, also twenty-eight, died leaving his relatives convinced that there was a connection between the film and his death. A plating-plant worker who had been stationed in Germany during a three-year army stint, he had recently purchased a videocassette recorder, and one of the first cassettes he bought was a copy of *The Deer Hunter*. Shortly thereafter, he invited his parents over to his home in South Holland, Illinois, to see the movie.

The technological cat has been let out of the bag, and both guns and violence in media are a part of the modern landscape.

Jackson, who worked nights, arrived at his brother's house around six o'clock one morning in January 1981. He was carrying an unloaded Colt .357 Magnum revolver, a powerful weapon. He woke his brother up, fixed himself a vodka and orange juice, and started to tell about having played Russian roulette in the service. He demonstrated with the unloaded gun, and then went back to his car and retrieved a hollow-point bullet. Back in the kitchen, he loaded the bullet into the cylinder, having a little trouble snapping it shut. Leaning against the kitchen counter and looking at his brother, he shot himself.

"*The Deer Hunter* seemed to hit home with a lot of people. Because the things the fellows did, the whole crowd that hangs around in taverns and things like that," says Elizabeth Jackson, Brian's mother. "I think it had a lot more meaning than the violence in other movies." She adds, "When I saw *The Deer Hunter*, I could see the young guys hanging around and the things they were doing. I could feel that that was part of my son, too—and his crowd." She describes her son as being "a close person; he held a lot in."

Although Mrs. Jackson believes the film had some connection with her son's fatal actions, she also notes that "film or no, you've got to have some common sense of what's going to happen to you. Hell, I'm a fatalist, but I don't run out in front of a car to see if it's my day."

Included in the NCTV and Handgun Control lists of alleged *Deer Hunter* Russian roulette shootings are the three survivors, one of whom is Stewart Robinson, a Muncie, Indiana, boy who was one day short of his twelfth birthday at the time of the episode. Stewart had seen the movie on HBO within a month of the time he played the game—June 1980. A healthy boy who is big for his age, Stewart was a bit of a show-off. He took three other boys to an upstairs bedroom in his home and showed them rifles that his father had in a gun rack. Trying to impress his friends, Stewart decided to show them the fully loaded .38 Police Special kept on the top shelf of a closet. He took out five rounds, spun the cylinder, put the gun to his head, and pulled the trigger.

The bullet entered Stewart's skull in the upper left portion of his forehead, at the widow's peak. It traveled through the frontal lobe of the brain and exited in the upper rear portion of the skull. Miraculously, Stewart survived. "He still doesn't have full use of his left side," reports Jan Robinson, the boy's father. "We didn't know if he could walk again for a while. He's made a remarkable comeback."

He adds that the rifles were unloaded but that the revolver was kept loaded for security. "I've had both my sons out shooting, trying to teach them gun safety, this kind of thing. I thought he was at the age when we wouldn't have to worry, that he'd know better than to play with it."

Stewart, who is still somewhat clumsy but continues to play energetically with his friends, hasn't said much about the incident. Doctors told the family that because of the trauma involved, he may never remember exactly what happened. His parents still don't know for sure if he was actually intent on playing the game or if it was an accidental pull of the trigger.

Stewart's father is convinced that the movie was connected with his son's actions. "In my mind," he says, "I'm sure that's where he got the idea. He never heard of Russian roulette or anything like that until he saw that movie. I've never been one to police them that much, because I always thought they were levelheaded enough and intelligent enough to take TV with a grain of salt, and not identify with the violence." The revolver, he adds, is "not available any more."

Just as television sets have become pieces of furniture as familiar as chairs and tables—indiscriminately spewing out an unending collage of images into our living rooms—guns have likewise come to occupy a familiar place in the American home. The gun is as common a household object as a spatula. The technological cat has been let out of the bag, and both guns and violence in media are a part of the modern landscape.

John W. Hinckley, Jr., the twenty-seven-year-old who shot President Ronald Reagan in the spring of 1981, found easy access to a gun and reportedly told his attorneys that the idea to assassinate the president occurred to him after he had seen *Taxi Driver*. Hinckley even claimed that his bizarre behavior was an effort to win the affection of Jodie Foster, the actress who starred as a young prostitute in that movie.

What appears to be a contagion of media-suggested self-destruction is not limited to the United States. Japanese youths have committed suicide in imitation of a puppet show that traces the tragic story of two lovers. And in prewar Europe young people reportedly killed themselves after hearing a sad tango called "The Last Sunday."

"Whatever we do is because of the stories we are told. These stories may be told by our grandmothers or maybe by our movies," observes Dr. George Gerbner, professor of communications and dean of the Annenberg School of Communications. "Indeed, we do formulate our image of the world and of proper and improper and other kinds of behavior according to storytellers. But it would be absurd and impossible to hold the storyteller responsible for someone acting out the story."

Michael Cimino was unavailable for comment on the contention that his film may have inspired the Russian roulette deaths. Joann Carelli, one of Cimino's producers, seems tired of answering this sort of question. "That's a joke," she says. "Let's get serious. If someone gets shot, does that mean that someone else watched a program on television and decided to shoot somebody?"

Dr. Thomas Radecki, chairman of NCTV, feels differently. "They can't wash their hands of the death their film is causing," he says about the syndicator of *The Deer Hunter*. (His media antiviolence lobbying group says that it wants MCA-TV to withdraw the movie in order to cut the crucial Russian roulette scenes.) Radecki, who is a psychiatrist and a faculty member of the Southern Illinois University School of Medicine, states that "the Russian roulette scenes in *The Deer Hunter* are clear incitements of imminent violence. The First Amendment was certainly not meant to protect gratuitous Russian roulette scenes that never occurred in reality."

There is no shortage of critics ready to saw off the legal limb Radecki has crawled out on. According to Nat Hentoff, *Village Voice* columnist and student of First Amendment controversies, "It is a First Amendment problem only if the government, the FCC or Congress, comes in [to censor broadcasts of the film]. You can't tell these days with the federal courts, but I don't think it would stand up." He says that a clear, systematic relationship of cause and effect would have to be proved, and that is impossible. On the other hand, Hentoff feels that NCTV is well within its rights to launch consumer boycotts against advertisers in order to pressure the media to lower the level of violence.

"The same kind of First Amendment rights that apply to the print medium should apply to cable and pay television," says Robbin Ahrold, director of public relations for HBO. NCTV has criticized the pay movie channel for showing *The Deer Hunter* as well as for the violent content of some of its other programming. "*The Deer Hunter* was one of the highest-rated movies we've ever played on HBO," Ahrold continues. "The pay television channel is something the individual subscriber brings into his home by his own free will. It is not an unidentified flying object; you actually have to write out a check each month."

The responsibility of the storyteller is to tell the story, and the responsibility for behavior lies with the individual.

But a broadcast channel is a different animal than a cable channel or a movie theater. Under licensed regulation, broadcasters have to be responsible to community standards. Do they have the right to show the Russian roulette scenes in *The Deer Hunter*? "I don't think there is any question that we have the right to run the movie," says Robert Hartman, vice-president and general manager of WFLD-TV in Chicago. Dr. Radecki sent him a letter predicting Russian roulette deaths if the station aired the movie. Nine days later there were two fatalities.

"I'm not qualified to explain what people did," says Hartman. "I don't know anybody who can state that because somebody watched a movie, they took their own life." He notes that eighty percent of the heavy mail and phone response to the airing was favorable and that *The Deer Hunter* had a phenomenal 25 rating and 35 share. "Those people told us unequivocally that they wanted that movie on television. Do you want me to make the decisions on the movies that you see? Or do you want to make the decision?" Neither FCC regulations nor the National Association of Broadcasters code was violated by the airing of the film, according to another station manager.

"Both the language and the violence were necessary parts of the movie and were probably pretty accurate reflections," says John Rose, station manager of WDCA-TV in Washington, D.C. He states that if a direct cause-and-effect relationship were ever established between media and the actions of individuals, the dissemination of books, television, radio, and other forms of communication would be impossible. Rose also points out that response ran two to one in favor of the showing of the movie. Of the negative reaction, "very few commented on the violence; they were all commenting on the language." It seems curious that in almost all instances when viewers complain about *The Deer Hunter* or other programming, they are more likely to be prudishly troubled by four-letter words than by pillage, mayhem, rape, and murder unfolding on their home screens.

Violence comes in different forms. The violence in *The Deer Hunter*, including the Russian roulette scenes, is necessary, organic, and effective. *The Deer Hunter* is a long way from a film like *I Spit on Your Grave*, which has made walk-outs of even the most hardened fans of grade-B gore movies. Before the sixties, violence in the media consisted of gangsters or cowboys with black, dime-size holes on white shirts to mark the bullet wound. These days, gaping, puffy pink flesh and buckets of mucous glycerin blood mark the spot.

Violence is no stranger to art and entertainment, having made its debut on the Western stage with Greek tragedy. Despite the escalation of violence in recent American movies, it seems foolish, shortsighted, and probably unconstitutional to hold the people who make these films responsible for what other people do after seeing them. The responsibility of the storyteller is to tell the story, and the responsibility for behavior lies with the individual. And that includes those unfortunate individuals who acted out their impulses in games of Russian roulette after watching *The Deer Hunter*.

IS ROCK THE MUSIC OF VIOLENCE?

John Rockwell

Eleven young men and women died at a Who concert in Cincinnati on Dec. 3. Most of the responsible commentary—and refreshingly enough, most of the commentary *has* been responsible—has dealt with questions of how rock concerts can be better organized and controlled. It would seem that so-called "festival" seating of the sort used in Cincinnati—unreserved tickets that lead to a buildup of impatient fans at the gates followed by a mad dash for the best positions when the hall finally opens its doors—will be curtailed. And legislation may be enacted to ensure a proper degree of concert security.

This is indeed a reasonable response, but there are two larger issues to be addressed in the wake of this tragedy: is there something inherently violent about rock music, and do rock concerts serve a constructive social function?

To begin with, one has to understand what rock music is and what it represents. Rock was born as an unprecedented free expression of adolescent sexual and aggressive energy. Before the advent of rock, the arts had never attempted to deal with such passions in quite so direct and democratic a way.

Pre-rock popular music had reflected the sturdier hierarchies of an earlier age, and the pieties of its dominant morality. If vaudeville and burlesque were allowed to get a little bawdy, that bawdiness was still sequestered from the mainstream. The mainstream—the Hit Parade of the early 1950's, for instance—was full of Moon-June songs and deliberately silly novelty numbers. The music was syrupy and bland, more an escape from social tension than an expression of it.

All that changed, dramatically, with the sudden—and, to older folk, shocking—advent of rock in the middle-50's. From the pelvic gyrations of Elvis Presley and the suggestiveness of early rock lyrics to the pounding beat of the music to the very name, "rock-and-roll," the new music and the very institution of the rock concert became part of our culture's way of dealing with teen-age rebellion.

This only reflected the new realities of mid-20th-century American life—the sudden coming of age of members of the post-war baby boom, the move of millions from tightly-structured rural America to a life of freedom and loneliness in the cities, the new self-assertiveness and social impact of black Americans, the loosening bonds of a previous century's social, moral and religious rigidities.

There are those who feel that the pre-rock attitude was as it should have been; that some things about human nature are best left alone, or repressed, or at the very least not encouraged. Some rock does indeed exploit sex and violence in a manner akin to pornography and exploitation films—and like them, is created for simple commercial gain. But the finest rock bands have had a higher aim; they have taken the sexual yearning and violent propensities of a newly assertive yet often frustrated adolescent social group and transformed them into art.

The best rock stands in relation to human experience as does all art, revealing us to ourselves. Rock art speaks directly to teenagers. It may be unhealthy that our society has tolerated the evolution of an isolated youth culture. But that culture exists: rock lives.

That doesn't mean, however, that rock only becomes "art" if it simply serves to tame violent energies. Art plumbs life more deeply than entertainment, and the Who and the Rolling Stones, the class of the hard-rock field, are better than lesser bands in part because they confront in the most unflinching manner the aggressive instinct of their audiences.

It is thus ironic, at least on the surface, that it was the Who, and not some lesser band, that was the catalyst of the events in Cincinnati. Because the Who, by the very nature of its music and career, might have seemed able to defuse the sort of violence that erupted in Ohio. And the nature of the Who still may be able to help us explore the ramifications of this tragedy.

Pete Townshend has always been the soul and the leader of this band—its guitarist, chief songwriter and principal spokesman. Nobody in rock has spoken more thoughtfully about what it means to be a teen-ager, and about the mystical relationship that exists between the true rock fan and his favorite band.

Mr. Townshend is an avowed mystic, a follower of the late Meher Baba, the Indian guru. In the days after Cincinnati, many thoughts swirled through Mr. Townshend's head, and among them was the notion that "the whole purpose of a rock concert is for people to forget themselves, to lose their egos in the crowd and to disappear—a temporary sort of flight."

It is an alluring idea, and one that helps explain not only the *positive* connection between rock and violence, but also the Who's own seemingly bifurcated image as the band that, on the one hand, introduced ritualized destruction to the rock stage—the smashing of guitars and drum kits—and, on the other hand, created an entire "rock opera" about transcendental experience in "Tommy." Mr. Townshend feels that young people will never accept preaching from the outside; he himself tried to make television commercials a decade ago warning against drug use, and felt them to be a ludicrous failure. Since then he has concentrated his energies on music—and, more recently, on films.

Right now a film called *Quadrophenia* is playing around the country. It was produced by the Who, and is based on Mr. Townshend's rock opera of the same name, about the riots between the Mods and the Rockers in England 15 years ago, when the Who was just beginning. What's interesting is that the film takes an empathetic but still bleak view of those riots, fueled as they were by amphetamines and ultimately expressive of little more than adolescent despair.

Mr. Townshend feels that what a rock band can do is evoke and sympathize with adolescent passions, and then try through the medium of music to transform them—to "help young people come out whole on the other side."

Sitting in a Cleveland Hotel room the other day, Mr. Townshend looked haggard and spoke with a quiet intensity. "If this had to happen at all, I'm glad it happened to us and not some other group," he said. "I think we're strong enough to turn it into something good—not just in terms of improving concerts, but of improving rock itself."

To summarize: the answer to the first question posed here is yes, there is something inherently violent about rock music. Moreover, there are groups that pander to such violence. But the best groups, while seeming to plunge most deeply into the heart of the violence, seek to transform it into an artistic or even a religious experience.

The second broader issue to be addressed in the wake of Cincinnati is whether rock concerts serve a socially constructive function. To begin with, there is no point in disguising the realities of the situation. Most rock concerts are reasonably well run, but at their worst, cost-cutting by promoters and hall managers turn concerts into anarchic pigsties—that more people aren't hurt at them is a tribute to the inherent good sense of the vast majority of our young people. At the worst concerts, the restrooms are disgusting, there is litter everywhere, the aisles are impassable and reserved seating a farce.

The justification for such squalor is that "the kids like it that way." That attitude suggests a toleration for teenage rowdiness at rock concerts that doesn't exist elsewhere in society. Rock concerts are places where young people are allowed to yell and shout, push and shove, drink and use both hard and soft drugs.

Yes, there is something inherently violent about rock music.

When a facility attempts to crack down on such behavior, the management quickly realizes the folly of its ways. A few years ago the Nassau Coliseum on Long Island made a fairly serious effort to prevent drinking and drug use at rock concerts; sometimes hundreds of teen-agers were arrested on a single night.

The result was widespread protests from young people, their parents and from the rock music business. Bands refused to play there because their fans were being "hassled," booking agents didn't include Nassau on tours, and attendance dropped off seriously at concerts that *were* scheduled.

Things are back to normal at the Nassau Coliseum now, and the reasons are two. On the one hand, most people prefer to look the other way at teenage drug use; until Cincinnati, at least, it seemed a victimless crime. Furthermore, there is big money in the rock concert business, and large facilities such as the Nassau Coliseum derive a considerable portion of their income from them.

Esthetically, rock concerts in arenas and stadiums leave a lot to be desired. The actual music in these environments is seriously compromised. The acoustics are generally terrible. The volume is screwed up to a roar. The difficulties of buying tickets and getting to an arena can be daunting. And with an audience dominated by loudly enthusiastic teenagers, an adult is almost assured of feeling awkwardly out of place.

On the other hand, there is generally not much wrong with an innocent little teen-age Saturnalia—except when something terrible happens. Naturally, there are invariably a few drunken, punkish louts in every such crowd, and sometimes the T-shirted security personnel can be downright brutal. But real physical conflict is rare (a lot rarer than at sports events, one suspects, on or off the ice); the more prevalent mood is of good-natured rough-housing.

Even so, it is not surprising that these concerts have helped bring about a split between record-buyers and concert-goers. Some people simply give up rock music as they grow out of their teens. More commonly adults keep buying the occasional record and listening to the music on the radio, but would never dream of going to a concert.

Given the realities of rock concert life today, as a tacitly licensed preserve for teen-age libertinism, what should be done? Even if a majority in this country should come to the conclusion that such formalized outlets are unnecessary or undesirable, it seems unlikely that they will be "outlawed," barring a nationwide wave of repression.

Thus we are left with the prospect of improvements in the regulation of such concerts. Rock concerts can and should be run in such a way that young people are encouraged to behave responsibly, rather than like cattle.

Still, there is a danger of overreaction on the local level. To avoid that, we must understand that rock carries with it the potential for a transformation of anti-social behavior into something that serves the highest of human ideals. But it can do so only by accepting the reality of human nature.

SUGGESTIONS FOR FURTHER READING

Anyone looking for articles condemning television violence will have no problem finding them; every edition of the *Reader's Guide to Periodical Literature* notes a few. The reports of George Gerbner and his associates are some of the best in this category. See, for example, G. Gerbner et al., "Television Violence, Victimization, and Power," *American Behavioral Scientist* 23, no. 5 (May/June 1980): 705–16.

It's more difficult to find articles that suggest TV violence might *not* be dangerous. Two that are still current are Max Gunther's "All That TV Violence: Is It Really So Harmful?," *TV Guide*, November 13, 1976, p. 34, and "TV Violence—A Red Herring?," Irving D. Harris, M.D., *Television Quarterly* 15 (Fall 1978): 34–36.

Students interested in the scandals associated with the Surgeon General's Report (1972) might want to read an article that was included in the first edition of *Mass Media Issues:* Harry J. Skornia, "The Great American Teaching Machine—Of Violence," *Intellect*, April 1977, p. 347.

Those interested in the reaction of viewers to violence on television news will want to read Jane Mayer, "TV Viewers Seem Increasingly Bothered By News Violence, Worrying Advertisers," *Wall Street Journal*, 25 June 1982, p. 19.

Also of interest:

H. J. Eysenck and D. K. Nias, *Sex, Violence and the Media*. New York: St. Martin's Press, 1978.

PART TWO

MASS MEDIA AND THE POLITICAL PROCESS

Free, unfettered mass media are, supposedly, necessary components of a working democracy. Yet more and more criticism is being leveled at the media for what the critics see as distortion of the democratic process. The four chapters in this section represent four areas of concern: mass media's influence on elections, media coverage of political issues, government secrecy, and international propaganda.

Mass Media and Elections

Observers of the democratic process pay careful attention to the effect of mass media on voting behavior. The first reading in this section, Larry Sabato's "TV Politics," lists several effects of television on election campaigns: the decline of political parties, the rise of "personality" politics and the "star" system, the emphasis on emotionalism, negativism and gimmickry, and the soaring costs of campaigns. Professor Sabato teaches at the University of Virginia, and this article appeared in the October 1982 issue of *Vital Issues*.

Elmer W. Lower's "Is Television Undermining Our Elections?" was published in *TV Guide* following the 1980 elections. Lower, who is a former president of ABC News and currently professor of journalism at the University of Missouri, argues that television is having a negative effect on elections because election-night coverage with its early projections of winners and losers discourages some people from voting.

In the last reading, Jeff Greenfield defends TV's role in elections. Greenfield is a CBS News commentator, a syndicated political columnist, and a former political consultant. His article appeared in *TV Guide* following the 1982 national elections.

TV POLITICS
The Influence of Television In Political Campaigns

Larry Sabato

The process of election has changed dramatically over the decades in the United States, and no change has been more important than the introduction of television into American life and politics. Television plays a crucial role in determining the conduct and even the results of U.S. elections.

The pervasiveness of television as a political force is undeniable. Virtually all American homes now have a television set; most have more than one. The average set is turned on between five and six hours each day, and today's Americans now receive most of their news from T.V. rather than radio, newspapers, or magazines.

The cumulative effect on politics of all this television watching is enormous. The basic political attitudes of voters are shaped in good measure by television's coverage of public affairs. Campaigns for public office are literally centered around the schedules and needs of television news programs. Press conferences are tailored to

From *Vital Issues* (Oct., 1982) Reprinted by permission.

contain "good visuals" for the cameras, and campaign activities become media events, often with a stress on style and motion, rather than issues and substance.

Television has had a particularly severe effect on the political parties. Firstly, television emphasizes candidate personality rather than the abstract party label, thus loosening the tie between a candidate's party identification and the voter's choice. Secondly, incumbents are especially strengthened by television over time; they secure repeated exposure that builds their name identification, thus discouraging lesser-known potential challengers and at the same time making incumbents less dependent for re-election on their parties. Most significantly of all, television essentially replaces the party as the middleman between candidates and voters. Whereas candidates once relied upon party organizations to communicate their message, now television accomplishes the same job, bringing the candidates directly into the voters' living rooms.

On commercial television there are two kinds of video time sought by candidates for public office: (1) so-called "free media" time, i.e., segments on evening news programs, debates, and documentaries for which the candidate pays nothing; and (2) advertising spots, designed and produced for the candidate by hired political consultants for which campaigns pay stations just like other advertisers (though usually at a somewhat reduced rate.)

Television at its best can inform and educate the electorate. News segments examining the candidates' stands on major issues, or a well-structured television debate, can focus voters' attention on matters of substance. Even advertising paid for by the candidates can be useful, crystallizing (as it *should* do) the best possible case for each contender. Unfortunately, neither television news nor campaign commercials have usually fulfilled their potential. Studies have indicated that news programs dwell on personalities, horserace polls, and the "brass bands" and razzmatazz of politics, not issues and position papers, while candidate advertisements frequently embody emotional appeals, employ image-making gimmicks, and prefer to simply attack the opposition.

The kind and quality of television's coverage of politics, then, has had a number of vital effects on the American electoral system. Of greatest importance, perhaps, has been the assist given the decline of political parties and the rise of personality politics. Other effects are significant, too, including television's development of a system of "star politics," its stress on emotionalism and negativism in politics, the video emphasis on gimmickry, style, and image instead of issues and substance, and the impact on campaign costs of televsion advertising. All of these consequences of television politics, and a few others, will be discussed in turn.

PARTY DECLINE AND PERSONALITY RISE

Television is a very personal medium, coming as it does directly into the inner sanctum of the American home. Long ago program producers learned the truth of political media consultant Tony Schwartz's description of effective presentation on television. The medium, said Schwartz, should be used "not as a large public address system, but rather as a *private undress* system." To fulfill the Schwartz prescription, those featured on television must become known as personalities; their characteristics and trademarks are developed so that viewers come to "know" them and feel comfortable with them in their living rooms.

It was inevitable that political consequences would flow from the medium's premium on personality. The political party is an abstract concept, its label diffuse and difficult to "package" in an eye-appealing way for viewers. The candidate, by contrast, can be developed as a personality.

Political advertisements are filled with pictures of, and glowing testimonials from, the mothers, wives, and children of candidates. Issues are complex and often divisive, while families and personalities are intimate and reassuring. One of Robert F. Kennedy's spots from his 1968 presidential campaign will illustrate. To counter Kennedy's "ruthless" reputation, his political consultant filmed Kennedy playing football with his children at Hickory Hill. As the warm sights and sounds of spring surround a playful and affectionate candidate, the narrator tenderly comments, "A man with ten children can't avoid a concern about the future. It's underfoot most of the time. Each day Robert Kennedy is surrounded by a lot of reminding that we must do something about tomorrow." Note that the advertisement never tells viewers *what* Kennedy will do about tomorrow. Substance is abandoned for the personal implication that a man with ten loving children cannot be ruthless. Kennedy, the viewer presumes, will do the *right* things once in power because he is a good family man and cares about his children's future. Similar techniques, used in most campaigns, have helped firmly establish the candidate-centered system of American elections—a system which relegates political parties to a lesser role.

THE DEVELOPMENT OF STAR POLITICS

Rare is the major political campaign today that does not include endorsements from well-known media stars in its advertising program. Political stardom is often conferred on those who marshall the most appealing and glittering associates. Most analysts attribute the 1978 election of U.S. Senator John W. Warner of Virginia to the attention his wife, actress Elizabeth Taylor, was able to attract to him. In the same state Charles S. Robb was in a position to run for office thanks to the fame generated by his marriage to the daughter of President Lyndon B. Johnson. Robb won first the lieutenant governorship and then the governorship of Virginia in 1981 by capitalizing on the media's attraction to his "star quality." There are many other examples, of course. Bill Bradley converted basketball stardom into a U.S. Senate seat from New Jersey in 1978. John Y. Brown won the Kentucky governorship in 1979 with a big assist from his wife, former Miss America and CBS sportscaster Phyllis George. George Murphy was catapulted into the U.S. Senate from California in 1964 from his stage and screen platform. And no list would be complete without the name of another California actor who met with political success, Ronald Reagan.

> Television plays a crucial role in determining the conduct and even the results of U.S. elections.

The line between politics and show business has been growing thinner in part because of television's influence. The qualities which help a program star to "project" to viewers are, in essence, the same ones that enable a television candidate to communicate his message effectively across the airwaves. Those who see this change as a good (or neutral) one argue that the effectiveness of office-holders is enhanced by communicative ability, and to the extent that television helps to elect better communicators, the relationship and general understanding between voters and their representatives is strengthened. Critics of televison's political power disagree, suggesting that television is helping to replace workhorses with showhorses. (As one observer has opined, what would the rather homely and unphotogenic Abe Lincoln—or the shy and stammering Thomas Jefferson—

have done in the television age?) Whichever view is correct, it is not surprising to find that an increasing number of local television news commentators and talk show hosts are being elected to Congress and municipal offices across the country.

THE EMPHASIS ON GIMMICKRY AND STYLE

Media researchers, in content analyses of the national evening news programs, have repeatedly found that campaign hoopla and a preoccupation with "who's ahead, who's gaining" polls tend to dominate news coverage of elections. Given the poor record of the news telecasts, it is only mildly surprising that political advertisements have been determined to be somewhat more substantive and issue-oriented than the evening news (though the low standard of comparison does not generate much of a compliment.)

In the place of issues, news shows and commercials often feature gimmicks designed by the campaigns precisely to lure the cameras. A perennial is the "walking candidate" who, clad in denim and boots, sets out to trek across the length and breadth of his state, along the way exchanging pleasantries (and little more) with voters and tourists in his path. Another much imitated gimmick is the "working" candidate, who spends a day or two a week performing tasks associated with various occupations. The "work days" candidate will be a high school teacher one day, a waiter the next, an oil rigger the following week. And all the while the cameras roll as the candidate establishes superficial identification with important voting blocs. Gimmicks like "walking" and "work days" are stylistically delightful, an image-maker's dream with tailor-made visuals for television. The problem then can be succinctly stated: they entertain, not educate.

PROMOTION OF NEGATIVISM AND EMOTIONALISM

Controversy and conflict are the stuff of television news. While a detailed position paper on health care is unlikely to generate much television coverage (even if the candidate releases it from a hospital bed for visual effect), an emotional and well-staged attack on the opposition will almost certainly draw television's attention. This is a fact of campaign life not overlooked by aspiring candidates and their managers. The tone of campaigns has become increasingly negative, partially as a result.

Far more influential in the trend toward campaign negativity has been paid television advertising. Over the past three decades, negative spots—that is, those commercials which primarily attack the opponent's character and record rather than supporting one's own—have comprised a growing proportion of the average campaign's advertising program. Whereas less than a quarter of a typical campaign's ads in the 1950s and early 1960s were essentially negative, about a third of the ads aired in a campaign of the late 1970s were negative. It is not unusual today to find campaigns where half or more of the advertisements are products of "attack politics." Political groups independent of the parties (such as the National Conservative Political Action Committee) are partly responsible, of course, since their advertising is entirely negative. Organizations like NCPAC "target" candidates for defeat, then can raise and spend unlimited sums for television commercial time as long as they do not coordinate their activities with the candidates they support.

Liberal PACS have begun to imitate the tactics of NCPAC and other committees of the right, thereby compounding the problem. Negative campaigns have gained a reputation for effectiveness, which partly explains their popularity. NCPAC's ad expenditures, for example, were given partial credit for the defeat of a number of incumbent U.S. senators in 1980. Yet the trend toward "attack politics" must be classed a disturbing one, for negativism is a corrosive quality that eats away at the foundations of the American system by destroying the necessary element of civility in politics.

Moreover, there is some evidence that the negative barrage of television commercials has helped to reduce voter turnout in a number of specific cases. One such case was the 1974 Ohio gubernatorial contest which pitted former two-term Republican governor James Rhodes against one-term incumbent John J. Gilligan. Rhodes' political consultants concentrated their candidate's negative commercials in the heavily Democratic Cuyahoga County (Cleveland area) media market. Democrats were puzzled by the tactic, since conventional wisdom suggested that one never wasted advertising dollars communicating with the other candidate's strong adherents. Once the results were in, however, the wisdom of the strategy became apparent. In the year of Watergate, when other Democrats were sweeping to victory in Ohio and across the country, Gilligan, to almost everyone's surprise, was narrowly defeated for re-election. Cuyahoga County's returns were the key to Rhodes' upset. In 1970 when Gilligan had first won election as governor, he had received 67.2 percent of the Cuyahoga vote (and 54.2 percent statewide). In 1974, after the Rhodes commercial onslaught, Gilligan's percentage in Cuyahoga dropped almost 9 percentage points (to 58.4 percent) compared to a drop in the rest of the state of only about 5 percent. Gilligan would still have won, though, if the voting turnout in Cuyahoga had kept pace with the statewide participation rate. While the statewide rate slipped only three-tenths of one percent, the turnout decline in Cuyahoga was a stunning 18.6 percent, a fall-off of about 105,000 voters from four years earlier. The negative advertising package had succeeded in moving many Democratic voters to the ranks of the non-voting by introducing doubts and damaging information about the Democratic party candidate. Strong Democrats were not going to vote *for* a Republican or even *against* a Democrat, so they exercised one of their other options, and abstained, in sufficient numbers to elect Rhodes by a wafer-thin 11,500-vote plurality in a turnout of more than 2.6 million.

IMPACT OF TELEVISION ON CAMPAIGN COSTS

Expenditures for commercial air time have been devouring an ever larger proportion of campaign budgets. In 1976 the Ford and Carter organizations spent about $17 million for television time and production in the general election—a shade under 40 percent of the $43.2 million in federal subsidies allotted to the major party candidates. Just four years later Carter's media absorbed fully 66 percent of his autumn budget, and Reagan's advertising claimed 56 percent of his general election war chest.

Partly, the growth of the media budget is due to mushrooming costs for air time, at a rate of increase that has considerably exceeded the inflation rate. Between 1972 and 1976, for instance, televison spot-time costs increased 64 percent compared to a Consumer Price Index rise of a much lower 36 percent. The price of one minute of network prime time doubled between the presidential elections of 1976 and 1980. On individual affiliates across the country, the increases were sometimes more staggering. A thirty-second prime time spot in Portland, Oregon, cost just $55 in 1974; in 1980, the figure was $3,000.

Further compounding the cost is the tendency for media advertising to begin earlier in a typical campaign. Just a decade ago television spots in a general election rarely appeared before mid-October. Now August and September airings are standard, and easily a quarter of statewide campaigns schedule some ads in the spring or summer preceding the November election. The 1980 presidential campaign on television began almost a year before the election date, and had the networks not objected, it would have begun even sooner. (A recent court ruling has reduced the networks' discretion in determining when the official media campaign period should begin, which will probably insure earlier advertising in the future.)

PROPOSALS FOR CHANGE

Ideally, the major commercial networks would operate under a system like Great Britain's. In the U.K.'s 1979 general election, for example, each major party was given five ten-minute television broadcasts sprinkled throughout the campaign, and lesser parties were allotted fewer slots based on the national percentage of the vote they received in the prior election. Moreover, each segment was broadcast simultaneously on all channels. While viewers could still turn their sets off (or, in the U.S., switch to cable TV), audience tune-out was held to a minimum. Furthermore, in apportioning time to parties instead of candidates, voters were reminded that they were making a choice between parties, not merely between personalities.

Regrettably, this sort of mandatory allocation system is no panacea. While it would be feasible at the presidential level in the U.S., it is much too simplistic to be applied at state, district, and local electoral levels. The constraints on stations include a fixed supply of air time, varying local conditions and market situations, and a multitude of candidates and offices being elected. For instance, many media markets reach dozens of congressional districts, while others incorporate only one or a few, so some stations would be deluged with demands for time and others hardly affected by a uniform guideline.

If large time blocks cannot be provided free to the parties, then television networks can at least make their coverage of campaigns more substantive. This they may be beginning to do. Content analysis of evening news broadcasts aired in the final weeks of the 1980 campaign suggested that, compared with earlier presidential contests, news reports were somewhat more issue-oriented and less obsessed with "horeserace" statistics.

The development of an extensive multichannel cable system will likely provide much richer opportunities for candidates to reach voters in the future. While any given cable audience will probably be considerably smaller than that watching an established network station, the costs will be far lower and the chances for extended discussion of campaign issues much greater.

> The line between politics and show business has been growing thinner.

Many reforms have been suggested in the area of paid poltical broadcasting. Some observers believe that purely negative ads should be banned from television outright, with so-called "contrast ads" substituted. Contrast ads are commercials that do not merely attack the opponent but also dwell specifically on how the candidate paying for the ad is superior. And to avoid excessive image-making and gloss, it has been suggested that candidates should appear in all of their own ads and speak simply and directly to the voters for at least half of each spot. To encourage substantive discussion and presentation, political commercials should preferably be five mintues in length rather than just 30 to 60 seconds in duration. (Costs and the unavailability of 5-minute slots in many locales make this reform a difficult one to achieve.)

Perhaps the most auspicious development for political advertising has been the recent activity of the national political parties in producing "institutional" advertising. The Republican party has been the leader, and the GOP has aired extensive commercial programs since 1978 designed to strengthen the public's identification of certain issues (such as tax cuts and reduction of government spending) with the GOP. A $9 million ad package in 1980, geared to a theme of "Vote Republican—For a Change", was considered particularly successful and was thought to have contributed to significant GOP gains in both Houses of Congress. The national Republican party has also produced complete ad packages for dozens of its congressonal candidates in 1978, 1980, and 1982, at a fraction of the cost charged by independent political consultants. These invaluable services, and the party's stress on consistent issue themes, have helped to draw GOP candidates closer together and closer to the party itself. The Republican party's services and television programs are partly responsible for the unusual degree of voting cohesiveness registered by U.S. House and Senate Republicans in recent sessions of Congress. The Democrats have been much slower to innovate with television advertising (primarily because of a lack of financing) but in 1982, for the first time, the party aired a small national advertising package. These party efforts demonstrate that television is not irrevocably a force for personality politics, and can actually promote a responsible party-centered system.

Overall, it is clear that, thanks to television, the modern American voter probably knows far more about candidates for public office than his counterpart just a few decades ago. Yet it is equally apparent that many aspects of television's political coverage are unsatisfactory. The critics of the medium are often sharp simply because television's potential for voter education is so great. The goal for television's future must obviously be the fulfillment of that political and educational potential.

IS TELEVISION UNDERMINING OUR ELECTIONS?

Elmer W. Lower

"We must reenfranchise our population living in the later time zones."

—SEN. JAMES MCCLURE (R-IDAHO)

"We don't think we ought to withhold information from people."

—JOSEPH ANGOTTI
NBC NEWS ELECTION PRODUCER

"The network polling methods have become so sophisticated we don't need anyone west of the Mississippi to decide a Presidential election any more."

—ART BUCHWALD
HUMORIST

Those comments were only three of the hundreds provoked by NBC News when on Election Night it declared Ronald W. Reagan the next President of the United States at 8:15 P.M., Eastern Time. West Coast and Rocky Mountain voters—also those in Alaska and Hawaii—still had from one to three hours in which to cast

From *TV Guide* (Jan. 17, 1981). Reprinted by permission.

their ballots. Many believed at that moment that they had lost their votes.

The arguments are certain to continue. Legislation has already been introduced. The questions that have arisen are not easily answered.

What effect do early projections have on voters who haven't yet cast ballots?

How do the networks make projections? What did NBC News do that ABC News and CBS News did not?

What effect do early projections have on Western voters who haven't yet cast ballots? Are projections based on key precincts accurate? What about those based on interviews with voters as they leave the polls?

Should Congress establish a uniform poll-closing time for all precincts in the 50 states and the District of Columbia? Or is there some other solution?

Since the early 1960s the three commercial television networks have projected the results of voting in each state—for President, senator and governor—by using a small sample of precincts that reflects the state's voting behavior. For example, ABC's 66 key precincts in Missouri have mirrored how the state's 4050 precincts vote.

The projections have usually been accurate. In 1976, the networks made only two incorrect calls all year; their records during the 1980 primaries were perfect, but they did make several incorrect projections on Nov. 4.

In 1980, all networks used extensive interviews outside selected polling places in an effort to tell their viewers why voters voted as they did. But NBC News carried these exit interviews one step further. It used them to make its projections of the results in each state, in some cases, reportedly, without waiting for the key precincts and the raw vote tabulated by the cooperative News Election Service.

This enabled NBC to project that Reagan would win Ohio's 25 electoral votes at 7:31 P.M., one brief minute after polls had closed, and to do the same in Missouri (with 12 electoral votes) at 8:02. Other projections were made so quicky that soon NBC anchorman John Chancellor announced—at 8:15—that Reagan would be the next President of the United States, having been projected to win more than the required 270 electoral votes.

NBC News trumpeted its victory in full-page newspaper advertisements, and Les Crystal, senior executive producer for election coverage, argued: "If tonight isn't proof that exit polls are useful, I don't know what is." NBC conceded that it had decided some states on exit polls alone, not waiting for the actual tabulation from key precincts.

ABC and CBS, both fielding exit interviewers at some 400 precincts, had similar information, but delayed their projections until they received the actual vote tallies from their key precincts. ABC called Reagan the winner at 9:52 P.M. and CBS at 10:32.

So what's wrong with being the first to tell American television viewers who their next President will be? The problem is that it may interfere with voting in nine Western states, not only in the Presidential race, but also in lesser—but still important—contests at the bottom of the ballot. Those states were still balloting when NBC announced that it was all over.

"Nobody goes to the ball game in the ninth inning when the score is 100 to 0," remarked Truman Campbell, California Republican chairman. Both he and Clinton Reilly, a California Democratic campaign director, felt that NBC's early call and President Carter's unusually early concession had turned voters from the polls and caused both parties to lose Congressional and state assembly races. A final CBS News-*New York Times* post-election poll reported that 10 per cent of those who didn't vote in the West said they didn't because they had heard either network projections or Mr. Carter's concession.

"What does exit polling do to further the democratic election process?" asked Reilly, arguing that laws should be passed to keep interviewers at least 500 feet away from the polls.

Other critics question the accuracy of exit interviews. In a Reagan landslide they were right on the money. But are they, in a close election? Do voters tell the truth as they leave the polls? Do the interviews represent a true cross section?

Reagan's landslide was not the first in the television era. Eisenhower won big and early in 1952 and 1956, Lyndon Johnson was an early victor in 1964, and so was Richard M. Nixon in 1972. After the networks' early projections of Johnson's 1964 landslide victory over Sen. Barry M. Goldwater, remedial legislation was introduced in Congress, but it died in committee.

So what are the solutions for the 1980s and beyond? Here are some of the proposals that have been made:

- That uniform poll-closing hours be established, so that all the 178,000 precincts in the 50 states and the District of Columbia would close simultaneously. Then network projections, however speedy, would no longer have any effect on voting in the West.
- That a law be passed requiring that news interviewers be kept at least 500 feet from polls. There is some doubt that such a law would be constitutional, but those who favor it contend that if party workers can be kept from electioneering too close to the polls, news interviewers can be required to keep at least a 500-foot distance. This would make it easier for voters to avoid being interviewed if they wished.
- That voting results in states that have finished voting early be withheld, and be released to news organizations only after all polls have closed.
- That Election Day be shifted from the first Tuesday after the first Monday in November to the first weekend in November, in an effort to produce a larger turnout; and couple this with uniform poll-closing time.
- That split-day voting be established in the Western states. Polls would open on the first Monday night of November to accommodate persons who vote after work, and then open again on Tuesday. Polls would close at 6 P.M. Tuesday, Pacific Time, to synchronize with 9 P.M. in the East. All polls in every state would close simultaneously.

Congress can take a big step in solving the problem in its next session. It can establish uniform poll-closing hours everywhere. That is the simplest immediate solution.

But even that would not restrain news organizations—notably those of the big television networks—from interviewing voters as they left the polls and making projections based on those results. As one Midwestern newspaper remarked, NBC "could have called the election at 10 o'clock in the morning if it had been brazen enough."

A law restricting the rights of reporters outside polling places might raise First Amendment objections and be bad public policy. Instead of legislation, the answer might be an act of network-news statesmanship: voluntary self-restraint. The networks could abandon the mad race to be first just to boast of it in full-page advertisements; let the voters everywhere cast their ballots without outside influence.

What form should voluntary restraint take? At the very least, all news organizations should withhold projections in states having staggered poll-closing hours until all the states' precincts have completed voting. (Thirteen states still have such staggered hours.)

All news organizations should agree not to use exit-interview polls as the sole basis for projections. They should use them only for developing demographic information about voting patterns.

If any news organization insisted on using exit interviews for projections, it should frankly reveal the precise data on which it based its predictions. An anchorperson might say, for example:

"XYZ News projects that Candidate A will win Missouri's 12 electoral votes. As the Missouri polls closed only 60 seconds ago, we do not yet have actual vote tallies. We base our projection on how 300 Missouri voters *said* they voted during interviews as they left the polls." The public could then decide whether to believe the XYZ News data.

> Do voters tell the truth as they leave the polls?

If Congress established uniform poll-closing hours and if news organizations ceased making projections based on exit interviews, there could be no possible interference anywhere with the voting process. But if voting hours remain the same, the problems will continue—even without projections.

The News Election Service tabulates the raw vote so swiftly that a Presidential winner in a landslide year is almost certain to be known by 8:30 P.M., Eastern Time, an hour at which seven to nine Western states are still balloting. And we have had *five* such races in the eight Presidential elections of the television era.

There are those who believe that neither legislation nor voluntary restraint will work. The solution will come, they say, when some news organization gets badly burned using exit-interview polls. What worked for NBC News in the Reagan landslide could lead to disaster in a close race.

As Idaho's Sen. James McClure says, "Our elections are much more important than a media event or a mere television spectacular."

SURPRISE! TV IS NOT RUINING OUR ELECTIONS

Jeff Greenfield

Now that the 1982 midterm elections are over, here's a short quiz to test your political IQ. What do these four statements have in common?

- In a mass-media age, big money always decides who gets elected.
- Television has made negative, nasty campaigns more successful than ever.
- Because of TV's emphasis on personality and imagery, the political parties are becoming more and more irrelevant.
- The voter is so turned off by the bombardment of political news and commercials that the turnout just keeps dropping.

All of these statements are widely believed by millions of American citizens and by many political experts. All of them represent the prevailing "wisdom" about how TV has altered our political life.

And every one of those statements proved wholly or substantially *false*, based on the outcome of the 1982 elections.

From *TV Guide* (Jan. 1, 1983). Reprinted by permission.

For years now—probably starting with the huge success of *The Selling of the President 1968,* which showed how Richard Nixon's advisers packaged the future President as if he were a product—observers have regarded television's impact on our political life with a mixture of fear and loathing. That the American voter might be getting more sophisticated about the electronic window on the world didn't stop the ceaseless shaping of new warnings, each designed to demonstrate that TV was wreaking havoc on the American political system.

So what happened in 1982?

First, most of the self-financed big-money candidates lost. Lew Lehrman spent more than $8 million of his own money to get elected governor of New York—and lost to a candidate who spent less than one-half of what the Lehrman campaign cost. Mark Dayton, heir to a department-store fortune, spent $4 million to win a Senate seat in Minnesota—and lost. Across the country, big money proved to have only a limited impact on the outcome of a campaign.

Of course, access to big money has clear political value: Lehrman, Dayton and others would never have won their parties' nominations without ready cash. And in close Congressional elections, candidates with a $50,000 or more edge over their rivals were successful almost two-thirds of the time. But, as Walter Staab, a prominent New York media buyer, explained shortly after the election, "Once you are able to make a creditable showing in the media, you can be outspent by two to one, and it probably won't make that much difference."

Second, the negative campaign, so much discussed and feared after the 1980 elections, turned out in 1982 to have its most devastating impact not on the *target* of the negative ad, but on its instigator.

In Tennessee, Republican representative Robin Beard, running against incumbent senator Jim Sasser, produced an ad charging that Sasser had helped ship American money to enemies of the U.S. In the ad, an actor impersonating Fidel Castro lit a cigar with American money and said, "*Muchas Gracias, Señor Sasser.*" The ad—whose charges, by the way, were false—had an immediate impact. *The Nashville Banner,* a staunch Republican journal, withdrew its endorsement of Beard, saying the ad "appalls the senses." Other publications strongly attacked the candidate, and he lost to Sasser in a landslide.

In 1982, the negative campaign had its most devastating impact not on the target of the negative ad, but on its instigator.

In California, Democratic governor Jerry Brown sought to dramatize his support for the nuclear freeze in his senate campaign by running this commercial: as various celebrities and citizens explained why they wanted to continue playing baseball or making music, a nuclear explosion filled the screen. The announcer said, "Pete Wilson opposes the nuclear arms freeze . . . . Jerry Brown supports it. Vote for your life." Instead of panicking voters to Brown's side, the ad triggered a renewed sense of Brown as arrogant and manipulative. Though it was withdrawn after a week, the damage was permanent. Brown lost by more than 450,000 votes.

For all of the hand-wringing over television's capacity to deliver negative messages, 1982 demonstrated that, after 30 years of living with the one-eyed wonder, Americans have grown more sophisticated, able to distinguish political hardball from political mud balls. In almost every case in which candidates crossed the line in their media advertising, they suffered severe political damage.

Even some of America's most highly respected

media consultants, men who make their living creating political advertising, agree that the American viewer is becoming steadily smarter.

"With each passing year," Republican media strategist John Deardourff says, "television viewers are becoming more sophisticated. They develop certain defense mechanisms to the material they see." Comments Democratic media consultant David Garth, "I think people are aware when you are criticizing fairly [and] when you're criticizing *un*fairly."

And what of the political parties, so often seen as dinosaurs in an age when candidates trot out family, dog and pony in a television spot?

In 1980, the Republican Party ran a series of brilliant ads that went right to the heart of the Democrats' blue-collar base. A "Democrat dollar" shrank to the size of a peanut as a commercial described 25 years of one-party domination of the Congress. A Tip O'Neill look-alike laughed off the energy crisis. And an out-of-work hard hat walked through an empty factory asking, "If the Democrats are so good for the working man, why aren't more of us working?"

The 1980 commercials effectively hammered home the message that, to change policy, voters had to change the Congress and the White House. In 1982, both political parties used television to convey their messages. Republicans urged Americans to "stay the course," and used bar graphs to demonstrate the decline in interest rates and inflation. Democrats showed us an elephant in a china shop smashing dishes marked "Social Security" and other social programs. And, in an effective dramatization of "trickle-down economics," a Democratic ad showed bejeweled hands pouring champagne from glass to glass while a few drops "trickled down" into a worker's metal cup.

Both political parties in 1982 woke up to the fact that television is the principal political forum in America—and began using that medium to get their messages across to the American voter. And, coincidentally or not, postelection comments by Republican and Democratic officials, as well as exit-poll data, showed a marked return to voting by party allegience—and party identification, according to many political scientists, is the key to an involved electorate.

Which brings up the last and perhaps most significant point: in every midterm election since 1962, voter turnout has declined. In 1978, the last off-year election, only 37.8 percent of eligible voters went to the polls. But in 1982, for the first time in two decades, the turnout in an off-year election was up—up by two and a half to three per cent—a substantial rise amounting to an increased turnout of some *four million* voters over 1978.

Americans have grown more sophisticated, able to distinguish political hardball from political mud balls.

Why didn't television coverage turn these voters off? Well, maybe because this year there were real, bread-and-butter issues on the table. Whether voters liked President Reagan's economic policies or not, no one could say they hadn't made any difference—the usual refuge of the politically lazy American. And maybe all of those political ads, talking about past Democratic programs and present Republican policies, actually got voters *interested* in politics. Maybe, just maybe, the much-maligned medium of TV proved that—when real issues are at stake—it can get voters turned on and turned out on Election Day.

Does this mean, then, that we should begin to see TV as an unqualified good? Hardly. Money still makes too much of a difference in our public life, and too many good men and women are kept out of the arena because they lack access to cash for TV time. Too many commercials still oversimplify. And 1982 doesn't ensure us against slipping back into the apathy that has characterized recent elections.

Still, it's encouraging to know that so many of the "truths" about television's influence on American politics took a bath this year. It demonstrates that this system—and the American citizenry—has a way of surprising those experts who decided that television had so scarred the process. Potentially, at least, television has the capacity to produce a more honest process and a more enthusiastic, informed voter. And that's the best 1982 election result of all.

SUGGESTIONS FOR FURTHER READING

Those interested in the debate over the political power of the media will be interested in two recent books: Jeff Greenfield's *The Real Campaign: How the Media Missed the Story of the 1980 Campaign*, New York: Summit Books, 1982, and David Chagall, *The New Kingmakers*, New York: Harcourt Brace Jovanovich, 1981. Greenfield claims that "television and the media made almost no difference in the outcome of the 1980 Presidential campaign." Chagall, on the other hand, claims that the media and the behind-the-scenes manipulators of the media are the "new kingmakers" of presidential politics.

Also of interest:

David Bloomquist, *Setups: Elections and the Mass Media*. Washington, D.C.: American Political Science Assn., 1982.

Robert C. Byrd, "Let's Have More Truth in Those Political Ads." *TV Guide*, October 16, 1982, pp. 21–22. "Those ads" referred to by Senator Byrd were those of the National Conservative Political Action Committee.

Charles U. Larson, "The Influence of Mass Media Coverage on Campaign '80." *USA Today*, March 1981.

D. Nimmo, "Ethical Issues in Political Campaign Communication." *Communication* 6, no. 2 (1981): 193–212.

Thomas E. Patterson, *The Mass Media: How Americans Choose Their President*. New York: Praeger, 1980.

Martin Plissner and Warren Mitofsky, "Voting Twice on Election Day." *Public Opinion*, August/September 1982, pp. 14–16. A defense of election polls, by two network news pollsters.

Robert Spero, *The Duping of the American: Dishonesty and Deception in Presidential TV Advertising*. New York: Harper & Row, 1980.

CHAPTER 6

Media Coverage of Politics

This chapter begins with comments from four historical figures. Thomas Jefferson's thoughts on the political coverage of his time are followed by further elaborations on that theme by Theodore Roosevelt, Edward R. Murrow, and Spiro Agnew.

In the final reading, Charles Krauthammer analyzes the significance of the current state of political "show business." Krauthammer is Senior Editor of the *New Republic*, where his article appeared in November 1982.

THOMAS JEFFERSON ON THE MEDIA OF HIS TIME

FROM A LETTER TO JOHN NORVELL

Washington, June 11, 1807

It is a melancholy truth, that a suppression of the press could not more completely deprive the nation of its benefits, than is done by its abandoned prostitution to falsehood. Nothing can now be believed which is seen in a newspaper. Truth itself becomes suspicious by being put into that polluted vehicle. The real extent of this state of misinformation is known only to those who are in situations to confront facts within their knowledge with the lies of the day. I really look with commiseration over the great body of my fellow citizens, who, reading newspapers, live and die in the belief, that they have known something of what has been passing in the world in their time; whereas the accounts they have read in newspapers are just as true a history of any other period of the world as of the present, except that the real names of the day are affixed to their fables. General facts may indeed be collected from them, such as that Europe is now at war, that Bonaparte has been a successful warrior, that he has subjected a great portion of Europe to his will, &c., &c.; but no details can be relied on. I will add, that the man who never looks into a newspaper is better informed than he who reads them; inasmuch as he who knows nothing is nearer to truth than he whose mind is filled with falsehoods and errors. He who reads nothing will still learn the great facts, and the details are all false.

From *The Complete Jefferson*, Saul K. Padover (Ed.), (New York: Duel, Sloan & Pearce, 1943).

FROM THE SECOND INAUGURAL ADDRESS

March 4, 1805

During this course of administration, and in order to disturb it, the artillery of the press has been levelled against us, charged with whatsoever its licentiousness could devise or dare. These abuses of an institution so important to freedom and science, are deeply to be regretted, inasmuch as they tend to lessen its usefulness, and to sap its safety; they might, indeed, have been corrected by the wholesome punishments reserved and provided by the laws of the several States against falsehood and defamation; but public duties more urgent press on the time of public servants, and the offenders have therefore been left to find their punishment in the public indignation.

Nor was it uninteresting to the world, that an experiment should be fairly and fully made, whether freedom of discussion, unaided by power, is not sufficient for the propagation and protection of truth—whether a government, conducting itself in the true spirit of its constitution, with zeal and purity, and doing no act which it would be unwilling the whole world should witness, can be written down by falsehood and defamation. The experiment has been tried; you have witnessed the scene; our fellow citizens have looked on, cool and collected; they saw the latent source from which these outrages proceeded; they gathered around their public functionaries, and when the constitution called them to the decision by suffrage, they pronounced their verdict, honorable to those who had served them, and consolatory to the friend of man, who believes he may be intrusted with his own affairs.

No inference is here intended, that the laws, provided by the State against false and defamatory publications, should not be enforced; he who has time, renders a service to public morals and public tranquillity, in reforming these abuses by the salutary coercions of the law; but the experiment is noted, to prove that, since truth and reason have maintained their ground against false opinions in league with false facts, the press, confined to truth, needs no other legal restraint; the public judgment will correct false reasonings and opinions, on a full hearing of all parties; and no other definite line can be drawn between the inestimable liberty of the press and its demoralizing licentiousness. If there be still improprieties which this rule would not restrain, its supplement must be sought in the censorship of public opinion.

MUCKRAKING

Theodore Roosevelt

Washington D. C. April 14, 1906

Over a century ago Washington laid the cornerstone of the Capitol in what was then little more than a tract of wooded wilderness here beside the Potomac. We now find it necessary to provide by great additional buildings for the business of the government. This growth in the need for the housing of the government is but a proof and example of the way in which the nation has grown and the sphere of action of the national government has grown. We now administer the affairs of a nation in which the extraordinary growth of population has been outstripped by the growth of wealth and the growth in complex interests. The material problems that face us today are not such as they were in Washington's time, but the underlying facts of human nature are the same now as they were then. Under altered external form we war with the same tendencies toward evil that were evident in Washington's time, and are helped by the same tendencies for good. It is about some of these that I wish to say a word today.

From *Voices of the Past: Key Documents in the History of American Journalism, Calder M. Pickett (Ed.)* Columbus, Ohio: Grid, Inc., 1977.

In Bunyan's *Pilgrim's Progress* you may recall the description of the Man with the Muckrake, the man who could look no way but downward, with a muckrake in his hands; who was offered a celestial crown for his muckrake, but who would neither look up nor regard the crown he was offered, but continued to rake to himself the filth of the floor.

In *Pilgrim's Progress* the Man with the Muckrake is set forth as the example of him whose vision is fixed on carnal instead of on spiritual things. Yet he also typifies the man who in this life consistently refused to see aught that is lofty, and fixes his eyes with solemn intentness only on that which is vile and debasing. Now, it is very necessary that we should not flinch from seeing what is vile and debasing. There is filth on the floor, and it must be scraped up with the muckrake; and there are times and places where this service is the most needed of all the services that can be performed. But the man who never does anything else, who never thinks or speaks or writes save of his feats with the muckrake, speedily becomes, not a help to society, not an incitement to good, but one of the most potent forces of evil . . . .

I hail as a benefactor every writer or speaker, every man who, on the platform or in book, magazine or newspaper, with merciless severity makes such attack, provided always that he in his turn remembers that the attack is of use only if it is absolutely truthful . . . .

"SEE IT NOW"—A LOOK AT JOSEPH McCARTHY

Edward R. Murrow

New York: March 9, 1954

. . . No one familiar with the history of this country can deny that congressional committees are useful. It is necessary to investigate before legislating. But the line between investigation and persecuting is a very fine one, and the junior senator from Wisconsin has stepped over it repeatedly. His primary achievement has been in confusing the public mind as between the internal and the external threat of Communism. We must not confuse dissent with disloyalty. We must remember always that accusation is not proof and that conviction depends upon evidence and due process of law. We will not walk in fear, one of another. We will not be driven by fear into an age of unreason if we dig deep in our history and our doctrine and remember that we are not descended from fearful men, not from men who feared to write, to speak, to associate and to defend causes which were for the moment unpopular.

This is no time for men who oppose Senator McCarthy's methods to keep silent, *or* for those

From Edward W. Bliss, Jr., *In Search of Light: The Broadcasts of Edward R. Murrow 1938–1961* (New York: Knopf, 1967), pp. 247–248.

who approve. We can deny our heritage and our history, but we cannot escape responsibility for the result. As a nation we have come into our full inheritance at a tender age. We proclaim ourselves, as indeed we are, the defenders of freedom—what's left of it—but we cannot defend freedom abroad by deserting it at home. The actions of the junior senator from Wisconsin have caused alarm and dismay amongst our allies abroad and given considerable comfort to our enemies. And whose fault is that? Not really his; he didn't create this situation of fear, he merely exploited it and rather successfully. Cassius was right. "The fault, dear Brutus, is not in our stars but in ourselves."

SOME COMMENTS ON TELEVISION NEWS COVERAGE

Spiro T. Agnew

Des Moines, Iowa Nov. 13, 1969

. . . How is this network news determined? A small group of men, numbering perhaps no more than a dozen anchormen, commentators and executive producers, settle upon the 20 minutes or so of film and commentary that's to reach the public. This selection is made from the 90 to 180 minutes that may be available. Their powers of choice are broad.

They decide what 40 to 50 million Americans will learn of the day's events in the nation and in the world.

We cannot measure this power and influence by the traditional democratic standards, for these men can create national issues overnight.

They can make or break by their coverage and commentary a moratorium on the war.

They can elevate men from obscurity to national prominence within a week. They can reward some politicians with national exposure and ignore others.

For millions of Americans the network reporter who covers a continuing issue—like the

---

Speech before Midwest Regional Republican Committee, November 13, 1969. From *Vital Speeches of the Day* XXXVI (December 1, 1969).

ABM or civil rights—becomes, in effect, the presiding judge in a national trial by jury.

It must be recognized that the networks have made important contributions to the national knowledge—for news, documentaries and specials. They have often used their power constructively and creatively to awaken the public conscience to critical problems. The networks made hunger and black lung disease national issues overnight. The TV networks have done what no other medium could have done in terms of dramatizing the horrors of war. The networks have tackled our most difficult social problems with a directness and an immediacy that's the gift of their medium. They focus the nation's attention on its environmental abuses—on pollution in the Great Lakes and the threatened ecology of the Everglades.

But it also was the networks that elevated Stokely Carmichael and George Lincoln Rockwell from obscurity to national prominence.

Nor is their power confined to the substantive. A raised eyebrow, an inflection of the voice, a caustic remark dropped in the middle of a broadcast can raise doubts in a million minds about the veracity of a public official or the wisdom of a Government policy . . . .

LIGHTS, CAMERA . . . POLITICS

Charles Krauthammer

> Suppose, then, that an individual clever enough to assume any character and give imitations of anything and everything should visit our country and offer to perform his compositions, we shall bow down before a being with such miraculous powers of giving pleasure . . . crown him with fillets of wool, anoint his head with myrrh, and conduct him to the borders of some other country.
>
> —Plato

> Take actors, for instance. The really good ones don't rely on mere technique. They also follow their feelings when they play a part. Like me, they are genuine.
>
> —Henry Kissinger

Plato had a problem with actors. He considered their talent for eliciting feeling rather than thought a threat to his well-ordered Republic. In his Republic of reason, to engage the citizenry in fictional contrivances, to appeal directly to the emotions, was an act of subversion. For Plato the choice was clear: politics, the active engagement

---

Published Nov. 22, 1982. Reprinted by permission of *The New Republic*

of man's highest powers in pursuit of the good, versus theater, a world of shadows where everything is possible and nothing is true. So Plato did the obvious. He banished theater from his Republic.

Several civilizations later, when theater was making a comeback, Rousseau drew inspiration from Plato's decisiveness: "What! Plato banished Homer from his republic and we will tolerate Molière in ours?" For Rousseau theater was bound to corrupt. Since its appeal was "founded on the passions," its fatal attractiveness would not only sap republican virtue but also confer enormous and unwarranted powers on actors. Of them he wrote:

> If they join a bit of art and intrigue to their success, I do not give the state thirty years before they are its arbiters. The candidates for office will be seen intriguing for their favor in order to obtain suffrages, the elections will take place in the actresses' dressing rooms, and the leaders of a free people will be the creatures of a band of histrions. The pen falls from my hand at the thought.

Granted, neither Plato nor Rousseau was much of a democrat. Plato found democracy "an agreeable form of anarchy," and Rousseau's republic was built on the idea of "forcing men to be free." But they had a point. Rousseau's nightmare has now become commonplace. Not only do politicians court actors, they have become actors. This, in turn, has inspired actors to take up politics. For the first time in history an actor has become the leader of a major country. The pen falls from no one's hand at the thought. On the contrary: Ronald Reagan has made a distinct political asset out of his ability to summon a tear on command, to introduce just the right hint of hoarse passion or controlled anger into his resonant voice. During his Presidential campaign, the "actor issue" never arose. It was considered irrelevant, even impolite, to bring it up.

Plato and Rousseau might have spared us an actor-king, but even those who deplore theater's invasion of politics will shrink from their harsh corrective. One needn't be a civil libertarian to resist the idea of banning theater; one need only be a realist. It's too late. Banning theater would no longer protect politics, it would abolish it, for the two have become indistinguishable. As Rousseau predicted, a citizenry captivated by illusion (one that watches television six hours a day, for example) loses interest in exercising its civic duties (voting, for example). Worse, it comes to demand that what little politics it does imbibe match the texture and taste of its usual diet of dramatic fictions.

> In politics the symbolic act corrupts when it substitutes for action.

The rush to meet that demand has transformed politics into theater, politicians into actors, and citizens into spectators. The process is now so advanced that the most striking manifestation of political theater, the terrorist seige—once so shocking, even confusing, as just another way of doing political business. Terrorists were the pioneers. Midway into the television age they discovered how to acquire such political commodities as legitimacy, visibility, and even power, and transform themselves from marginal conspirators languishing on the fringes of world attention to major actors commanding center stage. There was only one requirement—that they provide a spectacle or some other suitable entertainment—and they met it brilliantly, with such live thrillers as the Munich Olympic massacre and the Symbionese Liberation Army prime-time shootout.

Of course, political actors have always tried to grab the stage. But terrorists sought to put something peculiarly new on it: a morality play, a dramatic reenactment with live actors of their larger struggle. So they invented the most difficult and radical form of political theater: the politics of metaphor. Its rigid conventions make it easy to recognize. First, it substitutes demonstration for declaration, drama for discourse. Less marginal and less ruthless groups issue a statement; terrorists make one. Second, it is abstract. The terrorist act itself, having no intrinsic meaning, acquires meaning by analogy when it is seen as standing for something else—a principle, a feeling, a grievance. When Moluccans seized a train of Dutch commuters and began shooting them, the act was, on the face of it, senseless. The people they seized had never heard of the Moluccan problem, and even if they had, they could do nothing about it. But killing Dutch commuters, like more ancient forms of human sacrifice, is not intended to mean anything in itself. It is meant as a symbol of Dutch guilt, of Moluccan will, of what have you. Coming up with such interpretations is the job of the media, our Greek chorus. Media and audience are the final crucial elements of metaphorical theater, and the need for audience is absolute. Without audience, the gesture, like the sound of a falling tree in a remote forest, dissolves into air.

A good test of whether a political act is purely theatrical is to ask whether it would or could have existed without an audience. What distinguishes the assassination of Aldo Moro from that of Anwar Sadat is that eliminating Moro quietly would have been pointless; eliminating Sadat quietly would not have been. Moro's murder was purely symbolic; Sadat's too was symbolic, but it was more: it was an act of insurrection, an attempted coup, whose intention and reasonable expectation was to effect a dramatic transformation of Egyptian society.

In a similar way, those who sat in at the Greensboro lunch counter were not simply calling attention, by analogy, to the evils of racism, they were demanding to be served. Indeed, the entire civil rights movement scrupulously avoided the structures of metaphorical theater. It had drama, of course, but unlike guerrilla theater, the civil rights movement did not manufacture it. Its confrontations were planned, not contrived; they were real manifestations of the clash between black aspirations and white prejudice. Martin Luther King, who marched on camera and off, confronted not random bystanders pressed into duty as extras, but real racists. His means were the same as his ends, and thus enjoyed not only the same high moral standing but the same connection to reality.

A connection to reality can be confining. The first terrorist spectaculars managed to avoid such a constraint on their creativity. Their success inspired a rash of imitators, though none quite approached the absurd and abstract purity of the original. Not that they didn't try. A recent one-act production in Washington featured a band of men in battle fatigues who burst into the park at Dupont Circle, grabbed a woman lying on the grass, and began dragging her away. Before they could succeed, a squad of police with drawn pistols rescued the woman. She was incensed. They had missed the point: this is how people disappear in El Salvador. She and her abductors were acting, and they had a permit to prove it. But policemen are trained to look for criminals, not analogies, and no one had been there to explain to them what was going on. Metaphorical politics needs interpreters. Like all the avant-garde arts, this most severe form of political theater tends, in the absence of a medium, to lose its audience.

A citizenry captivated by illusion (one that watches television six hours a day, for example) loses interest in exercising its civic duties (voting, for example).

Not all varieties of political theater are so elaborate and demanding in dramatic structure. A popular alternative to metaphor is mime. Its statements are more direct, more accessible, more visceral. Unlike metaphor, it is not so abstract that without commentary it becomes incomprehensible. Disarmament marches today are schools for political mime. It is hard to find one that does not sport a legion of marchers decked out in death mask, skeleton costume, or bloody headband. (A few ghoulish exemplars grace the cover of the September/October *Mother Jones*.) Another popular form is the mass die-in, where thousands of people lie on the ground pretending to be victims of a nuclear attack. This not only gives the demonstrators a personal "feel" for what a nuclear holocaust would be like, it makes for a superb aerial shot of simulated destruction. Like the death mask, this image is meant to illustrate the proposition that nukes mean death. It is a simple message, meant, like all political mime, to be given and received viscerally.

The terrorist siege is now accepted as commonplace, as just another way of doing political business.

When it comes to sending visceral messages, however, there is no better vehicle than a baby. An index of how popular political mime has become is the epidemic use of babies as stage props. An inordinate attention to the welfare of babies has been the traditional pose of whistle-stopping politicians at election time. Now everyone is doing it. Helen Caldicott likes to raise an infant before a crowd to declare that this is what disarmament is all about. Yasir Arafat made the ostentatious baby-hug the culmination of each day's work during the Lebanese war, and assured the panting press corps that this is what the battle of Beirut was all about. Antiabortion fanatics wave horrific pictures of mutilated fetuses to tell us that this is what the pro-life crusade is all about. Since for everyone babies represent innocence and their protection a self-evident good, a symbolic identification with babies signals one's righteousness in a way that viewers everywhere will understand. Mime, like music and other wordless languages, is universal.

All this gesturing makes for a dismaying poverty of political discourse. In some parts of the world, like the Soviet bloc, where rich political discourse has been outlawed, sending signals is the only remaining means of communication. *Pravda* is not so much a source of information as of encoded messages. The way to know who is in favor at the Kremlin is to study the annual May Day picture from atop Lenin's tomb—the ultimate photo opportunity— and to see who stands nearest to Brezhnev. In such a system, even challenges to the monolith must adopt its methods. Solidarity has been criticized for pouring so much of its energy into symbols, like the great crosses at the Lenin shipyards and token work stoppages. But Solidarity leaders had no choice. They understood that when one faces an adversary who conducts political dialogue either in silence or with tanks, symbols are the only weapons.

In the West, political discourse is not conducted with tanks; language is permitted. Yet its use is dying, inexorably giving way to the politics of gesture. Dissidents—with their mime and metaphor—are only its most flamboyant practitioners. Those in power can do more than make faces at the camera. They can make policy, which allows them to practice a more subtle variety of political theater, the politics of symbolism. Symbolic politics turns policy into posture, into a means for projecting images. Its acts are empty of meaning; they are intended solely to send messages. Take the recent headline: PRESIDENT'S SANCTIONS AGAINST POLAND SEEN AS

SYMBOLIC. As the story made clear, denying Poland most-favored-nation status has no effect in the real world. Thus the headline should have read: PRESIDENT'S SANCTIONS SEEN AS EMPTY. But emperors know that nowadays it is safe to walk around naked, so long as their refusal to wear clothes will be "seen as symbolic."

Few events are as stripped of substance as the annual Western Economic Summit, an event of such transparent uselessness that it threatens to give symbolism a bad name. It is an occasion for Western leaders to kick each other under the table while reasserting, in the form of a group picture, Western unity. On the domestic front, the standard is set by the quadrennial national convention. Like the summit, it once had a real deliberative function, a condition it has outgrown. It is now, as every bleary-eyed viewer knows, a scripted display of choreographed enthusiasm and partisanship, whose rehearsed climaxes are timed to coincide with peak viewing hours.

We have an expression for manufactured happenings like summits and conventions that do nothing but play to the camera—the media event. But this expression, which gives the impression of some specialized *type* of event, misleads. The media event bears the same relation to a real event that a Potemkin Village does to a real village. However, in the age of television it makes no difference. By the time the cardboard scenery is taken down, the camera crews have gone home.

The rise of television is the most obvious and most important cause of the explosive growth of symbolic politics. Christopher Lasch traces its emergence (he calls it the politics of spectacle) to the first television President, John Kennedy ("No other President exemplified so completely the subordination of policy to . . . the appearance and illusion of national greatness," he writes). Lasch also astutely identifies "crisis management" as a creation of the media age, designed to turn politicians into heroes and decisions into "tests of leadership." Richard Nixon, Kennedy's debating partner and the man of six, then seven, crises, turned the political highwire act into a routine. But even Lasch must have been surprised by what followed: Hamilton Jordan's famous post-inaugural memo to President Carter pointing out that what counts in the end is perception, not substance; Carter's dimming the White House Christmas lights in response to the hostage seizure in Iran; his dramatic two-week, semisolitary mediation atop Camp David. Finally, though, Carter gave way to the ultimate fusion of theater and politics, Ronald Reagan, a man chosen to lead the conservative movement, not because of his demonstrated ability to think or lead, but because he could perform in front of the camera.

From the beginning of his Administration, when he denied the Soviet Ambassador his personal garage entrance to the State Department, Reagan has seemed obsessively attentive to the symbolic gesture. He lit a candle at the White House to protest the rape of Poland; he made a visit to an inner-city school in Chicago to show concern for blacks; he invoked an embargo against the Soviet pipeline (while acknowledging that U.S. sanctions could not stop it). He even sent a symbolic armed force to Lebanon with strict instructions not to fight. The problem with these symbolic gestures is what stands behind them. Authentic political symbols—those that represent, with concision and power, real policies—are important. For example, Jimmy Carter's cardigan represented, however clumsily, a real set of policies for energy conservation. On the other hand, Mr. Reagan's candle for Poland was backed by such pathetic measures as canceling twice-a-week Polish airline flights to the U.S. His visit to a black school in Chicago was coupled with an economic policy that ravaged poverty programs designed to help blacks. The pipeline embargo came shortly after the resumption of Soviet grain sales, where the real money lies. Even American soldiers in Lebanon are only a token, not a symbol; a truly symbolic force, like the U.S. Army in West Germany, will use its weapons if attacked.

Of course, there is nothing intrinsically wrong with political symbolism. Every society needs its triumphal processions, its inaugurations, its throne speeches. Ritual in politics, as in religion, is an indispensable communal practice, knitting society together, giving it common purpose and memories, and reasserting the legitimacy of its institutions. But just as religious piety becomes hollow when it substitutes for goodness, and offensive when it masks evil, in politics the symbolic act corrupts when it substitutes for action, or worse, when it conceals contradictory action. Yet that is the use to which political symbols are almost invariably put.

There is only one cause for hope, one circumstance that might spare us the worst effects of theatrical politics: the promiscuity of its practitioners. The images they produce have now become so numerous and ephemeral that they commit what nuclear strategists call fratricide: they obliterate each other. Washed over by thousands of images daily, the viewer retains very little. Some vague traces remain; that much advertisers of soda and footpowder have learned. But the total effect has become numbingly self-canceling. Does anyone remember even one episode of "America Held Hostage," the nightly hit television show (now known as "Nightline") spun off from Khomeini's siege?

Political theater has largely taken over real politics. It has made gesture a substitute for policy.

Yet even as overloaded circuits cause the spectator's attention span to dwindle, political impresarios show a dismaying capacity to rise to the occasion, producing ever more spectacular shows. Now that airplane hijackings are so common (and every disgruntled employee feels entitled to take a few hostages to air his grievances), Yasir Arafat had to invent a new genre—holding an entire city hostage—to make news. Now that every political rally has its Nobel Prize celebrity and rock group, the ERA campaign produced a political commercial that flashed nothing but a succession of famous faces, from Hawkeye Pierce's to Edith Bunker's, urging passage of ERA. Now that every sewer commissioner campaigns on smoke and mirrors, Ronald Reagan has made the empty gesture the touchstone of a Presidency—and succeeded: his personal popularity remains high even as that of his policies plummets.

The success of these actors (not a phenomenon unique to the U.S.: In India, one film star rules the state of Tamil Nadu, another has a good chance of winning the next election in Andhra Pradesh, and a third is a top political figure in Karnataka) and the rapid advances in the technology of dissimulation foreshadow the growing domination of political theater. An even more reliable way to ascertain where we are heading is to see where Jerry Brown has been. In 1980 he attempted the first hi-tech, multimedia, razzmatazz video political event, choreographed by Francis Ford Coppola, no less. It bombed because, as usual, Brown was slightly ahead of his time. For his recent Senate campaign Brown created a new act, a political ad that packed into thirty seconds every major device that political theater has spawned in the last twenty years.

First, the celebrities: Ron Cey (L.A. Dodgers, third base) says, "I want to keep on playing baseball"; Leonard Bernstein says, "I want to go on making music"; Candice Bergen says, "I want to go on doing it all."

Next, the symbol: a mushroom cloud.

Then the prop: a child, surrounded by other children, saying, "I want to go on living."

Then, crisis; "Pete Wilson [Brown's opponent]

opposes the nuclear arms freeze. Jerry Brown supports it."

And, finally, resolution by slogan: "Vote for your life. Elect Jerry Brown to the U.S. Senate."

Brown was again ahead of his time: he had to pull the ad after a week. All the conventions in thirty seconds is too heavy a dose. But he did show us the future.

It might still be argued that political theater is harmless, operating as it does in the world of perception across the metaphysical divide from the real world. That might be true if theatrical politics were just a bizarre variant of "real" politics. But it isn't. It has largely taken over real politics (about half of the Congressional campaign expenditures, for example, go to television and radio commercials) precisely because of its ability to present appearance as reality. It has transformed politics, and in doing so has given us more than just the die-in, guerrilla theater, and Ronald Reagan. In the hands of those in power, practitioners of symbolic politics, it has made gesture a substitute for policy. In the hands of dissidents, practitioners of political metaphor and mime, it has made gesture a substitute for argument. And in the minds of citizens, practitioners of the art of spectatorship, it has made politics a form of entertainment. None of this would have surprised Rousseau. The very thought of theatrical politics made him tremble. The pen may yet begin to fall from contemporary hands as well.

SUGGESTIONS FOR FURTHER READING

Articles of interest for a more general analysis of media coverage of politics include the following:

J. Garvey, "A Politics of Silence." *Commonweal* May 7, 1982, pp. 265–66. Garvey feels that "it is important not to let people who live on speed and on self-importance . . . define the limits of our world." He suggests we adopt a "politics of silence" that shifts attention away from mass media and public relations.

Walter Karp, "Subliminal Politics on the Evening News." *Channels* 2, no. 1 (April/May 1982): 23.

Michael Jay Robinson, "A Statesman Is a Dead Politician: Candidate Images on Network News." In *What's News*, edited by Elie Abel. San Francisco: Institute for Contemporary Studies, 1981, pp. 159–86.

Tom Hamburger, "How the White House Cons the Press." *Washington Monthly*, January 1982, p. 22. Presents further information on the Reagan administration's political public relations.

The following books are also of interest:

Michael B. Mackeun and Steven L. Coombs, *More Than News: Media Power in Public Affairs*. Beverly Hills, Calif.: Sage, 1981.

David L. Paletz and Robert M. Entman, *Media Power Politics*. New York: Free Press, 1981.

CHAPTER 7

Government Secrecy

One of the basic conflicts in rights arises when the government wants to keep a secret and the media want to make the secret known to the public. Former CIA director William Colby sums up the government's position when he says:

> **President Ford once said he would gladly share our government's secrets with all 212 million Americans if such information would go no further . . . . Some secrets, after all, do protect the nation. Secret technology to locate and shoot down foreign nuclear missiles could be jammed if known in detail by a potential enemy. Confidential give-and-take in diplomatic negotiations would be impossible under klieg lights. And disclosure of the intelligence pur-**

pose behind an apparently commercial venture can enable a foreign nation to thwart the operation.[1]

Ramsey Clark, the former U.S. Attorney General, does not share Colby's point of view. He states:

Democratic institutions are founded on assumptions, among them being the belief in the possibility of an informed public. That is why education has always been a major component in democratic theory. So, at the threshold, we see some conflict between secrecy in government and the idea of democracy. Secrecy in government deprives the public of essential information on important governmental matters . . . I have come to the conclusion—I came to it some time back—that there should be no acceptance of secrecy in government, that the risks of secrecy in government far exceed any possible benefits . . . It usually involves the need, or the desire, of authority to deceive the citizens whom it serves.[2]

This chapter's first reading gives former Press Secretary Ron Nessen's analysis of the balancing act the press must perform in order to self-censor news that might undermine national security and still give essential information to the public. The remaining readings represent a sampling of editorial opinion on two recent administration actions. An editorial from the *Portland* (Maine) *Evening Express* discusses the restrictions that were placed on contacts between government officials and the press, and the *Washington* Post and the Salt Lake City *Deseret News* editorials comment on an administration order that expands the category of "classififed" information.

NOTES

1. William E. Colby, "How Can the Government Keep a Secret?" *TV Guide* (February 12, 1977): 2.
2. Ramsey Clark, "The Case against All Forms of Government Secrecy," *Center Magazine* (January–February 1978): 70.

SHOULD TV NEWS *ALWAYS* TELL ALL?

Ron Nessen

"It would be like giving Anne Frank's address to the Nazis."

With that graphic argument, NBC News correspondent Richard Valeriani urged his network not to broadcast his discovery that six American Embassy officials in Iran had avoided being taken hostage in November 1979 and were hiding at the Canadian Embassy in Tehran.

NBC executives realized that the story almost certainly would have resulted in the capture of the fugitive Americans by militant Iranian revolutionaries, and so the story was not broadcast. The six American diplomats were later spirited out of Iran to safety on fake Canadian passports.

"That was an easy one to decide," Valeriani remembers.

But the choice of whether to suppress or broadcast a scoop on television news is not usually so clear-cut. The decision—on occasion literally one of life or death—places enormous pressures on correspondents like Valeriani and their network news superiors.

From *TV Guide* (June 27, 1981). Reprinted by permission.

On the one hand, they are mindful that broadcasting a sensitive story could undermine national security, endanger lives (as in the case of the Tehran fugitives), upset delicate diplomatic negotiations or provide comfort and propaganda to the Nation's adversaries. On the other hand, the networks are sensitive to their First Amendment rights and responsibilities, and to the need to resist pressure from Government officials who may wish to kill a legitimate story only because it is embarrassing or politically damaging.

Acting White House press secretary Larry Speakes foresees the time when the Reagan Administration "will have to ask reporters to hold back on using a story when exposure could cause an explosive crisis." Speakes says . . . that if the White House appeals on a case-by-case basis to the "best instincts" of journalists, the networks will voluntarily agree not to broadcast secrets that could harm the national interest.

He may be wrong. The TV networks—and the news media generally—have become less willing to withhold news stories since their bitter experiences with attempted press manipulation during the Vietnam War, the Pentagon Papers case, and, most of all, Watergate.

In the never-ending controversy over what constitutes improper censorship and what constitutes proper concern for national security, both sides cite dramatic episodes to support their arguments.

Those who claim that TV should broadcast what it knows in virtually every case point to President John Kennedy's famous lament after the 1961 Bay of Pigs fiasco. Kennedy expressed regret that the *New York Times* had bowed to his plea not to reveal in advance what they knew of the plans for the invasion of Cuba. Had the *Times* blown the operation's cover, Kennedy mused later, he might have reconsidered the ill-fated landing.

Those who argue on the other side, that the networks damage the national interest when they ignore Government requests to suppress sensitive secrets, cite the case of the *Glomar Explorer*, a sophisticated ship built for the CIA to raise a sunken Soviet missile submarine from the floor of the Pacific Ocean.

Says ABC's Jack Anderson: "I have a duty to report what the Government is doing, which is not always what spokespeople say it is doing."

The three networks and a number of newspapers learned of the Glomar and its mission in early 1975. But they voluntarily withheld the story at the request of then CIA director William Colby while the ship, which had already brought up half of the Soviet sub, prepared to grapple for the other half, believed to contain valuable Soviet coding equipment.

Then, in March 1975, Jack Anderson went on the air and broke the *Glomar Explorer* story. As a result, the CIA says, it canceled efforts to bring up the rest of the submarine for fear that the Soviets—their discomfiture spotlighted on TV for all the world to see—might feel compelled to flex their muscles by interfering with, or even sinking, the *Glomar Explorer*.

Anderson, now with ABC, explains his role in the incident this way: "I have a duty to report what the Government is doing, which is not always what the authorized spokesmen say it is doing." Yet, Anderson says, "Admittedly, reporters are not security experts and the publication of military secrets is always a thorny question."

Surprisingly, despite his experience in the *Glomar Explorer* episode, Colby is opposed to any legislation that would give the Government the power to prohibit the broadcast or publication of information by legitimate news organizations, even if authorities consider the information inimical to the national interest.

Legislation here similar to England's Official Secrets Act—which allows for censorship of classified information—would, Colby believes, violate the U.S. Constitution. The former CIA director feels that television and the press must be free from Government censorshp. "That's the cost to have this kind of free country," he declares.

In an unexpected reversal of the normal roles in this debate, NBC's Valeriani disagrees. "Britain has an Official Secrets Act," he points out, "and it's still a very good, functioning democracy." If TV correspondents and other reporters act irresponsibly—by divulging the identities of undercover intelligence operatives, for instance—then Valeriani thinks some restraints may be necessary.

"I don't believe in total freedom of the press," the veteran NBC correspondent explains. "I'm not a First Amendment absolutist."

Daniel Schorr *is* a First Amendment absolutist.

Schorr, a longtime CBS reporter who is now chief Washington correspondent for the Cable News Network, holds the strong belief that the Constitution prohibits the Government from imposing any kind of censorship on broadcast and print journalists, period.

"It's quite simple," Schorr says. "You don't impose prior restraint by law."

Schorr worries that certain laws and regulations, and a number of court decisions aimed specifically at broadcasters, have curtailed the First Amendment rights of television journalists compared with print journalists. He points to the Fairness Doctrine, the equal-time provision and the right of aggrieved parties to reply to personal attacks on the airwaves.

The justification for these Government-imposed limitations, Schorr notes, stems from the Federal Communications Commission's authority to grant or cancel licenses to stations for the exclusive use of the limited number of TV channels. Schorr would like to see instead the Government auction off the licenses. Then, TV stations would own their own channels, "just as newspapers own their printing presses."

Schorr strongly opposes legal restraints on TV news. But he does believe the networks can be talked into voluntarily withholding sensitive news stories on those occasions when the Government makes a persuasive case.

"Television newspeople are quite patriotic," Schorr insists.

"Television newspeople," insists Cable News Network's Daniel Schorr, "are quite patriotic."

For one network correspondent, patriotism outweighed his journalistic instincts when he had to decide whether to broadcast some highly classified intelligence data he had discovered concerning a new Soviet plane. (The material is still considered classified.) The reporter worried that his story would compromise intelligence sources and damage American relations with a third country that secretly had supplied the data. After talking it over with a high-level executive at his network, the correspondent decided that his story would harm the national interest and he kept it off the air.

Sometimes the decision goes the other way. Sander Vanocur, the NBC's White House correspondent, braved White House displeasure in 1961 when he broke the story that President Kennedy was secretly negotiating for a summit meeting with Soviet Premier Khruschev. (The following year Vanocur bowed to a White House request and kept another story off the air, only to see it revealed on the front page of the *Washington Post.*)

And sometimes the patriotism-vs.-journalism dilemma is settled by compromise. For instance, two days into the Iranian hostage crisis, Valeriani learned that the Carter Administration was about to send Ramsey Clark on a secret mission to Tehran to try to negotiate the release of the American captives.

Hodding Carter, then the State Department spokesman, pleaded with Valeriani not to reveal Clark's mission because the newscast might cause the unpredictable Iranians to cancel the negotiations.

Valeriani worked out a deal: he agreed to keep videotape of Clark boarding his plane off the air until the Iranians gave approval for the mission. As a result, viewers learned of the mission on the *Today* show the following morning, instead of on that evening's *Nightly News* program. (Clark's mission failed anyway.)

Perhaps the most troubling recent case involving media exposure of sensitive national-security secrets involved the broadcast and publication of a detailed description of the workings of an H-bomb. The article disclosing the above originally was written for the *Progressive* magazine by a young antinuclear activist, Howard Morland.The Government went to court to prevent publication, seeking the first prior-restraint injunction in American history based on grounds that the article would endanger national security by showing foreign leaders how to build an H-bomb.

Before the Supreme Court could issue a final ruling, the case was made moot when the bomb story turned up in a number of news broadcasts and publications.

Episodes like the H-bomb case produce periodic threats from security-conscious Government officials to forbid or exact retribution for the broadcast and publication of national-security secrets. The Carter Administration required about 20 officials to sign affidavits swearing that they were not the source of one particular leak of sensitive information. During the Ford Presidency, top White House officials once considered bringing criminal charges against a reporter for violating an obscure law against revealing intelligence data picked up by electronic surveillance. And, of course, the Nixon White House ordered wiretaps of its own officials, as well as reporters, to stop national-security leaks.

However, such heated reactions to TV and press disclosures normally cool off when the irate Government officials realize that (1) most disclosures are harmless, and (2) the First Amendment to the Constitution guarantees reporters the right to broadcast and print virtually any information they uncover, even if it might harm the national interest.

More than any other story in recent years, coverage of the American hostages in Iran drew complaints from Government officials and ordinary viewers alike that the networks placed journalistic competition ahead of the national interest.

The incident that seemed to anger TV-watchers the most was NBC's decision to allow the Iranian militant "Mary" to deliver an anti-American, anti-Shah harangue unedited, in prime time, on the network in exchange for an interview with one of the captives. The networks were flooded with protests that the continuing presence of their camera teams in front of the occupied U.S. Embassy in Tehran encouraged the militants to prolong the capitvity of the American hostages. Network news executives generally defended their coverage of the Tehran scene by arguing that they were pointing their cameras at legitimate news events and were not responsible for influencing the conduct of the militants.

However, George Sherman, a respected State Department public-affairs adviser, complains that TV coverage of the hostage crisis influenced the conduct of the American Government in several ways.

For example, Sherman says that by playing up what he believes was a *pro forma* threat by Ayatollah Khomeini to place the hostages on trial, the networks forced the United States to issue a stern response, which, in turn, forced Iran to issue an even tougher rejoinder. As a result, according to Sherman, public opinion in both countries was further inflamed and a negotiated settlement became more difficult.

> Television can broadcast everything it knows—but only at the risk of losing the good will and tolerance of its viewers.

On the other hand, many of the hostages' relatives have praised television for keeping the plight of the captives in the news and thereby keeping the pressure on the U.S. Government to secure their release.

The patriotism-vs.-journalism debate raises two questions:

(1.) *Can* television legally broadcast whatever it chooses, even if the story might damage national security or the national interest? Under the First Amendment, the answer is yes.

(2.) *Should* television broadcast everything it knows?

The answer here is: only at the risk of losing the good will and tolerance of its viewers.

Television news correspondents and executives often turn aside criticism about what they put on the air by insisting that they are only serving the public, giving it what it needs and wants.

However, a two-year research project examining attitudes toward television and the press by the New York-based Public Agenda Foundation discovered widespread opposition to the broadcast of top-secret information that might endanger national security. The report found that: "For many Americans, it is the media who may be the enemy of freedom of expression, since the media have the power to select and limit the information available to the public."

Television, like every other major institution in a free society, depends for its continuing viabilty on public support and understanding.

Legislators, regulators and judges will dare to chip away at the underpinnings of a free press only when they sense that they have the backing of an angry public.

Therefore, in order to preserve its current freedoms, television news should do a better job of explaining to its viewers why it shows what it shows and why occasional lapses should be excused as the price for retaining the blessing of an unfettered press.

At the same time, television news should exercise a greater degree of responsibility and a willingness to eliminate its worst excesses on a voluntary basis.

The alternative to such responsibility may be further alienation of the viewers and rising demands for Government controls.

EDITORIALS ON GOVERNMENT SECRECY

Restrictions on Official Contact With the Press

Evening Express

Portland, Maine, January 15, 1982

Two things can be said about President Reagan's attempts to stem the profusion of news leaks from the inner councils of his administrations.

One, Reagan is acting in the time-honored tradition of modern presidents in this regard. Two, the leaks will continue.

> The order is likely only to isolate the administration by encouraging an us-against-them mentality.

Citing national security interests, Reagan hopes to shut off the leaks by requiring administration officials handling classified material to obtain permission before talking with members of the press, and then to file reports of their conversations with reporters.

Aside from adding to the discomfort—and paperwork—of administration officials, the order is likely only to isolate the administration by encouraging an us-against-them mentality. But it is not likely to prevent the leaks from continuing, since they inevitably serve the purposes of the individual leaking the information as they do those of the press.

Past presidents have resorted to bizarre techniques in an effort to stop news leaks. Lyndon Johnson, for example, made it a policy not to appoint anyone to a top government post if the name of his nominee appeared in the press before he announced it himself.

Richard Nixon went a step further by bugging the telephones of those he suspected of passing information to the media.

But leaks are a normal condition of Washington life. Many news leaks are officially sanctioned, peddled by administration sources "on background," that is, under condition they not be named in news stories.

Ironically, the very White House aide who announced the president's anti-leak measures agreed to answer reporters' questions about the new policy only if he were not identified.

The aide's identity —communications director David Gergen—quickly leaked out.

On Increasing "Classified Information"

Deseret News

Salt Lake City, Utah, April 3, 1982

There's room for reasonable people to disagree over the wisdom of the action President Reagan took Friday making it easier for federal officials to stamp documents secret.

Just as disturbing as the increase in secrecy, however, is the manner in which it was accomplished.

Also disturbing is the fact that this step was taken contrary to statements by White House adviser Edwin Meese indicating the President was backing away from this very move.

By executive order, President Reagan allowed documents to be classified as secret even if possible damage to national security is not identifiable.

The Reagan order also drops previous requirements that officials determine if public interest in the disclosure outweighs any damage to national security and that classified documents be reviewed after six years for possible release to the public.

Moreover, the order creates a new area of classification for documents on "the vulnerabilities or capabilities of systems, installations, projects or plans that relate to the national security."

The upshot is to reverse a 30-year trend toward giving the public more access to public files. Instead, the government has now been given virtually a blank check for keeping secrets.

All this was done with the stroke of just one pen, the President's, even though the documents being stamped secret were produced by public employees paid with funds authorized by Congress.

These decisions are too important to be made by just one man, no matter how capable or well-intentioned. Congress ought to reconsider whatever provisions in the law allow the nation's chief executive to make such decisions single-handedly.

The Washington Post

Washington, D.C., April 2, 1982

President Reagan's new executive order on classifying national security information is good news for people in the rubber stamp and ink business. It is bad news for people who believe that the flow of information is essential to the health of a democracy. Mr. Reagan has in effect reversed a 25-year presumption that the public interest lies in maximum disclosure. His order shifts the presumption a long way toward secrecy. This is truly regrettable, not least because the president's counselor, Edwin Meese III, had assured anxious critics that the restrictive early drafts were the handiwork of "overzealous bureaucrats."

The final draft, published a few days ago, does show a few welcome second thoughts. It restores the requirement of the Jimmy Carter order to mark the portions of documents meant to be kept secret. It restores, too, the Carter prohibition against classifying basic scientific research not clearly related to national security. It drops a proposal to create a new classification of peripheral "restricted" information—this could have forced universities that won't do classified work out of certain types of research they conduct now.

In its main components, however, the Reagan order is bad. It eliminates the need for an official opposing declassificaton to identify the damage he claims would be done by disclosure—a unanimous Senate Intelligence Committee opposed this change. It wipes out the requirement that, in disclosure decisions, the government balance benefit against harm. It lets the government reclassify information sought under the Freedom of Information Act, even after the information has been released. It instructs classifiers, when in doubt, to apply the higher rather than the lower level of secrecy.

Mr. Reagan believes his order strikes a "proper balance" between secrecy and disclosure. Few in Congress appear to agree, and some are already planning to do something about it. Up to this point, it has been left to the president to decide what is secret and what is not. The Freedom of Information Act, for instance, defers to the president in the national security area. Now Sen. David F. Durenberger (R-Minn.), a member of the Intelligence Committee, says he will introduce legislation to remove the FOIA from exclusive presidential hands. Mr. Durenberger is no firebrand. He simply believes the president has gone too far. He is right.

SUGGESTIONS FOR FURTHER READING

Those interested in the issue of government secrecy may want to read Chapter 12 of the first edition of *Mass Media Issues*, which includes an analysis of the *Progressive* magazine H-bomb case.

Those interested in an anlysis of the public's "right to know" should read Eugenia Zerbinos, "The Right to Know: Whose Right and Whose Duty," *Communications and the Law* 4, no. 1 (Winter 1982).

Also of interest:

Arthur M. Cox, *The Myths of National Security: The Peril of Secret Government*. Boston: Beacon Press, 1975.

Itzhak Galmoor, ed., *Government Secrecy in Democracies*. New York: Harper and Row, 1977.

David Wise, *The Politics of Lying: Government Deception, Secrecy, and Power*. New York: Random House, 1973.

CHAPTER 8

International Propaganda

One of the most important and most studied political uses of mass media is international propaganda. The first reading in this chapter provides an historical overview of international propaganda techniques. The author, W. Phillips Davison, is professor of sociology and journalism at Columbia University.

Former Congressman John Le Boutillier discusses his views on the use of international propaganda in the second reading.

The final reading, originally published in the Soviet magazine *New Times*, gives a Soviet reaction to U.S. overseas propaganda efforts.

SOME TRENDS IN INTERNATIONAL PROPAGANDA

W. Phillips Davison

Those engaged in propaganda to further national goals have always used all channels available to them. Genghis Khan sent agents in advance of his Mongol armies to plant exaggerated rumors about the huge numbers and ferocity of his fighting men. Actually, the Mongol armies were often inferior in number to their opponents. Herodotus records that Themistocles had propaganda messages engraved on the stones at a watering place that he knew the opposing Ionian fleet would visit.[1] During the European Middle Ages, hand-copied leaflets and tracts supplemented sermons, speeches, songs, plays, and face-to-face conversation as weapons in the religious and dynastic struggles of the time.[2] With the invention of printing, a new flood of propaganda was unloosed. Both sides in the Thirty Years' War turned out massive quantities of leaflets, pamphlets, and line drawings—including vicious caricatures.[3] When, during this struggle, the coach carrying the chancellory records of Frederick of the Palatine (a Protestant leader) fell into the hands of the emperor's forces, the latter immediately made them public in a pamphlet entitled "The Secret Documents of the Principality of Anhalt." Shortly thereafter, the Protestant side came into possession of papers that concerned secret negotiations between the emperor and Spain. These, too, were promptly published.[4]

All available media were used by the French revolutionaries to spread their doctrines throughout the world at the close of the eighteenth century. They even hit upon a new means of exporting ideas: the use of clothing styles. Revolutionary sympathizers throughout Europe began to wear long trousers instead of the courtly knee breeches, long unshaped coats, Phrygian caps, and red collars. A conservative German prince, the Landgraf of Kassel, seeking to combat these subversive styles, ordered that all prisoners be dressed in them and then sent out in chains to sweep the streets. History does not tell us whether this counter-propaganda device was successful.[5]

The emergence of regularly published newspapers, and the increasing numbers of people who could read them, provided new opportunities for the propagandist. The press could be used to advance national policies in three principal ways: one could insert one's own material in existing newspapers; new papers could be founded, sometimes as overt organs of a particular nation or interest group, sometimes masquer-

From the *Annals of the American Academy of Political and Social Science* (Nov. 1971). Reprinted by permission.

1. Paul M. A. Linebarger, *Psychological Warfare* (second edition) (New York: Duell, Sloan and Pearce, 1954), pp. 7 and 15.
2. Wilhelm Bauer, *Die Öffentliche Meinung in der Weltgeschichte* (Potsdam: Akademische Verlagsgesellschaft Athenaion, 1929), chap. 7.
3. Elmer A. Beller, *Propaganda in Germany During the Thirty Years' War*, profusely illustrated (Princeton, N.J.: Princeton University Press, 1940).
4. Bauer, op. cit., p. 131.
5. Alfred Stürminger, *3000 Jahre Politische Propaganda* (Vienna and Munich, 1960), pp. 313–314.

ading as independent spokesmen; and overt or covert censorship could be exercised over the press under one's own control, thus ensuring a one-sided picture.

Napoleon proved expert at exploiting the press for propaganda purposes, surpassing all previous attempts along these lines. His government, like most governments up to that point, maintained domestic censorship. In addition, items serving French policies were planted in seemingly independent papers on the continent. The *Hamburger Korrespondent*, for instance, was persuaded to carry articles attacking the British government. Several new papers were founded by the French in occupied German territories, their content consisting largely of excerpts from the official French *Moniteur*.[6] In Paris there appeared *The Argus of London*, allegedly edited by an Englishman but actually produced in the French Foreign Office. The *Argus*, written from an "English standpoint," argued against the "war mongering journals" back in London.[7]

Napoleon's influence over the press was maintained largely by force, or the threat of force. Somewhat over a half century later, money was more important. We find governments of major powers spending large sums to assure that material they wanted to reach or keep from the public was published or suppressed. Napoleon III in France and Bismarck in Prussia both resorted to extensive bribery or to outright support of certain newspapers. The official handout also became common during this period, and ministries in many countries introduced offices to service the press. News management became somewhat more subtle and covert. Bismarck remarked in 1864 that certain papers were kind enough to provide the Prussian government with a quantity of "white paper," but this did not mean that the government took any responsibility for the articles that appeared in this space. Nevertheless, the Prussian government did not have complete control even of the Berlin press. When the desk of an Austrian diplomat was sold, drafts of articles that had previously appeared in Berlin newspapers were found in it. Not until then did the Prussian authorities know the origin of those unwelcome items. Napoleon III had even less thorough control over the Paris press. He could influence it, but it could also influence him, and it played an important part in projecting France into the disastrous Franco-Prussian war.[8]

TWENTIETH CENTURY PROPAGANDA

Bribery of the press continued to occur during the First World War. The Committee on Public Information, which conducted the worldwide propaganda of the United States, issued uniform instructions to its agents not to spend money on bribing or subsidizing newspapers and other information media; but the committee's files show that this rule was not strictly enforced, and sometimes the committee gave specific permission to break its own rules.[9] It is probable that all major powers spent substantial sums to influence the press in neutral countries, although specifics are difficult to document.[10]

In any case, means other than outright bribery were found effective in influencing the content of the press during World War I. These included not only carefully constructed handouts, but also the

6. Ibid., pp. 203–205.
7 Ibid., pp. 199–200.

8. Bauer, op. cit., chap. 16.

9. James R. Mock and Cedric Larson, *Words That Won the War* (Princeton, N.J.: Princeton University Press, 1939), p. 238.

10. George R. Bruntz, *Allied Propaganda and the Collapse of the German Empire in 1918* (Stanford, Calif.: Stanford University Press, 1938), p. 41. Bruntz notes that an anonymous booklet, allegedly written by a Paris editor, states that the French Government set aside 20 million francs to influence the neutral press. Bruntz, however, was unable to substantiate this charge.

provision of transportation and other services—for instance, office space—to journalists, as well as parties, conducted tours, and special "news scoops." The British arranged for neutral newspapermen to interview important public figures, knowing that many stories in the neutral press would find their way behind enemy lines.[11] George Creel, who directed American propaganda, reported that one of the most effective methods of the Committee on Public Information was to bring delegations of foreign newsmen to the United States so that they could make personal observations about American strength and morale. "These trips were of incalculable value in our foreign educational work. . . . "[12] A German embassy official, who came to Washington as a correspondent of a Berlin newspaper just before war broke out, claims that he was able to influence the publisher of the *New York Sun* to give more favorable treatment to Germany by promising preferential status for the *Sun's* Berlin correspondent and favorable access to the cable that Germany planned to lay to the United States.[13] The German cable did not materialize, and British control over major channels of communication from Europe to the United States proved important in insuring that the American press predominantly carried news that favored the Allies.

World War I also saw the greatly increased use of other propaganda channels: some old, some new. Leaflets, pamphlets, and posters were prepared in huge quantities. Some were sent to friendly and neutral countries, some were smuggled into enemy countries, and millions were dropped by various means on enemy troops.[14] Radio had not yet developed sufficiently to play a major role, but the American Committee on Public Information approximated the coverage of radio, at least on the home front, by mobilizing 75,000 "four-minute men" who were qualified to give brief, inspiring speeches on war-related subjects. Their oratory became a "nightly feature in virtually every movie house, and eventually in every place where Americans gathered for a communal purpose."[15] One is reminded of the even larger numbers of oral "agitators" later organized by the Soviet Union.[16]

All communications media are potential propaganda media.

Radio was, however, coming into its own. Toward the end of the war the Allies broadcast President Wilson's Fourteen Points to many parts of the world, and the Bolshevik revolutionaries in Russia recognized radio as a prime propaganda instrument. They broadcast the details of the 1918 Brest-Litovsk peace negotiations with Germany, in order to expose German annexationist ambitions, and soon after the end of the war Moscow's short-wave transmitters were sending out programs in German, English, Polish, and other languages.[17]

Short-wave radio became the dominant propaganda channel in World War II, although other channels were not neglected. Moscow, Berlin, London, New York, and Tokyo all blanketed major portions of the world with broadcasts in many

11. Sir Campbell Stuart, *Secrets of Crewe House* (London and New York: Hodder and Staughton, 1920), p. 98
12. George Creel, *How We Advertised America* (New York: Harper & Bros., 1920), p. 227.
13. Emil Witte, *Revelations of a German Attaché* (New York: George Doran, 1916), pp. 44–45.
14. Bruntz, op. cit., provides an excellent description of the leaflet activities of the Allies, pp. 41–67.
15. Mock and Larson, op. cit., p. 113.
16. Alex Inkeles, *Public Opinion in Soviet Russia* (Cambridge, Mass.: Harvard University Press, 1950), p. 67.
17. L. John Martin, *International Propaganda: Its Legal and Diplomatic Control* (Minneapolis: University of Minnesota Press, 1958), p. 7.

languages. The United States was late in developing short-wave propaganda but then proceeded rapidly. As of 1941, only 13 international short-wave transmitters were available, and most of those in operation beamed programs to Latin America. At the conclusion of the war, in 1945, the Office of War Information alone was using 36 transmitters in the continental United States and had installed 14 government-owned transmitters overseas. In addition, captured transmitters in Europe and Asia were pressed into service.[18] But the emphasis on recently developed electronic channels did not preclude the use of what is perhaps the oldest channel for international propaganda: infiltration of agents behind the enemy lines to spread rumors. All major powers employed rumor carriers and set up defenses against enemy-inspired rumors.[19]

When World War II ended, none of the victorious powers terminated their propaganda organizations, although in some cases names were changed.

Propagandists in both world wars made use of films to promote their doctrines, especially in Allied and neutral countries, but it was not until nearly twenty years after World War II that television became a major channel for international propaganda. Most industrialized countries now make substantial use of television in their efforts to reach foreign audiences, although the limited reach of direct television broadcasts has allowed short-wave radio to retain its pre-eminence in the international propaganda arena. Television programs intended for foreign audiences must ordinarily be taped and then broadcast from a friendly transmitter abroad, or else be carried over an international network such as Eurovision.[20] A major question facing students of international communication is how the rapidly developing capability of broadcasting from orbiting satellite transmitters to home receivers all over the world will be exploited. Will it offer an opportunity for increased consensus among nations, will it provide a new issue for international dispute and recrimination, or will it be stifled by domestic regulations prohibiting the reception of satellite transmissions?[21]

As the above brief account indicates, all channels, as they develop, are soon pressed into the service of international propaganda. An authority on the subject summarizes the situation by observing: "Of course, all communications media are potential propaganda media."[22] It is important to note, however, that new channels rarely displace old ones: they are merely added to the stockpile of available instruments and their use is coördinated with the use of previously existing channels.

18. Charles A. H. Thomson, *Overseas Information Service of the United States Government* (Washington: Brookings Institution, 1948), pp. 53–55.

19 Daniel Lerner, *Sykewar: Psychological Warfare Against Germany, D-Day to VE-Day* (New York: George W. Stewart, 1949), p. 267.

20. Televison does play a propaganda role in areas close to international boundaries. For instance, West Germany and East Germany direct TV programs to each other. It has been estimated that 70 percent of East German receivers can receive West German television, although during the last few years East German authorities have attempted to prevent this by building community antenna systems that receive only domestic broadcasts. (Bundesministerium für Gesamtdeutsche Fragen, *SBZ von A bis Z.* Bonn: Deutscher Bundes-Verlag, 1965, p. 128.) At the same time, about 140,000 households in West Germany can receive Austrian TV, and about 200,000 households in Austria can tune in a West German station. ("Sonderuntersuchungen zum Program des ZDF (Zweiten Deutschen Fernsehen) von 1963 bis 1969," *Schriftenreihe des ADF, #6*, Mainz, 1970.)

21. Paul L. Laskin, *Communicating by Satellite* (New York: Twentieth Century Fund, 1969).

22. Martin, op. cit., p. 200.

PROPAGANDA AS A REGULAR FUNCTION OF GOVERNMENT

The pervasiveness of international propaganda has increased not only as a result of the availability of new channels, but also because of the recognition of propaganda as a regular, permanent function of national governments, in peace as well as in war, and the expansion of the audience for international communication to include whole populations rather than only leaders, fighting men, or the educated classes.

Throughout most of history, communications from governments to citizens of other countries have been rather limited, except in time of war or international crisis. For this reason, most of the examples given above have been taken from crisis or wartime situations. Germany, France, England, and the United States all built up large propaganda machines during the First World War, but at the end of the war they dismantled them. Indeed, the U.S. Congress was in such haste to liquidate the Committee on Public Information that it cut off the committee's funds before its director had had a chance to dispose of his files and issue a final report.[23]

In the Soviet Union the situation was different. The triumphant Bolsheviks from the first recognized propaganda as a regular weapon of state power, and as early as 1923 we find Lord Curzon, the British Foreign Minister, vigorously protesting to Moscow about Bolshevik propaganda in various parts of the British Empire.[24]

As the Fascists and Nazis came to power in Italy and Germany, respectively, they, too, set up propaganda organizations. Italian broadcasts attacked British interests in the Middle East and appealed to Italian nationals in Latin America. The Berlin short-wave radio appealed to persons of German descent throughout the world.[25] Under Joseph Paul Goebbels, the Nazis established a propaganda ministry with enormous resources devoted to both domestic and foreign propaganda.[26]

Meanwhile, several colonial countries began to use radio to strengthen the bonds of empire. The Netherlands inaugurated an experimental service to the East Indies in 1927. France started broadcasting to its colonies in 1931. The BBC followed with its Empire Service in 1932.[27] In 1934, the British Council was established "to make the life and thought of the British peoples more widely known abroad," and also to strengthen the common cultural traditions of the British Commonwealth.[28]

In 1937, stung by Italian attacks in the Middle East, a British broadcasting station in Palestine undertook regular broadcasts in Arabic. Broadcasting in German and Italian commenced in the following year, and plans were made to erect two 50,000-watt transmitters that would make the British short-wave facilities the most powerful in the world.[29] When war came in 1939, a powerful British propaganda organization utilizing all media rapidly developed. The United States organized a Foreign Information service in 1941, and this was incorporated into the Office of War Information, which was established the following year.[30]

---

23. Creel, op. cit., p. 427.
24. John B. Whitton and Arthur Larson, *Propaganda: Toward Disarmament in the War of Words* (Dobbs Ferry, N.Y.: Oceana Publications, 1964), pp. 25–28. Whitton and Larson present an admirably concise history of international propaganda in forty pages. For a fascinating account of Communist propaganda in an American city during the interwar period, see Harold D. Lasswell and Dorothy Blumenstock, *World Revolutionary Propaganda: A Chicago Study* (New York: Knopf, 1939).
25. Whitton and Larson, op. cit., pp. 34–35.
26. Derrick Sington and Arthur Weidenfeld, *The Goebbels Experiment* (New Haven, Conn.: Yale University Press, 1943).
27. Whitton and Larson, op. cit., p. 35.
28. H. Schuyler Foster, Jr., "The Official Propaganda of Great Britain," *Public Opinion Quarterly* 2 (April, 1939), pp. 266–267.
29. Ibid.
30. Elmer Davis, "Report to the President," Ronald T. Farrar, ed., *Journalism Monographs* 7 (August, 1968), p. 7.

When World War II ended, none of the victorious powers terminated their propaganda organizations, although in some cases names were changed and budgets cut back. West Germany, Italy, and Japan, whose international propaganda activities had been terminated by defeat, built them up again rapidly. Mainland China became a major participant in international broadcasting and cultural activities, and its news agency, Hsin Hua, was able to rival the Soviet Service TASS in some areas.[31] Most smaller powers built up foreign information services, and today it is a rare nation that does not engage in at least some short-wave broadcasting.

Propaganda has thus become a standard arm of statecraft. "The great innovation of modern times is the frank recognition of propaganda as a regular branch of government, alongside economic and military departments."[32]

At the same time, propaganda has been directed to increasingly broad circles of the world population. The total nature of two world wars, in which the outcome was determined in part by the morale of whole populations—their will to work, to take orders, and accept deprivations—led propagandists to give more attention to mass audiences.[33] Nor could public opinion in neutral countries be disregarded. Following the conclusion of overt hostilities in 1945, the Cold War of the late 1940s and the 1950s brought continuing attempts by the major powers to influence the populations of hostile, friendly, and neutral countries.

Propaganda from abroad now reaches almost everyone, through almost all channels, almost all the time. There is no reason to believe that this trend toward increasing pervasiveness will be reversed.

31. W. Phillips Davison, *International Political Communication* (New York: Praeger, 1965), pp. 196–197.

32. John B. Whitton, "Propaganda in Cold Wars," *Public Opinion Quarterly* 15, 1 (Spring, 1951), p. 142.

33. Hans Speier, "Psychological Warfare Reconsidered," in *Social Order and the Risks of War* (New York: George W. Stewart, 1952), p. 436.

EXPENSE AND COMPLEXITY OF PROPAGANDA

While propaganda is cheap when compared with other instruments of policy, its costs are constantly increasing. George Creel reported that the Committee on Public Information spent about $6.9 million during the 18 months of its activity during World War I. But it earned $2.8 million from its films, war expositions, and various minor sources. So the net cost of the committee's activities, at home and abroad, came to about $4 million.[34] Elmer Davis found that the bill for Office of War Information operations for three years and three months came to about $132.5 million, of which some $12 million was for domestic activities. The net cost was somewhat lower, since OWI also realized about $2 million from such sources as the sale of publications.[35] By contrast, the U.S. Information Agency spent some $177 million in the fiscal year 1969 alone.[36] It can be assumed that costs of international propaganda operations have risen proportionately in other countries.

International propaganda is increasingly expensive, not only because it is produced in greater quantity than before but because modern communication technology requires the investment of more and more money, and propaganda staffs have become more specialized and complex.

Actually, we cannot be sure how much the expense and complexity of propaganda organizations have increased, since historical records give us few details about propaganda operations of ancient and medieval times. Certainly, Alexander the Great spared no expense to make sure that the Greek world received favorable accounts of his exploits in the East. With

34. Creel, op. cit., p. 13.

35. Davis, op. cit., p. 39.

36. U.S.I.A. Appropriation Hearings for 1970, Subcommittee of the Committee on Appropriations, U.S. House of Representatives (Washington: Government Printing Office, 1969), p. 423.

him on his campaigns he took a group of skilled Greek writers whose task it was to prepare news reports. The reports were then sped back to Macedonia by relays of swift runners. There they were copied and disseminated throughout Hellas. We do not know how much this operation cost, but it could scarcely have been cheap.[37]

Alexander also seems to have used the services of accomplished public relations advisers. His court historian, Callisthenes, who was constantly at his side, propagated the idea that Alexander was the son of Zeus. This politically important notion was confirmed by the oracle of Didyma, and we can assume that Alexander's propaganda staff had something to do with the oracle's pronouncement and also made full use of it subsequently. Callisthenes warned Alexander, however, not to try to introduce into Greece the forms of emperor worship then common in Asia.[38] Translated into modern language, his advice was "Respect the local cultures."

A Holy Roman emperor of the thirteenth century, Frederick II, offers another example of a monarch who built an extensive propaganda organization. His chancellory included a group of able young writers, who produced a stream of documents supporting the emperor in his struggle with the papacy. An indication of the skill of these publicists is that the emperor's manifestos were constructed so as to be most effective when read aloud—an important consideration in the days of limited literacy. Full use was made of repetition, contrast, rhetorical questions, rhyme, and alliteration. Particular attention was given to the beginning of each manifesto, what the modern journalist would call the "lead." Frederick also mobilized large numbers of traveling troubadours; they carried his propaganda in lyrical form from the Mediterranean to the most distant borders of the empire.[39]

37. Stürminger, op. cit., p. 386.
38. Ibid., pp. 61–62.

Napoleon organized a rather elaborate propaganda apparatus, but he seems to have directed this personally, and to have made extensive use of his existing administrative and diplomatic machinery for press control. Among the units that Napoleon set up specifically for propaganda or press-control purposes were a translation bureau which kept him informed of what was appearing in the foreign-language press, especially the English and German papers, and a directorate that was to monitor, influence, and (if necessary) suppress printed materials. The news service of the official *Moniteur* was greatly expanded, and all other newspapers were instructed to follow its lead in their news and commentary. Napoleon personally reviewed much of the material that went into the *Moniteur.*[40]

The propaganda organizations that took shape during World War I were considerably more differentiated. Furthermore, they were functional units of government directed by appointed administrators. The chief of state no longer exercised personal supervision over daily operations. By 1916, France had established a Maison de la Presse as the official agency for the conduct of French propaganda, under the control of the Minister of Foreign Affairs. This organization had sections to monitor the foreign and domestic press, to supply news and information to media in France and in friendly or neutral countries, to obtain information about public opinion in enemy and neutral countries, and to distribute propaganda leaflets, books, photographs, and films. The Maison de la Presse also had a radio division, which sent out dispatches eight times daily from the Eiffel Tower, from Lyons, and from Carnarvon, Wales.[41] Additional propaganda work was done by other government agencies, especially the War Ministry and the semi-official Alliance Française.

In England, a number of propaganda agencies

39. Ibid., pp. 135–138.
40. Ibid., p. 198.
41. Bruntz, op. cit., pp. 13–15.

grew up during the first years of the war, but most of these were gathered together in a Department of Information of the Foreign Office at the end of 1916. This department had four principal divisions: the cinema division, the news division, the political intelligence division, and a division that produced and disseminated material for neutral and domestic consumption. A later reorganization in 1918 resulted in the creation of a Ministry of Information, directly responsible to the War Cabinet, with divisions for enemy countries, neutral countries, intelligence, administration, and cinema. A separate National War Aims Committee concerned itself with domestic propaganda. As in France, the military establishment also conducted propaganda, and these activities were only gradually coördinated with those of civilian agencies.[42]

The American Committee on Public Information, in addition to its domestic branches, had three principal units in its foreign section: the Wireless-Cable Service, the Foreign Press Bureau, and the Foreign Film Division. Committee representatives in some twenty countries attempted to see that local media used the wireless and cable bulletins and the articles and photographs that were mailed abroad by the Foreign Press Bureau, and that foreign movie houses showed the committee's propaganda films. Information about public opinion abroad was supplied by the Military Intelligence Branch of the Army.[43]

Although propaganda organizations during the First World War were more complex than any the world had seen hitherto, they were simple in comparison with those that emerged in World War II. In the Office of War Information, for instance, operating bureaus were established for each major propaganda medium, for communication facilities, for intelligence, and for the support of field offices. In addition, deputy directors were in charge of regional staffs concerned with Europe, the British Empire, and the Far East, respectively. There were also various specialized planning, policy, administrative, and control staffs.[44] The joint British-American Psychological Warfare Division, the principal Allied Military propaganda organization in Europe, was almost as complex. Furthermore, it was responsible to various British and American civilian agencies as well as to the military command. A British member of the division later observed cheerfully that this unwieldy complexity carried an accidental advantage with it, since nobody had the final word and individual propagandists could enjoy considerable autonomy. An American participant was more gloomy: promising personalities wore themselves out in organizational battles and had little energy left for constructive activities.[45]

Whether or not organizational complexity results in more effective propaganda, it apparently is here to stay, and one may expect that propaganda machines of the future will contain even more moving parts. Whenever a new channel of communication is developed, or another country of the world becomes relevant to national policy, a new unit or sub-unit is added. Then new policy, coördination, and liaison units are necessary to control the conglomerate. The organization chart of today's U.S. Information Agency, and what is known about the structures of the Soviet and Chinese agencies for conducting propaganda abroad, do nothing to dispel this impression.[46]

42. Ibid., pp. 18–30.

43. Mock and Larson, op. cit., pp. 239–246.

44. Thomson, op. cit., pp. 37–48.

45. Lerner, op. cit., pp. 57–59.

46. Robert E. Elder, *The Information Machine: The United States Information Agency and American Foreign Policy* (Syracuse, N.Y.: Syracuse University Press, 1968); Frederick C. Barghoorn, *Soviet Foreign Propaganda* (Princeton, N.J.: Princeton University Press, 1964); Frederick T. C. Yu, *Mass Persuasion in Communist China* (New York: Praeger, 1964).

THE ROLE OF SOCIAL SCIENTISTS

There also seems to be a trend toward the inclusion of social scientists in propaganda organizations: first historians, then others. The names of historians are scattered through the record of past propaganda activities. Callisthenes has already been mentioned. The Roman historian, N. Junius, may have been the first to make historical research serve policy purposes. He averred that during the period of the kings in ancient Rome, the quaestors had been named by the citizens, not by the kings, thus assisting the political fortunes of his friend, Gaius Gracchus.[47] During the Middle Ages, rulers had frequent occasion to employ historians to show that their ambitions were sanctified by past practice. George Creel claimed that he could call on 3,000 historians to assist the Committee on Public Information, and a number of historians did in fact fill important positions in Creel's organization, including Guy Stanton Ford.[48] Charles E. Merriam, a political scientist from the University of Chicago, also held a strategic post, but Creel refers to him as an "economist and sociologist," thus suggesting that his professional expertise was not very salient to his superior. We also find a Captain Walter Lippmann of Army Intelligence, then known as a political scientist, in charge of editorial work at the American printing plant in Paris which was turning out propaganda materials. Colonel House, President Wilson's confidant, acted as unofficial adviser to the propaganda operation "because of his knowledge of German psychology."[49]

The behavioral science input in World War II was much more extensive. Top positions in the Office of War Information were held mainly by journalists, but psychologists, sociologists, anthropologists, and political scientists could be found in quantity at all levels below the top echelon. The same was true in the military psychological warfare organizations and, to an only slightly lesser extent, in British propaganda units. The basic questionnaire designed to collect psychological warfare intelligence in Europe was designed by a British psychiatrist (Henry V. Dicks) and an American sociologist (Edward A. Shils). One account refers to "historians and social scientists in abundance, including men of considerable professional standing" as populating the psychological intelligence set-up.[50]

The influence of social scientists on U.S. propaganda policy in World War II was considerable. This was partly because they helped to shape the policy papers that later were approved at higher levels as basic policy guidance, partly because they were the ones who collected and analyzed most of the information on which policy and output were based, and partly because distinguished social scientists served as official or unofficial policy advisers to the highest officials who were concerned with propaganda. An example of direct influence on policy is provided by the work of social anthropologists in the OWI, who recommended that the United States refrain from propaganda attacks on the Emperor of Japan and should leave his fate to be decided by the Japanese themselves after the war.[51] It is now routine for a substantial number of positions in the U.S. Information Agency and other propaganda organizations to be occupied by persons with social science training.

PROPAGANDA GOALS AND USES

Because international propaganda has been employed mainly in wartime and times of revolu-

47. Stürminger, op. cit., p. 79.
48. Creel, op. cit., pp. 6, 101.
49. Bruntz, op. cit., p. 62.
50. Lerner, op. cit., pp. 109–111.
51. Alexander H. Leighton, *Human Relations in a Changing World: Observations on the Use of Social Sciences* (New York: Dutton, 1949), pp. 55–56.

tion or crisis, its goals have been largely the same throughout most of history. On the basis of his analysis of World War I propaganda, Harold D. Lasswell finds that it had four principal strategic aims:

1. To mobilize hatred against the enemy.
2. To preserve the friendship of allies.
3. To preserve the friendship and, if possible, to procure the coöperation of neutrals.
4. To demoralize the enemy.[52]

If we look at the mission of the overseas branch of the Office of War Information, as stated in a directive early in 1943, we find substantially the same aims restated in slightly different language. The principal difference is that the OWI's mission also included the task of keeping alive hope of liberation in enemy-occupied countries and stimulating resistance to occupation forces.[53] If Alexander the Great, Ghengis Khan, or Napoleon had had a policy section of their propaganda apparatus, it is probable that they would have stated propaganda goals in much the same way.

Yet some international propaganda has always been conducted in peacetime, and now it is accepted as part of peacetime governmental structures. Clearly, the traditional goals as formulated in war are not appropriate. That international propaganda can serve peaceful aims probably was recognized in classical Athens, where word about the city's magnificent buildings and elaborate festivals was spread throughout the known world. This propaganda not only impressed allies but also attracted tourists.[54] French cultural propaganda during the nineteenth and twentieth centuries contributed to French prestige and helped to retain the preeminence of the French fashion industry.[55] Lasswell has observed that even wartime propaganda can serve to stimulate an international dialogue: "We are witnessing the growth of a world public, and this public has arisen in part because international propaganda has at once agitated and organized it."[56] Although it is probable that the bulk of official propaganda . . . still serves selfish political aims, a part of it is devoted to advancing international coöperation and promoting commercial interchange.

The great innovation of modern times is the frank recognition of propaganda as a regular branch of government.

The trend toward the use of international propaganda for peaceful, nonpolitical purposes is especially marked in the case of smaller industrialized powers. Sweden, for instance, is concerned about its national image abroad in part because this has been found to have a bearing on the acceptance of Swedish exports. One reason that Sweden took part in the recent Osaka trade fair in Japan was that surveys in Japan had shown Sweden to be regarded there as far behind the United States, England, West Germany, and Switzerland in its technical know-how. A Swedish official concerned with international information concludes: "Just for that reason it is of the greatest importance that there be a not too limited information activity about Sweden in those countries where we would like to be understood and find customers."[57] The Foreign Agents Registration Section of the U.S. Department of Justice, which registers persons and organizations

52. Harold D. Lasswell, *Propaganda Technique in World War I*, new ed. (Cambridge, Mass.: M.I.T. Press, 1971), p. 195.
53. Thomson, op. cit., p. 40.
54. Stürminger, op. cit., p. 34.
55. Ibid., p. 317.
56. Lasswell, op. cit., p. 6.
57. Tore Tallroth, "Sverige i Stora Världen," in Morgan Abrahamsson et al., *Vårt Ekonomiska Läge 1971* (Stockholm: Sparfrämjandet Förlagsaktiebolag, 1971), p. 154.

in the United States that conduct propaganda on behalf of foreign governments and political parties, observed in a 1960 report:

> The largest source of political propaganda has continued to be the official foreign government information and tourist offices, whose activities are intended to create good will toward their respective countries, promote tourism, trade, and investment, and present the positions of their governments on various international issues.[58]

As of the end of 1969, 450 active registrations of agencies distributing propaganda in the United States on behalf of foreign principals were on file, most of these concerned heavily with tourism, investment, or trade.[59]

As far as the United States is concerned, official propaganda activities by the government have been dwarfed by the commercial publicity of private enterprise. Already in 1953, U.S. advertisers were spending $280 million in other countries, more than twice the budget of the U.S. Information Agency.[60] Foreign advertising by firms in most countries has grown enormously since then. In 1955, West Germany was spending $20 million for international advertising, The Netherlands $50 million, and Switzerland $17.5 million.[61] It is probable that the foreign advertising expenditures of West European countries and Japan have in recent years increased at a more rapid rate than those of the United States.

A growing quantity of propaganda, political and non-political, governmental and nongovernmental, is also being transmitted by the international news media as a part of their day-to-day reporting function. A trend toward presentation of propaganda in the form of news through the regular news channels can be observed since the rise of the daily newspaper, and this trend can be expected to continue into the future. As a student of journalistic technique observes: "There are growing numbers of men who understand how news is generated, organized, and transmitted, and it would be unintelligent of them if they did not use it to their own advantage.[62]

A trend toward propaganda in the form of news can be observed, and this trend can be expected to continue into the future.

Propaganda in the coming years will be more pervasive in part because there will be a wider range of channels available to larger populations, and in part because more resources will be devoted by national states and private organizations to grinding out purposive communications. One of the major tasks of scholars is to suggest ways that it may be more fruitfully employed in the service of international harmony in a shrinking world.

58. Report of the Attorney General to the Congress of the United States on the Adminstration of the Foreign Agents Registration Act of 1938, as Amended, for the Period January 1, 1955, to December 31, 1959, mimeographed (Washington, D.C.: Office of the Attorney General, June, 1960).

59. Report of the Attorney General to the Congress of the United States on the Administration of the Foreign Agents Registration Act of 1938, as Amended, for the Calendar Year 1969, mimeographed (Washington, no date). These registrations do not reflect the propaganda activities of embassies or consulates, or activities conducted from abroad via international mail, short-wave radio, and the like.

60. "Annual Volume of U.S. International Advertising Continues to Expand," Sixth Annual Survey of the International Advertising Association, New York (no date).

61. "International Advertising Volume Continues to Grow," Seventh Annual Survey of the International Advertising Association, New York (no date).

62. Ben H. Bagdikian, *The Information Machines: Their Impact on Men and the Media* (New York: Harper & Row, 1971), p. 293.

HOW TO OVERTHROW THE SOVIET GOVERNMENT—WITHOUT FIRING A SHOT

John LeBoutillier

In 1975, a Long Island rabbi visiting Moscow decided to take a stroll through the local park on the outskirts of the city. He happened upon two men conversing in hushed tones. The rabbi's ears were not fooled; the men were speaking Yiddish. Approaching them, the rabbi introduced himself and then asked, "Aren't you risking severe punishment if caught?"

One of the Soviet Jews nodded his head and asked, "If you are so concerned with the way the government treats us, then why don't you in America do something about us?"

The rabbi replied, "Each year I lead a protest march in front of the Soviet mission in Glen Cove, N.Y. The newspapers write stories about it—and the Soviet Ambassador tries to ignore our existence."

The two Soviet Jews paused and listened, then one of them grabbed the rabbi's arm. With tears in his eyes, he said, "We've never heard of these protests. But knowing of such actions gives us hope, hope that somebody cares . . . that somebody is thinking of us."

From *USA Today* (Jan. 1982). Reprinted by permission.

This brief incident exemplifies a vital, missing link in our foreign policy as it relates to the Soviet Union. While relations deteriorate with the Soviet government, moving from detente to confrontation, we are ignoring a hidden ally—the Soviet people. As no less an expert than Aleksandr I. Solzhenitsyn has said, "The Kremlin leadership is immeasurably indifferent and remote from the Russian people."

Scholars of both the left and right agree that this new decade is fraught with danger. There is no question that America's once dominant position of military leadership has diminished, only to be replaced by a precarious security position. The Soviet Union has constructed the most awesome military machine in the history of mankind. They have eclipsed the U.S. in conventional weapons, greatly expanded their naval power, and have clearly decided to make space weaponry an integral part of their arsenal.

Of course, such a rapid and widespread buildup is not conducted without some internal, social cost. Indeed, the Soviet government has bled every drop of available resources from the Russian economy and spent those resources on military power. The result is an economy that limps along, barely able to sustain the population on much more than a minimal diet. In fact, Solzhenitsyn states that some peasant areas of the Soviet Union have gone 30 years without ever eating meat! The health of the working public is deteriorating, and alcoholism is at the highest rate of any nation in the world. Yet, despite these alarming conditions, the Soviet leadership persists in its desire to possess a war machine capable of enabling the Kremlin to exert its will anywhere in the world.

The U.S., as witnessed by the Reagan mandate, finally awoke from its post-Vietnam lethargy and recognized the severity of the world situation. The rise of the Ayatollah and our impotence in dealing with the hostage situation in Iran demonstrated for all to see our declining military capability. Unquestionably, Reagan and the new Congress are presently responding to that mandate by drastically increasing military spending.

It must be understood, however, that even a large increase in funding for the Pentagon will not appreciably alter the balance of power for years to come; present spending can not result in renewed strength for years. It takes time for new weapon systems to be constructed, tested, and manufactured.

Thus, it is generally agreed that the U.S.S.R. and the U.S. face an immediate future roughly equal on the strategic nuclear front, with the U.S. still superior at sea and the Soviets clearly ahead in conventional forces. This situation provides a military stand-off for the next few years, but the Soviets will continue to press their ground force advantage whenever and wherever they can.

REACHING THE SOVIET PEOPLE

Given this situation, I believe the real war of the 1980s will be the war of ideas. If the U.S. is to be successful in this "war of ideas," we must at once prepare to have our ideas heard. For that reason, I am proposing that we radically change the scope and nature of our two present communications arms in Europe—Radio Free Europe and Radio Liberty. These two broadcast operations are poorly financed, undermanned, and subject to both physical and qualitative pressures. Furthermore, the broadcasts themselves are sloppy, timid, and badly conceived.

First of all, I would like to see an increase in funds made available for the purpose of radio communications behind the Iron Curtain. Presently, we are unable to even reach Soviet Central Asia, nor can we be heard by the population in the far eastern sections of the Soviet Union. It is useless to spend any money whatsoever if we are not being heard. To correct this, we need to upgrade our broadcast facilities not only in Munich, but also in Oman and Taiwan so as to have blanket coverage of all of Eastern Europe and the entire Soviet Union.

The cost of such a project? Not much. In fact, by simply subtracting the cost of one new tank from the Administration's new Pentagon budget, we could build the necessary transmitters. We are talking about approximately $2,500,000.

I am a firm believer that we in the U.S. have the truth on our side. We do not need to lie, distort, exaggerate, and concoct as the Soviets do; we need only to let the Soviet people have access to all the facts their government refuses them. The recent events in Poland, for example, are a devastating sequence of mini-revolutions that could spread into the Soviet Union. The year-long massacre in Afghanistan also needs to be explained to the Soviet people; their government refuses even to acknowledge the presence of Soviet troops in that country.

Other forms of the truth also need to be supplied to the people, truths that have been barred by the Kremlin. Religious services, historical accounts, and audio transmissions of books banned inside Russia all should be incorporated in our broadcasts.

It is now almost 30 years since the creation of Radio Liberty. That organization's charter was to use radio transmissions into the Soviet Union in an effort to forge a line of communication with the Soviet people. Now, however, we must make use of the most modern medium—television. Almost everyone in the Soviet Union today has a radio; surprisingly, though, more and more people are acquiring television sets. We should take stock of this and prepare to reach the people through this powerful medium. I propose the creation of a visual counterpart to Radio Liberty—Television Truth.

Can anyone in America today deny the awesome power of a video image? Just imagine the reaction among Soviet farmers and laborers if they could see broadcasts from Poland each night featuring the members of Solidarity. Would it be long before Russian workers banded together for the same reasons as the Polish workforce?

The hidden attraction of television is something the Kremlin has yet to grasp. Not long ago, they began broadcasting nationally from Moscow, where the standard of living is appreciably higher than in rural areas. Before long, Moscow was besieged by an unexpected migration of peasants from the rural areas who had seen the "better life of Moscow" on television and decided to move. The Soviet government was taken by surprise.

We *can* broadcast and telecast into the Soviet Union. Presently, we utilize ground transmitters. I propose that we add a new dimension—satellite broadcasts. For the cost of four fighter jets, we could launch and deploy a communications satellite positioned directly over Russia. From this location, we could send both radio and television messages unimpeded directly into every radio and television in that nation. The Kremlin could not jam us. Indeed, with the recent success of the Space Shuttle, the cost of deploying this satellite will be reduced.

Of course, it isn't how much we spend that counts; it is how we spend it. The fanciest equipment in the world is not enough. The most important ingredient in this project is the substance of the broadcasts themselves.

If some in the U.S. are dubious about the effectiveness of this use of the truth as a bridge to the Soviet people, the Kremlin is not. Soviet leaders are paranoid about each and every one of these programs. As an example of this fear, compare our total broadcasting budget to their jamming efforts. While we spent just under $100,000,000 in 1980 on Radio Liberty and Radio Free Europe, the Kremlin spent $700,000,000 just to jam our broadcasts! Clearly, they are afraid of the truth.

Moscow's desire to stop our transmissions is not confined merely to electronic jamming. Indeed, our main broadcasting station in Munich was mysteriously bombed a few months ago. Traces of the explosive device revealed the use of plastique explosives made in Eastern Europe. The operators of that Munich station also have been personally threatened, and there are reports of attempts to poison the food in the cafeteria.

Even more alarming is recent evidence of Soviet disinformation and infiltration into the management of Radio Liberty. Syndicated columnist Jack Anderson recently reported that one of his associates discovered "broadcasts peculiarly in harmony with Soviet expansionism, as one containing the statement that the 1939 Soviet invasion of Poland 'extended Russia's borders to their natural limits' "; a broadcast "upbraiding Pope John Paul II for his support of the Uniate clergy in the Ukraine"; and one on "anti-Polish positions current in Soviet historiography."

It is uniquely American to believe in the power of truth. We have a duty and an obligation to provide that truth to peoples all over the world who are denied it.

Such indications of Soviet influence in the content of our broadcasts are not new. The publication *Kontinent* reported that "Radio Liberty tried the patience of its listeners with broadcasts of a frankly Marxist inclination" and Solzhenitsyn claims that a number of Radio Liberty messages are blatantly anti-Semitic.

The jamming, the bombing, the disinformation, and possible infiltration by the Kremlin are all examples of Moscow's fear of the truth. They know that, in the "war of ideas," they will lose, unless they distort the truth for their purposes and limit our means of reaching their people.

THE POLISH EXPERIENCE

In 1980, when the worker rebellions began in Poland, the government in Warsaw immediately restricted the flow of news reports in an attempt to isolate the trouble and prevent it from spreading to other regions of the nation. Radio Free Europe deserves great credit for assuming the responsibility of informing the Polish people of the latest events. Indeed, it can be said that, without our assistance, Solidarity would never have been able to achieve and maintain such a strong sense of unity in the face of extreme State pressure.

There is no reason why the same effectiveness cannot be achieved inside another country, such as the Soviet Union or Cuba. Since the Polish uprising began, we have evidence of labor strikes inside Russia. Only the vice-like grip over news dissemination by the Kremlin prevents this news from spreading throughout the U.S.S.R. We will have to be the ones who inform the Soviet people.

Cuba is a similar example of a repressive, domineering government that denies the truth to its people. Cuba is a country that harbors latent discontent with the Castro regime. Evidence of this can be found in the rapid exodus of so many unhappy natives and the tales of cruelty they brought with them.

A Radio Free Cuba, based in Southern Florida, would be a more effective anti-Castro device than all the military and economic aid we presently are shipping to Central American governments currently under attack by Cuban agents. In this case, the best defense is a good offense. Exploiting the internal weakness of a nation forces its government to retrench internationally.

Cuba and the U.S.S.R. have grave internal difficulties. Health problems, morale decline in the ranks of the military, labor unhappiness, and a repressive regime . . . are all sore points which we can exacerbate by our use of modern media techniques.

The use of Radio Liberty, Radio Free Europe, and a television program (Television Truth) to exploit these internal weaknesses places these programs in our national defense arsenal. They *are* weapons. However, they are not weapons designed to kill people; instead, they are tools to transmit the truth to populations long starved for it.

Richard Pipes, the noted Soviet expert and an extreme hard-liner when it comes to his appraisal of our military strength *vis-a-vis* the Soviets, recently said, "I would rather have this new communication program than have three new nuclear aircraft carriers." Pipes agrees that such a "truth" capability aimed at the heart of the Soviet Union is an "offensive" weapon in the truest sense of the word. However, it is designed to prevent a military war; rather, it will enable us to win the "war of ideas."

In a time of reappraisal of priorities in our society, we should not lose sight of our own Revolution. Could the early Americans have succeeded in confronting the King had not they had the truth on their side? Communicating that truth came in the flourishing media of pamphlets. Then, in the era of the Abolitionists, leading up to the Civil War, those brave individuals who fought slavery communicated in newspapers known for their political stances. In each of these instances, a just cause triumphed over evil because the truth was made available.

It is uniquely American to believe in the power of the truth. We have a duty and an obligation to provide that truth to peoples all over the world who are denied it. Why? Because we know that, armed with that truth, they will act accordingly.

SUBVERSION BY RADIO

V. Chernyavsky

Radio Liberty and Radio Free Europe are lavishly financed by the U.S. Government. In 1980 their budget amounted to $93.9 million. Their 1981 budget, the U.S. press reported, will be $113.5 million.

Why such munificence? A big-business Government is usually very stingy when it comes to public education and culture. The point is that Liberty and Free Europe are not ordinary radio stations. They are engaged in subversion and espionage against the Soviet Union and other Socialist countries.

And they are not secret agencies; the way they are directed and financed leaves no doubt that the two are official propaganda media maintained by federal funds, as are the CIA, the FBI, the Pentagon, the International Communication Agency, or any other U.S. Government institution. One can draw this conclusion on reading *Subversion by Radio* (Novosti Press Agency), a collection of convincing documentary evidence and facts exposing Liberty and Free Europe.

From *World Press Review* (Feb. 1981). Reprinted by permission. Originally published in the Soviet magazine *New Times*.

For many years Washington has tried to observe a semblance of decency, claiming that Liberty and Free Europe are "private organizations" which have nothing to do with the U.S. Government. It was only in 1971 that the Government took them under its wing.

Radio Liberty and Radio Free Europe are engaged in subversion and espionage against the Soviet Union and other Socialist countries.

In 1973 an international broadcasting council consisting of five members appointed by the U.S. President and of the executive directors of Liberty and Free Europe was established, and responsibility for the political activity of the stations was placed on the State Department. Formally this meant that the stations broke off their ties with the CIA. The first chairman of the council claimed that the stations were engaged only in exchange of information and ideas in full accord with the Helsinki Final Act.

Subsequent events belied this statement, writes Sergei Golyakov, a Soviet journalist and one of the authors of *Subversion by Radio*. Evidence gathered by a Czechoslovak intelligence officer who worked at Radio Free Europe proved that Radio Liberty and Radio Free Europe were still being used by the CIA for subversion against the Socialist community. A Bulgarian intelligence officer who worked at Radio Free Europe revealed that the U.S. Secret Service still controlled the Munich-based radio stations. And CIA director Stansfield Turner said in an interview that nothing had changed in Radio Liberty and Radio Free Europe; the top posts were, as before, held by Americans—mainly employees of the CIA or associated agencies.

The stations engage not only in subversive radio propaganda but also in "sideline" activities of great interest to U.S. intelligence, Polish journalist Julian Wilczynski writes. The *New York Times* has revealed that Radio Free Europe employees maintain constant ties with people in some of the "Soviet bloc" countries who collect information for the station. The research department of Radio Free Europe, the *International Herald Tribune* wrote, is regarded "as a uniquely comprehensive record of life in Communist countries."

Radio Liberty and Radio Free Europe glean information not only by sending their staff members to Socialist countries in the guise of tourists, businessmen, and scientists, but also by fishing it out of citizens of these countries who visit capitalist States. Having examined documents of the U.S. Library of Congress, the authors of the book conclude that Liberty and Free Europe annually "process" some 7,000 citizens of Socialist countries.

The secret information gathered by these stations is used not only by special services of the U.S. but also (with CIA approval, of course) by its Atlantic partners. This is not surprising, for closer coordination of Radio Liberty and Radio Free Europe activity with the "psychological war" departments of the NATO States was envisaged even in President Carter's March, 1977, report to Congress on international broadcasting.

Now that U.S. imperialism is pushing the world into a new cold war, creating a situation dangerous to international peace and security, the Munich radio stations have been given a powerful stimulus for their subversive activity. The *Washington Post* reported recently that the CIA had worked out new plans for intensifying subversion against the Soviet Union and other Socialist countries, partly by intensifying Radio Liberty and Radio Free Europe operations.

All people of goodwill—all who champion peace, social justice, and dĕtente—cannot but agree with the conclusion drawn by the authors of *Subversion by Radio*: there is no room for Radio Liberty and Radio Free Europe in the present-day system of news media or in the political life of the world.

SUGGESTIONS FOR FURTHER READING

One of the more confusing, complicated issues in international communications today is the proposed New World Information Order. For an in-depth analysis, see Kusum Singh and Bertram Gross, "'MacBride': The Report and the Response," *Journal of Communication* 31, no. 4 (Autumn 1981): 104–17. Also see Corydon B. Dunham, "On Government Control of the Media," *Communications and the Law*, 4, no. 3 (Summer 1982): 19–22.

Those interested in Voice of America may want to read "Propaganda Warts" in the May 1982 issue of *Harpers*, p. 19, or "Voices of Discord," in the January 2, 1982 issue of *America*, p.2.

Also of interest:

Julian Hale, *Radio Power: Propaganda and International Broadcasting*. Philadelphia; Temple University Press, 1975.

Maury Lisann, *Broadcasting to the Soviet Union: International Politics and Radio*. New York: Praeger, 1975.

Gladys Thum and Marcella Thum, *Persuasion and Propaganda in War and Peace*. Evanston, Ill.: McDougal-Littell, 1974.

GROCERY
Coca-Cola
VIRGINIA SLIMS.
MILK MAKES YOU
FAT

PART THREE

Mass Media and America's Perception of Reality

It has become axiomatic to point out that we live in a media-saturated age, surrounded by messages that change our perception of the world. Changing our perceptions is, after all, mass media's intended purpose, which underlies the commonly recognized media functions of informing, entertaining, serving the economic system, and influencing public opinion. So the issue here is not *whether* the mass media help mold America's perception of reality. They do. The issue is how they mold that perception, and if that molding is beneficial to American society.

The first chapter in this part of the book deals with the most direct forms of media manipulation of reality: advertising and public relations. The second chapter extends this examination to journalism, and the third chapter extends it to television news. The fourth chapter looks at television entertainment. The fifth looks at the media's depiction of sex, and how it affects us. The final chapter presents analyses and debates on the way media tend to stereotype according to race, sex, and occupation.

CHAPTER 9

Advertising and Public Relations

This chapter begins with articles on the topic of advertising. Some of the practices that have brought the most criticism upon the advertising industry include false "scientific" claims, phony demonstrations, phony secret ingredients, manipulated statistics, meaningless testimonials, meaningless comparisons, exaggerations, and out-and-out lies.

The first reading in this chapter is Rick Berkoff's analysis of some of the tricks of the advertising trade. The second reading is Curt Gentry's exposé of "wordsmithing" in advertising, and the third reading is an article that Vance Packard recently wrote as an update to his 1957 book, *The Hidden Persuaders*, which was an examination of "the games admen play." In the final reading on advertising, Jerry Goodis protests against one author's claim of a conspiracy to implant subliminal messages in ads.

The last two readings in this chapter concern the world of public relations. The first of these is P.J. Corkery's insider's view of the workings of a public relations firm. Mr. Corkery's article originally appeared in *Harper's* magazine. The final reading is the transcript of a speech given by a public relations executive on one of public relations' time-honored techniques: the press conference.

CAN YOU SEPARATE THE SIZZLE FROM THE STEAK?

Rick Berkoff

People in the advertising business like to say: "Don't sell the steak; sell the sizzle!" In other words, an advertisement should concentrate on selling not the particular product or service, in and of itself, but what is called its "end benefit."

What's an end benefit? Well, when you drink a Coke, it supposedly refreshes you. That feeling of being refreshed is the end benefit. Likewise, you don't buy a lawn mower for the sake of simply having a lawn mower (at least most people don't); you buy it because you want your grass cut. A trim lawn—and perhaps peer approval—are the end benefits here. And what about the dream merchants? Revlon isn't selling a face cream—it's selling beauty, youth and hope.

There's nothing wrong with emphasizing end benefits—within reason. But much of the advertising we see has a way of taking indecent liberties with these end benefits, carrying them to their absolute extremes. The result: lots of promises that can't be delivered. Sizzle that *oversells*.

Problems inevitably result when we allow our-

From the *Journal of Popular Culture* (Fall, 1981). Reprinted by permission.

selves to become dazzled by the sizzle, and romanced to a point where, as consumers, we forget ourselves, losing touch with reality just when we need our good judgment the most—when we're being motivated to buy.

In the two decades since Vance Packard wrote his now classic study of the role of motivational research in modern advertising, *The Hidden Persuaders,* much has been said and written on the subject of "M.R." But even today most of us take advertising too much for granted. We have little notion of how it's actually constructed, and we care much less. But our lack of apparent interest makes us no less susceptible to advertising's charms—and costly charms at that.

Hence this short guide to some tricks of the trade.

THERE'S NOTHING BETTER THAN A GOOD PARITY STATEMENT

When you've got nothing really unique to plug, sometimes the best you can do is make a parity statement. Especially if you're selling something you can't make any special claim for. (In advertising, that special claim is often called the "Unique Selling Proposition," or U.S.P.)

One example among many is the tagline used for years by Personna Double II, a twinblade razor made by a subsidiary of Phillip Morris. Personna Double II liked to say: "There's no finer razor made. Period." This is a seemingly strong and certainly a dramatic *sounding* statement, but what is it really saying? Only that Personna Double II is as good as its competition. Personna Double II never for a moment claimed superiority, only that their product was as good as the rest, and no worse. All the blades could claim was parity. They were equal to their competition, and nothing more.

Unfortunately even the cleverest parity statement lacks the appeal of the U.S.P. It might do to ask whether you really need any product about which its advertisers can think of nothing special to say.

WHAT LIZ TOLD JACKIE ABOUT BORROWED INTEREST

"Borrowed interest" is interest which exists in one thing, or person, and which is borrowed for use somewhere else, and for a different purpose. When advertisers use borrowed interest, they take a product or service which is inherently dull and *without* interest, and they give it some excitement by borrowing for their use something which in itself *has* interest.

A recent TV commercial for DuPont spends nearly all its time showing us a bride on her wedding day, in a world of white—white gown, white invitation, white carpeting even—all made lily-white and possible by virtue of the use of *titanium dioxide.* Consider the ingenuity of linking all the positive feelings we hold for a bride on her wedding day, or linking up that romance—that sizzle—to *titanium dioxide.* That's borrowed interest. And it does the trick very nicely. It gets us to watch the beautiful bride, even while the ugly bridesmaid—some chemical compound—catches the bouquet.

Typical of the most common ads and commercials using borrowed interest are those which take us to sea to sell us Nescafe coffee and to the moon to sell us Tang breakfast drink. And what about the spot which carries us to the eighteenth green and asks the memorable question: "Orange juice after a golf tournament, Arnold Palmer?" "Sure," says Arnie, "it isn't just for breakfast anymore." Question: Is Arnold Palmer some kind of expert on the subject of orange juice? Of course not. But what a stroke! And he sure can command attention. From an advertiser's point of view, that's a smart start for any TV spot.

PLAYING ON—AND PURGING—OUR GUILT AND FEAR

We all have our guilts and fears, and motivational studies have exposed many of these to advertisers eager to capitalize on them. The mother of young children is particularly vulnerable. A Pampers TV commercial, for instance, asks the question: "Doesn't your baby deserve Pampers dryness?" This question implies both that Pampers offers more dryness than its competition and that mothers who don't buy Pampers are failing to give their babies what they deserve. Another Pampers spot has a woman claim, "I'd wash a million cloth diapers myself if it meant they'd keep him as dry as Pampers." What an ingenious way around the guilt mothers feel for not using the more traditional—and time-consuming—cloth diapers!

Then there's the spot for the Playtex nurser, telling us that it ". . . gives mother one less thing to worry about." Now, what is that one less thing to worry about? Nursing itself? Or which substitute nursing device to use? The calculated vagueness works to this product's clear advantage.

And, finally, there's the commercial for toilet bowl cleaner which whispers the insidious words "People *will look!*" Spare us.

Kentucky Fried Chicken commercials now tell us how "It's nice to feel so good about a meal." This plays on the good psychological feelings you presumably will have if you buy their chicken. These words "position" K.F.C. as something quite different from, say, McDonald's hamburgers. The difference is that, while McDonald says, "You deserve a break today" (in other words, "Get out of the kitchen and out of the house for a change"), the chicken people *want* you to think of home, and home cooking, when you think of their product. Much as people love the convenience of eating at these fast food places, they suffer guilt because they're not cooking it at home. So in order to combat this guilt, K.F.C. tells us, "It's nice to feel so good about a meal." They sing it to us and we believe it, because we want to believe it.

We're also accosted by commercials which play on our fears—even our fear of making mistakes. H & R Block commercials now feature people saying, "I shoulda come here last year." They feel what can only be described as retroactive guilt. This campaign takes us enigmatically to task with the gnarled self-criticism: "It's already too late, so hurry!"

And what about the ever-growing number of smoke alarm spots, usually showing smoke and flames and families in crisis? One of these opens with a presenter—he appears to be a dangerous intruder with thoughts of arson on his mind, a flaming torch in hand—asking the unanswerable question: "Are you really safe there in your bed?" (Strings dramatically up.) Probably the only rule to come out of this is: Never rush out to buy anything while you're still in a cold sweat from the advertising you've been watching. Sleep on it. If you can.

THE CARDINAL SIN OF OMISSION

It's every bit as important to know what is *not* being said as what is, because it raises a pertinent question we should habitually ask ourselves: "Is this advertisement telling us the whole story?"

Example: TV commercials for American Express Travellers' Checks focus on hysterical people—who haven't been wise enough to use American Express checks, and have used other companies' checks, instead—suffering the loss of their money and belongings. These spots, with Karl Malden as their spokesperson, have, in the past, said: "What to do? Get American Express Travellers' Checks. If *they're* lost, you can get a full refund at over 600 places."

By committing the sin of omission, American Express created the impression—through implication—that its competition will not offer full refunds on lost or stolen checks. This is absolutely contrary to the truth, and a successful court suit brought by Thomas Cook Company has forced American Express to amend its commercials, which in their new versions now include the admission that other travellers' check companies also do, in fact, make refunds.

Eager to climb on the conservation bandwagon, Commonwealth Edison, the northern Illinois electric utility, ran an advertisement some time ago showing a female water chemist testing the water used to cool one of Com Ed's nuclear power facilities. The newspaper ad has this chemist say: "The water our power plants use is just as clean coming out as going in. It's my job to make sure of it." These words allay our concern about possible problems which could result from Com Ed's using millions of gallons of Lake Michigan drinking water to cool their engines. Most people feel good when they read that ad. But what they aren't told is that the water coming out of these nukes may be clean all right but it's also substantially *warmer* than it was before being diverted to the utility's use, and this warmer water can have the effect of changing entire eco-systems.

Sins of omission are like the black holes of space. They draw you in and swallow you whole. So watch where you walk. And what you hear.

DOIN' THE SIDESTEP OR LEAKY BALLOONS THAT DON'T HOLD UP

You'll never have problems recognizing this dandy, since your typical reaction is a double-take. You hear the pitch and nod in agreement; then you slap your forehead and curse the curve ball.

Example: "What's in Bayer is what doctors recommend most." Now what is that supposed to mean? Does Bayer contain an ingredient, the mystical workings of which we mere laymen cannot comprehend? Or is the truth, more likely, that Bayer contains precisely what every aspirin product, by definition, must contain: Acetylsalicylic acid?

The point here is that often the only difference between a brand name drug and its generic equivalent is the price. Trademark-advertised brand names often sell for 50% more than the generic pharmaceuticals which their names are designed to obfuscate. It is estimated that over a year's time, the average consumer can save up to $125 or more by buying generic drugs instead of the more heavily advertised brand names.

To show how cannily the Bayer words dance the sidestep, let's look at them from another angle. Let's pretend that we have created a product which is 99% water and 1% sugar. We call it Goodie Juice, and we sell it with words like, "You can't live without what's in Goodie Juice" or "What's in Goodie Juice can save your life."

It comes to this: If what's in Bayer is what doctors recommend most, then what's in Bayer is what I want. Not Bayer itself, necessarily, but *what's in* Bayer. And that's generic aspirin.

Rule: Carry your critical sickle always at your side, to cut away the camouflage. It's a jungle out there.

WHO'S THAT A-TUGGIN ON THOSE OL' HEARTSTRINGS O' MINE?

Into this giant category fall all those advertisements so hard to hate, because they are triggered to touch us way deep down. They play on our emotions, and unless we are cold or un-American, it's hard not to respond. Ma Bell's "Reach Out" campaign is a perfect example. We're told to "Reach out and touch someone." And we're shown all sorts of people, reaching out and touching those they love. Go ahead. Just pick up the phone. Nothing to it. But consider reality here. A monopoly utility is spending our money—it has recently upped the cost of phone calls in many areas—in order to increase service and make more money. Really, now, do most of us have to be reminded of the phone?

THE JELLYFISH IN SHEEP'S CLOTHING

The jellyfish is about as transparent as the aforementioned leaky balloon. Consider Orson Wells, for Paul Masson Wines, uncorking this beauty: "We will sell no wine before its time!" The drama, the vibrato, the strength of these words of commitment! But what is the Paul Masson Wine Company committing itself to? Do they promise us thirty-year old wine? No. Ten year-old wine? No. Not a word of it. All they say is that they will sell no wine "before its time." Now maybe that time is a year, maybe it's 6 months. Who knows? What we *do* know is that these words play upon our desire to gain prestige when we quaff wine. And they work. What could be more prestigious than to get your hands on a good vintage wine? Say a rich, robust 1980.

THE ADVERTISING OF JOY

Like the classic hearttuggers, the advertising of joy is usually mounted on behalf of those major companies which can afford to enhance their images with magical positioning words like "Coke Adds Life." Words like these, linked with pictures of happy people drinking Coke, work through the power of suggestion. Forget the fact that Coke cleans the rust off your fender panels. "Just give me a smile with everything on it, and I'll pass it on."

Advertising like this may require that we mentally take a step away from it in order to appraise it more objectively. But usually it's so well put together that we fall into it, taken by its charms. Perhaps we are underestimating Coke's value as a secret weapon in fixing our new relationship with China.

HOLY WORDS

These are words designed to sound not only believable but semi-sacred, words to be taken as gospel. Words like "Geritol every day." They have the fine fit of a rule of habit and behavior. Another example, again from American Express, is for the American Express card: "Don't leave home without it." Your American Express card is like your socks or briefcase or car keys or kissing your wife. At least that's how the folks at American Express want you to think.

SELLING YOU "WHERE YOU LIVE"

Finding out "where you live" is the specialty of the motivational researchers. What's your sex? Age group? Income profile? Are you female, 18–34? Virginia Slims sells to you by saying "You've come a long way, baby!" But most truly liberated females want to scream "Save us from the stereotyping!" After all, being cast as some pseudo-siren of '79 in a slinky gown is no less degrading than being cast as some pseudo-suffragette sneaking a smoke in 1919.

Are you America's typical macho male? You're gonna love it in Marlboro Country, a territory of the mind so well established in full-color magazine ads that the mere sight of one evokes the desired response patterns. Health hazard? What's that?

Many, if not most of the ads we see, play on our desire to conform. The popular "Dewar's Profile" of the average Dewar's whiskey drinkers shows us precisely the sort of person who drinks

Dewar's. Want to be like the skydiver or the rising young stockbroker? Drink his brand of alcohol. Do people really take to this approach? They do! They do! And companies can trot out sales figures to prove it.

CHARLEY THE TUNA AND OTHER RED HERRINGS

Charley the Tuna, as well as Tony the Tiger, the Jolly Green Giant, Snap, Crackle & Pop, the Pillsbury Doughboy, Ernie Keebler and all the rest of the netherworld of cartoon characters created by advertising agencies are simple symbols designed for the purpose of creating certain mental associations in our minds. Again, these little charmers are image-builders. The Giant, for example, isn't going to tell you that his niblets are on sale this week. What *he* wants you to know is that the vegies growing in his valley are the very best. The Giant is making what is called a "generic" sale. He's selling you the concept of overall quality.

Unfortunately, product quality is often outstripped by sheer "cartoonability." Take, for example, the advertising of kids' cereals, many of which use cartoon personalities like Tony the Tiger, Frankenberry and Count Chocula to hawk their sugar-laden wares to kids who, without the advantage of a discriminating judgment, know only that they like the taste of sugar, and who watch these same heroes adorning their cereal boxes come alive on Saturday mornings in TV commercials piped into their rooms.

The trick is to look beyond our own initial, subliminal, sympathetic reactions, in order to find the real product story. Let's go back to our friend Charley the Tuna. Charley's job is telling us what tastes good. He plays to our worries over having to make do with second best. The fact is that while tuna may vary somewhat from one grade to another, the difference is mostly in color, consistency and medium (oil or water). Canned tuna is—pretty much—canned tuna. Our "taste" is largely learned. Charley is helping to teach us to like the most expensive cuts—his boss's cuts.

When it comes to these seemingly innocuous little creatures, beware. The tasteful little tuna may be trying to hook you.

GREAT BIG IRRELEVANT ATTENTION-GETTERS (NOT RED HERRINGS—JUST A LOT OF CARP)

No area of advertising can claim to be innocent of this technique but somehow automobile dealers—particularly on the local level—seem to act as though irrelevancies are their special province. Noteworthy are those dealers who regularly take sledge hammers to new cars and vans. Although this wanton destruction is surely pitiable, it is more entertaining than all those dealers who play violins, sing for their supper, or put their little ones to work to show you what terrific family men they are. What does this tell you about their product? Goose egg zero.

DIGGING OUT THOSE BURIED WARNINGS AND ADMISSIONS

Back to those beautiful two-page spreads for Marlboro cigarettes, with the mustachioed macho-men and the horses and the wide-open spaces. It's time to reach into those saddlebags, partner, and grab your spyglass. Now scout the countryside. You'll find what you're looking for—eventually. There under the sagebrush and the boulders, in the lower corner of Marlboro Country, like a small headstone, rests the Surgeon General's warning that "Cigarette Smoking is Dangerous to Your Health." Of course this caveat is treated by the advertiser as completely incidental to the thrust of the ad as a whole, and that's how it comes off.

It's up to you to notice warnings, and pay attention to their true importance. When a company is required by law to print a warning, they're not going to give it any more prominence than they absolutely have to.

That also goes for what are called "qualifier words," which often appear in premium offers. You'll see the word "FREE," followed in substantially smaller type by the words which "qualify"—that is, limit—that offer. "FREE . . . with 2 coupons," for example, or "FREE . . . with purchase of regular size." Financial advertisements often include an abundance of qualifying words, like "Substantial Interest Penalty for Early Withdrawal," which flash on and off the screen in . . . a flash.

Admissions are ingeniously finessed by ad agencies, and the tired albatross hung around the company's neck can be made to come off like a soaring eagle, so pay attention. Especially when Ford Motor Company, under pressure of litigation growing out of its Pinto's lethally located gas tanks, ends up talking about the new '79 Pintos in terms of their bold new design, with no direct mention of the original problem whatsoever.

Likewise, Listerine brushes by its admission that it doesn't stop colds, an admission forced upon it by court order. Listerine promises less to us now than it did half a year ago, but do most of us pick that up?

UNTYING THOSE GORDIAN KNOTS

The words that win the Gordian Knot Award are so carefully turned that they turn in upon themselves, like a pretzel. They take you from A to B and back again to A. You know you've been travelling, but you suspect that you haven't gotten anywhere for your trouble. Take this award-winner: "The world needs more of what Allis Chalmers makes." The A.C. people don't want to bore you by telling you specifically what it is they make. They just want you to know that, whatever it is, it's important in our lives. But how can people who won't even tell you what it is they're in business to make expect you to take this leap of faith on their behalf? Words that take you nowhere ought to leave you cold.

MUSIC HATH CHARMS

(So Hath Marvelous Art Direction, Computer Animation, Clever Ideas and Snappy Editing)

Ad agencies often subcontract work to "jingle houses." These are production studios which make music, developing soundtracks for use in radio and TV commercials. These jingles are often built around important campaign words, or taglines, which are at the semantic roots of the campaign. For example, listen again to McDonald's popular "You deserve a break today." As you speak them aloud you can hear these words set to their familiar music. (Starting out much the same, incidentally, as Walt Disney's "When You Wish Upon a Star.")

It's hard not to love the well-coiffed results of expensive production, with its commissioned music, top directors, producers, editors and the finest commercial talents—composers, arrangers, musicians, designers, writers and animators—all working together on one project built to run probably 30 seconds—although on countless occasions. With all the talent a big budget buys you can clothe the barest idea in the finest raiment.

We end up looking at these beautiful print ads, listening to these clever radio spots and watching these overproduced TV commercials, and we can't help loving the actors, the sets, the story turns and production values, the very sureness and tightness of it all.

The question, of course, is whether we're loving the lady for her clothes or for her heart. Which takes us back to the sizzle on our steak. And our ability to separate the two.

WOMEN, BABIES, ANIMALS—

Even the least jaded among us must admit that advertising, *if only by virtue of its charge to get and hold our attention,* co-opts absolutely everything we hold most dear. Chief among these ideals are women, babies and animals. We see them in advertising everywhere. One good question to ask is whether their presence is contributing to our understanding of product benefits. Another question is whether their absence would damage our understanding, or only give us less to look at.

—AND STARS

The stars are out every blessed night. And every day, too. On every channel, from JoAnn Worley horsing around with her Kleenex boxes to Senator Sam Ervin drawling his pitch for life insurance. But what do the stars tell us? How have they legitimized the products being advertised? Does the fact that Neil Armstrong walked on the moon make him more believable as a spokesperson for Chrysler cars? The Chrysler commercial offers us the link, talking about Chrysler's respect for "machines solving problems." And Armstrong goes no further than to say that "Chrysler cars are exciting, innovative approaches to the needs we all have today." Now, when you look at these words on paper, it appears that they may belong several categories back, back among the jellyfish in sheep's clothing. After all, to say that your products ". . . are exciting, innovative approaches to the needs we all have today," is to use the safest, most nebulous words in the dictionary. Most—if not all—companies advertising hardgoods could feel fairly comfortable using those same words themselves. Words as general as that come pretty cheap.

IS THE NAME THE GAME?

Advertising people know the value of a well-chosen name for their product, and agencies go to incredible lengths to find that perfect name, using group interviews, questionnaires and other research tools in order to find the right words to attach to what is sometimes only an idea on the way to being born as a product on your grocery shelf. When an agency first takes on a new product assignment, that product may already have a position, a name, even a package. But, more likely, and especially if the agency has the opportunity to work in close creative association with its client company, that agency will have basic responsibilities for developing ideas, sometimes even from inception; taking them into test markets; finding the right names, packages, sizes, colors—everything. A good agency is continually testing and making changes, like a tailor custom-fitting your new suit.

Sometimes you can take a name and give it meaning; sometimes you can take a word or set of words that already have meaning and lay them on a product. It depends on what you're trying to accomplish.

Take "Hamburger Helper." From the point of view of the merchandiser, this is a solid gold name. It describes what is generally called a "food stretcher," and it describes it with just the right nuance. The two things this name tells you are really everything you need to know about the product; it works with your hamburger (not your steak); and it does something good to it. Yet any name, by itself, cannot answer all our questions. Using "Hamburger Helper" as an example, you might ask whether it really is helping your hamburger, or just your budget. You may end up deciding that, using food *quality* as an indicator rather than sheer stretchability, you can help your burgers more in other ways.

Often new product names do the real work of positioning. New products such as Heinz's "Chili Fixin's" and Swift's "Soup Starter" have the names they do so that consumers will recognize that they are intended not as end products, but as "ingredient" products. Most research indicates that homemakers reject the concept of instant dinners, even though they welcome convenience features. To circumvent this problem, merchandisers have wisely left a few things for consumers to do themselves. We are instructed to add an egg to the cake mix and ground beef to the Chili Fixin's. Presto! We've got dishes we can pretend we've prepared from scratch. And so these new products are positioned not as instant dinners, not as means in themselves, but as "starters" or "add-ons." The trick is to leave us with a sense of usefulness. Left only to add water, we rebel.

Insofar as naming goes, the promise held out by Hamburger Helper seems innocent when compared with hot little numbers like "Night of Olay." There are people sitting around, day and night, conjuring up names that capture our imagination and . . . fantasies. In sheerest ecstasy we buy the dream-soap. And what've we got? Soap. The dreams you can't buy.

Advertising undeniably packs a wallop. You can pretend to be immune to its influence, but unless you watch no television, listen to no radio, and read no newspapers or magazines, you are, more or less—and like all the rest of us—under its spell. No one is completely immune. That is why we need to develop our defenses through self-education as to how advertising works. It begins with our paying *more* attention, not less, to advertising.

WORDSMITHING

Curt Gentry

The object of advertisers is to capture the trust of consumers and, in so doing, make them spend their money. This is done through *wordsmithing*—arranging words and phrases in such a way that they (1) make a true statement and (2) at the same time convey, or, better still, suggest a meaning which they don't actually possess. For example, take this TV commercial of a few seasons ago:

> Arrid is one-and-one-half times as effective as any other leading deodorant tested.

We can assume this statement is true, and that Arrid's makers and advertising agency undoubtedly have evidence to support it if challenged. Nor are they to be blamed if the public chooses to misinterpret it. Yet, unless one were listening carefully—and who listens carefully to

From *The Vulnerable Americans* by Curt Gentry (New York: Doubleday, 1966). This reading was reprinted in the first edition of *Mass Media Issues* under the title "Of Course That Ad Is Lying."

commercials?—he just might come away with the impression that Arrid is one-and-one-half times more effective than any other leading deodorant. The catcher here, of course, is that word "tested." Giving it some thought, one might come up with a number of questions: How many other leading deodorants were tested? One? All? Who conducted the test or tests? How representative were they? Were they conducted scientifically, in a manner free from bias? The real catch is that few of us would give it that much thought.

Another:

> Three out of four doctors recommended the major ingredient in Anacin for the relief of simple headache pain

Once in a critical mood, this seems easy. How many doctors were interviewed? Were four doctors picked whose opinions were already known? Or were a number of doctors questioned, in sets of four, until three in one set so recommended? If your reasoning has followed this pattern you've been misled, for this part of the statement means exactly what it implies—if all the doctors in this country were questioned, at least 75 percent would make this representation. The catcher here is "major ingredient." Three out of four doctors *would* and *do* recommend the major ingredient in Anacin—but by the generic name by which that ingredient is best known: *aspirin*.

THE NEW (AND STILL HIDDEN) PERSUADERS

Vance Packard

People keep asking me what the hidden persuaders are up to nowadays. So, for a few months, I revisited the persuasion specialists. The demographers and motivational researchers, I found, are still very much with us, but admen today are also listening to other kinds of behavior specialists. It's a less wacky world than 20 years ago perhaps, but more weird.

Admen seek trustworthy predictions on how we the consumers are going to react to their efforts. Years ago they learned that we may lie politely when discussing ads or products, so, increasingly, the advertising world has turned to our bodies for clues to our real feelings.

Take our eyes. There is one computerized machine that tracks their movements as they examine a printed ad. This spots the elements in the ad that have the most *"stopping power."* For overall reactions to an ad or commercial, some admen have been trying the *pupillometer*, a machine that measures the pupil under stimulation.

The pupil expands when there is arousal of

From *Reader's Digest* (February, 1981). Reprinted by permission.

interest, although this can lead to mistaken conclusions. A marketer of frozen french fries was pleased by reports of significant dilation during its TV ad. But further analysis indicated that it was the sizzling steak in the ad, not the french fries, that was causing the dilation. What's more, the pupillometer cannot tell whether a viewer likes or dislikes an ad. (We are also aroused by ads that annoy us.) This caused some of its users to become disgruntled, but others stick with it as at least helpful. Arousal is *something*. Without it the admen are inevitably wasting money.

There are also machines that offer voice-pitch analysis. First, our normal voices are taped and then our voices while commenting on an ad or product. A computer reports whether we are offering lip service, a polite lie or a firm opinion.

In the testing of two commercials with children in them, other kids' comments seemed about equally approving. The mechanical detective, however, reported that one of the commercials simply interested the kids, whereas the other packed an emotional wallop that they found hard to articulate.

Viewing rooms are used to try out commercials and programs on off-the-street people. Viewers push buttons to indicate how interested or bored they are.

One technique for gauging ad impact is to measure brain waves with electrodes. If a person is really interested in something, his brain emits fast beta waves. If he is in a passive, relaxed state, his brain emits the much slower alpha waves. An airline has used brain-wave testing to choose its commercial spokesman. Networks have used the test to check out actors and specific scenes in pilot films that need a sponsor.

Admen also seek to sharpen their word power to move us to action. Some have turned to psycholinguistics—the deep-down meaning of words—and to a specialty called psychographic segmentation.

A few years ago Colgate-Palmolive was eager to launch a new soap. Now, for most people, the promise of cleanliness ranks low as a compelling reason for buying soap. It's assumed. So soap makers promise not only cleanliness but one of two gut appeals—physical attractiveness (a tuning up of complexion) or a deodorant (a pleasant smell).

Colgate-Palmolive turned to psychographic segmentation to find a position within the "deodorant" end of the soap field. The segmenters found a psychological type they called Independents—the ambitious, forceful, self-assured types with a positive outlook on life, mainly men, who like to take cold showers.

Their big need, over and above cleanliness, was a sense of refreshment. What kind of imagery could offer refreshment? Colgate researchers thought of spring and of greenery and that led them to think of Ireland, which has a nationally advertised image epitomizing cool, misty, outdoor greenery.

So the Colgate people hired a rugged, self-assured male with a bit of a brogue as spokesman and concocted a soap with green and white striations. The bar was packaged in a manly green-against-black wrapper (the black had come out of psychological research), and they hailed it as Irish Spring—now a big success in the soap field.

Advertising people have long fretted about not being able to say much in a 15- or 30-second commercial. So they experimented with faster talking. Typically, when you run a recorded message at speeds significantly faster than normal you get Donald Duck quackery. But psychologists working with electronic specialists came up with a computerized time-compression device that creates a normal-sounding voice even when the recording is speeded up by 40 percent. Research has also indicated that listeners actually preferred messages at faster-than-normal speed and remembered them better.

Meanwhile, at one of the world's largest advertising agencies, J. Walter Thompson, technicians forecast that by 1990 many TV messages will be coming at us in three-second bursts, combining words, symbols and other imagery. The messages will be almost subliminal.

The subliminal approach is to get messages to us beneath our level of awareness. It can be a voice too low for us to hear consciously. It can be a message flashed on a screen too rapidly for us to notice, or a filmed message shown continuously but dimly. It can even be a word such as SEX embedded in the pictures of printed ads.

Subliminal seduction has been banned by most broadcasters, but nothing prevents its use in stores, movies and salesrooms. Several dozen department stores use it to reduce shoplifting. Such messages as "I am honest, I will not steal" are mixed with background music and continually repeated. One East Coast retail chain reported a one-third drop in theft in a nine-month period.

The sale of imagery and symbols continues to fascinate admen. In one experiment, 200 women were questioned, ostensibly about color schemes in furniture design. For their co-operation the women were given a supply of cold cream. They were to take home and try out two samples. When they came back for their next advice-giving session, they would be given an ample supply of the cold cream of their choice.

Both sample jars were labeled "high-quality cold cream." The cap of one jar had a design with two triangles on it. The cap of the other jar had two circles. The cold cream inside the jars was identical, yet 80 percent of the women asked for the one with the circle design on the cap. They liked the consistency of that cream better. They found it easier to apply and definitely of finer quality. All because, it seems, women prefer circles to triangles.

The use of sexuality in the media has become standard. Interestingly, a research report stated that women now are more aroused by nudity in ads than men. This may account for one twist recently employed by admen. In 1980, a highly successful campaign for men's Jockey-brand underwear was aimed at women, based on the finding that women often buy clothing for their mates.

For this campaign the star was the handsome pitcher of the Baltimore Orioles, Jim Palmer. In the ads he was nude except for the snug-fitting Jockey briefs. Sales soared—as did Palmer's female fan mail.

Today, as when I first reported on persuasion techniques in advertising, our hidden needs are still very much on admen's minds. One need that has grown greatly in two decades—perhaps because of all the moving and the breaking up of families—is warm human contact.

The American Telephone and Telegraph Company used this need to generate more long-distance calls. Historically, such calls were associated with accidents, death in the family and other stressful situations. AT&T wanted long-distance calling to become casual spur-of-the-moment fun. Hence the jingle, "Reach out, reach out and touch someone," played against various scenes filled with good friendship.

Then there was a manufacturer of hay balers who sought more farmers to buy his machine. Psychologist Ernest Dichter, an old master at persuasion, came up with a technique based on the theory that instant reward is better in creating a sense of achievement than long-delayed reward—in this case a check for the hay two months later.

Dichter recommended attaching a rear-view mirror and a bell to the baler. Every time a bundle of hay was assembled as the machine moved across a hayfield, the farmer could see it in the mirror. And when the bale dropped onto the field the bell rang. Thus the reward was not only instant but visual and audible. Farmers loved it. And so did the manufacturer, who started ringing up the hay-baler sales.

HELP! THERE'S SEX IN MY SOUP
A Small Plea for an End to Subliminal Silliness

Jerry Goodis

When I was a schoolkid in Toronto, there was a joke going around about a psychologist who was testing a subject by holding up ordinary geometric figures and asking what they made him think of. Each figure—square, oblong, or rectangle—apparently made his subject think of only one thing: sex. Finally the psychologist could take no more. "Good God," he cried. "Does *everything* make you think of sex?" "You should talk," his subject retorted scornfully, "you're the one who keeps showing me all those dirty pictures!"

For years, every time I thought of that story, I believed it would take a very disturbed person or, conversely, some marvelously zany bunch like Monty Python's Flying Circus to see sex in such ordinary things. But, when I first read Wilson Bryan Key's book, *Subliminal Seduction,* subtitled "Ad Media's Manipulation of a Not So Innocent America," (New American Library paperback, $1.95) I realized that here was someone who *did* see sex, or at least *said* he did (in the understandable interest of selling more of his books), in virtually every picture, every illustration, and every advertisement in magazines, newspapers, films, TV shows, and other entertainment and communication media.

From *Quest* (February-March 1979). Reprinted by permission.

And Key didn't mean only suggested or subtly implied sex. Key saw the actual word *sex* spelled out in bold letters on whiskey glasses, on the faces and arms of infants, on Ritz crackers, in clouds, grass, and trees, in every curve and indent of pneumatic *Playboy* cuties, and of course, even on his own portrait adorning the dust jacket of his book. But this astounding discovery was mild compared to the utter maelstroms of depravity and deception Key could readily find worked into your average, run-of-the-fridge *ice cube,* in some of the most prestigious and expensive advertisements for soft drinks and liquor.

> Here was someone who *did* see sex in virtually every picture, illustration and advertisement.

"The right side of the ice cube above the lime slice," Key points out on page 100 of the paperback edition of *Subliminal Seduction,* as part of his clinical dissection of a Sprite ad which appeared in *Esquire* magazine, "forms the back of a large shaggy dog with a pointed nose, or quite possibly a polar bear."

> The animal's legs are extended outward to the left, parallel with the top of the lime. The animal's arms (or legs, as you will) appear to be holding another figure which is human with long, feminine hair. Her face is located just above the animal's head.
>
> The two figures, animal and human, are in what can only be described as a sexual intercourse position. The polar bear, dog, or whatever, is in sexual embrace with a nude woman.

> Bestiality may be illegal throughout most of the world, but, at the symbolic level, it appears to have sold a lot of Sprite. The Coca-Cola/Sprite advertisement was designed to sell around a subliminal theme of highly taboo sex.

This incredibly ludicrous excursion into the utterly absurd sent a chill up my spine. If it wasn't all so appallingly perverted, it might be mildly humorous.

My mind was still reeling when, a few pages later, Key claimed to have found, in a *fake* ice cube, something much more sinister:

> The primary symbolic device, subliminally perceived in the Bacardi ad, appears at first to be an ice cube in the center bottom of the glass. Look more carefully. The ice cube is a golden skull with a flattened nose, large eye sockets and jagged teeth. . . .The thematic implication . . . implies that one might richly enjoy dying if well fortified with Bacardi rum. . . .

On page 115 Key declares, in the authoritative, straight-from-heaven style he employs throughout his book:

> There is not even an outside chance, however, that major U.S. media embeds [Key's own term for hidden messages] inadvertently or without full knowledge of what they were doing.

What malicious effrontery!

Though Key specifically refers to American advertising agencies in his convoluted indictment, he is damning all advertising agencies, Canadian as well, as he later confirmed. And since I've spent most of my life in advertising and am fiercely proud of the work my agencies have done, I consider Key's allegations a *personal* insult.

Also, I have another cogent reason for leaving the sidelines and jumping head-first into the controversy Key precipitated with his ridiculous, disturbed fantasies. For some years I have been traveling to Canadian universities and community colleges (at their invitations), talking to students about what I do for a living and how I sincerely believe advertising benefits society. And I've had some rip-snorting, knock-down, drag-out arguments in many a college bear-pit.

The connection between these collegiate confrontations and Wilson Bryan Key is that by the time I got around to perusing his first book—he's since done another one containing even more bizarre claims of alleged media malpractices and misdirections called *Media Sexploitation* (New American Library paperback, $1.95)—he was snugly ensconced as professor of journalism at the University of Western Ontario in London.

His inauspicious term at that institution lasted only one year, at the end of which its administrators undoubtedly heaved a collective sigh of intense relief as he headed back to California. But even in that relatively brief interval, Key's fantastic theories, and the bland certainty with which he spouted them, infected a good number of impressionable young people. He convinced them that there really was a deep, dark plot to poison people's subconscious minds with all sorts of unspeakable messages and suggestions, and that large advertising agencies like mine were only the evil front-men for "the merchandisers and the culture controlled by merchandisers."

I first found it incredible that anyone would swallow the Key brand of foolishness, except possibly as basic training for a career with the CIA. But I had to face the fact that hundreds of Canadian post-secondary students, bemused perhaps by Key's undeniable gift for highflown rhetoric, had accepted his maniacal meanderings as valid research.

While Key was on staff at Western, he swore there was a secret room at the local daily paper, the highly respected *London Free Press*. Here, Key claimed, unknown even to the publisher himself, expert retouching artists allegedly earned the tainted money supplied by big advertising agencies, by superimposing or cunningly inserting their sordid, hidden commands or scenes of debauchery, bestiality, and other orgies on any photograph or illustration they could lay their filthy paws upon.

Further, on Key's own office wall, emphasized by its own special spotlight, was a *Time* magazine cover of Queen Elizabeth, on whose face and hair Key revealed he'd located the common, explicit word for fornication—not only once, but literally dozens of times.

But beyond these instances of Key's personal obsession as recorded by responsible people who knew him at Western, I think a statement of my own credo may help convince students and others that neither I nor my confrères could possibly be a party to such devilish plots against the public.

I am an advertising practitioner—a salesman, if you will—a man who does his damndest to persuade Canadians to buy the products people pay me to promote—Speedy Muffler, Hiram Walker, Alcan, London Life, The Permanent, Scotiabank, and Molson's, to name only a few.

All the time I've been in advertising, we've tried to produce *tasteful* ads, whether they were slated for magazines, television, newspapers, radio, kids' balloons, shopping bags, mountainsides, fireworks displays, or to be towed behind low-flying aircraft. And if possible, not only tasteful ads, but often ads with a bit of humor added for good measure.

A lot of people who had read David Ogilvy's book, *Confessions of an Advertising Man*, published in 1963, firmly believed this last whim of ours would be the downfall of our little Toronto firm, because David, senior partner in a very successful American advertising agency, had decreed that though humor undoubtedly had its place in the cosmic scheme of things, that place was definitely not the advertising business. Wrong, David.

In every ad campaign we launch, we know what segment of the public we are aiming at, and how we should go about reaching them, usually because we've done exhaustive market research beforehand—or as much research as the client's budget will stand. Even so, we're sometimes wrong. But not too often. Every word in the copy block, every illustration, the precise positioning of the text in relation to the illustrations, the choice of colors, models, and typefaces, the media to be employed, the amount of money to be allocated to each medium—these and a host of other details are all deliberately chosen to strike a balance between artistry and salesmanship. And always with good taste.

I consider Key's allegations a *personal* insult.

If anyone in my organization was "embedding" secret messages in our ads, I would certainly be aware of it. But what I must ask is this: what could possibly be the point of anyone inserting words like *sex*, death's-heads, earthy verbs, euphemisms for female fixtures, or artfully concocted scenes of wanton bestiality into their ads? What particular section of the consuming public would they be trying to reach with such messages? What possible financial gain would any sponsor hope to glean from the exhortation alleged by Key to be embedded in *Time's* portrait of Queen Elizabeth, urging everyone to rush out and fornicate?

And who is paying for all this? As I read Key, the art of "embedding" is a very complicated one, requiring experts to do the job properly. Experts cost money—piles of it. We use them only in dire necessity. Just arranging for the word *sex* to be embedded randomly a dozen-odd times across each Christie Ritz cracker, as Key claims, would cost thousands of dollars for the molds used by the bakeries alone. And has Key's own market research proved conclusively that you can slip a Ritz under ham or a Ritz under jam much more easily and tastily if it happens to be slathered with the word *sex?*

Our ads, besides being in what we consider to be good taste, are usually subtle, requiring a little thought on the part of the viewer/reader to grasp their full significance, but often rewarding this cerebral exercise on our client's behalf with a chuckle. But however we do it, everything we want to get across to the public is right out there for them to see. Why? Because otherwise they might not get the message at all, even after thinking about it. And that would mean we've failed miserably at our job and should lose the account and our franchise to operate.

Unlike Key's ads, which, to detect their full significance, usually have to be held upside down or sideways, viewed through the paper onto the next page—or at the very least, examined under a magnifying glass (according to his directions)—we liberally estimate that we have about 10 seconds at the very outside to get our message across. If we have to instruct our audience how to hold the paper or watch the screen, then we've lost before we've even begun.

It is noteworthy that Key is usually the only person able to see all these hidden messages. And even then, if I understand him, he is only able to do so by relaxing and letting his subconscious take command. The rest of us are obviously just too uptight and repressed, too brainwashed by the Machiavellian media and their lackeys, to see what to Key is exceedingly clear.

It astounds me that it has taken this long for someone to throw down the gauntlet to Wilson Bryan Key and expose his sick, perverted ideas.

What is even more disturbing than Key's infatuation with these ludicrous theories is that some misguided cynics actually believe them. And that *really* scares me.

FOR IMMEDIATE RELEASE;

The true story of an innocent journalist trapped inside a public relations firm

P. J. Corkery

In 1920, a young press agent named Edward L. Bernays testified in a trial involving his former client Enrico Caruso. Up until that moment Bernays, like his co-practitioners, had been content to describe himself as a "press agent" or "publicity director." But when the court asked him to name his occupation that morning, he said "counsel on public relations." No one had ever heard that configuration of words before. As a PR gimmick, it worked. The next morning the *New York World's* headline was FIND NEW PROFESSION IN CARUSO SUIT TRIAL.

Bernays then began a campaign—which he continues to this day—to convince people that there is a real profession called "public relations" and that its practitioners provide a valuable service to society besides getting free publicity for their clients. Bernays's first real triumph came in 1923, when he persuaded the predecessor of the New York City *Yellow Pages* to list "Public Relations" as a category. His greatest triumph came in 1946, when Boston University announced it was creating a "School of Public Relations" and would grant degrees in the new field.

Yet sixty-one years after Bernays's first salvo, newspapers in Los Angeles received the following press release from a PR firm called Hanson & Schwam:

> For Immediate Release
>
> Private airplanes interrupted sound recording of "They Call Me Bruce," theatrical feature starring Johnny Yune and Margaux Hemingway in the Newhall California desert Wednesday as pilots flew over to watch.
>
> Unfortunately the martial-arts comedy which Yune is producing must have been too diverting. Result: plane crash in nearby San Fernando with pilot Jan M. Vinson and passenger Andrew M. Carlson killed.
>
> Cast and crew of the Gold Pine Productions film were unaware of the tragedy at the time.
>
> "They Call Me Bruce" also stars Ralph Mauro, Pam Huntington, Keye Luke, Tom Dreesan, Bill Capizzi and Martin Azarow among the 117 actors with speaking roles. Screenplay is by David Randolph, Yune, Elliot Hong and Tim Clawson from a story by Yune and Hong. It will be released next summer.

The "profession," clearly, has a way to go. Last year, I decided to offer it my humble services.

The waiting room of this large Beverly Hills public relations firm (*not* Hanson & Schwam) looks as if it had been decorated by a moneyed aristocratic packrat with an odd interest in TV stars. Chintz sofas, Chippendale tables, rifle stands, and other artifacts of British country life fill the room. The walls are covered with red silk flocking. On them hang nineteenth-century prints side by side with glossies of current celebrities. Cathy Lee Crosby next to the Epsom Derby. The Lone Ranger next to Bulwer-Lytton. Tony Orlando and Max Beerbohm. Queen Victoria and Rona Barrett. On a copper-topped coffee table are current copies of *People, Parade, Us, Good Housekeeping, The Ladies' Home Journal,* and the two daily mainstays of the entertainment industry—the *Hollywood Reporter* and *Variety*.

Staffers roam by. The women, and there are plenty of them at all levels of the firm, wear expensive clothes—designer silks, big puffy Nancy Reagan outfits, matching scarves and shoes, designer bags. Most of the women are small, with the tiny figures and modest proportions that are favored in Beverly Hills businesswomen. But even the bite-sized ones walk purposefully; you could get an elbow in the face walking up against one of these striders. They make little eye contact with strangers, though their eyes are constantly surveying the scene. Smiling at one is like smiling at the camera in the bank; it looks at you and looks beyond at the same time. This look is considered cosmopolitan.

If an item is printed in a paper, it's considered to have been "planted," and a letter announcing this achievement is sent to the client.

Top male executives strive for something British in their appearance. Total-life air conditioning (homes, cars, offices) makes it possible for Los Angeles PR men to wear clothing made for people in cold, damp climates. Tweeds denote class. "Idea men" add what's called "an eccentric touch" to their presentation of self. One account executive, for example, never wears shirts. Instead he wears embroidered sweaters. Even at formal events he can be seen in a tux and a special white turtleneck sweater embroidered with propeller airplanes flying across his chest. Another executive affects baseball caps. These touches are considered the mark of a creative or unconventional mind.

Beyond the waiting room is a large room occupied by junior staffers who ape the dress of their seniors. These people are called "planters." Each day they write and distribute scores of "items" about the firm's various clients. If an item is printed in a paper, it's considered to have been "planted," and a letter announcing their achievement is sent to the client. One planter concentrates exclusively on the gossip columns of *Variety* and the *Hollywood Reporter*, which together will print twenty-five or so items. Another ten will be picked by other papers. The rest are recycled to gossip columns in papers around the country until someone prints them or age destroys them.

A typical item will announce that "Brush Fire, the vibrant young star of Lookma Television's searing miniseries *The Rise of the Dutch Republic*, has been named Humanitarian-of-the-Year by the Inflation Club, a philanthropic organization of Los Angeles bankers, for his forceful dramatic presentation of the role of Hans Money, the first bank teller, whose life and loves transformed Holland and the world. He'll receive the traditional plaque and scroll at the club's dinner next week." Contract signings, new projects, and other deals make good items, but awards are the best. That is why Humanitarian-of-the-Year, Man-of-the-Year, Woman-of-the-Year awards are handed out in Hollywood by the hundred, all year long. Public relations firms actively court the sponsors and nominate their clients for prizes.

Near the planters' room is the bookers' room. The walls here don't bear prints of the Ashmolean Museum at sunset or of Ye Olde Cheshire Cheese. In the bookers' room the walls are made of cork—each wall is a bulletin board. The boards are broken up into segments, each segment representing a different television talk show—*Merv Griffin, Phil Donahue, John Davidson*, and so on. The names of clients booked on the shows are pinned up on the boards in an appropriate slot. (There's no bulletin board for *Johnny Carson*. Johnny calls you. You don't call Johnny.)

The shrewd and well-respected booker is one who can turn a talk show's request for a certain client into a bonanza for other, undesired clients. One nice lady booker in her fifties became a legend by once parlaying one hot client into bookings for three less desirable ones on a big talk show. She received a "job well done" memo from the head of the firm. There's nothing like placing a client on a talk show to convince the client that he's receiving his money's worth for his fee. And the fees here, like those at all major firms, start at $2,500 a month, with a three-month minimum.

About half this firm's clients are individual actors and actresses. About a quarter are independent producers who don't have in-house publicity departments for their movies and TV shows. The rest are a varied collection of corporate and individual clients ranging from a champagne maker to aspiring politicians. The champagne maker wants to see his champagne used at prominent local parties, and has provided champagne for charitable events. For his money, he gets references to his product in the society columns. The politicians, and some of the newer stars also, are paying to be introduced around town, to be put on invitation lists.

The planters and bookers have no windows. These are reserved for executives, whose offices overlook the mountains and the greenery of Beverly Hills. The top executives prefer offices decorated to look like a den or living room. Sofas and televisions, yes. Desks and typewriters, no. My office had a typewriter, however. I've been hired not to babysit clients but, in the words of the head of the company, to "generate some copy." The firm isn't getting enough of its press releases printed in the daily papers around the country. Using my newspaper experience, I'm to write copy that more closely approximates what editors need.

This is a radical innovation. Although PR people deal with newspapers and magazines daily, most of the staffers—thanks to Edward L.

Bernays's campaign to create a separate "profession" with its own credentials—have no experience working for the press. They are hired directly out of school, with their degrees in public relations, and are put to work planting items. After a few years, they are entrusted with the care of clients.

Sometimes, of course, there are different career patterns. As I am settling into my office, an executive I'll call Mr. Duck, because of his voice, waddles in and says, "You'll be sharing this place with another new guy for a while. He's the nephew of a studio boss and wants to get started in the PR game." Almost immediately, the office mate arrives. He can't be older than seventeen, a scrawny kid in jeans, running shoes, and a Hawaiian shirt. Sullen, he sits down at his desk, smokes three or four cigarettes, stares at the walls, and then dials his telephone.

"Get me So-and-so's office," he says, naming his famous uncle, a mogul of years' standing.

"Doris," he says, "is Unk in? I need to talk to him."

In a moment Unk is on the line. This adolescent has done what agents, producers, stars, and lawyers spend days unsuccessfully attempting: getting Mr. Big on the phone. This is an awesome accomplishment. Studio bosses don't usually take calls from their own issue, let alone from nephews.

"Unk," the nephew says, "this place is kind of formal. I need new clothes."

Unk does some talking and the nephew closes with, "So you'll have Doris call over there. Thanks, Unk!"

He hangs up the phone, gets up, walks to the door, and out.

Protocol is everything, even in the garage under the office. It's 11:30 on a Wednesday morning, and twenty of us are lined up in ten cars, about to drive to a private screening room on Sunset Boulevard in Hollywood. We are waiting for the chairman to get into his white Rolls Royce and lead our procession across town. He'll be the first car. The second car is Mr. Movies, who is the president of the movie division of our company. (In other words, he's the account executive in charge of movie producers. But of necessity titles are inflated. If he were merely a vice president, his phone calls wouldn't be returned.) Mr. Duck is the third car. Another executive, named Trixi, is fourth. I'm fifth. We are lined up in the order of our parking spaces. Finally, the chairman descends from the elevator. He is wearing a hunting jacket with leather rifle patches on the shoulders. Sort of Mr. Chips on holiday, except for his California tan.

Mr. Chips backs his car out of the stall, winds up the ramp, and heads north toward Sunset. In our ten-car convoy, only two cars are American-made. Most are Mercedeses, BMWs, with the occasional Volvo. Mr. Movies is driving a Cadillac, and I'm driving a Thunderbird. Why take abuse from valets? Mr. Chips gets a thrill out of these convoys to corporate appointments. All we need are flashing blue lights and flags on our fenders, and we'd be just like a Ronald Reagan motorcade, the standard by which stylish travel is judged nowadays in Los Angeles.

The screening room is in another office building, with underground parking. We park and ascend (having avoided all contact with untreated air), clutching our parking tickets so the screening-room lady can "validate" them with her rubber stamp, a key Los Angeles ritual that means we won't have to pay for parking. The movie producer and director are here, along with a man from one of the major studios, which will distribute the independently made movie.

We take our armchairs. The top executives to the rear, the juniors down front, close to the screen. Each armchair has a small table and ashtray beside it. On each table is a small light for taking notes. The screening-room lady hands out coffee and bottled water and soda. She also passes around candies in a tin with a picture of Lady Di and Prince Charles on it.

"Shall we watch it?" says Mr. Chips, and the

movie begins. Today it is a thriller set in the Middle East. Why some of the victims are murdered is unclear and why the heroes seek the trophy they seek is also unclear. It seems to have something to do with a race against time to decipher some hieroglyphics.

One hundred minutes after it starts, the movie ends. What will happen now? Everyone smiles at the clients. Mr. Chips breaks the silence. "This is a marvelously interesting movie," he says. "It has some great qualities. It's so difficult to predict in a film like this what the critics will say and what the public's reaction will be." This is his all-purpose speech for delivery on such occasions. But before he can finish it, one of our staffers pipes up with, "It's very unusual for me to become sexually aroused in a movie. This one did it for me." Mr. Chips hastens the producer, the director, and the distributor out the door so they won't have to listen to any more about the peculiar responses of his personnel.

"Making this movie must have been a great challenge to you," Mr. Chips concludes as the four step out the door. They are off to have lunch, and Mr. Chips will return to the office at four to discuss how to promote this movie.

At 3:30, Trixi, Mr. Movies, and I gather to "brainstorm" before Mr. Chips arrives. Most of the other staffers who were at the movie aren't involved. They drove forty-five minutes each way and spent two hours at the screening as window dressing.

"This is a real dog," Mr. Movies says about the picture.

"Just go for radio contests," says Trixi. Radio promotions are her specialty. Trixi arranges to give tickets to radio stations, which give the tickets away to listeners who call in at the right moment. The process involves frequent mention of the movie's name. "Teenies are the only ones who go to movies now," she says—often.

"We can try and get some of the actors on talk shows," offers another, creatively. The best idea I have to suggest is that we put up billboards entirely in hieroglyphics and then alert editors to the presence of these inscrutable texts. As weeks go by, we could translate the boards bit by bit, until they revealed the message: "See this movie."

Mr. Chips strolls in. "We can get four pictures a year at $75,000 a picture from these people," he says, "so let's keep them happy."

We pour out the ideas we've been developing.

"No, no, no, no," Mr. Chips says to each one. "The idea is to make the client *happy*."

"These ideas won't do it?" a staffer asks.

"Nothing will promote this movie," he says. "So let's have a party," he then offers.

"Marvelous idea," says Mr. Movies.

The idea now is to come up with a party to celebrate the premiere of the movie that will be so star-studded and soignée that the client will come back for more even after his movie inevitably flops.

"Too Marvelous!" says Mr. Movies. "It's so *Now*—that's why I like it. It's so *1981*!"

Party schemes are tossed around. Finally it's concluded we need a charity to sponsor a celebrity premiere of the movie. After the premiere, hold a party in a museum with an Egyptian motif.

"And a junket," says Mr. Chips. He issues instructions to plan a junket to the Middle East on behalf of the movie. Staffers are told to look for a Middle Eastern government willing to supply air fare and hotels for a group of international celebrities in exchange for sharing in the publicity. A classy guest list of international celebrities is drawn up. They are to be sounded out about participating.

"See if you can get Sadat and Begin," says Mr. Chips. "And on the flight," he says, "no critics. Just space."

"Space" means writers who will provide entirely positive, uncritical pieces about whatever project we're asking them to write about. They recognize the rules of a junket: we show you a good time, take care of all your expenses, and in turn you write us a story that says nice things about the project. "Space" writers are usually not to be found on big papers or widely circulating magazines, so they don't provide much in the way of wide-ranging publicity. But what they do provide is nice publicity clips to send the client. So if you've got a real dog, hold a party and invite "space."

Mr. Chips leaves to play racquetball. His parting words are, "Make sure everything gets 'activity-ed.'"

To "activity" something is to record an effort on a client's behalf on a special form. Each "activity" is a separate page. One staffer even "activity-s" calls to directory assistance. At some regular interval, all the "activity" sheets are found in a fancy folder and sent off to the client. Should a piece of "activity" result in "space" or "ink," the clipping is also sent along to the client, accompanied by a "merchandising" letter explaining just how this feat was accomplished and how impressive it is.

I'm still sharing my office with the mogul's nephew. These days he is wearing three-piece suits. Now he is reading a book published by a client, a self-made millionaire who wants to be vice-president of the United States. He wants to be vice-president because a psychic on a talk show predicted he could become vice-president if he wanted it. Later he ran into one of our executives on a plane and was signed on. For $75,000, we're helping him to realize his destiny. His book, an autobiography, is supposed to be a source of ideas for publicity about his political and social insights. I've looked at the book. His insights might be suitable for the op-ed page of the *National Enquirer*, if the *National Enquirer* had an op-ed page.

The nephew spends most of his time listening to the radio, or just staring at the wall in silence. He shows enterprise on behalf of only one client, a disco in Hollywood. Just now, as I walk back in the room, he asks for a piece of notepaper. On this he draws a stick figure with a smiling face. Under the figure he scrawls the word "daddy" with the last *d* backward. Then he tapes up the drawing on the wall in front of his desk and walks out of the room.

The press kit is the oldest tool in public relations, yet it is still the industry staple.

There's a new file on my desk, involving a charity client (they do charity work, but we don't—they pay full fare). The charity recently held a lunch for its board of lady advisers—ladies from Beverly Hills and Bel Air. Mr. Chips and Trixi attended on behalf of the firm. In his notes, Mr. Chips has listed the names of the women who were there, where the meal was (a member's home), what the menu was, who prepared the food (a Beverly Hills restaurant), what the floral arrangements were, and what florist did them. He describes the party favors (leather bags from a boutique and matching leather desk sets). He also provides detailed descriptions of the gowns the women wore, writing with perfect mastery of the incomprehensible jargon of clothes designers: Mrs. So-and-so wore a morning gown by Rudy of Rodeo that featured cahuenga shoulders of genuine pico and a sepulveda bag by Pacoima, with matching green topanga-skin pumps by El Segundo, and so on. The memo also supplies one-sentence quotes from the ladies about their work.

Attached to this information is a note from Mr. Duck. "Write up for Suzy," says the note. "Send in pouch for New York office tonight." I call Mr. Duck.

"What Suzy am I writing this up for?" I ask.

"Suzy the columnist in the *Daily News*," he says.

"What is it you want me to tell Suzy?"

"Just write up the lunch," he says and hangs up.

Suzy is the highly idiosyncratic chronicler of what passes for American society in the New York *Daily News*. So I write up the information in the notes—the menus, the attendees, the witty remarks, the designer labels, the hopes for the charity—in a fashion that I think will appeal to a busy columnist like Suzy who receives scores of press releases every day. I organize it in good form and send it upstairs with a note saying that if I were an editor or a columnist this is the kind of press release I'd pay attention to.

"I hate it," Mr. Duck says to me five minutes later on the phone.

"What's wrong?" I ask in my best weary-pro tone, pencil poised.

"It doesn't sound like Suzy," he says.

"It's not supposed to," I say. "It's for her to use as a resource."

"No!" he says. "You have to write it like Suzy writes."

"No," I say. "You don't understand. It would be an insult to Suzy to write it like that."

"No, *you* don't understand," he says in an angry voice. "You have to write it just the way the columnist writes it, or she won't use it. We don't call it planting a column for nothing. It won't get printed unless she can throw it right in."

"You're kidding," I say, "canned columns went out with Walter Winchell. No one writes canned columns for columnists anymore. That's thirty years ago."

"Do it my way."

I rewrite the column, using the last six Suzy columns as a guide, and send it back. Nothing from Mr. Duck. This time a memo comes down from Mr. Chips himself, saying job well done.

Around the office I gain a reputation as someone who can mimic a columnist. I try to explain that based on what I've seen, columnists don't accept canned columns anymore, but to no avail. I watch Suzy's column. The item, of course, never appears in any form. But my star is rising.

It's Thursday afternoon and I'm in Mr. Duck's office. He has an advance copy of next Sunday's *Calendar*, the hefty entertainment weekly of the *Los Angeles Times*. Advance copies are hard to find; it's a tribute to Mr. Duck's connections that he has one this early in the week. He is reading an interview with a prominent British actor. In this interview, the British actor heaps praise on a client, an American director who has just finished shooting a movie with the British actor. On the set, the actor despised the director and said as much in an interview with a British paper. In *Calendar*, however, the actor has nothing but praise for the director. Mr. Duck is talking to the American director on the phone. After reading him the interview, Mr. Duck says, "Isn't that nice? Didn't he come through for us? Well that's what we're here for." He hangs up.

"I earned my fee on that one," he says to me, "getting that guy [the British actor] to come across took some doing."

"What did you do?"

"I can't tell," he says.

Trixi, the movie specialist, calls me in to see her. She has her own celebrity aura and likes to be greeted in restaurants and stores like a star. She works with a number of top celebrity clients on their own personal publicity. When I arrive in her plant-filled den of an office, she is on the phone. She is always on the phone. In keeping with her status, however, she doesn't have a phone. She never has to dial a number or hold a receiver. She has a secretary who cowers at her right hand, at a tiny table, to dial and a squawk box to yell and listen through.

Trixi's life is her job. She is about thirty-five and has wrapped her entire existence in her work. Now that she's making big money ($65,000 and generous expenses), she's recently moved from a small Hollywood apartment to a new condominium in Beverly Hills. When I walk in, she's ordering new phone service for the apartment.

"I don't love that number," Trixi says out loud to the speaker phone. "I don't want that number. I don't like it. It's wrong and it's bizarre."

The phone-company lady starts to explain. Trixi twirls impatiently in her big chair and shoves across her table a mimeographed five-page biography of a starlet from one of the top-rated jiggle-and-guns shows on network television. Swannie is about to divorce her husband. "We'll need to rewrite Swannie's bio to incorporate the divorce," Trixi says, "and you've got to think up some new lines for her to say about it."

"Huh?" says the squawk box.

"Put on your supervisor," Trixi says. "I won't accept that number."

The phone company, I gather, is trying to give Trixi a phone number for her new condo that doesn't have the classic Beverly Hills prefix of "27-." Trixi's having none of it. She hasn't worked hard to move to Beverly Hills only to end up with a phone that might as well be from Studio City or El Segundo.

Apparently it's my turn to speak. "We can make it sound like they're both very sad to be divorcing," I say. "But they're both growing as persons with differing needs, and the demands of their expanding careers are such that they can't spend much time together and they're awfully glad for the years . . . ah, the *time* they've had together."

"That's great," Trixi says. "That's it exactly. We'll put that line out right away." God knows why Swannie and Walter really were divorcing. As she became more famous, he grew more sickly and bitter-looking. She began affecting a punk look and occasionally they'd take swings at each other in restaurants. My guess is that one of their psychiatrists put on his brain-cop cap and blew the whistle.

"Call me back," Trixi says to the squawk box now, "with an acceptable number. I've got other things to do than make sure you phone-company people do your jobs right."

Now Trixi places a call to a wire-service reporter who has wanted to interview Swannie. "I need a reward," she says as the secretary dials. "Lovey, what's doing? You never call me."

The reporter repeats his request for an interview with Swannie.

"Well, I don't know," says Trixi. "She's been awfully busy with her new play. I hear she's just great, just, just great, great, great."

"Well, that's fantastic," says the squawk box. "I'd love to have her talk about that. It'd be a great story."

"Well, don't ask her about her personal life," Trixi says, winking at me. "You know, she's so sad that she and Walter are just too busy now with their own careers to even have the time to get together."

"Oh, I don't want to talk to her about her personal life."

"It's out of the question, lovely. But I'll see what I can do. You'll probably have to go out to her house at the beach. She's just too busy to come into town." Now she calls Swannie.

"Swanniesweetie, I've been working all day to get an interview for you, and I think I've got something set up."

"Does he want to talk about the play?"

"Yes, but you've got to expect some questions about you and Walter. P.J. here will talk to you later and help you organize your thoughts."

"Okay."

"But in the meantime, have your secretary hire a bungalow at the Beverly Hills Hotel. Order Wednesday lunch for three, and we'll do the interview then. I'll be there, so don't worry about anything." Swannie clicks off.

"That's my reward," Trixi says to me. "I'm going to spend next Wednesday by the pool at the Beverly Hills."

She calls the wire-service reporter back and delights him with the news of the interview.

The telephone company calls back with good news, too. They've located a Beverly Hills number for Trixi that begins with the proper "27-" digits.

"That's much better," Trixi says expansively. "That's a good number. All those other numbers were very bizarre."

"Under what name shall we list the number?" the phone-company lady says, through the speakerphone.

"List the number?" Trixi barks at the squawk box. "I don't want that number in the book. That's to be a Beverly Hills *unlisted* number."

Word comes in that the Egyptian cultural attaché in Washington is not thrilled with the Middle East thriller, and will not recommend that his government pick up the plane fare and hotel bills for a junket. The junket is dead. That means our major effort on behalf of this movie, for $75,000, will be to prepare a "press kit." A press kit is a collection of photographs and canned stories about a movie that is sent out to newspapers and magazines. The movie's producer dislikes the stories the firm has fabricated for the kit, and it has fallen to me to try to improve them. He wants more about events during the filming. Unfortunately, not much happens that is even plausibly newsworthy during the filming of a movie. Fortunately, though, on almost every movie set somebody dies, either through an accident or from natural causes. Movie crews can number hundreds of people, so it isn't surprising. When this thriller went on location in Egypt, three people died—two in a collapse of scaffolding, and one drowned. Later, after shooting, some others died. It strikes me that all this slaughter must have something to do with an ancient curse of disturbed mummies who have vowed to inflict evil on all who distress them. I get to work.

The press kit is the oldest tool in public relations, yet it is still the industry staple. You would think (and many PR people apparently do think) that journalism still works the way it did in the 1860s and 1870s when Jerome Eddy, American's first press agent, roamed the country in advance of circuses and traveling shows, supplying canned stories to the local newspapers. In those days, most newspapers lacked editors and reporters. The newspaper reporter, indeed, is an invention not much older than the linotype machine, which came in around 1880. Until then, most newspapers were simply advertising sheets issued by jobbing printers, who were grateful for free copy to fill in the space between ads. According to Richard Maney's memoir, *Fanfare, the Confessions of a Press Agent*, a Boston-based press agent for the Shubert theaters around the turn of the century—one A. Toxen Worm—sent out each week, for each play he represented, "twenty feature stories, page-long blurbs for each Sunday drama section, opening-night and seat-sales announcements, daily paragraphs for drama columnists, fashion stories, women's page stories, suggestions for features and interviews." Most of this material would be printed verbatim.

> Although PR people deal with newspapers and magazines daily, most of the staffers have no experience working for the press.

Ivy Lee was the first press agent to expand beyond the theater. In 1906, some coal-mine operators—a group with a perennial bad press—hired him to plant stories on their behalf. By 1914, Lee had been hired by John D. Rockefeller, another image-problem perennial. In a seminal PR stunt, Lee advised Rockefeller to start handing out dimes to average citizens. This produced hundreds of favorable stories and photographs, and got Lee listed in *Who's Who*.

Press agents were not considered suitable material for *Who's Who* in those days. There were, however, about a dozen people who identified themselves in that volume as "publicist." Publicists were well-to-do progressives dedicated to municipal reform and other advanced political ideas. They devoted their energies to promoting causes in newspaper articles and on the lecture circuit. Early in this century, before Bernays had invented "public relations," press agents began appropriating the term "publicist" to lend some dignity and panache to their work. The appropriation was so successful that today "publicist" connotes a low-rent public relations person—a press agent, in other words.

In 1922, Walter Lippmann published his book *Public Opinion,* with a long section on the role of press agents. Lippmann wrote, "The development of the publicity man is a clear sign that the facts of modern life do not spontaneously take a shape in which they can be known. They must be given a shape by somebody." Edward L. Bernays read this book, was inspired, devised the term "public relations," and began his crusade to establish that his was a function essential to the operation of the modern world.

Basically, however, it is still a matter of manufacturing press kits, and I decided that this was not my life's work.

On the morning of my last day at the firm, I discover that the mogul's nephew is also packing his belongings. This is a surprise. He's been working very hard these last few days, organizing a charity event for the disco client, phoning suppliers, stars, agents, and so on. It sounded as if it would be a great success, with a lot of local TV coverage of the stars donating Christmas toys for the needy at this disco. This uncharacteristic burst of activity has drawn the firm's attention to the fact that the disco was not the firm's client. Nephew was doing this on his own, using the firm's name.

In this final hour, my eye is drawn to the enigmatic stick figure still taped above his desk. I ask him what it is all about.

"I wanted them to think I had kids. More mature. Just thinking."

"I should do a half hour of that every day," I say.

"It never hurts," he says, and strolls out.

On my way out, I stop at a press conference we're holding in honor of one of Hollywood's oldest and most beloved stars, a tiresome comedian who makes mildly dirty jokes. The room is full of reporters waiting for interviews. The occasion is some sort of anniversary of his. Many of the reporters are reading a long, eulogistic article about the comedian in that morning's *Los Angeles Times."* I congratulate Trixi, who manages this account, on the *Times* coup.

"How did you do it?" I ask.

"Unfortunately, sweetie," she says, "we had nothing to do with it. It just happened. This oldtimer is hot and the *Times* called him up directly. It was just good luck."

The aged comic's manager comes over. He's in a fury. He doesn't want the reporters to have individual interviews with his star. "It's undignified," he says. "Ronnie Reagan doesn't talk to people like that. He makes all the reporters sit inna big room and then he picks out who gets to talk."

Trixi tries to explain the enormous publicity value of private interviews. Each reporter will be flattered by this chance to spend a few minutes with the star. And if a reporter can tell his editor the quotes are exclusive to their paper, the story will get more space and better display.

But the manager insists. "If it's good enough for Ronnie Reagan, it's good enough for us," he says. "We're not going to knock ourselves out like a road company."

In the hallway I run into Mr. Duck. He has the *Los Angeles Times* story in his hand and is walking into the press conference.

"Great ink," I say.

"It sure is," he says, "and I planted it myself."

THE PRESS CONFERENCE
Its Uses and Misuses

Joseph J. Duome

Nothing ever happens when there is no communication.

You would not have been sitting out there and AT&T would not have become a most successful and flourishing world entity if news of a tinker's toy had not been communicated to the world.

I have a letter here written by Alexander Graham Bell on April 10th, 1876, to his good friend and laboratory assistant, Thomas Augustus Watson. I believe it further illustrates my point:

> Dear Thomas Augustus:
>
> I pray that this letter finds you in the best of health. I do miss your most valuable assistance in my experiments with the multiple harmonic telegraph. It was most enjoyable to succeed in such a transmission and when you told me that you had heard me speak the words: "Watson, come here I want you," I knew somehow that we had reached a new frontier in communications and that we would be able to transmit messages of longer duration in the future.
>
> I will work on this and hope, too, that you may return in time to help me develop it further. The excitement is almost as self-fulfilling as working with my wonderful deaf students and making my school on vocal physiology succeed.
>
> I don't think, dear Thomas Augustus, my friend, however, that I want to demonstrate my new invention at the American Academy of Arts and Sciences in Boston on May 10th, this year. I know you insist that I do, but to what advantage is it to publicize such a product? Suffice to say it exists.
>
> Yes, even Mrs. Bell tells me that the telephonic instrument is a most significant one and should be shown at the Philadelphia Centennial Exposition. I say no: and I will positively not form a company bearing my name: "The Bell Telephone Company." Indeed!
>
> At any rate, there is no need to generate any more unnecessary excitement. Oh, I will still enjoy working with my telephone (and how do you like that for its name? Mrs. Bell helped suggest it to me.)
>
> Keep well my good friend, you and your family. I will still be at the old stand tinkering with my little voice machine. Promote its use? Heavens no! It would do no good, I am sure.
>
> Warmest regards.
>
> Your obedient servant,
>
> *Alexander Graham Bell*
> East Braintree, Mass.
> April 10, 1876

Well, as you can see the letter is self explanatory. If indeed Mr. Bell truly felt this way, as indicated in this apocryphal letter, we all wouldn't be able to, as Bell's TV commercials say, "reach out . . . reach out and touch someone . . . "

There is nothing arcane or obscene about public relations and, contrary to many beliefs—in Hollywood and yes, even in some corporate circles—there is little or no "black magic" about it.

From a speech delivered at AT&T's Executive Conference Center, March 11, 1980. Reprinted from *Vital Speeches of the Day* (May 15,1980). Reprinted by permission.

In the basic sense public relations is the effective use of communications—most often the printed or spoken word—to achieve the most favorable impression or image for the enterprise with the financial/business community, Washington D.C., plant communities, or the general public.

Public relations is one practical means by which American business puts its best foot forward. Utilizing what he considers the right techniques, a public relations professional will, by his efforts, correlate the company's sales and marketing efforts. As markets grow more competitive and products more standardized, the importance of a company's reputation and prestige, as a sales factor, increases.

Simply put, public relations *complements* the marketing, sales and advertising efforts with a more penetrative, deeper and lasting effect.

The twin goals of a company like AT&T are profits and prestige. If they were always of equal import, one perfectly balancing off the other, the public relations professional's work would be vastly simplified. But objectives shift and change: profit and prestige come into momentary conflict. To decide where emphasis must fall requires the best judgment available to management. The P.R. man, as an integral part of management, should, and is expected to, implement corporate policies. He is management's representative with the public, whether the company is introducing a new or a newly improved product, changing its management structure, building a new plant, holding its annual meeting, or announcing its earnings.

Should the public be apprised of the new product, the new service, the management changes? Should the construction of a new plant be revealed? Or should we keep out the press when a company's earnings are down and sales are not all they seem to be? Should we keep quiet when the news does not seem too favorable?

Each decision involves a risk. By proper use of public relations techniques the chances of favorable reception and sustained acceptance by the public are greatly enhanced. A public relations professional, as a top echelon corporate officer, is expected to be keenly sensitive to public moods and reactions. His advice and counsel are needed on all important matters, whether it is determining the attitude of a company in a crisis or the seemingly mundane timing of a corporate announcement.

As a rule, the public usually does not know whether the news and information it gets is accidental, incidental or planned—as long as it is interesting and true.

Major expansion plans, acquisitions, installations of new equipment and similar corporate developments are of definite interest to the community, to the trade, to the financial community and the general public, especially if a company is a relatively large one with many shareholders, far-flung plants and markets and services. How then, after we have assessed all aspects of a project—its corporate ramifications, such as relationship to sales, earnings, markets—do we take the news to the public?

In cases where the news is of substantive importance and the news treatment would be improved by providing the media an opportunity for further information, a corporation may want to consider holding a press conference. The press conference, a special form of releasing news, is particularly appropriate for news of *major* importance. It provides a platform for a more formal presentation of the news and can be expected to result in a substantially longer and more detailed story on the company.

This technique, however, should be used sparingly and only in cases of significant developments. Once bitten, the newsman or woman will be twice shy of invitations to a press conference that does not warrant his time and trouble.

The press conference, in which the company's top officers meet newspaper, radio and TV reporters face to face, has the great advantage of establishing personal relationships. These are invaluable. A scientific demonstration or a machine of any sort is far more interesting once one has touched it, seen it, watched it work. And a person is always more real when he has seen and heard: he becomes more than a faceless voice on the phone, more than a name in print.

A few simple rules should guide the decision as to whether a given news story warrants a press conference:

1. One does not hold a press conference unless there is a genuine news story.
2. One does not hold a press conference until you've taken a hard, objective look at what you're going to give reporters in the way of news. Wear the reporter's mocassins and walk in them for a mile.
3. One does not hold a press conference unless top corporate officers are available to meet with and present the news story to the invited press.
4. One does not hold a press conference unless enough background material is available to buttress your news story.
5. One does not hold a press conference unless you've had a "dry run" or "rehearsal" with corporate spokesmen prior to the scheduled day (even in emergencies and hastily called conferences a prior run-through or briefing would be smart.)
6. One does not hold a press conference unless you are prepared to offer *all* news to the press "on the record." There is no such thing as "off the record." This can be likened to a judge instructing a jury to disregard a very revealing bit of testimony. And, not unlike jurors, reporters have retentive memories.

This, then, is the basis for a press conference scenario, your blueprint for the pronouncement. You are well prepared. Nothing can go wrong. Or can it? Let's examine a few of the past press conferences.

A New Paint Product. The press conference was being held by a major paint manufacturer at Gallegher's Restaurant. We reporters were *not* given news releases or press kits. Instead we were immediately seated for lunch. The news presentation was made at the conclusion of the lunch just as a curtain to a freshly painted wall was being drawn.

Why? Simply this: the company wanted to dramatically show us that their brand new paint product was indeed odorless, that we were able to partake of our food without any semblance of odor. We were indeed impressed with the clever presentation and the product.

Unbreakable Dinnerware. This press conference was sponsored by a leading chemical and plastics maker at a local hotel. The company introduced for the first time unbreakable dinnerware made of a material called melamine. It was a good product story; that is until one of the top officers, determined to show the quality of the product, suddenly stood up on a chair and with a Falstaffian gesture held up a dinner plate. "See," he shouted, "it won't break." Whereupon he tossed it to the floor.

You guessed it. It smashed into a thousand pieces.

> There is nothing arcane or obscene about public relations. There is no "black magic" about it.

A Mutual Fund. A small group of newsmen were this time gathered at a venerable bankers' club of dear, departed memory. They were there to listen to a unique mutual fund success story. The entire party lunched at one large table. After the presentation the newsmen began asking questions of this proper Bostonian Mutual Fund executive. Following the fifth or sixth query he suddenly and abruptly jumped to his feet and cried: "Who the hell are you people to be asking me such questions?" It's none of your business!

What nerve!" Whereupon he turned and stalked out of the room leaving a bunch of hardened newsmen completely flabbergasted—and a new P.R. person petrified.

Joe Namath. This press conference was called at an early hour in the morning at a major bank in the Wall Street area. It featured the irrepressible Joe Namath, who, at that time, was the quarterback for the New York Jets. An investment banking firm was underwriting Joe's Florida hamburger stand with an eye towards franchising it throughout the U.S. Now, ordinarily, underwriting of this sort—about $5 million dollars—is rather routine news procedure. But look who we had here: Broadway Joe!

Well, a press conference was called for both the financial and sports press for the official presentation of the check. To insert a little touch of the theater a true facsimile of the check was realistically drawn on an official National Football League football.

Fortunately — or unfortunately — our underwriter signed the football making it entirely negotiable!

What did the public relations man do? He asked Joe to cash it. And Joe promptly did. Well, that photo with Joe waiting in line surrounded by other bank customers, was carried by newspapers around the world. Oh, by the way the lovely young lady behind the counter almost suffered cardiac arrest when she looked up at handsome Joe with his $5 million football.

Fire Engines. My client? Ward La France, one of the major makers of fire engines. In an industry where there are not too many press conferences.

One day I discovered while doing research that red was *not* the traditional color for fire engines—that the first 1812 was blue, the next white, *and in the late 20s red came into vogue.* Further search revealed that an oculist had written:

1. More firemen killed to and from fires because of color at dusk.
2. Lime yellow most visible color on spectrum.

Now, one can have the greatest idea in the world but will not be able to do anything with it if the head man turns it down.

The head of Ward La France agreed to invest in special Du Pont paints and an $80,000 fire pumper.

We held this press conference amidst fierce competition at the Annual Firemen's Convention—riding with the Cleveland Fire Dept. to and from a couple of fires in the new lime yellow fire pumper.

The story broke in newspapers all over the world—on front pages. By the end of 1971, 15 percent of all fire engines were lime yellow, 35 percent by 1972, and 48 percent in 1973, 1974 and 1975.

Now, more than at any other time in the history of the free enterprise system, our nation's leading businesses and the men who direct them must speak out. The press conference, used wisely, is one of the most *effective* means of filling the excessive lack of effective communications between top corporate decision makers and their publics.

Remember, however, that you're dealing with sophisticated news gatherers who are not looking for gimmicks, not seeking out junkets any longer, but want *hard,* cold news. It makes them look good . . . and makes *you* feel good.

A press conference is a two-way method of communications: the reporter seeks information; the corporation wants to get the word out. The press conference is a truly valuable medium in today's complex and highly competitive world. As John Milton once said:

"Good, the more communicated, the more abundant grows."

SUGGESTIONS FOR FURTHER READING

Pertaining not only to this chapter, but also to Chapter 17 (on stereotyping) is James U. McNeal's "Advertising's Disparagement of American Workers," in *Business Horizons*, January/February 1983, pp. 7–12.

Those interested in subliminal advertising may want to read the excellent research summary provided in Timothy E. Moore's "Subliminal Advertising: What You See Is What You Get," in *Journal of Marketing* 46 (Spring 1982): 38–47.

Also of interest:

Stuart Ewen, *Captains of Consciousness*. New York: McGraw-Hill, 1976.

Ken Hornsby, *The Padded Sell*. New York: St. Martin's Press, 1980.

Vance Packard, *The Hidden Persuaders*. rev. ed. New York: Pocket Books, 1981.

CHAPTER 10

Journalism and Truth

The first reading in this chapter is E.W. Scripps's 1908 statement on the conflict between a newspaper's big-business identity and its honesty. Scripps was the founder of America's first newspaper chain.

Recently, the credibility gap that Scripps suggested has increased. Newspapers have been accused of slanting news, ignoring news, and sensationalizing news more than at any time since "objective reporting" became the standard for American journalism. Most of the arguments that arise over bias in reporting are simplistic, and hinge on the question of whether the newspaper intentionally misled its readers. However, as the second reading, by Richard A. Kallan, illustrates, the differences between news and truth are more complex than that. Kallan is a professor of communications studies at the University of Nevada, Las Vegas. He says that today's problems of journalistic veracity arise from the failure of journalists to properly analyze news data—what he calls the noncritical posture of American journalism.

In the third reading Kurt Luedtke, a scriptwriter who is a former newspaper editor, presents a third view: he believes that the public's lack of faith in today's journalism is a direct result of journalists' abuse of their freedom and power. Luedtke, whose screenplay *Absence of Malice*, was nominated for an Academy Award, was previously the executive editor of the *Detroit Free Press*.

The next six readings constitute a sampling of editorial opinion from around the country on the *Washington Post* Pulitzer Prize scandal of 1981.

The final reading is an editorial ad from Mobil Corporation that deals with one of the perennial problelms of journalistic truth: the emphasis on bad news.

IS HONEST JOURNALISM POSSIBLE?

E. W. Scripps

November 29, 1908

. . . There are tricks in all trades, especially in our trade. I am a newspaper owner. Newspaper owners do not like competition. They want as few newspapers in existence as possible. It is but natural—even if to be natural is to be dishonest—for newspaper owners to desire to create the impression that it requires tremendous sums of money to found a newspaper, and that even when founded a newspaper is not a very profitable property.

Yet, as a matter of fact, although I do not know the full history of all of the great newspapers in the United States, and only know in a general way the history of a large majority of them, I can say that I am not personally acquainted with the history of a single great and successful and influential American newspaper, the first cost of the founding of which has been equal to the cost of founding any third- or fourth-grade business in the locality where the newspaper was founded, at the time of the founding of that paper.

As a matter of fact, no great newspaper has

From Oliver Knight, (Ed.) *I Protest: Selected Disquisitions by E. W. Scripps:* (Madison: University of Wisconsin Press, 1966).

been founded by the aid of large capital. As a matter of fact, no more substantial obstacle to success can be presented to the founder of any newspaper, than the possession of abundant capital . . . .

In journalism, money does not make money. In journalism, money makes for failure . . . .

The possessor of great wealth may be, and frequently is, corrupted. No matter how good or moral a man may be, the possession of great wealth must have a certain amount of corrupting influence upon him. The possession of wealth isolates a man to a great extent from his fellows. This isolation results in a constantly diminishing sympathy for human kind. The duties connected with the administration of a large property are so absorbing and so strenuous as to permit a man, who is the possessor of wealth, no time to think of even his own misfortunes, and much less of the misfortunes of others. Perhaps only the very rich men are those who fully appreciate the fact that the most unhappy men are those who are farthest from the center of the general average. The very rich and the very poor are, if not equally unhappily situated, at least far more unhappily situated than the great mass of men who occupy the intermediate space between wealth and poverty.

THE NONCRITICAL POSTURE OF AMERICAN PRINT JOURNALISM

Richard A. Kallan

Attacks on American journalism are anything but new: editors, columnists, reporters and even cartoonists have a long history of being second-guessed by their readers. What *is* new is the pervasiveness and sophistication of that criticism. Whereas "misrepresented" public officials once ostensibly led the foray, today they are joined by political activists, racial and social minorities, law-enforcement agencies, special interest groups, athletes, celebrities—to mention only a few. Each increasingly in recent years has voiced dissatisfaction with its coverage and treatment by the press. And while much of the criticism echoes familiar charges of bias, distortion and sensationalism, more probing analyses also surface with greater frequency. Journalism reviews, press councils and the writings of academicians in particular have led the way in rejecting simplistic, stimulus-response explanations and indictments of the news media in favor of more thoughtful, process-centered views. In short, we have begun to look at journal-

From the *Journal of Popular Culture* (Fall 1981). Reprinted by permission.

ism with both a greater vigor and a more sustained rigor.

Presented here is but another perspective. The concern centers not on lamenting the ills of newsgathering and writing *per se*, as does much previous commentary; rather, I wish to focus on that "middle" step—news *analysis*—and argue that the philosphy of newsgathering and the pragmatics of newswriting *affect* the ability of print journalists to critically interpret news data. The absence of critical posture, I believe, substantially accounts for bad journalism.

I

My thesis first should be distinguished from the seemingly-similar position advanced by Edward J. Epstein in his excellent book, *Between Fact and Fiction: The Problem of Journalism.*[1] Epstein contends that journalism "cannot serve as a credible investigator" of truth.[2] Even if the now operating newspaper constraints of time, space and money were lifted, according to Epstein, genuine *investigative* reporting still would not transpire—owing to the training of journalists and the conventions of newsgathering. Journalists, he notes, "are rarely, if ever, in a position to establish the truth about an issue for themselves, and they are therefore almost entirely dependent on self-interested 'sources' for the version of reality that they report."[3] Unfortunately, journalists have no "acceptable procedure for examining, testing, and evaluating [such] evidence."[4] They cannot force a source to give them information; nor can they rigorously cross-examine, lest risk offending and losing the source; and they certainly cannot always identify their sources (which might allow for possible corroboration). What emerges, then, is a "daily journalism [which] is largely concerned with finding and retaining profitable sources of prepackaged stories."[5]

> Journalists, to be sure, may be ineffective at establishing truth, but not because they are ignorant or impotent.

The merits of Epstein's argument notwithstanding, I find it faulty primarily because he overstates his case. Factual verification is not quite the task he would have us believe. Increasingly, journalists specialize and develop areas of expertise. One may find political reporters with strong academic backgrounds in history and political science, financial editors possessing college degrees in business and economics, science reporters who actually know science and of course sports writers with more than just vocational interest in athletics. And in those instances where reporters do not have the training necessary to judge the veracity of their data, avenues exist: sources can be intelligently questioned and many "put-up" with the questioning—despite Epstein's contrary claim—if they believe they otherwise would not gain media access. (Many sources, in fact, all too willingly cooperate with reporters in return for press coverage.) Also, not every source or corroborative source speaks from vested interest. Journalists, to be sure, may be ineffective at establishing truth, as Epstein argues, but not because they are ignorant or impotent.

The problem stems from the journalist's inability to interpret facts meaningfully and thus provide an accurate and complete rendering of

1. *Between Fact and Fiction: The Problem of Journalism* (New York: Vintage, 1975).
2. Ibid., p. 18.
3. Ibid., p. 3.
4. Ibid., p. 6.
5. Ibid., p. 9.

truth. The earlier noted inherent constraints of time, space and money aside, most journalists *cannot* exercise interpretive reporting given the anti-intellectual nature of newspaper journalism. Hence, the crux of my argument: journalism does not teach or encourage journalists to think. It promotes a noncritical posture whereby even the best trained and most powerful journalists seem incapable of analyzing, synthesizing, theorizing or presenting data in anything other than the reportorial narrative.

Look at the whole structure of journalism and you realize that newsgathering assumes primary status, easily eclipsing newswriting and news analysis. The golden ring every aspiring reporter reaches for is the "big" story, i.e., anything significant as yet unrevealed. It is an ancient if not somewhat archaic tradition dating to when newspapers represented the only daily mass communications medium and the world appeared considerably less complicated. News by itself, the barons of the Penny Press period soon realized, interested an America more absorbed with discovering its environment than making sense out of it. But information discovery and dissemination, ironically, became in time so spectacular that yet another public evolved: one yearning not just for new information but for some explanation of the old. In response, newspapers have become more interpretive; but the emphasis today still remains on collecting not explaining data, with peer praise still reserved for the scoop, the exposé, the exclusive. None of which is surprising considering the heroes of reportorial journalism were heroes because of *what* they discovered and not *how* they presented it. Thus, the Pulitzer Prize winners remembered are the investigative journalists, the persistent muckrakers who persevered and got the "ungettable" stories. Pedestrian writers like Bob Woodward and Carl Bernstein became the darlings of America's young journalists not because they could write or reason, but because they possessed the skills of good private detectives.[6] Their successors, from the moment they enter their first newsrooms, similarly will have had inculcated the value of fact-ferreting and its transcending importance.

Despite preoccupation with gathering data and cultivating sources of information, journalists usually along the way acquire without much effort—because of the relative easiness of the literary form—at least the minimum writing skills required of the profession. But developing a mind capable of logical query and inference is another matter: without continual training and self-application, the talent proves elusive. As shown, often that becomes the case because of journalism's philosophy of newsgathering.

The pragmatics of newswriting further add to the problem. Some worry whether the summary lead, inverted pyramid style and short simple-sentence paragraphs stacked one upon another without benefit of serious transition do not lead the reader to accept a facile, black-white view of the world. But I worry how the style affects the *writer* and whether it encourages simplistic thinking.

Take, for example, the convention of short-paragraphing which probably epitomizes the style's defects. Because journalists believe that short paragraphs are typographically easier to read, news stories seldom contain paragraphs with more than two or three sentences and often single sentence paragraphs abound. In journalism no such thing prevails as the topic sentence supported by subsequent sentences; sentences stand by themselves, paragraphically set off from

6. Here again I disagree with Epstein who even minimizes Woodward's and Bernstein's investigative talents by maintaining that they "only leaked elements of the prosecutors' case to the public in advance of the trial." and that "it was the investigative agencies of the government and not the members of the press who assembled the evidence" (pp. 25, 10). But that argument forgets the simple fact that Woodward and Bernstein were clever and persistent enough to get their sources to talk—an accomplishment which cannot be minimized.

others, and often without relationship to one another. Statements which naturally follow, entail, support or elaborate one another are severed into separate, isolated paragraphs. The journalist consequently seldom acquires the keen sense of logical order and development afforded by learning the traditional concept of paragraphing. A paragraph after all is a miniature argument: to know how to write one well is to know how to reason well. Journalists, unfortunately, daily immerse themsevlves in an "anti-paragraph" writing style which blurs the differences between a thesis, overview, contention, subcontention, piece of evidence, transition and summary. As such, journalists never learn the components of an argument, let alone the skills necessary for clear thinking.

Moreover, because journalists write in a style lacking significant structure and sequence, they never come to appreciate the logical interaction and interdependency of variables in the function of the whole. A package of unassembled units at best, the news story pictures a world devoid of articulation—a relationshipless environment lacking unity and cohesion. Prevented from explaining context, deciding causality, shading tone, positing solutions or even authoring a conclusion, the journalist ultimately accepts a shallow, simplistic view of the universe. Indeed, the conventions of newswriting obviate the burden of critical thinking and leave unchallenged altogether the journalist's intellectual capabilities.

II

Although numerous examples of the journalist's lack of critical posture come to mind, I have selected three—each because it represents a slightly differing aspect of the problem, and collectively because they cover a wide spectrum: news, editorial and sports.

The first example deals with press coverage of Gerald Ford's pardon of Richard Nixon and is borrowed from David Shaw's provocative book, *Journalism Today: A Changing Press for a Changing America.*[7] According to Shaw, "Press reaction to the pardon of Mr. Nixon was, in most cases, harsh, subjective and speculative, at times giving the impression that the act was, above all, a personal affront to (and a betrayal of) the press itself."[8] But the press, ironically, observes Shaw, described Ford *prior* to his pardoning of Nixon as a highly partisan but compassionate man who did not view Nixon guilty of any serious wrongdoing relating to Watergate. Why, then, did the pardon shock the press and why were they, by their own admission, caught off guard? Everything in Ford's political and moral character, as described to us so thoroughly by the press, dictated it.

> Newspapers have become more interpretive; but the emphasis today still remains on collecting, not explaining data, with peer praise still reserved for the scoop, the exposé, the exclusive.

Now some press members seemed surprised not at the pardon *per se* but at its timing, i.e., it coming less than two months after Ford assumed office. But Shaw rightfully points out that Ford had set the stage with other actions. Upon taking office he and various Republican leaders more than once suggested that Nixon had suffered enough. Further, his offer a few weeks before of amnesty/leniency toward Vietnam evaders and deserters could be viewed as laying the philo-

7. *Journalism Today: A Changing Press for a Changing America* (New York: Harper's College Press, 1977).
8. Ibid., p. 115.

sophical and psychological groundwork for an imminent Nixon pardon. Too, if Ford was set on pardoning Nixon, as apparently he was, and if Ford was the politically-minded politician described by the press, surely an *early* pardon would be more expedient than one closer to election time.

The *validity* of the pardon aside, the press should have interpreted existing data sufficiently to know and report that the pardon was in the offing. Reporters did not perceive or simply refused to accept a logical progression of events, as well as the logical inconsistencies of their reporting of the Ford presidency before versus after the pardon. The contradiction of observing that Ford remains loyal and compassionate to Nixon and on the other hand expressing surprise that Ford would exercise loyalty and compassion to his personal and ideological friend and former President seems extraordinary. Shaw might argue, I suspect, that such slipshod reasoning stems not from any inherent press deficiencies, but rather from intense biases against Richard Nixon interfering with normally good judgment.

> It is almost impossible to convey to anyone outside Washington just how deep and intense the press's bitterness toward Mr. Nixon runs—and how pervasively, albeit subconsciously, that bitterness colors some of their perceptions. . . .
>
> Throughout the 1960s, many editors say, the press had been criticized for reporting racial and campus unrest. Then came Agnew and Watergate and Mr. Nixon—and more criticism.
>
> When Mr. Nixon resigned, the press felt a sense of justification. They were grateful. And Mr. Ford was the beneficiary of that gratitude. But when he pardoned Mr. Nixon, he deprived the press of their ultimate public vindication. They felt shortchanged, and they took it out on him.[9]

Press hatred of Richard Nixon may account for dubious logic shown in reporting and analyzing his pardon; however, as borne out by other examples, even in the absence of such bias the press is sometimes something less than thoughtful.

Let us move to a different arena and consider how the press's fascination with newsgathering yields a significant corollary attitude which adversely influences editorial opinion. More specifically, belief in the overriding importance of newsgathering appears to correlate with the notion of defining intelligence primarily by how much a person *knows*, as opposed to how well a person *thinks*. The perspective repeatedly influences journalistic opinion. It underlies, for instance, the frequency with which newspapers editorially endorse political incumbents, often despite lackluster performances. (Only when the incumbent seriously and continually blunders, it seems, does editorial support wane.) "Journalistically," the major advantage the incumbent possesses is *experience*—if only by virtue of the incumbency—at least it appears, since endorsements frequently cite experience as the deciding factor.

The adulation of experience follows from the importance the journalist places on knowing: someone experienced is someone *in the know*. Experience, after all, is *knowledge* sensorily achieved; "to have experience" means to have acquired a base of experientially-learned facts. An experienced candidate represents someone "factually seasoned," someone who may not know necessarily what to do but recognizes what to expect. But history certainly has not proven the highly experienced politician any more or less effective than the marginally experienced. Some of our best *and worst* presidents were politically experienced, and some of our best and worst were not. One's experience admittedly bears consideration, but to judge one solely or predominantly on experience is to dismiss the significance of other ideal attributes, e.g., commitment, integrity, industry, fortitude, vision and creativity.

9. Ibid., pp. 119, 121.

The obvious shallowness of the facts equals intelligence equation does not merit extended comment here. Suffice to remember that probably every significant question has been not of fact but of value and judgment. Almost anyone, Richard M. Weaver implied, could retrieve the facts, but knowing what to do with them required a more advanced intellect.[10] For pure facts by themselves seldom yield any significant answers beyond the immediate and superficial; as starting points for discovery, they must be interpreted synthesized and related to one another. Genuine intelligence is problem-solving, the ability to make sense out of one's data via inference and extension, hypothesis and theory. The press by narrowly defining intelligence as equalling experience promulgates a simple-minded view of society . . . .

My final example is one with which I am particularly familiar. I think it aptly demonstrates how the press may fail to draw insightful conclusions even after the necessary premises are in full view.

In 1971 the National Collegiate Athletic Association (NCAA) launched an investigation of the University of Nevada, Las Vegas (UNLV) to determine if UNLV's basketball program violated NCAA governing rules. On August 26, 1977 the NCAA placed UNLV's program on two years probation and ordered the University to suspend its basketball coach, Jerry Tarkanian, for the probation's duration. The University reluctantly did; Tarkanian, however, immediately sought and won a court injunction prohibiting the suspension, and he continued coaching. There followed legal appeals, congressional hearings and oratory—all of which received in addition to expected local coverage, considerable national press attention.

The NCAA charged UNLV with 38 recruiting violations of which about half occurred during Tarkanian's tenure, with fewer still assessing blame specifically to Tarkanian.[11] The other half, and by far the more serious infractions, transpired during the reign of Tarkanian's predecessor, John Bayer. Nevertheless, the press invariably pitted *Tarkanian* against the NCAA, while relegating other key UNLV figures to background material. That was somewhat understandable since Tarkanian is a nationally recognized personality, and the NCAA seldom suspends coaches—who much less fight back and accuse the Association of having a vendetta against them, as Tarkanian did. I am not criticizing, then, the press for covering Tarkanian, but I question whether he deserved top billing.

On one level, I wonder if the public would not have been served equally well had the news media probed more fundamental questions. Some continually need asking: How important is winning? Can there be such a thing as a student-athlete? Should college sports become more or less professional? Who should control college athletics? Some, a bit fresher: What constitutes fair and legitimate punishments for those guilty of NCAA violations? How does due process function in a voluntary organization? To whom and for what is a head coach responsible?

---

10. According to Weaver, facts are determined scientifically whereas truth is decided dialectically (*The Ethics of Rhetoric* [Chicago: Regnery, 1953], pp. 15–17; ch. 2 passim). "Positive terms" describe phenomena (facts) existing in the objective world; these facts are located and reported via "a rhetoric of simple description, which requires only powers of accurate observation and reporting" (Ibid., p. 188). "Dialectical terms," however, are concepts "defined by their negatives or their privations"; they reflect judgment of value (truth) and "depend on something more than the external world for their significance" (*Ibid.*). For Weaver "there is never an argument, in the true sense of the term, about facts. When facts are disputed, the argument must be suspended until the facts are settled. Not until then may it be resumed, for all true argument is about the meaning of established or admitted facts. And since this meaning is always expressed in propositions, we can say further that all argument is about the systematic import of propositions" (Ibid., pp. 52–53).

11. See "University of Nevada, Las Vegas, Placed on NCAA Probation," National Collegiate Athletic Association press release, 26 Aug. 1977, pp. 5–10.

Questions arising specifically out of this case also could have been addressed. One in particular remains especially intriguing: To what degree did UNLV as an institution profit—yes, *profit* by the press's preoccupation with Tarkanian? Potential harm to UNLV was well reported: revenue lost because imposed sanctions prohibited any NCAA-sponsored televised games; UNLV forbidden from NCAA playoffs—which, when coupled with the television blackout, meant players denied national exposure; UNLV's bid to enter the Western Athletic conference possibly jeopardized; and perhaps most significantly, the University stigmatized athletically and academically. All true. Yet the press never realized that by focusing on Tarkanian and implying that the whole NCAA investigation revolved around him, they removed the University from any perceived culpability and directed the reader's attentions away from judging *UNLV* and instead to judging *Tarkanian*.

The journalist seldom acquires the keen sense of logical order and development afforded by learning the traditional concept of paragraphing.

The press knew enough to question at least whether the University was but an innocent victim of a Tarkanian/NCAA battle. One could argue that Tarkanian actually represented a minor figure in the story, and that blame should have been aimed at UNLV's highest academic administrators, whose indiscretions were well documented. Remember that many of the more serious infractions contained in the NCAA's investigative report occurred under Tarkanian's predecessor, a man relieved of his duties, according to UNLV's president, once the University discovered his wrongdoings. His punishment? Far from banishment, he eventually received tenure and became Chairperson of the Department of Physical Education, while his aiding and abetting assistant coach was given another university job and also later tenured. UNLV then hired Tarkanian, who they knew was already under NCAA investigation at California State, Long Beach! And when UNLV themselves came under NCAA scrutiny, they conceded virtually nothing, and defended themselves sometimes with the most ludicrous of arguments.[12]

Circumstantial evidence suggests the plausibility of UNLV's highest administrators knowing all along about corruption in the school's past and present basketball programs. Hence, the media attention Tarkanian received benefited the University by diffusing the public review of its policies. In commanding the bulk of news coverage, Tarkanian funneled attentions toward *his* possible wrongdoing, while the University was perceived as an unfortunate bystander who just happened to employ a coach disliked by the NCAA. Had they tried, the University could not have created a better fall guy than Tarkanian.

Whatever Tarkanian's failings, they were equalled if not surpassed by a greater moving force, the mentality of his superiors. Why were journalists oblivous to this? The press *knew* that even in the pre-Tarkanian era the University committed serious NCAA violations (in fact they often defended Tarkanian by labeling his predecessor as the real culprit); they *knew* that UNLV realized that Tarkanian was under NCAA investigation when UNLV sought to hire him; they *knew* that the University had not honestly investigated itself as required by the NCAA. By what reasoning, then, did the press choose to write extensively about Tarkanian? The real story lay under their noses.

12. For a summary of the University's defense, see "Memorandum of the University of Nevada, Las Vegas: Case No. 443," memorandum to NCAA, 13 Aug. 1977.

III

Not every journalist commits the sins outlined above nor are the guilty always guilty. Good journalism exists, but enough bad prevails to warrant some suggestions for solutions.

First we must reconsider the formal training journalists receive. Although some professionals still advise against the college journalism major in lieu of a supposedly broader liberal arts background, I find that many journalists do not know *enough* about journalism and the intricate questions/issues/problems raised by its daily practice. Journalists need to think more about the theoretical perspectives underpinning the profession and the assumptions underlying their own work. Similarly, journalism skills should be taught with greater emphasis on data analysis; too, more thoughtful writing might result if within the journalism curriculum and required of every journalist were courses in argumentation, logic and criticism. Overall, journalism instruction must reject a slavish devotion to garnering facts and recognize that they serve as a means not an end in the process of establishing truth. Adherence to that perspective ideally might produce a more discriminating group of journalists who "consult a greater number of sources, but quote fewer of them."[13]

But for journalists to change so must newspapers. They must show less interest in soliciting *attributable* statements and more concern for locating sound, probable information capable of confirmation. I agree with Dennis Chase that newspapers should decide "to unite news and truth, to stop publishing the lies of official sources and the unvalidated opinions and doctored stories of the new journalists, and to allow into our journals only demonstrable truths that can be independently verified."[14] Perhaps reporters could spend more time on their stories and write with greater depth if newspapers required from them *fewer* stories. The suggestion may seem radical if not heretical, but given the hypothetical choice of reading ten poor stories or five good ones, most people, I think, would choose the latter. After all, is every news story really newsworthy? Or perhaps newspapers simply could enlarge "In Brief" sections and summarize more articles into one or two paragraphs. Whatever direction, one thing is certain: it matters little if journalists learn to think if not *allowed* to think.

> Good journalism exists, but enough bad prevails to warrant some suggestions for solutions.

This essay has not meant to demean journalism. Quite the contrary. I believe few professions to be as significant to the public interest. The journalist shoulders an honorable yet awesome burden requiring the best of minds and the strongest of integrities. The need for reliable information mandates we set these standards and reject anything less. For like Will Rogers, most of us know only what we read in the newspapers. The question this paper addresses and which periodically needs asking is whether that knowledge accurately reflects truth.

13. Alex S. Edelstein and William E. Ames, "Humanistic Writing," *Nieman Reports*, 24 (1970), 15.

14. Dennis Chase, "From Lippmann to Irving to New Journalism," *Quill*, Aug. 1974, p. 21.

AN EX-NEWSMAN HANDS DOWN HIS INDICTMENT OF THE PRESS

Kurt Luedtke

How many of you truly believe the public is really capable of making important decisions for this society?

OK. Then let me ask you this: Are you willing to put your definition of the role of the press to a popular vote? Will you let your readers decide how useful you really are? Let the public will determine the extent of your rights and privileges?

Because if you won't, what do we do to protect ourselves against an institution grown so powerful and become so undisciplined that we are defenseless against your ability to affect our lives?

On your discretionary judgments hang reputations and careers, jail sentences and stock prices, Broadway shows and water rates. You are the mechanism of reward and punishment, the arbiter of right and wrong, the roving eye of daily judgment. You no longer shape public opinion, you have supplanted it. There are good men and women who will not stand for office, concerned that you will find their flaws or invent them. Many people who have dealt with you wish that they had not. You are capricious and unpredictable, you are fearsome and you are feared because there is never any way to know whether this time you will be fair and accurate or whether you will not. And there is virtually nothing that we can do about it.

So how do you think the referendum will go on Times versus Sullivan?* Joint operating agreements? Reportorial privilege before the grand jury? Prior restraint of the publication of government secrets? Premature disclosure of criminal investigations? Publication of the names of juveniles and rape victims? The right to make use of stolen documents? To violate the law in pursuit of a story?

If you lost the vote—if it were the law that damages would be awarded whenever false publication caused injury, if the anonymous source could speak only with the knowledge that his identity might one day be revealed, if it were left to the courts to weigh the societal value of publishing a fact against the societal cost of doing so—would *the people* be worse off? There's a risk, certainly, but is a corrupt judge more dangerous than a reckless newspaper? What if a man *does* have a right to confront his accusers? What if it *ought* to be against the law to publish the plans for a hydrogen bomb?

If you lost that vote, would America be less free? Are we more free than Britain, France, the Scandinavian countries? Their *press* is less free—they have already decided every question on your ballot and elected to restrict—but their citizens are every bit as free as we are. The near-absolute freedom which you enjoy is *not* essential to a functioning democracy: every society in the world has found it useful to exert a greater measure of control than we do.

They can do it, you know, the mob out there. It's not likely, thank the Lord, but there is nothing in our law to prevent public regulation of the

From a speech presented before the American Newspaper Publishers Association. This speech was excerpted in the *ASNE Bulletin* of May/June, 1982. Reprinted by permission of Mr. Luedtke.

* Editors Note: In which the Supreme Court found that a public figure must prove "actual malice" to recover for libel.

American press if enough Americans get het up about it. I wouldn't endorse any constitutional conventions if I were you.

For the record, I happen to think that the First Amendment is far too important ever to be allowed to become a public question. But you are pushing awfully hard.

You seem to be oblivious of the fact that any expansion of your rights necessarily results in a constriction of mine. And you badly underestimate how naked we feel and how resentful we are now that it is clear that we have no remedy for inaccuracy.

Times versus Sullivan was a very bad case and, as a matter of heresy, let me say that I think it made very bad law. If public discussion cannot survive without libel, then it ought not to survive at all. As a matter of fairness, there is just nothing wrong with paying compensation to someone who can show falsity and damage. The burden on the press was not at all excessive; the "chilling effect" which the threat of libel action posed chilled exactly what it was supposed to.

Times-Sullivan and the subsequent decisions which flowed from it swept away five hundred years of libel law and however damaging the new law has been to the poor souls who are wrongfully accused, it has been equally damaging to the press. It is simply too easy to get it wrong these days, to let the professional leaker find his way into print in the cloak of the usually reliable source. Under the burden of *star decisis,** the Court itself has been wrestling with Times-Sullivan for almost twenty years and has made a hash of it so you still don't know where you stand.

And Times-Sullivan was sufficiently incredible as a guidepost of public policy that it badly muddied the water as to just how sacrosanct our already free and already unfettered press ought to be. If it encouraged you to think too well of yourselves, and I think it did, the fault can at least be shared with the high court.

Times-Sullivan was a gift but your reaction has not been a grateful one. Now you are forever inventing new rights and privileges for yourselves the assertion of which is so insolent that you apparently feel compelled—as I certainly would—to wrap it in the robes of some imaginary public duty and claim that you are acting on my behalf. If I am indeed involved, then I would like you to do a little *less* for me. But of course I'm not. Your claims of privilege have nothing to do with any societal obligation because you have no societal obligation: that is the essence of what the First Amendment is all about. Meantime, we have bred a whole generation of newspaper people who without apparent difficulty hold simultaneously in their heads the notions that they are armed with a mandate from the public and are accountable to no one save you. You ride whichever horse suits you in the situation until eventually you are persuaded that whatever you choose to do with your newspaper is somehow done in the service of the Republic. The press is full of itself these days, and frequently, it is simply full of it.

There is no such thing as the public's right to know. You made that up, taking care not to specify what it *was* that the public had a right to know. The public knows whatever you choose to tell it, no more, no less. If the public did have a right to know, it would then have something to say about what it is you choose to call news. At which point, bring on the First Amendment, Charlie, these guys are trying to tell me what to print.

Neither does it make much sense for you to tell me that you are, self-appointed, my watchdog. If I could get you to say who the senior administration official is who sounds so much like my secretary of state or if I could get you to squeal on the creep whose salary I pay who's running around leaking grand jury information, I would be somewhat more persuaded that you are

* Editors Note: Latin phrase which means "to stand by decided matters," or the policy of following principles laid down in previous judicial decisions.

watching what I want you to watch. But you aren't and you don't have to. The First Amendment says so.

Your rhetoric not withstanding, there are a lot of things the First Amendment does *not* say. It does not say that the freedom to print means that we are obligated to make it easy for you to gather news, which is what your access argument comes to, and it sure as hell does not say that a journalist—whoever and whatever that is—does not have to talk to a grand jury. It is inconceivable to me that you do not see the violence that such a position, if maintained, would do to the most basic individual rights of our citizens. Its promulgation makes a mockery of the role you claim as defender of the democracy.

There is no such thing as the public's right to know. The press made that up, taking care not to specify what it *was* that the public had a right to know.

The publication of a newspaper is in itself a pretentious act: it should come with a daily apology. We are met instead with your firm insistence that you must be uncontrolled so that you can perform—unbidden—an essential public service which is so essential that the people for whom it is being performed must not be allowed to control it. That is wonderfully circular but not very endearing. Such thinking must inevitably lead to arrogance, and it has.

By a reasonable standard, the American daily print press turns in a performance that is simply competent. It is highly motivated, usually well-intentioned, frequently accurate, and occasionally useful, and when it combines with the moral indignation for which it is notorious a correct perception of what it is that's really relevant to those it swears to serve, it is then, in those instances, a prime mover in the betterment of the society. I'd give it a B and vote to keep it.

But your continued claims to special privilege and your rigorous refusal to acknowledge that you do a difficult job imperfectly require that we measure your performance against a much higher standard. It is then clear that while you may be good and useful, you're not *that* good and useful. You're asking for more than you're entitled to.

Your shortcomings would be more tolerable if we had a sense that you were willing to listen but you do not suffer your critics gladly and surely not with humility.

There is, of course, the fact that you own the presses, which has raised a question in some minds about who will have the last word in any discussion of your virtues. I think it is fair to say that you are disinclined to listen to any complainant who seems to have an ax to grind, a category which of course includes most of those who make news regularly and so are in a good position to have an opinion. It seems to be your notion that any criticism which springs from one who seeks the readers' favor is somehow polluted at the source. The dismissal of all politicians, bureaucrats, businessmen, judges and police chiefs seems to me somewhat preemptory but I must admit that it does control the size of the crowd. That leaves only the little guys and it is an article of faith among you that the lay public simply cannot understand what news is, how a newspaper works and why newspapers sometimes do things which hurt people.

Your dismissal of your critics is not very subtle but it is certainly efficient. The silence which results may be soothing but it is easily mistaken for approval. It is a personal opinion of mine that reporters really don't realize how inaccurate they are simply because they assume, as I must say I would, that a story is correct until someone complains. Left out of that equation are all of those who don't want to make waves, or who are afraid of offending you, or who don't know how, or who cool down and don't bother, or who are brushed off by whoever answers the phone. Call your city desk anonymously some time and see if you like the feeling.

If reports of your rectitude are somewhat exaggerated, what about your utility? Are you really an essential part of our lives? I think you can go to the marketplace for an answer to that.

Were you in fact as useful as you sometimes claim to be, a grateful nation would reward you with circulation penetration beyond the security analysts' wildest dreams. The fact, of course, is that circulation has not kept pace with population growth in almost forty years. We don't need you quite as much as you tell us we do.

Whatever it is that the industry is doing, you are not creating a reason to buy. You have become not an essential product but a discretionary one and well more than half the households in the country have elected not to participate.

You are editing newspapers for people as you think they ought to be, not as they are. They ought to be interested in the daily processes of the multiple governments which serve them, but they aren't. They ought to be following what's going on in the United Nations, but they don't. They ought to keep particular track of what their Congressman is up to, but they won't. They are largely apathetic about their roles as citizens, defeated by their apparent inability to make their governments respond to their wishes. You can reach them with news of war and Social Security and not much else. Voter participation has dropped every election year for the last twenty years; in 1980, only half of those eligible to vote bothered to do so.

You can justify your abundant and rather overstaffed coverage of America's political processes philosophically, but you cannot do it as a matter of reader appetite. It continues because you believe in it, because you've always done it that way and because it is, relatively speaking, cheap. In every governmental building in the land, Monday through Friday, some tax-supported something or other is staging an event for you to cover with whoever happens to be available. It looks like news, it feels like news and nobody reads it. Creating detailed information which the reader can actually use is substantially more costly in both time and newsprint.

Event-centered news which the reader in fact acts upon is almost non-existent: if an event has appeal, it's appeal is that of entertainment. Man bites dog is an entertaining event; so is dog bites man if either creature is somehow special. It is awkward and very nearly cynical for me to say out loud that news isn't news unless it's entertaining but that, I think, is a fact of the marketplace. One interesting thing about television is that it takes its customer exactly as he is. The TV people don't like it either, but they live with it and they reach a lot more people than you do.

There is in my mind a clear distinction between news and information and it is there, I think, that your opportunity lies. Americans are hungry for information, material that they can put to use in their immediate lives. If you search through your newspaper for information that the reader can actually act upon, you will find very little of it that isn't advertising. There is the TV book, the weather and the food pages; at most newspapers, that's pretty much it.

If you tell Americans how to do things, if you give your readers information they can put to work, they will buy your newspaper. They may even read a little bit about government in the process.

My time is gone. It's not my place to give advice but since that didn't bother me twenty minutes ago, I guess it won't inhibit me now.

Lower your voices. Be useful. I'll respect your rights if you'll respect mine.

ON THE PULITZER PRIZE HOAX

THE NEWS AND COURIER

Charleston, S.C., April 20, 1981

Little sympathy can be detected in newspaper circles for the principals in the winner-loser affair in which the *Washington Post* gave back the Pulitzer Prize it had won for a story that turned out to be fiction instead of fact. Little sympathy is deserved.

The *Post's* editors are losers. They were taken, but everything written and said of the circumstances strongly suggests they had reason to be suspicious but failed to take normal editorial precautions.

The reporter who wrote the story is a loser. She is out of the prize and out of a job. That is where she should be, because she is a deceiver. She passed off as truth a figment of her imagination. She violated a journalistic canon.

The Pulitzer Prize board is a loser because disclosure of the hoax focused attention on the curious manner in which the *Post* story was selected, creating new doubts about how winners actually are picked—the jury system notwithstanding.

The only losers entitled to sympathy are the *Washington Post's* readers. They were given information about a young drug addict that purported to be factual. Now they have been told the story was made up of whole cloth. Their confidence has been shaken. For a while, at least, many will read each *Post* article with skepticism, wondering if they are being accurately informed or fooled again.

THE WASHINGTON POST

Washington, D.C., April 16, 1981

WE APOLOGIZE. This newspaper, which printed Janet Cooke's false account of meeting with an 8-year-old heroin addict and his family, was itself the victim of a hoax—which we then passed along in a prominent page-one story, taking in the readers as we ourselves had been taken in. How could this have happened? What does it say or imply, if it says or implies anything at all, about the reliability of other stories? An embezzled bank may point out that the heist was an aberration, that other accounts remain safe and sound. But it will immediately examine its system of internal controls to see how such a thing could have been allowed to happen.

So too will we. In some way, it is already plain, the sheer magnitude and breathtaking gall of the deception—its *size*—made it harder to detect. Reporters are often challenged by their editors, grilled on elements of a story or on their construction of some event. And, paradoxically, it is more probable that you will be able to catch and correct less ambitious distortions or errors than the massive falsehood that underlay the "Jimmy" story. For the rock-bottom element of trust and the assumption of good faith that must exist in any professional relationship diminish the chances that you will spot a huge scam right away. You just do not read a many-paged memorandum from an apparently reliable reporter, relating her visit to and prolonged conversation with several people in great detail, and then inquire: "Say, did any of this actually happen?" Like some giant weapons system that can come in under the radar, Janet Cooke's invention eluded detection by the normal protective procedures and techniques that are designed to catch far less spectacular but more commonplace slides and lapses.

In fact, it will be an error and a shame if serious students of the press take the "Jimmy" episode as the model of what's wrong with us or as evidence that stories are largely fabrications. The fact is that the shortcomings we in the business are continually fighting against, the shortcomings that can threaten our prized credibility and that we recognize in all their danger are far more subtle and insidious than some out-and-out made-up story.

It will also be a mistake if the disproof of the fictional "Jimmy" is taken as disproof of the existence of a hard drug problem being spread to and imposed upon very young children. And it will be another if it is used to try to discredit the various First Amendment protections that were activated and called into service when the conflict sharpened between the paper and the authorities on the question of identification of sources and the rest. Those protections and the constitutional values they embody and reflect were abused by Miss Cooke in the reporting and aftermath of her story, but they are no less vital today than they were before for that.

In truth, just as readers may feel maltreated by publication of the "Jimmy" tale and all the subsequent hullabaloo it created, so we at this newspaper feel at once angry, chagrined, misused ourselves, determined to continue the kind of aggressive reporting Miss Cooke's story only purported to be and determined also to maintain and honor the highest standards of straight and fair reporting. We feel, as well, something else: enormous sorrow for the burden this young woman created for herself and deep hope that she will find her way out of trouble.

All this is an analysis, not an excuse. It seems to all of us around this newspaper that warning bells of some kind *should* have sounded, that procedures *should* exist, if they don't now, for smoking out a weird and atypical hoax of this kind. You may be plenty sure that there will be lots of self-examination, that the episode will be written about and explained in this paper and that more of the skepticism and heat that our colleagues traditionally bring to bear on the outside world will now be trained on our own interior workings. One of these episodes is one too many.

ST. LOUIS POST-DISPATCH

St. Louis, Mo., April 17, 1981

The American press, and to a lesser extent, the Pulitzer Prizes have been dealt a cruel blow by the disclosure that the prize this year for feature writing was awarded to an entry that was a fabrication. Understandably, consternation arose in press circles when *the Washington Post* announced that its reporter, Janet Cooke, could not accept the award because her prize-winning story about an 8-year-old heroin addict named Jimmy was "a composite" and that quotes attributed to the child were fabricated. The *Post*, to its credit, apologized to Washington officials and to its readers for the hoax.

In order to make amends, the Pulitzer Prize board promptly withdrew the award. Although the board was also victimized by the hoax, it could hardly be expected to maintain a screening mechanism sufficient to verify the authenticity of all prize submissions. The same thing, however, cannot be said of news organizations, whose mission obligates them to take special pains to ensure the accuracy of their reports. In this case,

Post editors were not alert enough. Even though they did not discover the hoax before the article was printed, should they not have been induced to conduct a thorough internal investigation when the Washington Police Department, after an exhaustive inquiry, reported its conclusion that the child was fictitious?

Unfortunate though it is, this case—said to be the first of its kind in Pulitzer Prize history—should not be seized upon as the basis for a general attack on press credibility and for the forced disclosure of confidential press sources, such as were reputedly used by Ms. Cooke. Still, the press cannot afford to be self-righteous about the episode. It teaches the lessons that editors must redouble their efforts to be certain that published articles are genuine and accurate and that they should rely on confidential sources only when they are absolutely necessary to obtain socially useful news reports.

THE INDIANAPOLIS NEWS

Indianapolis, Ind., April 17, 1981

A faked story, an over-ruled panel of judges, an ineffective personnel department—these facts have cast a cloud over what is supposed to be the most prestigious award in journalism—the Pulitzer Prize.

Janet Cooke, a reporter for the *Washington Post*, was awarded the coveted prize for a story about an 8-year-old ghetto child hooked on heroin. Now she says it was a "serious misrepresentation" which she deeply regrets. The *Post* has allowed her to resign—surely a soft sentence for such a professional crime—and has returned the $1,000 award and the plaque.

Two of the Pulitzer jurors, however, have related other irregularities in the judging process. Joel Dreyfuss, executive editor of *Black Enterprise* magazine, says the article in question was entered by the *Post* as a local news story, but that someone transferred it to the feature category when it seemed certain it was not going to be a winner in the news category. "We (the judges) never saw the story," Dreyfuss said.

The Pulitzer judges in the feature category, however, did not choose Miss Cooke's entry a winner, but the Pulitzer board overruled them. Juror Robert Maynard, editor of the *Oakland* (Calif.) *Tribune*, said "certain friends of the *Post*" manipulated the prize.

It is a serious charge remaining to be proven. But the *Post*'s record in the case is clouded in any case.

Janet Cooke misrepresented her experience and education when she was hired by the *Post*. She said she was a Vassar graduate, the holder of a master's degree from the University of Toledo, and a former student at the French university, the Sorbonne. The actual record of her education appears to extend only to one year at Vassar. It seems indeed strange that a modern personnel department could not have ascertained the truth about her records.

Beyond this reprehensible breach of professional ethics, there are unanswered questions about the procedure for choosing Pulitzer winners—and this is not the first time such questions have arisen. We suggest that Pulitzer officials clear the air by doing what all good newspaper people advocate—and most of them practice—full disclosure.

TULSA WORLD

Tulsa, Okla., April 17, 1981

A former *Washington Post* reporter's admission that her Pulitzer Prize winning story was mostly fabrication may go into the history book as U.S. journalism's most embarrassing moment.

The reporter, Janet Cooke, must bear primary responsibilty for her own deception, of course. But the embarrassing thing for the news business in general is that Cooke was allowed to use the 1st Amendment as a cover for her ruse. She used it in a way that should have sounded alarm bells and raised all sorts of questions about the story. Yet neither the *Post's* editors nor members of the Pulitzer board were bothered by the obviously suspicious use of the 1st Amendment.

In her contrived story about an 8-year-old heroin addict, Cooke claimed to have seen the boyfriend of the child's mother inject the child with heroin.

When District of Columbia authorities sought the name of the victim, Cooke refused to cooperate, claiming a 1st Amendment right not to reveal the names of news sources.

Thus, if the story had been true, Cooke would have been a party to a serious crime—perhaps even homicide if the child had subsequently died of heroin usage. Incredibly, the *Washington Post* went along with the secrecy and saw nothing questionable about the reporter's willingness to leave a child in danger in the name of the 1st Amendment.

The idea that a journalist has special privileges and exemptions not available to other citizens under the 1st Amendment is at best debatable. Many Judges and lawyers hold that a journalist has the same rights and the same responsibilities under the Constitution as any other person—no more, no less. But suppose for argument that reporters are Constitutionally permitted to "protect news sources" by refusing to cooperate with law enforcement officials. It is still hard to believe that the privilege could be sensibly invoked in this case.

When the reporter insisted on trading the safety of an eight-year-old for her own right to protect her news sources, both the *Post* editors and the Pulitzer board should have smelled something very fishy.

This is the sort of thing that gives not only journalism, but the 1st Amendment itself, a bad name.

THE MILWAUKEE JOURNAL

Milwaukee, Wisc., April 17, 1981

Janet Cooke, the *Washington Post* reporter whose prizewinning news story turned out to be a fabrication, has damaged much more than her own reputation.

By giving her readers fiction in the guise of fact, she has harmed the credibility of the *Post*. And we fear that she has made it harder for the news media in general to retain the public confidence essential for a free, vigorous press.

Appropriately, Cooke has been forced to return the Pulitzer Prize and to resign from her job. No less could have been asked; she had grossly misrepresented facts not just in the news columns but in her job application as well.

Many will wonder if the competititve nature of journalism, particularly on such aggressive newspapers as the *Post*, may tempt certain reporters to stretch their stories or cause certain editors to be less persistent than they should be in demanding verification of facts. The pitfall should be acknowledged. However, competition also fosters genuine excellence.

Moreover, we believe that the public would be favorably impressed if it could know what pains are taken by most newspapers, the *Washington Post* included, to assure accurate and faithful reporting. While the press has shortcomings, they are not nearly as serious or widespread as much of the public assumes.

As for the performance of *Post* editors in the Cooke affair, they seem mainly guilty of misplaced trust. The trouble would have been averted if the *Post* had followed its standard procedure, under which information is not used when a reporter refuses to tell editors its source. (That also is the practice of the *Milwaukee Journal* and many other papers.) An exception was made for Cooke because she claimed she would be killed if she told anyone, even her editors, the names of the purported sources.

A particularly unfortunate aspect of the case was the *Post's* original assertion of First Amendment immunity to keep authorities from questioning Cooke about criminal activities depicted in her story. Some critics undoubtedly will seize on the incident to argue (unfairly, so far as most journalists are concerned) that the press uses the First Amendment as a shield for irresponsible reporting.

All in all, the Cooke episode is deeply distressing. Its only potential bright spot is the probability that the *Post's* embarrassment will cause journalists across the country to put an extra measure of caution, precision and thoroughness into their work.

Some news is good news

It's a wonder sometimes that Americans ever venture out of their homes. If they don't fall victim to violent crime, they're sure to be caught up in the maelstrom of a mass demonstration. If they survive that, they still have to live through the daily neighborhood explosion on their way to catch a bus which is certain to careen over an embankment. Such, after all, is life as portrayed by the news media.

Since the President is, by tradition, the nation's first citizen, he speaks for all of us when he says that he's sick and tired of nothing but bad news. When President Reagan recently called upon the media to observe "National Volunteer Week" by concentrating on the brighter side of life in these United States, he had not only catastrophes in mind. He also addressed himself to the relentlessly pessimistic assessments of just about everything that happens on the international and domestic scene: Isn't there anything redeeming to be said about world events?

Like the President, we think there is—although you'd never know it from the media.

During one recent week, three New York TV channels devoted one-quarter to one-half of their newscasts to crime stories. An earlier, more formal study in *Public Opinion Quarterly* compared CBS news coverage with that of the Canadian Broadcasting Company. It found that "aggressive news"—violence and protest—accounted for 36.5 percent of the U.S. network's broadcasts over a three-week period compared with only 17.8 percent on the Canadian broadcasts, even though both had access to the same pool of reportage and film clips.

We recognize that more TV viewers may stare at scenes of a body being dragged from a bloodstained sidewalk than at pictures of children dancing around a maypole. And it's common wisdom that headlines about violence, corruption, and bedroom proclivities may sell more newspapers than accounts of garden club meetings. But what about media responsibility?

Skewed news selection distorts the perceived temper of this country. It cheapens human values to the danger point—people may more readily resort to violence since "everybody's doing it." Finally, it erodes the trust the public has in established journalism because most people are loath to accept such a high degree of aggressiveness.

The constant diet of bad news is already beginning to backfire on the media. A *Harris Survey*, comparing attitude changes, showed that TV audiences trusted television news reporting less in 1981 than they did in 1969. A similar pattern emerged for faith in the veracity of newspaper reporting.

We doubt that these surveys are an indictment of reporting as such. But they do put into question the judgment of those who determine the emphasis to be given different types of news events.

Most Americans, we're convinced, believe that, with all our problems, America remains a far better place than the media would have us think. It follows that—without censorship and without slanting the news—it should be possible for the media to keep the big picture in better focus.

After all, some news is good news.

Mobil®

SUGGESTIONS FOR FURTHER READING

The following articles should interest those pursuing the issue of journalism and truth:

David L. Eason, "Telling Stories and Making Sense." *Journal of Popular Culture* 15, no. 2 (Fall 1981): 125–29. Eason feels that the best "new journalists" reconstruct reality for their audience in such a way that they recognize the separate realities of any story.

N.E. Isaacs, "America's Growing Dissatisfaction." *USA Today*, October 1982, pp. 3–4. The chairman of the National News Council gives his views on the reasons for the decline in media credibility.

William Greider, "Reporters and Their Sources." *Washington Monthly*, October 1982, p. 10. Asserts that the relationship between reporters and their sources assures "mutual seduction."

Also of interest:

Edward Jay Epstein, *Between Fact and Fiction: The Problem of Journalism*. New York: Random House, 1975. One chapter of this book, "Journalism and Truth," was reprinted in the first edition of *Mass Media Issues*.

CHAPTER 11

TV News

Although newspapers have received their share of criticism for distortion, far more such criticism has been directed toward television news programs. TV news is criticized mostly because of distortion caused by superficiality, and the print media have been the loudest critics.

In this chapter's first reading, David Brinkley argues that TV news, unlike newspapers, ought to present only news that is interesting to its audience. In the second reading, J. M. Sullivan, a teacher, editor, and free-lance writer, responds directly to Brinkley's ideas.

In the final reading, Carey Goldberg, a free-lance writer, analyzes the effects of TV medical news coverage.

A QUESTION FOR TELEVISION NEWSMEN: DOES ANYONE CARE?

David Brinkley

Television is a mature and serious news medium, and it is time we who work in it had our own standards of news judgment, instead of those handed down to us from the newspapers.

It is time to do things our own way, to meet the needs of our audiences and the strengths and the weaknesses of the medium we work in.

Why should we develop our own standards? Those we inherited are pretty good. They've served the newspapers well for a long time, and the public is used to them.

And, if it is news in a newspaper, is it not also news on radio and television? No.

No, it is not, and for a basic reason we all know but tend to forget. The basic reason we are different is that in a newspaper you can skip around, read what is interesting to you, and ignore the rest. While on a news broadcast you have to take it as it comes, in order.

A newspaper can print items most of its readers don't care about, because those who don't care about them can skip them, and go on to something else. We can't.

So, what does that mean? In my opinion, it means we should not put a story on the air unless we believe it is interesting to at least 10 percent of the audience. Preferably more. But at least 10 percent.

For example, one night last summer we put on the *NBC Nightly News* a two-minute story about the Lebanese civil war. There was a little military skirmish on the front line, and we ran two minutes on it with great confidence and assurance that this was important news.

But was it? That night I spent a little time thinking about it. Why did we put that on the air? Who, in this country, really cared about it?

Who really cared about it? Lebanese living in the United States? Even if they do, they're a tiny fraction of 1 percent of our population. Americans who have business or other interests in Lebanon? How many can that be? A fraction of 1 percent? Foreign-policy specialists, government and private? How many can that be? A fraction of 1 percent?

Ordinary working Americans like the rest of us? A fraction of 1 percent? That is not enough.

The Middle East is of great interest to Americans, but Lebanon is peripheral to the area we're concerned about. It has very little effect on the lives, hopes, problems, needs, fear, or future security of Americans sitting at home looking at television. In my judgment, 99.9 percent of them did not give a damn.

What I concluded in thinking about it that night was that practically nobody was interested in our story from Lebanon and that the two minutes we devoted to it were an utter waste of effort, money, and air time.

So why did we put it on? Because nobody stopped to ask all these questions. Because the decision was made by habit, by rote, unthinkingly. Wars are always news, aren't they?

Well, no, they aren't. It depends on who's fighting whom and what they're fighting about and what the consequences are likely to be.

We couldn't even use the excuse that the story

was easy to get. It wasn't. It was hard, dangerous work for a correspondent and a camera crew and it was sent to the United States by satellite, which is expensive.

And in the end, after all the work, danger, time, and money, who really wanted to see it? In my opinion, almost nobody.

But even so, we do that kind of thing frequently, if not every day.

Because we continue—in radio and television—making news judgments by habit, by rote and formula developed over the years by the newspapers and inherited by us.

This is not to be critical of the newspapers. I enjoy reading them, have worked on them, and may sometime do so again. The good ones do their job very well.

We should not put a story on the air unless we believe it is interesting to at least 10 percent of the audience.

But their structure and format are so totally different from ours that very few of their rules and habits are relevant to broadcasting. We follow them, nevertheless. We really ought to stop it.

The Lebanon story is only one example. We could all think of many more.

If news is something worth knowing that we did not know already—as it is—then the appropriate test is: Worth knowing to whom? And to how many? The right question to ask is: Who really cares about this? Does anyone care and should anyone care?

It's a question we often forget to ask ourselves. If we did, and built our programs accordingly, we'd have bigger audiences, better served . . . which is supposed to be our job.

Obviously, applying this little test would not eliminate foreign news and shouldn't. It would not eliminate any particular kind of news. It would not eliminate news our viewers are not informed about but which they would find interesting if we did inform them.

But it would eliminate a lot of stuff, like the Lebanon story, that we put on without really thinking about it because it sort of looks like news, or sounds like it, even though when you get down to it, it is not.

Of course, there are days, as we all know, when material of any kind is scarce, and we have to use what we can get, including some we know is not great, but air time is air time and it has to be filled.

On those days we all just do the best we can.

But on the days when we have a choice, I don't want to see a news program filled with jokes and laughs and light stories about children and cats and dogs and the reporters elbowing each other in the ribs and laughing it up. We have more than enough of that.

I do not suggest more light or frivolous news or more laughs. What I do suggest is that the news judgments the newspapers and wire services have developed over the generations may be fine for them, but not for us. We should stop using their habits and practices and develop our own.

We should not bore the audience any more than necessary.

TV NEWSMEN—STOP CHEATING MY CHILDREN!

James Michael Sullivan

For some time now, David Brinkley, the NBC newsman who spends a half-hour each night in many of our homes, has been writing and lecturing on a particular media issue. It is an issue which demands a strange kind of professionalism from his colleagues. Brinkley is claiming that news stories should not be broadcast which do not "interest" 10 percent of the audience.

Thus does Brinkley plead for the final cop-out of his news industry. We already have the glamorous and golden-tongued, making the TV newscaster the consummate cosmetic image. Now, we are to reach even greater professional depths and present only that news which lends itself to the same cosmetic appeal. Let us not, Brinkley has decided, involve ourselves in that complicated, yet critical, area of values and social judgment. Let us pretend that the only news there is is the news we want—a clear value judgment to be sure.

Brinkley's notion will probably receive wide support, however. It fits hand in glove with the contemporary American social philosophy—whatever turns you on is good and deserves to be propagandized; whatever does not make you thrill should be ignored as if it did not exist.

As Brinkley has mentioned, and quite correctly, a civil war in Lebanon is probably of interest to only a fraction of 1 percent of the population. He goes on to draw the logical, if simplistic, conclusion given our social norms today—forget it. It does not interest people, therefore it is not worth reporting. Let the newspapers handle it.

A quarter-century ago, that argument, given the competition between the media for their shares of the American audience, was defensible. Profit, after all, is still the name of the game when you are running a business.

> Television is not simply a business anymore. It is a powerful social force which has yet to define limits for itself.

Two important factors have come into play in recent years, however, which poke a few holes in this argument. First, television is not simply a business anymore. It is a powerful social force which has yet to define or have defined limits for itself. Second, if people did, indeed, supplement their news intake from other media, TV could surely make some case for determining what, for it, is newsworthy. Yet, polls consistently show that the great majority of people, if they do take in news at all, take it in from TV and not from newspapers, magazines, or the radio, as they did in yesteryear.

Brinkley may look at this as a chance to narrow his sights and his responsibilities. It may, on the other hand, be regarded as fantastic opportunity and challenge.

Television is in the values business, like it or not. Network presidents may not intend it to be so, and their networks are run as if it were not so, but the evidence is too overwhelming to deny that, regardless of intent or actual management, the effects of television on an individual and on a society must be considered in full and frightening range.

I want my children to have, as part of their TV diet, as many issues and opinions as can possibly be presented to them. Children believe that little machine far more than they should. However, as long as it is there and unavoidable in its social scope, I want television to do a job parallel to its influence. Yes, I want them to know of a tiny, forgotten civil war in a tiny, forgotten country—so that they'll turn and ask me what it is all about and so that their father, in turn, will feel put upon enough to try and find out the answer.

The TV newsman represents a business and a tradition greater than television. I don't care what *medium* Joseph Pulitzer or Walter Lippmann or Edward R. Murrow worked in. Theirs was not a tradition of radio or TV or magazine or paper—it is a tradition of *news reporting* and it is a tradition that has a right and a responsibility to endure.

SUPERFICIALITY

Television news today suffers from much more than a "tell them what they want to hear" syndrome, however. The narrowing scope of news coverage has been quickly followed by an easy superficiality. Network bosses argue that, in the average 22 minutes per broadcast in which they have to deliver the news, full justice cannot possibly be done to each story, feature, or issue. Expand the broadcast? The idea has been toyed with, yet the conclusion is always the same—the *people* won't stand for it. They want their news fast and simple. Thus, in yet another way, do network "leaders" jettison their responsibility to that cornerstone of audiovisual communication—creativity. Where is the experimentation, the studies, the pilot projects, the trial and error incorporating all different possibilities which might offer some proof that more than 22 minutes of an evening news show is completely unworkable? It is such failure of creativity in areas where it counts the most that poses a serious threat to our children's understanding of their world and contributes to our own superficialty as a people.

Polls consistently show that the great majority of people, if they do take in news at all, take it in from TV.

There isn't enough time in a few minutes of nightly news to address the causes of specific issues. The complex fabric of social, political, and economic factors which create a race riot or a religious war or a Third World revolutionary movement is not explored—not because it is impossible, but because it is not expedient for network management. It is this continual insistence on controlling and manipulating the news so that it might be neatly packaged into two-minute presentations that is so dangerous. Content with the illusion of control such news packaging gives us, we are unchallenged to probe deeper into the problems of our day, searching meaningfully for a solution or at least some grounds for hope. Our politicians, moreover, have sensed our contentment with the superficial and have responded to it in kind.

The news broadcaster's lack of sensitivity to root causes, then, has implications which echo through our social and political system. When no parallels are drawn, when no context is established, we may as well be watching *I Love Lucy* reruns, for, although information is imparted, it does not challenge us with the consequences of the history we are a part of. We are not learning or growing or understanding. Even that video violence of the century, the Vietnam War, seems to have taught us little about war or history or ourselves. What TV news coverage of that war did do was confirm that even violence at its most hideous could lull us into apathy.

At its most simplistic, television consecrates competition of opposites—success or failure, Democrat or Republican, win or lose, guilty or innocent, yes or no. As Harris has noted, "A conflict must always be established, a race, a contest; and, whenever possible, someone must be drawn into the trap saying something provocative about someone else. Addicts of the media become confined to limited alternatives. No third, no fourth, no limitless possibilities exist, or even shades of those we have. There isn't time."[1]

Thus does television news remain part of our contemporary problems, rather than part of our solutions. In its refusal to challenge and upset, it feeds existing prejudices. The very criteria it uses for judging a story newsworthy necessarily coincide with a predetermined value system and a particular view of economics and social philosophy. Let us not forget that it is network sponsors, with their own particular value systems and world views, who pay the bills.

We must never overlook the fact that television news considers itself bound to values only of its own choosing. Of course, the values of honesty, fair play, etc. are first in line and taken for granted—television fortunately inherited what consumers had traditionally demanded of other media—but sponsors measure a program's "effectivenes" in dollars and cents, and it is the overriding value of profit which can cause great harm to any so-called "unbiased" and "impartial" reporting. As Harris notes: "During the months of Watergate, thousands of people suffered starvation; the world was progressively endangered by military expansion and ecological neglect. By what corruption of values were the crises of Richard Nixon a million times as newsworthy as the facts of human starvation? . . . Starving people are bad box office."[2]

We have demanded little of television or its newscasting in the nearly three decades of its history. It has, in turn, demanded little of us. Too often, it assures for us only a measuring up to our least common social denominators, hindering our maturity as individuals and as a society. It cannot be denied, that some attempt to raise reporting standards and coverage has been in evidence (documentaries and specials on the oil industry, energy crisis, forced busing, etc.). These deserve praise as far as they go—which, unfortunately, is not far enough. Included in this number is *not* the pseudo-documentaries on pornography and violence—sensationalism masquerading as journalism. Nor is intensive television coverage to be confused with the reporter who crassly jams a microphone into the face of a grieving widow or a terminally ill cancer patient. This too appeals to the more base dimensions of our psyches, distracting us from the more vital issues of our day.

We have not, in this brief article, touched on all the dangers and disappointments of television journalism. Hopefully, we have focused on a few core issues that point out what is keeping TV news from becoming the positive social force that it has the potential to become. We could write whole other articles on the news reporting of other media which have long neglected their commitment to the public. Yet, until a more powerful medium comes along, this is the day of television. It is an extremely difficult and demanding enterprise. What we ask of the Brinkleys and the Cronkites, the Chancellors and the Walters, and the host of "news consultants" who so critically influence the industry is a sense of responsibility. On behalf of our children and their

1. Mark Harris, "The Last Article," *New York Times Magazine* (October 6, 1974).

2. *Ibid.*

futures, we seek from these people an accountability proportionate to television's all-pervasive influence.

WHO KNOWS BEST—THE DOCTOR OR THE REPORTER?

Carey Goldberg

Last spring, ABC News made mention of a new antiarthritic drug called Oraflex. The report suggested that Oraflex not only might relieve arthritic pain but also might stop the crippling process. Following the Oraflex piece, many patients urged their doctors to prescribe the new drug—and many cautious doctors, leery of the side effects they'd read about in medical journals, resisted.

Recently, Oraflex was taken off the market after being linked with deaths from liver and kidney failure in England. Was ABC at fault for repeating controversial claims based on inconclusive evidence? Or were the viewers who demanded the new drug and subsequently suffered side effects to blame for second-guessing their physicians?

The Oraflex dilemma was followed this fall by the tragic Tylenol mystery, in which bottles of the painkiller were found to contain cyanide-laced capsules that killed several unsuspecting people. The Tylenol case, of course, was clear-

From *TV Guide* (November 22, 1982). Reprinted by permission.

cut medically. But it served to underscore that, like medicine itself, medical news can be a life-or-death business. And as TV's medical coverage expands, it raises many unique questions for doctors, journalists and television viewers alike.

In the past, a doctor could expect to be his patient's sole source of medical information except, perhaps, for a few mass-circulation magazines. Now, in the face of more national medical news and an entire cable network (the Health Channel, founded by Dr. Art Ulene of *Today* show fame) devoted to health and science programming, doctors have become only one of many sources, and not always the most current. When it was discovered that toxic-shock syndrome was linked to tampon use, for example, TV blitzed the public with warnings long before most medical journals could go to press with detailed case reports. In this instance, doctors, too, were initially alerted to the new developments by the media. These television-induced pressures are forcing physicians to ask: "How can I interpret media medical reports, admit to controversy and still retain my authority as the final judge of what's best for my patient?"

As coverage of controversial medical issues increases, so do the questions about what is safe . . . and what isn't.

One answer is to modify the doctor-patient relationship, suggests Dr. Malcolm Rourk. In a recent article, Dr. Rourk, clinical director of the Cystic Fibrosis Center at Duke University, told a classic tale of TV's effects on medicine: last year, *20/20* aired a segment entitled "New Hope or False Hope?" that focused on a scientist's theory that cystic fibrosis, a fatal childhood disease, might be caused by selenium deficiency instead of bad genes. Selenium is toxic if taken in large doses. In the weeks following the show, dozens of patients complained that Rourk's staff never told them about selenium, and some decided to take the drug despite their doctors' doubts. Because the *20/20* segment was "balanced," allowing room for the possibility that the selenium theory was right, it not only raised false hopes but reduced some patients' trust in their doctors. The theory was eventually disproved.

The moral of the story, says Dr. Rourk, is that physicians must assume the responsibility for delivering fast, accurate critiques of the media's medical coverage. Even more important, they must adopt a less authoritarian role and be willing to discuss controversy more openly, offering informed, not infallible, opinions. "Of course, that assumes a doctor is *willing* to be informed," he adds. "You can't just present the decision between laetrile and chemotherapy, for example, as a coin flip."

That's asking a lot of doctors, Rourk admits. The amount of medical information has been snowballing for years, and with it the amount of controversy. Nowadays, even such accepted treatments as coronary-bypass surgery and aspirin for children's ailments are being challenged on TV, and debates continue to rage over herpes and the causes of cancer. In response to the strain, some doctors just sigh and quote Thomas Jefferson: "It is better to know nothing than to know what is wrong."

If medical news burdens doctors, it's even more of a burden on journalists who have to keep up with it, understand it and—hardest of all—present it correctly. Invariably, their reports are carefully worded: "Researchers *believe* alcohol causes birth defects"; "Aspirin *might* prevent strokes"; "Interferon *promises* a cure for cancer." But such qualifiers slide by easily, and many viewers hear what they want to hear.

"We are very protective because we're dealing with vast populations of people who are desperate, and desperate people grasp at straws," says George Strait, an ABC News medical correspondent. And the dangers of self-prescribing are compounded by the common attitude that "If some is good, more is better." After the selenium segment, for instance, pediatricians feared that some of their cystic fibrosis patients might be poisoned by the potent substance.

Alleged medical advances that reach the screen prematurely foster false hopes and fears.

The visuals that accompany most TV reports also add to viewer misinterpretation. Charles Crawford, Strait's counterpart at CBS, notes: "At the height of the laetrile controversy, the cameras tended to run after the couple who took their 3-year-old son with leukemia to a Mexican clinic. Even though the copy put it in perspective, to *see* a little boy dying adds too much emphasis to one part of the story. As soon as you *see* something, it has more impact."

The fact that so many alleged medical advances reach the screen prematurely also fosters false hopes and fears. Normally, a researcher reports his findings in a professional journal following peer review, even though his conclusions may well be tentative. The networks all subscribe to the major medical journals. They regularly pick up the lead stories, squeeze a half-dozen pages of text into a minute and a half, add a dramatic gloss and air them—at the rate of about three stories per network news show per week. But because they prefer to report "news," TV journalists sometimes select items too new or speculative to be interpreted, even by experts: the latest research on cancer-causing genes, for example.

In the opinion of Dr. Timothy Johnson, *Good Morning America's* resident physician, covering medical news calls for a special kind of reporter—one who has some working knowledge of the principles of epidemiology and biostatistical analysis. Aware of the need for such experts, the major networks and stations in the top 10 markets have begun hiring more specialty reporters like Crawford and Strait specifically to cover science news and signing on more doctor-consultants like Johnson. Art Ulene's Cable Health Network, programming 24 hours a day and shown on about 450 systems, is attempting a mix of science and health news combined with advice and self-help shows like *Keeping Fit; Nutrition, Diet and Eating Well*; and *Healthy Relationships*. One doctor who has seen the Cable Health Network gives it reasonably high marks. Dr. Allen Douma, a New York-based health consultant, says the service's reports are "valid and credible" and adds, "They're a good compromise between giving details the audience will sit still and listen to, and giving a full exposition of the subject."

The medical profession is responding to the communications challenge, too: hundreds of doctors are involving themselves in radio and TV. Sarasota, Fla., cardiologist Dr. Robert Windom may be a typical example of the real TV doctor. Every week (well, every Saturday morning at 6:30—it *is* public-service time) he is host of *Medical Viewpoint*, a half-hour local talk show covering everything from sunburn to CAT scanners. Once largely the domain of pop psychologists and diet doctors, TV news and talk shows are providing more and more physicians the opportunity to express their more accurate, less self-serving views.

But as doctors and journalists are finding common ground, the hardest questions are still left for the viewers. Whom can I believe? Whose word can I trust more—a national network correspondent's or a local doctor's? Does my doctor *always* know best? In the end, most sensible people play the short odds; although no doctor knows everything, and precious little absolutely, he or she remains the best bet for reliable personal advice. Most doctors agree that a patient can legitimately ask for an appointment merely to solicit information on a new drug or treatment. But he should be prepared to pay the customary fee, since all that doctors really have to sell is their time and knowledge.

Meanwhile, between appointments, the best prescription for medical-news watchers is: one large grain of salt, to be taken every evening at 6 and 11.

That is, unless you have high blood pressure, of course. Then again, you may be one of the 50 percent of hypertensives who don't react to dietary salt, and may suffer from a calcium deficiency. Or . . . (stay tuned).

SUGGESTIONS FOR FURTHER READING

Those who are interested in the criticism of TV news documentaries may want to read Michael J. Arlen's "The Prosecutor," from *The Camera Age: Essays on Television*, New York: Farrar, Straus, & Giroux, 1981, pp. 158–79.

Other recent works of criticism on TV news include:

David L. Altheide, *Creating Reality: How TV News Distorts Events*. Beverly Hills, Calif.: Sage, 1976.

Herbert J. Gans, *Deciding What's News: A Study of CBS Evening News, NBC Nightly News,* Newsweek and Time. New York: Random House, 1980.

Julius Hunter and Lynne S. Gross, *Broadcast News: The Inside Out*. St. Louis, Mo.: Mosby, 1980.

Stephen Lesher, *Media Unbound: The Impact of Television Journalism on the Public*. Boston: Houghton Mifflin, 1982.

Mark Crispin Miller, "How TV Covers War." *New Republic*, November 29, 1982, pp. 26–33. Crispin asserts that TV "muffles and muddles" the facts of war.

Av Westin, "Inside the Evening News." *New York*, October 18, 1982, pp. 48–56. "A candid, anecdotal look at broadcast journalism and its limitations, as well as the things it does the best." This article is an excerpt from Westin's book by the same title.

CHAPTER 12

TV Entertainment

It seems that every person who has learned to write has written at least one essay deploring the sorry state of television entertainment and the way it is warping us as individuals. The readings that follow are a small but representative sample of this body of literature.

The first reading, by English author Anthony Burgess, presents a fairly strong indictment of television drama. In the second reading, philosophy professor Paul Kurtz of The State University of New York at Buffalo discusses possible implications of the distortions caused by television's docudramas. In the third reading, Richard Hawley, a high school dean, takes a look at how television influences his students' norms of behavior and taste. The final reading, by Benjamin Stein, author of *The View from Sunset Boulevard*, gives some reasons why television tends to distort everyday life.

TV IS DEBASING YOUR LIVES

Anthony Burgess

Vigdis Finnbogadottir, the charming President of the Republic of Iceland, recently said: "I look at the *Dallas* TV program and I feel deep pity. They never seem to read a book and they have such problems." In a country where even a volume of poems sells 10,000 copies (and consider how small the population is), such an observation was to be expected. But those who live in less literate European countries have noticed the same thing about the television series America feeds us: nobody reads, nobody thinks, nobody generates an idea other than a money-making or murderous one. In fact, we are very rarely presented with a whole human being. A good deal of the cerebral cortex of the average TV character seems to have been cauterized; the emotions are primitive; the motives of action are oversimple.

I once worked at Warner Bros. on the script of a film (never made) based on the life of William Shakespeare. Now, presumably Shakespeare had one of the most complex personalities of all

From *TV Guide* (September 18, 1982). Reprinted by permission.

time, but the head of the script department was insistent that he be simplified in the interests of popularization. This meant that we should see plenty of jealousy, greed, lust and power hunger, but very little of the self-contradictory mental mixture that could produce a play like *Hamlet*. When, in my script, I made Shakespeare do something or go somewhere, I was always asked to stress the motivation and make it simple. *Motivation* was the big word, but it had more to do with the winding up of a mechanical toy than the huge jungle of the unconscious mind, of which the conscious mind is merely a sunlit clearing.

The "cardboard characters" on U.S. shows may be dangerous to our way of life.

It is true that the vast majority of watchers of American TV series want their stories to be daubs of poster paint rather than delicate pieces of impressionism. In Shakespeare's own time, playgoers wanted mostly revenge, revenge, revenge: *The Spanish Tragedy*, a garish play about a vendetta, was far more popular than *Hamlet*. Yet what makes *Hamlet* fascinating is the perpetual putting off of revenge. The prince can't act, and he doesn't know why. In other words, he is a complex human being. He is much more like ourselves than the characters of *Dallas*.

Among the most popular American TV exports to Europe is *Columbo*. I watch it in French every Saturday and in Italian every Sunday. Now, the appeal of Lieutenant Columbo is not quite a Hamlet appeal, but he is a good deal more complex than the suave murderers he brings to book. His complexity starts off with a contradiction between appearance and reality: the sharp deductive mind contrasts with an amiable, scruffy eccentricity. There are mysteries in him. How, for instance, with his stoop and his shuffle, did he get into the Los Angeles police force in the first place? God knows, these mysteries are not much, but they serve to make Columbo human. They also serve to make *Columbo* popular.

Columbo is not, however, typical TV fodder. Much more typical are those attempts to reduce, or exalt, human beings into bionic machines. It is far easier for scriptwriters, or their masters, to deal with characters compounded of sexuality and power. If you want artistic and psychological complexity, you can always watch British series on the public channel.

Perhaps it is unfair to ask of a popular entertainment medium the seriousness and complexity we associate with high art. But television has become, for most Americans (and Europeans, too), their sole purveyor of drama. Unless we do something about educating the great American viewing public into taking a more civilized view of dramatic art, there is a grave danger that the quality of American life will be debased.

A good deal of the cerebral cortex of the average TV character seems to have been cauterized; the emotions are primitive; the motives of action are oversimple.

This sounds melodramatic, but few will deny that television forms part of the educative process that makes adults out of children, and that they are induced to impose television values on their lives. We are all made of what we read, hear and see; and what we read, hear and see had better be good, else we are in trouble. We may conceivably put to rule over us a President whose image we first encountered in a B film (not a production of *Hamlet*) and whose simplistic characterizations we identify with reality. Reality is not *Dallas*, but we are in danger of wanting reality to be *Dallas* because of our hankering after simplicity. Life, of course, is far from simple.

Talk about suppressing certain television representations of life as mere money and violence and sex is, of course, stupid. We should not suppress; we should merely seek to change. The current philosophy of television entertainment is highly colored, easily segmented for commercial breaks with contrived cliffhangers, mere simplistic pabulum. And yet this great medium of television is wasted if its highest achievement is *Dallas* or *The Bionic Woman*. To regard intellectual excitement or human complexity as dangerous is in order for the Soviet Union, but hardly for the greatest democracy the world has ever seen.

"SOME PEOPLE BELIEVE ANYTHING THEY SEE" ON TV

Interview With Professor Paul Kurtz of the State University of New York

Q: Professor Kurtz, is the American public increasingly mixing fact with fiction as a result of stories on TV and in films?

A: Yes, regretfully. I say "regretfully" because we are the most advanced scientific and technological society in the world and we face very complex problems that require the use of critical intelligence. Yet a whole new generation of people are being confused and overwhelmed by the electronic media and are finding it increasingly difficult to distinguish fiction from reality.

Q: Can you give some examples of what you're talking about?

A: A number of scientists I've been associated with in the last few years are especially concerned about the growth of belief in the paranormal and the occult.

One example is the *Bermuda Triangle*, which has been packaged and sold on TV and in books and magazines as true. There are millions of people who believe that there's something mysterious south of Bermuda—that more ships and planes go under or disappear there than anywhere else. But that's not true. If you do a careful scientific analysis, you find that it's largely science fiction at work. No greater number of ships and planes go down, proportionately, south of Bermuda than any other area of heavy traffic, and all that have can be given natural explanations.

The revival of the belief in exorcism, demonic possession, and reincarnation also is incredible. I've taught in universities for 30 years, and until five years ago almost no student would have expressed a belief in reincarnation or devil possession. But now I find that as many as 30 percent of the students, as I lecture around, claim that they believe in this.

When you ask them what their source of information is, they often cite TV shows called "docu-dramas" that mix fact with fiction—sometimes very, very loosely, but so cleverly that it is hard for the layman raised in the television age to sort things out. He thinks it's all true.

> A whole new generation of people are being confused and overwhelmed by the electronic media and are finding it increasingly difficult to distinguish fiction from reality.

Q: Do drama and comedy alter a viewer's ideas of reality?

A: Definitely. Many scriptwriters warp reality by portraying the world from their own personal points of view. The abuses of scientific technology are exaggerated, but its bountiful contributions to modern life are rarely extolled. The bad guy is often the big businessman and never the poor kid from the slums. In real life, of course, there are some good businessmen and some bad guys from the slums, but you'd hardly know it if you only watched movies and television.

These shows don't indicate that writers are committed to any particular political ideology. It's more that their stories reflect the thinking of a primitive social romanticism. They have helped to create in the media a general atmosphere of antitechnology and antiscience and a lack of appreciation for traditions such as the free-enterprise system.

Q: Which shows, specifically, have contributed to this?

A: People have been so inundated by movies such as *The Exorcist* or *Audrey Rose* that they tend to believe in prior lives or the operation of mysterious and demonic forces in the universe.

Q: Might this reflect a deep need to believe in something that these people don't find elsewhere?

A: Perhaps to some degree, although it may be nothing more than a fad. What really happens is that fashions and moods develop, and these are furthered by the skillful use of propaganda—conscious or unconscious. These beliefs are something like the ideological religions that were popular in the '20s, '30s, and '40s in many parts of the world. We're witnessing a growth of occultism, and this is being sold to the gullible public. People are fascinated by it. It strikes their imagination and fancy.

It may very well be that the breakdown of certain aspects of traditional religion is more than some people can bear, and so they slide to this new belief in the paranormal.

Q: What sort of belief?

A: There was the case of a rumor that an unidentified flying object had landed and that its occupants were ravaging the countryside. The "proof" offered was that cattle were being mutilated by these creatures—that they were removing the eyes from the cattle and leaving them dead. The truth was that cattle die of diseases in the open fields, and their carcasses are eaten by predators such as rodents. It's a very natural process, but nobody could dissuade the believers in UFOs, fed by the movies and TV.

Cases like that show that some people who need meaning and purpose in this rapidly changing technological world are getting their answers in the wrong places. For millions of Americans, the electronic media have replaced the university as a revered institution for learning. Now the media are also replacing the church. The media have become sacred because they deal with the realm of imagination.

Q: How dangerous would you say this trend is?

A: Very dangerous. When people watch TV for entertainment, that's fine. But it's more than that now; it's the main source of information and education for the American people. The average child spends approximately 50 to 60 hours a week before the tube, and the adult isn't far behind. This is the only kind of knowledge that they get: imagery in color, with sound, shock, horror. If it's not situation comedies and violence on the one hand, it's the paranormal and science fiction on the other.

That's all right if it's labeled and people can make distinctions. What bothers me is that critical judgment is being perverted and polluted. Watching the tube is replacing analysis. Imagery is replacing language and symbols. That is dangerous to a society because it means people can't tell what the truth is. That can be carried over to religion and politics.

Q: What do you mean?

A: The danger is that some people will believe anything they see and that they will buy political or ideological positions the same way. I am afraid of what may happen if there is a further decline in objective or critical thinking—if people are not willing to be skeptical about what they hear or read.

A notable example is the tragic case of the Rev. Jim Jones and his followers in Guyana. He claimed to be a faith healer, and he used paranormal tricks. He performed psychic surgery—supposedly performing an operation without cutting. What he actually did on the stage before his gawking onlookers was to put his fingers in somebody's throat and pull out chicken gizzards dipped in Mercurochrome—which he had palmed—and then say, "Look, I've cured him of cancer!"

Look at all the gullible people who fell for him. What would happen if a new Reverend Jones comes along on a white horse and assumes political power? That is a possibility that we should not discount, especially since the media are changing our perceptions of the truth.

Q: Why do you think these problems are more serious on TV and in the movies than in books, newspapers, and magazines?

A: Today, books and magazines are aping television. Unfortunately, television is leading the way. The electronic media are far more powerful in intensity; they can really seize a person and capture him. Reading skills are declining. We know how poorly students are doing in the schools and the colleges. People read less and watch more, and it's undermining their ability to judge ideas.

It doesn't have to be this way. Television could be used for constructive means, and the electronic media have the potential for this. It's the abuses that cause so much concern.

Here is an example: I lecture in various universities throughout the country, and many students tell me that they go to fortunetellers or that they believe in psychic detection. About 80 percent of the students I have met believe in extrasensory perception—receiving information outside the ordinary senses. Something like 56 percent believe that unidentified flying objects come from outside the earth. And most of these students base their beliefs on what they have seen on TV and in the movies.

For millions of Americans, the electronic media have replaced the university as a revered institution for learning. Now the media are also replacing the church. The media have become sacred because they deal with the realm of imagination.

Q: How should we combat media-induced misconceptions?

A: The only solution, I think, is to encourage more diversity, to have more give-and-take of ideas, especially on TV and radio. Now we don't have sufficient debate. The electronic media, for example, do not present sufficient conservative or radical opinion; most of what is presented is lukewarm liberalism. We really don't have—as we should have—a wide range of ideas. We need more dialogue, more debate, more criticism. The segment of the public that is still sophisticated and educated is surely entitled to it. Television is talking down; it should be talking up to the people.

The great difficulty here is that it's almost impossible to deal with this concentration of power in the electronic media. I'm afraid that the fairness doctrine—which is supposed to guarantee that opposing points of view are presented equally on the air—has failed and is not being applied by the Federal Communications Commission. We're not getting balance in the presentation of controversial ideas. Conservative as well as liberal ideas have to be expressed, and at present they're not very often.

Q: How do you think that should be changed?

A: Cable TV, which will open up thousands of channels nationwide, will help to provide alternative voices. Maybe when cable TV is more widespread, we will get more hard-hitting, in-depth treatments of issues, which will enable people to make rational judgments. We need to encourage people to read more and watch less.

Q: Have you sensed in your visits around the country that any particular area is especially willing to accept fiction as fact?

A: One place stands out above all others: Southern California.

Q: Why?

A: I don't know, except that maybe that's where the people go who most believe in these things. The trend is nationwide now, but there seems to be a greater concentration in California than anywhere else.

I was in San Diego last year, and I was taken to a meeting hall which had been rented to a group of believers. Here were 300 people, many of whom were holders of advanced college degrees, who believed in UFOs and creatures from outer space. A woman walked in who was dressed in a very strange costume and told everybody she was from Venus and that she communicated with our "space brothers" on outer-space ships. This was soon after the films *Close Encounters of the Third Kind* and *Star Wars* had appeared, and belief in spacemen was very current.

I asked some of her disciples: "You don't really believe in this, do you? You know, the temperature is at least 800 degrees on Venus. Don't you think she'd burn?" They said: "No, no, no. You don't understand. She's on an ethereal plane." I was floored!

That's what the electronic media are doing to us—making it possible for anyone to believe anything. Indeed, unfortunately, this is becoming the age of believing the unbelievable.

TELEVISION AND ADOLESCENTS: A TEACHER'S VIEW

Richard A. Hawley

Ever since its novelty wore off in the fifties, we have all known, really, that television in its commercial form wasn't up to much good. This isn't to say that millions of people don't still depend on it, but dependency is hardly a sign of virtue. Except for Marshall McLuhan's grab-bag theoretics, few claims have been advanced for the improving effects of television. In fact, recently there has been a flurry of publishing activity, most notably Marie Winn's *The Plug-in Drug*, about television as a cause of downright mental erosion. But what I think Marie Winn and others need is a concrete, closely observed, and intensely felt illustration of the larger thesis. That's what I offer here.

Television has a way of intruding into our lives, and last year it intruded into my life and into the life of the school where I work in a way that many of us there will never forget. We had all taken our seats for morning assembly. The usual announcements were read, after which the morning's senior speaker was introduced. Like many independent schools, ours requires each senior to address the student body in some manner before he graduates. Since public speaking is not a widely distributed gift these days, the senior speeches are infrequently a source of much interest or intentional amusement.

As the curtains parted, we could see that the speaker had opted for a skit. On the stage were a covered table and a number of cooking implements. Out stepped the speaker wearing an apron and chef's hat, which very quicky established that he was going to satirize one of my colleagues who has a national reputation as a gourmet chef. Since this colleague is also a man who can take a joke, the prospects for the skit seemed bright. But not for long.

At first, I think almost all of us pretended that we didn't hear, that we were making too much of certain, possibly accidental, double entendres. But then came the direct statements and a few blatant physical gestures. Then it was clear! This boy was standing before 500 of us making fun of what he suggested at some length was the deviant sexual nature of one of his teachers. The response to this was at first stupefaction, then some outbursts of laughter (the groaning kind of laughter that says, "I don't believe you said that"), then a quieting, as the speech progressed, to periodic oohs (the kind that say, "You *did* say that, and you're in for it").

When he had finished, there was a nearly nauseating level of tension afloat. As the students filed off to class, I made my way backstage to find the speaker. It had by now dawned on him that he had done something wrong, even seriously wrong. We met in my office.

He expressed remorse at having offended a teacher whom he said he particularly liked. (Before the conference I had checked briefly with the teacher and found him badly flustered and deeply hurt.) The remorse was, I felt, genuine. But something was decidedly missing in the boy's explanation of how he came to think that such a presentation might, under any circum-

From *American Film* (October 1978).

stances, have been appropriate. He hadn't, he admitted, really thought about it, and some of his friends thought the idea was funny, and, well, he didn't know. When it occurred to him that serious school action was in the offing, he protested that in no way had he intended the sexual references to be taken sexually—they were, you know, a joke.

I pointed out to him that the objects of such jokes have no way to respond: To ignore the insinuation might affirm its validity; on the other hand, to object vigorously would draw additional attention to the offense and sustain the embarrassment connected with it. I pointed out further that sometimes innocent parties *never* regain their stature after being offended in this manner, and that the injured party was, at the very least, in for a terrible day of school.

The boy became reflective and said, "Was it *that* bad? You can see worse on *Saturday Night Live.* I told him I doubted this, but if it were true, and were I in a position to judge, I would be in favor of expelling *Saturday Night Live* from the air. He left the office, and subsequently endured the appropriate consequences.

For my part, I resolved to turn on *Saturday Night Live,* and when I did, I realized the student had spoken truly. The show's quick-succession, absurdist comedy spots depended for their appeal on establishing an almost dangerous sense of inappropriateness: exactly that sense created by our senior speaker. To me, for some years a lapsed viewer, it seemed that both the variety and specificity of sexual innuendo had developed considerably since, say, the once daring Smothers Brothers show of the sixties. What struck me more, however, was how many punch lines and visual gags depended on suddenly introducing the idea of injury or violent death.

I happened to tune in the night a funny caption was put over the documentary shot of Middle Eastern political partisans being dragged to death behind an automobile. Was this funny? I asked my students. They said it was "sick" and laughed. Does this kind of fun trivialize crisis? Trivialize cruelty? Inure us to both? Or is it, you know, a joke?

The right things were said, I think, to our students about the boy's speech. But I can't say the situation improved. Not more than a couple of weeks later, a speaker garbed in a woman's tennis dress took the podium and began to talk humorously about the transsexual tennis player Renee Richards. I can't think of a subject harder for an adolescent to discuss before an adolescent audience. Rarely noted for their confidence and breadth of vision in matters of human sexuality, adolescents are unlikely to be objective, sympathetic, or (let me tell you) funny about so disturbing a phenomenon as sex change. This particular boy, whose inflection is very flat and whose normal countenance is especially stony, managed to convey almost a sense of bitterness in making his string of insulting and, in his references to genitals and to menstruation, awfully tasteless cracks.

> I was suddenly struck with the realization that he was using television as an arbiter of taste—that is, as *an arbiter of good taste.*

So there it was again: the inappropriateness, the tension. This time the injured party was remote from our particular world, so the hastily arranged conference with the boy turned on general considerations of taste and judgment. This time, however, the speaker was recalcitrant: We could disapprove of his speech and discipline him if we chose, but we ought to know that we could hear the same thing on television.

At that moment something clicked for me. Not only did my brief exposure to *Saturday Night Live* convince me that, yes, I would hear the same thing on television, but I was suddenly struck with the realization that he was using television as an arbiter of taste—that is, *as an arbiter of good taste.* I began to see in this premise a common ground upon which he and I could at least argue. Both of us were in agreement that what is broadcast over television ought to be acceptable; our point of disagreement was his feeling that broadcasting something over television *made* it acceptable. Alarming as such a feeling is to me, it is not hard to see how it has developed over the past few decades.

Until the middle sixties, with the exception of the very earthiest plays and novels, the values of home and school and the values of the popular culture were fairly continuous; if anything, radio, television, and motion pictures were more staid than real life. Of course, all this would change very quickly—not because change was requested or even consented to, but because it wasn't, perhaps couldn't be, resisted. And suddenly there it all was at once: the most embarrassing expletives as common speech; every imaginable kind of sexual coupling depicted in ever increasing candor; obsessively specific wounds, mutilations.

These formerly unacceptable kinds of stimulation made their way more easily into the relatively insulated world of print and film than they did into the more communal world of the television set. Television is typically viewed in homes, and what is communally seen and heard must be communally integrated, or there will be friction. Since American households—setholds?—share this communal experience for an estimated two to seven hours per day, the potential for friction is considerable. This is why, on grounds of taste, criticism of television programming tends to be more bitter and more relentless than criticism of books and films.

Television foes and partisans alike continue to advise, with some reason, that those who object to certain programs ought not to watch them. But given the impossibility of monitoring the set at all hours, control over the amount and quality of viewing is difficult to maintain even in principled, surveillant households. Too, some viewers will insist on being their brother's keeper. Not everyone who is convinced that what is beaming over the national airwaves is inhumane, unscrupulous, or scurrilous is going to fight to the death for the networks' right to be so.

For many people, television is no longer on the polite side of real life. This is an obvious observation about a novel development, one whose consequences are only just dawning on us. A realist or an existentialist may argue that the unflappably suburban world of "Father Knows Best" revealed none of the complex, ambivalent, and often irrational forces at work in real families: But it is hard to argue that "Father Knows Best" in any way *contributed* to those dark forces. On the contrary, it is possible to argue—although one hesitates to carry it too far—that the theme of Father Knowing Best serves as a psychologically soothing backdrop to the prickly dynamics of real family life. And while today's most highly rated shows suggest that the prevailing seventies' theme is Nobody Knows Anything, there are still apparently enough viewers who like Father Knowing Best to support series like "The Waltons" and "Little House on the Prairie."

Sometimes the theme is compromised in a typical seventies' manner, of which *James at 16* provides a good example: The parents are cast very much in the Robert Young–Jane Wyatt mold, but their son James is, to borrow a phrase, kind of now. By far the most interesting thing he did was to lose his virginity on prime time. The 15-going-on-16-year-old boys I work with, many of them at least as sophisticated as James, typically hold on to their virginity a bit longer, until the disposition of their sexual feeling is under surer control. The best clinical evidence maintains that the process of bringing newly emergent sexuality under control is *inherently* delicate and troublesome. James's television plunge planted the anxiety-provoking notion in the mind of the adolescent viewer that he was sexually lagging behind not only the precocious kid down the block, but the Average American Boy character of James. (One was allowed to be less anxious when Father Knew Best.)

> Both of us were in agreement that what is broadcast over television ought to be acceptable; our point of disagreement was his feeling that broadcasting something over television *made* it acceptable.

Why shouldn't television make people anxious? say the producers of programs that make people anxious. After all, the *world* is anxious. (An awfully self-serving position: Programs that arouse anxiety are relevant; those that don't are enjoyable.) Before long, this line of argument begins to lay claim that programs which bring up irritating subjects in an irritating manner are performing a valuable social mission. Norman Lear, the producer of comedies such as *All in the Family* and *Maude*, makes such a claim. According to the Lear formula, a controversial topic will be raised, tossed around for laughs, then either discarded or resolved. Resolution occurs when one of the characters tolerates or forgives the controversial person or practice, while some other character, usually a combination of lovable old coot and ass, does not.

As many critics have pointed out, this is only apparent resolution. Nothing much really happens to a racial or sexual conflict when it is laughed at (a device that is supposed to soften outright slurring and stereotyping), discarded, tolerated, or forgiven. The idea that "if we can joke about it this way, we have taken a humanitarian stride" is mistaken. There is plenty of evidence, particularly among the student population, that, for one thing, race relations are more strained today than they were a decade ago. No one would want to claim that racism among youth disappeared during the politically active sixties; however, a claim can be made that when a student was confronted then with having made a racial slur, he seemed to be aware of having violated a standard.

Who is to say that Archie Bunker hath no sting? More and more television comedians, in the manner of Don Rickles, seek *only* to sting. It is really an empirical question, not a matter of taste, whether or not it is harmless, much less healing, to denigrate everybody, including oneself. A hit song by Randy Newman insults small people; this is no parody of unkindness or bigotry, but the real thing. My students understand it perfectly and parrot it enthusiastically. Rebuked, they grimace in exasperation. Nothing in their youthful experience tells them that bigotry is a sign of cultural regression ("It isn't bigotry; it's, you know, a joke"). They prefer to see whatever wicked delights crop up in the media as a progressive casting off of prudish inhibitions. According to such a view, progress is whatever happens next.

Toleration of the intolerable is always worrying, but it is especially so when it takes place among the young, in whom we want to invest so much hope. Tolerating the intolerable is part of a dynamic, not a static, process; the intolerable, when it is nurtured, grows.

Which brings me back to the senior speeches. Two so thoroughly inappropriate presentations in a single year represented a high count for us, so we were not ready, at least I wasn't, for the third.

This time the talk was about a summer spent working on a ranch, and the format was that of a commentary with slides. No apparent harm in this, but there were a number of factors working against the speech's success. The first was that the speaker was renowned for being a card, a reputation the welcoming ovation insisted he live up to. Second, he had not adequately rehearsed the projection of the slides, so that they tended to appear out of order and askew, the effect of which was to provide a subtextual comedy of visual nonsequiturs. Third, he chose to capitalize on the audience's nearly unrestrained hilarity by playing up certain questionable references.

The speaker made a fairly good, not too inappropriate crack about a slide which depicted a bull mounting a cow—"Sometimes the corrals get so crowded we have to stack the cattle on top of one another." But he chose to exploit his references to the gelding of bulls. There were, in all, four jokey and brutal evocations of this process which served to keep the image of bull genitalia before our minds for quite a few minutes. Since laughter had already been spent, the castration jokes were met with a kind of nervous applause. Bolstered by this, the speaker closed with a coda to the effect that he would be available after assembly to anybody who wanted tips on "cutting meat."

Since I happened to be in charge that day, I sent him home. It seemed to me, in light of the various reprisals and forewarnings connected with the previous speeches, that this particular performance, though perhaps less offensive in its specific references than the other two, ought to be the last straw. The speaker had clearly exceeded anything required by either schoolboy or cowboy saltiness. He had created an anything-goes atmosphere, and then he had let it go—for which he was applauded. "That was great!" said the boy next to me on the way out of the auditorium.

That morning and afterward scores of students, most, but not all, of them civil, hastened to let me know that they felt it was unfair to have sent the speaker home. Not one of them failed to remind me that I could see worse on television. Had I never seen *Saturday Night Live*? That afternoon an opinion poll went up requesting signatures from those who disapproved of the action I had taken and, in an opposing column, those who approved. Within the hour, hundreds expressed disapproval, only one approved.

For a day or two at school there was an animated atmosphere of martyrdom (the speaker's, not mine), but it dissipated rapidly, possibly because the right to make castration jokes from the stage was not, as a cause, very catalytic. The banished speaker, a very likable boy, returned, was received warmly, and apologized not at all cringingly.

In the calm that has followed, my colleagues and I have taken pains to stress to our students, especially at the commencement of the new school year, that whenever somebody addresses an assembly, it is a special occasion. Speakers are expected to observe definite standards when they speak or perform; audiences are expected to be courteous and restrained. Humor at someone else's expense is out, unless it is prearranged with the party lampooned, and even then it ought not to be inhumane. Excretory and copulatory humor is out; it's too easy. Preparation is important. Being persuasive is important. Being controversial is important. Being funny is a delight to all, though it is harder than it looks.

Perhaps these expectations are high. However, schools, especially parochial and independent schools, are gloriously unencumbered in setting such standards: Schools are often *chosen* for the standards they set, the difference they represent. One of the things schools have an opportunity to be different from is television, for although we are all wired into it and it feels public, like the law, it is actually private, like a door-to-door salesman. We don't have to buy the goods.

Since children who watch a fair amount of television will quite naturally assume they are being told and shown the truth, it seems to me crucial that they are exposed to models who view it selectively and critically, who judge it by criteria other than its potential to engage. My own experience has been that students are surprised, but not hostile, when television programming is harshly judged. I think they may even come to like the idea that they themselves, at their discriminating best, are in the process of becoming people television ought to measure up to.

HERE'S WHY LIFE ON TV IS SO DIFFERENT FROM REALITY

Benjamin Stein

There is, on prime-time television, a unified picture of life in these United States that is an alternate reality. For hours each day, people can leave the lives they are compelled to lead, lives whose limitations and frustrations hardly need to be detailed, and enter a different world that is more pleasant and less difficult in almost every way—life on television.

Most TV shows are set in the present or in a time within the memory of the viewers. Their characters are supposed to be types we are familiar with. While that familiarity may be more imaginary than real, we do see a world on television with which it is not difficult to feel a distant kinship. More than that, we see a world that is extremely appealing in a whole variety of ways. These ways have to do largely with simplification.

The alternate reality that television creates is not a coincidence or a result of random chance. It is the product of the thinking of TV producers and writers about life. We can see reflected on our video screens the attitudes of TV creators. More than that, we can sense the experience and "feel" of a city replicated on television. For what we see on prime-time television is nothing less than the apotheosizing of Los Angeles, and the spreading of the Los Angeles experience across the TV screens of America.

No show displays a kind of life that is anything but immaculately clean and neat, in which people are anything but well-groomed and hygienic and their motivations anything but straightforward.

Today's television is purer, in terms of backdrop and story endings, than the lines of a Mercedes convertible. Every day's shows bring fresh examples. A while ago, I saw an episode of *Charlie's Angels* about massage parlors that were really houses of prostitution. The three beautiful "angels" of the show were compelled to pretend they worked at massage parlors in seamy areas. Anyone who has ever passed by a massage parlor knows that they are invariably dirty, shabby places, with pitiful and degraded denizens. On *Charlie's Angels*, the Paradise Massage Parlor compared favorably in terms of cleanliness with the surgical theater at Massachusetts General Hospital. The girls were immaculate and well-groomed, soft of speech and clear of eye and skin.

On *The Waltons*, we are supposed to believe that we are in a Depression-era farming town in backwoods Virginia. Anyone who has been to a backwoods farming town in the South knows that, whatever else may be said about them, they are invariably dirty and bedraggled. On *The Waltons*, even the barnyard is immaculate. Marie Antoinette could not have asked for more agreeable play-farm quarters.

The grittiest TV show, when it was on, was generally believed to be *Baretta*. Yet even there, the supposedly shabby boardinghouses are neat, bright, and cheery. Even the junkies wear fresh clothing and sport recent haircuts.

Why is television so clean? The answer is simple. TV writers and producers replicate the world in which they live in their art, and the world they live in is the superclean, superbright world of Los Angeles, where even the slums are spotless and have palm trees in front.

> The alternate reality that television creates is the product of the thinking of TV producers and writers about life.

Until I moved to Los Angeles, I had no idea where the images of television came from. Where on Earth, I wondered, were pastel drugstores, low stucco apartments with balconies overlooking artificial waterfalls in the poor neighborhoods and bars with almost pitch-black interiors, opening onto glaringly bright sidewalks, utterly without litter or refuse? Drive along any boulevard in Los Angeles. There is block after block of pastel drugstores and apartment houses with balconies and artifical waterfalls. Close by are the bars with pitch-black interiors.

When I lived in Washington and in New York, I wondered where in America were all cars bright and shiny, unspattered by mud, with their original colors gleaming in the sun. Where did people have new cars even if they were secretaries or rookie policemen?

In Los Angeles, where everyone spends a few hours a day in a car, everyone has a shiny new auto, even if it is a financial sacrifice. In Los Angeles, where the sun shines every day and rain never falls, cars never get muddy.

Where are policemen handsome, thin, neatly dressed, and polite? They certainly were not in New York or Washington or New Haven or Santa Cruz or anywhere else except in Los Angeles. In Los Angeles, the policemen look like male models, except that they do not look effeminate. They are the models for the ruggedly modish cops on a dozen TV shows.

Among the TV writers and producers I interviewed, whenever people spoke of Los Angeles they spoke of a "fantasy land," "plastic paradise," "wonderland," "sterile concrete," "lotus land," and similar hackneyed phrases that are nevertheless accurate. The writers and producers see and experience a life of cleanness and emphasis on good appearance that would be unbelievable to anyone who did not live in Los Angeles. That has become their image of life, so that when a world is re-created on television, the Los Angeles world, the one in the creators' minds, is the one that comes out. However much the writers and producers may mock and decry the sterility and cleanliness of Los Angeles, it is Los Angeles they are broadcasting around the world as the model environment. The faces, clothes, haircuts, and cars of people on television are the faces, clothes, haircuts, and cars of people walking down Rodeo Drive in Beverly Hills.

On television, everything ends happily, which might be a way of summarizing the TV climate.

But this applies only to the question of appearance. There is also a moral and philosophical world on television, and that, too, has to come from somewhere.

Beyond the physical and visual cleanliness on television is an attitude appealing far beyond most of what real life has to offer. On television, everything ends happily, which might be a way of summarizing the TV climate. There is far more, however. Every problem that comes up on television is cured before the show is over. No one suffers from existential terrors. They are not even hinted at.

On a smaller scale, people on television are not small-minded, nasty folks. No shopping-bag ladies, reeking of urine, stalk a traveler in a crowded subway. No snarling teenagers threaten and mock on a deserted sidewalk. Instead, people move along rapidly on highways and byways. Impediments are cleared out of the way, both visually and psychologically. At the end of 60 minutes, at the most, everything has come up roses, even if there were a few minor thorns along the way.

On television, people get things done. No one spends all day in a windowless office going over musty volumes of figures and regulations, seeking to comply with guidelines and plans laid out by persons long since dead. No one on television spends all day in bed, too lethargic or depressed to get up. On television, in fact, there is no such thing as depression. That most widespread of modern psychic ailments simply does not exist in the alternate world of television. Everyone, good or bad, is charged with energy. If someone wants to do something, he or she simply goes out and does it.

Further, people on television think big. They are no longer concerned with telling Ricky Ricardo how much they spent on a hat. Instead, they think about making a million by selling heroin, or about ridding Los Angeles of the most vicious killer of the decade. In a comedy, a poor family thinks of getting rich. A middle-class family thinks of getting into the upper class. A black family thinks of overcoming racism.

"Out there," for the folks on television, is a big world, full of possibilities. Here, a sharp distinction needs to be made between social activism and personal ambition. The people on television are never interested in social movements. They want money and happiness. They want to be great sleuths or great criminals. They have big plans and hopes for themselves, but not for society.

This entire psychic galaxy is, as far as I can tell, a reflection of the psychic makeup of the Hollywood TV producer and writer. Before I came to the world of TV production I never would have imagined that a group of people as psychologically successful and liberated as TV writers and producers existed. It is their mental world that is up there on the TV screen.

In the world of television are people who are financially successful, creative, living in comfortable surroundings, and generally quite happy. Around a successful TV production company (and the unsuccessful ones quickly vanish), there is an air of confidence and self-satisfaction that is rarely encountered anywhere else.

Those people are highly unusual folk, operating in a highly unusual milieu, and it shows. In the eighth decade of American life in the twentieth century, the working situation of Americans has become steadily more bureaucratized. Almost everyone coming out of school goes to work for a large enterprise of some kind, finding a spot on a bureaucratic ladder. The worker must flatter everyone over him and worry about everyone under him. His real rewards come not from producing anything, but from pleasing those above him on the ladder.

Workers derive their security and status from the bureaucratic structure in which they find themselves. They are cogs in a vast machinery. There is little or no creativity in their daily lives. Advancement comes with infuriating slowness. To reach a position of financial independence or modest wealth is impossible. Getting that extra few thousand a year in wages becomes the key goal, and few see further than that.

On the other hand, the bureaucratic structure provides a protection against having to actually produce anything. Simply serving one's time at the office is all that is required to get by. Eventually, however, that too takes its toll. The realization that one is doing nothing but serving out a life sentence results in devastating blows to one's self-esteem.

The whole process of the engorgement of institutions and the swallowing up of the individual into large enterprises leads, in my experience, to a smallness of mind. Bitterness and pettiness are generated by the unmixed frustration that is each day's portion.

Imagine, on the other hand, the world of Hollywood. It is a throwback to the world of individual entrepreneurs. Each writer sinks or swims on the basis of his product. Those people do not have to wait in a bureaucratic holding pattern all of their lives. If their product is good, they become successful and important immediately. They are not judged by how well they can accommodate themselves to a paranoid boss's suspicions. Rather, they move along or fall out depending on what they get done. They are immediately able to make themselves independent by having a skill that is in great demand and correspondingly highly paid. They float from contract to contract. Each time they begin a project, they have the opportunity to become millionaires, and many of them do.

The people on television are never interested in social movements. They want money and happiness.

A story about Bob Dylan comes to mind. When Dylan started out, he wrote about depressed, crazy people suffering daily crises. After a few years, when his income had risen to eight figures left of the decimal point, he started to write only about happy, cheerful subjects. When asked about the change, he is reported to have said, "It's hard to be a bitter millionaire."

So it is with the people in television. They have many firm and negative opinions about various groups within the society, but they are basically fairly satisfied with life. There may be, and probably are, starving would-be TV writers in North Hollywood and Studio City who are filled with rage and anger. But the ones who have made it, the ones who are working regularly for many thousands a week, are quite content for the most part.

The successful TV writer and producer is a person who gets things done and who feels good about it. After spending years in bureaucracies of various kinds, I found it staggering to see how much each individual writer and producer got done each day. In Norman Lear's T.A.T. Communications, there is a full-time staff of fewer than 50 to get out hundreds of millions of dollars' worth of TV product. If the government had a department of TV comedy, there would be at least 75,000 employees—and they would do nothing. Naturally, each of those few people who are producing so much feels good about it and about himself. The opposite of small-mindedness is generated.

No one is completely or even mostly happy, but the Hollywood TV writers and producers that I met went a long way along that line. They were, and are, people who take risks and live successfully. Their horizons are broad. The small annoyances of life do not faze them unduly. They see life not as a prison sentence but as a garden of rich potentialities.

TV writers and producers are not starving in garrets. They lead fulfilled, productive lives, by most standards. They live those lives in an attractive, uncluttered world of immaculate sidewalks and gleaming new cars, pastel storefronts and artificial waterfalls. They have been a party to striving and success in their own lives, and they have not missed the lesson of the possibilities of life. And it is this way of life that has been translated into the flickering colorful images on hundreds of millions of TV screens.

SUGGESTIONS FOR FURTHER READING

Some recent major pieces on the effect of TV entertaiment include:

Parents, "What TV Is Doing to Your Kids." June 1981, pp. 55–60.

US News and World Report, "What Is TV Doing to America?" August 2, 1982, pp. 27–30.

Harry F. Waters, "Life According to TV." *Newsweek*, December 6, 1982, pp. 136–41. A report on the most recent study by the group of researchers headed by George Gerbner at the University of Pennsylvania.

One of the best-known criticisms of television entertainment is FCC Chairman Newton Minnow's "Vast Wasteland" speech: *Vital Speeches of the Day*, June 15, 1961, pp. 533–37.

An interesting personal perspective on the effects of TV on young people can be found in Joyce Maynard, *Looking Back: A Chronicle of Growing Up in the Sixties*. New York: Doubleday, 1973, pp. 51–58.

Also of interest:

Sally Bedell, *Up the Tube: Prime Time TV in the Silverman Years*. New York: Viking Press, 1981.

George Comstock, *Television and Human Behavior*. Beverly Hills, Calif.: Sage, 1980.

George Goethals, *The TV Ritual: Worship at the Video Altar*. Boston: Beacon Press, 1982. According to Goethals, TV has taken over the four functions of religion: divinity school, ritual, ceremony, and sacred symbols.

Benjamin Stein, *The View from Sunset Boulevard: America Brought to You by the People Who Make TV*. New York: Basic Books, 1979.

CHAPTER 13

Sex and the Media

"Sex and violence" are often grouped together as a single problem—media's biggest problem. Actually, they are very different types of problems, which excite the interest of different groups. Protests against violence come chiefly from academics and intellectuals, while the protests against sex come mostly from religious groups. Media violence is disturbing because of its effect on societal aggressiveness, whereas media sex is feared for its effects on our morals.

The readings in this chapter focus on some of the current controversies surrounding the media sex issue. In the first reading Howard Polskin gives us an update on the controversy surrounding pay TV's offerings in pornography. In the second reading

Larry M. Lance and Christina Y. Berry analyze the sexual revolution from the perspective of popular music.

In the third reading, Phyllis Schlafly analyses a popular song's messages about sexual behavior, and comments on some of the reactions it provoked. Her article first appeared in the conservative magazine, *Human Events.*

The final reading is an editorial ad from Planned Parenthood that addresses media's power to influence viewers through the depiction of sexual behavior.

SEX ON PAY TELEVISION—THE BATTLE LINES ARE FORMED

Howard Polskin

Mike Klein gets paid to watch pornographic movies.

Every day he settles into his small, uncluttered office in a corporate mall on Long Island and screens at least four sexy films. As a film evaluator for a two-year-old cable-TV network called Escapade, he must pick approximately seven films each month to be shown to the network's 278,000 paying subscribers. Klein estimates he saw almost 1000 sex films last year.

"People think I have the greatest job in the world and that it's a real breeze," says the 24-year-old bachelor, who was graduated from Boston University in 1980. "But I tell you, it's a lot of hard work."

It's also very tricky. Klein must choose films that are erotic enough to satisfy the varied sexual interests of his nationwide cable subscribers and tame enough not to provoke the wrath of city councils that have the power to revoke the franchises of cable systems that carry the service. More often than not, Escapade and the almost two-dozen similar adult pay-TV services (both

From *TV Guide* (October 30, 1982). Reprinted by permission.

cable and over-the-air) are leaving their subscribers like long-distance runners at a barely functioning water fountain—panting and wanting more.

Every two months, Escapade polls 600 subscribers with an eight-page questionnaire. The surveys reveal some surprising information: 42 per cent of the viewers are female. The original programming produced by Playboy Productions (a partner in the network), like Playboy's titillating profiles of its magazine's Playmates, is, in most cases, more popular than adult movies. But one overriding theme emerges from the raw data: Escapade subscribers want raunchier movies.

So far, Escapade has been cautious. The service, which costs subscribers $6 to $11 each month, does not present movies that show explicit sex. (Only one small cable-TV system in the country—Twin-County Cable in Allentown, Pa.—offers hardcore X-rated films to viewers.) Escapade, for instance, will not show films that include close-up shots of genitals. But Escapade does get away with saucy scenes such as a man kissing a woman's breasts or a naked man in bed with a naked woman.

Still, for many viewers, it's not enough.

"Sure, we get complaints about Escapade," notes Brian O'Neill, until recently general manager of United Cable TV of Eastern Shore in Ocean City, Md. Approximately 1000 of United Cable's 16,000 homes choose to subscribe to Escapade. "About 10 subscribers each month phone up and say that Escapade isn't explicit enough," says O'Neill. "Nobody has told me that the service is objectionable."

Which is not exactly surprising. Cable-industry research indicates there is an appetite for sexy movies in the privacy of the home. For instance, in a 1981 survey commissioned by a Buffalo, N.Y., cable system, 68 per cent of the subscribers said they would consider purchasing an adult service if it were available.

But despite the public's apparent desire for hot, erotic programming, only about 500,000 of the Nation's 27.8 million cable homes purchase an adult service. The reasons for the dearth of subscribers are many, ranging from price resistance to poor marketing. And many cable homes haven't yet had a chance to subscribe.

The response to Escapade, for instance, has been cool. Where the service is offered to cable viewers, only 10 to 35 percent subscribe. Many cable operators have chosen not to offer it to their customers. That may change soon. On Nov. 19, Escapade will become the Playboy Channel. Then, say cable-marketing experts, the service will be easier to sell to cable operators and, ultimately, to subscribers who are familiar with the Playboy name and reputation.

However, in some markets, adult films have proven so popular they even challenge the drawing power of the highest card in the pay-TV deck: The Hollywood blockbuster.

On Warner Amex's Qube cable-TV system in Columbus, Ohio, subscribers can view sports, concerts and instructional programs as well as adult films and Hollywood movies on a pay-per-view basis. (When subscribers select certain programs, they are usually charged anywhere from 50¢ to $4.50 per viewing.) According to internal Warner Amex documents, more subscribers paid more money to watch soft-core pornographic films (which Qube edits) than any other type of programming, including recently released Hollywood films, in the first two months of 1980. Films like *Massage Parlor Wife* and *Erotic Delights* proved more popular than established hits like *Norma Rae* and *Moonraker*.

The most popular film in January 1980 was Russ Meyer's *Beneath the Valley of the Ultravixens*, which was purchased by 4259 subscribers who paid about $3 per household. In one month on Qube, the film grossed nearly $15,000. In comparison, the most-watched feature film was *Moonraker* in that period. Only 3344 subscribers paid the regular price of $2.50 to watch it.

Although the information from the memos is almost three years old, Warner Amex is still showing the same types of adult films and Hollywood hits on its Columbus pay-per-view service. Although the company has refused to comment about any current or past Qube viewership figures, Warner Amex contends that Hollywood films are more popular than adult movies on Qube.

But where adult films have made a bigger hit (albeit with a much smaller potential audience) is on over-the-air subscription-television channels. Such services charge subscribers about $20 a month to receive a single encoded signal. There are 29 STV stations in the country with about 1.5 million subscribers. Thirteen of those 29 stations offer a late-night package of soft-core sex films for an additional fee.

STV adult services have achieved what's unblinkingly referred to in the television industry as a higher penetration level than cable TV: it's estimated that close to 80 per cent of STV subscribers take an adult service when it's available.

A major factor is cost. STV subscribers can purchase an adult service for as little as an additional $4 per month.

Another reason for the popularity of adult films on STV is that STV stations show more explicit movies than cable. Unlike their cable cousins, STV operators are not granted franchises by local governments and therefore do not have to worry about reprisals by city officials. Some stations offer films with detailed genital shots. Other stations air lightly edited versions of hard-core pornographic classics like *The Opening of Misty Beethoven*.

In Ann Arbor, Mich., 14,500 of Ann Arbor STV's 15,000 subscribers pay the additional $3.95 each month to view the late-night adult-film service.

"Our people really want adult movies," says Kip Farmer, former general manager of Ann Arbor STV and now executive vice president of its parent company, Satellite Syndicated Systems. "But they don't want just wall-to-wall sex"—badly produced, badly acted, no storyline. "Between the lines, they say they want good erotic movies."

Farmer says that the Ann Arbor system will keep showing harder and harder films until subscribers say, "Enough."

"They keep saying 'More! More!' I'm uncertain how far to go," Farmer muses. "There's a fine line that I won't cross. If I do, I'm a purveyor of smut. But nobody knows where that line is."

Wherever that line may be, it has not stunted the growth of STV adult subscribers. In 1981, only 30,000 STV subscribers received adult movies. This year, the figure has swelled to 300,000.

But there are obstacles that threaten to block the spread of soft-core movies on STV and cable. The most vocal opponent of sex on cable is Morality in Media, an ultraconservative 20-year-old organization that serves as a nationwide clearinghouse for research on obscenity laws and the $5-billion-a-year pornography industry. Recently, Morality in Media turned its guns on cable television.

Its first salvo was fired more than a year ago when the group mailed 400,000 letters, signed by former Dallas Cowboy quarterback Roger Staubach, asking citizens to write their mayors and tell them not to tolerate "smut on television."

In part, the letters said, "I can't let another day go by without alerting you to the danger that may invade your home. . . . Movies that have been judged obscene in some of our Nation's courtrooms and are now being broadcast over some pay-cable systems and fed into our homes."

Soon after the letters were mailed, Morality in Media accelerated the attack. The organization's monthly newsletters began running regular stories about the dangers of the adult cable-TV networks, with headlines like "Sex Offender, 14, Blames Pay-TV." Then, last fall, the group's general entered the fray. In October 1981, Father Morton Hill, S.J., president of Morality in Media and a former member of Lyndon Johnson's Presidential Commission on Obscenity and Pornography, launched a six-month, 44-city speaking tour during which he vigorously campaigned against cable pornography.

Today, Father Hill still sees sexy films on pay-TV as a threat to the moral structure of the country. "It's not like there's a pornographic film in some seedy theater downtown. . . . The pornography is downstairs . . . on television . . . in the living room . . . where the family can see it!"

The cable industry doesn't buy that argument. The standard reply is simple: if viewers find the programming objectionable, they won't subscribe.

Still, while most pay-TV programmers recognize the potential threat of an organization like Morality in Media (which recently drafted a model cable obscenity law for local communities), the general industry feeling is that it won't be an activist group or conservative city council that could doom the adult pay-TV business. Ironically enough, the programmers fear that the public could tire of soft-core pornographic movies. After the initial thrill of seeing naked bodies wriggle around the screen for a few months, the attraction may wear off, especially if the movies lack decent production values.

"You'd be surprised how awful some of these films are," says Mike Klein of Escapade. "I've screened some European sex movies where the actresses are so fat I hoped they wouldn't take their clothes off. Some movies are so bad that I wanted to call up the directors and yell at them."

His boss agrees. "There's a dearth of good sex films," explains Jeanne O'Grady, director of Escapade's film acquisition. "The major studios don't produce those kinds of movies. The only films that make money theatrically in the sex genre are the hardcore films. Not many companies are making a good soft-core product like *Young Lady Chatterley*. That leaves us in a bind."

To remedy the problem, Escapade has begun producing its own programming in conjunction with its partner, Playboy Productions. The results have not met with much critical acclaim. One show in particular, *Everything Goes*, in which contestants remove an article of clothing every time they answer a question incorrectly, was described by the *Los Angeles Times* as "the worst game show ever."

As Escapade sinks more money into original productions, Mike Klein finds himself looking harder and harder to find the perfect adult cable-TV movie: tastefully erotic, well produced, decently scripted and filled with a plentiful supply of beautiful bodies.

Some days, Klein wades through a sea of soft-core movies—he says he sometimes screens 20 daily—to find the right pictures. On days like that, his fellow workers sometimes drift into his office and ask him how many cold showers he's taken that afternoon. Or his girl friends call him and kiddingly ask him if he's learning anything new.

Usually he replies with his standard line, "Hey," he tells them, "it's a tough job but someone's got to do it."

Sometimes it comes off as a joke and his friends laugh. Other times, it's just the plain truth.

HAS THERE BEEN A SEXUAL REVOLUTION?: AN ANALYSIS OF HUMAN SEXUALITY MESSAGES IN POPULAR MUSIC DURING THE 1960s AND 1970s

Larry M. Lance and Christina Y. Berry

Social changes in the sexual scene have been considered so rapid as to justify that the American society is presently in the process of a sexual revolution. Using mailed and group administered questionnaires, interviews, participant observation, and content analysis of books, magazines, and films, social researchers have analyzed changes in sexual attitudes and behavior. Sexual changes pointed out include increased premarital sex, extra-marital sex, swinging, group sex, group marriages, living together, homosexuality, female and male nudity, recreational sex, explicit discussions of sexual acts, and changes in male and female roles and expectations in sexual relations.

While many approaches have been taken to gather knowledge about contemporary American sexual changes, one socialization agent has been overlooked—music. Music provides daily communication of sexual roles, sexual behaviors, and sexual relationships to Americans. The opportunity to have the same popular music repeated many times daily enables easy memorization of sexual messages. What sexual messages have been transmitted? What changes in sexual messages have taken place in popular music during the sexual revolution? Are sexual messages becoming more popular in music?

From the *Journal of Popular Culture* (Winter, 1981). Reprinted by permission.

BACKGROUND LITERATURE

Discussions and studies pertaining to the sexual revolution, generally considered to refer to a rapid rise in the frequency with which people become involved in several diverse types of previously proscribed or restricted sexual behavior (Kando, 1978:375), have been published for years. In the following summary of relevant literature we will seek to determine if there is empirical support for a sexual revolution and what changes in sexuality there have been in the media.

It has been maintained that the term revolution is not appropriate for describing changes in sexual behavior. Those who take this position would argue that the sexual changes which have taken place were not as revolutionary as conveyed by sensationalist media and alarmist moralists (Kando, 1978:376). Since a revolution refers to a very rapid and profound change which would constitute a break with the past, there are those who would propose that we have been experiencing a sexual evolution rather than a sexual revolution.

Others would take issue with the sexual revolution from another point of view. They would argue that sexual changes which have taken place involve standards and attitudes rather than behavior. What sexual changes have previous studies pointed out and how fast have sexual changes been?

Corry (1966) maintained that sexual change is generally talk rather than action. Studies have pointed out that there is generally more approval of various sexual behavior than actual participation (Kando, 1978:376). Moreover, rather than indicating moral decay, attitude changes reflect an emerging ethic of autonomy and responsibility for one's behavior (Reiss, 1973). Rather than revolutionary or decadent, the thinking behind these studies would view this new morality as wholesome progressive change which has not increased indiscriminate and promiscuous sex (Kando, 1978:376).

Supporters of this position contend that the incidence of sexual intercourse, premarital virginity and coitus has stayed fairly steady. The report by Kinsey (1953) that about 20% of unmarried college females weren't virgins was said to be upheld about one decade later (Corry, 1966). At the end of the 1960s about 60% of the male population participated in premarital coitus, which was consistent with reports since 1900 (Kaats and Davis, 1970). Therefore, it is maintained that the sexual activity of youth today is about the same as that of the youth during the 1920s (Cuber, 1972).

> Studies have pointed out that there is generally more approval of various sexual behavior than actual participation.

However, sociological studies over the past couple of decades have reported evidence of revolutionary sexual changes. Obsolete now are descriptions of youth as sexually conservative (Reiss, 1961), the persistence of the double standard, and the major difference between attitudes and behavior (Ellis, 1968). Recent studies have reported the decline of premarital virginity, the increase of premarital coitus, and disappearance of the double standard (King, et. al., 1977).

By the end of the 1960s the incidence of premarital coitus among college females had more than doubled the 20% repeatedly stated since World War I (Kaats and Davis, 1970). By the beginning of the 1970s, less than half the people were virgins when they were first married (Kando, 1978:377). Conventions like engagement became looked upon more frequently as anachronisms (Bell and Chaskes, 1972). During the 1970s, cohabitation and other alternatives to marriage became popular on the college campus as well as in the community (Kando, 1978:377). Sexual activity in the 1970s has been the continuation of a revolution which started in the 1960s (Hunt, 1973–1974). During this period the double standard with regard to male-female differences has been disappearing while full equality of sexual rights has been advanced for youth, the aged, for homosexuals, transsexuals and others (Mazur, 1977).

In summary, a number of empirical studies have pointed out that sexual changes are taking place. Scientific surveys have reported sexual changes such as the greater acceptance of masturbation (Reiss, 1967:56), increased premarital coitus (Leslie, 1973:384–389; Packard, 1968: 160–162; Bell and Chaskes, 1970; Christensen and Gregg, 1970), extramarital relations as more commonly occurring (Bagueder, 1973:123), erosion of the double standard and increasing acceptance of a more equalitarian standard (Mirande, 1975: 342–343; Byrne, 1977).

Changes toward increased sexual explicitness and permissiveness in mass media have been found to be paralleled by analogous change in scientific surveys on human sexuality (Byrne, 1977:12). Since the research in this article is concerned with one form of mass media (music), other forms of mass media examined for sexual changes will be discussed in this section.

An analysis of sexuality in fiction has pointed to changes over the past 40 years. Novels in the early 1940s treated sexuality with caution, as indicated by Kathleen Winsor's *Forever Amber* (1944). In post-World-War-II novels sex became more openly treated but caution was given to sexually explicit details and words (Byrne, 1977:

14). For example, Norman Mailer was restricted in his word choice in *The Naked and the Dead* (1948).

In the 1950s restrictions on the spoken word were reduced and by the 1960s there were few limitations on words used and explicit writings of increasingly varied sexual behaviors became widespread. Changes in sexual fiction during the 1970s have continued toward greater permissiveness. There now appears to be little chance of additional increases in sexual candor, since all restraints have been left behind (Byrne and Byrne, 1977:16).

In terms of changes in magazine photographs, it has been noted that photographic sex has continually lagged behind written descriptions in the past with respect to permissiveness. Even now, the U.S. Customs will permit any and all written matter to enter this society without question while "lustful" photographic displays of sexual behaviors are regularly intercepted (Byrne and Byrne, 1977:17).

Prior to *Playboy* in the early 1950s, sexual photos were generally nonexistent in widely distributed magazines. However, between the early 1950s and the present time changes in sexual photos are as great as sexual changes in novels.

In the early issues of *Playboy* airbrushing about the nipples was used to soften any erotic details about the breasts, and the genital area remained concealed. However, during the 1960s frontal nudity started appearing and erect nipples were shown. In the 1970s changes have included the showing of pubic hair, nude male centerfolds, female models glancing at their breasts, then touching their breasts, then glancing at their genitals, then placing their hands suggestively near their genitalia, and then taking part in explicit masturbation. Photos started presenting two females, followed by both sexes, kissing, touching and embracing in nude poses, (Byrne and Byrne, 1977:17–18).

Magazine photos now appear to be at a stage similar to that of fiction in the late 1940s and early 1950s. This conclusion is suggested since today there is some simulated or suggestive sexual intercourse and other sexual behaviors that fall short of hard-core pornography by the lack of erect penises and the lack of pictures showing bodily penetration by the penis. (Byrne, 1977:18).

As with other forms of media, explicit sexuality in the movies is not new. However, following early attempts with nudity, Hollywood developed a production code of ethics in 1934 spelling out a restrictive and detailed list of what could and could not be stated and done on the screen for the respectable moviegoing public. In the 1930s and 1940s movies indicated that married couples sleep separately and presumably chastely in twin beds, that kisses involve only non-prolonged lip contact, that one foot was always on the floor when two people even talk to each other in the same bed, and that reckless or immoral individuals who became involved in nonmarital sexual intercourse (not shown) would become parents and would suffer for their misdeeds with physical and psychological miseries. Partial nudity was unthinkable (Byrne, 1977:19).

By the early 1950s there was a movement toward relaxing the restrictions on movie content and a rise in the permissiveness of what was stated and done in the movies. This movement continued into the 1960s with more explicit sexual scenes, partial or total nudity, and the frequent use of themes such as premarital sex, rape and adultery. This widespread movement toward the use of sex in the movies contributed to the elimination of the production code in 1968 and the introduction of the rating system (Byrne and Byrne, 1977:19).

With the advent of this rating system there became an implicit implication that anything could be shown in an X-rated movie. This brought about explicit sexual behaviors such as masturbation, cunnilingus, fellatio, and intercourse in varied positions (Byrne and Byrne, 1977:19–20).

Beyond the mass media of books, magazines and movies there have been many other avenues through which sexuality has become more explicit. Other avenues include the theater, television, and music. This study will trace recent changes in sexuality through the medium of music.

Research Design

To determine what changes in sexual messages have taken place in popular music, *Billboard Magazine's* 100 top hit rock and roll single records for each year from 1968 through 1977 were chosen for analysis. Popular songs which pertained to human sexuality were selected from the 100 top rock and roll single records for each of the years in the past decade and content analyzed. For each top rock and roll single record dealing with sexuality a content analysis was conducted to determine the type of sexual activity, the gender of the initiator of the sexual activity, the type of personal relationship in which the sexual activity occurred, and the evidence of objections to the sexual activity described.

> From 1968 to 1977, an increasing number of top hit rock and roll records involved sexual intercourse.

Following is a list of top rock and roll songs by year from 1968 to 1977 dealing with human sexuality which were content analyzed:

1968 Sunshine of Your Love
Love Child

1969 Honky Tonk Women
Lay Lady Lay
This Girl Is a Woman Now
Ruby Don't Take Your Love to Town

1970 Make It with Me

1971 Maggie Mae
Help Me Make It Through the Night
Gypsies, Tramps and Thieves

1972 My Ding-A-Ling
Go All the Way
If Loving You Is Wrong

1973 Let's Get It On
Pillow Talk
I'm Gonna Love You Just a Little More Baby
Me and Mrs. Jones
Touch Me in the Morning
The Night the Lights Went Out in Georgia

1974 Rikki Don't Lose That Number
On and On
Feel Like Making Love
Sundown
Dark Lady
Midnight at the Oasis
You're Having My Baby

1975 Love Won't Let Me Wait
I Don't Like to Sleep Alone
Third Rate Romance
Angie Baby
Get Down Tonight
Midnight Blue
Chevy Van
Lady Marmalade
Cut the Cake
Swearin' to God
Poetry Man
Only Women Bleed

1976 Love Hangover
Love to Love You
More, More, More
Let's Do It Again
December, 1963
A Little Bit More
Moonlight Feels Right
Afternoon Delight
Sweet Thing
Fooled Around and Fell in Love
Island Girl
All By Myself
Kiss and Say Goodbye
Evil Woman

1977 Got to Give It Up
Don't Leave Me This Way
Undercover Angel
Night Moves
Tonight's the Night
Right Time of the Night
Angel in Your Arms
Smoke from a Distant Fire
Cold as Ice
Lucille
After the Lovin'
Do You Wanna Make Love?
Looks Like We Made It
I'm in You
I've Got Love on My Mind
Heard It in a Love Song

Findings

From 1968 to 1977 there has been an increase of rock and roll hits pertaining to sexual activities. As indicated in Table 1, the number of records concerned with sexual activities increased from a total of 13 hits from 1968 to 1972 to a total of 55 from 1973 to 1977.

Traditionally rock and roll songs very rarely presented sexual feelings in anything other than very vague or highly romantic terms, with implications of sexual intercourse being avoided. However, from 1968 to 1972 there were 10 hits which used well-known slang to refer to sexual intercourse (see Table 1), including three records in which women initiated the activity. In the next five years, there were over four times as many hit records concerned with sexual intercourse.

Changes in the reference to extramarital sex in the hit rock and roll songs analyzed were also found. Between 1968 and 1972 two records concerned extramarital sex, while 10 in the period from 1973 to1977 dealt with it (Table 1).

Another change within this period in rock and roll hits pertained to the gender of the intitiator of the sexual activity. In the 13 hits between 1968 and 1972, in nine the initiator of the sexual activities was a male while four were initiated by females. In the period 1973–1977 females became more aggressive, 26 times compared to the males' 22 times (Table 1).

In an analysis of the type of personal relationship in which sexual activity occurred, there was evidence of a shift in emphasis from casual involvement to emotional involvement. From 1968 to 1972 the number of records dealing with casual relations and emotional involvement were almost evenly divided (Table 2). Analysis of the records 1973–1977 indicates emotional involvement almost twice as often as casual relations.

There was little evidence of objections to sexual activities described in hit records between 1968 and 1972 by either males or females. However, while there were also few objections to sexual activities described between 1973 and 1977 from females, there was an increase in male objections in the messages in the records from 1973 to 1977 (Table 2).

Between 1968 and 1972 only two of the ten records referring to sexual intercourse by unmarried couples presented the subject negatively: in one a girl refused sexual intercourse for fear of pregnancy, and in another a girl became

TABLE 1 Type of Sexual Activity and Gender of Initiator of Sexual Activity in Rock and Roll Hit Single Records, 1968–1977

	Type Of Sexual Activity			Gender of Initiator of Sexual Activity			
Year	Sexual Intercourse Between Unmarried Persons	Extramarital Sex	Other Sexual Activity	Male	Female	Not Specified	Number of Records
1968	2			2			2
1969	3	1		2	2		4
1970	1			1			1
1971	3			1	2		3
1972	1	1	1	3			3
1973	4	2		2	4		6
1974	4	1	2	2	4	1	7
1975	9	1	3	4	5	4	13
1976	12	2		5	7	2	14
1977	12	4		9	6	1	16

TABLE 2 Type of Personal Relationship in Which Sexual Activity Occurred and Evidence of Objections to The Sexual Activity Described, 1968–1977

	Type of Personal Relationship in Which Sexual Activity Occurred			Evidence of Objections to The Sexual Activity Described			
Year	Casual	Emotional Involvement	Not Specified	Male Objections	Female Objections	Society Objections	Number of Records
1968		2			1		2
1969	2	2		1			4
1970			1				1
1971	2	1					3
1972	1	1	1			1	3
1973		4	2	1		1	6
1974	2	3	2		1	1	7
1975	3	6	4			1	13
1976	6	4	4	5			14
1977	4	9	3	3	1		16

an unwed mother. In these same 10 records, in one a man, and in two women, initiated casual sex.

Of the forty-one records involving sexual intercourse by unmarried couples between 1973 and 1977, women initiated having sex in 19 songs. There were 18 hit records in this period in which a man proposed or told of having sex, and of these, two records were mainly exclamations and instructions to a lover during sexual intercourse. There were no instances in which a female regretted sexual activity, but in three records a man criticized a woman for sexually exploiting men, and in another three a man regretted his own sexual exploitation of women. Four records simply referred to couples having sex, and only one, which concerned two strangers, was critical of the situation.

With regard to the two records concerning extramarital sex between 1968–1972, a husband in one record was self-critical but continued his affair, while in the other record a sexually disabled man begged his wife to stop seeking sex elsewhere but did not criticize her for doing so. From 1973 to 1977 there were 10 hit records dealing with extramarital sex: two referred to a husband, seven referred to a wife, and one referred to a husband and a wife who were not married to each other. Eight of these songs presented negative attitudes or actions concerning the activity: one husband and his lover were shot dead, another husband found his wife seeking revenge by having an affair herself, a wife and her lover were shot dead and in four records men were critical of wives who had extramarital sex. In one record in which two married people were having an affair together, the man decided to end the relationship because of their primary obligations to their spouses.

In terms of other sexual activity besides intercourse between unmarried persons and extramarital sex, in 1968–1972 there was one record which referred to a penis, both in its title and subject, by use of a well-known slang term. Between 1973 and 1977 one song depicted a homosexual supportive of a man who had trouble accepting his own homosexuality. Another record referred to a couple conceiving a child, but made note of the fact that the woman could have chosen to get an abortion but did not. In a third record a man alluded to oral-genital sex with a woman, and in another a boy, who attempted to seduce a mentally ill girl, was instead held captive by her for her own sexual pleasure. A final unique song in this period referred to menstruation in slang terms, to criticize women who feel they are helpless and utterly dependent on men.

Conclusion

Rapid changes in sexual attitudes and sexual behavior during the past decade have led many to characterize this period as a sexual revolution. In the last ten years attitudes toward human sexuality have changed, so that the subject is examined and discussed more openly than in the past, and a wider variety of sexual behavior is recognized and/or endorsed. From 1968 to 1977, but especially from 1973 to 1977, an increasing number of top hit rock and roll records involved sexual intercourse either between married people or in extramarital relationships. Records between 1973 and 1977 portrayed slightly more females than males initiating sex. While songs referring to sex between unmarried persons were generally not presented in a negative manner, songs concerning extramarital sex were generally presented with a negative view. There were more instances found in which men rather than women were critical of sexual activity, especially extramarital sex.

Evidence was also presented which indicted a change in the personal relationship for sexual activity. A shift was noted from an emphasis on casual relations to more concern with emotional involvement.

The increasing number of songs pertaining to sexual activity together with findings mentioned above indicate a more liberal attitude toward sexual activity in general, and more sexual freedom for women in particular. As in other popular art forms, the sexual attitudes and activities presented in rock and roll top hit records reflect, and in turn influence, what is socially acceptable.

Thus, changes in the sexual messages in the popular songs over the past decade, like the sexual changes found from scientific surveys of members of the American society, support what has been termed the sexual revolution. As previously indicated, there was a striking increase in the number of popular songs involving sexual intercourse from 1968–1972 and 1973–1977.

The question still remains as to how much influence sexual messages have on the sexual attitudes and sexual behaviors of members of American society. Do people who buy hit records with sexual messages pay attention to what is being said? Do people who learn the words of popular sexual songs, such as those who sing along with *American Bandstand*, subscribe to their sexual messages? Does the close identification with a popular singer persuade a person to follow the sexual messages sung by the singer? Further research needs to be conducted to determine exactly how much influence popular songs with sexual messages have on American society.

REFERENCES

Baguedor, Eve. 1973 "Is Anyone Faithful Anymore?" *McCall's* (February):73, 123–126.

Bell, Robert R. and Jay B. Chaskes. 1970 "Premarital Sexual Experience Among Coeds, 1958 and 1968." *Journal of Marriage and the Family* 32 (February): 81–84.

Bell, Robert R. and Jay B. Chaskes. 1972 "Premarital Sexual Experience Among Coeds, 1958 and 1968," in *Intimate Lifestyles: Marriage and Its Alternatives*. Joann S. Delora and Jack R. Delora, eds. Pacific Palisades, Cal.: Goodyear Publishing Co., pp. 53–66.

Byrne, Donn and Lois A. Byrne. 1977 *Exploring Human Sexuality*. New York: Crowell.

Byrne, Donn. 1979. "A Pregnant Pause in the Sexual Revolution," in *Human Sexuality in a Changing Society*. Graham B. Spanier, ed. Minneapolis, Minn.: Burgess, pp. 135–137.

Christensen, Harold T. and Christina F. Gregg. 1970 "Changing Sex Norms in America and Scandinavia," *Journal of Marriage and the Family* 32 (November): 616–627.

Corry, John. 1966 "Current Sexual Behavior and Attitudes," in *An Analysis of Human Sexual Response*. Ruth and Edward Breecher, eds. New York: New American Library, pp. 283–289.

Cuber, John, 1972 "How New Ideas about Sex are Changing Our Lives," in *Intimate Life-Styles: Marriage and Its Alternatives*. John S. Delora and Jack R. Delora, eds. Pacific Palisades, Cal.: Goodyear Publishing Co., pp. 112–118.

Ellis, Albert. 1968 "The Ambiguity of Contemporary Sex Attitudes," in *Problems of Sex Behavior*. Edward Sagarin and Donald E. J. McNamara, eds. New York: Crowell, pp. 5–30.

Hunt, Morton. 1973–74. "Sexual Behavior in the Seventies," *Playboy* Oct., Nov., Dec., Jan., Feb., Mar.

Kaats, Gilbert R. and Keith E. Davis. 1970 "The Dynamics of Sexual Behavior of College Students," *Journal of Marriage and the Family* (Aug.) 390–399.

Kando, Thomas H. 1978 *Sexual Behavior and Family Life in Transition*. New York: Elsevier.

King, Karl. et al. 1977 "The Continuing Premarital Sexual Revolution Among College Females," *J. Marriage and the Family* (Aug.): 455–459.

Kinsey, A.C., W.B. Pomeroy, C.E. Martin and P.H. Gebhard. 1953 *Sexual Behavior in the Human Female*. Philadelphia: W. B. Saunders.

Lelyveld, Joseph. 1979 "The New Sexual Revolution," in *Human Sexuality in a Changing Society*. Graham B. Spanier, ed., Minneapolis: Burgess, pp. 75–76.

Leslie, Gerald R. 1973 *The Family in Social Context*. 2nd ed. New York: Oxford.

Mailer, N. 1948 *The Naked and the Dead*. New York: Holt, Rinehart & Winston.

Mazur, Ronald. 1977 "The Double Standard and People's Liberation," in *Marriage and Alternatives: Explaining Intimate Relationships*. Roger W. Libby and Robert N. Whitehurst, eds. Glenview, Ill.: Scott, Foresman, pp. 205–215.

Merton, Robert K. and Robert Nisbet, eds. 1976 *Contemporary Social Problems*. 4th ed. New York: Harcourt Brace Jovanovich.

Mirande, Alfred M. 1975 *The Aged of Crisis: Deviance, Disorganization and Societal Problems*. New York: Harper & Row.

Packard, Vance. 1968 *The Sexual Wilderness: The Contem-*

porary Upheaval in Male-Female Relationships. New York: McKay.

Reiss, Ira L. 1960 *Premarital Sexual Standards in America.* New York: Free Press.

Reiss, Ira L. 1961 "Sexual Codes in Teen-Age Culture," in *Ann. Am. Acad. Pol. and Soc. Sci.* (Nov.): 53–62.

Reiss, Ira L. 1973 "How and Why America's Sex Standards are Changing," in *Sexual Development and Behavior.* Anne McCreary Juhasz, ed. Homewood, Ill.: The Dorsey Press, pp. 139–148.

Stoll, Clarice Stasz. *1978 Female and Male: Socialization, Social Roles and Social Structure.* 2nd ed. Dubuque, Iowa: Brown.

Winsor, K. 1944. *Forever Amber.* New York: Macmillan.

POPULAR "MESSAGE" SONG ON MOTHERHOOD UPSETS LIBERALS

Phyllis Schlafly

One of the top-10 rock records at the present time is "I've Never Been to Me," sung by Charlene and issued by Motown Records. And thereby hangs an amazing tale of ideology, timing, social trends and censorship.

The song was released in 1976. Its timing was wrong and it didn't catch on. Recently, a disc jockey played it one night and all his phone lines lit up with immediate enthusiasm. The song became an overnight sensation.

In the first two stanzas of the song, Charlene sings about her exotic life enjoying sexual encounters all over the world. She was living in a liberated "paradise" on earth. When she "ran out of places and friendly faces" in the United States, she continued her travels to Greece and Monte Carlo because she "had to be free." As she sings it, "I've been undressed by kings, and I've seen some things that a woman ain't s'posed to see."

But all the sexually liberated paradise didn't make her happy. She's all alone now and she's "crying for unborn children that might have made me complete." Hence, the refrain of the song, "I've been to paradise, but I've never been to me."

The lyrics give Charlene's personal advice to

From *Human Events* (June 5, 1982). Reprinted by permission.

the "discontented mother and the regimented wife" who fantasizes about the exciting life she doesn't have. Charlene wishes someone had told her the truth about real love before she wasted her youth on "lies."

Anyone who has been watching the lifestyle sections of metropolitan newspapers and the national magazines knows that stay-at-home motherhood now is "in"—especially for feminists in their 30s and 40s who have discovered that the calendar is catching up with them and that there is more to life than just having a well-paying career.

But this rock tune goes even farther. It implies that having a baby is necessary to make a women "complete." Even more remarkable, it says that real "truth" is not only in having a baby but in loving and living with only one man.

For years, teen-age girls have been taught just the opposite. Through a combination of peer pressure, classroom sex courses, "X"—and "R"—rated movies, suggestive TV programs, soft-porn literature and rock music, they've been taught that sex with any partner is okay if you feel comfortable about it, that housewives lead dull and unrewarding lives and that fulfillment for women means liberation from home, husband, family and children.

Now, at last, young women are hearing about the joys of a husband and children from a rock record. Times surely have changed. But, wait a minute, there's more to this story. As soon as "I've Never Been to Me" became a hit song, the liberals and the feminists caught on to its clear pro-family message and they set out to silence it.

A columnist for the *Washington Post* wrote an indignant column about it. He is all upset because "the pendulum is swinging back" to motherhood. He concludes that the song's popularity is a social commentary which proves that a "reaction has set in" to the feminist movement (which he says was good because it "shattered stereotypes" and it "liberated women").

Now comes the most interesting part of this story about the "motherhood song." After it became so popular and its message so clear, Motown Records accommodated the liberals by issuing a censored version of "I've Never Been to Me." Of course, Motown and the radio stations don't use the word "censored"; they call it the "edited version."

Now, at last, young women are hearing about the joys of a husband and children from a rock record. Times surely have changed.

If you tune in on your local adult rock radio stations, you will probably hear the song within a couple of hours of listening. You will find that some stations play the original version and some play the censored version. What has been censored out of the edited version is the middle part where Charlene interrupts her singing to talk straight to the housewife who thinks she is missing out on liberated living.

In the censored passage, Charlene says: "Hey, you know what paradise is? It's a lie, a fantasy we create about people and places as we like them to be. But you know what truth is? It's that little baby you're holding and it's that man you fought with this morning—the same one you're going to make love with tonight. That's truth; that's love."

"Censorship" is the current chic slogan of the liberals who today are trying to intimidate pro-family activists who object to obscenity, profanity, blasphemy, immorality and violence in textbooks, other school materials and television programming. It is clear that the liberals are like the thief who tries to conceal his crime by crying, "Stop, thief!" The pressure groups against motherhood and against traditional moral standards are really the most ruthless censors of all.

Photograph: Larry Robins

THE 1 MILLION TEENAGERS WHO GET PREGNANT EACH YEAR HAVE SOMETHING ELSE IN COMMON.

They watch 19½ hours of television a week.

Some of these teenagers bear unwanted children for which they are neither mentally nor physically prepared. Some seek an abortion. All of them will never be quite the same again.

We as concerned adults share a responsibility. To educate. To counsel.

Through the years, you as television programmers have filled them with a lot of information. Much of it good.

There's a lot of sex on television every day. Through you they may learn about sex. But through you they could also learn about sexual responsibility.

If you would like to help educate them through television, give us a call. Planned Parenthood helps to teach teenagers one of the most important lessons of their lives: how to be sexually responsible adults. And that makes us one of the best resources on this subject in the country.

So contact Planned Parenthood in your community, or call Timmi Pierce, vice president for communications, at (212) 541-7800.

After all, who else but you has 19½ hours of a teenager's undivided attention every week?

SUGGESTIONS FOR FURTHER READING

The following articles pertain to media depiction of sex:

Steven H. Chaffee and Michael J. Petrick, "Mass Communication and Sex." In *Using the Mass Media: Communication Problems in American Society*, New York: McGraw-Hill, 1975.

Robert Love, "The Retreat of the Skin Mags." *Washington Journalism Review*, November 1981, pp. 33–35. Love suggests that the baby boomers might be past the state of rapt interest in "girly" magazines.

Barry S. Sapolsky, "Sexual Acts and References on Prime-Time TV: A Two Year Look." *Southern Speech Communication Journal* 47, no. 2 (Winter 1982) pp. 212–26.

Tony Schwartz, "TV Pornography Boom." *New York Times Magazine*, September 13, 1981, p. 44.

J. N. Sprafkin et al., "Reactions to Sex on Television." *Public Opinion Quarterly*, 1980.

Also of interest:

H. J. Eysenck and D. K. Nias, *Sex, Violence and the Media*. New York: St. Martin's Press, 1978.

CHAPTER 14

Stereotyping

Media distortion of reality is especially troublesome when it leads to stereotyping of the sexes or minorities (racial, religious, and occupational).

Many people think that such stereotyping results from underrepresentation of the group in question. The first reading in this chapter shares this point of view: Christopher Connelly of *Rolling Stone* magazine feels that the segregated format of rock radio is a form of racism.

The second reading also addresses racial stereotyping. Its author, Mark Crispin Miller, is the television critic for the *New Republic* magazine. He feels that television aggravates the problem of racial tension by portraying racial problems in an overly sentimental and simplistic way that obscures current realities.

The third reading deals with one facet of sexual stereotyping: Mary Alice Kellogg of *TV Guide* points out that television almost always portrays blondes as dumb.

The final reading is a full-page editorial ad placed by United Technologies Corporation in several publications. The ad protests the stereotyping of business people.

ROCK RADIO: A CASE OF RACISM?

Christopher Connelly

Rock & roll radio, known as album-oriented radio or AOR, has become racially segregated. In the words of one programmer, AOR stations across the country have "bleached the airwaves" by refusing to play black music in any form. "There is what appears to be a color line," says Clive Davis, president of Arista Records. "It's woeful." "It's unconscionable," echoes Ron Fell, managing editor of *The Gavin Report*, a radio trade publication. "It's the single largest blemish on the face of American radio."

On the typical AOR station, you can hear the Rolling Stones' version of "Going to a Go-Go," but not Smokey Robinson's; Journey, Styx and Foreigner, but not Prince, Michael Jackson or Diana Ross; the funk experiments of Talking Heads or Queen, but never Rick James or Chic. With only a few exceptions—Jimi Hendrix, Gary U.S. Bonds—the door appears shut to black performers. "The very format that lobbied for tolerance . . . in its first days," wrote Mike Perkins, program director at Pittsburgh's WYDD, in a

From *Rolling Stone* (December 9, 1982). Reprinted by permission.

blistering piece for an industry journal, "has produced a 'master race' mentality regarding the pigmentative desirability of musical roots."

Though AOR advocates argue that their lily-white format attracts a more affluent listener, thereby making their stations more appealing to advertisers, the existing evidence does not support their contention. In fact, it seems that AOR stations could *improve* their ratings by programming black music. In several areas, including New York City, stations that air a combination of black and white music—"urban contemporary" stations—have notched higher ratings than their AOR rivals.

It's the single largest blemish on the face of American radio.

AOR programmers also claim that any attempt to mix in black music meets with resounding—and racist—disapproval from their audience. They say that radio is a mirror, not a leader, of an audience. But a growing sentiment within the music and advertising communities suggests that to survive in the coming years, AOR will have to change dramatically.

The situation is deeply troubling to black artists who are eager to have their music heard by a white audience. Lionel Richie, whose records are played on every radio format except AOR, recalls that one Washington D.C. music director told Richie's group, the Commodores, that she couldn't play their record because it was "too black." Says Richie, "I turned to the guys in the group and said, "'Gentlemen, we don't have a chance in radio, 'cause there ain't nothing here *but* black.'" One-time Jackson Five member Jermaine Jackson, whose "Let's Get Serious" was seen by some as the inspiration for Olivia Newton-John's smash "Physical," says he's baffled by the racial separation. If Michael McDonald can get airplay on black stations, he asks, why can't black artists be heard on AOR?

This trend doesn't only affect black performers; it also extends to white acts that make music some consider black-sounding. Artists from Blondie to Hall and Oates have had difficulty getting their funk-flavored compositions played on AOR. Daryl Hall, in fact, seems rather upset about it: in a recent interview in *Musician* magazine, Hall termed the "disco sucks" movement of a few years back "a real racist statement. . . . And what's going on in AOR right now, too. Which is a dinosaur. This heavy-metal revival . . . that's not rock & roll. That's *part* of rock & roll. What we do is just as much rock & roll as what they do."

AOR programmers admit that the music they play is made almost entirely by white people, but they reject the charge of racism. "It comes down to a style of music," says Chuck Du Coty of WIYY in Baltimore. "Our audience won't go for anything funk-oriented."

"If you play [Stevie Wonder's] 'Sir Duke' or something like that," adds WYDD's Perkins, "you get people calling up and saying, 'Get that nigger music off the radio.'"

For those who grew up listening to radio in the sixties and early seventies, this racial schism is shocking. In the heyday of Top Forty radio—roughly from the arrival of the Beatles to the arrival of disco—black music happily coexisted with white music on the hit-singles format. Meanwhile, "progressive FM" stations aired everything from Frank Zappa to Earth, Wind and Fire. Racial considerations were unimportant; the FM stations played anything they liked, and Top Forty stations played anything that was a hit.

Many attribute today's problem to the polarizing effects of the disco phenomenon of the late seventies. The disco stations that sprang up in response to that music's overwhelming popularity took most of their listeners from Top Forty stations, practically obliterating Top Forty overnight. Meanwhile, many of those who disliked the insistent, beats-per-minute disco sound were white progressive-FM listeners, who tended to lump all black music into the disco category. The strong reactions to disco—and to a lesser extent, the punk movement of the same era—led to a dramatic fragmentation of the radio audience and drove listeners into strictly defined musical camps. Disco fans listened to urban-contemporary stations; softer music, both white and black, turned up on "mellow" stations, known as adult-contemporary; and AOR became the province of young white males whose favorite song was "Stairway to Heaven."

Bill Hard, editor of the *Friday Morning Quarterback Album Report*, a widely read radio tip sheet, remembers the old days. "The feeling was that if you played a lot of different types of music, you had a shot at a legitimate eighteen- to thirty-four-year-old audience. And it worked: we'd play Stevie Wonder and the Brothers Johnson and LTD, and it would be fine. But by the late seventies, the philosophy became super-serving your core audience, eighteen- to twenty-four-year-old white males." Other authorities say the actual demographic is lower, perhaps twelve-to twenty-four-year-olds.

"We were playing Harold Melvin and the Blue Notes, Van McCoy, unbelievable stuff," recalls Larry Berger of WPLJ in New York. "We were also playing James Taylor, Joni Mitchell and Carly Simon. Then along came the adult-contemporary format, and Carly Simon and James Taylor became its main thrust; and along came the urban-contemporary stations, and their thing was Harold Melvin and way beyond that. Radio became more specialized."

But AOR's specialized format may, in fact, be hurting it, at least in terms of ratings. In New York City, admittedly an atypical market, all three AOR stations finished well behind three urban-contemporary stations in the summer Arbitron ratings. Maye James, music director of WBLS, an urban-contemporary station in New York, avers that AOR's reluctance to stretch its musical boundaries has significantly helped her station. "With all the people going to the clubs, we're almost forced to play what we play. It doesn't matter if it's black or white."

Because of their larger audience, urban-contemporary stations can charge more for their commercial time—and they do. But perhaps more significant is the fact that urban-contemporary stations are very strong in the demographic areas most important to AOR: eighteen- to twenty-four-year-old men. In New York, WBLS was significantly outrated only by WAPP, an AOR station that was commercial-free during the summer. And in the more frequently used demographic segment, men eighteen to thirty-four, all three urban-contemporary stations outperformed their AOR rivals.

AOR advocates argue that their lily-white format attracts a more affluent listener, thereby making their stations more appealing to advertisers.

AOR boosters argue that their average listener is likely to be more affluent than an urban-contemporary one, and thus more attractive to a potential advertiser. But Charles Trubia of the Ted Bates Advertising Agency, which does commercials for Panasonic components and the U.S. Navy, maintains that the only difference is an ethnic one. "For the kind of goods we have, the buying power will cover either format. We're not selling big-ticket items to eighteen- to twenty-four-year-olds."

But some observers, like the *Album Report's* Hard, don't think AOR stations feel threatened enough to change. "A lot of AOR stations have done quite well with a white-rock approach," says Hard, "which doesn't make them interested in broadening their base. They feel that as long as they've got competition that is pretty white or pretty rock & roll, they're not willing to take a chance."

Trubia, though, thinks AOR stations are asking for trouble by *not* stretching. "AOR is a shrinking format," he declares. Could AOR add new listeners by playing black music? "If they expand, they're gonna lose a lot of their core audience. But they'd probably be better off doing that, because I'm not too sure such a narrow audience has the buying power the advertisers are looking for. Why compete with other AORs for the shrinking amount of market when a station could expand and generate an audience that other advertisers would be interested in?"

Radio consultant Lee Abrams agrees. "The rocker crowd is getting smaller and younger," he says. "If stations want to get anybody over eighteen, they're going to have to open up." New types of AOR formats are the answer, in Abrams' view, such as the new-music philosophy pioneered by Rick Carroll at KROQ in Los Angeles. Abrams himself is developing a similar format at WLIR in New York and KFOG in San Francisco. These stations emphasize the dance-oriented Anglo synth pop of such groups as Yaz, the Leisure Process and the Human League—formats, says Abrams, that are made-to-order for the reintroduction of black music on AOR. "We're going through a real renaissance," he says. "In five years, a lot of programmers will be out of business."

Until then, though, the struggle continues. Donna Summer has a song entitled "Protection" on her new album. It was written by Bruce Springsteen and features him on lead guitar. What has it done for AOR? "Nothing," says Hard, who says he personally likes the song. "It takes more than Springsteen's name and guitar to get Donna Summer on AOR."

BLACK AND WHITE

Mark Crispin Miller

The word "racism" ought to be as complex as the tangled thing which it denotes; and so it should be handled carefully, as a delicate gauge to help assess an old and varied problem. All too often, however, the word is used as a blunt instrument, cutting conversations short and making people circumspect. Thus wielded, it is not an analytic or descriptive term, but mere accusation, based on a limited conception of racism. It is, first of all, a reduction of the whole range and history of our interracial struggles to the crude oppression of one side by the other. And this "racism" is as abstract as it is one-sided. It is not a social or historical phenomenon but merely a dark impulse, atavistic and irrational, lurking in every white heart and nowhere else.

Although the charge of "racism" is ostensibly intended to expose the secret thoughts and deeds of bigotry, it is actually a means of concealment. It inhibits frank discussion of what really happens between blacks and whites today; it demands the suppression of any experience that

From *New Republic* (October 28, 1981). Reprinted by permission.

might contradict the sentimental myth of simple, unilateral persecution. The charge of "racism," in other words, forces us to ignore the very conflicts that have kept racism going: it demands not that we resolve our differences, but that we repress them, and this insistence on repression has perverted all our thinking about race. What we often consider "racist" nowadays is not the mistreatment of one race by another, but the mere acknowledgment of differences between blacks and whites—different histories, different cultures, unequal origins within these borders.

There are more middle-class blacks than there used to be, and whites often are very tolerant. There are other important improvements besides. But old conflicts remain. By repressing those qualities, we have not simply failed to eliminate them—we have actually made them worse, maintaining the old inequities under an up-to-date disguise. In dying to escape the uneasy deadlock of slaves and masters, we have stereotyped ourselves back into it, thanks to that simplistic "racism" which we all abhor. Many blacks now present themselves as angry victims of (white) racism, and as nothing more; and many whites, guilt-ridden and uncertain, eagerly defer to that black self-image, taking all responsibility, as masters must. This national psychodrama may seem like a sign of progress, but it perpetuates the worst aspects of a racist society—all blacks as victims, all whites as victimizers, the two neurotically united forever.

Strong contrasts, lots of pathos, easy distinctions between weak (good) and strong (bad)—this is the stuff of television, which reflects (and half creates) these crude impressions. Television illuminates our racial woes, just as it illuminates our other social problems: inadvertently, by exemplifying (and so prolonging) the very flaws which it purports to analyze.

Take *America—Black and White*, a 90-minute documentary on our racial problems produced by NBC and broadcast on September 9. The title couldn't have been more fitting. For one thing, it summed up the program's conclusion that "America still remains, in many ways, two nations," that blacks are still outcasts in this free country. And, unfortunately, the title also provides an apt critical judgment of the show itself, which turned the recent history of race relations into prime-time melodrama reducing complexities to black and white.

"Reported by Garrick Utley, with Emery King," the show swept far and wide across American society, moving from the suburbs of New York to Harvard University, from the rural South to Watts and Detroit, and elsewhere. And yet, despite its travels, the show got nowhere. Its conclusion was a simple one: that America's blacks are still suffering because of "racial attitudes—prejudice, racism."

Although this doesn't explain much (at the end of 90 minutes, we might expect more complicated arguments) this evocation of a vague "racism" does have a certain aesthetic advantage for the purposes of video. Like many other shows, *America—Black and White* used "racism" as the basis for a series of contrived dramatic situations, featuring blacks and whites as two crude opponents: villains and victims. It was social criticism at the low level of *Roots*. Although the program told us little about racism in our society, it revealed a lot about the subtle sort of racism that pervades television news. The program, in fact, was typical of television (news and "entertainment" shows alike), which usually belittles blacks in the very act of taking their side, while dismissing whites entirely. It may be the most dangerous sort of racism, because it is subtle, seems benevolent, and is often expressed in shows that come across as true reflections of "the way it is."

This sentimental racism works through dual caricature. All of America's whites, we infer, are equally devious, heartless, and remote, united in their groundless "prejudice." White students at Harvard, white parents in New York were not to be distinguished from the likes of Strom Thurmond and the Ku Klux Klan. And while the whites came across as a pitiless horde, the blacks were, time and again, embodied in some single pitiable figure—The Black, an eternal victim who suffers beautifully.

Of course, this broad device demanded that the whites be utterly dehumanized. The show began with a report on Rosedale, New York, a once "all-white community" whose original residents now feel themselves hemmed in by a growing black population. First we saw the bad guys. "These are some of the white voices of Rosedale," Utley said, introducing some grainy footage of several tense, middle-aged whites sitting around and complaining about affirmative action. Utley provided the background. In 1977, he said, the local school "had three black students for every white one. White parents said the school was overcrowded, that their children were being harassed by blacks." The whites kept trying to start another school, with a black enrollment of only 40 percent, and the blacks, assisted by the federal government, defeated all those efforts. With implicit disapproval, the program showed a few more snippets of white discontent. "I won't send my child into a school where he's going to be a token white," one woman protested. "Why? I don't feel it's a healthy atmosphere."

This is, obviously, a case of "prejudice." Isn't it? Consider Utley's formulation of the whites' grievances: "*White parents said* the school was overcrowded, that their children were being harassed by blacks." By compressing the charges into a sort of list, the sentence implies that the whites were coming up with a lot of desperate excuses. Its emphasis is not on the atmosphere at school, but on the white parents' claim that the atmosphere was bad; such emphasis has the effect of making the claim seem dishonest. And was it? Were the children being harassed? It would seem to be a crucial question, one that a good reporter would pursue, and yet the makers of this documentary (who can afford to send their children off to private schools) did not bother to address it.

"In the past," Utley hurried on, the whites "would have moved out," but today "they can't afford to. Since they cannot escape blacks, they have to face them—face David Fleming." Cut to Fleming, a youngish and attractive black man, talking in his living room: "I call them the Archie Bunker Syndrome group," he smiles. "They are afraid of any change." Fleming is "a salesman of surgical instruments," Utley said, who came to Rosedale "looking for a larger home for his growing family." With Fleming as its momentary hero, the show began cross-cutting from Fleming as he talked about Rosedale to Fleming as he drove his son to Little League, coaching all the way (" . . . and *never* take your eye off the ball!") After this fancy bit of montage, the program took us to "the graduation ceremony at a school for gifted children," where Fleming's daughter gave the valedictory: "We should set our goals high and strive to meet them," etc.

So these were some of the blacks whom Rosedale's whites "cannot escape"! Now why should anyone want to "escape" such people? Is it possible that David Fleming and his gifted daughter like to roam the school grounds, wielding surgical instruments? Obviously not. What we were meant to think, however, is equally absurd, and much more destructive.

Fleming was used as Sidney Poitier was used in *Guess Who's Coming to Dinner?*, and as so many blacks have been used in films and on television: not as a sterling character who might make racists feel ashamed, but as a means to deny what whites find most terrifying about blacks. The image of Fleming was meant as reassurance that blacks are never violent, that the black underclass is not dangerous, because blacks and whites are exactly the same, "under the skin." Fleming seemed, in fact, whiter than the whites—peppy entrepreneur, family man, owner of a house and car, etc.; a solid citizen, as opposed to those "white voices" that refuse to vanish. If it weren't for "racism," in other words, Our Way of Life could contain all differences, by painlessly erasing them. And yet, in fact, it is not our System that erases differences, but television, with its constant repressions of the unpleasant.

In shows like this, television represses the real effects of slavery, even while purporting to lament that institution. By insisting that blacks and whites are entirely alike, television denies the cultural barriers that slavery necessarily created; barriers that have hardened over years and years, and that still exist, exacerbating all those complicated hatreds that must endure between masters and slaves. These hatreds have never been more intense and debilitating than they are now, as blacks and whites commingle in our cities, many blacks becoming more frustrated, many whites discovering what it feels like to be openly menaced by the other side. In other words, both races suffer. Television, meanwhile, constantly simplifies these hatreds, calling them "racism" and blaming them all on one side: *America—Black and White* presented whites as the detached authors of black suffering, as if this country were no different from South Africa; and all that's needed, the show implied, is for whites to have a change of heart, as in some old Frank Capra movie. It is not a useful message, or a timely one. While many of yesterday's white liberals are now edgy and disillusioned, feeling they have learned a bitter lesson, this "documentary" merely preached these misconceptions: that blacks are the only ones in pain, that whites are the only ones who hate.

The real crime of Rosedale's whites, then, was that they called attention to those differences which television labors to repress. They had the gall to feel menaced by a black majority, when we all know, from watching television, that blacks are incapable of the sort of resentment that can turn violent; that blacks, in other words, aren't really human. For this inconvenient behavior, the whites were appropriately punished by the program, which presented them as irrelevant, ludicrous, "prejudiced," "the Archie Bunker Syndrome group," "afraid of any change." If "racism," as we often hear, entails the demotion of some ethnic group to the status of nonpersons, then this program was racist in its presentation of the whites.

And yet, as broadly "pro-black" as the program seemed, its depiction of the blacks was entirely offensive, and far more damaging than the dismissal of those dim "white voices." The show offered us a series of black protagonists, each one a sort of tragic hero, slightly overplayed. Fleming was the first of these noble underdogs. He emerged as the star of Rosedale in the opening report's last scene, a bitter school board hearing where the whites tried, once again, to regain the *status quo* ante. The show's partisanship was now unmistakable, the cameras following the proceedings from the blacks' points of view, and clearly lionizing David Fleming. He was shot from a very low angle, so that he seemed gigantic, overpoweringly righteous, as he orated to his allies in the familiar pulpit-thumping style: "You will walk," he intoned, with biblical passion and unclarity, "and you will serve as juggernauts! And no Dolores Grant, or poor other ignorant, bigoted racists, whether they be on this school board, or whether they be walking with white sheets in dark alleys!" After finishing, to wild applause, Fleming sprang up to the table at the front of the room, where the school board members were sitting, and got into a shouting match with one of them, as the camera followed close behind him, catching all the fuss. And then the meeting broke up acrimoniously, blacks and whites exchanging jeers and shrill charges.

Who won? It is another crucial question. The images suggested black defeat—black people shouting at those dour whites up on the dais, blacks leaving the room, bitterly denouncing their apparent persecutors—and, more importantly, David Fleming, the blacks' representative, was acting like a loser. Clearly egged on by the presence of the camera at his stomach, he struck the familiar pose of noble struggle; and when he leapt to confront his oppressors, he appeared to be acting from a sense of uncontrollable frustration. It seemed a familar spectacle: the blacks going down in glorious defeat as usual. It was therefore downright jarring, and almost incredible, to hear Utley say that the blacks had won, that the whites had lost—because television teaches us that blacks don't know how to win.

The other reports were similarly cast. At Harvard, we learned, most of the 502 black students were recently angered by the release of a document called the Klitgaard Report, drafted by a special assistant to the president: "Blacks and women scored high on entrance exams," the report concluded, "but did not perform well once admitted to the university." Harvard should therefore "not compete so heavily for blacks," who might do better at "slightly lesser institutions."

The release of this report was represented as another act of cruel racism, and, here again, the point was made through strokes of drama. Was the Klitgaard Report inaccurate? Or just impolitic? And does it have to mean that blacks and women are dumber than white males? Rather than deal with such questions, our reporters simply found themselves another personable underdog: a pretty coed named Rosalynn Roos, who spoke at length of her depression. Of course, her lonely sorrow had to appear against the backdrop of a cold white multitude, and so there were shots of various white undergraduates—more "white voices"—questioning the wisdom of racial quotas; these were "conservative whites," said Emery King, without explaining what that meant. The report ended with a group of black students singing dolefully on some steps.

The show's final segment was the strangest. There was footage of some vicious geeks at a Klan rally in Connecticut, and then we saw what was presumably a corrective to such atrocity: Dr. Charles King, "president of the Urban Crisis Center in Atlanta," goes around "conducting sensitivity seminars on race," and we saw some of his work. King, a towering boor with a voice like the blast of a hostile tuba, stood before a mixed group of college students, provoking the whites with theatrical explosions of self-pity. "What do you mean by 'oppressing'?" asked one earnest white type. "Am I oppressing black people?" "Yes, because you asked, 'What is oppression?'" King bellowed illogically. "Since you don't *know* what oppresson is, *you* are one of the persons doing it through your damn ignorance, *fool*!" King's purpose, Utley chimed in, is "to get whites and blacks to face their own racial attitudes," which is one way of putting it, although it looked like just another est-type scam, with King mooing belligerently at his shifty white viewers: "If *you* would *feel* the problem, then *we* would not *have* a problem as a *race*!"

Between the dramas of Fleming, Roos, and King, there were other, sadder moments, as various destitute persons came and went, none of them star material—young men who seemed old and broken, people who can't learn to read. The show punctuated these appearances with shots of nasty-looking politicians (Strom Thurmond, Ronald Reagan, Orrin Hatch), which made the villains/victims thesis seem pretty accurate. All the show's blacks, in other words, were meant to come across as *poignant* figures, whether charismatic or pathetic, whether well-to-do or on the brink.

Although contrived with the best intentions, this sort of presentation can only work against black progress. Watching such shows, we begin to assume that blacks can't ever win, that their plight is eternal, a fact of nature. Apparently, David Fleming and Rosalynn Roos, for all their personal successes, still inhabit that nether region of shanties and welfare. And, conversely, the black poor are not remarkable for their poverty, their membership in a certain social class—a condition which could, presumably, be changed—but for their blackness, a condition of permanent woe.

As presented in this and other programs, the blacks seem unlikely to improve their lot because they seem to take to suffering with such soulful gusto. The show consistently aestheticized the black plight; the Harvard students sang, in their unhappiness; B. B. King sang "There's Got to Be a Better World"; and there were those rousing theatrical moments when King and Fleming hammed it up. This kind of thing may be inevitable on television, which will always use the best (i.e., broadest) shots; and, to their credit, the makers of such programs surely want to make a strong impression. But whatever the reasons, it must be recognized that television has impaired the black movement by turning the various black styles—behavioral, rhetorical, musical—into stereotypic signs of authenticity. Television seems "right on" for bringing us, say, shows like *Good Times* or the ranting of a Dr. Charles King. Such hopped up displays give the false impression that progress has occurred simply because blacks appear on television.

No one is innocent in this process. If television has transformed black politics into a stale docudrama, it is because blacks have enjoyed the opportunity, and whites have enjoyed the show. Indeed, to explain it any differently—to say that blacks have simply been "oppressed" by the medium—would be inexcusably racist, suggesting that blacks are too passive and too feeble to be held accountable for their behavior. It is an odious assumption, and a familiar one; and it was the guiding assumption of this show.

"If *you* would *feel* the problem, then *we* would not *have* a problem as a *race*!" Not only is this formula naive, implying that one's emotional response can overcome political and cultural realities; but it is profoundly slavish. It suggests that blacks are obsessed by whites, the weak waiting angrily for the strong to do something; and so it bespeaks the surrender of all responsibility in an outburst of blame and self-pity: "All my problems are your fault!"

The program did not just provide a forum for these sentiments, but actively encouraged them in its quest for the pathetic. However, the program exploited these displays of bitterness for more than merely sensational purposes. These images helped to convey the show's real message, which was that blacks are weak and need to be protected—by the white viewer, by the television industry, by the government. If the villains/victims structure places all the blame on the villains' side, it looks there too for all effective action. Blacks are like unto little children, the show implied throughout; they can't do right, and so, of course, they can't do wrong.

"Meet Augustus Williams's family," said Utley somberly over footage of some children in a squalid shack. "He and Betty, the woman he lives with, have ten children." "This is the home of Carrie Washington," he said at another such point. "She is 31 years old, has nine children, and no husband." These reports on black poverty in Mississippi made very clear that these people are in real distress; but Utley seemed to exploit those sufferers to make a condescending point. He simply took for granted the existence of all those hungry children, never asking the parents why they had so many little ones under such circumstances, never bothering to analyze those circumstances. He implied in short that these people were absolutely helpless, so lame that it was pointless to suggest that they try to help themselves, even a little. Such reports were meant as a pitch for further government assistance, but they went too far, depicting the poor as gentle, feeble animals.

Thus Utley, all unknowing, helped to perpetuate the very misery which he was trying to redress, by endorsing, perhaps even celebrating that helplessness which is the basic problem. The show itself was implicated in the same contradiction. It actually exalted itself as the protector of those huddled masses, who, it appeared, would have curled up and died if it weren't for the intercession of the news people; the show, in other words, seemed to be standing in for the reluctant government. This was the general sense of the documentary, with its eagerness to champion the blacks, and at times it became explicit. We followed an illiterate youth named Cortez Walker as he looked despondently for work. "On this day," said Emery King, Walker "was turned away from two other locations before he tried a Burger King downtown."

"What kind of trouble do you have?" asked King. "I have trouble, like, pronouncing some of the words on the application," Walker answered. Then, in voice-over, King made this heartrending revelation: "His only experience—some culinary training in reform school. But, had we not been there, the management would never have known about it," because Walker couldn't read the word "culinary." Then, under the camera's watchful eye, Walker turned in his application, albeit half-heartedly.

It was a sad scene, and it was very noble of the crew to step in and help; but this was small compensation for the general destruction which television has helped to bring about among its young black viewers. If they can't read, it may have something to do with their having grown up watching hours and hours of television, which, *Sesame Street* to the contrary, does not do much for literacy. If they feel powerless and bitter, it may have something to do with that flood of bright commercials, which tempts them endlessly with visions of a million things they can't hope to buy. If they feel that their anger is meaningless, it may have something to do with that television world that shines on forever, without showing the slightest trace of their unbearable rage. And if they feel isolated, and have no feeling of community outside the gangs, it could have something to do with the general disappearance of all community into our gray-lit living rooms, and with the hastening disintegraton of the black movements, which television has helped to bring about. In short, the subtlest unpleasantness which television has repressed in its years of "covering" the racial issue may be television itself, which makes slaves of those who entrust it with their freedom.

WHY BLONDES AND BRAINS DON'T MIX

Mary Alice Kellogg

First, a confession: I am a blonde. A real blonde (yes, they do exist). Since 1955, I have been searching my television dial, looking for fair-haired role models. I can tell you that this has not been a happy quest. All the women who are intelligent, level-headed, wise, happily married/well adjusted—those TV women who embody virtue, truth and beauty—have all been . . . brunette. Jane Wyatt. Marlo Thomas. Mary Tyler Moore. Rhoda. For starters.

By contrast, TV blondes (Marie Wilson, Donna Douglas in my formative years) are embarrassingly underdressed, miraculously overdeveloped, intellectually void and distressingly gullible. To use the term "dolt" is an act of charity; "airhead" is almost a compliment. It is time to tackle seriously the issue of why Joyce DeWitt is reasonably smart in *Three's Company* and Suzanne Somers jiggled. Why did Kate Jackson and Jaclyn Smith get all the brilliant lines and Farrah the wet T-shirt? In one of the darker days in history, *Mary Tyler Moore*'s blonde Georgette was so supremely stupid she married Ted Baxter.

On television, age does not necessarily lead to wisdom. Jiggle TV may be giving way to giggle TV these days, but the result is sadly the same: the fair-haired are still not getting a fair intellectual shake (nor a fair wardrobe shake: no wonder blondes jiggle; they're usually so skimpily dressed they have to jump up and down just to keep warm). Private Benjamin's cutesy antics set the cause back 200 years. In *Bosom Buddies*, fellas pursue Donna Dixon, a sexy, breathy blonde whose jump suits are often two sizes too small. *Too Close for Comfort* deals my cause the ultimate blow: multidimensional Dad has silver hair, sensible Mom is a redhead, serious career daughter No. 1 is a brunette and daughter No. 2—she of the tight sweaters, loose lip and teeny brain is . . . you guessed it.

In desperation, I talked to network executives, producers, casting directors and writers, asking them one burning question: Why? Their first reaction was one of universal embarrassment, followed by a spate of wells, ers and . . . come-to-*think*-of-its. With the exception of an NBC spokeswoman and a Warner Bros. executive who were downright hostile (this sort of thing just doesn't exist, they sputtered), the chagrined majority admitted the validity of my observations. "A lot of this stems from the Marilyn Monroe era sexpots and the image just stayed that way," explained Geri Windsor, executive director of talent for MTM. "Actually, I never thought about the blonde question before."

Michael Ross, executive producer of *Three's Company*, hadn't either, but nonetheles gave a lofty interpretation. "As far back as we all go, the dizzy one was always a blonde. Just look at the *colors*. There is a lightness, an airiness, about blond. There is a somberness about brunette. That's it, psychologically."

Howard Gewirtz has been on both sides of the flaxen fence. He was story editor for *The Associates*, the only series in recent memory that featured an intelligent blonde (Shelley Smith, taste-

From *TV Guide* (February 20, 1982). Reprinted by permission.

fully dressed, played a lawyer in that one) . . . and yes, the series folded. Gewirtz was also a producer of *Bosom Buddies*, where it was assumed that a blonde would play the not entirely bright love object. "People just seem to be comfortable with blondes being in the Marilyn Monroe image," Gewirtz sighs. "It seems to be a much-utilized, well-worn stereotype in American culture."

Gewirtz also brought up the television demand for quick typecasting. "There is a great degree of stereotyping in television characters, which goes beyond the blonde/brunette thing, and this is a larger problem." Hugh Wilson, executive producer of *WKRP in Cincinnati*, agrees, and says that this happens because "it's a sink-or-swim-in-three-airings situation, and the characters that catch on quickly are, unfortunately, the stereotypes."

The real fun began when, after blaming history and the limitations of the industry, those interviewed started to blame each other. Using a logic that by comparison would make the most vapid TV blonde look like a philosophy Ph.D., network executives said that the production companies that supply programs are at fault. The producers, in turn, blame the networks. "Networks for sure have the idea that the blonde is a sex symbol," says Michael Ross, "and the networks, of course, influence cast approval." Howard Gewirtz says, "I've never seen it written down that someone should be played as a blonde, but the networks might specify what they want in factors that are alost computerized stereotypes. The producer would never specify."

Producers also blame casting directors, who blame the writers. "Many times we get our directions from the scripts," says MTM's Geri Windsor, "but often their input comes down from the networks. If one show is successful with a dumb blonde, they'll want more." Writers agree with this last, and the argument comes full circle back to the network doorstep.

All interviewed said the situation was deplorable, of course. But only one brave soul was candid enough to admit the practice was going on in his immediate vicinity. Says Peter Greenberg, producer for ABC Circle Films: "Many of the blonde actresses who come in tend to be a little dippy—not because they *are*, but because they feel they have to be."

Loni Anderson's *WKRP* character may be the only current exception to the dumb-blonde rule. Jennifer is memorable because, as the smartest character at the station, she is also blonde—a direct contrast to stereotype. "Going in, we didn't want a blonde bimbo in that role," says Hugh Wilson. "We wanted her to be smart and we didn't specify she should be a blonde, just that she be 'shockingly beautiful'." Anderson herself says, "That's why I wanted to do it so badly, to fight that whole stupid blonde image." Anderson admits that, after 30 years as a brunette, "the lighter my hair got, the more work I got." She still sees an uphill fight for the fair-haired to come into their TV intellectual own because "there's something more vulnerable, less threatening and more cuddly about a blonde. You do have to prove yourself more."

Jennifer may be smart, but she still sports the airhead's clingy knit/fishnet/spandex wardrobe. Office dressing this isn't. Those who create, write and cast television series seem sincere enough and contrite enough on this issue. Yes, they are working in a medium that latches onto stereotypes. But if they really were helpless in this department, Orientals would play only houseboys and blacks only dimwitted domestics. Those stereotypes were blown away years ago; why is there a double standard for blondes?

The eternal optimist, I still await the day when a brunette will play a real cretin. But I'm not holding my breath—all the industry movers and shakers I interviewed, even the baldish ones, were dark-haired. You figure it out.

Crooks and Clowns on TV

See the dastard. Hiss at him. See the dolt. Hoot at him. They're both businessmen, TV variety.

In the skimpy fare served up as network entertainment night after night, the business world is peopled mostly by ne'er-do-wells and nincompoops. Likely as not, businessmen and women are portrayed on the tube as schemers and lawbreakers, a la J.R. Ewing, or else they're bubbleheads bumbling about and mouthing off for laughs, in the manner of Archie Bunker.

Such are the key gleanings of a study, first of its kind ever done, looking into the way television depicts people in business. The study found that two out of every three businessmen on television come across as foolish, greedy, or evil. In the prime-time view, over half of all corporate chiefs commit illegal acts, ranging from fraud to murder. Some 45% of all business activities are shown as illicit. Only 3% of TV business people behave in ways that are socially and economically productive.

The study, titled *Crooks, Conmen and Clowns: Businessmen in TV Entertainment,* was done by The Media Institute, a Washington-based research organization that seeks to improve the level and quality of media coverage of business and economic affairs. If the institute's researchers wound up their work bug-eyed and babbling, that's understandable. They peered at 200 episodes of the top 50 series on ABC, CBS, and NBC: sitcoms, shoot-'em-ups, dramas, and the like. The sample excluded all specials, sporting events, and news programs.

Analyzing the shows' content and characters, the institute confirmed what some of us in business have long been squirming about: As pictured by the floppy-necked quiche nibblers who dream up network series, most businessmen are either blackguards or buffoons. "Businessmen on prime-time television are consistently shown in an unflattering light," The Media Institute said. "Sixty-seven percent are portrayed in a negative manner—as criminals, fools, or greedy or malevolent egotists—while only 25% are shown in a positive light."

The bigger the business, the more unfavorably its practitioners are painted. The leaders of large companies tend to be cast as out-and-out crooks, lesser executives as mere miscreants, and small businessmen as dimwits. In TV's vision of business, ethics are about as rare as rowboats in the Sahara.

Why the perverse portrayals? Leonard J. Theberge, president of The Media Institute, points out that TV entertainment adheres to a simplistic format of good versus bad. In years past, "bad" was personified by such societal stereotypes as minorities, ethnic groups, and women. Happily, such stereotypes have all but been eliminated. Still, the bad-guy slot remains to be filled Business folks, it seems, make suitably handy villains and knuckleheads.

Theberge notes, too, the existence of "cultural reasons which might explain a bias by TV writers against businessmen. For example, it is not a new phenomenon for creative artists to look down on the commercial sector."

Two ironies obtrude. One is that the networks whose shows project businessmen as scoundrels and jesters are themselves commercial enterprises run by, yes, businessmen. The other is that the programs denigrating business are supported by advertising dollars from—you guessed it—business.

SUGGESTIONS FOR FURTHER READING

There is a large body of literature on the stereotyping of women and minorities. Interested students might want to read Chapter 8 of the first edition of *Mass Media Issues*, especially E. Simson's "Stereotyping of Women on Television." Simson analyzed the first-run serialized crime dramas from one recent television season and found that "in general, women were present less frequently than men. When present, they were more incompetent, silly, dependent, and passive—much less likely to be either the heroine or the villain." She also found that "the most prevalent occupation was prostitution."

Many critics feel that the role of women has improved significantly, at least in some areas. See, for example, Mary B. Cassata and Niki Scher, "You've Come a Long Way, Baby . . . from Minnie Mouse to Wonder Woman." In Mary B. Cassata and Molefi K. Asanti, *Mass Communication: Principles and Practices* New York: MacMillan, 1979, pp. 203–17. Also: Delores Mitchel, "Women Libeled: Women's Cartoons of Women," *Journal of Popular Culture* 14, no. 4 (Spring 1981): 597–610, and Molly Haskell, "Women in the Movies Grow Up," *Psychology Today*, January 1983, pp. 18–27.

Conflicting viewpoints on the stereotyping of blacks are presented in the first edition of *Mass Media Issues*: Roscoe C. Brown's "Let's Uproot TV's Image of Blacks," and John J. O'Connor's "Toward Balancing the Black Image." Another interesting article on race issues is: John De Mott, "White Racism in the Newspaper," *Masthead*, 33, no. 4 (Winter 1982): 6–11. This professor of journalism describes what he calls "our country's most common form of mental illness" and how the press is affecting it.

Those who are interested in a more in-depth view of the depiction of business people in television and the other entertainment media can read Linda S. Lichter, S. Robert Lichter, and Stanley Rothman, "How Show Business Shows Business," *Public Opinion*, October/November 1982, pp. 10–12. The authors find that "the portrayal is overwhelmingly negative."

Also of interest:

Arthur G. Miller, ed. *In the Eye of the Beholder: Contemporary Issues in Stereotyping*. New York: Praeger, 1982.

Bernard Rubin, ed., *Small Voices and Great Trumpets: Minorities and the Media*. New York: Praeger, 1980.

Frederick Williams, et al., *Children, Television, and Sex-Role Stereotyping*. New York: Praeger, 1981.

PART FOUR

Rights in Conflict

The authors of the Bill of Rights knew that it provided for so many rights that it was inevitable that some of them would eventually overlap. So they set up a judicial system that could constantly examine those rights and, possibly, reinterpret them over time.

In recent years, the rights claimed by government, the public, and the media have tended to conflict with alarming frequency. The government demands the right to withhold information from the public and the media, and, on the other hand, the right to force journalists to reveal sources and testify in court and congressional hearings. The media demand extra privileges for news gathering and protection from privacy laws. The public is torn between the desire for the right to personal privacy and the desire to know about the lives of others. And that's just a sample—the list of overlapping rights is extensive.

This part of the book examines some of the more important cases of conflictng rights in the media. Chapter 15 looks at the conflict between a defendant's right to a fair trial and the public's "right to know." Chapter 16 examines the conflict between the public's "right to know" about crime and terrorism and law enforcement's "right" to withhold information, if necessary, during the course of an investigation. Chapter 17 examines the conflict between the public's right to know and the individuals's right to privacy. Chapter 18 treats conflicts inherent in copyright, Chapter 19 treats libel, and Chapter 20 examines the conflict between broadcasters' First Amendment rights and the public's right to have broadcasters operate in the "public interest, convenience, and necessity."

CHAPTER 15

Free Press/Fair Trial

The free press/fair trial issue is one of the most clear-cut media controversies in America today—and therefore one of the most difficult to resolve. The First Amendment to the Constitution guarantees freedom of the press, and the Sixth Amendment guarantees the right of every defendant to a trial by an impartial jury. As many observers have pointed out, the two amendments are very likely to come into conflict during media coverage of a trial.

The first reading in this chapter is by Lyle Denniston, a legal reporter for the *Baltimore Sun*. He examines the current state of the free press/fair trial controversy. The remaining readings take up three issues that are part of this controversy: cameras in court, trial publicity, and the disclosure of sources.

THE STRUGGLE BETWEEN THE FIRST AND SIXTH AMENDMENTS

Lyle Denniston

As the trial of John W. Hinckley Jr. for the attempted assassination of President Ronald Reagan neared its end, an unsettling sequence of events unfolded.

An unpaid volunteer, who was helping a United Press International reporter, followed one of the jurors home in an effort to learn her name and address. UPI wanted to be able to talk to that juror and others after the verdict was in, and the trial judge had kept the jurors' identities secret. They were not sequestered.

The juror complained at the courthouse, and word of the incident reached Judge Barrington D. Parker of the U.S. District Court for the District of Columbia. The judge had two obvious options: a contempt citation, or referral to the U.S. attorney for possible prosecution for jury-tampering. He did neither.

Instead, he told U.S. marshals to keep two UPI reporters, Gregory Gordon and Judi Hasson, out of the courtroom. For one full trial day, Gordon and Hasson could report the story only from the

From *California Lawyer* (November, 1982). Reprinted by permission.

corridor; the 457 newspapers that buy only UPI's wire service got second-hand accounts. The judge relented at the end of the day, but never explained what he had done.

To most judges and attorneys, no doubt, what was unsettling about the incident was the behavior of the UPI aide (and of UPI itself) in telling someone to learn the identities of jurors, in an apparent violation of the judge's protective order. To the press the incident was unsettling for a different reason. It illustrated how swiftly and summarily a reporter's access to a courtroom can be restricted by the trial judge.

Much of the impetus for closing courtrooms comes from attorneys, especially defense counsel, but the judge, with virtually unlimited control over the courtroom, always has the final say. Many judges seem to view access largely as a privilege, not a right. The press, like the public spectator, is seen as a visitor to the courtroom, who is expected to obey the rules of the house. And the judge makes the rules.

It is true that the U.S. Supreme Court has said—beginning with *Richmond Newspapers* v. *Virginia* in 1980—that some access for the public, including the press, is a right. But it also has said that, like the other rights drawn from the First Amendment, it is not absolute. In reality, the right expands or contracts at the discretion of individual trial judges. At present, that discretion is not monitored very closely.

Much of the difficulty (aside from the opacity of the Supreme Court opinions on the subject) is due to uncertainty about theory. The theories of "openness" that emerge from First Amendment analysis are thought to be in conflict with the theories of "fairness" that come from Sixth Amendment analysis. Judges are naturally preoccupied with their obligation to make criminal trials as fair as possible. But when they give Sixth Amendment values precedence over First Amendment values, they forget Chief Justice Warren E. Burger's admonition in *Nebraska Press Association* v. *Stuart* (1976).

> The authors of the Bill of Rights did not undertake to assign priorities as between First Amendment and Sixth Amendment rights, ranking one as superior to the other: . . . If the authors of these guarantees, fully aware of the potential conflicts between them, were unwilling or unable to resolve the issue by assigning to one priority over the other, it is not for us to rewrite the Constitution by undertaking what they declined to do.

(*Nebraska Press*, it should be noted, did not involve access to courtrooms. Rather, it involved a judge's "gag" order forbidding the press to report as news in the pre-trial period some information thought prejudicial, even though some of it had come out in preliminary hearings in open court, observed by press and public spectators. The order came in a Nebraska murder case, and was upheld by the Nebraska Supreme Court. The U.S. Supreme Court reversed.)

> There is a right to receive ideas about courts and how they work, the court made clear in *Richmond Newspapers*.

Even if judges do not give the Sixth Amendment precedence, they still have to resolve potential conflicts between rights under the two amendments. But in this process the issue of comparative rights is often confused with the comparative interests that are at stake. The press has an interest in publishing information without regard to its admissibility at trial; the accused has an interest in confining the information that is circulated to that which will be admissible. But the interests of the press and of the accused may both be satisfied, under a different interpretation of the relation between the First and Sixth Amendments. Under this interpretation each amendment is viewed separately, as serving its own constituency. According to this approach, the press could be allowed absolute right of access to courtrooms—including access for television cameras—without impairing the right to a fair trial.

The jurisdiction of the two amendments, according to this approach, can be divided at the courthouse door. The Sixth Amendment serves the community within, the First Amendment the community without. The rules of evidence and decorum apply inside the courtroom, but not outside.

What might be called the "internal community of the law" should be defined for each particular trial. It includes the judge, the attorneys, the other trial participants, and that segment of the public that might be summoned for jury duty. It does not include the remainder of the public—including the press—except while they are inside the courtroom. The "external community" is the public outside the courthouse, including the readers of newspapers and listeners and viewers of radio and television.

Within the "internal community," the right to fairness is of paramount concern. If there is any hint of prejudice there, it can be dealt with there: by the process of jury selection, by the rules of evidence, by the discretion of the court to postpone, to transfer or change venue, to instruct the jury, to control the entire trial process. If a juror, or a witness, brings prejudices in from the outside, it can be discovered and controlled if not eradicated. To believe, as some judges apparently do, that prejudice cannot be handled without resorting to limits on press access is to underestimate the capacity of the court to neutralize prejudice and to overestimate the moral corruptibility of juries.

The Supreme Court, in *Nebraska Press*, trusted judges to deal with prejudice without resorting to controls upon the press. Clever defense attorneys have demonstrated that they, too, can protect their clients, especially by careful jury selection. Moreover, there is evidence that adverse publicity about an accused person does not create lasting prejudice in the minds of jurors.

In the "external community," the process of communicating ideas will go on, both by commercial, organized means and by private, informal methods. Speculation, inference, guesswork, even fantasy, bigotry and possibly lunacy will be indulged in by that community. The press will contribute its share. But its excesses can no more be cured by the judge than can those of neighbors gossiping about a case across a back fence. Short of maintaining a ubiquitous force of communications police, there is no way for a community to rid itself of all error in thought or utterance.

This rather rigid separation of the two communities has the simple virtue of recognizing the peculiar competence—or incompetence—of the controlling power structures within each community. And it does allow an arena in which the Sixth Amendment can be superior, and a separate one in which the First can be.

As the constitutional theory behind fair trial-free press issues has developed, it has become something of a "public utility" concept. Public access is thought to serve the good of the public and of the government. It lets the people observe the proceedings and thereby help keep them right, honest, effective and just.

That theory is refined through a subtheory, the "right to receive" ideas about public affairs—that is, governmental affairs. There is a right to receive ideas about courts and how they work, the court made clear in *Richmond Newspapers*. It is, however, a "public" right, not to be exploited by the press for private commercial gain. It is the citizen who needs the information, and thus has a constitutional right to it, under the First Amendment.

Even the most devoted proponent of public access to governmental affairs, Justice William J. Brennan Jr., favors its extension only insofar as it is deemed necessary to make the governmental process work. Consider his concurrence in *Rich-*

mond Newspapers: "What is crucial in individual cases is whether access to a particular government process is important in terms of that very process." That is about as plainly as the "public utility" concept of press access can be stated.

This is what the court majority had in mind when Brennan wrote the decision in *Globe Newspaper Co.* v. *Superior Court* (June 23, 1982).

> The First Amendment is . . . broad enough to encompass those rights that, while not unambiguously enumerated in the very terms of the Amendment, are nonetheless necessary to the enjoyment of other First Amendment rights. . . . Underlying the First Amendment right of access to criminal trials is the common understanding that 'a major purpose of that Amendment was to protect the free discussion of governmental affairs' . . . By offering such protection, the First Amendment serves to ensure that the individual citizen can effectively participate in and contribute to our republican system of self-government . . . [T]he 'expressly guaranteed freedoms' of the First Amendment 'share a common core purpose of assuring freedom of communication on matters relating to the functioning of government.'

The press itself has long embraced its own theory of a "public right to know." And no civics teacher (or Supreme Court justice) could muster more passion than the press for its "public service" role. It is close to heresy within press ranks to suggest that the press should not feel an obligation to make the government and society function better. It is not much less audacious to suggest that if government or something else in society is made better by the work of the press, that ought to be accepted as merely coincidental, not causal.

Most of the press has rarely, if ever, thought about the logical conclusion toward which a "public right to know" (protected by the sentinels of the press) is moving. The Supreme Court has already embraced a constitutional equivalent of the "public right to know": the "right to receive" ideas about government, implemented through a "right of access" to at least some governmental processes (see "Right of access: the birth of a concept," p. 276). In defining that right in a case-by-case process, the court is defining what the public "needs" to know—and by exclusion, what it does not need to know.

No civics teacher could muster more passion than the press itself for its "public service" role.

In *Gannett Co.* v. *DePasquale* (1979) the court refused to recognize a right of access to pre-trial hearings in criminal cases, seeing no need for the public to know what goes on there as it occurs. "Our adversary system of criminal justice," said the court, "is premised upon the proposition that the public interest is fully protected by the participants in the litigation." That statement has never been repudiated. *Gannett* involved a request by a defendant accused of murder, robbery and grand larceny that the public and press be excluded from a pre-trial hearing on a motion to suppress confession and physical evidence. The order was granted and upheld by the New York Court of Appeals. The U.S. Supreme Court affirmed.

In *Richmond Newspapers*, and even in *Globe Newspaper*, many qualifications were imposed on the right of access. A criminal trial need not be open, the court said in *Richmond*, if the trial judge decides that there is another overriding interest. Parts of trials may be closed, it added in *Globe*, "under appropriate circumstances." *Richmond* involved closing the entire trial in a Virginia murder case at the request of defense counsel. The Virginia Supreme Court upheld the closing, but the U.S. Supreme Court reversed. In the *Globe* case, an entire trial on charges of a sexual assault upon victims under the age of 18 was closed as required under a state statute in

Massachusetts. The state Supreme Judicial Court, however, interpreted the statute to require the closing of the courtroom only during the testimony of minor victims. The U.S. Supreme Court ruled against the mandatory closing of the trial, holding that no compelling government interest had been shown.

The court's reservations about how far to extend First Amendment rights make it obvious that the court does not accept the idea that the public has a "need" to know everything that can be learned about governmental proceedings, in court or elsewhere. During the past term, the court's decision in the Globe case was offset by its refusal even to consider access in other court settings. It denied review of a Washington Supreme Court decision that permitted a trial judge to bar a newspaper's access to a pre-trial hearing in a criminal case because of the paper's refusal to sign a written promise not to violate "voluntary guidelines" limiting press reports on criminal cases. That was the case of *Federated Publications* v. *Swedberg* (1981) involving a pre-trial hearing on a motion to suppress evidence against a woman accused of attempted murder. A reporter for the *Bellingham Herald* in Washington was barred for refusing to make a commitment to abide by bench-bar-press guidelines which urge the press not to report confessions, make references to police tests, offer comments about guilt, or state opinions about the quality of evidence or the credibility of witnesses.

The court denied review of a California appellate ruling that permitted a trial judge to deny public and press access during questioning of potential jurors in a capital case. In *Press-Enterprise* v. *Superior Court* (June 30, 1981), a murder trial had been transferred from Riverside County to San Diego County. Reporters for Riverside and San Diego newspapers were barred from the courtroom during the entire time that potential jurors were being questioned.

The court also denied review of a ninth circuit decision permitting a trial judge to bar the press when lawyers were discussing in open court whether evidence would be admitted in a narcotics trial. In this case, *Sacramento Bee* v. *U.S. District Court* (1981), a federal district court judge had twice excluded the press during "sidebar conferences." In one of those instances, public spectators were allowed to remain when the press was not. Each time, the jury was out of the courtroom.

Review was also denied of a Texas Supreme Court order permitting a judge to close a pre-trial hearing in a civil case because an attorney for a bank involved said the case touched on "sensitive and confidential matters." That case, *Cox Enterprises* v. *Vascocu*, (1981), involved a stockholder lawsuit against the directors of a bank, seeking damages for alleged mismanagement. A reporter for a newspaper in Lufkin, Texas was excluded from the pre-trial proceeding.

> One cannot escape the suspicion that access is, in fact, a form of control that judges use out of frustration over their constitutional inability to "gag" the press directly.

In each of those cases, the trial judge either gave no reason for closing the trial or issued a conclusory assertion not subject to challenge or review. Pressed to say why a topic in court should not be aired outside it, many judges reply only that they think the press will misrepresent the case and the judicial process, thereby undermining the latter.

The Supreme Court, however, has given one broad hint that the manner and style of press coverage may not be irrelevant to the issue of access. In *Chandler* v. *Florida* (1981), two police officers accused of breaking and entering a Miami Beach restaurant unsuccessfully sought to exclude television cameras from the trial. Only two minutes and 55 seconds of the trial were broadcast on television, and all that was shown was on the prosecution's side of the case.

By the time that case had reached the court, technological advances in television videotaping had made the presence of electronic eyes and ears in the courtroom no more intrusive than human eyes and ears. Courts in many states had begun to experiment with cameras in the courtroom. *Chandler* freed the states to go on with that experimentation, but the court's opinion made it clear that the justices were by no means endorsing such coverage themselves. The opinion did not even mention the earlier *Richmond Newspapers* ruling, so the constitutional right of access evidently was not extended to television and radio.

But the chief justice's opinion for the court posed the serious question of whether the highly selective, perhaps over-simplified portrayal of a trial on a television news show might give the community at large a flawed view of criminal justice to the detriment of the accused, by inflicting "a form of punishment before guilt."

There appears in that opinion at least the implied conclusion that, however well-mannered a television crew might be while inside the courtroom, the programs that it broadcasts afterward could be a factor affecting future access. If *Chandler* is taken seriously by trial judges, "prejudicial" broadcasts might lead to a denial of further access to the broadcast press.

Conferring access according to press performance is tantamount to content regulation, which television and radio have always been subject to under broadcast licensing regulations and federal communiciations law. But there is nothing in currently prevailing legal theory to suggest that content regulations through the restriction of access can or will be limited to the electronic media. When the Washington Supreme Court decided the Swedberg case, it said that denying access to a newspaper because it would not commit itself in advance to editorial restraint in its reporting of the case was not a form of prior restraint in violation of the First Amendment. After all, that court said, the judge did not tell the paper what it could or could not say. The *Bellingham Herald* nonetheless was obliged to cover the proceedings from the corridor.

One cannot escape the suspicion that access is, in fact, a form of control that judges use out of frustration over their constitutional inability to "gag" the press directly. When press credentials are handed out and then withdrawn because of the way a story is covered, only an insensitive reporter will not conclude that that is punishment. In recent years there has been little sign of hesitation among judges to use what powers they do have whenever the press enters—always by invitation—the "internal community of the law" inside the courthouse.

Most reporters are not only capable of giving judges full respect in their courtrooms; they do it as a matter of routine. Long before cases like *Gannett* reached the Supreme Court, reporters learned courtroom etiquette—and lost access when they forgot it. They have long known that they are, as Justice Potter Stewart wrote in *Gannett*, "strangers" in the courtroom.

But they also know that the workings of the judicial mind are indeed "strange" and should not be relied on as the premise for editorial judgment. To the press, a story about a criminal case is just another story. There are no special rules, and can be none, for defining what the "external community" may find interesting or readable. News, in short, is not law.

Right of access: the birth of a concept

Lyle Denniston

Among the newly born constitutional rights, none has a more peculiar ancestry than the "right of access" to government information. It is, in fact, the constitutional stepchild of another new "right": the right to gather information. Both emerge from the First Amendment, and they are the common creation of seven different justices of the Supreme Court.

It took 15 years, from 1965 to 1980, for these rights to grow from mere hints into constitutional reality. Their exact scope, though, is still largely uncertain, and the kind of governmental activity or information toward which they may be extended in the future is even less certain.

The right of access and the related right to gather information are an amalgam of the views of Justices Harry A. Blackmun, William J. Brennan Jr., Lewis F. Powell Jr., John Paul Stevens, former Justice Potter Stewart, and, to a lesser extent, Chief Justice Warren E. Burger and Justice Byron R. White.

Eight of the present nine justices have written or signed opinions embracing some version of both rights. The newest justice, Sandra Day O'Connor, did so with some reservations, in the recent decision in *Globe Newspaper Co.* v. *Superior Court* (June 23, 1982).

Blackmun, Brennan, Stevens, and Justice Thurgood Marshall have been fairly consistent in their views (with notable exceptions for Blackmun and Stevens). Powell, White and Stewart have accepted these rights inconsistently. The chief justice did so belatedly. Only Justice William H. Rehnquist has refused to accept them as constitutionally valid in any context.

The first hint that these rights might someday exist came in a case that has had a great deal to do with limiting the philosophical reach of the First Amendment. In *Zemel* v. *Rusk* (1965), the late Chief Justice Earl Warren, upholding the denial of the right of U.S. citizens to travel to Cuba, wrote: "We cannot accept the contention . . . that it is a First Amendment right which is involved. . . . The right to speak and publish does not carry with it the unrestrained right to gather information."

That was apparently the court's first explicit mention of something like a "right of access" or a "right to gather information." It would be seven years before the court first intimated that it might acknowledge such a right. In *Branzburg* v. *Hayes* (1972), Justice White picked up the theme: "We do not question the significance of free speech, press, or assembly to the country's welfare. Nor is it suggested that news gathering does not qualify for First Amendment protection; without some protection for seeking out the news, freedom of the press could be eviscerated."

The words, "news gathering is not without its First Amendment protection," appeared again in the opinion, but White also added: "It has generally been held that the First Amendment does not guarantee the press a constitutional right of special access to information not available to the public generally."

He then quoted Warren in the *Zemel* opinion

regarding the absence of an "unrestrained right to gather information" and a further remark from that opinion suggesting that the public has no First Amendment right to enter the White House uninvited to check up on the government.

Dissenting in *Branzburg*, Stewart found the phrase had a different meaning. He emphasized the word "unrestrained" in *Zemel* and said in a footnote, "The necessary implication is that some right to gather information does exist."

Strangely, however, when Stewart wrote the opinion in *Pell* v. *Procunier* in 1974, limiting press access to prisons, he relied upon the *Zemel* statement to support the proposition that "(t)he Constitution does not . . . require government to accord the press special access to information not shared by members of the public generally."

In dissent in *Saxbe* v. *Washington Post Co.*, a companion to *Pell*, Powell treated the *Zemel* thought as reflecting "no more than a sensible disinclination to follow the right-of-access argument as far as dry logic might extend." Burger imitated Stewart's interpretation in *Pell* (and White's in *Branzburg*) to justify a denial of access to prisons in *Houchins* v. *KQED* in 1978, only to provoke a retort in dissent by Stevens picking up the Stewart interpretation in *Branzburg*.

In *Gannett* v. *DePasquale* in 1979, the first case directly testing a right of access to pre-trial proceedings in a criminal case, Stewart's opinion for the majority said the court "need not decide in the abstract . . . whether there is any such constitutional right."

It was not until 1980, and *Richmond Newspapers Inc.* v. *Virginia*, that a majority of the court was ready to hold that there was such a right in the Constitution. In an opinion by the chief justice, the court opened criminal trials generally to the public and press, leading Stevens in concurrence to suggest that this was a"watershed case . . . (N)ever before has the court squarely held that the acquisition of newsworthy matter is entitled to any constitutional protection whatsoever."

In doing so, however, Burger's opinion took care not to label it either as a "right to gather information" or a "right of access." The decision was based on a galaxy of constitutional rights that included but was not limited to free speech and press guarantees. At that point, moreover, access was recognized only where governmental proceedings were open either by a policy choice of legislature or court, or by tradition or long-standing custom.

Finally, in the *Globe Newspaper* decision at the close of the 1981–82 term, Brennan's opinion for the majority appeared to have eliminated the condition of long-standing history. In doing so, the Brennan view provoked the chief justice into dissent. Burger noted that the opinions of a majority of the justices in the *Richmond* case had "emphasized the historical tradition of open criminal trials." He cited Brennan, too, to that effect, and added: "Today Justice Brennan ignores the weight of historical practice." Rehnquist joined that dissent. In an opinion concurring only in the judgment, O'Connor also interpreted *Richmond* as resting upon "our long history of open criminal trials."

The Brennan view, putting the "right of access" on strong First Amendment footing, commanded a clear majority without O'Connor. Blackmun, Marshall, Powell and White joined the opinion unreservedly. Stevens, who had favored a right of access in prior cases, dissented on a procedural issue. Even the Brennan opinion allowed, in a footnote, that "in individual cases, and under appropriate circumstances," the right of access in order to gather information about courts might be set aside.

CAMERAS IN COURT: THE VERDICT IS YES, BUT . . .

Max Gunther

There is an air of contentment and relief around the Rhode Island Superior Court these days. Earlier this year, the wealthy Claus von Bulow was convicted in this court of trying twice to murder his wife. It was one of the most notorious criminal trials in the state's history. What made it still more noteworthy was that, as part of a one-year experiment, it was televised.

"It worked out fine," says Andrew Teitz, a court research technician who doubled as press-liaison man during the trial. "My impression was that TV got a lot of compliments from the public and very few complaints. I think the need to compress a long trial into short news excerpts will always cause some distortion, but on the whole, the networks' coverage was fair and balanced. The public got as accurate a picture of the trial as it could get, given the time compression."

As for sensationalism, Teitz saw none and heard no complaints of any. The trial had highly emotional moments—for instance, the moment when Von Bulow's teen-age daughter watched him being sentenced—but if TV was guilty of exploiting that heart-wrenching scene, so were newspapers such as the august *New York Times*, which ran the picture on its front page.

The view from inside the courtroom was equally good. "We had a lot of fears before we started this experimental year," says the Superior Court's presiding justice, Anthony Giannini. "We were afraid the cameras would make judges and others behave differently, but I haven't seen it happening. I haven't seen lawyers grandstanding more than usual. I haven't found witnesses more timid. The cameras haven't been annoying or disruptive."

Rhode Island's experience reflects what has happened in other states. The national verdict on TV in the courtroom is: with reservations, it seems to work.

This verdict is no surprise to the man who may be the nation's fiercest crusader for courtroom TV: Norman Davis, vice president of WPLG-TV in Miami. "The less experience courts have with TV, the more they fear it," says Davis, who travels about the country tirelessly haranguing bar groups and others on the topic. "There's this standard litany of fears that you hear in every state where cameras are still banned: TV will scare witnesses, bring out the worst showoff instincts in judges and lawyers, disrupt everything. People are *sure* of this. But as soon as they try it, the fears start to die away. We've had courtroom TV in Florida for longer than almost anybody, and I can't overstress how ordinary it seems now. There simply is no issue any more in this state."

Davis hopes the issue will similarly evaporate throughout the nation. He feels optimistic, for Rhode Island's type of experiment is being tried all over the nation.

"It's a pretty tentative experiment in some cases, but at least it's better than a plain no," he says. As such things go, the change from the negative to the experimental mood has been startlingly sudden. For its first quarter-century as a major news medium—up to the late 1970s—

From *TV Guide* (August 14, 1982). Reprinted by permission.

TV was flatly and rudely banned from all Federal and nearly all state courtrooms. When Norman Davis and WPLG first got cameras into the Florida courts in 1977, only Colorado, Washington and Alabama showed similar tolerance for TV. Today, the Radio/Television News Directors Association counts 38 states that allow some form of broadcast coverage, though often under severe restrictions.

The remaining 12 states still forbid all audio or camera coverage. So do the Federal courts—with the single exception that a Federal judge may, if he likes, let cameras in on a purely ceremonial proceeding such as an investiture. The highest Federal courts are the least hospitable to TV. "As far as I know," says Barrett McGurn, chief spokesman of the U.S. Supreme Court, "this court has never allowed a camera into one of its working sessions in all the 150-odd years since photography was invented."

Not even optimists like Norman Davis expect that attitude to change fast. But there could be rapid changes in the group of 12 reluctant states. "There are pro-TV movements in many of those states," says Steve Nevas, First Amendment counsel for the National Association of Broadcasters (NAB) and a dedicated crusader. "We're working with a study commission in Virginia, for instance. You could see the numbers change very soon.

Why are three-quarters of the states making friendly gestures to TV after rejecting it so long? Nobody is sure. "The idea just seemed to catch fire spontaneously, and the fire spread," says Catherine Arnone, who handles TV arrangements for the New Jersey state courts.

The U.S. Supreme Court added fuel to the fire in 1981. It heard a case involving two Miami Beach policemen. The two had been convicted of a burglary, and some short segments of their trial had been shown, despite their objections, on TV. They appealed, contending that the camera's presence made the trial unfair.

The Supreme Court disagreed. The justices were unanimous: they saw no evidence that the trial had been "tainted" by TV. The mere presence of a camera, they held, does not automatically rule out a fair trial.

Still more impetus came from development of the so-called ENG (electronic news gathering) breed of TV cameras. These are very much smaller and less obtrusive than standard studio cameras, they run silently and they can make do with ordinary courtroom light. "Until they came along," Nevas says, "many judges and others were put off by the clumsiness of the gadgetry itself."

These factors helped push the movement forward—but it did not move at the same speed on all fronts. "There's a lot of hanging back," says Norman Davis.

The Supreme Court, for example, definitely did not say in its 1981 decision that TV has a Constitutional right to get into court. Nor did the justices invite the nosy medium into their own proceedings.

The American Bar Association (ABA) has also failed to show any enthusiasm for TV. Its unfriendly posture could be softened somewhat at this summer's ABA convention. Even if it is, however, few expect ABA's unwelcoming attitude to disappear quickly. "The fact is," Steve Nevas says gloomily, "judges and lawyers tend to think of the courts as their private preserve. They don't really want TV looking over their shoulders."

The fear of TV is shown in the states' preliminary caution. Most, like Rhode Island, have insisted on a tryout period before making a permanent rule change in favor of TV. Many, too, have paid for expensive studies of the medium's impact on the trial process.

California, for instance, in a tryout period that will end this December, has had a consulting group handing out questionnaires and observing people's behavior at trials. One of the consultants is Gerald Miller, communication professor at Michigan State University and a widely known court-TV authority. He has attended trials such as last year's dispute between Carol Burnett and the *National Enquirer*. Results? "TV seems to have no detectable effect on anybody," Prof. Miller says.

Those are precisely Rhode Island's results. "Those are *everybody's* results," Norman Davis says. No tryout period to date has ended with a state's turning TV away. Despite that, the suspicious attitude remains, and each state feels it must run its own tests.

The fear of TV is also evident in the restrictions with which the dangerous-looking newcomer has been shackled. Afraid that TV can expose people to unwanted publicity, many states allow it into court only with permission from defendants and other trial participants. Since this permission is not often granted, NAB's Nevas grumbles that these states have only half-opened the door. "We're very disturbed by this particular restriction," he says. He and the NAB are happier with the setup in Florida, generally felt to be the state with the widest-open door. Florida TV people need no special permission from anybody to go into court—not even the judge. A participant can object if he likes, but he has the burden of proving that the TV coverage will do some tangible harm.

Some states, fearing coercion or vengeful acts against jurors, permit jurors to forbid any photography that shows their faces. Other states have rules about the kinds of trials at which TV is unwelcome. For instance, Pennsylvania permits coverage at civil trials only. Others ban the camera from some criminal trials and some civil ones. New Jersey forbids coverage of cases involving rape, child custody, trade secrets or marital disputes.

There are also some fears that cannot so easily be exorcised with rules. The most widespread is the fear that TV, by selecting only the most emotional or shocking parts of a trial, will turn what is supposed to be a dignified process into a cheap peep show. One man who harbors this worry is William Bruce, a professor at the New York Law School. He recalls that he was upset by last year's Supreme Court decision in the Miami burglary case. "The danger," he says, "is prurient coverage, the kind that would make a trial into a circus of victims' pain and humiliation."

He admits that he has not seen this happening to any great extent so far. Indeed, he found the coverage of the Von Bulow trial "for the most part quite sensitive." Yet he worries about the way that material will be reused in the future. Emotional scenes could be exploited, he suggests. For example, they could be glued into a patched-up melodrama based on the case.

Though 38 states now allow some TV coverage of trials, many jurists still worry about its impact.

Another fear is that innocent defendants might be hurt when the charges against them are broadcast. TV people reply that the same danger has always existed with newspaper coverage. "Emotional reactions to a trial can happen with or without a camera," says Andrew Teitz. He points to the overheated public reaction to the trial of John Hinckley, the would-be presidential assassin. Hinckley was found innocent by reason of insanity, but a large and loud segment of the public finds him guilty. This hot reaction was not caused by TV. The trial, in Federal court, was not broadcast.

Still another fear is that an unpopular judge, defendant or witness can be hurt by selective coverage. The TV argument, again, is that this danger is nothing new. "Unfair selectivity is something all news media have to guard against," Norman Davis says. "But in the normal course of events, TV will give you a more complete picture of reality at a trial than any other medium. Only TV shows the facial expressions, voice tones, gestures."

"TV can show the public what really goes on in the courts," says Carol Cotter, producer of news and documentaries for WHA-TV in Madison, Wis. She speaks from experience. Three years ago, just after Wisconsin adopted a permanent pro-TV rule, she placed a camera in the courtroom of a Milwaukee judge, Christ T. Seraphim. Lawyers had been complaining about overflamboyant behavior by this judge for a long time, but the public had never actually seen what the grumbling was based on. Shortly after WHA's documentary was broadcast—"The judge came across as quite colorful," Carol Cotter says mildly—he was suspended from the bench for "misconduct."

Many observers thought this outcome was a direct result of the public exposure on TV. Carol Cotter modestly declines to take that credit. "But I do think our show was a good example of what TV can do," she says. "The court system is mysterious to a lot of people. TV can go in there and open it up to the light of day."

Does Cotter look forward to more coverage like that? "Yes," she replies cautiously, "but I'll be very selective. If you want the truth, most trials are pretty dull."

She echoes the feelings of many other TV people, perhaps most. Prof. Miller recalls that California judges were buried in inquiries from TV producers when the state first opened the court doors in 1980. "In those first few months," he says, "the TV people wanted to cover everything—it didn't matter what. Then the novelty wore off. Today, they want to cover only what's genuinely newsworthy, a trial like the Burnett-*Enquirer* affair. In California, at least, the day is gone when a camera in a courtroom is news by itself."

Or, as Catherine Arnone reports from the New Jersey court offices: "We get a pretty steady stream of TV inquiries around here. But I don't think you'll ever see your favorite news show filling up with back-to-back trials."

SHOULD THE COURTS CONTROL TRIAL PUBLICITY?
A Newsman's View

Richard Oliver

Gagging the press is the chic thing these days in courtrooms from New York to California. But in reality the gag order is as old as tyranny itself. And, like tyranny, it is a threat to everyone.

Let's take a closer look at this judicial fad that has been called into use recently in two murder trials—the Sonny Carson murder case in Brooklyn and a Nebraska case now before the U.S. Supreme Court.* And the press was barred from the courtroom during jury selection in the Patty Hearst case.

The issue in all these cases is now more than simply the innocence or guilt of the defendants, but whether the public, through its free press, is entitled to know what is happening in its courts. In the Brooklyn and Nebraska cases, the press was ordered not to publish matters of public record, facts, and background material that had come out in open court and had been published previously.

The (appeals) courts struck down the gag order in the Brooklyn case, although that ruling

From the *New York Sunday News* View Section (February 1, 1976).

*In the Nebraska case (1976) the court severely limited the use of gag orders, which was seen as a major victory for the press.

appeared to leave the door open for gag orders under certain circumstances. The Nebraska case has resulted in an appeal to the U.S. Supreme Court by the press.

The judges in these gag-order cases contend that publication of certain background information—facts deemed necessary to make news stories understandable to readers—could prejudice the jury and jeopardize the defendant's right to a fair trial. So, without even showing that the forbidden material would actually prejudice a jury, some judges turn to the gag-order gimmick.

Never mind the First Amendment, freedom of the press, and the public's right to know, the advocates of gag orders are really saying. Forget the words of Supreme Court Justice William Brennan: "The First Amendment tolerates absolutely no prior judicial restraint of the press (based on the fear) that untoward consequences might result."

THERE ARE WAYS

Forget about the established tools of the court to keep jurors from being influenced by the press:

- Admonition—the judge cautions the jurors that they are bound by law from reading or listening to news accounts.
- Change of Venue—shifting the trial to another city or county.
- Continuance—delaying the trial until the publicity has worn off.
- Sequestering—keeping the jury in private, "locked up," to avoid exposure to the news media.

And there are other ways, such as bringing in a jury panel from another area, or excluding jurors before they are accepted on the panel. The remedies, according to recent studies, are rarely used. Some judges find it easier to gag the press.

Leaving aside for a moment the highfalutin' words and phrases of the continuing conflict between the news media and the legal establishment, let's look at the confrontation itself. The headline on these stories usually says something like: "Free Press vs. Fair Trial." The implication is that you have to take sides—that if you are for one, you must be against the other.

Well, that is hogwash. In truth, you cannot have one without the other. We need both, and we should cherish both.

Those judges who find themselves lured by the gag-order gimmick might well consider the recent admonition of New York's top judge, Chief Judge Charles D. Breitel. He cautioned the courts, the legal profession and the news media not to assume that any single group is the exclusive protector of the public interest.

One thing is clear, however. In the words of another top judge, Warren Burger, the Chief Justice of the United States: "For better or worse, editing is what editors are for."

A Judge's View

Burton B. Roberts

A controversy, which by no means is insoluble, has arisen between the media and the courts. On one hand, there is the constitutional right of the media to print the complete background of a defendant in order to guarantee the public's right to know what is happening during a criminal trial.

On the other hand, the court must, also under the Constitution, guarantee the rights of a defendant to a "public trial by an impartial jury," a jury that cannot be influenced by anything outside the courtroom.

In a few extremely rare and unusual cases, courts have asked the media to use restraint in reporting certain background information in order to protect this Sixth Amendment right of a defendant. The use of that kind of restraint order has to depend on the facts and circumstances of the individual case.

No general rules can be established other than to say it is a remedy of last resort. But I can see why it might become necessary to make such a request to the press in a rare circumstance.

In my opinion, the First Amendment, guaranteeing freedom of speech and press, is the darling of the Constitution's nursery. But the primacy of the First Amendment is not absolute. It was settled long ago that the Constitution does not provide for an unfettered right of expression. One cannot shout "fire," when there is no fire in a crowded theater.

> I do not advocate adopting the British system, which certainly curtails the right of the media to cover trials. But I do advocate that in certain rare instances the court has the right to direct that the media exercise restraint.

In a criminal case, a defendant is presumed to be innocent until a jury unanimously agrees that his guilt has been established beyond a reasonable doubt. This is a real right, applicable to a "sinner" as well as a "saint." Both are presumed to be innocent. Indeed, both may be innocent.

If a defendant elects not to take the stand, his unsavory past, his criminal record, cannot be brought to the attention of a jury.

Only in the rarest instances will a court direct the media not to write anything either about a case or the defendant's background. For, after all, the court directs the jury not to read anything about the case, or it can even sequester a jury.

The first remedy, practically speaking, however, is often ignored. Jurors are human, and they will read newspapers or have articles brought to their attention.

SEQUESTERING IS COSTLY

The second remedy is rather expensive. Sequestering a jury costs at least $2000 a day; in a month-long trial that means $60,000 in taxpayers' money, and to what avail. In addition to the expense, sequestering a jury can cause great inconvenience to jurors and their families and create imbalances in the pool of jurors due to lack of availability.

In those extremely rare instances that a court directs the media not to publish something in the interest of a fair trial, cannot the press reveal that background after the verdict is in? I do not advocate adopting the British system, which certainly curtails the right of the media to cover trials. But I do advocate that in certain rare instances the court has the right to direct that the media exercise restraint. If the court has abused its discretion, certainly a higher court can correct this in short order.

I believe that guidelines fair to both the defendant and the press can be worked out if the two sides get together. The issue should be resolved in light rather than heat.

MUST REPORTERS DISCLOSE SOURCES?

Yes—"Reporters Have to Obey the Law Like Everyone Else"

Interview with Philip B. Kurland

Q: Professor Kurland, why do you believe newsmen do not have the constitutional right to keep sources and information confidential?

A: I feel that way for two reasons: one, because the Supreme Court has said there is no such right. Reporters can live in a dream world and say, "We know what the Constitution says, and the Supreme Court doesn't." But as the law exists today, the press doesn't have that right.

Second, because the right of freedom of speech and press is given to everybody, not just the institutional press. The use of the word *press* at the time it was put into the First Amendment did not denote newspapers or magazines but anybody who was engaged in the printed rather than the spoken word. So there's no reason to say there's a greater privilege for the institutional press than for the individual who seeks to publish his views.

Q: Aren't journalists entitled to have a privilege comparable to lawyers and doctors?

A: The privileges to which you refer, and which the newspapers from time to time speak of as constitutional privileges, are not constitutional privileges. The doctor-patient privilege, the priest-penitent privilege—they're all dependent on statute.

There's nothing in the Constitution that forbids either state governments or the national government from effecting a statute which would create this kind of privilege for the press.

Q: Isn't the public well served by enabling reporters to protect their sources?

A: Not under all circumstances. What you've got is a problem of balancing. The courts recognize this. There is an obligation on the part of anybody who seeks information from reporters to justify access to the information. In the case of *New York Times* reporter M. A. Farber, there's some question whether access to secure his private notes has been justified.

Q: Do you contend that news reporters are acting above the law when they refuse to turn over confidential information to the courts?

A: Not long ago, the press maintained that even the President of the United States can't be a judge in his own case. The same thing holds true for the press. Reporters have to obey the law like everyone else.

Q: Don't reporters run the risk of being used as an arm of the state, as an investigative tool of government?

A: No more than any witness to an event whose testimony is necessary for a trial. I don't become an agent for the government because I've witnessed a crime and am called on to give testimony.

Q: Critics say that some lawyers use the press as a ploy, actually preferring that reporters refuse to give information so the lawyers can claim that their clients have been denied fair trials—

A: I don't think the courts have been stringent enough in imposing ethical standards on either prosecution or defendants in the abuse of these matters—either the abuse of trying their cases in the newspapers or of abusing subpoenas. There are cases in which lawyers don't really want witnesses' testimony but only want to make a public issue of it.

Q: Do judges often order reporters to turn over information without first determining that the information is essential to the outcome of the case?

A: There may be some cases like that. The rules should be clear that judges should not issue such orders unless good cause is shown that the reporter is in possession of unique information of importance or relevance to the processes of the criminal law and not elsewhere available. That kind of judgment is dependent on the discretion of the person who's making the judgment, obviously. Whether the judges have made that judgment correctly in most cases, or incorrectly in most cases, I can't say.

Q: Are there ways that reporters could protect sources while not impairing the right of an individual to a fair trial?

A: An individual's interest in a fair trial is not abused or violated unless the reporter's data are proved to have a likelihood of weightiness and there's a necessity for them. If those items are shown to be not only relevant but substantial, I do not see a way for the reporter to avoid meeting the command of the court.

Q: Is there a way around many of these confrontations between the courts and the press?

A: There's a clear way around it—and it's one that the press has obviously recognized. And

that's to go to Congress and ask for the creation of a legal privilege, often called a "shield law." I'm a great believer in the notion that public policy is primarily to be made by our legislatures and not by our courts. I think that's the forum to which the press will have to go if it's going to get the kind of relief that it wants.

Q: Is there growing hostility toward the press by the courts?

A: In the last Supreme Court term, the press lost a substantial number of cases. They're not used to that. None of the issues decided against the press were reversals of a prior position by the Court. These were new questions, not a change of position with regard to the old ones. I see great sensitivity on the part of the press. The notion of the press as the ombudsman for American government—which the press continues to repeat—is not necessarily shared by all the citizenry, and not even by the courts.

I think the question that has to be asked is: What are the responsibilities of the press to the government and to society? It is not a question whether the press has a right to be free of restraints by government and society.

No—"We Have to Have Confidentiality or We Can't Do Our Jobs"

Interview with Jack C. Landau

Q: Mr. Landau, why do you believe newsmen have the constitutional right to keep sources and information confidential?

A: The First Admendment to the Constitution says that the press is supposed to be immune from government. By requiring reporters to disclose sources, government hampers the press from collecting information. If you can't collect it, you can't publish it. This is clearly contrary to the First Amendment.

While the press has always made this First Amendment argument very strongly, it seems to me there's also another First Amendment argument relating to freedom of association. A reporter should be free to circulate through the community. He should be free to talk with people and to have those people have the assurance that their identities aren't going to be disclosed.

Q: What will happen to the press if the courts continue to try to force reporters to reveal confidential information?

A: People will not provide information to the press in sensitive cases if they think their identiies are going to be made public.

The highly publicized case of *New York Times* reporter M. A. Farber is a perfect example of what could happen. If the courts force Farber to disclose confidential information and sources, the next newspaper reporter who comes across a situation where there may have been a crime committed may not be able to disclose it to the people in New Jersey or New York.

Q: Don't the First Amendment claims of the press collide with other constitutional rights, such as a defendant's right to a fair trial?

A: I'm not sure there is a conflict. Furthermore, there are lawyers all over the country who have in their files information which would clearly acquit or convict people. But those lawyers have an attorney-client privilege. No one has argued that the country is going to fall apart because of that privilege. I don't understand why, when it comes to the press, all of a sudden it becomes a cosmic disaster for society to protect sources.

Q: Critics contend that the press is trying to put itself above the law by protecting confidentiality—

A: We are not putting ourselves above the law any more than a major law firm is putting itself above the law when it asserts its attorney-client privilege.

The lawyers say, "We have to have a confidentiality privilege or else we can't do our job." The press says, "We have to have a confidentiality privilege or we can't do our jobs."

If you want to look at the social impact, the lawyer is protecting only a single individual. But in a case like Watergate, the reporters may be protecting thousands, maybe millions, of individuals.

Q: Hasn't the U.S. Supreme Court said there is no such privilege for the press?

A: This Supreme Court has said that. And the Supreme Court a hundred years ago said that blacks could be discriminated against, and that women were nonpeople.

Q: Doesn't the press already have protection in many states by "shield laws" that are designed to protect reporters from revealing sources or confidential information?

A: So far, 26 states have such laws. In California, New Jersey, and New York, judges have pretty well ripped them up through their rulings. But, in general, they are working. There is a question, however, as to whether perhaps we need a national shield law that would override any state constitutional bounds.

Then, of course, there comes the next question: Would the Supreme Court uphold such a federal law? That I don't know.

Q: Are the courts riding on a wave of press unpopularity with the public?

A: Yes. The attitude of the courts is pretty reflective of what one might call the moderate, conservative business establishment. In 1970, Vice-President Spiro T. Agnew came along and touched a very sensitive nerve all over the country. He made attacks against the press politically respectable.

Corporations started going out and being more aggressive. The bar started serving more subpoenas. The critics of the press became more popular. I think it was a whole movement of which the courts are only one part.

Q: Are you saying that there is a broad trend to penalize the press?

A: There's a broad trend to try to use the press as an important information resource. The state wants to use the press as an investigative arm, or the defense wants to use the press as an investigative arm, or the judge wants to use the

press as an investigative arm. It's a general movement to try to take away the independent standing of the press and really make it an appendage of the government.

As a result of recent court decisions, I think editorial independence and privacy are in terrific danger. They can take all your files. They can march into your office. They can seize your telephone records. So I don't think that we are exaggerating the danger that these cases are posing.

Q: Will the press continue to fight these decisions?

A: Reporters are willing to go to jail, and publishers are willing to pay extraordinary amounts to defend the First Amendment. The press is not used to being unpopular—not with the courts, not with politicians, and not with the local business community. But we may have to become unpopular for a while and take the heat in order to defend something which is really crucial.

SUGGESTIONS FOR FURTHER READING

Law journals are good sources for in-depth treatments of the free press/fair trial controversy. See, for example, P. Douglass, "Media Technology, Fair Trial, and the Citizen's Right to Know," *New York State Bar Journal* 54 (October 1982): 364–69.

Also of interest:

Kenneth S. Devol, ed., *Mass Media and the Supreme Court.* 3d ed. New York: Hastings House, 1983. Discusses a variety of Supreme Court First Amendment cases, including those pertaining to "trial by newspaper and television."

Lyle W. Denniston, *The Reporter and the Law: Techniques of Covering the Courts.* New York: Hastings House, 1980. Day-to-day technique of legal reporting, including the special legal risks that confront the reporter on the courthouse beat.

Fred Friendly, *Minnesota Rag.* New York: Random House, 1981. "The dramatic story of the landmark Supreme Court case that gave new meaning to freedom of the press."

Harold W. Sullivan, *Contempt by Publication: The Law of Trial by Newspaper.* 3d ed. Littleton, Colorado: Rothman, 1980.

Morris Van Gerpen, *Privileged Communication and the Press: The Citizen's Right to Know vs. the Law's Right to Confidential Evidence.* Westport, Conn.: Greenwood, 1979.

CHAPTER 16

Coverage of Crime and Terrorism

Crime coverage has always been a difficult issue for the media, and in recent years the coverage of terrorism has become an even bigger concern. In this chapter's first article, Marvin Kitman offers his opinion that terrorist activities should be covered—if at all—only in a very limited way. In the second reading, the editors of *Editor & Publisher* explain why, in their opinion, each decision has to be made on an individual basis.

DANGEROUS COVERAGE

Marvin Kitman

We had a fascinating hostage case on our local news shows the week of October 20. A prisoner broke away from his guards at a Brooklyn hospital and locked himself in the basement of the institution with six employees who were playing cards there. He had plenty of non-negotiable demands. First, he wanted a print reporter on hand, his own Boswell. Then radio coverage. Then an appearance on WABC-TV's *Eyewitness News*. By the third day he was requesting air time to issue statements: five full minutes on conditions in New York state prisons, and more to expound his theory that the rich are society's real criminals. No doubt he thought this would be educational television, on a par with Dostoevsky reading from the manuscript of *Crime and Punishment*. Another few days and the lunatic in the locker room at Kings County Hospital would have been insisting on his own weekly series. Or at least a guest shot, so to speak, with Merv, who would ask the only question he ever really asks anyone: "How does it feel to be a celebrity?"

The guy's knowledge of the media and his ability to manipulate everyone were frightening. He had the authorities send down a TV and a radio so that he could see and hear himself. After all, there's no point being a superstar if you can't enjoy the big show. He almost went berserk when he heard the reporters describe him as a "snitch" and an "informer."

Watching this media freak's bizzare performance, I was reminded of the puzzler raised by Bishop Berkeley long before the electronic age: If a tree falls in the forest and nobody hears the crash, did it really fall? Unfortunately, the tree did not go unheard in the New York TV market. For three or four days and nights one could not escape the story. My local NBC affiliate even broke in on sitcoms with the latest bulletins. (I can remember when a bulletin meant war had been declared, or something important.)

Someone holding hostages can ask for practically anything from the media today and get it.

After the flap was over, we were treated to discussions of propriety: Was TV wrong to grant the madman's every whim? The question was presented as a genuine dilemma. WABC-TV had the most explaining to do, since it wound up giving the perpetrator the most attention. (It was the only major network affiliate he could tune in down in the basement—stations at the lower end of the spectrum were unreceivable without a roof antenna.) Channel 7 righteously claimed it was saving the hostages' lives by granting their captor air time. Knowing the way the minds of television executives work, I would have to say that at best this may have been a passing thought, once they finished tallying their ratings.

The important point, though, is that someone holding hostages can ask for practically anything from the media today and get it. I think that's wrong. Covering such stories at all is a big mistake. As you may have noticed, I won't even mention the name of the guy in the Kings County case, let alone his various aliases.

The fact is that the coverage breeds imitators. A few days before October 20, there were breathless TV reports about a hostage taken on a train in North Carolina. Next came the Kings County melodrama. Within 20 minutes, it seemed, a similar incident occurred in the Bronx. "The sparks jump," psychoanalyst Dr. Erika Freeman noted on WPIX-TV in the only examination of the psychological impact of the media's role that I saw at the height of the hostage circus. "The criminal mind is most receptive to this kind of story." What is worse, she pointed out, is that the copycat criminals learn the latest hostage intervention techniques from TV. Every move is revealed to them before they begin their own escapades.

I also worry about the impressionable young people watching what happens when you take hostages these days. Suddenly you are in the limelight. Everybody is talking about you, Mr. Nobody. You might even be able to coax newscaster Sue Simmons into a room and make her whistle Dixie. Sure, you could get shot and killed, but it's better to be a media star and prove to your girlfriend, family and the guys on the corner that you are really somebody for at least a brief while than to live out your life in wretched obscurity. As Andy Warhol observed, pretty soon everybody in America will be a celebrity for 15 seconds.

The networks' excuse for glorifying the bad guys is that the public wants this sort of thing. The public wants nudity and sexual intercourse, too, yet we do not see that on, say, WNBC's *Live at Five*. In covering most crime the stations also tend to use discretion in not displaying the contents of body bags. Nor do they feature the heads that are blown apart in the nightly killings that figure prominently on the local news. If they can snip out the gore, they can snip out other harmful elements as well.

The free press issue here may make a civil libertarian's heart beat faster. But it is something of a joke in the realities of local TV reporting. The bottom line with a hostage story is that it provides the opportunity to cover a "live" event. The stations yearn for a break from the glut of lackluster, silly live remotes. ("Here we are, standing at this bus stop. A bus went by five minutes ago. Another is due in five minutes. Now back to you, Chet.") If you've seen one traffic jam or pothole, you've seen them all, as the news directors well know. A madman threatening to harm innocent people is different. They can trundle out their minicams, microdishes and other expensive toys to come up with riveting visuals. It is a triumph of technology over the common good. The likelihood of perpetuating antisocial acts and endangering many others does not faze the stations so long as the ratings are high.

> Copy-cat criminals learn the latest hostage intervention techniques from TV.

The way the powers that be at WABC-TV played up the Brooklyn hostage-taker, you'd think he was a member of the *Eyewitness News* team. They made it in their story, their exclusive: "Your official hostage station. Come to us first." This was blatant exploitation of the worst kind. I wouldn't be surprised if the next crazy asks for bids to the rights to his siege, auctioning his crime off like the Olympics.

Such stories have, in effect, taken the media hostage. The TV executives claim they're news, and therefore they must be covered. Are the viewers going to stop watching the summary of the day's events because it doesn't include a hostage drama? They wouldn't even be aware of what they were missing if not for the bulletins. Moreover, I would suggest it is the unpredictability—the not knowing what you will see on a news program—that is the governing principle of audience interest.

Okay, that's how I feel. Others say that once you start tampering with the public's right to know, no matter how pure your motives, you are violating the First Amendment and asking for big trouble. As Ted Koppel of ABC News' *Nightline* eloquently argued, if the government could muzzle news about kooks, nothing could prevent it from doing the same when it came to political protests (which helped get us out of Vietnam), the Bay of Pigs invasion, the Pentagon Papers.

TV attention is society's biggest reward. It should not be squandered on low lifes.

Well, I have an open mind on any issue. Maybe the solution would be to ban hostage stories from the local news and require them to be shown on public television. My thinking is as follows:

Public TV is an underutilized resource. It is not significantly involved at the present time in any socially useful function, other than reruns of British programs and old Hollywood movies. Yet it has a more intelligent audience that would perhaps be better able to cope with violence. Similar logic already guides the showing of sex and other subjects of a mature nature forbidden commercial TV. Frontal nudity, for example, has been permitted on public TV for years—so long as it is costumes in an 18th- or 19th-century drama that are coming off, because this is thought to be less incendiary.

I don't mean to imply that everybody who watches public TV is sane. But numbers are a factor, too. A commercial station can get a rating of 45 for *The Godfather*. The average public TV station is happy and is considered very successful with a rating of 2. The percentage of nuts in a small audience is bound to be smaller than in a large one.

Further, most public TV viewers read books, and literate types are less likely to take hostages or need to fulfill themselves on a local news show. Can you imagine any psychotic media freak turning himself in on *MacNeil-Lehrer*?

My scheme should satisfy Ted Koppel and other civil libertarians. Our democracy would get the news it needs to grow, and simultaneously public television's ratings would improve.

Another noninflammatory way to satisfy the public's need to know about every violent act occurs to me, using commercial outlets. The networks could be limited to reporting stories of this kind in print. For instance, a slide on *Eyewitness News* might read: "ANOTHER HIJACKING TOOK PLACE TODAY." Period. Or, "THE FOLLOWING PEOPLE WERE MURDERED IN NEW YORK DURING THE LAST 24 HOURS," followed by a list. No elaboration. The gruesome particulars are not necessary. Television news is largely a headline service anyway.

The reporting package today consists of a superstar newsreporter on the scene, accompanied by a minicam. This is needlessly dangerous. By adjusting the medium, perhaps the bomb can be defused. The message to the bad guys should be: Drop dead, get lost. You will be thrown in jail, ignored until you get your fair trial, etc. I wouldn't permit a single glimpse on the tube of the worm who allegedly did the deed, whether taking a hostage or shooting a President. If he devotes his life to serving mankind after his parole, maybe then I'd give him a little publicity. TV attention is society's biggest reward. It should not be squandered on low lifes.

None of these reforms are likely to happen by themselves, particularly when there is good reason to worry that the other station will use a gruesome event to feather its own nest. TV has not developed a social conscience to accompany the new technology. A genuine code of ethics is needed, a revolutionary concept in a business that has no standard besides the dollar. The next time the television and radio news directors meet in Las Vegas, it would be nice if in between playing 21 and sticking coins into slot machines they adjourned to a closed room and searched their souls. They should unite to ban certain practices that they all know in their hearts are bad for society. When in doubt, don't.

Newspapers are guilty of the same shoddy practices as TV, of course. But I don't have to apologize for what the papers do. And TV is far more powerful than print. Criminals don't read—they look at pictures.

SIEGES, HOSTAGES, AND THE PRESS

Editorial from Editor and Publisher (October 23, 1982).

Hard and fast rules on how the press should respond to demands from hijackers, terrorists, and others who demand their unedited messages be printed or broadcast under threat of harm or death to hostages are not only impractical but unwise.

The subject is a re-occurring one as individuals or groups adopt the technique believing they have found a new way to air their grievances.

The purely ethical rule accepted by most responsible journalists is that news people should not permit themselves to become part of the story they are covering and editors should not permit their columns to be used and exploited by outsiders for their own personal reasons.

In practice, however, the rule has been overlooked by editors who have felt that circumstances involving human lives have been compelling enough to make exceptions in the public's interest. Editors have demonstrated time and again that they are neither so arrogant or hard-boiled as not to be influenced by the human tragedy confronting the community requiring compassion rather than adherence to high ethical principles.

Each case must be judged individually.

The latest incident involved a gunman holding hostages at a Brooklyn, N.Y., hospital. He demanded that a certain newspaper reporter act as intermediary and further demanded that his statement be broadcast, which was done. In the opinion of almost everyone these two acts violated the basic principles we have referred to but in doing so the newspaper, the reporter and the broadcaster placed human lives and the community's interests first and acted admirably.

There have been many incidents where reporters have been requested to act as intermediaries, or mediators, between criminals and the law enforcement authorities. It is a compliment to the integrity of these news people and their media that they should be thought of in this regard. And, there have been many instances where terrorists and others have demanded access to print or broadcast to air their grievances. In the case of the Croatian nationalists who hijacked a plane and held 52 hostages, media gave in to the demand. In the case of the Venezuelan terrorists who had kidnapped an American businessman, they did not.

Each situation must be judged in terms of the problems involved and the threat to humanity. Each case must be judged individually. None of these cases in the past have presented easy solutions either to the press or to law enforcement agencies. It is to the credit of both, it seems to us, that each case has been treated individually and separately and fairly, and to the best of our recollection, lives have been saved not lost.

SUGGESTIONS FOR FURTHER READING

Those who are interested in a more in-depth analysis of the terrorist coverage issue may consult either of the following:

M. Cherif Bassiouni, "Media Coverage of Terrorism; The Law and the Public." *Journal of Communication* (Spring, 1982): 128–143.

James W. Hoge, "The Media and Terrorism." In *Terrorism: The Media and the Law*, edited by Abraham H. Miller. Dobbs Ferry, N.Y.: Transnational Publishers, 1982.

Also of interest:

Richard Clutterbuck, *The Media and Political Violence*. London: MacMillan, 1981.

Alex Schmid and Janny de Graff, *Violence as Communication: Insurgent Terrorism and the Western News Media*. Beverley Hills, Calif.: Sage, 1981.

CHAPTER 17

Privacy

The first reading of this chapter addresses the question of individual privacy in an age of electronic communication. Arthur Miller, a Harvard University law professor, is an outspoken advocate of the right to personal privacy. His comments first appeared in a symposium on privacy published in The *Center Magazine* in 1982.

The next two articles address a specific question within the privacy issue: publication of the names of rape victims. Michael Rouse, managing editor of the *Durham* (N.C.) *Morning Herald*, explains why he is in favor of printing the victim's name. Zena Beth McGlashan, a journalism professor at the University of North Dakota, gives an opposing opinion; that printing the victim's name amounts to a second victimization.

In the final article, David Perdew, photo editor of the Gannett Rochester Newspapers, discusses his professional concerns about printing photographs that might be invasions of privacy.

THE RIGHT TO BE LET ALONE

Arthur R. Miller

The conflict between the individual's right of privacy and the public's right to know is of enormous dimension and there is no intuitively obvious or ultimate, legally correct or socially proper way to resolve it.

Here is an illustration of it. Several years ago, President Gerald Ford was on a street in San Francisco, when, in the middle of a crowd around him, an arm raised up, with a gun in hand. It was the arm of Sara Jane Moore. She was about to shoot President Ford. An ex-marine, Oliver Sipple, was standing nearby. Instinctively he lunged forward, struck her arm, and the bullet went astray. Whether he saved the President's life or not, it was a heroic act. A few days later, a prominent San Francisco newspaper columnist wrote an article about Oliver Sipple and revealed, for all of the news agencies of the world to pick up, that the hero is a homosexual.

Now, by the performance of a heroic act, does one forfeit one's right to privacy? Does the public have the right to know the sexual preference of Oliver Sipple?

From *the Center Magazine* (September/October, 1982). Reprinted by permission.

Everybody knows what free speech is. It is the First Amendment, the first among equals. It is the holy of holies. It is, according to the press, absolute. What I prefer to talk about is the other side of the issue, namely, privacy.

The right to privacy is, it is alleged, a young right. It was discovered ninety-two years ago in a famous *Harvard Law Review* article by Samuel Warren and Louis Brandeis. It is imperfectly accepted by the courts. Some courts reject it totally. It is subject to diversion and tort categorization. Indeed, the law profession's most prestigious organization, the American Law Institute, now accepts the analysis which asserts the legal right of privacy against (1) intrusion; (2) appropriation; (3) false light; and (4) publishing of private facts.

By the performance of a heroic act, does one forfeit one's right to privacy?

I reject all that. I do not think that is what the right of privacy is in mid-twentieth-century America. To me, the right to privacy is much more than a particular tort categorization in the law. The right to privacy is the right to be let alone. It is the right of autonomy, of individuality, of self-determination, of spatial privacy, of associational privacy, of ideological privacy, of bodily privacy. All these values have one thing in common: by and large they are subjective. And therein lies their great weakness. What is private to me may be public to you. There is just no homogeny of thought about where the penumbra—or even the core—of the right to privacy lies.

That right has deep roots in the law. They reach far beyond that *Harvard Law Review* article of 1890. It is a fact of American history that, with an open frontier, with an agrarian society, with newspapers that were no more than ma-and-pa operations, and with illiteracy throughout America until this century, one never ran into any major difficulty protecting one's privacy. When Horace Greeley advised, "Go west, young man, go west," he was talking about the economic opportunities that existed in the West. But one could also go west and get away from one's bankruptcy record in the East. One could slip into the frontier without any fear that one's prior life would follow. In some loose sense, there was always the opportunity for redemption.

All that has changed. Newspapers are no longer ma-and-pa enterprises, they are Times-Mirror, Inc. And we now have these funny little signals that come through the air. You don't even have to know how to read; you can listen to NBC. And we have computers. If Horace Greeley were to tell me to go west, young man, go west, from Boston, it would be a cruel joke, because we all know that my credit record would have arrived in Los Angeles or San Francisco seven hours before I got off the plane. We live in a different world. There is no longer a frontier, there is less space, there is no illiteracy, there is massive information-gathering and maintenance, and there is worldwide communication. We live in a society that can send information from the earth to the moon in less than two and a half seconds. It is a society in which there are no time, space, or quantitative limits on the movement, transfer, and manipulation of information.

To me, the modern concept of privacy does not relate to intrusion, misappropriation, embarrassing private facts, or false light. Those things constitute the work of lawyers in their quest to get things within rigid limits. I know an embarrassing fact and misappropriation when I see them.

But to me, the modern sense of privacy and growing interest in privacy stem from four concerns. The first is data collection. More and more institutions in our society are collecting more and more data about more and more Americans and more and more aspects of their lives. You cannot travel on a plane without being computerized. You cannot check into a hotel without being computerized. You cannot even pay your taxes without giving any informational scientist a profile of your last year. Indeed, if you were to compare this year's 1040 tax return with a 1040 of twenty years ago, you would be stunned at the increased data you now provide the government in exchange for the privilege of paying your taxes.

What is private to me may be public to you.

I am not saying that is bad. I am very upset that many of you around this table are not paying your fair share of taxes, so I am delighted that the government has been improving its enforcement techniques. I am simply observing the fact that the Internal Revenue Service, along with every other organization, including the University of California at Santa Barbara, is now collecting more data about its constituent group than at any other time in our history. So, concern number one is the womb-to-tomb dossier on each of us, and the sense that we are simply an alter ego of our records.

The second concern flows from the first: it is that all those organizations that are collecting information about us are making decisions affecting us that are based on that data. We all know that with 220,000,000 people in this country there is no such thing as face-to-face credit or face-to-face banking. That is the price one pays for living in a mass society. The truth is that insurance, employment, credit, benefit eligibility, even admission to a university, are transacted almost exclusively on the basis of information, not person-to-person encounters. This creates enormous anxiety as to the accuracy of the information, the currency of the information, the relevance of the information, and the wisdom of the middle-level bureaucrats who manipulate and make decisions based on the information. I often wonder, whenever I am turned down for credit or when my BankAmericard comes back at me, whether the file is on the real Arthur Miller, or some deadbeat playwright or deadbeat law professor who happens to have my name. Do we have any existence other than these files?

A third concern is that not only are more decisions being made about us on the basis of information, which most of us do not even know exists, let alone have access to, but increasingly that data is being used out of context. The same technology that sends information to our astronauts on the moon moves information about us from its point of generation to distant files in institutions which probably have no sense of the conditions under which the original data were generated, the purposes for which they were generated, and the standards—especially the evaluation standards—of the initiating organization. But the information is moved. We all know, for example, that a grade of A at UC-Santa Barbara is not the same as a grade of A at Siwash University. So why should we assume that any evaluative data, collected by any organization, are intelligible to any other organization distant from the point of creation?

Here is a case in point. In my judgment, one of the most dangerous forms of information that gets transferred in this country is arrest data. Such data are generated by thousands of law enforcement agencies throughout the country. The information is funneled through the Federal Bureau of Investigation, by and large by the FBI's National Crime Information Center, an on-line, computer-driven criminal justice information system. Even the title of that system is emotionally loaded. It is called the Criminal Offender Record Information, even though forty percent of the people in that file are never prosecuted. Therefore, under our system, they are not criminals. But we call them "criminal offenders" because their names are put in that arrest file so labeled. Simply having one's name in that file is a stigma.

Now, in some states these arrest records circulate not only within the law enforcement community, but also to licensing organizations. If you want to be a croupier in Las Vegas, an arrrest-record check will be made on you. If you want to be a beautician in Florida, the same check will be made. And if you want to work in the securities industry in New York, you will have to go through New York's link on the FBI's arrest-record system. Thus, a system that was generated for law enforcement purposes is suddenly and curiously deemed relevant to the question of whether or not you can comb hair in Florida, sell securities in New York, or drive a taxicab in other states.

> More and more institutions in our society are collecting more and more data about more and more Americans and more and more aspects of their lives.

If you are black, male, eighteen or nineteen years old, and live in the Bedford-Stuyvesant or Harlem area in New York, the chances are eight out of ten you have been arrested at least once. So, in effect, eight out of ten urban, male, black teenagers are blacklisted from the securities industry in New York. Who says we know what we are doing?

The fourth concern is, to me, the big one philosophically. It is the role played by large and powerful organizations in our society, starting with the United States government, and including United States Steel, International Business Machines, Times-Mirror, Dow-Jones, the National Broadcasting Company, what have you. These are power institutions. Is there a place in a democratic society—whether one is part of the government or part of the military industrial complex—is there a place for information surveillance? Do we want a society in which every sound one makes and every thought one thinks is the object of surveillance? That is a deep concern of many people, and not simply those in the American Civil Liberties Union. People in Orange County, California, are also concerned. The two highest rates of nonresponsiveness on the national census are inner-city blacks and the residents of Orange County. Both have the same concern about being recorded, watched, counted, interrogated.

We saw that kind of society during the Vietnam war and only now are we beginning to understand what it means. It means the cameramen at the peace rallies who everybody knew were from the FBI. It means the benign activation of the domestic military intelligence network by President Lyndon Johnson to try to solve the inner-city disturbance problem. It also means that the more you know you are being recorded, the more you are deterred subliminally from engaging in constitutionally protected conduct. It is not the rabble-rousers who are deterred, but average people, majoritarian people.

"Come to the rally tonight on nuclear energy." "No, I understand they'll be taking pictures."

"Sign this petition on the draft." "No, you never know whether the Justice Department or the Department of Defense will get a copy of that." In effect we have been subtly terrorized by the threat of surveillance.

The real message of George Orwell's *1984* is not that a Big Brother on the television screen is watching you; it is that you think there is a Big Brother on the television screen watching you. The reality is irrelevant. If you think someone is watching, listening, and reporting, you will modulate your behavior. You want to look good in Big Brother's eyes, whether Big Brother is Ronald Reagan, the FBI, or the editorial-page writer of the *Los Angeles Times*. That's human nature. We want to look good for the record-keeper.

Now, to the degree that society does not put rational limits on the keeping or use of records, then it is tolerating the most dangerous threat to democratic society, that is, behavior modification.

These four developments—massive record-keeping, decision-making by dossier, unrestricted transfer of information from one context to another, and surveillance conduct at one level or another—relate to the mid-twentieth-century American concern for privacy.

RAPE

Michael Rouse

Those newspaper editors lacking the benefit of divine guidance usually call upon their own objective judgment when deciding such matters as the handling of crime stories. They consider how much information a reader wants and how much of it is important. What happened to whom? Did the police arrest anyone? The editors insist that their newspapers answer these questions.

That is what newspaper editors do usually—but not always. Not when rape is involved. It is here that many of us go out in search of divine guidance. We should not. We should treat rape much the same way we treat other crimes. (I do not claim divine guidance. Still, I cannot resist the opportunity to evangelize. It's the Southern in me.)

Blasphemy, you may say. Rape is different. It is stigmatic. Like no other crime, it leaves its victim in shame. The stigma undergirds in some way nearly every argument for giving rape special handling in newspapers.

From the *ASNE Bulletin* (February, 1982). Reprinted by permission.

Bowing to it, many newspapers allow prosecuting witnesses in rape cases to bring their charges against a man anonymously. In some jurisdictions, where rape is a capital offense, they will not identify the chief accuser of a man who is on trial for his life. They are all-protective of the rights of the accused in every other instance. There is, rightly, no end to their suspicion of the police, the courts and other forces of the state which are against him. But if his charge happens to be rape, their faith in the system is absolute. It is so complete that they can lay aside for his case basic, objective news judgment. They do not consider that a man accused of rape can be innocent, that perhaps he is a victim, and not a perpetrator, that someone has made an honest mistake or for some reason is prosecuting him maliciously.

Newspapers should assume in rape cases, as in other crimes, that the accused is innocent. They do not convey that assumption when they identify him and grant a special privilege of anonymity to his accuser.

And, in the long run, they are not helping rape victims at all. Their practice tends to legitimize any stigma still attached to rape. Granted, we can't end an unjust stigma overnight simply by identifying rape victims. But the more we ignore the stigma, the more it will go away. We do not help matters by allowing it to control the policies of our press and other institutions.

Rape victims will be better off when rape is brought out of the closet.

Professor Gilbert Geis, a sociologist at the University of California in Irvine, conducted a study on media reporting of rape. By granting anonymity to prosecuting witnesses, he concluded, the media are "further imparting to the act of rape a particularly dirty, shameful nuance, rather than serving to portray it and its victims as no more than part of the criminal scene. . . . Anonymity is founded in the view that there is something degrading about being raped. . . . (Anonymity) suggests that the public will in some subtle manner conclude that the victim in a way contributed to her own fate. . . . "

In any case, the stigma once attached to rape has abated. That is evident, at least, in Durham, N.C., in the Arlington, Va., area and in Winfield Kan. In those communities people have arisen in heroic proportions against what they regarded as unfair treatment of rape victims. The objects of their wrath were the local newspapers. I do not agree that the newspapers treated the rape victims unfairly, but these protesters showed a realization that rape victims deserve sympathy, not censure. That attitude is more widespread than ever. Few people continue to believe that rape is degrading to a woman, that it makes her somehow a dirty person. Because of a stigma that isn't even there, most newspapers in covering rape allow critical, unfair exceptions to good reporting.

The Winfield case went to the National News Council on a complaint from two rape victims quoted by the *Winfield Daily Courier* in a report on a hearing. The *Courier* did not identify the prosecuting witnesses, but they complained that its description of their testimony was too explicit. The News Council found properly that the complaint was unwarranted.

The *Courier's* report included such testimony as "I . . . kept moving my pelvis so he couldn't penetrate," that the rapist "went ahead with what he was doing" when an alarm clock went off, that after intercourse with one victim the man "entered her rectum." That, frankly, is more than I would have said in my paper, but I am second-guessing. One must consider seriously what *Courier* Publisher Dave Seaton told the News Council. The council's report quoted him as saying that during the hurried moments in which he was considering the story before publication "two thoughts were strongly in mind. One was his feeling that the paper had often been criticized for being too cautious and protective of the community. The other was a concern that the citizens of Winfield needed 'to know how severe rape cases are. . . . It seemed to me that there was a sound case to be made for having people face the harsh realities.'"

Amen, brother. Rape to many of our readers is but an abstract concept. A good purpose is served by describing its horror, by putting it in perspective. The *Courier* put it in perspective.

John Rains, editorial page editor of the *Durham Morning Herald*, was a heavy contributor to an 18-part series of editorials in the *Herald* in 1978 when our paper was targeted for protests, pickets and boycott because of our policy on rape coverage. In the Winfield case, Rains wondered what would have happened if the hearing had been televised, a practice that might become widespread. Would the testimony have been bleeped out, as offensive words on talk-shows are sometimes censored? If TV coverage of trials ever becomes common, to what degree should the trials be censored? Who will do the censoring?

To what degree should newspapers censor court proceedings?

If you decide that your newspaper will censor less, you might be in for the fight of your life. Hostility toward full reporting of rape knows no bounds among some readers and some public officials.

At the *Northern Virginia Sun*, Publisher Herman J. Obermayer was faced with a resolution by the Falls Church City Council withdrawing any city advertisement from the *Sun* "so long as" it persisted in identifying prosecuting witnesses in rape cases at the point of trial. (The council members substituted "so long as" for "because of" in the motion so it would not appear that they were trying to coerce the free press!)

Also seeking to coerce the free press was the tax-supported Commission on Women in the Arlington area, which assisted in a drive to persuade readers to cancel their subscriptions to the *Sun*.

Like those in Winfield and Durham, these protesters believed divine guidance was on their side. They undoubtedly were not discouraged by editorials in some of the larger newspapers in the area which were critical of Obermayer's policy.

Although Falls Church continues to withhold legal ads from the *Sun*, which is more dependent upon such advertising than most dailies, Obermayer persists in his policy. "I do not see how you can have a type of crime in which the accused is denied the protection of the law, and I cannot sit by and accept the premise that there is a crime where an individual can go to prison for life without the witnesses being publicly identified," he told the National News Council.

When rape is involved . . . many of us go in search of divine guidance. We should not. We should treat rape much the way we treat other crimes.

The *Northern Virginia Sun* does not identify prosecuting witnesses in rape cases until the cases reach the trial stage. At the *Durham Morning Herald* and its sister evening paper, the *Durham Sun*, the policy is to identify an adult prosecuting witness at the time a person is charged, not when the rape is merely reported. Our reasoning is that when a warrant is drawn, and not until then, the witness places a specific person in jeopardy. If she is 16 or under we do not identify her.

In 1978 police arrested a man on 11 rape charges after a series of attacks over several months. No names had been used when the rapes were reported but, in accordance with its policy, the *Herald* named the prosecuting witnesses when the man was charged. And while rape is not normally a front-page story, this arrest was.

The story ignited Durham's Rape Crisis Center, which organized the campaign to force us to change our policies. There were pickets, petitions, canceled subscriptions, a threatened boycott of our advertisers and, as at the *Winfield Courier* and the *Northern Virginia Sun*, an untold number of letters to the editor. We printed the letters for a while, then finally called a halt.

We met several times with our critics, including rape victims, to allow them to give us their views. Then we held a series of in-house meetings involving people from all departments of the newspaper to get other opinions. Finally, each newspaper established a committee from its own newsroom, chaired by the managing editor, for the final discussions and decision.

The policy that resulted was like our old one except for one change. Rape victims had said that after their names and addresses were published they were fearful that their attackers, or friends of the attackers, would return to punish them for prosecuting. We stopped publishing specific addresses of the witnesses, and now we use addresses that are less specific, such as Jane Smith of East Main Street. We felt that some address was needed for proper identification but that we could yield to some degree to relieve the fear of the victims. (That has caused us no problems, and we are considering extending the practice to other types of witnesses who become involved involuntarily in crimes.)

Then we had our say in the 18-part series of editorials. The series was intended mainly to convey our reasoning. We wanted also to demonstrate that our policy was not adopted capriciously but with concern for everyone involved in a rape charge and with concern for our responsibility to report the news.

There has been no widespread campaign against the policy since then, but we continue to have problems with law-enforcement agencies. We usually end up getting the names from warrants, which are public records.

If you consider publishing the names, you will surely be asked whether you would want your own daughter's name in the paper if she were raped. But, of course, newspapers must base policy on professional judgment, not personal feelings. Otherwise you might reply, "Maybe not, but if my son were accused I certainly would want his accuser identified. Someone might come forth with important information about the case."

Of the arguments that we heard against our policy, the most common was the statement that publishing the names discouraged women from reporting rape and prosecuting rapists. If that is true it is an unfortunate but necessary trade-off. But it is not necessarily true.

Some women are reluctant for many reasons to report a rape—even to tell a close friend, much less describe it in detail to a stranger from the police department.

Once a person reports a rape, most of the people who are close to her probably will learn of it whether or not the newspaper prints her name. And of course the people close to her are the ones who matter to her.

As the stigma continues to subside, rape victims will be more inclined to call in the police. And facing the people close to them will be easier.

I am glad Professor Geis agrees with me. And I am particularly gratified if my paper's policy helps, even just a little, to lessen the stigma against innocent victims of rape. Still, I am a newsman, not a sociologist. And newspaper editors are supposed to report the news, accurately, fairly, and thoroughly. We are not supposed to recognize stigmas; we are not responsible for what simple-minded people might do with news once it is reported.

Note: Results of Professor Geis' study are in the book Deviance and the Mass Media, *edited by Charles Winick and published by Sage Publications in Beverly Hills, Calif.*

BY REPORTING THE NAME, AREN'T WE VICTIMIZING THE RAPE VICTIM TWICE?

Zena Beth McGlashan

Rape has indeed come out of the closet—as an issue which still needs thoughtful, frequent coverage. Rape victims, however, are still in that closet, edging their way toward the light.

Michael Rouse's self-labeled evangelical appeals to editors to adopt the policy of his paper—the *Durham* (N.C.) *Morning Herald*, which prints the names of victims as well as the accused when rape charges are filed—indicates Rouse to be a devotee of the "bullet theory" of communication. Because newspapers and other media have responded to the most recent wave of American feminism by running feature stories, first-person accounts (both anonymous and from women who have been willing to identify themselves) and news stories replete with rape statistics, Rouse would have us believe that only the "simple-minded" still attach some stigma to this crime and its victims.

A decade or so of public information doesn't re-mold society's biases. If change occurred on the tidy schedule which partially forms the basis for Rouse's argument, then women would have won the right to vote about 1858, ten years after the Seneca Falls Convention. History—and common wisdom such as that gained by being in the newspaper business for any length of time—tells us that society doesn't change its attitudes rapidly.

Important gains are being made in respect to women's willingness to report. According to the FBI Uniform Crime Reports, experts estimate that the more than 82,000 rapes reported to police in 1980 may represent only a small part of the number of rapes committed. However, that figure represents a 45 percent increase in reports from the 1976 total, which is encouraging to those dedicated to rape counseling and prevention. The FBI attributes this significant rise in reports to the growing number of rape crisis centers and an increased sensitivity by police in dealing with victims.

The number of rapes reported is not mirrored in the number of arrests, which totaled 49 percent—up less than 1 percent from 1979 and just 18 percent from 1976. Reluctance on the part of victims to sign arrest warrants—thus placing themselves in jeopardy—their inability to identify their assailants and police successes in carrying through on arrest warrants are among factors explaining the fact that slightly less than half the reported rapes resulted in arrests.

Federal guidelines for Uniform Crime Reports define forcible rape as a "women-only" crime. Apparently—and not surprisingly—government regulations may be caught in a "culture lag," evident in Rouse's and, to be fair, probably most people's thinking. We do tend to label rape as a crime inflicted solely on women.

However, men are also rape victims, as reflected in a recent *New York Times* story. Dr. Margaret McHugh, director of the child abuse team at Bellevue Hospital and an associate professor of pediatrics at New York University Medical Center, was quoted: "Sexual victimization of

From the *ASNE Bulletin* (April, 1982). Reprinted by permission.

males is much more common than most people recognize, but we don't talk about it in our culture." Male rape, inflicted primarily by other men and not limited to children and adolescent boys, may be far more prevalent than we now realize, adding another layer to the sensitivity required of the press when helping the public learn about social problems. We may soon have to abandon our attitude toward male rape and sexual abuse as being a problem confined to prisons.

Rape counselors agree that chief among the reasons for not reporting rapes are the victims' fear of publicity, of attracting other potential rapists and of dreading the isolation that comes with the role of victim. Stigmatization still prevails. A well-educated friend of mine, when he learned about the rape of a woman we both knew, ruefully admitted to me later that his first thought was to "wonder what she had done to invite it."

Rape counselors agree that chief among the reasons for not reporting rapes are the victims' fear of publicity, of attracting other potential rapists and of dreading the isolation that comes with the role of victim.

Even for the strong victim, concern for others may have a chilling effect on whether she reports the crime. A student once told me that the reason she had not pressed charges against her attacker, whom she recognized, was not fear of confronting the man in court—"I'd really like to get that bastard"—but worry over what she anticipated would be her parents' traumatic reaction.

For most victims, going to court "is as much of a crisis as the act of rape," according to Ann Wolbert Burgess and Lynd Lytle Holmstrom, both of Boston College. In their book, *Rape: Crisis and Recovery,* they relate the court delays, the public setting and, in some instances, a continuing tendency to treat the victim "as if she were the offender" as stresses which victims must endure. Burgess, a professor of nursing, and Holmstrom, a sociology professor, also say that because the victim's character is examined as closely as that of the accused, then the victim must live with the "silent suspicion" that she was not raped after all, if the defendant is found not guilty. She may be considered by some to be psychotic, in search of attention. False accusation cases do happen. But these are overwhelmed by the number of cases in which the charge is firmly established, even if the accused's guilt is not proven well enough—for any of a number of legal reasons—for a jury decision to conflict.

Counselors also agree that rape victims are far more liable to be threatened than are victims of other crimes. This undermines Rouse's condescending to print only general, not specific, victims' addresses with rape charges. Even in a metropolitan area, that policy may not provide a shred of protection. For example, when I lived in Los Angeles, mine was the only such name in the phone directory.

Rouse suggests that a victim's friends will know anyway. "Friends" is a broad term—like a rock dropped into a pond, the circle from its wake spreads farther and farther. If I were raped, I would not hide it from my family and close friends. But would I feel comfortable having all the people I know—from passing acquaintances at work to the man who okays my check at the supermarket—aware that I had been raped?

Margaret T. Gordon, chairwoman of the advisory committee to the National Health Institute's National Center for the Prevention and Control of Rape, says, "Prosecutors have made it clear that when newspapers print the names of rape victims, it discourages other victims from reporting rapes." This chilling effect of publicity relates to what Professor Gordon, director of the Center for Urban Affairs and Policy Research at Northwestern and a former news professional who also teaches courses at Northwestern's Medill School of Journalism, says is vital to the victim's psychological recovery: "She needs to be able to control who knows about the rape."

In one case, when a suburban newspaper printed the name of a victim without her consent or knowledge, the victim's son found out about his mother's rape when he was taunted by grade-school playmates, Gordon said. The newspaper editor was persuaded by an aroused community to abandon her policy which was based similarly to Rouse's—that the stigma will disappear more rapidly if the press provides equal treatment to the accused and the accuser.

Beverly Kees, executive editor of the *Grand Forks* (N.D.) *Herald* and a former associate managing editor of the *Minneapolis Tribune*, says she has known women who have made the personal choice and talked to the press about their rapes. "I wish more women would," Kees said. But as for newspapers making that choice for rape victims, "I don't think we've gotten to that point yet," because publication of a victim's name means that the "victim has become victimized twice."

Victims of rape are not traffic offenders. Johnny Carson, picked up for driving while intoxicated, can say on television: "I've learned my lesson; I sure won't do that again." Everyone understands. But what "lesson" is the rape victim supposed to learn from the publication of her identity? Is she supposed to come forward and say: "I've learned my lesson. I won't be raped again?"

For editors who may have found themselves swayed by Rouse's argument, reading Professor Gilbert Geis's article, which the Durham editor cites as support for his policy, may be helpful. The research, supported by funding from the National Center for the Prevention and Control of Rape, is a sociological review and interpretation of legal restrictions on rape coverage in the United States and Great Britain. Geis, who has done extensive research about rape, does conclude, as Rouse reports, that giving equal treatment of the accused as well as the accuser may result in the "best redress of injustice," because society will be "fully informed about those processes and persons involved in and victims of injustice." Geis, however, also qualifies his conclusion by saying his opposition to anonymity is "perhaps, but hopefully not, based on wishful thinking. . . ."

We may soon have to abandon our attitude toward male rape and sexual abuse as being a problem confined to prisons.

Concerning professional standards, one of my students here at the University of North Dakota insightfully observed that, just as we recognize both the law and the "spirit of the law," so should there be a "spirit of reporting" as well as the "law" of reporting. And a Durham resident told me, "If Mike Rouse wants to be fair, he could go the other way and choose not to reveal either name."

Rouse seems to want editors to believe that they're between a rock and a hard place: either choose "divine guidance" (heavenly beams directed to the newsroom?) or "objectivity." The editors I've been fortunate enough to work for have factored into their decisions such things as community standards and the "public good," as well as the difference between what the public "needs to know" and what isn't really necessary.

I learned a good deal from Walter Nelson, editor of the *Butte* (Mont.) *Standard,* 20 years ago. As an idealist fresh out of journalism school, I wondered why the local folks had not voted in favor of a governmental reform issue for which the paper had eloquently campaigned. Nelson, silver-haired and wise with decades of newspaper experience, smiled and told me: "One thing I've learned in this business is that people always do what they want to do."

Rouse's battle with the residents of Durham has not ended but has been fired up again by protests from the Duke University student body which sponsored a week-long rape education program in February. The policy of the Durham papers, both the *Herald* and the *Sun,* which leads directly to a decline in women's willingness to report rapes—much less go on to prosecute—is one which Rouse calls a "necessary tradeoff."

I would like to believe such lack of "censoring" does influence the rapid removal of any stigma rape has, adds to the education of the public and does not damage a victim seriously; that, in fact, it will be helpful toward having rape victims view their sexual violations as they would any other crime. But, I keep returning to Walter Nelson's words about human nature. Editors, like their readers, are human. But they are also, I believe, generally more humane and careful with the power they wield to damage other human beings.

Society should be rid of its "hangups" about the criminal act of rape and its edgy attitudes toward rape victims, just as women should become stronger physically and in their attitudes toward themselves. In reality, we aren't there yet. And the weight of evidence indicates it's going to take a long time and much more counseling, education and judicious reporting about both victims' ordeals and rapists' motives before rape becomes a routine news event. By then—after many years of concentrated effort—perhaps we'll see substantial attitude change and, even more ideally, a significant decline in the incidence of the crime itself.

EDITORS FACE THE TOUGH QUESTION: SHOULD THE PHOTOS RUN?

David Perdew

The old woman's face was pressed against the windshield. She had been pinned between the dashboard and the front seat after an oncoming motorist slammed into her car. Her face was twisted with fear and agony.

It was the summer of 1976. I was a photography intern with the *Louisville Courier-Journal* and *Times.* This was the first time I had encountered a spot-news situation.

I often thought about spot news and even dreamed of winning awards with dramatic news pictures. All I needed was the right situation.

The woman in the car seemed to afford the opportunity for a dramatic, award-winning picture. Her face, the windshield, the pain—all were elements of an easy photograph. Easy to see, easy to take.

But I didn't take it.

She saw me. And with her eyes asking me not to take her picture, not to humiliate her by putting her misfortune on page 1, I walked away.

But I always regretted that. Did I not take the

From *Editorially Speaking* (April, 1982). Reprinted by permission.

picture because I was sensitive to human suffering, because I was sensitive to the woman's unspoken wishes? Was I intimidated by being caught in the act of stealing a person's image—invading her privacy (dignity)?

Or did I just shirk my duties as a news photographer?

Ask a picture editor what I should have done. Many will say, "Make the picture; worry about it later."

SHOOT FIRST; ASK LATER

That's the safe way. It's also the most difficult approach for the photographer: Shoot first; ask questions later.

> A picture that lets readers feel what the person in the picture feels takes a toll not only on the photographer but also on everyone who comes in contact with the picture.

Editors push photographers to take pictures in tough situations, just as reporters are asked to call the surviving families for obituaries. It's the business.

But a picture that lets readers feel what the person in the picture feels takes a toll not only on the photographer but also on everyone who comes in contact with the picture. Editors must accept the responsibility for including such a photograph in the day's news report.

When there is a big story such as a gunman holding hostages at a bank, editors hope for the dramatic picture that illustrates the terror and insanity of the situation. Rochester photographer Jim Laragy captured that moment when a bank teller ran—screaming—from a Security Trust Bank branch in Rochester. Windows were shattered behind her by the gunman's shots.

A bank teller runs from a bank after being held hostage in Rochester,N.Y., by a gunman who killed another teller, then was killed himself by police sharpshooters. The photo is by Gannett Rochester Newspapers photographer Jim Laragy. Writes Photo Editor David Perdew: "When there is a big story . . . editors hope for the dramatic picture that illustrates the terror and insanity of the situation."

All the legal torts were on the newspaper's side: public place, newsworthiness, being thrust into the public eye. The picture was used dramatically in both Rochester newspapers and, through The Associated Press, dramatically in newspapers across the country. (See photo, above.)

But three days later, when Rochester photographer Burr Lewis was sent to a slain bank teller's funeral, he knew the situation would be tense and emotional. He sat inconspicuously for two and a half hours at the front of the church, camera pointed toward the dead woman's son and his father, waiting for the right picture. And Burr asked himself why he was there.

Certainly that is a legitimate question—and one that editors must always ask, because they can be sure that readers will. Why would we use the very dramatic and emotional picture of the son crying on the father's shoulder? Why does the public need to see that?

SOME GUIDELINE QUESTIONS

There is no book we can open to determine whether the picture should run or whether it is invading someone's privacy. We have to rely on the gut.

Here are some questions for editors to keep in mind to help them decide:

- What's the scope of the story?
- Who is affected?
- Does it convey a sense of loss, of tragedy?
- Is it honest?
- Would we be serving the readers by running the picture? Or could we be accused of censoring or softening the news if we don't run it?
- Is it important?
- Does the gruesomeness of the death outweigh the reasons for running the picture?

The answers to those questions can evoke very subjective, honest and often different responses among editors. No one will have the absolute, correct answer.

It is the picture editor's job to explain why the newspaper should run pictures or not run them. But it is also his job to listen, to gain a perspective on the story by talking to reporters and photographers involved, to show the pictures to people and get their reactions.

At the funeral of a slain bank teller in Rochester, N.Y., photographer Burr Lewis took this photograph of the dead woman's son and the boy's father. Writes editor Perdew: "Why would we use the very dramatic and emotional picture . . . ? Why does the public need to see that?"

A FINE LINE

Pictures that have substance and impact should run; pictures that are sensational shouldn't. But often there is a very fine line between the two. Consider these instances:

- A fireman is carrying a dead baby to an ambulance. The photographer takes a picture. At this point, the newspaper has a dramatic—and by accepted photojournalistic standards, a good—picture from a fire scene. But what is the impact that picture will have on readers? How would a photo of a dead baby help our readers understand the importance of the news?

But the ambulance driver starts mouth-to-mouth resuscitation, and the child is revived. Now we have a story—something to tell the readers through photographs that is more than another picture of a fire victim.

Establishing rules that say "we do not run pictures of bodies or death" is as irresponsible as running every picture of lifeless bodies. That is what makes newspaper photography difficult; editors and photographers have to produce and evaluate. Each picture has to help us understand the story, not just shock us.

Sometimes pictures of death are the only means by which we understand the impact of a story. (Remember the charred bodies from the failed U.S. rescue mission in Iran; the grotesque firing squad executions of the Kurdish rebels in Iran; the My Lai massacre; the Jonestown suicides; and other situations often closer to home?)

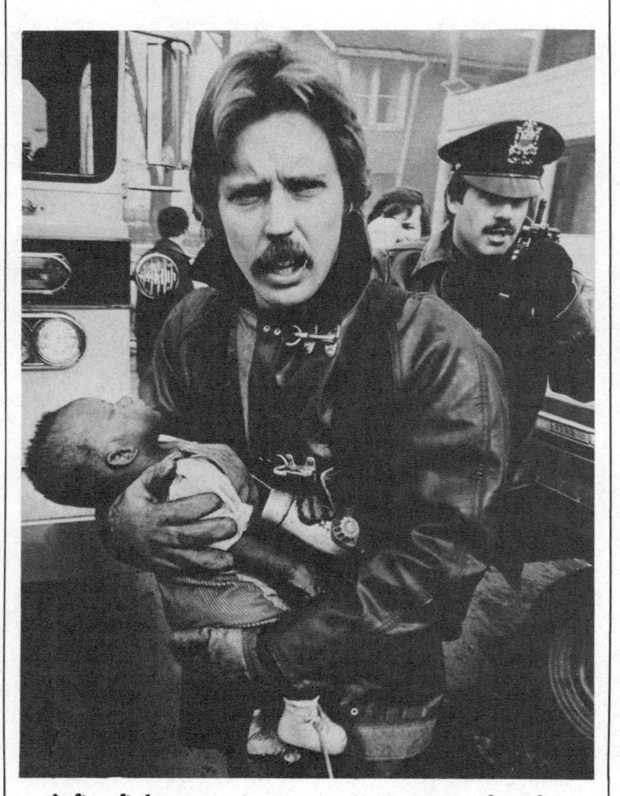

A fire fighter carries a young victim in the photograph by Burr Lewis (above). And a young child (in photo above) breaks into tears as he, his father and brother are met by newspeople at the Rochester airport. The photograph is by Reed Hoffman of the Rochester newspapers. Writes Perdew: "Pictures that have substance and impact should run; pictures that are sensational shouldn't. But often there is a very fine line between the two."

- A school principal returns to town from Texas after locating his former wife who had run away with their two sons. It's the climax of a two-year search. The school principal talks freely with reporters about the ordeal—even appears on live television.

But at the airport, with his two young sons in tow, he is met by about 20 reporters and photographers. The youngest child, anxious about the whole ordeal, begins to cry. The photographers shoot furiously. The editors ponder the photographs and consider the impact, the purpose and the content.

What damage are the newspapers causing the family? How can the newspapers not show the readers what the effect of the two-year trauma is on the children?

> Would we be serving the readers by running the picture? Or could we be accused of censoring or softening the news if we don't run it?

- Two men contemplate suicide: One is atop the 10-story parking garage downtown; the other is on the ledge of a bridge over a river.

Hundreds of people watch the man atop the parking garage for an hour or two as he talks with police and a girlfriend and finally is rescued.

Police have cordoned off the bridge where the second man is leaning over the water. Police identify him as a former mental patient; he is talked back on the road in a few minutes. Several police hurry him away.

The newspaper's photographers have recorded emotional moments from each event. Is the public-place rule enough to warrant publication of both pictures? Do we run them because we have them?

The suicide attempt at the parking garage affected more people and was potentially more dangerous—more newsworthy. It was an event of some importance in the day's events.

Photographer Burr Lewis catches the moment when police and a girlfriend grasp a man who threatened to jump from the roof of a municipal garage in downtown Rochester, N.Y. Editor Perdew writes that from the agony of determining whether to run such pictures "evolves a responsible newspaper with substance."

The other affected only a few and didn't have the same impact.

But, more importantly, the circumstances were different. While anyone can contend that someone who tries to end his life is a potential mental patient, the confirmed mental history of one man must make an editor look at the pictures differently. The outcome may be the same; the editor may run them both (or only one or neither). But the photograph of the former mental patient certainly is more questionable and probably less newsworthy.

All of these situations were actual, agonizing

decisions faced by several people at the Rochester newspapers. But from such agony evolves a responsible newspaper with substance, rather than a sensational scandal sheet.

And that agonizing and decision making begin when a photographer feels the pain as he presses the shutter button.

SUGGESTIONS FOR FURTHER READING

Those who are interested in the privacy issue might want to read some articles in the first edition of *Mass Media Issues*: "The Press, Privacy and the Constitution," Floyd Abrams's analysis of the four types of privacy actions; "The Press and Privacy," Arthur Miller's explanation of why he believes privacy to be more important than the public's "right to know"; and James Alexander Thom's "The Perfect Picture," a personal perspective on privacy.

Another analysis of the privacy controversy can be found in Theodore L. Glasser, "Resolving the Press–Privacy Conflict: Approaches to the Newsworthiness Defense," *Communications and the Law* 4, no. 2: 23–42. Glasser compares three legal approaches to newsworthiness and concludes, "there may be only a limited constitutional privilege to pander to vulgar curiosity by publishing lurid gossip."

Another interesting privacy issue surfaces when a film is produced about a live celebrity without that celebrity's permission. See Tamar Lewin, "Whose Life is It, Anyway? Legally, It's Hard to Tell," *New York Times*, November 21, 1982 sec. 2, p. 1. This article analyzes the issue in light of the Liz Taylor case—she threatened to sue CBS when they announced their intention to make a movie of her life.

Also of interest:

Trudy Hayden and Jack Novick, *Your Rights to Privacy*. New York: Avon, 1980.

Jethro K. Lieberman, *Privacy and the Law*. New York: Lothrop, 1978.

Don R. Pember, *Privacy and the Press: The Law, the Mass Media, and the First Amendment*. Seattle, Wash.: University of Washington Press, 1972.

James Rule, Douglas McAdams, Linda Sterns, and David Uglow, *The Politics of Privacy*. New York: NAL, 1980. A study of the invasion of privacy in America.

CHAPTER 18 Copyright

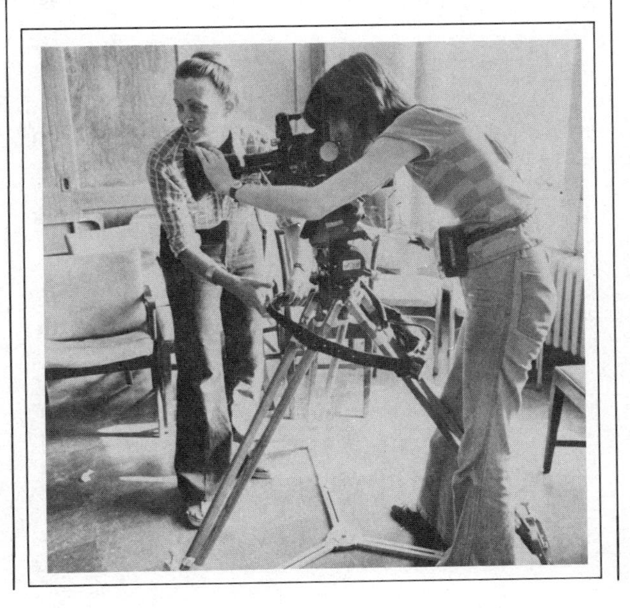

Copyright is currently one of the most disputed areas of mass communications law. This chapter's first article, by David Ladd, U.S. Register of Copyrights, explains the background of the current home-videotaping controversy. Mr. Ladd's article appeared in the *Wilson Library Bulletin* of December, 1981.

The second article is film critic Stephen Farber's analysis of the copyright conflict between film producers and authors of nonfiction who work with the same topic. The article appeared in the May 1982 issue of *American Film*.

The third reading, Peter Shaw's "Plagiary," is an insightful analysis of the societal and personal implications of plagiarism, an issue that arises on college campuses nearly as often as it does in the world of mass communication.

PRIVATE USE, PUBLIC POLICY: COPYRIGHT AND HOME RECORDING

David Ladd

Nowadays, above all else, technology dictates the content of our copyright laws and plots their course into the future. In the last twenty years, more than ever, copyright specialists have been preoccupied with problems falling under the heading of "new technology." The problems arising from the relationship between copyright and new technologies are, however, not new.

Copyright originated in technological change—the printing press—and at each stage in the history of copyright law, technological innovation has been a central problem to policy makers. However new the computer may seem, however strange or exotic laser holography, the videodisc, and direct satellite broadcasting, the central questions they pose for authors, disseminators, and users have been with us a long time.

The contemporary attitude toward our generation's copyright problems with new technology is ambivalent: optimism over the prospects of new markets, new modes of education,

From *Wilson Library Bulletin* (December, 1981). Reprinted by permission.

and new sources of consumer satisfaction is tempered by anxiety over the dangers of irretrievable loss of control over copyrighted works because of that technology.

Videocassette recording technology is only a simple and clear example: educators are eagerly and imaginatively exploiting this new tool, the prospect of large video sale and rental markets is excitingly attractive, yet the motion picture and television production industries sense that recording equipment can blight markets for rentals and sales to consumers, and even the broadcast market as well. In short, in the area of new technologies and elsewhere, domestically and internationally, copyright is pressed to keep pace with changes for the benefit of authors and proprietors; and, in some quarters, questions are raised about whether copyright can keep pace at all.

This is unfortunate, because copyright, as the principal instrument for protection of author's rights, is widely accepted throughout the world. The principle is clearly stated in the preamble of the Universal Copyright Convention: that a universal copyright system "will ensure respect for the rights of the individual and encourage the development of literature, the sciences and the arts. . . . "

And throughout the world, under the international conventions, copyright has extended and expanded to accommodate that principle to new kinds of works and to new uses of works. Whatever its basis anywhere—reward or incentive, privilege or natural right—the exclusive rights of the author have always been rooted in economic realities. Protection for the creations of authors may be based upon recognition of the special role of creative artists in shaping national or human culture. The nature of such protection, however, depends upon the marketplace in given societies. We may dwell in the sublime realms of Don Quixote's vision only if we also are properly mindful of Sancho Panza's more earthly concerns.

ADAPTING COPYRIGHT TO NEW TECHNOLOGY

Applying this instrument of copyright to contemporary conditions has not always been easy. The adaptation of copyright rules to technology began with piano rolls and jukeboxes, then with motion pictures, broadcasting, sound recording, and television, and recently with computers, cable television, and photocopying machines.

The questions that arose were varied and difficult. The marvel is that the adaptation occurred in the United States as efficiently as it did, since it was largely accomplished by judicial decision. But courts can only go so far, particularly when they are forced to compromise conflicting interests when statutory guidance is absent or unclear. The market-place of the 1920s and '30s was smaller and more amenable to gradual, judicial expansion of copyright. Today we may not have the luxury of assessing technological impact at our leisure.

Technology now presents copyright with especially troublesome problems of adaptation. The rate of technological change has accelerated, and accordingly, the strains on copyright have intensified. There has also emerged a new problem different in kind: how to control uses of copyrighted works that are not readily detectable and therefore not readily policeable. Until recently, nearly all infringements of copyrighted works were public and so visible at their source that enforcement of copyright presented no special problems, particularly after the appearance of collecting societies.

Take, for example, the cinema market of the 1930s. Replication was strictly controlled; distribution was only through a limited number of theaters, and filmmakers did not even part with ownership of their prints. Contrast this with the multitiered markets for motion pictures today: theaters, television, cable, MDS, cassettes, special educational, and 16mm markets. The same reproduction devices once used only by the copyright owner are now widely owned, and copyright owners are confronted with the problem of controlling unauthorized copying of protected works with these devices. Now, in these new problem areas, we must decide whether we can devise and use the equivalent of the theater-era box office to collect payments for use, or whether we must throw up our hands and accept all home copying as lawless but uncontrollable, or lawful because it is uncontrollable.

CURRENT AUDIO AND VIDEO TAPING PRACTICES

Audio and video recording equipment are used by many different groups including unauthorized commercial "pirates," schools, libraries, archives and other nonprofit organizations, and private individuals. Each of these uses presents different concerns, interests, and potential dangers. While this article focuses on private home taping, a few words about each kind of taping may be useful.

Unauthorized commercial recording In recent years, there has been rapid growth in the unauthorized reproduction and distribution of copyrighted sound recordings and audiovisual works in copies or phonorecords. It poses a threat not only to the recording and motion picture industries, but to the public.

In fact, film and record piracy has become epidemic around the world, as participants at the World Intellectual Property Organization Forum on the Piracy of Sound and Audiovisual Recordings well know. In the United States, this form of unauthorized recording is clearly an infringement under section 106 of the copyright law. Sanctions, both civil and criminal, are available under chapter 5 of the law to deal with this situation. However, with the recent developments in technology, experience indicates that the present criminal sanctions, especially the length of the prison terms, should be increased in the hope of restraining those who illegally interfere with the legitimate market for sound recordings, motion pictures, and other protected works. Legislation to achieve that purpose is now pending before Congress.

Educational recording Educational uses of television and radio programming is *not* a subspecies of the larger issue of home taping. Educational off-air taping is not merely a matter of personal convenience. Film and video are so much a part of world culture and modern history that education without the moving image would be incomplete. Educational off-air taping can take several forms: spontaneous taping for a single use or collecting for repeated use, perhaps by several cooperating educational institutions. The materials taped off-air may be unavailable from authorized sources, or they may in fact be works specifically created for sale, rental, or broadcast to schools.

Private home recording Home recording by individuals for their own personal, private use has flourished in the United States. Its scope and growth have caused concern to copyright owners. While recording of both audio and audiovisual works represents potential harm to copyright owners, the varied reasons for recording and the possible legal response to different cases warrant separate analysis.

People record audio works at home primarily to build a library for repeated enjoyment. Audiovisual works, on the other hand, by their length and nature, have a limited reuse value. This difference, when coupled with the current high cost of blank videotape (as opposed to blank audiotape), somewhat reduces the immediate prospects for extensive collecting of audiovisual works.

Why, then, is home video recording increasing? Two reasons have been mentioned in public discussions: people want to avoid commercial advertisements and to shift programming times. Commercial broadcast stations today charge advertising rates according to the popularity of their particular programming. And because copyright owners' royalties are tied to audience size, unmeasured time-shifting and commercial advertisement avoidance are important to the program supply industries. This looks merely technical, but it cuts to the very heart of our system for determining broadcast value of films and television programs. The price of freeing the viewer from the constraints of broadcast scheduling creates uncertainty in audience measurement by present sampling methods and also risks reduction of audience size for later broadcast reruns.

THE LEGAL RESPONSE TO COPYRIGHT VIOLATIONS

How are all these diverse interests and activities treated under the 1976 Copyright Act? What structure does it provide to guide market evolution? Section 106 of our new law enumerates five fundamental and exclusive rights. Three of these rights—distribution of copies and phonorecords, performance, and display—are limited to public uses. No such limitations are present with respect to the right of reproduction and adaptation.

The statute sets forth these rights in broad terms, unlimited by general requirements of commerciality or profit, and then provides express and specific limitations, qualifications, and exemptions to these rights in the twelve sections that follow. The very architecture of the statute thus has compelling advantages in explicitly demarcating the legislature's balance between the rights of ownership and the rights of use.

By the same token, the statute avoids wholesale exceptions, such as "not-for-profit" uses, that entail too great a risk of eroding the copyright monopoly. Furthermore, it makes possible that claims for additional limitations, qualifications, or exemptions can be subjected to the legislative process and there assessed upon the whole evidence from all interests, instead of a limited litigation record between a few private parties.

> A universal copyright system will ensure respect for the rights of the individual and encourage the development of literature, the sciences and the arts.

The structure of the statute is central to the home taping issue because of one obvious fact: none of the twelve sections *expressly* recognizes home taping as permissible. Instead, attempts to balance interests in this area center around section 107 and the doctrine of fair use of copyrighted works. Regardless of the context—commercial, noncommercial, educational, or private—the question in the United States so far has boiled down to two lines of inquiry: whether the use is "fair" or infringing, and whether the unqualified right of reproduction in section 106 is inherently limited to exclude private reproductions.

First, a few words about the doctrine of fair use in United States law.

"FAIR USE" IN U.S. COPYRIGHT LAW

For 188 years, before the 1976 Copyright Act came into force, the principle of fair use was devised, applied, and elaborated by courts. Some see it as a policy-based defense, or waiver, for infringing use. Others view it as an inherent, indwelling limitation on the author's right, which, in a given case, bars a conclusion that infringement has occurred.

The absence of a statutory definition of fair use may have posed difficulties in applying it prospectively to certain activities; but, as a judicial instrument utilized in litigation, it was a flexible way of adjusting the reach of the copyright monopoly to fit the needs of justice in practical situations. Adding up particular holdings to reach a single definition of fair use was, however, a speculative business. It still is.

> Because copyright owners' royalties are tied to audience size, unmeasured time-shifting and commercial advertisement avoidance are important to the program supply industries. This looks merely technical, but it cuts to the very heart of our system for determining broadcast value of films and television programs.

The new law sets out the principle of fair use in section 107, with four tests (here paraphrased) to guide its application in specific cases: (1) quantity—that is, how much of the protected work was taken; (2) the nature of the work; (3) the practical substitutability of the copied portions for the original work; and (4) the possibility or degree of risk that the copy poses to the market for the copyrighted original—that is, the impact of the copying on the potential market for or value of the work.

The tests were developed from commercial litigation. From a canvass of this litigation as a whole, it appears that in ninety-nine percent of the reported cases, courts applied "fair use" to assure that the copyright monopoly in one work would not be so overreaching as to prevent a second, otherwise original work from becoming available to the public. Less than a half-dozen cases deal with noncommercial, educational uses, and only one deals with private, noncommercial reproduction. Yet, under our new law, "fair use" is the cockpit of conflict over educational and private copying privileges.

LEGAL RESPONSES TO EDUCATIONAL OFF-AIR TAPING

Scattered throughout the law are a number of limited exceptions to the exclusive rights of the copyright owner that involve noncommercial or classroom uses of protected works: for example, archival preservation of audiovisual news reporting and ephemeral recording of non-dramatic literary and musical works in educational broadcasting. But only the doctrine of fair use would appear to insulate educators from potential liability for the kinds of off-air recording activities they wish to routinely pursue.

On this question, the Congress, in enacting the 1976 revision, noted only that:

> The problem of off-the-air taping for nonprofit classroom use of copyrighted audiovisual works incorporated in radio and television broadcasts has proven difficult to resolve. The Committee believes that the fair use doctrine has some limited application in this area, but it appears that the development of detailed guidelines will require a more thorough exploration . . . of the needs and problems of a number of different interests affected and of the various legal problems presented. . . . [T]he Committee . . . urges the representatives of the various interests, if possible under the leadership of the Register of Copyrights to continue their discussions actively. . . .

"Guidelines" are a curious U.S. invention: they raise the well-known "gentlemen's agreements" to a somewhat higher, publicly endorsed status. Standing somewhere between these "gentlemen's agreements" and law, they can symbolize consensus and enhance definition in the application of abstract principles like "fair use." They can exercise the kind of influence that one hopes good common sense always has; and they can be changed, as experience exposes their flaws, more readily than legislation can be amended.

In 1979, during the course of an oversight hearing, Congress selected a small number of individuals drawn from among educators, copyright owner interests, public broadcasting, and artists' guilds to negotiate guidelines on educational fair use of broadcast audiovisual works. After nearly three years of work, during which negotiations were stalemated and almost terminated, guidelines have been produced.

I will not belabor you with their details. I'll note only that the thrust of the guidelines is to give individual teachers the freedom to make tapes or to request that taping be done in more or less spontaneous fashion; that a fixed period for retention and classroom use is permitted, followed by a period during which the work recorded may be evaluated (previewed) for possible longer term retention and use; and express recognition that, for longer term use or retention, the permission of the copyright owner is required.

The negotiation of these guidelines may have been, in some degree, influenced by copyright litigation. In the case of *Encyclopaedia Britannica Educational Corp. v. Crooks* (known as the "BOCES" case), a preliminary injunction was issued on behalf of the plaintiffs, copyright owners of educational audiovisual works. The injunction enjoined a noncommercial educational media center from systematically videorecording copyrighted programs off-the-air and subsequently distributing the copies to schools in a number of districts. Two crucial facts should be noted: first, the copying was done at a copying center whenever it was determined that a program of educational value was broadcast on television, and the copies were then offered to the teachers in the various schools by use of listings in a catalog; and second, the copy center did not require that the copy be returned or erased after use.

The court stated: "The scope of BOCES' activities is difficult to reconcile with its claim of fair use. This case does not involve an isolated instance of a teacher copying copyrighted material for classroom use but concerns a highly organized and systematic program for reproducing videotapes on a massive scale." A final decision on the merits of this case is expected soon.

PRIVATE HOME RECORDING AND THE LAW

To consider the extent to which "fair use" is applicable to the home recording of television programming in the United States, one must begin with the already famous "Betamax" case of *Universal Studios, et. al. v. Sony Corp. of America, et. al.*

The case held that the noncommercial home recording of copyrighted material broadcast over the public airwaves, under the circumstances of the case, was not an infringement and was permissible as fair use under the Copyright Acts of 1909 and 1976.

Several points about the "Betamax" case raise the question of whether litigation and court decisions can satisfactorily resolve such complex issues. It must be said, however, that the court had to decide, because statutory law may not have.

First, in finding an implied limitation of the exclusive right of reproduction, the court gave significant weight to the legislative history of the Sound Recording Act of 1971, despite the differences in the types of works involved and the different commercial markets for them.

Second, in applying fair use, the court emphasized that the programming involved was broadcast *freely* over the public airwaves, and expressly refrained from addressing home recording from either pay or cable television. Nor did it rule on the legality of either tape swapping or tape duplication.

Third, the court found that the plaintiffs had failed to establish any present or past harm as a result of off-air taping, and that plaintiff's allegations of potential harm were too speculative to provide a basis for relief.

The "Betamax" court gave vent to its feeling that the problem was not well suited to judicial resolution:

> The ramifications of this new technology are greater than the boundaries of this lawsuit. A court reviewing the limited claims of specified parties in a particular factual setting cannot and should not undertake the role of a government commission or legislative body exploring and evaluating all the uses and consequences of the videotape recorder.

THE LIMITATIONS OF JUDICIAL DECISIONS

What does it mean when courts emphasize how little law they are pronouncing, acknowledge how blunt a tool for policy-making litigation is, and glance pointedly at the national legislature?

When law, and broad policy, are created judicially—and make no mistake, in America nowadays they undeniably are so made—policy emerges piecemeal by small accretions of precedent; or, in an effort to achieve legislation-like results, courts issue broad declarations that really rest on the particular facts of the given case. These shortcomings need to be carefully considered, because the courts are already moving to apply the test of fair use to private taping and other copyright problems created by new technologies. The result may be the emergence of broad policies without any clear legislative guidance.

A relatively small number of households with videotaping equipment may not be enough to create immediate palpable harm to copyright owners—whether one views markets broadly or narrowly. But a national viewing public that has integrated videocassette technology into its home entertainment habits is, cumulatively, quite another thing. A single family making a single copy of a free television program may not seem too much; but, as one observer remarked: "Babies are born one at a time, but can result in overpopulation."

INTERNATIONAL EFFORTS TO PROTECT COPYRIGHT

The international copyright community has recognized that legislation, not case-by-case adjudication, is necessary to deal with home video recording. Several agencies have called attention to global compensation systems that could provide revenue for all rights holders from both home audio and video recording. They have recommended legislation to prevent inevitable harm to creators, with emphasis on the idea of a levy upon either videotape hardware or blank cassettes. Whether or not one calls this a tax, levy, or fee, it must be recognized that its essence is a license.

Doubtlessly the interest over a levy—a global compensation system—is partly due to the tremendous difficulties of enforcing private rights in private homes. However, the fact that several states have, or are considering, this system raises hopes that experience will demonstrate its political feasibility and its justness to the public and creators. The jury is, however, still out.

The German Copyright Act, which was enacted September 9, 1965, and went into effect January 1, 1966, contains the first legislative provision that provides compensation to copyright owners for the private home audio and video taping of their protected works. As a pioneering effort, it has attracted great interest and considerable commentary. Already, on the basis of experience under the law, amendments to it have been proposed. There have also been proposed changes to Austrian copyright laws.

The British government recently published its "Green Paper" relating to copyright, designs, and performers' protection. Without drawing any final conclusions, the paper noted that the government "has still not received convincing evidence that the introduction of a levy on audio or video equipment or blank tape would provide an acceptable solution to the problems or potential problems." The document did suggest, however, that the industries continue research "aimed at finding a technological solution to the problem." It further offered to consider supporting legislation making illegal any anti-spoiler devices that might be developed to circumvent technological solutions. Although it may be possible for spoiler devices to discourage home taping in the short term, it appears likely that the only result of building a better mousetrap, in the form of spoiler devices, will be the education of smarter mice.

Legislation of the German and Austrian types has its defenders and detractors. Whatever their defects, the German and Austrian laws are grounded on a crucial premise: copyright owners need not demonstrate serious market damage *before* some form of protection or remuneration will be provided.

In the United States, there is not yet any congressional action on this question, but there is no doubt in my mind that academicians, copyright specialists, broadcasters, creators of television programs, and the professional unions are beginning to stir. In the United States, off-air educational taping absorbed our attentions first; the time to deal with home taping is fast approaching.

As I see it, in the United States we should move on the legislative front on home taping. I would rather heed our courts' calls for legislative solutions than attack their efforts to discharge their duty. There are even more severe tests ahead on our commitment to copyright and on our ability to adapt copyright to innovation of market change.

Consider the home communications center of the future, where data, images, and performances will all flood into the consumers' home entertainment and information center with all its capabilities. What then becomes of the bundle of rights? Where then is the box office? Our response to the problems of home taping will test our resolve to enrich society by rewarding and protecting authors, and our ingenuity in fashioning adaptations for copyright as ingenious as the innovations in technology itself. And the experience will be needed in the tests to come.

WHOSE LIFE IS IT ANYWAY?

Stephen Farber

When William Arnold, a young film critic for the *Seattle Post-Intelligencer*, went to see a revival of *Come and Get It* in the summer of 1973, he could not have guessed that a casual night at the movies was about to engender an obsession that would dominate his life for the next decade. But that night he came under the spell of Frances Farmer, the film's long-forgotten star, and he resolved to learn more about her. Five years later, McGraw-Hill published his book about Farmer's tragic life and death, *Shadowland*. From the time he began researching the biography, Arnold says, he imagined it as a movie; he was excited by the cinematic possibilities in this story of a beautiful and talented young actress persecuted because of her fiery temperament and her radical politics, and eventually committed to a mental institution, where she was abused and probably lobotomized. Writing the book was for him a means to an end; he hoped one day to work on the screen version of Frances Farmer's story.

From *American Film* (May, 1982). Reprinted by permission.

Now, almost nine years after Arnold's obsession took hold, the Frances Farmer story has indeed been turned into a major motion picture, starring Jessica Lange. But Arnold, who believes that his book awakened interest in the subject, has no credit line in the movie. Mel Brooks's company, Brooksfilms, made *Frances* without buying *Shadowland*. The story of how this happened is the nightmare that every author fears, one that raises questions for all writers who deal with biographical or historical material. As Hollywood looks to real people and real incidents for the inspiration for more and more films and television movies, debate over the legal rights of authors who provide the original research on these stories will intensify. The courts are likely to be clogged with lawsuits by biographers and historians who believe that producers have capitalized on their research without acknowledging their contributions.

This is not a new problem, but in the past, it was resolved without litigation. One famous instance was that of the two *Harlows* in 1965. Joseph E. Levine paid $100,000 for Irving Shulman's biography of Jean Harlow and planned an expensive, big-screen version starring Carroll Baker. But before the Levine *Harlow* was completed, promoter Bill Sargent announced that he was making a black-and-white Electronovision movie called *Harlow*, starring Carol Lynley. Sargent's *Harlow*, covering the same basic story as Levine's, was filmed in eight days and rushed into theaters two months before the Levine opus.

Levine fumed publicly, but there was not much he could do except take out full-page ads crying: "Let there be no confusion! The only 'Harlow' produced by Joseph E. Levine and Paramount Pictures will open August 11. It's the *only* 'Harlow' starring Carroll Baker, the *only* 'Harlow' filmed in breathtaking Technicolor, the *only* 'Harlow' produced at the world-famous studios of Paramount Pictures." But the only lawsuit filed in the case was by Sargent against Paramount and five theater chains for allegedly keeping his quickie *Harlow* out of movie theaters.

After the Andes plane crash in 1972, when the survivors resorted to cannibalism in order to stay alive, United Artists paid a hefty sum of money for the rights to *Alive*, a best-selling book on the crash by Piers Paul Read. John Schlesinger was hired to direct. At the same time, producer Allan Carr got hold of a Mexican film called *Survive*, based on another book about the plane crash. Carr re-edited and dubbed the movie, Paramount released it, and that killed the projected film of *Alive*. The people who had hoped to make *Alive* had no legal recourse.

The outcome of these disputes has not discouraged others from seeking redress. The *Shadowland* case, for example, is currently in federal district court in Los Angeles, where William Arnold and producer Noel Marshall, to whom Arnold had sold the movie rights to his book, have filed a $5 million suit against Brooksfilms and the movie's producers, Jonathan Sanger and Marie Yates, charging them with copyright infringement as well as violation of contractual relations. The judgment in the case may well affect future rulings in this thorny field of authors' rights in regard to factual material.

Arnold has read the script of *Frances*, and he thinks he has an open-and-shut case. "They actually used dialogue that I had constructed in the book," he says. "It amazes me that they were so stupid; but maybe they know something I don't. In the book I advanced several theories about Frances Farmer. I argued that her case grew directly out of the left-wing labor movement in the Pacific Northwest, that she was committed by a right-wing judge, that she was not really insane but was a victim of the psychiatric and legal establishment. They incorporated all of those ideas into the screenplay.

Arnold's lawyer, Jay Plotkin of Los Angeles, acknowledges that "as a general rule of law, you cannot protect facts, per se. Those become part of the public domain. But *Shadowland* is not purely factual. It has certain things in common with a work of fiction, which *is* protectable. There are a lot of things in the book that Bill conjured; he took the facts and imagined scenes that *might* have taken place. Our contention is that the producers lifted the whole concept of Bill's book as well as some specific details that he had invented himself."

In affidavits on file in federal court, Brooks and Sanger state that they were familiar with *Shadowland* but that they instructed screenwriters Eric Bergren and Chris DeVore to take a different approach to the Farmer case. Sanger says he told the screenwriters that he wanted to downplay the theory of a political and psychiatric conspiracy, which is at the heart of Arnold's book. To establish a fresh slant on the material, Sanger approached Lois Kibbee, a friend of Farmer's, and got a signed release from her for exclusive use of her reminiscences. The screenwriters conducted additional research in Seattle and interviewed a private detective, Stewart Jacobson, who claimed to have had a close relationship with Farmer; they created a character based on Jacobson, who had not appeared in Arnold's book.

Questioned about the case, Sanger says, "I was interested in the Frances Farmer story long before I read Arnold's book. I never considered it a particularly well written book, and there was nothing special in *Shadowland* that we wanted to use. The reports of her arrests and commitment are part of the public record. As for the book's conspiracy theory, I don't think there are easy villains or heroes in this story. Frances was as much responsible for her fate as the people around her."

The director of the film, Graeme Clifford (the film editor on *The Man Who Fell to Earth* and the recent *Postman Always Rings Twice*), says that he also has been interested in Farmer for many years. As a matter of fact, other film projects on the actress's life had been considered even before Arnold's book appeared. In 1974 a film on

Farmer was announced, with Glenda Jackson starring and Ida Lupino directing, but it never materialized. Two television movies, one for CBS and one for ABC, were in the works at various times, but neither got the go-ahead. The CBS movie was to be based on Farmer's autobiography, *Will There Really Be a Morning?*, published in 1972, two years after the actress's death. In one of the amusing complications of the case, an attorney representing Sama Productions, the company that originally owned the rights to *Will There Really Be a Morning?*, threatened Arnold's partner, Noel Marshall, with a lawsuit if he made a film of *Shadowland*. Sama Productions claimed that *Shadowland* infringed the copyright of the Farmer autobiography.

All of this appears to verify the defendants' claim that Frances Farmer is not the exclusive property of William Arnold or any single writer. However, there are special circumstances in the *Shadowland* controversy that would seem to strengthen Arnold's case. As Jay Plotkin points out, "In many lawsuits regarding copyright infringement, it is difficult to establish that there was any contact between the two parties to the suit. Here there is an incredible bridge between the two camps." Plotkin intends to introduce documents to try to establish that Marie Yates, the coproducer of *Frances*, acted as Arnold's agent, helping him to get *Shadowland* published and to sell the movie rights to Noel Marshall. Yates also is said to have brought the book to the attention of Sanger and even to have set up a meeting between Arnold and Mel Brooks.

Arnold describes his own relationship with Brooks: "I first interviewed Brooks in late 1977, when *High Anxiety* was released. I was with him for ninety minutes, and it was a great interview. At the end of the interview, he actually kissed me. During the course of that interview, another reporter who was there mentioned *Shadowland*, and Brooks said he would be interested in reading it. I told Marie Yates to get him a copy of the manuscript." Some time later, Arnold met again with Brooks. That meeting did not go well, and they parted on a discordant note. "The next thing I knew," Arnold says, "Brooks and Marie Yates were working together on their own Frances Farmer movie." (Brooks has declined to discuss the case.)

In their affidavit, Brooks and Yates acknowledge their contact with Arnold, and this may help Arnold to prove his charges of contractual violations. In many cases of suspected plagiarism, the courts are inclined to dismiss the charge of copyright infringement but still award the plaintiff some damages under the separate charge of breach of contract.

As movies turn to the lives of real people for inspiration, authors and producers battle over the question: Can history be copyrighted?

But Arnold and his attorneys want to win on the copyright charge as well. They believe this case could be a landmark in the field of copyright law. "I think Mel Brooks wants to set a precedent," Arnold says. "He is trying to prove that the author of a work of nonfiction has no rights at all."

Actually, that is pretty much the conclusion that the courts have already reached. Judges have consistently held that "ideas are free as air" and that "factual information is in the public domain." Richard E. Marks, an agent and attorney with Ziegler, Diskant Inc., a major literary agency in Los Angeles, agrees that "the law is definitely in favor of the free flow of information and ideas." John Diamond, an attorney who handled copyright cases for Simon & Schuster for seven years, adds, "It is almost a truism that a book based on fact is unprotectable. Of course, you cannot lift huge portions of the text, huge portions of dialogue. But when two writers simply use common facts, the courts have found that there is no infringement.

Two recent court decisions give a strong indication of where the courts stand on the copyright of biographical or historical material. The first case revolved around the movie *The Hindenburg*. In 1962, A. A. Hoehling published a book called *Who Destroyed the Hindenburg?* in which he hypothesized that the dirigible was sabotaged by an anti-Nazi zealot who wanted to embarrass Hitler's regime. Ten years later, Michael Macdonald Mooney published another book, *The Hindenburg*, which also advanced the theory of sabotage; Mooney acknowledged that he had read Hoehling's book before writing his own. Universal bought Mooney's book and eventually made a film about the Hindenburg directed by Robert Wise. Hoehling sued both Mooney and Universal for stealing his ideas.

In rejecting Hoehling's claim, Judge Irving R. Kaufman of the U.S. Court of Appeals in New York declared that in situations where "the idea at issue is an interpretation of an historical event, our cases hold that such interpretations are not copyrightable as a matter of law. . . . Such an historical interpretation, whether or not it originated with Mr. Hoehling, is not protected by his copyright and can be freely used by subsequent authors." Judge Kaufman concluded, "In works devoted to historical subjects, it is our view that a second author may make significant use of prior work, so long as he does not bodily appropriate the expression of another."

This principle was further clarified in a recent case. Gene Miller had written *83 Hours Till Dawn*, a true story about a woman who was kidnapped and buried alive. He put in a great deal of original research, including extensive interviews with the victim. Then Universal produced a "Movie of the Week" for ABC called *The Longest Night*. Although it was based on the same story, Universal had not purchased the book. Miller sued, and the lower court ruled in his favor. But a U.S. court of appeals reversed that ruling, declaring, "Labor of research by an author is not protected by copyright." In other words, the appeals court argued, the mere fact that Miller had done original research did not give him exclusive rights to the story.

> ". . . a book based on fact is unprotectable," argues a copyright attorney.

Mel Brooks and Jonathan Sanger were involved in a related case a year before they embarked on the Frances Farmer movie. They made *The Elephant Man* while the Broadway play on the same subject was running, but they did not buy the rights to the play. Sanger insists that he had hired screenwriters to work on the story of the elephant man before the play appeared: "Our script was registered in March of 1978, and the play opened in January of 1979." Besides, John Merrick's story had already been the subject of several books, and so it belonged to the public domain. The only real controversy revolved around the title. The producers of the play sued Sanger and Brooks to prevent them from calling their movie *The Elephant Man*. "We finally reached a settlement with them," Sanger says. "They *had* made the title popular, and even though I think we probably would have won the case in the end, it might have dragged on and there was always the chance that we might lose. We wanted to use the title, so we agreed to give them a modest fee."

ABC Motion Pictures is currently preparing a theatrical movie on the life and death of Karen Silkwood, to be directed by Mike Nichols and to star Meryl Streep. Two books about Silkwood have already been published, one by Richard L. Rashke and one by Howard Kohn. Others are in the planning stages. But the producers have bypassed all of the authors. "We used primary sources," says Robert Bookman, vice-president of ABC Motion Pictures. "The film is based on research, court records, and interviews that we conducted ourselves. We did not feel that it was necessary to buy a book. Besides, most of the books take a strong point of view. We want to present all the information and let viewers draw their own conclusions." Howard Kohn, for one, says he wishes that he had been involved in the film project but recognizes that he has no exclusive rights to the subject matter.

Is there, then, any protection for an author who puts in years of labor telling a true-life story? Richard Marks of Ziegler, Diskant, which represents a number of journalists and authors who try to sell nonfiction books to the movies, says, "We advise our writers to create some unique slant on the story. And, of course, if you get an exclusive release from the subject of the story, that helps, too. Even then a producer could still sidestep the author of the book. But often it's an advantage for a company to buy the book. Usually a movie company wants to hang its hat on something concrete before embarking on a film."

In many instances, it is more convenient to buy the book. "The reason you go to an author," suggests attorney John Diamond, "is to avoid a lawsuit. Even if a studio expects to win the suit in the end, it's frequently cheaper to buy the book and avoid all the court costs."

The issues in these copyright cases are extraordinarily complex, and it is impossible to make absolute judgments about right and wrong. Attorney Kenneth Kulzick, who frequently represents the studios in such cases, makes a compelling case for the free flow of information: "Wouldn't it be terrible if we had only one history? I think any First Amendment lawyer would cringe at the prospect. That would be like Russia. I find it disturbing when a writer tries to fence off a historical figure. Who's to say that his book is definitive? I think we all benefit from having access to different viewpoints of the same material." Kulzick, who is not involved on either side of the *Shadowland* case, says, "I know a lot about Frances Farmer, and I've never read that book. Just because a writer opens up a subject doesn't mean he owns it. Someone else might come along and do it better."

As Kulzick suggests, there are strong legal and ethical arguments for allowing considerable leeway to the media to offer as many perspectives on factual events as possible. At the same time, one can sympathize with the anger of an author like William Arnold, who immersed himself in his subject for years and now feels his work has been exploited without being acknowledged. "When I read the script of *Frances*," he recalls, "I got physically ill. I felt as if I'd been raped."

In the copyright field, perhaps there's one law that everyone would agree on: Author beware.

PLAGIARY

Peter Shaw

In the past few years a number of prominent writers have been accused of plagiarism, among them Norman Mailer (for his first book on Marilyn Monroe), Alex Haley (for *Roots*), John Gardner (for a biography of Chaucer), Dee Brown (for *Bury My Heart at Wounded Knee*), Penelope Gilliatt (for her *New Yorker* profile of Graham Greene), Ken Follett (for his spy novel, *The Key to Rebecca*), and Gail Sheehy (for *Passages*). More recently, Martin Amis, the son of Kingsley Amis, charged that his 1973 novel, *The Rachel Papers*, had been plagiarized by Jacob Epstein, a twenty-three-year-old first novelist.

As far as one can tell, none of these writers suffered from the resultant publicity. Instead, a universal reluctance to render judgment meant that even those of them who confessed were never publicly disgraced. As Edgar Allan Poe was the first to observe, "When a plagiarism is detected, it generally happens that the public sympathy is with the plagiarist." It can be added that most of the embarrassment in such cases is ordinarily experienced not so much by the accused as by those who have been confronted by his deed. Thus reporters and editorialists tend to replace the word "plagiarism" with uneasy euphemisms. *Newsweek*, for example, put it that Alex Haley "acknowledged *lifting* modest portions of *Roots*"; that the film critic Penelope Gilliatt was caught "appropriating another author's eloquence"; and that John Gardner "was discovered to have *borrowed lavishly*" (all italics added).

In the past few years a number of prominent writers have been accused of plagiarism. As far as one can tell, none of these writers suffered from the resultant publicity.

After an initial flurry of discussion, most charges of plagiarism tend to disappear from public view. If a suit and trial follow, the result is usually a private, unrecorded settlement, part of which is an agreement not to publicize the outcome. The writings in question remain extant, of course, but no one is eager to evaluate them.

The contrast could not be sharper between the literary world's failure to render judgment and the draconian code imposed by the scientific community. When Dr. Vijay Soman was recently discovered to have plagiarized some sixty words in a medical paper, for example, he was forced to resign his position at Yale University. Soman, it is true, was at first given only a mild rebuke. But the persistence of the researcher who had accused him led to an investigation in which it developed that he had faked data in addition to plagiarizing, and as a result he was asked to leave.

Later, Soman's superior, Dr. Philip Felig, had to resign his recent appointment as chairman of the department of medicine at Columbia's College of Physicians and Surgeons. Although Dr. Felig was not himself accused of either plagiarism or faking data, the people who had interviewed him for the Columbia chairmanship felt in retrospect that he had kept his faith in Soman for too long a time and had given a too generous account of Soman's improprieties. Dr. Felig was eventually rehired, but by Yale, not Columbia.

To be sure, one senses in Dr. Felig's delayed response the same reluctance to come to terms with the problem as that displayed by humanists. In numerous cases of scientific plagiarism and fraud over the past few years, as Alan F. Westin of Columbia University has shown, the perpetrators have suffered less than those who exposed them. When a plagiarism is detected, it seems, the public's sympathy for the plagiarist is often matched by its disapproval of the victim. Nevertheless, even the most reluctant authorities cannot avoid taking action when science is in question, whereas in literary studies it is possible to avoid the unpleasant responsibility of dealing with a breach of ethics.

This avoidance would seem to be related to the attacks on literary standards that have come from various sources in recent years. One school of literary critics, for example, has argued that all professional literary interpretations are merely subjective, so that no critic or criticism is really any better than any other. Another school has seized on a contention put forward by the critic Harold Bloom, who maintains that poets are so much influenced by their predecessors, unconsciously as well as consciously, that no poet can be called original. Commenting on Bloom's list of six ways in which influence supposedly exerts itself in poetry, one sympathetic scholar, Thomas McFarland, has logically suggested that "he might have added a seventh, 'plagiarism.'"

McFarland elsewhere voices the "hope" that modern relativism has so far freed us from the "rigid certainties of Victorian moralism" as to make it no longer necessary to be terribly concerned about plagiarism. In contrast, it was not very long ago that a historian of the subject could still regard plagiarism as both a moral and a cultural issue. In *Literary Ethics* (1928), H. M. Paull posited the importance of knowing the extent to which plagiarism is being practiced at a given time. Furthermore, "the extent to which it is condoned," he argued, "is a still more valuable indication of the state of the literary conscience of the period."

Currently, the tendency in the literary world is either to deny or to extenuate the commission of plagiarism. Where the act in a given instance proves to be too overt to be denied, it is typically described as an exception—a plagiarism by technicality only. In effect, plagiarism has come to be regarded as a relative phenomenon—one to which disgrace no longer attaches. Writers have always plagiarized, it is said. Shakespeare and other greats, we are reminded, explicitly justified themselves with the concept of "imitation," by which writers were positively encouraged to model their works on those of their predecessors. In accusing Jacob Epstein of plagiarism, Martin Amis himself, for reasons that will appear, softened his indictment by remarking that "the boundary between influence and plagiarism will always be vague." All in all it begins to seem that plagiarism amounts to no more than the invidious relabeling of practices that were once perfectly acceptable.

How much, in fact, has the definition of plagiarism changed through history? At present, plagiarism is defined as the wrongful taking of and representing as one's own the ideas, words, or inventions of another. In the ancient world and through the neoclassical period of the seventeenth and eighteenth centuries, imitation was admittedly the prescribed mode of composition. Writers were expected to adopt models for their work and to follow these with regard to plot, characters, and even versification and expression. It was only with the Romantics of the late eighteenth and early nineteenth centuries that originality came to be valued over imitation. Not surprisingly, concern about plagiarism greatly increased during the Romantic period and continued, along with the high valuation of originality, down to the quite recent past.

Yet it does not follow, as some have argued, that plagiarism is a strictly modern concept. The poet Martial complained of being plagiarized from in the first century A.D. The term *plagiary* itself entered the English language in the sixteenth century, along with bitter accusations by writers against one another. The concept of plagiarism, therefore, existed alongside that of imitation, so that there have always been acceptable and unacceptable modes of using the work of one's predecessors. What has not changed through time is the ethic of borrowing. Throughout history the act of using the work of another *with an intent to deceive* has been branded as plagiarism. As Lord Chesterfield pithily phrased it in the eighteenth century, a plagiarist is "a man that steals other people's thoughts and puts 'em off for his own."

> Can plagiarism take place inadvertently, unconsciously? The feeling that one may unconsciously be a sinner oneself makes writers especially hesitant to pronounce judgment on other writers who have been accused of plagiarism.

There will always remain certain gray areas resistant to definition. Not every act of copying from another author is the same, for example, since a wider latitude is traditionally allowed for imitating authors of the past. This was the case with Shakespeare's use of Plutarch, and also with John Updike in an example cited by *Newsweek* as evidence that plagiarism is virtually universal among writers. "Even John Updike," *Newsweek* noted, "recalls comfortingly that 'my first published novel was very clearly an imitation of Henry James.'" Yet one can imagine Updike's following his well-known, virtually classical model as closely, say, as Joyce followed the *Odyssey* in *Ulysses* without raising any question of plagiarism. On the other hand, equally extensive, unacknowledged use of a contemporary's work—with the intent to deceive—would have to be labeled plagiarism.

> Giving the game away proves to be the rule rather than the exception among plagiarists.

When one turns to recently publicized accusations of plagiarism, the authors' explanations at first seem to support the notion that plagiarism cannot be satisfactorily defined. For example, Alex Haley was sued by two novelists, Margaret Walker Alexander and Harold Courlander, the latter the author of *The African*. Haley swore that he had not read *The African* but admitted that three passages from it had "found their way" into *Roots*. Jacob Epstein was more forthright about the accusation that he had taken more than fifty passages from Martin Amis's novel. But though Epstein freely admitted having "taken another writer's imagery and language for my novel" (*Wild Oats*, 1979), he blamed his doing so on faulty record keeping. Similarly, when Dee Brown was accused of improperly taking materials (for *Bury My Heart at Wounded Knee* in fourteen separate instances) from the historian Lawrence Kelly, he admitted only that "six sentences were taken from Kelly, and omission of the source was an oversight of the typist."

Both Haley and Epstein said that they had collected passages in notebooks without keeping track of where they came from. Then, long after copying them out, they had inadvertently used them in their books. Haley said that he used notebooks containing passages originally copied by his research assistants as well as by himself. Epstein added that he himself had discovered his borrowings after publication, and had in fact removed thirteen of them from the second American edition of his novel.

All of these cases at first appear to offer insuperable problems of definition—until it is noticed that each of the explanations contains an admission of wrongdoing. Those accused do not actually deny that plagiarism took place; instead, they suggest that extenuating circumstances should make us hesitate to render judgment. At issue, they in effect argue, are nothing but a few inadvertent, unconscious slips. Thus if there was plagiarism, it was not extensive and it was not intended.

Can plagiarism take place inadvertently, unconsciously? Certainly every writer worries that he may unconsciously be echoing, or even repeating, phrases or ideas that have somehow stuck in his mind. Similarly, researchers fear that inadvertent mistakes in footnoting may have resulted in their failure to credit all of their sources properly. The feeling that one may unconsciously be a sinner oneself makes writers especially hesitant to pronounce judgment on other writers who have been accused of plagiarism. But while it is theoretically possible for anyone to breach the rules inadvertently, for the most part the incompletely or improperly attributed passages in the working author's manuscript somehow are caught by the time his work sees print. It may happen that an observer will later point out an uncredited idea or phrase, but there will be no implication of plagiarism.

This is because an accusation of plagiarism normally arises only where there has been a *pattern* of improper conduct. Practically speaking, authors are sued, not for single acts of plagiarism, though technically they could be, but for having committed *dozens* of such acts. Any one failure to acknowledge a source might be defended, were it not that the pattern of which it is a part points to an intent to deceive. Accordingly, the accused plagiarist, along with offering excuses, ordinarily proceeds to reduce the number of instances of wrongdoing that he has been accused of. Thus Haley reduced Courlander's "more than eighty passages" to three; Dee Brown reduced fourteen to six; Epstein reduced more than forty to thirteen. The writers plagiarized from—reasoning that, having extracted a confession of plagiarism, they have no need to quibble—often silently agree to the reduced number. At this point, the two or three or six instances can again begin to present a problem of definition—unless the larger pattern from which they have been cut is remembered.

When that pattern is kept in mind, one notices, for example, that it does not matter exactly when Jacob Epstein copied passages from Martin Amis's novel into his notebook. In the case of Amis's passage containing a reference to the English advice-columnist, Marje Proops, Amis had written: "I always tried to look tranquil, approachable, full of dear-Marje wisdom." Epstein changed this to read, "Billy . . . tried to appear sensible and approachable, full of Ann Landers wisdom, but with no result." (The passages are taken from Amis's article in the London *Observer.*) If Epstein made the substitution while copying from his notebook to the manuscript of his novel, the English columnist's name would have had to identify the passage to him as not being his own. If he substituted the American columnist's name as he copied from Amis to his notebook, it can only have been with the intent to plagiarize.

Not only are multiple plagiarisms within a single book common, but it frequently turns out that the plagiarist will eventually violate some other literary or extraliterary rule. The disputed meaning of Dr. Vijay Soman's six plagiarized sentences, for example, was suddenly clarified when his faked data were exposed. In the same way, the charge of plagiarism against Alex Haley took on a different coloration when it was followed by a serious charge that Haley had faked *his* data.

In a recent discussion of scientific fraud in the *New York Times*, Dr. Elliott Osserman of Columbia University's College of Physicians and Surgeons remarked: "One goes on a presumption of honesty for the first time. If a given investigator has been suspect in his previous work, then I think it's a whole new ball game. Once suspect, always suspect."

> The psychology of plagiarism begins with the plagiarist's act of stealing material of the sort that his talent and intelligence would appear to make unnecessary for him.

It was difficult not to take this attitude in a recent case in which John Gardner was charged with plagiarism in what appears to have been an unfair manner. Some years ago a scholarly reviewer of Gardner's *Life and Times of Chaucer* had pointed out in *Speculum*, the journal of medieval studies, that Gardner "frequently"—and properly—cited the well-known authority, *England in the Fourteenth Century* by May McKisack. In numerous instances, however, Gardner copied long passages nearly verbatim from the same book without any acknowledgment. There could be no doubt that Gardner understood and accepted the conventions of attribution. Yet in the passages in question he copied McKisack in "close paraphrase"—that is, with slight variations of phraseology—without providing either footnotes or any other hint of what he was doing.

Here what at first might appear as a case too full of anomalies to be comprehensible actually fits two typical patterns. First there is the repeated use of and even oblique identification of a single, prominent book (though Gardner used other books in the same alternatingly proper and improper manner, according to the *Speculum* review). In such cases an odd but unmistakable tendency toward self-incrimination makes itself apparent. Secondly it develops that another charge of wrongdoing arises some years later. In such cases an objective observer cannot help but cast a jaundiced eye back on the *first* charge.

Initially, most observers find it difficult to believe that clues strewn about in an obvious manner can be anything but misguided attempts to give proper credit. Indeed, the cover-up is usually so flimsy that the term *plagiarism* hardly seems appropriate. Surely, it appears, the particular charge of improper copying that happens to have come one's way must represent some kind of exception. The truth, though, is that plagiarism remains what it is no matter how inexplicable the manner in which it may have been carried out.

As it develops, giving the game away proves to be the rule rather than the exception among plagiarists. Both in the commission of the original act and in the fantastic excuses that follow it, plagiarism is often calculated above all to result in detection. Though the means vary, one or another kind of hint, slip, or other suspicious gesture usually manages to call attention to the improper act. And here the common excuse that the act was unconscious offers a clue to the operative psychology. What was unconscious, it seems evident, was not the plagiaristic act itself, the deceptions surrounding which testify to a plentiful awareness of what was being done, but rather the desire to be caught. Martin Amis called the hints that give away the plagiarist a kind of honesty. He speculated that Jacob Epstein "in some half-conscious way, was too honest not to give a clue to his own imposture. Plagiarism is one of his book's principal themes."

Odd as it may seem, Amis's attack on Epstein

itself fits into the category of inadvertent, yet somehow purposeful, self-exposure. For the fact is that Amis's own novel, *The Rachel Papers*, from which Jacob Epstein is alleged to have plagiarized, also contains the theme of plagiarism. One of the features borrowed from Amis by Epstein has to do precisely with this theme. Epstein followed Amis in making his hero what could be described as a verbal plagiarist: in both books the central character has the habit of collecting impressive things to say to girls. Amis's hero, who memorizes and repeats the words of others, is eventually caught committing a genuine plagiarism. On an English literature admissions paper he pretends that two phrases he has memorized from well-known critics are his own, and he cleverly applies these to the authors he has been assigned to write on.

Amis, too, it appears, is telling something both about plagiarism and about himself through the use of this theme in his novel. For in the course of exposing Epstein, he obliquely admitted to two plagiaristic acts of his own. In the first instance, Amis revealed that one of the phrases copied from him by Jacob Epstein actually came from Dickens. Closely following Amis, Epstein had described a man's hair as appearing like "two gray-colored, wiry wings on either side of his otherwise hairless head." Amis explained: "I am something of an idiom-magpie myself—to a reprehensible extent, perhaps. That bit about 'wiry wings,' for instance, was stolen by me from Dickens: Podsnap in *Our Mutual Friend* has 'two little light-coloured wiry wings, one on either side of his else bald head.'"

So disarming was Amis's manner that no one seems to have noticed that his revelation about the source of the "wiry wings," together with the following passage, amounted to a public confession: "I once lifted a whole paragraph of mesmeric jargon from J. G. Ballard's *The Drowned World*, and was reproved by the publisher via an alert Ballard fan. In fact, I had belatedly got verbal permission from Mr. Ballard, who is a friend and colleague. But the lapse was evidence of laziness, and a kind of moral torpor." Amis failed to specify exactly what kind of moral torpor was involved, but it can be observed that he claimed only a "belated" securing of permission. All in all it would be hard to improve on Amis's own conclusion that "the psychology of plagiarism is fascinatingly perverse: it risks, or invites, a deep shame, and there must be something of the death wish in it."

And yet it is not quite enough to speak of a death wish or some other psychological mechanism at the heart of plagiarism—any more than it is enough to demonstrate that the act can be satisfactorily defined and evaluated. For even as one calls for humanists to emulate the objectivity of scientists in dealing with plagiarism, one cannot help sympathizing with their reluctance to deal with the problem of plagiarism.

> At all times, to belittle a breach of professional ethics is to belittle one's profession itself.

Such reluctance itself, in fact, can be shown to represent a part of the psychology of plagiarism. That psychology begins with the plagiarist's act of stealing material of the sort that his talent and intelligence would appear to make unnecessary for him. There follows his strewing of clues to bring about detection. After detection, the plagiarist offers excuses that testify to the unconscious motivation of his original act, though ordinarily without acknowledging either its breach of ethics or its obvious self-destructiveness. Finally there comes the sympathetic reaction of the public mentioned by Poe, followed by uneasiness, ambiguity, and eventual abdication of responsibility on the part of those called upon to render judgment.

Not all of this is unique to plagiarism. Similarly self-destructive behavior characterizes the social crime that plagiarism most closely resembles. This is kleptomania. The plagiarist resembles the kleptomaniac both in his evident wish to be detected and in the circumstance that what is stolen may not be needed. (With kleptomania, lack of need, we are told, is absolutely central.) Because kleptomania so evidently issues from an uncontrollable compulsion, furthermore, it tends, like plagiarism, to inspire understanding and sympathy. The comparison, though, stops here. For kleptomania does not result in any confusion over whether or not goods were stolen.

There is something at once fascinating and repellent about both of these acts. The normal response to them tends to be an instinctive recoil accompanied by a shudder of uneasiness or an uncomfortable feeling in the pit of the stomach. These are reactions that resemble nothing so much as the experience of the uncanny. In novels and short stories the uncanny is often conveyed through a character who is first mesmerized by some horrible apparition or evil deed and then overcome by an urge to flee. (Henry James's "The Jolly Corner" is such a story.) Freud pointed out that a reaction comparable to the one represented in such fictions is sometimes experienced in real life when we encounter psychological disturbance in others. In such cases, he wrote, the ordinary person has seen "the workings of forces hitherto unsuspected in his fellow-man but which at the same time he is dimly aware of in a remote corner of his own being."

In contrast to the uneasy responses of ordinary people to plagiarism, plagiarists themselves tend to be unequivocal. For example, modern scholarship has revealed that Edgar Allan Poe was a plagiarist—most dramatically in his book-length fiction *The Narrative of Arthur Gordon Pym*. Yet Poe himself regarded plagiarism as a "detestable" act and a "sickening spectacle." Similarly, Jacob Epstein, in his novel, treated a waffling response to plagiarism as a form of weakness. When the minor character, Professor Russo, who knows all about the "racket" of selling term papers, discovers that he has been handed two such papers, he ruminates: "Who the hell am I to set myself up as some moral paragon, as if I know right from wrong." Russo's failure publicly to expose his two student plagiarists is viewed by the narrator with contempt.

Plagiarists also tend to suffer from the delusion that they have been plagiarized from. Poe exhibited a perfect obsession on this point as with the subject of plagiarism in general. Over the years he collected materials for a book to be entitled "Chapter on American Cribbage," in which he planned to expose his contemporaries. His essay "Mr. Longfellow and Other Plagiarists" was full of wild accusations against some of America's most respected literary figures. The existence of a class of people, some plagiarists themselves, who spread false charges of plagiarism enormously complicates the problem, for the fear of being associated with false accusers often makes those whose work has actually been plagiarized from hesitate to say so.

Just as plagiarists differ from apologists in their moral attitudes toward plagiarism, so do they differ in being attracted to, rather than repelled by, the uncanniness of the subject. The scholar Burton R. Pollin showed that Poe, for his *Arthur Gordon Pym*, plagiarized from the travel book *A Narrative of Four Voyages* by Benjamin Morrell. Unbeknownst to Poe, this book, which was actually in large part the work of a ghostwriter, contained many faked incidents. Uncannily, one might say, Poe relied "heavily" on the very material that Morrell and his ghostwriters had "borrowed." More recently, according to the *New York Times*, a writing instructor at San Diego State University belatedly discovered that a student had plagiarized the entire Janet Cooke Pulitzer Prize story, "Jimmy's World." Unaccountably—uncannily—the student had fastened on this particular story *before* it was exposed as an imposture.

Perhaps the most important and instructive case of plagiarism in English is that of Samuel Taylor Coleridge, who was first exposed as a plagiarist immediately after his death in 1834. During the next century and a quarter, a series of studies revealed that Coleridge had doggedly committed plagiarism from the beginning until the end of his career, in both obscure instances and in connection with some of his best known and most influential works, especially those in literary criticism. Coleridge's stature as a poet is shaken, but not destroyed, by these revelations. This is because his reputation rests on a very few poems written over a short span of time. Although many of his other poems were plagiarized, his three great works—"Kubla Khan," "The Rime of the Ancient Mariner," and "Christabel"—cannot be called plagiarisms. But Coleridge's reputation rests almost equally on his literary criticism, most notably his *Biographia Literaria* and his lectures on Shakespeare. And these writings contain particularly extensive plagiarism, including some of the passages for which Coleridge is most famous.

Surprisingly, it was not until the appearance of Norman Fruman's *Coleridge, the Damaged Archangel* in 1971 that any of this became a serious issue. Today the general reading public remains for the most part unaware that Coleridge was a plagiarist, while literary critics and professors of English—outside of those who specialize in the study of Romantic poetry—are largely unaware of the extent and significance of his plagiarism. The manner in which the present state of ignorance came about bears directly on the literary world's current unwillingness to deal with contemporary cases of plagiarism.

Norman Fruman's study reflected badly on scholars of Romanticism. Its information had long been available to them, as he pointed out, yet they rarely confronted it. Fruman remarked in the introduction to his book: "Except for a few lonely dissenters, the overwhelming majority of authorities in the field dismiss the charges of plagiarism and intellectual dependence against Coleridge as mistaken, or, at best, so partial a truth as to be grossly misleading."

Thomas McFarland was one such authority. His *Coleridge and the Pantheist Tradition* (1969) contained a chapter entitled "The Problem of Coleridge's Plagiarisms," which amounted to a compendium of scholarly defenses of Coleridge. Writing a short time before Fruman, McFarland observed that, in twentieth-century discussions of Coleridge, "there has been a curious and very widespread tendency to gloss over, and even to suppress, the fact of the plagiarisms." Nevertheless, he himself attempted to make the charge of plagiarism appear absurd, and he proceeded to cast aspersions on those who made it. His arguments, it is worth noting, have reappeared in the writings of apologists in connection with several recent cases of plagiarism.

McFarland's defense of Coleridge displayed an evident ignorance of typical plagiaristic practices. Thus, where Coleridge plagiarized from some of the very works that he mentioned, McFarland satisfied himself by asking rhetorically why Coleridge would be "determined to help his accusers by supplying the names of both the author and the book to which he is indebted." To be sure, this was before the appearance of John Gardner's book on Chaucer. But as a scholar of English Romanticism, McFarland should have known that earlier, in 1965, Albert Goldman, in *The Mine and the Mint*, had shown that Coleridge's contemporary, Thomas De Quincey, yet another plagiarist, had followed exactly the same pattern. In fact, Coleridge's case exhibited the typical anomalies of plagiarism—from guilt-ridden, self-incriminating gestures in the commission of the act, to a tainted exposer, to professional apologists, and finally to a highly moralistic attitude on the part of the plagiarist himself toward the very crime secretly being committed.

Coleridge—as McFarland noted—gave himself away "by using the words 'concealment' and 'plagiarism'" (a circumstance that McFarland found indicative of a confident innocence in Coleridge). Furthermore, Coleridge devoted himself to accusations of plagiarism in others. "It is doubtful," Fruman wrote, "whether any other writer in the history of letters has accused so many writers of plagiarism, and so many so falsely." It was altogether fitting, therefore, that Coleridge should have been first exposed by another plagiarist, Thomas De Quincey, and that he himself should have entertained an honest affinity for the works of still another plagiarist, the Polish poet, Casimir. Coleridge revered and openly imitated Casimir without suspecting what has only recently been revealed about him—that Casimir in turn had "'stolen *en bloc* and without acknowledgment from a contemporary Italian' the world-famous series of poems called the *Silviludia*." (Whereas Coleridge is known to have imitated Casimir, it is not yet known if he plagiarized from him as well.)

In McFarland's view, what called for analysis in Coleridge's case was not his plagiarisms themselves but rather the fact that a succession of nineteenth-century critics should have chosen to publicize them. He pointed out that several of the critics in question were Scottish, and theorized that their interest in the subject derived from "the traditional antipathy of the Scots toward the English." McFarland commented in particular on the exposures made by the Scot, J. C. Ferrier, regarding plagiarism in Coleridge's *Biographia Literaria*. McFarland wrote: "While on the one hand it is impossible not to be impressed by the relentless documentation of Coleridge's pilfering, on the other it is surprising and rather anti-climactic to find that when the firing is over Ferrier has discovered no more than nineteen pages of plagiarism in the hundreds that make up the *Biographia Literaria*." If nineteen pages are anticlimactic, it is not clear what would have impressed McFarland in the circumstances—twenty-one pages copied? Twenty-five? Fifty? Nor is it clear what McFarland would have made of Ferrier's case had he been, say, a Turk.

But the point is that McFarland was hardly alone in his tortured apologetics. When Fruman's book appeared two years after McFarland's, scholarly reviewers made no mention of their failure to have dealt forthrightly with Coleridge's plagiarisms. Instead, they dismissed Fruman for being "trivial" and "presumptuous." On the other hand, the same reviewers had to admit that Fruman's book was "formidably . . . well documented" (L. C. Knights), "thorough, well-written and well-documented" (Owen Barfield), and "carefully proofread" (Thomas McFarland, with perhaps a hint of regret). In the end, rather than deal with the case put by Fruman, these otherwise intelligent, even distinguished, critics preferred to accept the propositions that lack of need proves the absence of theft and that outright, unconcealed plagiarism proves the absence of plagiarism.

Inasmuch as these attitudes have spread out beyond the academy, it is worth recalling their intellectual origins in the Romantic doctrine of originality—a subject that has been of special interest to both Harold Bloom and Thomas McFarland. If the spectacular cases of Coleridge and De Quincey represented a kind of hysterical revolt against the tyranny of originality, then one can speculate on the phenomenon of sympathy for this revolt among modern specialists of Romanticism. Romantic refusal to be fettered by rules, it can be said, finds its modern equivalent in a relativistic questioning of the rules themselves by these specialists. In this perspective it makes sense that the scholar who wished the world free from the rigid certainties of Victorian moralism should have been Thomas McFarland himself. And it follows that McFarland should have gone on to conclude of Coleridge that "if translating some pages from his German contemporaries was his worst and blackest fault, then surely he was a prince among men."

At all times, to belittle a breach of professional

ethics is to belittle one's profession itself. But in a period such as the present, when there is considerable doubt about the importance and dignity of humane letters, the refusal to render judgment has particularly unfortunate results. Today it is difficult to imagine a plagiaristic act, or indeed any other breach of literary ethics, that would go undefended. It hardly seems an accident that along with this particular devolution, literature, in general, went from a position where it could claim for itself the highest morality to one in which many are claiming that it is no more than a marginal entertainment.

A vendetta against plagiarists will hardly set things right again. The specific harms that plagiarism may cause are, after all, of far less importance than the act's threat to the moral climate of literature. It is therefore on this level that the problem should be addressed. Where there is an injured party, or where professional advancement over others has been gained through the employment of plagiarism, the issue must be brought out into the open. But where no one has been hurt, those privy to the circumstances, usually the plagiarist's colleagues and peers, ought to be counted on to inflict punishment enough with their personal disapproval.

Such an approach can be effective, however, only so long as the steady judgment of contemporaries and the objectivity of history can be counted on. While private judgment remains confused and scholars continue to treat literary wrongdoing as they have Coleridge's, there can be no confidence in the private handling of plagiarism. As long as such confidence is lacking, more and more cases are likely to be dragged into the courts and given wide publicity. Thus it is that the attempt to evade professional responsibility when a case of plagiarism arises only makes for further complications.

Ideally, plagiarism ought to be treated as one of those areas, like manners, where the enforcement of right behavior belongs to society at large. Given the present situation, it seems clear that literary critics and scholars must bear the responsibility to affirm that there is indeed such a thing as plagiarism and that they are capable of identifying it if necessary. When they come into contact with a charge of plagiarism, moreover, they must accept the responsibility to determine whether or not literary norms have been violated. With literary standards thus reasserted, it may become possible once again for the general opinion quietly to settle most cases of plagiarism by itself.

SUGGESTIONS FOR FURTHER READING

The following articles provide further reading on copyright issues:

W. Anderson, "Taxing Tape." *Stereo Review*, July 1982.

D. B. Hopkins, "Ideas, Their Time Has Come: An Argument and a Proposal For Copywriting Ideas." *Albany Law Review* 46, no. 2 (Winter 1982); 443–73.

Charles H. Lieb, "The Sony Betamax Case–Winds of Change" *Communications and the Law* 4, no. 2 (Spring 1982): 17–22.

New York Times, "George Harrison Guilty of Plagiarizing, Subconsciously, a 62 Tune for a 70 Hit." September 8, 1976, p. 50.

Jack Wayman, "Home Taping: Scapegoat." *Billboard*, July 10, 1982, p. 12. Wayman gives his own account of the record industry's problems.

The following books are also of interest:

Donald Dible, *What Everyone Should Know About Patents, Trademarks, and Copyright.* Reston, Va.: Reston, 1981.

John S. Lawrence and Bernard Timberg, eds., *Fair Use and Inquiry: Copyright Law and the New Media.* Norwood, N.J.: Ablex, 1980.

CHAPTER 19

Libel

Recently there has been a spate of highly publicized libel cases. The readings in this section analyze the significance of those cases. First, William M. Carley of the *Wall Street Journal* analyzes the libel cases that have resulted from more aggressive TV news tactics, such as the ambush interview. In the second reading, Tony Mauro of the Gannett News Service suggests that the punishments incurred by the press might be too heavy, and that it might be time for some reforms—if only in the form of a uniform libel law for all fifty states.

The last three readings are a sampling of editorial opinion following Carol Burnett's libel victory over the *National Enquirer*. The editorials from the *Hartford Courant* and the *Pittsburgh Post-Gazette* present a rather negative view of the decision, recognizing the chilling effect of such libel awards. The *Union Leader* of Manchester, N.H., however, disagrees. It is entirely in favor of the award and says that libel laws should be made even stronger.

LIBEL CASE LOSSES STING MEDIA; CONSTITUTIONAL BATTLE FORECAST

Tony Mauro

WASHINGTON—As juries continue to sock the nation's news media with multimillion dollar libel verdicts, lawyers in the field are beginning to forecast a major constitutional showdown on the issue.

One media lawyer is even raising the possibility of congressional action to help stem the tide of damaging judgments against the press.

With the likes of Watergate conspirator E. Howard Hunt winning libel suits, and with juries giving no second thoughts to punishing the press with million-dollar verdicts, the news media are worried.

One company that insures newspapers against libel has threatened to pull out of the field if the trend continues. Mutual Insurance Co. Ltd. of Bermuda took out a full-page ad in a trade journal to scold the press: "Too many reporters appear to have assumed that the way to get ahead is to permit their personal predilections to enter into their stories with concomitant results of malice and error in the stories."

From the Rochester New York *Sunday Democrat and Chronicle* (November 14, 1982). Reprinted by permission.

Richard Schmidt, lawyer for the American Society of Newspaper Editors, sees the libel binge as the result of a "kill the messenger syndrome" on the part of the public. "Juries see the press as fat and arrogant," said Schmidt. "They feel the press can afford to lose a few dollars to learn a lesson."

More and more it has become the ironic truth that judges are the media's best ally in protecting them from juries, which are, after all, made up of their readers, listeners and viewers.

It was a jury that awarded Wyoming beauty queen Kim Pringel $26.5 million for a fictional *Penthouse* magazine article that fantasized about a hypothetical Miss Wyoming. It took a federal judge to reduce the verdict, and a panel of appeals judges to reverse it altogether, just last week.

Media defendants lose four out of five libel cases that go to trial, and lose at an even higher rate in jury trials.

It was a jury that awarded Mobil Oil President William Tavoulareas $2 million in damages for an article in the *Washington Post* that suggested he set up his son in a lucrative business. The *American Lawyer* magazine interviewed five of the six jurors in the case and found that they had a fundamental misunderstanding of libel law. People at the *Post* are betting that a judge will reduce the verdict or reverse it.

"Judges can discern the constitutional rules of the game, and juries cannot," said libel expert lawyer Bruce Sanford. Sanford's handbook on libel has been a best seller among reporters increasingly worried about the problem.

Sanford is a lawyer for the Society of Professional Journalists, Sigma Delta Chi, which is meeting in its annual convention in Milwaukee, Wis., this week. The convention's main speaker is Tavoulareas.

A study in August by the New York City-based Libel Defense Resource Center found that media defendants lose four out of five libel cases that go to trial, and lose at an even higher rate in jury trials. Damage awards and especially punitive damages have increased sharply, according to the study, but four out of five damage awards are reduced or overturned by judges after trial.

"There is cause to be troubled by the poor performance of media defendants at trials, and even greater cause for concern over the grotesque, outrageously large damage awards that have been imposed by juries in all too many of these cases," said Henry Kaufman of the center, which draws funding from several media groups.

Many of the large awards result from the increasing tendency of juries to punish the media—by awarding high punitive damages—in addition to making the usually lower-level dollars-and-cents calculations of actual losses suffered by the libel victim, as reflected in compensatory damages.

It is those punitive damages that could produce the courtroom confrontation that many see coming.

"Libel cases are always going to be there," says Sanford. "The problem is wildly excessive punitive damage awards. It is absurd and inconsistent to punish speech when the speaker had the honest belief he was justified.

"We need the Supreme Court to say that the only time punitive damages can be awarded is when there is overwhelming evidence of a deliberate, calculated lie."

Media Lawyer Floyd Abrams also sees an upcoming battle over "the constitutionality of punitive damage awards and what limits the First Amendment places on the award of punitive damages." He asks, "Can we have the same standard of proof for compensatory and punitive damages, or shouldn't you have to prove more for punitive damages—ill will, bad feelings, as well as actual malice?"

In other words, in addition to the First Amendment issue of whether high punitive damages have the effect of impeding freedom of the press, fairness questions may be raised: Is it fair to the press to use the same standard of proof for both compensation and punishment, and is it fair to punish the press in addition to compensating the victim when the press believed it was doing its constitutionally-protected job?

"It's time for Congress to pass a uniform libel protection law."

Jack Landau of the Reporters Committee for Freedom of the Press thinks that the possibility of getting Congress involved should be considered. "It's time for Congress to pass a uniform libel protection law," says Landau, noting that all 50 states have different libel laws and standards.

"For a national publication, do you know who controls what you can write?" asks Landau. "It's Alabama," with probably the least favorable libel law. "Why should Alabama control the news? News is now a national commodity."

A uniform law, Landau said, could set minimum legal protections for the media in libel suits, for example barring punitive damages for public figures.

BAD RECEPTION: AS TV NEWS REPORTING GETS MORE AGGRESSIVE, IT DRAWS MORE SUITS

William M. Carley

CHICAGO—Tall and mustachioed, ABC-TV newsman Geraldo Rivera prowls through charred ruins on this city's North Side during a *20/20* program titled "Arson and Profit." He discloses "circumstantial evidence . . . that a small group of Uptown Chicago businessmen are making money (from insurance payments) as their buildings burn and their tenants die. . . . "

Mr. Rivera then gets specific: "The early-morning hours of Dec. 29, 1979. . . . Yet another fire in still another building owned by Charles Roberts and his associates. Before it's over, seven people are dead. . . . ABC News has learned that Charles Roberts and his associates stood to benefit from this tragic fire" because of potential insurance payments.

Contending that this 1980 broadcast falsely portrayed him as an arsonist and murderer, Mr. Roberts has sued ABC in Illinois state court. Though ABC sticks by its story, a later investigation by the Chicago U.S. attorney cleared Mr. Roberts. In a statement, the federal prosecutor said there is "no substantial or credible

---

Reprinted by permission of the *Wall Street Journal* (January 24, 1983).

evidence to support charges that Mr. Roberts was guilty of either arson or murder, or that he participated in a scheme to burn rental buildings in Uptown in order to collect insurance proceeds."

INCREASING RETALIATION

Like Mr. Roberts, a growing number of people claiming to have been damaged or falsely accused by television news are retaliating in court. Obscure citizens and well-known public figures alike are suing the networks and stations for defamation or invasion of privacy, or both. Though records of the total number of such suits aren't kept because so many initial filings are frivolous, it is clear that the volume of serious suits heading toward trial is surging.

As TV news reporting gets more aggressive, it draws more suits.

"When I came to CBS in 1974, we hardly ever tried a case," says Ronald Guttman, associate general counsel of the company. "But in the last few years we've tried half a dozen cases, and there are more coming." Attorneys for other networks share his impressions.

Television news isn't the only target of litigation, of course. In recent years, the print media, too, have been hit by a spate of libel suits. In one celebrated case, Mobil Corp.'s president won more than $2 million in damages from the *Washington Post* after the paper reported he had "set up" his son in a business that benefited from Mobil shipping contracts. The Post is seeking to reverse the verdict.* And the *Wall Street Journal* currently faces a lawsuit filed in federal court in Washington, D.C., by two federal prosecutors who, the *Journal* reported, had put heavy pressure on a federal prisoner to testify against others.

*This verdict was reversed on appeal.

TV AND THE LAW

Still, lawyers and press critics say that the nature of television—its visual immediacy, its power, its capacity to inflame emotions and the punishing time constraints it imposes on news people—makes its brand of journalism particularly vulnerable to legal counterattack.

To cite a few examples:

Philadelphia's Mayor William Green sued CBS after the CBS-owned station there had broadcast, incorrectly, that the mayor was a target of a federal investigation. The network eventually settled out of court, paying the mayor around $300,000.

In Davenport, Iowa, Garo Lauderback, an insurance salesman, has sued ABC and Mr. Rivera over another *20/20* program broadcast in 1981, that purported to expose "unscrupulous insurance salesmen cheating the elderly." Singer Wayne Newton sued NBC in federal court in Las Vegas over a newscast that, Mr. Newton says, falsely linked him to the Mafia. Retired Gen. William Westmoreland is suing CBS in federal court in New York over a 1982 documentary that stated that the general's staff falsified estimates of enemy strength in Vietnam.

AFTER WATERGATE

It has only been in the past few years that TV news regularly undertook the sort of aggressive reporting likely to make waves—or inspire lawsuits. "You go back 10 years and you had *60 Minutes* and that was about it," recalled David

Boies, an attorney with Cravath, Swaine & Moore in New York who is defending a case against CBS. Then came Watergate, he says, "when the TV people, for the most part, were reduced to reporting what ran in the *Washington Post*." Stung by this indignity, TV news executives began ordering more investigative stories.

Some TV reporters, however, were ill-equipped for the new role of muckraker, and their lapses, critics say, have spawned suits. One attorney suing a network calls TV investigative reporters "a bunch of hip-shooters . . . who don't know what they're doing, and they ought to be taught a lesson." Though, as a plaintiff's attorney, he is hardly a detached observer, some on the other side of the fence have similar misgivings. "You tend to have people with more of a showboat background on TV," says a prominent New York attorney who defends networks. "'Will it sell in Peoria?' is a different mind set than 'Are the facts right?'"

TV reporters concede the pitfalls of doing investigative stories requiring rigorous documentation in a medium where a premium is placed on brevity. Don Reuben, a Chicago attorney who defends networks, observes that TV reporters "have to sumarize everything; it's like the TV bulletin that 'Moses has come down with the Ten Commandments, the most important of which is . . .'"

Others are critical of the rush by broadcast journalists to get on the air with exposés. "They're so fast—like a shark that's smelled blood," says an attorney who defends the networks. Adds James Dahl, a Chicago attorney who represents a client suing a network: "The pressure on TV investigative reporters to produce—to come up with the weekly exposé—is leading to errors."

TV reporters hotly deny that their work is sloppy. "In addition to myself, there's a reporter and a researcher on every story, so we have three people doing the basic donkey work," says Mike Wallace of *60 Minutes*, where it takes at least three months to produce an investigative story. As a result, Mr. Wallace says, *60 Minutes* has never lost a suit nor paid a plaintiff in an out-of-court settlement.

Nevertheless the enormous reach and influence of *60 Minutes* and other television news programs make them increasingly tempting targets for lawsuits. Nearly 40 million people watch *60 Minutes* on Sunday evenings, compared, say, with the 6.3 million who read the *Wall Street Journal*, the nations biggest daily newspaper.

Beyond that, TV news, being visual, is often more inflammatory than the printed word. TV packs "an enormous emotional wallop," says Floyd Abrams, an attorney with Cahill Gordon & Reindel in New York who has been defending NBC. Mr. Abrams notes that a few years ago, a rape scene in an NBC movie prompted 5,000 letters of protest—as well as a lawsuit that the network eventually won.

Defamation and other cases multiply, some as a result of the ambush interview.

There is some evidence that television executives are taking some of the criticism to heart. After a *CBS Reports* segment alleged that the military "conspired" to falsify enemy strength in Vietnam—and after TV Guide magazine criticized the program as a "smear"—CBS conducted its own investigation.

In a memorandum to his staff after the investigation, Van Gordon Sauter, the president of CBS News, concluded that *CBS Reports* shouldn't have used the word "conspiracy" and should have interviewed more people who disagreed with the broadcast's premise. He also noted that the program had violated some of CBS's own standards by, for example, failing to identify a paid consultant as such. Following this investigation, the network appointed a vice president for news practices to, in Mr. Sauter's words, "further ensure that our journalistic efforts are sound."

Television news executives also are screening new reporters and producers more rigorously. "We won't hire anyone now unless they already have a solid news background," says one network's news vice-president.

When they do err, networks and stations move fast to retract. NBC News recently reported that John Fedders, the chief of the Securities and Exchange Commission's enforcement division, was the target of a grand-jury investigation. Actually, according to the Justice Department, Mr. Fedders was a cooperating witness—not a target—in the investigation, which was probing payments made by a company Mr. Fedders had represented while he was still a private attorney. NBC retracted its story the following night; Mr. Fedders isn't planning to sue.

THE NEWTON SUIT

Lawsuits involving the broadcast media often pose particularly thorny issues for the courts. For if newspaper cases are restricted to the printed word, TV journalism contains the complicating, highly subjective dimension of video. A case in point is Wayne Newton's $6 million suit against NBC, an action so complex and bitter that even before trial, it has generated 14 volumes of arguments by attorneys.

In the 1980 newscast at issue, NBC broadcast a picture of Guido Penosi, whom the network identified as "from the Gambino Mafia family." Next, Wayne Newton was shown performing, while a voice-over reported that he and a partner were about to buy the Aladdin Hotel in Las Vegas for $85 million. Then, while a still shot of Mr. Newton was juxtaposed with a separate shot of Mr. Penosi, NBC related that Mr. Newton had telephoned Mr. Penosi for help with a "problem." Mr. Penosi, NBC said, contacted one Frank Piccolo, whose picture then appeared on the screen. According to police, the NBC report continued, this "mob boss . . . told associates he had taken care of Newton's problem and had become a hidden partner in the Aladdin Hotel deal."

NBC argues that the statements in its newscast were all accurate. But Mr. Newton contends that the impression conveyed by the video, taken together with the words of the script, defamed him. An attorney familiar with the case says: "You flash a picture of Newton, side by side with a picture of this Mafia guy, and then a picture of another Mafia guy, and the overwhelming impression is that Newton is indeed tied up with the Mafia."

(In the year following the broadcast, Messrs. Penosi and Piccolo were indicted in federal court on charges of conspiracy to extort money from Las Vegas figures, among them Mr. Newton. Before that trial, Mr. Piccolo was shot to death. Later, Mr. Penosi was acquitted of the extortion charges.)

COURT CHANGES

While the courts ponder the audio-plus-video question that a number of recent suits hinge upon, journalists and their attorneys are bracing for more suits to come. Their wariness, in part, stems from what they view as the Supreme Court's antagonistic stance toward the media. A lawyer who defends TV networks says; "In earlier days you had (Justices) Brennan, Black and Douglas, who championed and voted for First Amendment rights (of the press), but now you have (Chief Justice) Burger, who thoroughly dislikes the press, and (Justices) Rehnquist and White, who are less than sympathetic." According to another lawyer, Mr. Boies of Cravath,

Swaine & Moore, this change in the high court's complexion is "encouraging more suits against TV."

So worried are media lawyers about the Supreme Court that they go to lengths to avoid it. After NBC broadcast a "docudrama" about the "Scottsboro Boys"—black men who allegedly raped a white woman during the 1930—the woman involved sued the network, charging defamation. Two lower courts held that after 40 years the woman remained a public figure in relation to the notorious event. (As such, she faced a more demanding legal test to prove defamation.)

> TV reporters have to summarize everything: it's like the TV bulletin that "Moses has come down with the Ten Commandments, the most important of which is. . . . "

After the Supreme Court agreed to review the case, NBC, fearful that the court would overturn the lower-court rulings, settled out of court for an undisclosed sum.

THE AMBUSH INTERVIEW

To critics of TV news, perhaps the most controversial technique is the so-called ambush interview, in which reporter and cameraman descend on an unsuspecting individual and badger him with accusatory questions. Until fascination with this device wanes, the critics say, stations and networks will continue to be inundated with litigation.

The ambush interview figured prominently in a 1979 newscast by WCBS-TV, the network-owned New York station, that resulted in a lawsuit. A tipster had alerted the station that chemical wastes had been dumped in a New Jersey vacant lot. The next day a crew sped to the scene, found drums of chemicals strewn about and headed for an adjacent plant operated by Flexcraft Industries, an adhesives and coatings maker. Cameras rolling, the crew encountered the plant manager.

MANAGER: Get that damn camera out of here.

REPORTER: Sir . . . Sir . . .

MANAGER: I don't want to be involved with you people. . . .

REPORTER: Why are the chemicals dumped in the back?

MANAGER: I don't want—I don't need—I don't need any publicity.

REPORTER: Why are the chemicals dumped in the back?

MANAGER: We don't—we didn't—dump them.

The interview appeared on that evening's news—even though, as acknowledged in the broadcast, Flexcraft officials had actually reported the dumping, had themselves denied dumping the chemicals and didn't own the adjacent lot. Flexcraft and its owner, Irving Machleder, are suing CBS and its station for invasion of privacy and defamation. They charge that the reporter's "accusatory questions . . . were phrased and delivered in a manner so as to imply that plaintiffs were guilty of the alleged dumping. . . . " CBS denies any wrongdoing.

THE 'ARSON' DISPUTE

Ambush interviews helped touch off the controversy over ABC's "Arson for Profit" broadcast. About a year after the *20/20* program, Chicago's CBS-owned station, WBBM-TV, broadcast an unusual follow-up that questioned the facts presented in ABC's arson story and the journalistic techniques employed in its preparation.

In a subsequent rebuttal program, ABC's Mr. Rivera defended the accuracy of the original program and his ambush interviews of the landlord Mr. Roberts and his associates: "Obviously if we had asked them by invitation to sit down to a formal interview, they would have swapped information and prepared their responses." Later, he added, Mr. Roberts was offered three times—but declined—the opportunity for a formal interview. In any case, four people in addition to Mr. Roberts are suing ABC over the program.

Mike Wallace of *60 Minutes*, who helped pioneer its use, now advocates the surprise interview only as a last resort. "First we write letters, we phone, we do everything" to obtain a formal interview, he says. Even then, he says, "60 Minutes" uses the technique sparingly. "If you're after light rather than heat," he says, "there's not much point to it."

Critics suggest that unless news broadcasters strive for more light and less heat, their credibility will decline along with their audience. "Ten years from now I don't think we'll see much investigative reporting on TV," says Mr. Dahl, the Chicago attorney suing a network. "We'll be back to nothing but *Laverne and Shirley*."

THE HARTFORD COURANT

HARTFORD, CONN., MARCH 29, 1981

The *National Enquirer*, which loves to purvey sleazy news about celebrities, got its comeuppance last week at the hands of one of its celebrity subjects, Carol Burnett.

> Free press rights, like free speech and free assembly rights, are not confined to those in our society who behave "responsibly."

It was undeniably gratifying when the news came over that an 11-person jury in California decided that the *Enquirer* must pay Miss Burnett $1.6 million* for libeling her. The tabloid published an article containing false, defamatory information about her behavior in a Washington restaurant, knowing that it was false, the jury decided. So the *Enquirer* got its just deserts.

*Miss Burnett's award was reduced to $800,000 on May 12, 1981.

The newspaper did behave irresponsibly and its invocation of the First Amendment in its defense is both obnoxious and self-serving. But the defense has some relevance, and may ultimately win the day on appeal.

Free press rights, like free speech and free assembly rights, are not confined to those in our society who behave "responsibly." They apply also to the extremes, however much they are disdained by most of the public.

The outcome of the Burnett case could unloose an avalanche of other celebrity libel suits against the *Enquirer* and similar publications, possibly driving some out of business. Most people—including most journalists—probably wouldn't care, even though the wide circulation of such publications suggests that they are serving some needed social function.

The delight most people must feel for Miss Burnett should be tempered by an awareness that one more subtle tether has been attached to the ideal of a free press.

PITTSBURGH POST-GAZETTE

PITTSBURGH, PA., MARCH 23, 1981

In California, where so much that is imprudent seems to become a matter of jurisprudence, a court case of trivial substance and serious implication has been heard with attendant theatrics. Comedian Carol Burnett seeks the last laugh in suing the *National Enquirer* for $10 million over an article that implied she had too much to drink at a Washington restaurant in 1976.

In emotional testimony, Miss Burnett denied the truthfulness of the report in such terms as almost to conjure up violins playing dolefully in the background. Meanwhile, Johnny Carson used his own show as a witness stand to say from personal experience that the people at the *National Enquirer* were liars who printed unsubstantiated gossip. The judge in the Carol Burnett case was forced to excuse two jurors who had watched Carson's outburst.

It is hard to argue against the righteous sense of indignation held by such public figures presenting themselves as Virtue Outraged. Certainly, no responsible newspaper taking pride in its ethical standards can condone flagrant untruthfulness—if that, indeed, turns out to be the case. And there is great embarrassment when the lowliest among us cites the First Amendment in its defense. The difference between the mainstream press and the *National Enquirer*—we presume to think—is the difference, for example, between pharmacists and people hawking snake oil off the back of wagons.

In dignifying such nonsense with a lawsuit, Miss Burnett puts a strain on the legal bulwarks protecting other newspapers and magazines.

Yet the entertainment quotient in the back-of-the-wagon approach must be understood. The *National Enquirer* is really a sort of adult comic book with print instead of panels. It is a chronicle of fatuousness with exclusives on UFOs, amazing diets, astrology, and the latest non-pronouncements of celebrities. To the bored people its headlines seduce at the supermarket checkout, it offers an escape into a fantasyland of cheap thrills set off with exclamation points.

Because the world according to the *National Enquirer* is not a serious one, the revelation (erroneous or otherwise) that a public figure like Carol Burnett had a drink or two at a Washington restaurant bothers nobody in this context except the most cretinous—and they, by definition, have short memories anyway.

The publicity mills of Hollywood take diverse forms and the *National Enquirer* is but one of them. It is not the sort of publicity Miss Burnett would wish, no doubt, but in the end it may even be helpful for at a certain level all publicity is good publicity.

That she indirectly bites the hand that feeds her is not our concern. It is far more serious that, in dignifying such nonsense with a lawsuit, Miss Burnett puts a strain on the legal bulwarks protecting other newspapers and magazines which do their jobs responsibly.

THE UNION LEADER

MANCHESTER, N.H., MARCH 28, 1981

And for the eleven men and women of the jury which gave Carol Burnett a $1.6 million verdict for the libel involved in the untrue story which *The Enquirer* had printed about the actress: the jury is to be congratulated for not falling for all the drivel about freedom of the press by which the defense tried to free *The Enquirer* from liability.

As so often happens in life, the Supreme Court thought they were doing the right thing when, several years ago, in the so-called *New York Times* case, they changed the laws of libel which previously said a plaintiff could collect if something untrue was written about him. Truth, in other words, was the only defense for libel.

The Court said, in the interests of broadening freedom of discussion, that if the individual who said he was libeled was a politician or a public figure, he or she could not collect against the publication even if what had been said about them was untrue, unless the politician or public figure could prove that the untruth had been printed either because the person doing it was malicious or had utter disregard for facts that could have been checked.

It sounds like a good idea on the face of it, but what the Supreme Court didn't realize was that there are a great many scurrilous and dishonest writers who would take advantage of this ruling in order to say anything they wanted about a political or public figure on the grounds that it would be almost impossible for the politician or public figure to win a libel suit. That is actually what has happened in most cases.

The Supreme Court would be well advised to return the libel law to where it was before, in which case truth is the only defense for libel.

Politicians and public figures therefore have decided in most cases that there is no use in suing for libel no matter how much they are lied about. Carol Burnett, fortunately, is made of other stuff. Fortunately, too, she also has the financial means to fight a large publication. Carol is supposed to have spent $200,000 on legal fees and other expenses in connection with the suit. She might have lost all this if the jury hadn't come up with a verdict in her behalf.

Very few politicians or public figures have that kind of money to use in a lawsuit to defend themselves and correct a wrong.

The Supreme Court would be well advised to return the libel law to where it was before, in which case truth is the only defense for libel. In other words, if you say something about somebody and it isn't true, even if you have the best intentions, you are liable to pay damages to the individual hurt.

Meanwhile, the Los Angeles jury has really

made one of those great landmark decisions which will have effect for years to come.

Other individuals, such as the well-know movie actor Rory Calhoun can now proceed with his suit with some hope of success. In Calhoun's case *The Enquirer* published a story saying he had cancer. As a result, Calhoun lost some valuable contracts because nobody wanted to hire a dying man.

It is one thing to criticize individuals as this newspaper does quite strongly at times, but it is something else entirely to lie about their activities.

So, congratulations to Carol Burnett on her gutsy performance and her willingness to put her money up for a good fight, and congratulations to eleven jurors.

SUGGESTIONS FOR FURTHER READING

The following articles provide background to the libel issue:

Business Week, "How Media Are Fighting Back." June 1982, p. 120.

Seth Kupferberg, "Libel Fever." *Columbia Journalism Review*, September/October 1981, p. 36.

Bruce W. Sanford, "Fairness and the Recent Trend in Libel Law." *Wall Street Journal*, December 15, 1982, editorial page.

The following books are also of interest:

Robert D. Sack, *Libel, Slander and Related Problems*. New York: PLI, 1980.

Bruce W. Sanford, *Synopsis of the Law of Libel and The Right of Privacy*. New York: Newspaper Enterprise Assn., 1980.

CHAPTER 20

DEREGULATION

As FCC chairman Mark Fowler points out in this chapter's first reading, we are currently in an era of broadcast deregulation. Radio has been largely deregulated, by FCC order, and it seems that television will follow. Fowler lays out the philosophy behind deregulation in a speech to a group of North Carolina broadcasters, as he tries to convince them to support a user fee and the "print model" approach to broadcasting.

The other readings in this chapter take up the question of whether to follow the suggestion of Fowler and others to drop the fairness doctrine, which requires that broadcasters give both sides of controversial issues. Corydon B. Dunham, vice-president and general counsel of NBC, argues for the elimination of this law. In the final reading, John D. Dingell, Democratic congressman from Michigan, gives his views on why the law should remain intact.

FREE THE BROADCASTING 10,000

A Marketplace Approach to Broadcasting

Mark S. Fowler

We in Washington are enjoying a new season. This fall marks the second season of our unregulation. We point to it with considerable pride.

We've managed to turn around the thinking of the agency in many areas. We've been successful in areas critical to broadcasting's future.

The theme of this turnaround in broadcast regulation takes its cue from the marketplace. I've endorsed a transition, a transition from a trusteeship approach to broadcast regulation to a marketplace approach. What's the difference? Under the past trusteeship model, the Commission attempted to determine the rules of the game by which a broadcaster served the community.

Under our marketplace approach, the Commission favors competition as a way to ensure service. We won't try to second-guess broadcasters as to how you serve your communities. Instead we should defer to your market judgment as you compete for viewers and listeners. The public's interest, then, becomes the public inter-

From *Vital Speeches of the Day* (December 1, 1982). Reprinted by permission.

est. The public interest is measured by the success or failure of broadcasters in the marketplace, against each other, and against other competing technologies.

The goals of our national communications policy are best served when we allow the marketplace to function whenever possible. Government meddling, however well meant, *must* be avoided.

In the last year, we've worked hard to implement this policy. Let me share a few of our successes.

We've been able to take significant steps to reduce unnecessary paperwork. Last spring the Commission got rid of Form 324, your annual financial report. Here were literally pounds of paper collected by the government that was not put to any regulatory purpose.

As you know, we implemented immediately, rather than on a graduated basis, longer renewal terms for television and radio licensees that Congress approved in 1981.

We've reduced the filings requested to transfer broadcast stations.

We've authorized the first new over-the-air service in 20 years, low power television, and allowed existing broadcasters to operate these new facilities.

We finally came to a decision in AM stereo. Our marketplace approach has in fact made AM stereo a reality. Already several AM stations are broadcasting in stereo. By going marketplace I believe we avoided a lengthy, potentially devastating court delay that selection of a single system might have led to.

We've proposed eliminating operating and maintenance logs for all broadcast licensees.

We've proposed greater flexibility in licensing auxiliary spectrum as well as sharing the excess capacity of auxillary spectrum with others.

We've removed the cloud hanging over AM/FM combinations. From now on, you can co-own two stations in the same market without the FCC jeopardizing your investment.

We've affirmed the earlier elimination of first class radiotelephone operators' licenses and examinations.

We've asked Congress to repeal the Fairness Doctrine and equal time laws because they violate your First Amendment rights. And we're part of an administration whose President, Ronald Reagan, is the first to call for full First Amendment rights for broadcasters.

We've begun an intensive review to deregulate television along the lines of last year's radio deregulation order.

Looking to the future, we've proposed eliminating the "trafficking" rule which requires an owner to hold a station for three years before he can sell it.

We'll also be looking at our attribution rules for ownership purposes and simplifying the character qualification in licensing. These rules are ready for pruning, to say the least. Generally speaking, they retard competition in the marketplace with very little concern for marketplace effects. While I withhold my right to decide the future or non-future of these existing policies, I believe that they are not entitled to a presumption of validity.

All of these efforts, I think, reflect a commitment by myself and others on the Commission to end needless regulation and to promote a competitive spirit within the radio and video delivery industries. Some of the reforms accomplished in this past year were major; others are not likely to shake up the world. But all of them, I think, go toward the theme I have been stressing during my watch as Chairman of the FCC: that the Commission allow broadcasters to play in the marketplace, not plod among our rules. I say, serve your markets, not your regulators.

A most significant and long-term development that we've launched during the past year is our First Amendment initiative. I want to see the day that the broadcast and the print media are treated the same under the First Amendment.

Simply put, I don't find the reasons that have

been set forth to justify different treatment of the media sufficient to allow the rules that evolved. Neither the "scarcity " rationale, nor the "impact of television" rationale mandates all of the regulations we have on the books.

I do not accept either of these arguments, particularly in light of the clear, sure language of the U.S. Constitution and the heavy burden it imposes on those who try to regulate the press.

As to scarcity of spectrum space, in many markets there has never been a shortage of channels, simply a shortage of advertising or other revenues to support more outlets. In those markets where, say, an additional VHF television channel can't be added under existing interference standards, you have to ask—scarcity compared to what? In these major cities, newspapers, not television or radio, form the scarcer medium. Fortunately, advocates of greater content regulation have not managed to lower the standard of protection given newspapers to match that given broadcasters.

The second argument for leaving radio and television vulnerable is the impact of the two media. According to this theory, the electronic media are too powerful, because they may influence decisions in the political arena or shape values in the home. This "power," however ill-defined by its discoverers, is reason enough to treat broadcasting differently from print. The more effective the speech, the less protection it needs from the First Amendment.

But many forms of expression, from hit movies to newspapers' exposés, have a great impact in society. If we start to regulate media according to impact, we set a national policy favoring the bland, not the bold. This logic turns the First Amendment on its head.

Some would like to see a policy toward television programming based on the inverse of the child-proof bottle cap: Only what's fit for children will be available over the air. Now, it's one thing to schedule adult-oriented programs late at night or to provide suitable warnings; it's another to dilute the content of radio and television fare until it's on a par with browsing material in a pediatrician's waiting room.

Freedom of speech and press is to my mind the basic and most important underpinning of our system of government. The founding fathers made themselves clear and unmistakable when they told Congress 200 years ago it could make "no law" abridging freedom of the press. "No law" means "*no* law"—*no* fairness doctrine, *no* content guidelines, *no* political speech rules. Zip.

What Thomas Jefferson said in 1786 holds true today. "Our liberty" he said, "depends on the freedom of the press—it cannot be limited without being lost."

On this I think we all agree. The question is how to get from today to tomorrow, . . . and that tomorrow means broadcasting and newspapers will be indistinguishable—that's right, indistinguishable, from a regulatory perspective. One starting point has already been provided by Jim Broyhill. Two bills he introduced last term, HR-5584 and HR-5585, would remove content controls over broadcasting, including the Fairness Doctrine and political speech rules. Broadcaster support for this legislation is important.

In addition to Jim's efforts earlier this year, over the last several weeks I've passed along another approach to getting the job done. I'd like to review it with you now.

Start with the proposition of freeing broadcasters entirely from special regulations—in short, making a broadcast property indistinguishable from the print model.

What do I mean by a print model? I mean that you, the broadcaster, should be as free from regulation as the newspaper you share the press table with and compete with for advertisers. No renewal filings, no ascertainment exercises, no content regulation, no ownership restrictions beyond those that apply to media generally, free resale of properties, no petitions to deny, no Brownie points for doing this right, no fingerwagging for doing that wrong. For instance, if a broadcaster plays fast and loose with an advertiser or a ratings service, it'd be a matter for a local court, not a federal agency.

I believe that the print model is the right ultimate aim of broadcast deregulation. And why? Because in the last two hundred years, it's worked. It's served the American people well. Oh, there've been the narrow-minded bullies from their pulpits of pulp, using papers in mean ways for small ideas. And there have been virtuous newspapers that, for one reason or another, are now as extinct as the Dodo bird. But over the long course, the American newspaper and magazine model has worked. And it's worked without a Federal Newspaper Commission administering hundreds of rules and policies, with the power to padlock the door and sell the company for the value of its physical assets.

> I've endorsed a transition from a trusteeship approach to a marketplace approach.

Now, I will continue to do everything in my power at the FCC, consistent with legislation on the books, to accomplish deregulation. But there is a limit under the existing law. There is just so far that the agency can go. And whatever *we* do can be undone by a later Commission.

So, I pledge myself to take deregulation to the limits of existing law. But we need a new statute, passed by Congress, to get the job done, finally, and to prevent a different Commission from turning the clock backwards.

It's in this context that I proposed to "break the ice" in the deregulation debate a few weeks ago through adoption of a modest user charge by Congress. The fee might be one way to make deregulation stick. For some feel that a modest fee is a fair return for print model regulation.

This user charge would be imposed not on broadcasters alone, but on all users of the spectrum. This way, the charge on broadcasters might be lower than otherwise. It'd be consistent with others being applied to government services, from airport landing rights to waterway patrols.

If adopted by Congress in connection with deregulation, the fee would replace the old *quid* for *quo* under the trustee regime—content regulation and other "taxation by regulation" in exchange for a likelihood of license renewal.

I'd also suggest that Congress consider setting aside funds collected by this charge to support public broadcasting programming. What kind of programs? Not rock music or soap operas, but program types that might be displaced under a marketplace scheme. Economists recognize that some goods and services in society may not be supported by the marketplace. But society still may want them, whether they're museums, public parks, or universities.

Instructional programs and documentaries, for instance, have not been marketplace success stories, although there may be a need for them. Congress could mandate that public radio and TV do the job they were intended to do—to program for these unmet needs in the market—not to draw away viewers, but to fill in the gaps.

To some, the user fee may seem like a lot for a little. I think, in hindsight, it may well appear like a little for a lot. The fee absolutely must be modest. I'm about as fond of big fees as I am of big government. And I oppose even considering a fee so long as the trustee concept remains intact.

Yet a modest fee in connection with deregulation could be a big payoff for the public and for broadcasters. You'd achieve guaranteed renewal from the government—in short you'd get a property interest in your station. In a way, it's like switching from an apartment that you rent month to month to a condominium you own, with modest condominium fees. Right now the landlord—that's us—can and does evict the broadcast tenants.

The landlords may be friendly these days, but they haven't always been. Sometimes they go about evicting without a lot of notice or even reason, and even engage in multiple evictions.

It's the present law that makes these evictions possible—whenever a challenger decides to file against an incumbent. What other business is subject to this system? What other business would put up with such a zoo parade, where a businessman's handiwork and life's labor can be snatched away by adminstrative fiat, like a monkey grabbing a bag of peanuts from a passerby? Indeed, it would be comical, if it weren't so true, if it didn't happen. But it did happen, and it does happen. It's the type of dead-of-the-night seizures that may belong in Moscow, but not on Main Street, U.S.A.

I want to see the day that the broadcast and the print media are treated the same under the First Amendment.

Broadcast deregulation signifies the maturing of your industry *and* the maturing of governmental philosophy toward broadcasting. User fees may make it possible for you to move from being renters to being owners, lock, stock and barrel . . . or more accurately, mike, transmitter and tuner. Like the newspaper, the broadcaster's only concern with the FCC is technical operation.

In closing, let me say that I am not a cheerleader for user charges. I believe they're a starting point, a way to approach the problem. It's a time for flexibiity, for thoughtfulness about how best to get to where we all agree you should be. It's also a time to look beyond the ideal of the perfect and focus on the art of the possible. Clenched fists can pound on tables pretty well. But I've never found one very useful when you're sincerely trying to shake on a deal.

Parties truly interested in the broadcast reform effort might consider the difficult—but solvable problem of what appropriate fee levels could be. It's something we'll be thinking about at the FCC, but only if the parties think it makes sense.

Ultimately, though, it's up to you, the broadcasters, to decide whether such charges are sensible in the deregulation effort in Congress. You, not I, must decide whether to support them. For practically speaking, if you don't, Congress most likely won't. For my part, I think they're worth a look.

For years, you've tried many ways to break the legislative deadlock. Those bills, not to mention the thousands of hours, and dollars, spent trying to get Congress to consider them, lie gathering dust in the basement of Congress. The midnight hour of the trusteeship regime is approaching. The new dawn of a more vigorous communications marketplace is arriving. You, the broadcaster, and the people of America deserve a system of regulation—or more accurately, unregulation—worthy of this bright new day.

All I say is, isn't it time to consider a fresh approach? We at the FCC stand ready to facilitate this process of legislative reform. My office is open five days a week, and more if necessary, to try to help reach a consensus on a new communications act.

In the meantime, we'll continue to pursue our deregulation philosophy at the FCC to the limits of the existing law. There are about ten thousand commercial broadcasters in the United States today. And I say, it's time to free the broadcasting ten thousand!

THE FAIRNESS DOCTRINE DEBATE:

Can the marketplace guarantee your right to be heard, or is it necessary for the government to take a hand?

The Fairness Doctrine is based on the notion that the airwaves are a valuable resource held in trust. When Congress passed the 1934 Communications Act, it regarded broadcast licenses as no more than leases of space on the publicly owned airwaves. The Federal Communications Commission was created to regulate broadcasting in the public interest. In general terms, the Communications Act held broadcasters responsible for keeping listeners and viewers informed. The Fairness Doctrine, which requires broadcasters to air balanced presentations of controversial issues, developed out of this concept.

In the forties, the FCC forbade editorializing on the air in an effort to restrict broadcasters from using their licenses for political purposes. The commission reversed the policy in 1949, and, in the ruling, the first "fairness" language emerged as a compromise between broadcasters' First Amendment rights and the right of the public to hear all sides of important debates. Access to the airwaves is limited, the FCC reasoned, and government must try to ensure the broadcast of minority viewpoints.

In 1959, Congress amended the Communications Act to require broadcasters "to afford reasonable opportunity for discussion of conflicting views on issues of public importance," making the Fairness Doctrine law. Ten years later, in the *Red Lion* case, the Supreme Court affirmed broadcasters' responsibility to air contrasting opinions.

Since then, the growth of FM radio and the promise of cable technology to develop hundreds of television channels have challenged the scarcity assumption that underlay the Fairness Doctrine. The FCC is contemplating sweeping changes in broadcast regulation, and Congress is preparing to rewrite the Communications Act to reflect the present deregulatory climate. The following opinions outline the opposing sides of the argument. NBC vice-president and general counsel Corydon B. Dunham leads off the debate with his case for the elimination of the Fairness Doctrine. Representative John D. Dingell, Democrat of Michigan, chairman of the House Energy and Commerce Committee, counters with his opinion that the public still needs the protection it offers.

From *American Film* (January/February, 1982). Reprinted by permission.

Pluralism Guarantees Access

Corydon B. Dunham

The electronic press—the news source the public turns to most—isn't a free press. Unlike print media, news presented electronically must comply with Title 47, Section 315, of the Communications Act. This is the Congress's "fairness" statute, enforced by the Federal Communications Commission and applicable to all broadcast programming, particularly news and information.

The Fairness Doctrine provides that the presentation of any view on a controversial issue must be balanced by opposing views so that the public is not left uninformed. The point is to promote robust debate. No journalist disagrees with that objective.

But the Fairness Doctrine does not promote open debate and good journalism: it discourages them. Investigative reporting, for instance, often triggers government inquiry—but into the reporting rather than the conditions reported on. This has been the aftermath of many searching documentaries, such as *The Selling of the Pentagon* and *Hunger in America*, and news programs on subjects like welfare problems, gambling and official corruption, sex education in schools, and government aid to education.

"The FCC has no way to reward you for bold, controversial journalism. All it has is a way to harass you," Bill Monroe of NBC's *Meet the Press* argues. "And you can be almost certain that if you engage in hard-hitting, investigative journalism, you will make important people mad, they will complain to the FCC, the FCC will ask you for an explanation, and you'll have to spend as much time on a carefully researched and prepared document of explanation as you did on the original news project."

In the FCC inquiry, truth is not sufficient. Although truth is always a defense to a libel suit, a Fairness Doctrine inquiry treats it as irrelevant. That the report is fair comment is not sufficient. While fair comment constitutes a privilege for court proceedings, the commission recognizes no privilege. The commission's requirement of a balance of opposites has led to such absurdities in reviewing news judgments as an FCC count of the number of lines of broadcast scripts and number of minutes taken to air them.

> The Fairness Doctrine does not promote open debate and good journalism: it discourages them.

When NBC exposed the failure of some pension plans in an award-winning documentary, the FCC ordered the broadcast of offsetting programming about successful plans, to be "fair"—despite a near unanimous Senate vote for a pension reform bill.

Confrontation with every government agency which grants broadcast licenses is an inhibiting burden. There are also legal costs. NBC appealed the *"Pensions"* case—and won—but the legal costs were substantial. For those with fewer resources, this may not be an option.

NBC's *Holocaust* dramatized the Nazi effort during World War II to exterminate the entire Jewish population of Europe and other civilian "enemies" of the Third Reich. Although a complainant failed in his effort to have the FCC require the broadcast of a view that there had not been a holocaust, the complainant has appealed and the case is still in court. In another instance, a small western station could find no spokesman to present an opposing view to a local bond issue, despite repeated invitations. The commission put the station through a long defense of its actions—costing much of that station's profits for the year.

The injury to the public will be very real if the broadcasters shy away from controversial issues. The more significant the problem being reported, the more important that society learn of it. But the more disturbing, unusual, or provocative, the more likely the report will trigger complaints—either about the point of view broadcast, or about the absence of other points of view from the broadcast.

The journalist's report becomes an occasion for government inquiry and regulation. And a blander form of journalism becomes less troublesome and more attractive. Broadcasters and professional broadcast journalist associations have warned of the inhibiting tendencies caused by such government inquiries into news. They see what the public does not—provocative film which winds up on the cutting room floor.

The government's Fairness Doctrine is unfair to the public. Repeal of the doctrine would end the inhibition and the wasteful harassment. It would permit the free flow of news that is essential to self-government. News (and other) programs would remain, of course, subject to privacy and libel laws, and it is hard to imagine that significant points of view on current issues would not be aired on the thousands and thousands of news broadcasts by radio and television in this country.

In 1969 the Supreme Court upheld the Fairness Doctrine in *Red Lion*, saying that Congress could pass laws affecting the press where there was a scarcity of news outlets. But there certainly is no such scarcity in the electronic media today. There is a burgeoning of radio, television, cable, and other new electronic media. Yet many in Congress would continue or even expand the Fairness Doctrine to cover all over-the-air and wired distribution of news and information to the home.

The government's Fairness Doctrine is unfair to the public.

History teaches that government oversight of news will be used at some point to deny to people knowledge they should have about government and its abuses. News delivered to the public—by whatever means—must have the benefit and protection of the public's Constitution. News in the *Washington Post* should be protected whether delivered by foot, bicycle, truck, or electronic transmission.

The First Amendment states, "Congress shall make no law . . . abridging the freedom of speech or of the press." The FCC itself has now asked for repeal of the fairness statute. What is the threat to our republic that entitles Congress to suspend our nation's First Amendment and regulate its news?

Scarcity Precludes Access

John D. Dingell

Deregulation is part of the Reagan administration's new cure-all for the eighties. The idea is that minimizing the burden on the private sector, combined with tax and budget cuts, will spur the private sector to create new jobs and revitalize our economy. Riding the crest of this wave, the Federal Communiciations Commission, led by Chairman Mark Fowler, has proposed repeal of the Fairness Doctrine. Chairman Fowler, and other proponents, assert that the Fairness Doctrine is unnecessary in view of the diversity available through new video technologies and, therefore, it imposes an unjustifiable burden on the broadcast industry.

Repealing the Fairness Doctrine in the spirit of deregulation would be like throwing the baby out with the bathwater. The Fairness Doctrine remains an important protection to the First Amendment rights of the public, and it is now administered in a manner which minimizes both the burden on the broadcast industry and the intrusiveness of government.

We have yet to see the tremendous new diversity in video sources with which Chairman Fowler justifies the repeal of the Fairness Doctrine. Today, only one in four U.S. households receives cable services; less than one percent of these homes had subscription television (STV) at the end of 1980; and less than one-half of one percent received the Multipoint Distribution Service (MDS, a microwave system). Projections are that in 1990 roughly fifty percent of the U.S. households will still be without cable services.

Direct broadcast satellite (DBS), designed to provide new diversity in programming to rural areas too remote for cable, is still several years away, and it is unclear how quickly subscribers will sign up for new service at $25 a month. In addition, the cable systems now operating transmit mostly broadcast signals from affiliates of the three major television networks and some nonaffiliated stations, pay movie channels—such as HBO and Showtime—and sports channels. Very little new programming is now created for cable systems, and most of that which is available is not raising local or national issues of concern or presenting different viewpoints—the basic objectives of the Fairness Doctrine.

What these factors suggest is that even if optimistic projections on the growth of cable, MDS, STV, and DBS eventually became reality, we will continue to operate in a climate of scarcity for some time to come. Hence, we will continue to need the protection afforded by the fairness provision against abuse caused by that scarcity.

The argument that the Fairness Doctrine places an undue burden on the broadcast industry is equally without merit. The FCC requires that a person who files a complaint meet a heavy burden before the licensee is placed in the position of having to account for its practices. In 1980 more than twenty thousand complaints or inquiries were made to the FCC's Political Broadcast Division, roughly equally divided between fairness complaints and complaints about the denial of access by a political candidate. Of these, only twenty-eight cases were brought by the FCC to the attention of the stations involved, resulting in a total of six admonitions to the stations, five regarding political access. The penalty for a violation is not that the broadcaster pay a fine or lose his license—only that the broadcaster air more discussion of the issue. The FCC administration of the Fairness Doctrine and political-access requirements is thus picking up only the most abusive cases and is not placing a heavy burden on the broadcasters.

> The Fairness Doctrine now works to protect the public from the broadcaster who might air his personal views on controversial issues and refuse access to those who disagree.

The Fairness Doctrine now works to protect the public from the broadcaster who might air his personal views on controversial issues and refuse access to groups or individuals that disagree. Although the Fairness Doctrine has been attacked as the government's exercise of editorial control over the media, in practice, the requirement that some air time be given to a fair presentation of public issues leaves television and radio broadcasters wide discretion as to what issues are discussed, how they are presented, by whom, and the format in which they are discussed. In doing so, the doctrine protects the public's First Amendment right to be exposed to a diversity of views. As the Supreme Court so forcefully emphasized in the landmark *Red Lion* case: "It is the [First Amendment] right of the viewers and listeners, not the right of the broadcasters, which is paramount."

The broadcaster is a "public trustee," and the airwaves are a public resource. A television or radio broadcaster receives licensed access to a scarce public resource—the airwaves—so that the public can reap benefits from the use of its resource. In return for a government license granting exclusive use of a portion of the spectrum for private profit, the broadcaster takes on the obligation to operate in the public interest.

Regulatory reform and deregulation are worthwhile goals, but they should not be undertaken without thoughtful review of why the regulatory programs were created in the first place. Congress established the Fairness Doctrine because the development of the television networks and relative scarcity of channels in most communities dictated a need for some controls to ensure that audiences were provided with a diversity of views through this most powerful medium. The growth of cable television and other alternative video sources has begun to change the situation. But today this change has begun in only *some* of the many communities in this country. The proof isn't in yet. Until the time that there is real and robust diversity among the channels available to a large share of the population, the Fairness Doctrine should remain in place.

SUGGESTIONS FOR FURTHER READING

Those who are interested in FCC Chairman Fowler's views might want to read his article, "The Public Interest," in *Communications and the Law* 4, no. 1 (Winter 1982): 51–58. This is an adaptation of his September 1981 speech to the International Radio and Television Society.

James Traub, in "Radio Without Rules," *Columbia Journalism Review*, January/February 1982, pp. 36–38, looks at how radio stations have adjusted to deregulation.

The Fairness Doctrine is not the only regulation currently being debated. A debate on FCC media ownership rules can be found in the *Journal of Communication* (Autumn 1982), p. 48. The debate includes "FCC Media Ownership Rules: The Case for Regulation," by Henry Geller, and "FCC Media Ownership Rules: The Case for Repeal," by Harry M. Shooshan II and Catherine Reiss Sloan.

An in-depth examination of the fairness issue can be found in Fred W. Friendly, *The Good Guys, the Bad Guys, and the First Amendment: Free Speech versus Fairness in Broadcasting*. New York: Random House, 1977.

CNN CABLE NEWS NETWORK
CNN
CNN

PART FIVE

THE NEW ELECTRONICS AND THE INFORMATION AGE

The "new technologies" have created some of the most pressing media issues of our time. As many of the previous readings have shown, the new technologies have created problems: privacy, copyright, fair trial, the effects of media on politics, and others. In fact, anything that was a problem for the older media often proves to be a worse problem for the newer electronic media.

The first chapter in this section, "A Field Guide to the New Electronic Environment," attempts to sort out some of the new technologies and provide a framework for their analysis. In the final chapter some of the implications of the information age are discussed.

CHAPTER 21

A Field Guide to the New Electronic Environment

Introduction

Les Brown

We call this a field guide, instead of a guidebook or handbook, to stress a point: what we are dealing with is not a line of products but an environment.

It grew up around us rather suddenly the last few years, an electronic forest springing from the union of four technologies: cable-television, computers, satellites, and telephone. If this new landscape eluded almost everyone's notice, it was because it is mostly invisible, made up of such things as

All readings in Chapter 21 are from *Channels Magazine* (December, 1982). Reprinted by permission.

microwaves, laser beams, data bits, microcomputer chips, and digital impulses running through wires.

Yet the electronic environment surrounds us every minute of our lives. For these wires, chips, and radio waves combine in a profusion of new media, some of which by now have entangled themselves inextricably with business, education, politics, law, and our popular culture. Indeed, this electronic wonderland already makes a greater claim than the natural environment on the attention of children.

Ever since the Stone Age, the efforts of humans to understand the environment have had three main purposes: survival, opportunity, and enjoyment. These purposes apply as well to the Electronic Age. Survival is the prime issue because the new systems taking root—from two-way cable to cellular radio—portend change in practically every aspect of life. Opportunity, meanwhile, abounds for entrepreneurs in quest of new wealth and influence, as well as for ordinary citizens seeking convenience, security, and greater personal productivity. As for enjoyment, it is implicit in technologies that put images on a television screen and encourage viewer participation.

The barrier to understanding this new environment, oddly, is language. Everything about it sounds intimidatingly technical—gigahertzes, bandwidths, transponders, addressable converters, upstream and downstream signals, bits and bytes, digital and analog. Adding to the bewilderment of the uninitiated is the industries' habit of reducing every newly named system, technique, or service to a set of initials. Thus the landscape has become littered with esoteric shorthand: MDS, MTV, DBS, HVN, MSO, CBN, CNN, ENG, HBO, SMATV, HDTV, LPTV, VCR, ESPN, SPN, SIN, and scores more.

In fact, there is no more reason to be put off by technology in this instance than with jet planes, automatic dishwashers, or old-fashioned radios. Millions of us drive cars without the merest notion of why they run or what goes on beneath the hood.

This Field Guide sorts out the families, species, and subspecies of the new electronic media and describes them in everyday language that, we trust, will demystify the jargon and dispel fear of the technology. Our aim is to illuminate the expanding electronic forest so that more may explore it for reasons of survival, opportunity, and enjoyment.

TWO-WAY CABLE: Television in the Active Voice

James Traub

The arrival of two-way, or "interactive," cable television in Pittsburgh has opened the way for, among other novel experiences, electronic match-making.

Every Tuesday evening at 7:30 Steve Hansen, host of *Singles Magazine*, asks searching questions of bachelors and bachelorettes. Then he turns the decision-making over to the viewers. On a recent evening some 300 folks at home pressed buttons on their consoles while a computer at the transmission center of Warner Amex Cable instantly tallied their responses. A fellow named Phil was overwhelmingly the people's choice for a night out with Nancy.

Warner Amex's newly built Qube cable system in Pittsburgh, with sixty-three (of a potential eighty) working channels providing virtually every kind of programming service yet devised, defines the state of the art in cable television. The feature that makes it stand out among large cable systems is interactivity.

Participatory romance is only the most whimsical of the many uses of this versatile technology. It is also used for "instant polls" on political issues and speeches, college exams, and quiz shows. Two-way capacity vastly simplifies "pay-per-view" programming, and even opens up the new business of cable-monitored home-security systems.

Ordinary cable systems connect the home to the source of programming with a single wire; interactive technology uses two wires so that information can flow in both directions. The wires are hooked up to a large central computer that checks each home in the system every six seconds, "reading" communications from viewers. And the viewers, in turn, make their preferences known on a hand-held console that also serves as the channel selector. To choose a date for Nancy, for example, the viewer pressed a "Response" button, and then hit "1," "2," or "3" (for Chris, Phil, or neither).

Warner's first commercial experiments with interactivity were with its Columbus, Ohio system in 1977. Since that time cities soliciting bids to build cable systems have routinely demanded two-way capacity, and other operators have developed their own versions of the technology.

In Columbus, Warner has emphasized the role of two-way systems in promoting "electronic democracy." After President Carter's 1979 energy speech, for example, subscribers were asked to offer instantly their opinion of his performance. On another occasion, consumer advocate Ralph Nader asked viewers whether they would support his petition to change children's advertising.

In Pittsburgh, Qube has edified as much as entertained. Besides the somewhat tongue-in-cheek *Singles Magazine*, the local interactive Channel 59 offers quiz games for both school-age children and adults, a talent show in which viewers act as judges, and a program in which moral choices are dramatized by actors, after which viewers indicate their solutions to the dilemmas.

But in the long run, for most cable operators, the interactive channel may be a good deal less important than the pay-per-view opportunities of two-way cable. When an ordinary cable system, or a subscription-television channel, wishes to offer a program for a one-time charge, it must advertise well in advance and distribute special decoders to unscramble the signal. The system's popularity, despite this cumbersome procedure, was proved in September of 1981, when 500,000 homes paid up to $25 to watch the Sugar Ray Leonard-Thomas Hearns boxing match.

With two-way cable, however, the viewer simply indicates his preference on his console, the computer supplies the signal, and the viewer is automatically billed. In Pittsburgh, Qube offers four pay-per-view movie channels charging from $2.50 to $4 a title, and one channel offering lessons-for-pay in softball, home repair, guitar playing, and the like.

Two-way cable also lends itself to teleshopping, although it is as yet unavailable in Pittsburgh. A teleshopper can pore over televised descriptions of products and buy them without ever leaving home simply by punching in catalogue numbers on the console.

On the eighty-channel cable system of the future, twenty channels may well be devoted to retailing; at least one analyst predicts that by the decade's end 20 percent of America's shopping will be accomplished electronically.

Finally, two-way cable is revolutionizing the security business. Smoke detectors, burglar alarms, and other home-security devices can be connected to a home computer that is in turn connected to a master computer at the cable system's transmission center. The computer sweeps subscribers' homes every few seconds, alerting the police or fire department to changes recorded by the sensors. Cable security services have become another fixture in bids for franchises. In Columbus, more than 5,000 subscribers have already paid $1,100 to equip their homes with sensors, and are paying monthly fees ranging from $14.50 to $16.50 for the cable surveillance.

Gustave Hauser, the chairman of Warner Amex Cable Communications, predicts that home security and pay-per-view will become the two major sources of profit for cable operators in the near future.

PUBLIC ACCESS: The Anybody Channel

Ben Brown

The last, best hope for the plugged-in soap box may well lie with homemade television: with the amateur television freaks in a Detroit suburb who produce a dog-obedience school-of-the-air, and with artists, church groups, cops, senior citizens, librarians, rock 'n' rollers, political ax-grinders, exhibitionists, and just plain folks around the country who have something important or entertaining to show to their neighbors.

The public-access movement, from which all this homemade television flows, is anarchic and intentionally amateurish, struggling along in relative obscurity until one of its more inspired members drops his drawers on camera or threatens to overthrow the government. Yet the idea of providing public access to privately controlled mass media is alive and more or less well in hundreds of American communities. And as bothersome as such access seems to those who make policy and profits in modern telecommunications, the movement's success may be essential if citizens are to salvage anything resembling individualized freedom of expression in the wired nation.

It won't come easily. George Stoney, the New York University professor many consider the father of community-access video, readily admits it's "a David and Goliath movement." In this culture, network programming has established what television should look like—so public-access television looks decidedly bush league. But the problem is not the unprofessional look of the programming—at least not as far as Stoney's concerned. For him, amateurism lies at the heart of the movement.

From 1973 to 1978, Stoney directed the internship program on cable access at New York University's Alternate Media Center, which contributed most of the strongest leaders in public access; he remains the inspiration for what Sue Miller Buske, a former student and now executive director of the National Federation of Local Cable Programmers (NFLCP) calls "the gut philosophy" behind the movement.

"It's got to be a volunteer movement," Stoney says, "not something you're going to make a real living in. It's in the hands of people who have a real interest in their communities and who can afford to devote the time."

Stoney and other community-access enthusiasts want to set aside, for the free, relatively unrestricted use of the public, a few lanes on the new superhighways of telecommunications. They want time on the air, space on the satellites, and channels on the cable systems. But their opponents say that the people who own and run cable systems have the right to decide—free from government interference—how they are used. And everybody claims to have only the public interest at heart.

The issue gets blurred because the cable industry and many of the volunteer groups now using local cable channels make little or no distinction between *access* programming and *locally originated* programming. But there is a crucial difference.

The operator owns and controls the local-origination (LO, in cable talk) channels, which are equivalent to cable-only broadcast stations, complete with commercials. Public-access channels, in contrast, belong to the citizens of a community according to the terms stipulated in its franchise with the cable company. And citizens, through access committees or boards, make the rules.

In the hands of a benevolent cable company, the process of making noncontroversial LO television might feel very much like public access. Local folks come into a community video center, learn how to use the gear, round up a crew of volunteers, and set off down the street to become their neighborhood's answer to *60 Minutes* (or *The Gong Show*). Since the cable company controls LO, however, it has final say over what goes on the air.

> The public-access movement is trying to preserve freedom of expression in the wired nation.

Public access is different, because neither the cable company nor local government can legally interfere with programming (except when there are scheduling problems, or when programs violate obscenity laws). This independence suggests a peculiarly pure notion of free speech—the only glimmer of such a notion, in fact, in the Electronic Age.

In sought-after suburbs and major cities, companies typically offer many access channels, millions of dollars' worth of equipment, full-time staffers, and even mobile vans—all for community use. With all those goodies in the offing, it's tempting to think that access might finally be coming of age.

But advocates of access say the companies are unlikely to keep their promises. "They're talking out of both sides of their mouth," says George Stoney. Individual cable companies may be upping the ante in the competition for franchises, but at the same time the National Cable Television Association is busy trying to free them from regulatory requirements.

For the last two years, the NCTA has been lobbying fiercely for sweeping cable legislation in federal communications bills, including a provision that would prohibit local and state governments from regulating cable rates or mandating access channels. So far, the National League of Cities and the NFLCP have been able to dilute the proposals before they've been voted on. But if the industry's wishes ever become law, the access people fear that all the cable companies' grandiose promises will be meaningless.

"Things have gotten so out of line with all these promises," says Sue Buske of the NFLCP. "It's all going to backfire. What worries me is what happens *after* the franchise is granted." It's always possible, she says, that communities and cable companies, frustrated by the difficulties of setting up a workable access center from scratch, will ditch the whole idea when it gets more complicated than anyone thought.

To help cities and towns design reasonable approaches to access, the NFLCP acts as a consulting service and tries to put community leaders in touch with others who've gone through the same experience. The group publishes a franchising primer, offers sample bylaws for access corporations, and distributes demonstration tapes. In November, it launched a series of workshops and internship sessions for community-access coordinators.

The success of programs such as the internship plan and much of the NFLCP consulting depends in part on the cooperation of the cable companies, which have raided NFLCP ranks for experts on local programming (including some of Stoney's old students), and are kicking in the money for the access-coordinator training.

Stoney approves: "If we don't get inside the industry," he says, "we're licked." But other access people aren't so happy about cozying up to the operators.

Most don't trust the cable industry to remain friendly when the going gets tough, and many are worried that an NFLCP alliance with cable companies will effectively prevent the organization from leading the fight in the communities. Others are simply tired of community organizing and ready to pursue their own interests in filmmaking or video. They'd like to play down the celebration of amateurism and encourage the NFLCP to make as much room for independent film and video people as it has for cable operators and librarians.

A struggle clearly lies ahead. But the access people have already survived quite a struggle. "We've always sounded like radicals," Stoney told a group in Atlanta. And maybe a little crazy too. "If it were an absolutely rational process," says the movement's senior member, "we'd have given up long ago."

SATELLITES: The Birds That Make It All Fly

Jonathan Miller

In 1962, the tiny, experimental Telstar communications satellite inaugurated transatlantic telecasting—and changed the perceptions of a generation about the limits of telecommunications. Along with its gift of instantaneous global communication, the satellite brought visions of a "global village." Twenty years later, the importance of satellites has become so widely recognized that when the British sailed for the Falkland Islands last April, for instance, they took a satellite transmitter with them.

In the last few years satellites have begun to work profound changes in the communications environment. The global-scale expansion of the satellite industry now underway will more than quadruple the world's capacity for long distance communications in this decade. No longer simply another tool in the communications game, used mainly for such things as international news and sports relays, satellites are becoming a major force in the creation of an entirely new information environment. Communications scarcity, dictated by the big three networks and the Bell System's monopoly, is being replaced by communications abundance.

You cannot read or watch a satellite, but as a powerful distribution technology the satellite greatly expands the power of a host of other technologies and can even spawn media hybrids, such as cable networks and *USA Today*, the new national newspaper beamed by satellite to printing plants across the country.

In 1975, when Time Inc.'s Home Box Office began to transmit its programming on Satcom I, satellites began irrevocably to change the structure of the nation's television system. Before then, restrictive regulations, imposed largely at the behest of broadcasters, had confined cable to the role of passive relayer of broadcast signals; satellites shattered these limits. Suddenly cable programming could be instantly and economically transmitted nationwide. Cable systems, themselves proliferating rapidly, began to install dish-shaped "earth station" antennas to receive transmissions. And HBO has been followed by a wild profusion of networks offering cable programming. There are arts channels, children's channels, "superstations" such as Ted Turner's WTBS in Atlanta, foreign-language channels, "adult" entertainment channels, news channels, and ever more movie channels. As more cable networks have appeared, more satellites have been sent up beyond the atmosphere to handle the electronic traffic. Indeed, competition for space on the most coveted satellite, Satcom III-R, has become so intense that leases to its channels have been sold for tens of millions of dollars.

Satellites are starting to make other inroads on network dominance. The three major networks' historic monopoly over instantaneous program distribution to broadcast stations, via webs of leased AT&T long lines, has been overthrown. The Public Broadcasting Service and Spanish International Network have already equipped their affiliates with earth stations, and independent, commercial TV stations are starting to install dishes as well. Hundreds of hours of programming now are being delivered to stations by satellite each week, and even network affiliates are "cherry-picking" some of this fare from satellites as an alternative to the offerings of the networks. A "fourth network," long talked about, has not yet come to pass. But a new system is falling into place: Any television station can become part of an ad hoc program network that can pit its national programming against the offerings of the big three.

> The global-scale expansion of the satellite industry now underway will more than quadruple the world's capacity for long distance communications in this decade.

But the use of satellites is not limited to broadcasters and cable operators. Some 30,000 home owners have installed satellite receiving dishes in their backyards, at a cost of between $3,000 and $10,000. Dish owners can feast for free on any of the fifty or so program services currently up on the satellites (though the legality of doing so is unclear).

Another recent development of interest to those who can't afford a dish, or don't have access to a municipally franchised cable system, is something called SMATV—satellite master-antenna television—which, in effect, is a mini-cable system serving just a single building, or complex of buildings. SMATV installations—including an earth-station receiving dish connected by coaxial cable to individual homes—are being installed in apartments and condominium complexes at the rate of hundreds per month, and provide many of the same movie channels and sports services as conventional cable.

Just as satellites are breaking the networks' dominance over broadcasting, so they are making it possible to challenge the familiar telephone and data-communications monopolies. In the past five years, more than a million American individuals and businesses have started using non-AT&T long-distance services, such as MCI, which use satellites to relay phone calls between major cities. This number is expected to increase rapidly, although another emerging technology —fiber optics—may in a few years challenge satellites for some of this business.

A growing number of companies have begun using satellites as a substitute for executive travel, creating two-way satellite "videoconferencing" or meeting systems able to transmit audio, video, and even documents. Today's Xerox machine, with appropriate modifications, could be tomorrow's mail terminal. Connected to a satellite dish, a copier at one location can rapidly transmit documents to similar machines thousands of miles away. Without much fanfare, large corporations are increasingly relying on satellites for instantaneous internal communication.

Also little publicized, but of enormous commercial importance, is the rapid development of mobile communications services using satellites. More than a thousand ocean-going ships have already installed satellite equipment to permit direct-dial telephone and telex links; soon these capabilities will be extended to aircraft and surface vehicles. Something resembling Dick Tracy's two-way wrist radio-TV system could be along before the end of the century.

While the technology of satellites is frequently described as sophisticated, the reality is that today's birds are crude affairs compared to the giant space stations being planned for the next decade. When the space shuttle begins routine operations it will be capable of hauling into orbit an entirely new generation of satellites much larger and more versatile than those now aloft. These systems will in effect be orbiting switchboards, efficiently relaying huge amounts of information and possibly reducing the price of an overseas telephone call to that of a call across town.

One proof of the power and importance of satellites has been the fierce debates to which they have recently been subjected. Public-interest advocates argue that satellite technology, underwritten by billions of taxpayer dollars, may already have become a captive of corporate interests indifferent to the public's needs. These complaints are likely to become more insistent following the deregulation of satellite carriers now being undertaken by the Federal Communications Commission. Though originally "common carriers" were required to lease transponders on a first-come, first-served basis, some satellite owners have recently been selling them to the highest bidder.

Internationally, satellites have been targeted by the Third World in its demand for a "new world information order." Developing nations fear that a few rich countries will gobble up the limited number of orbital positions and space communication frequencies so quickly that space will be filled by the time the poor countries are ready to launch satellites of their own. The technologically advanced countries, meanwhile, have resisted limits on their ability to launch new satellites at will.

DBS: A Dish on Every Roof?

Julie Talen

If a satellite dish were something you could carry home under your arm, would you buy one and stick it on your roof? What if it cost only a few hundred dollars, and allowed you to receive several brand-new channels of movies, sports, and cultural programming—some of them free, some of them scrambled and available for a monthly fee? And if you already had cable, would you still buy the dish?

These and other questions swirl around the sudden arrival of direct-broadcast satellites on an already chaotic television landscape. Direct-broadcast satellites use a newly available span of frequencies—the 12 gigahertz band—and transmit a signal up to forty times more powerful than those of current communications satellites. They send a television beam so strong it can be picked up by a dish smaller than an umbrella—roughly two feet in diameter. (This stronger signal is also narrower than conventional ones; hence it takes as many as four DBS satellites to "cover" an area the size of the United States, as compared

A Satellite Primer

Satellites serve as radio relay stations in the sky. They receive transmissions from the ground, beamed to space from an "uplink," and retransmit them to a receiving dish called a "downlink" or an "earth station." The satellite always remains in the same position relative to ground stations because it has been placed in "synchronous" orbit 22,300 miles perpendicular to the equator, where objects revolve around the earth at the same speed that the planet revolves on its axis.

The most important element of a satellite is the "transponder," the name given to a single receive/transmit system. Typically, each transponder can relay a single color-television channel, or about a thousand simultaneous telephone connections (although satellite operators are developing systems to double or triple this capacity). Most satellites can carry two-dozen transponders today; those planned for later in this decade will carry forty or more.

The nation using the most satellites is the United States, which currently has fifteen—owned by RCA, Western Union, Comsat, and Satellite Business Systems (a partnership of Comsat, IBM and Aetna Life & Casualty Co.)—in orbit. Although the U.S. has long dominated satellite communication, the Europeans are building birds of their own, and both European and Japanese companies are competing to sell satellite systems in Asia, South America, and Europe. One recent study commissioned by NASA predicted that the total number of transponders in use by all countries could grow from fewer than 1,000 today to more than 6,000 by 1997.

to one satellite on the current frequency.) By reaching viewers directly, DBS poses a threat to television stations as well as to cable systems.

Spearheaded by Comsat's proposal to the FCC in the winter of 1980 for a three-channel subscription service, to be operated by a subsidiary, Satellite Television Corporation, the field of DBS now includes at least eight corporations, among them CBS, RCA, and Western Union. With the FCC encouraging the development of DBS, the first American DBS service began in 1983, when United Satellite Television started beaming four channels of movies, sports, news, and pay-per-view events from Canada's Anik-C3 satellite. This service uses a relatively weak signal, requiring a somewhat larger dish than do the DBS systems due in the mid-eighties.

Among the eight American contenders for DBS authorization, one wants strictly common-carrier status—to sell its time in lots to any takers. Most propose a mix of advertiser-supported "free" services and subscriber-supported pay services carrying uninterrupted movies, sports, and specially targeted programming, much as pay-cable systems now do. Two hope to become the fourth national network, reckoning that cable systems and local stations could pick up and rebroadcast the DBS signal. RCA and Western Union intend to lease out DBS time, but want the right to select their clients, presumably to insure room for their own programming.

The FCC is pushing ahead on DBS with uncommon speed because the new technology stands to be the alternative to cable in the sparsely populated areas that will probably never be wired by cable companies. The commission opened the docket for DBS applications in the spring of 1981, issued licensing guidelines in June the following year, and seems ready to approve construction permits for existing and possibly new applicants. The corporations involved have already begun negotiations with satellite manufacturers; Comsat has even reserved the space shuttle for satellite launches in late 1985 and early 1986.

However, any final decisions on how the spectrum will be divided must await the 1983 Regional Administrative Radio Conference, which will determine how DBS frequencies will be apportioned among all countries in the hemisphere. Already, American companies' requests for bandwidth exceed even the most optimistic predictions of the amount of spectrum space to be allocated to the United States.

To make matters more complicated, the FCC has agreed that part of the DBS spectrum should be set aside for experiments with high-definition television (HDTV), 1,125-line television, which requires five times the bandwidth of a normal 525-line picture.

DBS systems are expensive to build (Comsat's alone will cost $1 billion), but on a per-household basis they figure to cost considerably less than cable. For consumers who already receive cable, DBS offers mainly the novelty of receiving television programs directly by satellite. But some 20 million homes—30 percent of American households—are in areas too remote to be wired economically. For these people, DBS would provide an otherwise unavailable multi-channel pay service—the first national television service in America with no local middleman.

PAY TELEVISION: The Happy Medium

Michael Schwarz

Not many years ago, the sages were saying that people would never pay for television programs when so many were already available free. They weren't just guessing: All the experiments with pay television in the fifties and sixties—in large cities such as New York, Chicago, Los Angeles, and London; in smaller cities such as Palm Springs, California and Hartford, Connecticut, and in little towns such as Bartlesville, Oklahoma, and Etobicoke, Canada—were dismal failures.

Yet today, Americans living where pay television is not available in any form feel sorely deprived. In urban communities, the demand for cable can be traced directly to the desire for those premium pay channels that show movies, sports, and other special entertainment not presented on conventional television. It is nothing short of a monumental change in our culture that people now wish to pay for television fare that comes unabridged and without commercials.

Since 1975, pay television has grown into a billion dollar business and become a medium in its own right. With five routes into the viewer's home—over the air, on cable, on microwave systems known as multipoint distribution service (MDS), on master-antenna systems that can receive satellite signals (SMATV), and on direct-broadcast satellites (DBS)—it continues to expand.

It is nothing short of a monumental change in our culture that people now wish to pay for television fare that comes unabridged and without commercials.

Mainly, pay-television services are sold to subscribers on a monthly basis; their scrambled signals are decoded in paying households. Home Box Office (HBO), the leading pay service, which pioneered national distribution by satellite in 1975, proved that a subscription network could make huge profits with a mere fraction of the audience drawn by ABC, CBS, and NBC. Two years ago it started a second pay network, Cinemax, which offers an array of movies never intended for mass audiences.

The other leading pay-cable services are Showtime, owned by Viacom, and The Movie Channel, the only twenty-four hour all-movie channel, which is owned by Warner Amex. New to the pay-cable sweepstakes is The Entertainment Channel,* a deluxe television network featuring Broadway shows and the pick of the British Broadcasting Corporation's output, among other fare. Joining the field next spring will be the Disney Channel, viewed by the industry as a potential blockbuster. And Group W Cable operates

*The Entertainment Channel folded early in 1983.

Home Theater Network (HTN), a pay-cable service specializing in movies suitable for family viewing.

HBO's extraordinary success has linked pay television to cable television in the public's mind. Indeed, of the 14 million households that currently subscribe to a pay service, some 11.5 million receive it on cable, paying about $10 a month for each pay network in addition to a monthly fee for basic cable service. The remainder receive their pay service over the air on one of the STV stations (1.5 million subscribers nationally), via MDS (750,000 subscribers), or by SMATV and DBS technologies that are just becoming important.

These forms of monthly subscription television, however, may seem primitive in the latter half of this decade as two-way cable—typified by Warner Amex's Qube system—and "addressable converters" proliferate. These technologies allow people to buy individual programs rather than an entire monthly service. In the long run, pay-per-view television may prove more expensive for consumers than paying monthly fees for pot-luck channels, but the expectations are that viewers will be better satisfied if they can decide for themselves which programs are worth paying for. Pay-per-view opens a new frontier for promoters of special events and holds great new profit opportunities for the various pay-television systems.

Pay cable is now growing faster than basic cable. It appears that paying for television is a habit not very hard to acquire after all.

MDS: Movies By Microwave

Seth Goldstein

MDS, or multipoint distribution service, which operates in the superhigh frequency broadcast band, came out of obscurity as a communications medium with the advent of pay television in the mid-seventies. Today it is the non-cable conduit for such services as HBO and Showtime, and has a national subscriber count of more than 750,000.

With a microwave signal that travels a distance of only twenty-five miles, MDS had set out initially to become a common-carrier distribution service for business, lending itself primarily to data transmission and teleconferencing in metropolitan areas. MDS struggled as an industry until Microband Corporation of America, which holds the largest number of MDS licenses, decided in 1975 to use the evening hours for the transmission of pay-television fare to hotels and apartment complexes in major cities. Refinements in the technology soon made it possible to include single-family dwellings in suburban communities. Since then, home entertainment has become an MDS mainstay.

Like subscription television (STV), MDS has succeeded by entering markets ahead of cable. Typically, a subscriber faces an initial cost of less than $150 for the installation of a special rooftop antenna, and then must pay monthly fees of $10 to $15 for the program service. The MDS "feed" is routed into a vacant channel on a standard television set.

MDS provides opportunity for local commercial broadcasters to get into the pay-television business as a sideline, without violating FCC rules of cross-ownership. CBS, for example, has announced its intention to provide an MDS pay-television service in the five cities in which it owns and operates television stations. It can do this because it will not own the MDS licenses, but in effect will be leasing the channels from the owner, Contemporary Communications Inc.

Meanwhile, Microband has asked the FCC for authorization to provide five channels of service in its markets, instead of a single channel. To do this, Microband would take over some of the frequencies previously allotted—but rarely used—by Instructional Television Fixed Service, a microwave television service intended for educational use. If the commission approves, MDS conceivably could grow into an over-the-air version of cable.

STV:
A Different Kind of TV Station

Seth Goldstein

STV (subscription television) is the least exotic, and the oldest, of the "new" technologies. It is simply pay television transmitted over the air by local television stations that have chosen to offer a subscription service rather than conventional advertising-supported programming. The only thing new about STV is its right to operate.

The technology dates back to 1950, when the first STV test was conducted in New York. For the ensuing twenty-seven years, largely in response to lobbying by commercial broadcasters and theater owners, the Federal Communications Commission suppressed the medium's growth. Today, thanks to the success of pay cable, virtually all restrictions on STV have been lifted.

STV stations, most of them on the UHF band, send out a scrambled picture that a device on subscribers' TV sets can unscramble. The fare is similar to that on pay cable—current movies, entertainment specials, and sporting events—and the monthly charge approximately the same. The great difference is that pay cable comes with all that basic cable has to offer—from all-news to evangelical channels—while STV offers only movies and other typical pay-television programming. But this hasn't proven a handicap. Wherever cable has been slow to get started—in the large cities, mainly—STV has prospered.

Cable companies require several years to wire a city, but STV stations can enlist subscribers as quickly as they can install decoding devices in homes. Moreover, STV enjoys an economic advantage over cable. By current estimates, each subscribing household may cost an urban cable operator around $1,000; the costs for STV are only $200 per household.

After some five years in the marketplace, STV has captured more than a million subscribers nationally and continues to grow in such cities as Los Angeles, New York, Dallas, Washington, Detroit, Phoenix, and Miami. Even in areas where cable has finally arrived as competition—offering its abundance of channels and services—such single-channel STV operators as Oak Industries, SelecTV, and Wometco Home Theatre have managed to hold their ground.

Whether these companies can continue to withstand the march of cable may well depend on new tehcnological developments that would increase program selection for STV subscribers. And, in fact, there is a new decoder that will bring in more than one pay channel. Dallas, with three STV stations on the air, could be the first city to try it.

SMATV: Mini-Cable Systems Get Good Reception

Seth Goldstein

For years, builders routinely equipped their new apartment complexes with master-antenna systems (MATV)—special wiring to insure good television reception for all tenants. In effect, they created miniature cable systems, for the MATV installations connect all dwelling units of the building to a single transmission center capable of originating closed-circuit programming. A few years ago, someone thought of hitching the MATV system to a satellite receiving dish, and overnight what had been a residential convenience was transformed into a brash competitor to cable.

Today these installations are known as SMATV, satellite master-antenna systems. They pull down signals from the satellites, including the pay channels, and provide them to tenants paying monthly subscription fees. Wherever SMATV exists, cable has little chance of entering, because the two services are quite similar.

The development of SMATV has brought anguish to the cable industry, since it threatens to skim the cream off cable's choicest residential areas even before many cities are wired.

The cities themselves are also frustrated by SMATV because these systems, unlike their cable counterparts, pay nothing to the municipalities. Because cable operators are franchised by cities and use the public rights of way, they are obliged to pay up to 5 percent of their gross revenues (obstensibly to cover the municipalities' administrative and supervisory costs). Moreover, they are usually required to provide public-access channels and production equipment for community use. SMATV is outside municipal jurisdiction and free from such obligations.

SMATV operators have corralled close to 500,000 subscribers so far, but their chore has grown tougher. Some of the pay-cable networks—Home Box Office, for instance—are faithful to the industry they depend on, and have begun rallying to cable's cause by refusing to let SMATV use their services. A SMATV operator in Phoenix has filed suit against the pay-cable networks and local cable operators, claiming they have conspired to put him out of business.

But this conflict has provided an opportunity to some entrepreneurs. They are racing to develop programming expressly for SMATV, and for the hotels and motels that have installed satellite receiving dishes to provide their guests with added television service.

PAY-PER-VIEW: Opening Nights at Home

Savannah Waring Walker

In the summer of 1986, when the sequel of, say, *ET, the Extra-Terrestrial* opens and the family is dying to see it, you won't have to wait until the lines die down, or fight the crowds and arrive too frazzled to enjoy the film. Instead, even before its theatrical release, you may hear of its television release—a special, one-shot, well-hyped presentation that can be watched at home for less than the cost of a family movie outing.

By 1990, estimates the advertising firm of Ogilvy & Mather, as many as half of all U.S. households could be equipped to receive such "pay-per-view" events. At least 2 million homes already have the capability. Since the first large-scale pay-per-view venture in 1978, consumers in Los Angeles, Phoenix, Chicago, and other cities have been given the opportunity to see prizefights, concerts, Broadway shows, and football games as they happened, for fees of around $10. Since 1977, subscribers to Qube, Warner Amex's interactive cable experiment in Columbus (and now in several other cities), have been offered pay-per-view telecourses. Group W, the nation's third-largest cable-system owner, also offers weekly pay-per-view events to 2,500 of its subscribers. In late September, Twentieth Century-Fox timed a widespread pay-per-view release of *Star Wars* to occur just after the nationwide theatrical reissue.

While perhaps only interesting to the consumer because of the convenience it affords, pay-per-view is wildly exciting to business because of its vast—and easily tapped—money-making potential. "Consider a blockbuster film like *Star Wars*," crows one study. "A 25.0 rating among 50 million homes at $10 is a $125 million box office [overnight]." This jumps the gun a bit, since not even one-tenth that number of homes is ready for pay-per-view. Nevertheless, even the most popular first-run movies don't make $125 million in a week's theatrical run. It's clear what the excitement is about.

That excitement runs in many quarters, too: Film studios such as MGM/UA and Columbia, multiple cable-system owners such as Cox Cable, and manufacturers of addressable converters and other equipment designed to make "impulse purchasing" easy for the television viewer—all have begun jockeying for a part of the new market.

But certain problems must be overcome. Especially difficult for cable operators, for instance, has been the defining of pay-per-view for customers already confused by the alphabet soup of the new technologies. "I had a hard time explaining pay cable to my subscribers," one cable operator told *Variety*. "Now I'm going to have to explain pay-per-view."

Another major problem is technical. Attempts at upgrading older cable systems—making them addressable and thus more compatible with pay-per-view—have been foiled in many cases by equipment malfunction. The leading producers of addressable converters and similar hardware have been grappling with all the bugs of this relatively untried technology. Equipping the nation's cable systems may take years.

But that doesn't preclude our hearing quite a bit on the subject meanwhile. As one-shot presentations of big-budget films and concerts become more common, the purveyers of pay-per-view will doubtless become skilled in their art, adding a whole new dimension to the word "hype."

VIDEOTEX: The Electronic Word

Stephen Fenichell

A television set is transformed into an information-age appliance as soon as it's connected to a computer. That computer can be a small one in the same room, or a giant one a continent away. *Videotex* is the generic name for the two new technologies that arrange this transformation over long distances.

One of these technologies makes the connection through telephone or two-way cable lines and thus is interactive. It is know as *videotext* (with the final "t"), and allows the user to perform various transactions with the main computer, such as banking, shopping, and even sophisticated research, using the television screen and a keyboard attached to the set.

The other is a one-way technology that relies on signals broadcast over the air by television stations. Called *teletext*, this system promises to be cheaper and more widely available than videotext, but its information can flow only from the computer to the television set; transactions are not possible. A small keypad is used to select "pages" of information on the screen.

The teletext user, for example, could call up on his screen a theater directory to learn what shows have tickets available, but he could not reserve tickets through the television screen. The videotext user, on the other hand, not only learns what shows are not sold out, but could call for reviews and even to place his order for seats.

The 1980s began with four incompatible videotext formats, each developed in a different country with substantial government funding. Each now competes for a share of the world market.

Prestel, the world's first full-scale commercial videotex service, was introduced in 1979 by the British postal service. France's post office and broadcast authority created the Antiope teletext system, which spawned the more elaborate, two-way service, Télématique. The Canadian Department of Communications sponsored the radically different Telidon system, and Japan in 1980 introduced its own system, Captain.

> Videotex is essentially a hybrid of mass-communications and computer technologies.

These governments funded the development of videotex services because they also control their countries' postal, telephone, and telecommunications services; they regard the provision of video information as a logical component of a comprehensive public-communications utility. The United States, in contrast, has left the development of videotex to a "free" market—dominated by large communications, broadcasting, publishing, and financial concerns—on the ground that it is not a public utility but rather the technical basis for a new and exciting (if still somewhat vague) commercial enterprise known as electronic publishing.

All four foreign videotex formats are being tested by American entrepreneurs, while other companies are working entirely with American-made hardware and software.

In any format, videotex is essentially a hybrid of mass-communications and computer technologies. Combining television, print, and data processing, it blurs the traditional distinctions between publishing a message, broadcasting a message, transmitting a message, and reporting a message. As a result, videotex defies easy categorization: It can come into the home over the air, by cable, or by telephone; it can be a form of banking, publishing, newspaper reporting, entertainment, shopping, classified advertising, or a host of other "information services." The variety of transmission methods and the range of activities and services encompassed by videotex make it exceedingly difficult to regulate. How the various forms of videotex should be regulated, and who should be responsible for the decisions, are pressing issues of public policy.

Videotex Glossary

Videotex—The generic term for systems that transmit textual information for display on television screens.

Videotext—An interactive videotex system that uses either two-way cable or telephone lines to connect a central computer to a home television set, allowing for information retrieval and transactions.

Teletext—A one-way videotex system that transmits textual material as part of the standard broadcast or cable-television signal.

Ceefax—British teletext system operated by the BBC.

Oracle—British teletext system operated by ITV (commercial TV).

Prestel—British videotext system operated by government postal and telephone service.

Antiope—French teletext system.

Télématique—French videotext system operated by government postal and telephone service.

Captain—Japanese videotext system operated by government postal and telephone service.

Telidon—Canadian teletext system.

VIDEOTEXT: Putting the TV Set to Work

Stephen Fenichell

Videotext is the difference between watching television and using it. Yes, using it: to retrieve textual material on the screen when you want it, and to make various kinds of transactions. You might, for example, summon up an airline's schedule, make your flight reservations, and then instruct your bank to issue a check for the tickets—all at the television set.

You could buy theater tickets in the same manner, make restaurant reservations, call for the latest stock-market prices and place an order, or select a shirt from an electronic catalogue. With videotext, television also becomes a research library and electronic newspaper.

You make all this happen with a keybord hooked into your television set. In effect, it connects you to a bank of computers and data bases at the transmission source, either through telephone lines or two-way cable, allowing for many kinds of transactions at home.

Two videotext services, home banking and home shopping, seem to have the greatest potential for making television something you use rather than watch. They thus receive special attention here.

HOME BANKING

Anyone who has ever waited for the next available teller knows that banking in banks is no fun. In cities the banks are invariably crowded, and in rural areas, the're often a long drive from home. So it may prove a stroke of universal good fortune that banks themselves are disenchanted with the local-branch system. Once an effective way of increasing clientele by making banks more convenient, branches have now become uneconomical to build and operate. This is why more and more banks conduct their business electronically today, offering customers not only the convenience of sidewalk cash machines but, increasingly, the ability to bank at home.

"Banks see electronic services as a means of opening up new markets without a massive investment in bricks and mortar," says Janet Norman, director of the Center for Technology and the Consumer. "Videotext presents them with the opportunity to become a financial-services supermarket, in which the home terminal represents the shopping cart."

Through videotext, bank customers can check the status of their accounts, pay bills, transfer funds, check interest rates and money-market funds, or request more general financial information.

Although most bank-at-home services are still in a testing stage, Alan Lipis, president of Electronic Banking Corporation, a consulting group, predicts there will be approximately a million home-banking terminals by the mid-eighties. "There is a tremendous potential for new accounts, new services, new territories," claims Lipis, "but this will require a major investment not just in technology, but in getting people to know it's there, getting them to sign up, and getting them to use it."

TELESHOPPING

Teleshopping is a way of putting department stores on television—an electronic version of the mail-order catalogue. In October 1980, Federated Department Stores (owners of Bloomingdale's and Abraham & Straus) bought an interest in Comp-U-Card, the nation's first and most extensive electronic shopping service. For an $18 yearly membership fee, 1.5 million Comp-U-Card subscribers can use cable television, home computers, or telephone lines to get access to a product list of more than 50,000 items.

> Videotext is perfectly suited to providing an unprecedented knowledge of the mundane details of life.

In conjunction with Times-Mirror, Comp-U-Card has tested The Shopping Channel, a two-way-cable shopping service reaching some 150,000 subscribers in six Times-Mirror cable-system test markets.The Shopping Channel's only competitor has been the *Home Shopping Show*, produced by Modern Satellite Network. But it won't be long before the competition stiffens. Warner Amex Satellite Entertainment tested its own shopping service, ShopAmerica, in 1983. Theoretically, people watching ShopAmerica should be able to order products by telephone, charge them to their American Express accounts, and have them delivered from regional warehouses within a few days.

All these shopping services are examples of an entirely new form of commercial programming known as the "infomercial." Based on a largely unproven marketing premise, such television spots can entertain consumers while informing them about the merits of specific products.

But unlike home banking, which has proven readily adaptable to a pure data-processing technique (with a few notable exceptions, such as electronic bill-paying and cash withdrawals), any home shopping service must overcome a number of significant logistical obstacles in devising low-cost systems for order entry, accounting, and delivery. The fastest ordering setup in the world could easily be crippled by a reliance on the post office for speed. Setting up an alternate distribution system would daunt companies whose business is the provision of information. But teleshopping still figures heavily in nearly all videotext trials, including the CBS/AT&T test in Ridgewood, New Jersey and Times-Mirror's two-way cable test in the Los Angeles area; it is projected as part of Warner Amex's Qube operations in Columbus, Cincinnati, Pittsburgh, and Dallas.

"The point of videotext is to help the consumer get through a very complex, noisy world," says John Warwick, director of the Times-Mirror videotext experiment. "We help them to make a decision and act on that decision. Videotext is the only medium in which the user is in total control; we've given the consumer back the level of choice he had before the advent of the electronic age."

"The things videotext does best are ultimately boring," observes Pat Montague of the Birmingham *Post & Mail*, which is active in England's videotext trials. "Videotext is perfectly suited to providing an unprecedented knowledge of the mundane details of life. But it is those mundane details, the transactions, the record-keeping, the storage of information, that do, in fact, seem to make the modern world go round."

TELETEXT: Grabbing Pages Off the Air

Gary Arlen

That heavy black line that bobs up annoyingly on the television screen when the vertical hold needs adjusting is not as innocuous as it seems. It holds a hidden treasure, the promise of a new kind of broadcasting known as teletext.

In back of the black bar are twenty-one little-used lines of television signal that can do some amazing things. For these lines can carry specially programmed textual material—news headlines, sports scores, restaurant and theater directories, television listings, stock-market reports, airline schedules, recipes, horoscopes, classified ads—that the viewer may call up at will, either on a blank screen or superimposed on the television image.

Moreover, each of these "pages" of information can be sponsored. The border may read: "Pepsi Presents the Weather Report." Teletext, then, is potentially a new source of income for a television station, which is why technologists now call the black bar hiding below the screen "the most valuable piece of real estate on the electromagnetic spectrum."

The black bar is known as the vertical blanking interval, and before the invention of teletext its main purpose was to guide the electron gun in the television set. That gun shoots a beam of electrons horizontally for 525 lines, going from left to right and top to bottom, to create one picture. The process takes one-thirtieth of a second. When the beam hits the 505th line—the start of the vertical blanking interval—it is sent back to the top and starts the process anew. The blanking interval needs only one line to signal the end of a video frame, yet there are twenty-one lines in the band.

Some of these lines are now being used in sets that have automatic color adjustment, and line twenty-one is reserved as a closed-captioning service for the hearing-impaired. (Specially equipped television sets can display superimposed captions over the regular picture.) Teletext, in the experiments now underway in the United States, uses two other lines of the blanking interval to transmit a "magazine" of some 100 pages of topical information. This information is digitally encoded into the blanking interval by the broadcaster; households equipped with a decoder are able to call up any of the pages to their screens with a waiting time of no more than seven seconds.

Teletext—as opposed to videotext—is one-way, meaning that consumers cannot request specific information, but can only receive what is being sent. Using a hand-held keypad, a viewer punches in a page number from a subject index, and the television set "grabs" that page for display the next time it whizzes by in the cycle of pages being broadcast. Since the sender decides what the pages will contain, teletext is similar to a regular magazine. But teletext enjoys one important advantage over its print counterpart: Information can be continually updated.

The first full-fledged teletext service was Britain's Ceefax, which was started by the BBC in 1976 and now has about half a million subscribers using its television listings, news headlines, basic video games, and sports scores. Oracle, a similar system, also operates in Britain on the independent (commercial) network and is the world's first advertiser-supported teletext service. The French entered the market with the Antiope system, which is technically more flexible than the British versions, since it can be broadcast over FM radio as well as the standard television signal.

But perhaps the most sophisticated teletext system of all is Canada's Telidon, which offers more detailed graphics than competing systems. In the United States, Telidon has the additional advantage of conforming to a technical standard adopted by AT&T and CBS. Nevertheless, each of the teletext systems has picked up proponents in the U.S., and it remains unclear which will prevail.

This question is just one of many that a series of trials around the country is attempting to answer. Assuming people are willing to read their television screens, what will they want to see? Will advertisers be willing to sponsor "pages"? Who is in the best position to "publish" teletext—the networks, local affiliates, or newspapers? What effect will the new service have on conventional broadcasting? And finally, is there a large enough market for electronic publishing to support both teletext and videotext?

Since most of its hardware is already in place, teletext has the advantage of being cheaper and easier to launch. By the end of 1982, Keyfax started the first commercial teletext service, transmitting 100 pages of news, information, and advertising to cable subscribers who receive superstation WTBS, for a monthly fee of $20 (which covers rental of a decoder and keypad). And both CBS and NBC have announced that, pending FCC approval, they will launch national teletext services sometime next year.

ELECTRONIC MAIL:
Very Special Delivery

Martin Koughan

Anyone who has spent countless days waiting for that important piece of mail to arrive knows that rain, snow, sleet, and hail are often the least of the post office's problems. By the turn of the century, though, there will be no more waiting. Important mail will arrive not in days, but in seconds—directly into your living room.

Electronic mail (EM) could turn out to be one of the most widely used offspring of videotext as home terminals become common household appliances. Sending a letter will merely require typing the message on a home-computer keyboard. The words are transformed into bursts of digital data, which are transmitted as electrical signals over telephone lines or interactive cable television. Central computers sort and deliver the message to the "electronic address" of the recipient's home computer, where the signal is reconstructed into words on a screen or printed on paper.

By replacing the mail carrier with computer-to-computer chatter, EM will handle personal communications faster and more reliably than the post office ever could. But the benefits of EM go well beyond speed and efficiency. Electronic mail will extend the benefits of telecommuniciations to some groups that have previously been excluded. The hearing-impaired, for instance, were untouched by the miracle of the telephone, but EM will give deaf users, for the first time, instantaneous access to a distant network of friends and business associates. EM will also allow user groups with common interests to link up and share the latest information instantly and inexpensively. Professionals ranging from accountants to zoologists, adoption and disaster-relief workers—all will create their own open-party lines, electronic bulletin boards serving their individual interests.

Currently, home use of EM is limited to subscribers of such services as The Source and Compu-Serve, networks that offer anyone with a computer terminal access to information banks through telephone lines. But eventually, you will be able to compose a wedding invitation on your home terminal and transmit it simultaneously to the entire universe of your friends and relatives—and the machines will keep track of the RSVPs. If that strikes you as a saver of time and money, then imagine how eager the executives at your local bank or utility will be to mail monthly statements, which are already computerized, directly to their customers with a single command.

The huge volume of business communications makes EM a natural for corporations, and not just for their bills and monthly statements. Internal company communications, such as memos, charts, or reports that must circulate among offices and factories all over the world, can be distributed by EM and updated instantly. GTE's Telenet, a pioneer in business EM, provides a service called Telemail, which allows traveling executives to tap into their personal "mailboxes" from any location using a briefcase-size portable terminal and a telephone. So promising is the commercial potential of business EM that the competition in that field is fierce and strictly blue-chip. Joining GTE and Tymshare in the office-communications market are Exxon, Xerox, ITT, and IBM. Other computer manufacturers are expected to enter the fray, but the one player watched by everyone is the sleeping giant of the communications field, American Bell. Among the first words Ma Bell's unregulated child utters will be electronic mail—spoken through Western Electric's "smart" telephones, which will communicate over the company's long-line system.

All these developments spell big trouble for the U.S. Postal Service. Eighty percent of all first-class mail comes from business; according to recent estimates, one-quarter of first-class mail volume could shortly transfer to EM, thereby crippling the USPS. Enter ECOM (Electronic Computer-Originated Mail), USPS's $40 million counterattack against the telecommunications giants that would dare steal their lucrative business customers. ECOM allows bulk mailers to transmit their messages electronically over phone lines to computers in twenty-five specially equipped postal centers across the country. The computers sort the mail by postal zone and transmit it to the appropriate ECOM post office.

But that's where ECOM's resemblance to electronic mail abruptly ends. As the messages arrive at the local ECOM office, they are printed out, stuffed in special blue-and-white envelopes, and delivered by mail carriers. Delivery is guaranteed within two days. In concessions to postal unions and potential competitors, USPS has vowed never to extend ECOM's reach directly to any recipient's terminal, a fatal limitation for any EM service. As a result, the bulk mailers who were expected to use ECOM to send nearly 30 million pieces of mail per year have been staying away in droves; in the first ten weeks of operation, ECOM's volume did not even reach 1 percent of projections. As business customers begin to defect to commercial EM suppliers, postal revenues will plunge and service will worsen. By the

year 2000, we may not have the post office to kick around any more.

FIBER OPTICS: Through a Glass Lightly

Eric Scheye

Impressive as the capabilities of coaxial cables are, fiber optics could soon make them obsolete. A single strand of optical fiber no thicker than a human hair can transmit the entire broadcast spectrum or more than 100,000 telephone calls. A bundle of these fibers may eventually bring the whole array of communications media—radio stations, telephone calls, and hundreds of television channels—into the home through a single wire.

Unlike present-day television sets and telephones, whose electronic impulses travel through the air or on copper wire, fiber-optic technology involves digital pulses of light sent through flexible strands of glass. Since light waves are much higher on the spectrum than radio waves, a much greater amount of information can be transmitted through an optical fiber than through a conventional wire. And since the main ingredient of optical fibers is sand instead of copper, they should become much cheaper to produce.

If fiber optics seems a blessing to the cable industry, it is a decidedly mixed one, because the telephone company also has plans for the technology. Fiber optics would allow Bell to do what cable does—bring video signals into the home. The French government already has plans to wire part of Biarritz with a fiber system that will combine voice telephony, color video, and data transmission. In this country, the cable industry may have to race Bell to get the fiber optic wire into the home.

LOW-POWER TV: Broadcasting in a Minor Key

James Traub

When the Federal Communiciations Commission solicited applications in 1981 for licenses to operate low-power television stations, then-chairman Charles Ferris called the technology "the first new broadcast service in twenty years offering the same intriguing possibilities as the advent of commercial-television broadcasting in the late 1940s."

The mechanism for low-power television has been around since the early days of television. Low-power transmitters, known as "translators," have been used in rural areas to pick up distant signals and rebroadcast them into nearby regions that otherwise would have been bypassed. Until recently, translator operators were forbidden to broadcast their own material. When the FCC lifted this restriction, low-power television became possible. LPTV, as it is called, raised hopes for a new kind of television—small-scale, populist, adventurous. But some of the initial optimism has faded as the reality of economic and bureaucratic obstacles has sunk in.

LPTV uses very weak signals to broadcast over a small area without interfering with other signals. Every city keeps segments of its broadcast spectrum empty to avoid such interference. Philadelphia, for example, cannot use Channel 2 because that channel has been allocated to New York. Stations on the same channel must be 170 miles apart. Limited to only 1,000 watts of power (as opposed to as many as 5 million watts for some standard broadcast channels), the low-power signal will travel only ten or fifteen miles in any direction. The FCC has promised wary broadcasters that should an LPTV channel impinge on an extant signal, it will be hustled off the airwaves.

LPTV has been greeted with enthusiasm by ethnic minorities and community-oriented groups owing to a belief that it was especially intended for them. One "intriguing possibility" is the opportunity for a geographically defined community to speak to itself over the airwaves—blacks in Harlem, American Indians on a reservation, small-town citizens anywhere. Nonprofit groups could get involved. And so they all have: The FCC received applications from black and Hispanic groups, from unions and religious bodies, from radical television-for-the-people types, and from small-town folk of all descriptions.

But it also received carloads of applications from such big companies as Turner Broadcasting, the Gannett newspaper chain, ABC, and NBC. The FCC received 6,593 applications in all before the stunned commission declared a freeze on applications from all but the most rural areas. Neighborhood TV, a firm for which Sears Roebuck (through its subsidiary, Allstate Insurance) provided major financial backing, submitted applications for 141 LPTV stations. Its hope was to establish a "fourth network" whose programs would "show what is great about small-town life on a national scale." The FCC has since, however, given notice that applicants with no other LPTV stations will be given preference.

Perhaps more than that of any other communications technology, the future of LPTV rests with the federal government. The FCC will decide who gets the 4,000 or so licenses, though it is not clear when or how the decision will be reached. In the summer of 1981 Congress authorized the FCC to choose winners by lottery, after having figured in a preference for minorities and small owners. The FCC dillied and dallied and finally refused altogether—in large part, some critics suspect, because it did not want to favor little guys at the expense of large corporations. A second piece of legislation has now passed Congress, but until the lotteries are held no one can know who will finally benefit by LPTV.

A further problem for LPTV owners is their current exclusion from the "must carry" rule. The FCC requires that cable systems carry all local stations and "significantly viewed" broadcast stations within a thirty-five mile radius. As a result, people who hook up to cable for its better reception, greater diversity, and increased local programming won't be able to watch LPTV unless the rules are changed or the cable operator voluntarily carries it. The prospects for this are decidedly poor: Small cable systems won't have room for LPTV channels, and large ones may well view LPTV as competition, especially if the low-power station engages in pay television.

The independent LPTV operator—the determined neophyte with a station or two—faces one final problem that the government cannot solve: where to find programming. A station may cost only $50,000 to build, but the costs of original programming are immense for stations with limited revenue potential. This awkward fact has spawned partnerships like that of Gene Autry's Golden West Broadcasters and a black group called Community Television Network; CTN gets the daytime hours and Golden West prime time.

But independent LPTV stations may have great trouble providing the kind of community-based programming they have in mind. An official of SelecTV, which provides movies and special events for over-the-air subscription television, reports the company has been "virtually swamped with inquiries" from would-be owners. The force of economics just might turn LPTV into another fast-buck game. Intriguing possibilities have, after all, been overlooked before.

SUGGESTIONS FOR FURTHER READING

The technology explained in this chapter was also treated in the first edition of *Mass Media Issues*. Of particular interest are Les Brown's "Comes the Revolution," which originally appeared in *Keeping Your Eye on Television*, New York: The Pilgrim Press, 1979, and "Wired City, U.S.A.: The Charms and Dangers of Two-Way TV," by John Wicklein, which originally appeared in the February 1979 issue of *The Atlantic Monthly*.

Also of interest:

Vincent Mosco, *Pushbutton Fantasies: Critical Perspectives on Videotex and Information Technology*. Norwood, N.J.: Ablex, 1982. Examines four perspectives that shape our understanding of a communications revolution: post-industrialism in the workplace, mass society in the home, pluralism in government, and developmentalism in international relations.

Dan Schiller, *Telematics and Government*. Norwood, N.J.: Ablex, 1981. Systematically assesses the role of government in the convergence of U.S. and worldwide telecommuniciation and computer technology.

Jennifer Daryl Slack and Fred Fejes, eds., *The Ideology of the Information Age*. Norwood, N.J.: Ablex, 1981. A collection of articles that critically examine the concept of the information age.

CHAPTER 22

Implications of the Information Age

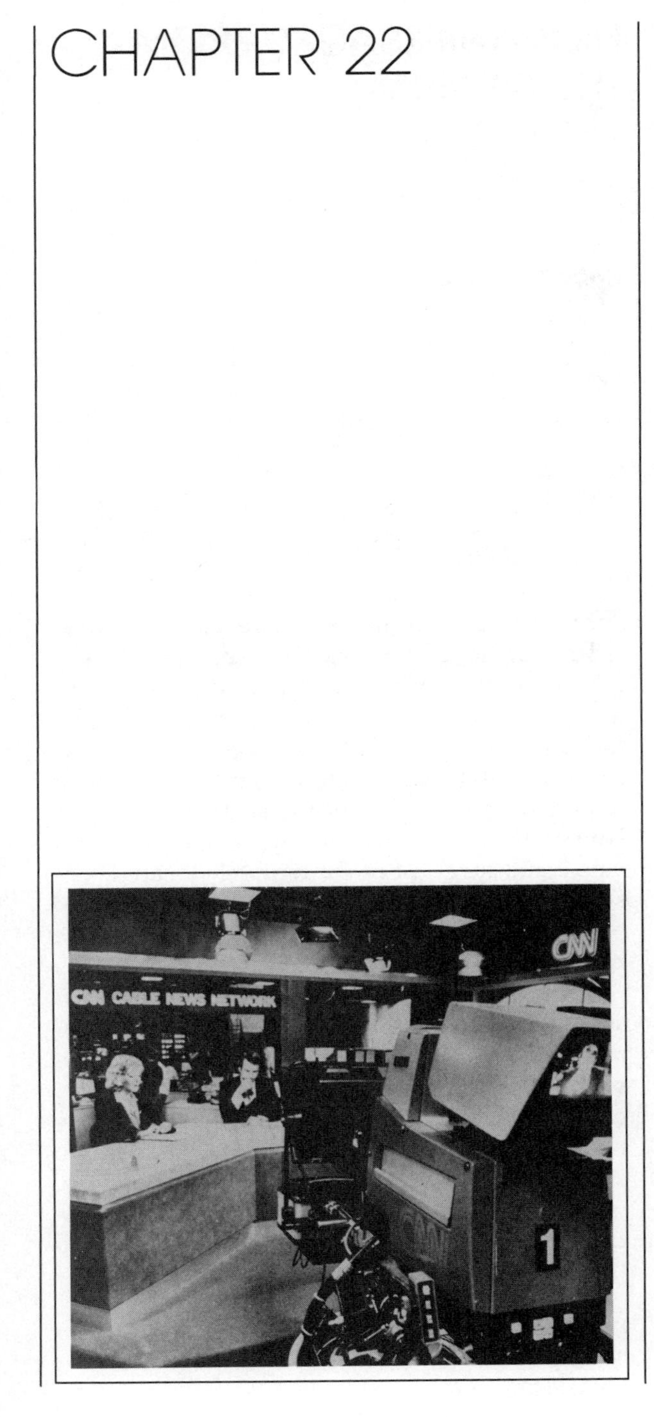

This chapter presents a variety of views on the implications of the information age. In the first reading, Robert D. Kahn of the Davis (Calif.) Cable Cooperative board of directors outlines some of the basic issues that arise out of cable technology. In the second reading, Martin L. Ernst takes up the issue of cable's economic impacts, and in the third reading Nicholas Johnson, the former FCC commissioner and outspoken media critic, discusses the need for cable regulation. All three of these articles appeared in the January 1983 issue of *Technology Review*.

In the fourth reading Richard A. Blake, a Jesuit priest and managing editor of *America* magazine, reviews Marshall McLuhan's predictions for a "global village" and finds that the new technologies have had just the opposite effect.

B. G. Yovovich then discusses the effect of the information age on magazines, and Karen Stabiner examines projected changes in the movie industry.

An essay by Kurt Vonnegut, the popular and critically acclaimed novelist, rounds out the chapter with a comment on the novelist of today.

MORE MESSAGES FROM THE MEDIUM

Robert D. Kahn

The earliest automobiles were called "horseless carriages" because that was the only way people at the time understood the new technology. This is not very different from calling today's cable systems "television." And just as the automobile went on to alter American life in important and lasting ways, so too may cable communications. Historically, cable has provided quality reception for remotely located consumers, but today it is the purveyor of myriad programming and services that redefine what we mean by, and expect from, TV.

Cable began to expand in the mid-1970s when several court decisions obliged the Federal Communiciations Commission (FCC) to relax some serious constraints. Until then, cable companies could not rely on national cable program sources but had to function on a local basis. In addition, space satellites were opened to commercial use, offering the cable industry an opportunity to establish its own national networks and to "cablecast" programming that broadcast TV—

From *Technology Review* (January, 1983). Reprinted by permission.

the established networks—either could not or would not offer.

Cable programming was linked to satellite transmission for the first time in 1975 when Time, Inc. established the first national network to distribute cable programs to local operators. And innovations such as all-movie channels—which showed current, uncut, commercial-free feature films—made a great impact on urban markets. In the three years from 1977 to 1980, cable subscribership went from 11 to 14 million households. Today that number stands at approximately 28 million, and the industry reports that 250,000 households per month are being wired for cable. Approximately 34 percent of U.S. residences now receive cable, with half the homes having access to cable subscribing to it.

Cable differs from broadcast television in three fundamental ways:

Cable offers expanded channel capacity. Cable systems installed today promise upwards of 100 channels, offering local communities a varied, and unprecedented, communications menu. Not only do these channels offer today's mass-oriented broadcasting, but cable also offers "narrowcasting"—special programs going out to special-interest viewers.

Cable offers two-way communication. While the majority of cable systems are now limited to conventional one-way communication, newer systems also offer the option of consumer-originated messages. These may take the form of polling, emergency calls, or requests for information.

Cable can easily be coupled with other communications technologies. Cable is one medium that can carry virtually all others: newspapers, radio, film, books, even still pictures. While cable can't really substitute for a visit to the movies or a museum, it can distribute images widely and inexpensively. Linking computer technology with cable—in transmitting data, for example—is especially powerful.

One sign of cable's maturity is the profusion of new networks. A recent count by the National Cable Television Association identified 51 national satellite-distributed cable networks, including three all-news channels, two all-sports channels, four religious networks, three movie channels, a health network, a Spanish-language network, and numerous others. Soon cable systems will even carry an electronic-games channel.

Cable has begun to cut into the historic dominance of television programming by the nation's three broadcast networks. In some cable-serviced communities, the major networks combined attract only 70 percent and less of the audience. In the United States overall, the three networks' share of prime-time ratings declined from 92 percent in 1979 to 81 percent in 1981.

In the fierce competition for local franchises, a cable company presents itself as a "common carrier," available to serve much of the host community's needs.

Cable offers three kinds of programming: basic programming, pay programming, and two-way services. "Basic" is covered by the monthly subscription fee paid by the customer. This "first tier" closely resembles conventional television and must (under federal law) carry local broadcast-TV stations. The first tier also frequently includes so-called "superstations" such as WGN-Chicago or WTBS-Atlanta—independent broadcast stations that specialize in sports and entertainment and are transmitted by satellite to hundreds of local cable systems. Basic services also include "community-access" programs generated within the cable-served community, under franchise terms negotiated between the operator and the local political jurisdiction.

"Pay TV" is the second tier: the system operator can offer subscribers numerous networks, in addition to the basic set, at additional cost. Moreover, special one-time programs such as concerts and boxing matches may be charged to subscribers on a "pay-for-view" basis.

Pay-TV programming accounts for much of cable's popularity and certainly contributes to its profitability; many subscribers appear willing to pay for the uninterrupted programs unavailable on commercial broadcast networks. Revenue from pay-cable channels has been rising steadily. According to Paul Kagan Associates, a leading cable analysis firm, approximately 19 million subscriptions to cable programs were sold in 1982. A conservative estimate of overall industry revenue for the year just ended is $4.36 billion. Kagan projects overall industry revenues to reach $16.6 billion by 1990, fueled largely by pay services.

But there are limits to pay cable's popularity. A 1981 study conducted by Benton and Bowles, Inc., a marketing research firm, determined that nearly half of those cable subscribers who presently reject pay TV would buy it if it were less expensive, even if this meant that advertising would have to accompany programming. In fact, cable viewers can expect to see more and more advertising over both basic and pay-cable channels. According to *Marketing News*, 70 percent of cable stations already seek advertising.

Two-way services constitute the third programming form that cable-TV systems make available. These services are now offered to only a fraction of the communities wired for cable, but they are becoming standard as new cable systems are installed. The offerings range from home banking, energy management, and security alarms to medical referrals and information-retrieval systems.

The best-known two-way system is Warner-Amex's Qube, used by 38,000 residents of Columbus, Ohio. Using the five-button keyboard distributed to every household served by Qube, consumers transmit elementary messages that are processed by a computer at the "headend" (the operator's central facility). For example, viewers may request a copy of a recipe demonstrated on a cooking program by flicking a switch on their home terminal; they will later receive a copy of the recipe by mail.

Qube has polled viewers for their opinions on everything from politics to TV shows, and once had them collectively "quarterback" a local football game. Warner-Amex loses money on Qube in Columbus, but the two-way channel seems to have paid off in the highly competitive "franchise wars"—where cities must choose among competing cable companies before granting a monopoly contract. By breaking new ground with Qube, Warner-Amex won a reputation for state-of-the-art technology, which likely helped it go on to win franchises in Cincinnati, Houston, Dallas, Pittsburgh, and St. Louis.

Not everyone is enthralled with cable's two-way capabilities: the potential for abuse is considerable.

But not everyone is enthralled with cable's two-way capabilities: the potential for abuse is considerable. Accounts of the pay-TV programs individual subscribers watch, from special entertainment events to pornography, are monitored routinely. Operators of two-way systems are privy to polling results, purchase decisions, personal schedules, and whatever household and commercial transactions subscribers make. Like the old-time village switchboard operator, today's cable operators could know more about us than we wish, with far more serious consequences.

In the fierce competition for local franchises, a

cable company presents itself—in effect—as a "common carrier," available to serve much of the host community's communication needs. According to Michael Dann of ABC Video Enterprises, "Cable must be seen as a new utility, a utility people will use when they need and want it, not so much for entertainment but for information and services."

But cable does not operate as a utility—cable operators decide independently what programs to carry and what two-way services to provide. For example, if an entrepreneur develops an improved way to offer security and emergency services over cable, the operator that offers a security option of its own can either deny this competitor access to the system or charge prohibitive rates.

The issue of equal access to cable, and whether it should be defined as a common carrier, was actively debated last spring in the California legislature. Assemblyman Richard Robinson, a moderate Democrat from Orange County, introduced a bill to regulate the California cable industry—the nation's largest—as a public utility. Robinson argued that the installation and operation of a cable system should be separate from the control of its programming. The bill included a series of equal-access provisions to stimulate the use of cable by California's "knowledge industries," and to promote widespread reliance on cable as an alternative to the phone company. Robinson's measure was soundly defeated after industry opposition was mobilized. For now, California remains among the nation's 39 unregulated cable states.

"Information equity," like equal access, is another issue suggested by defining cable TV as an information utility. With the advent of some cable services, viewers pay for what used to be free. For example, a whole new set of children's programming, adult-education offerings, and information services will be available only to those who can afford it. Les Brown, editor-in-chief of *Channels* magazine, quips that society may eventually be required to provide "information stamps," akin to today's food stamps, to establish minimum access to information.

Questions of information equity, equal access, and privacy safeguards arise from the cable industry's embryonic moves into the "information age." But the industry is approaching a watershed: it may soon have to choose between continuing exclusively in entertainment—eventually competing with the major broadcast networks—and evolving to provide information services such as data transmission and teleconferencing in competition with AT&T.

If cable firms continue to move in the latter direction—that is, if they function like utilities—the more they will be treated like utilities and face frequent political challenges. Such a cable industry must accept regulatory oversight and content itself with the bargain Americans have traditionally made with their utilities—equitable and affordable services in exchange for fair and protected profits. But so far, the industry has resisted even the thinnest local regulation, and Washington and the state houses have yet to seriously assert themselves.

CABLE'S ECONOMIC IMPACTS

Martin L. Ernst

After Gutenberg invented printing, massive amounts of information could be made widely available, often at little or no direct cost to users. Disseminating information no longer depended on the scarce resource of skilled and dedicated copyists; instead, information could be provided by a greater supply of far more productive labor. Fulfilling the print revolution required many other innovations, however. New industries had to supply paper, ink, and printing and binding equipment. Writers, publishers, and printers had to establish new business practices to work together effectively. New laws, such as copyright, were needed to provide economic incentives to create information. And new institutions, such as libraries and compulsory education, evolved as nations recognized the economic and social values of literacy and widespread knowledge. The result was that information was democratized—and, of course, copyists and parchment makers disappeared.

Cable systems and related technologies may well contribute to an equally significant set of changes. Large multichannel cable systems, low-power TV (permitting closer geographic use of the same broadcast frequencies), direct-broadcast services (whose authorization involves expanding the portion of the electromagnetic spectrum devoted to TV services), and, eventually, fiber-optic networks (that can provide multichannel capabilities far exceeding those of current coaxial cable) may convert a scarce resource—broadcast-TV channels—into an abundant commodity. And coupling these systems with advances in electronics, such as in computers, videotape systems, and videodiscs, may yield enormous impacts.

Historically, the scarcity of local broadcast-TV franchises, especially those for the higher-quality VHF channels, made them very valuable business properties; because the choice of channels was limited, the audience was highly concentrated. Networks and local stations competed for this audience by appealing to the broadest possible segments. At least for prime viewing periods, they could afford to produce elaborate and expensive programming. Advertising, the system's means of financial support, similarly focused on goods and services with mass appeal. As the viewing population grew, advertising rates per broadcast minute also grew. Ultimately, television advertising rates became the standard, or "umbrella," for other media rates, including those of major newspapers and national magazines.

The early cable systems had little impact on the structure of the broadcast industry. Few cable channels were available, programming was restricted to locally produced materials, and the systems tended to be regarded simply as grandiose antennas for providing better reception.

But the large-capacity systems now being put in place, free from programming restrictions and offering 50 or more channels, are a totally different kind of proposition. Because of the large profits anticipated from pay TV and other new

From *Technology Review* (January, 1983). Reprinted by permission.

types of programming, local cable franchises have increased greatly in value. This has permitted local authorities to make far better bargains during franchise negotiations—bargains that usually involve lower basic connection charges for a larger set of free broadcast services and more channels for commmunity use. Moreover, though early cable systems were priced to recover their costs entirely from basic connection charges, newer ones will likely require additional monthly revenues of at least $25 to $30 per connection from either viewers or advertising if they are to be profitable.

Because of the large profits anticipated from pay TV and other new types of programming, local cable franchises have increased greatly in value.

The differences between traditional broadcast operations and future cable systems may be quite striking. Cable-system operators will have to recover greater investments but will have more direct relationships with viewers and better records of their interests. Most important, operators will be able to deliver programs at very low marginal cost per additional channel. Broadcasters can offer only one "page" (that is, one program) at a time, and must compete with other broadcasters, each of whom is also offering a "page" that usually has similar contents at the same time. Cable operators will be able to deliver 50 or more "pages" simultaneously—provided they can acquire the programming—and will face no direct competitors with equivalent capabilities. Where broadcasters had little choice but to cater primarily to mass audiences, and broadcast advertisers could justify promoting only those products with mass appeal, cable operators can provide highly specialized programming and seek advertising that will appeal to particular audience segments.

As a result, broadcast franchises are likely to decrease in value; they may lose viewers seeking more specialized entertainment and information. Advertising directed at mass audiences will bring in less revenue as these audiences diffuse. New forms of advertising directed toward specialized consumer segments, already being delivered by cable, will grow, incorporating far more details on products and how they are used. Another attraction to advertisers will be the ability to conduct market research at the same time.

Other likely losers in this realignment will be the traditional print media. Although newspapers and magazines have responded flexibly to new competition in the past, and although they have many advantages over electronic media in terms of portability, display quality, and durability, they are quite vulnerable to loss of advertising. This source provides more than 60 percent of the total revenues of most mass-audience print publications. The major newspapers may well remain the superior means for receiving in-depth news, but loss of advertising revenues may force them to raise prices and thus lose readers. This, in turn, may force owners to make major changes in the size, format, content, and even social function of newspapers.

If broadcasters and traditional print media turn out to be the losers, who will be the winners? What new industries will have to arise to support cable TV and allow it to be fully used? This is an area of much controversy, but many of the forces at work are already visible and provide a basis for speculation. Here are a few possibilities:

• The great increase in the number of channels will lead to major economic incentives for lower-cost production of high-quality programs. The costs for basic equipment, such as color-TV cameras, have already dropped to a fraction of earlier levels. Prices for associated devices, such as computer-controlled editing and graphics equipment, are following the same trend. Particularly valuable would be the development of large videodisc archives (the "library" of the future?) indexed by content, visual details, and other characteristics. With access through computer, a wealth of quality material would be available.

• Because more people will become participants in television as well as spectators, cable will help "democratize" the provision of entertainment and information, much as printing did their availability. Schools and training in program production and performing arts are likely to grow. Some cable systems already offer opportunities for local amateur groups to use community channels and even provide assistance in preparing material. Thus, the programs offered on such channels will gradually become more professional.

• Because cable TV is in many ways more analogous to publishing than to film production, successful publishing formats will be applied to the field. Specialized "program-of-the-week clubs" will likely evolve, comparable to book-of-the-month clubs. Owners of videocassette recorders will be able to pick up such programs at their convenience. Packages combining video programs with supporting print materials could be developed. And the video equivalent of indexes and abstracts will be produced. The wealth of material that can be transmitted will tax the effectiveness of printed program schedules; these may have to be replaced by computerized schedules that offer brief samples of programs instead of written abstracts.

• The tremendous demand for materials by both audiences and advertisers could lead to a variety of new forms of entertainment and recreation. Even the limited two-way features available on cable systems today are already being used to provide interactive games, and expansion of such activities is limited only by people's creativity.

• Video education, whether basic or refresher courses, offers unusual opportunities. At first, cable systems may be used to present and upgrade correspondence-type courses. The next step could involve lectures transmitted to the home, "classroom questions" answered over the telephone, and local facilities established for doing laboratory and practice work. Eventually, fully accredited schools based on such systems could be established.

Business practices and relationships must evolve to support these kinds of services. But there are impediments. The first may be the cable operators themselves, who have complete control over the content of everything they deliver other than programs on community channels and the basic free services. While these operators have financial incentives to use their system's full capacity, restricting usage might increase profits in some situations. For example, if cable-system owners develop some of their own programming, they may seek to limit competition with these products. In many cases, cable operators receive a percentage of program providers' income from advertisers and subscribers. The alternative approach—leasing channels to the providers at specific, time-based rates—is unpopular with operators because they lose control. But the revenue-sharing approach can prompt operators to discriminate against low-fee providers because audiences from higher-fee programs might be diverted.

Numerous other business practices will have to be changed or established before cable's potential can be realized. Means of payment for access to video archives will have to be developed. These mechanisms may be more complicated than those for print media. Growing participation in program development may blur the distinction between amateur and professional production, with important implications for stage, film, and televison unions. Copyright practices are already a subject of much controversy because photocopiers and videotape recorders have become widely available; it is not yet clear whether the outcomes of these debates will expand or limit the range of programs available on cable.

But the most fundamental long-term regulatory problem relates to the roles of, and competition between, cable operators and the telephone network. Cable systems can deliver a great variety of materials to homes but they have only limited capabilities in the reverse direction. The telephone system, when associated with home computers, offers clear advantages in transaction services such as the ordering of goods or the paying of bills. This capability, already being used, will probaby grow rapidly in the next decade. As a result, two very different sets of sophisticated information-related services will soon be available to large numbers of households.

But questions will certainly arise over why it is necessary to have two sets of wires running into households—one a pair of low-capacity copper wires and the other a high-capacity coaxial or glass-fiber cable. The phone service could develop the switching necessary for direct video communications among households, but it won't have adequate incentive to make the necessary investments without the authority to offer video entertainment as well. Cable systems will have the video home-delivery capacity but will lack the switching authority and capability.

Current laws treat cable systems as an overlay on our existing "information infrastructure." And cable-system operators are granted monopoly privileges to induce them to make major investments. But eventually, fundamental changes in the older institutional patterns will be necessary if the full benefits of cable are to be realized. Such conflicts may be difficult to resolve since owners of both the phone and cable systems will have already made massive capital investments.

THE MYTH OF THE MARKETPLACE

Nicholas Johnson

Consider this imaginary conversation:

"Is this the phone company?"

"Yes."

"I'm new in town. Do you have phone lines available?"

"Perhaps. But if we were to put one in, what kinds of things would you be talking about on the phone?"

The conversation is absurd because the phone company doesn't control content. At least, not yet. Anyone can get access to the system. Freedom of speech by phone is so fundamental that people can organize protests over telephone rates—and use the phone to do it. Any alternative would be so outrageous we don't even think about it. But the ground rules we take for granted with the telephone are unique among communications networks—and fast eroding.

First Amendment rights have to be rewon with every new communications technology. And right now it looks as though Thomas Jefferson is getting the worst of it.

From *Technology Review* (January, 1983). Reprinted by permission.

Consider broadcasting. You have no legally enforceable right to a local radio or TV station. The station's management *does* ask you, in so many words, "Suppose we were to let you use our radio or television station—what kinds of things would you be talking about over the air?" Individuals have no right to appear if station management would rather censor them; the only exception is candidates for federal office.

First Amendment rights have to be rewon with every new communications technology. And right now it looks as though Thomas Jefferson is getting the worst of it.

Cable television was supposed to change all that. Broadcasting's "economy of scarcity" (with one to five stations per community) would become an "economy of abundance," with cable's 12, 20, 35—and now over 100—channels.

What about regulation? According to the cable industry, there was no need: with dozens of empty channels, the "marketplace" would see to it that all people and ideas got access. It would be safe to abandon the FCC's "fairness doctrine" (that controversial issues be covered, and some time provided for a range of views) and other legal guarantees of diversity. And it would not be necessary to limit the number of cable systems one company could own.

These ideas sounded plausible, and many Washington policymakers were persuaded. The volume went up on the rhetoric of cable "deregulation." The only problem was one enormous oversight, one leap of logic. The arguments simply assumed that access to cable was open to all, like access to the telephone network.

But whatever the virtues and vices of "marketplace regulation," one thing is certain: without a marketplace, the rhetoric becomes hollow. At a minimum, a marketplace enables a willing buyer and seller to exchange goods and services for money. That is not possible with today's cable systems. Here's an example:

Ted Turner offers cable subscribers a 24-hour news service called Cable News Network (CNN). He charges them 15 cents a month. CNN is distributed nationally by communications satellite. Every cable system receives it, but not all use it.

In Iowa City, Hawkeye CableVision has been asked to supply subscribers with CNN, but Hawkeye has stalled for two years. Hawkeye is owned by ATC, headquartered in Denver. And ATC is owned by Time, Inc. in New York. Time, Inc. also owns a pay-cable service called Home Box Office (HBO). HBO is on its Iowa City cable system; CNN is not. Time, Inc. does not own CNN.

Ted Turner wants to sell CNN in Iowa City. Subscribers want to buy. Why is there no sale? Where is the "marketplace"?

When a company controls all cable channels in a community—TV plus data, banking, and security systems—the potential for abuse becomes alarming.

Simple—there is no "marketplace." Cable is just not available to enterpreneurs, Hollywood producers, or ordinary citizens if the company doesn't feel like it. (Hawkeye also denied access to a local candidate for county commissioner.) And when a company controls all cable channels in a community (TV plus data, banking, and security systems), the potential for abuse becomes alarming.

Cable is not only the most immediate and dramatic of the censored communications technologies. Similar censorship threats occur with videodiscs, direct-broadcast satellites, videotex and teletext (electronic database services via telephone and television, respectively), and computer conferences.

The issue cannot be ignored, and the answer is seemingly simple: to legally guarantee access and separate distribution and content. Don't let Time, Inc. own both Hawkeye (distribution) and HBO (content). Don't let Comsat own both satellites and network programming. Keep the phone company out of "the knowledge business."

Guarantee the right to buy access to any communications distribution system the way we now guarantee access to the telephone network—for you and me as well as for Ted Turner, Norman Lear, and Mobil Oil. Ensure that the quest for profit drives distribution systems to move as much information as possible rather than choke it off.

If we're actually going to apply the conservative doctrine of regulation by the marketplace, not just use it as a fraudulent cover for unrestrained greed, "access" is an idea whose time has come.

CONDOMINIUMS IN THE GLOBAL VILLAGE

Richard A. Blake

Two full decades have passed since *The Gutenberg Galaxy* was published in 1962 and H. Marshall McLuhan became an academic cult figure whose writings many thought at the time would create the Copernican revolution of our age. As a professor of literature—and several other things as well—at the University of Toronto, he published a book on advertising techniques, *The Mechanical Bride,* as early as 1951 and had edited with the anthropologist Edmund Carpenter a short-lived periodical entitled *Explorations,* some of whose essays appeared as an anthology, *Explorations in Communiciation,* in 1961.

There is no doubt, even now, that Marshall McLuhan was on to something important. As a man of many interests, he was able to send out "probes"—unmanned space probes were the miracles of technology at the time—in many directions at once. He was aware that the human environment, even our thought and sense patterns, had been undergoing enormous changes

From *America* (June 5, 1982). Reprinted with permission of America Press, Inc., 106 West 56th Street, New York, N.Y. 10019.

because of the development of communications technologies, and he had the temerity to ask what these shifts were. If, he reasoned, historians and anthropologists could chart the change when a society moves from an oral culture to one with a written language and then moves from a manuscript tradition to mechanized printing, then he believed they should be able to discover the changes taking place as contemporary society moves from a print-dominated society to the age of radio, television and film. In the 1960s this notion of a generation gap between old breed and new breed was a hot topic, and McLuhan believed it had something to do with the way we communicate to one another.

> The global village, an optimistic projection of the McLuhan era, probably never did exist in fact, and if it was the logical goal of a trend apparent at the time, that trend has long ago hit a detour.

Despite the importance of his search, Marshall McLuhan was sadly an unwitting assassin of his own ideas. His prose poured out like water from a firehose with knots in it. He had an irrepressible lust for the catch-phrase, which he later mauled into puns that mocked the original concept. From the vantage point of the 1980s these phrases are quaint and oh-so 1960ish, hula hoops for the mind, Mickey Mouse ears for the intellect. For example, in *Understanding Media* (1964), the book that brought McLuhan celebrity and the rest of us headaches trying to understand what he meant by "hot" and "cool" media, he gave one chapter the catchy title, "The Medium Is the Message." By 1967, the phrase became the title of a book, *The Medium Is the Massage*, which dealt with the importance of tactility in communication—along with many other topics. By 1969, in *Counterblast*, it became an inset heading, "The Medium Is the Mess Age," highlighting the proposition that one medium absorbs another, and both become changed or "messed up." People who read, for instance, have speech patterns different from those who do not; people who watch television write differently from those who do not. Our own media-loaded culture is going through the media mixmaster: It is the mess age.

What is regrettable is that some of these ideas, torpedoed by the cleverness of their creator, deserve a better fate. Some of these key concepts should have remained alive so that they could be seriously tested and refined in the light of new data and new trends. After all, McLuhan was dealing with man in confrontation with his rapidly changing technological environment. Even the mustiest, library-bound scholar should be able to admit that technology continues to change and that its ongoing impact on the race should continue to be monitored. What would Marshall McLuhan be able to tell us, if he were still alive, of the meaning of the videogame, the desk-top home computer, the digital alarm wristwatch, or even that computer in Japan that last year stabbed a worker to death on the assembly line? When he was writing, space probes, those unmanned ventures into outer space, were exotic projects. He called his own essays "probes" because he fired them off into space with no idea what they would turn up. The data he uncovered always invited further exploration and refinement; they were rarely the final chapter.

One such probe, still intriguing but clearly in need of revision, is his concept of "the global village." Unlike some of his other aphorisms, like "The medium is the message," the global village keeps a certain ring of currency about it. It is still used by many organizations, especially religious ones, to describe a growing sense of awareness and responsibility for global problems, such as hunger, violence or the need for evangelization. It is a convenient term but a dangerous one, since injecting an old term into a contemporary situation can be misleading. On a practical level such a miscalculation can lead to a misreading of the signs of the times, to oversimplifications, to misdirected strategies and to a great deal of frustration.

The global village, an optimistic projection of the McLuhan era, probably never did exist in fact, and if it was the logical goal of a trend apparent at the time, that trend has long ago hit a detour. Technology, which McLuhan was ever sensitive to, has moved in like a greedy landlord and broken the global village into condominiums. Since the time of McLuhan's initial insight, the world has become less a tribal village and more an urban apartment building, where people in adjacent flats cannot recognize one another.

What kind of change took place? For Marshall McLuhan the notion of the modern postliterate world as a global village was a long time coming. It grew out of his major thesis that people raised in an age of print see reality as segmented and ordered, like letters of the alphabet on a line of type. Preliterate people, coming from an oral tradition, tend to apprehend the whole without awareness of individual components. Literate people rely on vision, and try to see connections between parts as though they were letters in a word; they feel secure in their understanding only when they can objectify something "out-there," even at times reducing reality to an outline or diagram, like a roadmap. Preliterate people make no sense out of maps and diagrams. They are involved with the topography and prefer to think of their environment in terms of hills, stars, ocean currents or dead trees.

Modern man, McLuhan observed, is in the process of returning to the sight and sound world of the preliterate. Even in academia, the clear, precise and diagrammatic answers of scholastic philosophy have become less interesting and less satisfying than the tentative answers based on the empirical data of the sociologist, novelist or psychologist. The age of the electronic media has retribalized us.

By 1967, in *The Medium Is the Massage*, McLuhan pointed out the effects of this new tribalization on a world scale. He announced: "We now live in a global village. . . . We have begun to structure this primordial feeling, these tribal emotions from which a few centuries of literacy have divorced us. . . . Electronic circuitry profoundly involves us with one another." He felt that it is no longer possible for pockets of humanity to remain isolated from one another; electronics was binding the race together. What seemed particularly attractive to religious people was the implication he drew from his observation: "Our new involvement compels commitment and participation." In another place in the same book, he returned to the theme: "Electric circuitry has overthrown the regime of 'time' and 'space' and pours upon us continuously the concerns of other men." Like it or not, electronics has made us, in the words of the Gospel, our "brother's keeper." The signs of the time, another catch phrase of the era, pointed to the social Gospel. Off to the inner city, the picket lines and the demonstrations!

Two of McLuhan's concepts must be distinguished. First, technology was providing more information about remote peoples and places, and, second, our postliterate sensibilities have conditioned us to respond differently. The first is self-evident. There is more news available, and it comes to us more quickly than ever before. As for the second, according to McLuhan, we are more involved with the hungry or the politically repressed because we cannot reduce them to discrete units of reality, separate from our own world, out there, objective and at a distance. When, for example—and this is not an example McLuhan gives, since he rarely gives examples—we see on television a black demonstrator at Selma attacked by guard dogs, we are personally involved and there is a visceral response because our own world is being subjected to the violence and oppression. Thus, the passionate radicalization of thousands of comfortable middle-class students during the civil rights movement was a result of both television information and television sensitivities.

For the religious person reading McLuhan, the one world of peace and harmony was becoming a reality through the miracles of modern technology, God's gift to His creature of intellect. The world of the future would be the ideal forum for extending the work of the Gospel.

Although Marshall McLuhan was a serious Catholic, he did not deal with these religious questions himself. He left such reflections to those who read his essays while they were reading the works of Pierre Teilhard de Chardin, S. J. Between Teilhard's "noösphere" and McLuhan's "global village" there are many congruent notions, but McLuhan chose not to explore in depth the theological implications of his ideas. It is doubtful that he ever thought that the global village, drawn into a tighter and tighter unity by the power of modern communications, would ever lead to the "recapitulation of all things in Christ."

As an interesting parenthesis, McLuhan did, however, include a brief chapter on liturgy in *The Gutenberg Galaxy*. This was 1962, when liturgical reformers were already stirring in their cocoons, but before Vatican II loosed a stampede of butterflies upon the church. Even then, McLuhan knew that the Tridentine Mass, with its emphasis on the literate person's reliance on the visual, on detachment, fragmentation and solitude would not serve the postliterate generation. After skipping through the works of Louis Bouyer, Thomas Merton and several other liturgical writers, he concludes: "The 'simultaneous field' of electronic information structures today reconstitutes the condition and need for dialogue and participation rather than specialism and private initiative in all levels of social experience." Thus this secular prophet warned us about the coming of the dialogue homily and the ever on-going effort to increase participation, even by downgrading the role of the remote, "visual" celebrant if necessary.

McLuhan's rather rosy picture of the dawning age of the global village should not be surprising. He was, as each of us is, a product of his times. (Even his relentless use of the word "men" and masculine pronouns dates his work as pre-women's movement.) His was an optimistic time for media analysis. As he looked to the future, communications satellites were just beginning to tie the world together with instantaneous relays. Television and telephone transmissions could reach any point on the globe. The paradigmatic event, of course, was the funeral of John F. Kennedy in 1963, when the world seemed bound together in mourning through television. By then virtually every household in the United States "had television," and instructional television had invaded many of the classrooms, promising an end to the drudgery of learning and perennial shortages of teachers. Families viewed television together. The set was called the "electronic hearth," and magazine writers praised the new "togetherness." The evening news was making civil rights an American issue, as a few years later it would make Vietnam the world's first television war. It was believed that the nightly newscast was turning the American people against not only that war but against all wars. It was a cheery time for media futurologists.

Things did not turn out as predicted, however. In a very few years the happy promise of the global village fell apart. Mass communication, as it penetrated the inner cities of the United States in the 1960s and the third world in the next decade, brought a sense not of participation but of exclusion. The image of the good life, available so readily to middle-class Americans on the gray-blue screen, was not accessible to everyone, and the result was outrage and violence. Murder on the streets became as insignificant as murder on the screen; heavy viewers became sociopaths.

Instead of a new generation searching for "participation and dialogue" the 1970s brought the "me-decade," with the solitary jogger monitoring his heartbeat and fiber intake in private rather than sharing feelings in "small-group discussions."

Clearly, something went wrong with the prophecy, but what or how? Why are the media apparently desensitizing us to the needs of the rest of the world when we had expected them to heighten our sensitivities? If Marshall McLuhan were alive today, he would have to revise his projections on the basis of new data and new trends, and for him that always meant beginning with the technology of communication. In fact, he can be faulted for focusing too narrowly on this area to the exclusion of other social and historical factors. However, since the "global village" is his creation, it is only fair to retain his methodology.

Why are the media apparently desensitizing us to the needs of the rest of the world, when we had expected them to heighten our sensitivities?

In McLuhan's time, every development in communications technology pointed toward greater unification, but in the last 10 years every development has led to greater fragmentation of the world-audience. Equipment is an obvious example. First the transistor made radios cheap, portable and accessible to everyone in every environment. Stereo radios and cassette decks increased the volume, thereby ending conversation. Radio listening has become an essentially private experience. No longer do people gather around the radio, but each person creates a private acoustical shell. Finally, the new lightweight headphones isolate the individual from his surrounding environment completely. Watch a group of the new wired listeners standing elbow-to-elbow on the corner waiting for the light to change, each following the beat of his own drummer, with street noise and fellow listeners effectively filtered out.

The Ayatollah Ruhollah Khomeini understood this during the worst days of the Iranian revolution. He did not have to block out information from communication satellites, rather he supplied his followers with tape decks and cassettes of his speeches. He may have been the first prophet to realize that mass communication, even from a satellite, is becoming obsolete. The future belongs to the tiny tape deck, with its private, personal message enhancing the importance of the individual listener.

When McLuhan was formulating his theories, the networks were at their peaks. One might complain about the types of programs American audiences were watching, but there is little doubt that *I Love Lucy* or *Laugh In* did provide a source of common, shared and unifying experience. Everyone knew Fred and Ethel, Ricky and Lucy, and what it meant when someone received a "fickle finger of fate" award at the office.

In the last few years, the trend toward unifying television experience has been reversed. On both networks and on local nonaffiliated stations, advertisers pinpoint their target audiences for age, sex, earning power and geography. This segmenting of the audience has developed even more drastically with the arrival of the cable with its capacity for 40, 80 or even 120 different channels. As of March 1982, 23.7 million households in the United States, that is 29 percent of all television homes, had cable, and the industry is adding a quarter of a million new subscribers each month. There are separate channels for sports, music, drama, movies, public affairs and even pornography. Every language group in the community has its own programming.

The cable, however, is still a medium for more affluent neighborhoods, where enough subscribers can pay the fees immediately and thus make the installation of the system profitable in the near future. For the present, at any rate, the poorer and less educated will remain with the networks, a fact that can be expected to influence programming decisions. In other words, network television will become even more vapid, and the quality material that is available will be on the cable, where the viewers can afford to pay for it.

Developments in over-the-air broadcast technology are also in the process of fragmenting the audience. The Federal Communications Commission is currently sifting through 6,500 applications—the number is expected to reach 12,000—for new low-power stations that can be received on a non-cable set. These will have a very limited broadcast range, and thus will serve a specific local community. The industry now speaks casually of a "narrowcast" concept rather than broadcast, to indicate its desire to pinpoint particular target audiences for its advertisers.

The cassette and videodisc business is booming, and as the prices tumble further, the growth rate will accelerate. Rental libraries of videotapes are springing up in shopping malls around the country. Combining videotape and cable technologies, ABC has even devised a system for transmitting films and other specials over the cable at night to a cassette recorder with an automatic timer. For a fee, the owner can play the tape back through a special decoder. For people using these services, viewing television has become as private and idiosyncratic a pastime as reading a book. In fact, by year's end Sony will begin marketing a pocket-sized television set no bigger than a paperback romance novel. Its two-inch screen is mounted in a case an inch and a half deep, and it will have the same lightweight headphones Sony made famous on its Walkman portable radio/tape deck components. The private acoustical shell will become visual as well.

A similar trend has been going on in radio. With the opening of the FM spectrum, radio, too, has been segmenting its audience. Of the 8,000 stations now operating in the United States, nearly half are associated with some kind of network, if only for news, but even the networks—and there are now 30 of them operating in the country—have become directed at specific target audiences. Some have nothing but talk, and the music networks are directed to a particular type of listener.

There is more news on television, but the happy-talk format that most of the stations have adopted means that there is less time for information on most broadcasts. With deregulation, limits for news broadcasting on radio have been dropped, so many people will no longer have even the five minutes of headlines and weather that used to break up music schedules.

There is more information around, but fewer informed people. As the media audiences become more fragmented, communicators spend more time talking to like-minded people.

As a result of these developments, it follows that there is more information around, but fewer informed people. As the media audiences become more fragmented, communicators spend more time talking to like-minded people, or at least those with similar interests. A church professional, for example, is likely to be inundated by information about the third world, while the congregation he or she deals with is likely to remain disinterested or apathetic simply because of a lack of effective information. The exchange of news releases among interested parties has become not only overwhelming but incestuous.

The growth of neoconservative groups, even within religious congregations whose leaders are vocally liberal, is not a product of hardening of hearts or callousness or perversity but a lack of effective communication. Religious elites are talking to one another, and their congregations hear little of the conversation. If these elites issue a call for mobilization on behalf of a specific social program, they cannot presume that their congregations are informed or interested, even though the topic might be belabored to the point of cliché in the communications networks the church professionals are tuned into.

If the media are now leading us to greater fragmentation rather than unity, the liturgical renewal might have to stop to reassess its assumptions and goals. Many of the current reforms were put in during the 1960s with the presumption that worshiping congregations actually wanted, as McLuhan said, "participation and dialogue"—or at least would want it once they became accustomed to it. Perhaps now that the global village has been fragmented into condominiums of privacy, worshipers now want their own sense of the sacred. Congregational singing and the kiss of peace may be as alien to the sensitivities of the 1980s as benediction of the Blessed Sacrament was to the sensitivities of the 1960s.

The churches then might be faced with a problem in trying to transfer the wisdom of the 1960's into strategies of the 1980s. Should we then give up the goals of social involvement and worshiping community? Of course not. The Gospel has clearly mandated a mission "to all nations" and "to feed the hungry." We would, however, be wise to admit that the concept of the global village, which appeared so clear in the 1960s, never did materialize. Any strategies that take it for granted then run the risk of serious frustration. Steps to inform, to raise the consciousness or to build community cannot be omitted. If they are, the gap between church professionals and their congregations will widen, as the church people overload one another with information and the people they serve drift further away, into other concerns and other information networks.

Three centuries before Marshall McLuhan, John Donne wrote: "No man is an island." If he could see youngsters standing mesmerized in front of a videogame screen, he just might want to give that sentence a second thought. Despite the information explosion, people are becoming more and more "islands." The global village may soon become the global archipelago, with isolated tribesmen speaking in peculiar languages only to one another. If, on the other hand, people realize that they are living on a tiny island, they should have enough sense to build canoes to reach those other islands. Without that awareness, the world's loftiest projects, even evangelization itself, will remain a collection of photocopied notes, duplicated by the hundreds and written in a peculiar language understood only by the like-minded.

MAGAZINES: OF MORE THAN PASSING INTERESTS?

B. G. Yovovich

Where do special-interest magazines go from here?

Their achievements during the last decade certainly have been impressive. At the same time that industry giants with the names of *Life, Look* and *The Saturday Evening Post* were dying, and *Esquire* and the traditional women's books were having serious problems, a slew of new categories of special-interest magazines were springing into life and prospering: Dozens of city and regional magazines; science magazines; magazines for working women and for women executives; magazines for entrepreneurs and magazines for small businessmen—not to mention hundreds of trade publications and titles aimed at other, even more highly specialized audiences.

But the 1980s give every indication of producing a very different kind of magazine environment, one in which the growth and prosperity of the 1970s could prove difficult to match. Many of the fastest-growing special-interest magazines of the 1970s are beginning to come up against the limits to growth that specialization generally implies. Competition within the magazine industry also seems to have sharpened, with new magazines finding it harder and harder to break into increasingly crowded newsstand and magazine racks.

Developments outside the magazine industry also are having their effects, including changes in consumer attitudes and life styles that threaten to erode support for some of the successes of the 1970s. And always on the horizon looms the challenge from narrowcast cable TV programs.

"The 1980s will be a period of shakeout and consolidation," predicts publishing consultant Christine D. Urban of Urban & Associates, a Sharon, Mass.-based company. "In the 1970s, the successful magazines simply had to take advantage of the growth. In the 1980s, the special-interest magazines will have to earn their growth."

Any discussion of the prospects for special-interest magazines in the 1980s has to begin with an examination of the forces that fostered their explosive growth in the 1970s. The production side, for example, saw two technological developments combine to play particularly important roles. On the one hand, advances in offset printing technology lowered the fixed costs of printing and made it easier for small circulation publications to survive.

At the same time, computer technology—especially the availability of computerized mailing lists that spurred the growth of the direct mail industry in the 1970s—helped make it easier and less expensive for publishers to identify potential subscribers for their special-interest magazines.

Special-interest publications also benefited from marketers' efforts to implement more precisely targeted marketing strategies. With their sharply defined audiences and their ability to produce detailed readership profiles through subscriber surveys, special-interest magazines were perfectly positioned to take advantage of advertisers' increased interest in getting more precise audience data—in sharp contrast to the difficulties that the broadcast media have had in trying to categorize and identify their audiences.

Finally, special-interest magazines also benefited from the multitude of social changes that occurred in the 1970s. The focus on self and the self-indulgent values connected with the much-heralded "Me Decade" created an environment that fostered a willingness among consumers to buy magazines that would enable them to pursue their hobbies and interests. The decade's cultural pluralism and the rise of a variety of new life styles—the growth in the number of women business executives, the increased interest in fitness and the heightened interest in science and technology—also created entirely new magazine audiences, and made possible the birth of entirely new categories of specialized magazines.

More recently, however, things have tightened up considerably and, maintains Ms. Urban, "Most of the factors [that contributed to growth] have reached their peak and stabilized."

For example, further technological improvements may promise additional reductions in production costs, but the economies realized are expected to be far less dramatic than those of the 1970s.

Recent trends in consumer interests, values and life styles also suggest a change from the heady growth of the 1970s and portend a new set of challenges. Take today's typical consumer. He or she exhibits a very different profile from the 1970s' large group of young, unmarried individuals who were experimenting with a variety of new hobbies and interests. In particular, with more working women and the ever-tightening time constraints faced by baby boom members starting families, special-interest magazines are facing more intense competition for readers' increasingly limited leisure time.

Marcella Rosen, senior VP-media director with NW Ayer, points out that recent magazine research shows that the average consumer continues to buy the same number of magazines as in the past, but is spending less time with each one.

"If affluence grows," adds J. Kendrick Noble, a media analyst with Paine Webber, "the number of magazines bought per capita probably will grow, but people will become more specialized within the magazines that they buy, buying magazines not for the entire issue, but for specific articles" or features that they are especially interested in.

On the other hand, argues Ed Weiner, media director at Geers Gross, there were significant numbers of consumers in the 1970s "who read everything from *Field and Stream* to *Car and Driver* to *Stereo Review* to *Popular Photography* when they were trying to develop their personal interests.

After they've shopped around, they may discover that they "no longer are committed to four or five different interests" and are likely to cut down on the number of special-interest magazines that they buy.

"My definition of a true specialty magazine is one whose readers do what the magazine is about, like a *Popular Photography*," explains Harvard media researcher Benjamin M. Compaine, whose book *The Business of Consumer Magazines* was published earlier this year.

On the other hand, magazines like *Discover* and *Sports Illustrated*, whose readers do not directly participate in the subjects covered in the magazines, are what Mr. Compaine calls limited-interest publications.

"In the 1970s, the big growth was in specialty publications," says Mr. Compaine, but considering the anticipated continuation of time constraints, "perhaps the 1980s will turn out to see more growth in limited-audience publications."

One consequence of such a shift could be the increased vulnerability of such magazines to economic and social changes. Because consumers are generally less involved and less committed to subjects covered in limited-audience magazines (when compared with specialty magazines), "Most of the limited-audience magazines are heavily dependent on newsstand sales, and tend to be more of an impulse buy," points out Ms. Urban.

"Their sales tend to be more cyclical and more volatile, whereas real specialty magazines may have a smaller, narrower audience, but it is more committed to the publication," she said.

Experts also expect shifts in consumer life styles to spur changes in many of the relatively new special-interest publications.

"Look at what *Apartment Life* did when it changed to *Metropolitan Home*," points out Laurel Baer, VP-media director at Marsteller Inc. "Or take something like *Rolling Stone*. It started out relating to kids and what kids do, but as its audience got older and the kids weren't there, it had to change."

"A person can be part of a special-interest group for only a short time," adds Roger Baron, vp-media director at D'Arcy-MacManus & Masius, San Francisco. "How long are parents interested in how to change a baby? The greatest interest is when they have just had their first child.

"*Savvy* or other magazines that go to young women executives are of greatest interest to the woman who has just been promoted and is suddenly finding herself with management responsibility. These kinds of magazines are likely to have a lower level of loyalty than you might expect from a *New Yorker*, *Reader's Digest*, or even a women's service magazine that a person can live with for 20 years."

As a result, say some media experts, magazines that enjoyed prosperity during the 1970s by appealing to women who had just become junior executives may find it difficult to sustain their growth, as the demographics of the 1980s dictate a steady decline in the number of women moving into entry-level management positions.

TOTAL REVENUE LEADERS IN SELECTED FOLIO 400 CATEGORIES
(Figures represent total revenues, in millions, in 1981)

Affluence	
Business Week	$159.0
Fortune	90.0
Forbes	74.2
The New Yorker	69.9
New York Times Magazine	69.8
Automotive	
Car & Driver	$23.7
Road & Track	22.9
Hot Rod	20.1
Motor Trend	18.0
Car Craft	10.0
Health & Fitness	
Prevention	$38.2
Self	25.3
Health	10.9
Weight Watchers	9.4
Home service	
Better Homes and Gardens	$161.8
Southern Living	63.0
Sunset	47.4
House & Garden	40.4
Architectural Digest	39.3
Men's life style	
Playboy	$200.9
Penthouse	155.1
Oui	22.6
GQ	20.5
Esquire	16.8
Men's service	
Popular Mechanics	$38.6
Popular Science	37.0
Mechanix Illustrated	28.1
Family Handyman	13.4
Popular Electronics*	9.7

Outdoor	
Field & Stream	$39.7
Outdoor Life	28.2
Sports Afield	12.9
Guns and Ammo	10.1
Bassmaster	7.9
Sciences: General	
Scientific American	$34.1
Omni	29.8
Discover	18.0
Science 82	12.6
Science Digest	10.9
Sports	
Sports Illustrated	$229.9
Golf Digest	28.4
Sporting News	19.4
Golf	18.8
Sport	17.3
Women's fashion	
Glamour	$79.2
Vogue	68.4
Mademoiselle	39.7
Harper's Bazaar	25.6
W	12.7
Women's life style	
Cosmopolitan	$121.6
Glamour	79.2
Vogue	68.4
Mademoiselle	39.7
Self	25.2
Women's service	
Family Circle	$174.6
Good Housekeeping	166.4
Better Homes and Gardens	161.8
Woman's Day	159.3
McCall's	126.6

**Popular Electronics* changed its name to *Computers & Electronics* in November, 1982.
Source: Folio 400. Total revenues defined as ad revenues added to circulation revenues.

Of course, changes in consumer life styles and interests in the 1980s are likely to spur creation of entirely new kinds of magazines.

"Take a woman who is 32 or 33, who has been working for 10 years and is a VP with Chase Manhattan, and now has decided to begin raising a family," says Mr. Weiner of Geers Gross. "She's had a radical change in her life style, and the big question is: How have her needs changed from when she was a fulltime career woman? What's going to make her feel good about herself?

"She now needs to know how she can pick schools for her children or daycare one or two days a week so that she can get out of the house or maybe do some parttime consulting work." And she is likely to find that existing magazines do not address her new needs and interests.

Media experts also see room in the near future for consumer-oriented magazines about computers, particularly publications that would provide a more lay-person alternative to the buff-oriented computer magazines currently available.

At the same time that the audience environment is changing, there also are new advertising challenges facing special-interest magazines.

"Special-interest magazines have a deep but narrow audience segment, and it is easy for them to get boxed in and limited in the kind of advertising that they attract," says Ms. Urban. "If they can't break out of that box, it pretty much puts a cap on their growth."

According to Ms. Urban, publications like *Architectural Digest* whose readership profiles are distinctive and desirable to advertisers will be able to "break out of the box." After one gets past the few such exceptional publications, however, "you get down to 500 titles that offer pretty much the same thing."

"That explains why the smart magazine groups are trying to sell their magazines as a cluster," says Ms. Urban. "If you want to do more than just get the natural advertising that comes with the depth you offer in covering your narrow segment, then it behooves you to get together with other magazines that have depth in their own segments . . . [in order to get] more leverage with general advertisers.

"The network approach will become even more important in the 1980s."

Despite all the constraints and new challenges confronting special-interest magazines, there is good news for them as well. Demographics and increased consumer educational levels suggest increases in the population groups that traditionally have been the heaviest consumers of magazines. Most media observers also see the increased time constraints as working to their advantage when compared with the effects on other media.

"TV is a non-self-selecting medium," points out Mr. Weiner. "You can't say, 'I don't want to watch the next 10 minutes, let's get on with it,' the way you can just skip pages in a magazine."

"One of the great advantages of magazines is their ability to communicate great amounts of detail about a subject and many facets of a subject," adds Roger Baron of D'Arcy-MacManus. "I don't see the broadcast media being able to offer the kind of in-depth coverage that the true hobbyist is going to want to get."

Special-interest magazines also should continue to benefit from "the long-term trend in society toward wanting special-interest information," says Mr. Noble of Paine Webber. "The trend can be traced back for centuries, and is the result of the increasing complexity of civilization and the increasing affluence of the population, which makes it possible for them to be able to afford to pay for useful information."

"The over-all outlook for specialty magazines over the decade of the 1980s is encouraging," concludes Mr. Compaine. "Magazines have proven their resilience in the face of changing life styles and competition. Theirs is a history of dynamism, and the long-term outlook for the industry is good."

THE SHAPE OF THEATERS TO COME

Karen Stabiner

The Aero Theater in Santa Monica, California, is a monument to the joys of moviegoing. Built in the fifties, it is the perfect neighborhood house: Beneath the small marquee is a peaceful, carpeted lobby where everything works, including the pay telephone (not an easy thing to find in vandalized Los Angeles). The sparkling clean refreshment stand even features one hundred percent butter, not butter-flavored vegetable oil, for your popcorn. Inside the auditorium, the floors are free of sticky soda pop residue, the seats are maintained, the show starts on time, and the print and sound are good.

When you call the Aero, you get a *person*, not a tape loop, telling you what time to catch the feature you missed at a first-run house in some grid-locked neighborhood where parking costs a dollar for the first half hour. General admission tickets are three dollars, sometimes for a double feature, and there's a fair amount of free, on-street parking. The usual complaint—that a film ends up costing twenty-five dollars by the time a

From *American Film* (September, 1982). Reprinted by permission.

couple pays for tickets and parking and a babysitter and a snack—does not apply at the Aero.

But as you settle in to consider the charm of this exemplary neighborhood theater, consider also what the wise men of the entertainment industry have to say about the future of the Aero, and other single-screen, second-run houses like it across the country. The sages may disagree on the causes, but they speak in a single, united voice on the effect: The Aero and its peers, in all likelihood, are doomed to extinction. The future of theatrical exhibition lies elsewhere: first, in the explosion of the multiplexes; second, in technological innovations that cannot be duplicated on the home screen; and third, in the careful tending of the big first-run houses.

The owners of the more than eighteen thousand movie screens in this country are now faced with an inescapable economic truth: There is not enough business to support that many screens. What exhibitors call the "sub-run theater" gets the unsuccessful films all too quickly and the successful films only after they've been wrung dry at the first-run houses. And, meanwhile, they can hear the sound of pay, cable, and home video snapping at their heels. The "window"—the amount of time between a film's theatrical release and home exhibition—is closing, and in the new era of exhibition, the last theaters to get the product will be the first casualties.

For the distributor, there is an economic, as well as a technological, imperative involved here. Film budgets, and the accompanying interest rates, have ballooned in the last few years. Given a choice between letting a film languish in a second-run theater and turning new profits by selling the film to ancillary markets, a studio will be tempted to go for the fast payoff.

Whether the villain is the video explosion, inflated costs, or, more likely, a combination of the two, the impact is the same, and exhibitors are scrambling for ideas that will lure audiences away from their increasingly lavish home entertainment centers. Within the National Association of Theatre Owners is a small but visionary group already committed to improving the way we see films.

Speaking for the multiplex approach is Garth Drabinsky, president of the Toronto-based Cineplex. He and partner Nat Taylor—who was credited with being the first to "twin" a theater, back in 1948—are bullish about creating a "shopping" environment to entice filmgoers into a theater. In the last few years, Cineplex has made a quick fortune setting up what vice-president Linda Friendly calls "film bazaars," blocks of up to twenty-one screens, usually situated in shopping malls of upscale urban areas across Canada. Cineplex has just established its first beachhead on U.S. shores with a sixteen-screen setup, complete with café and all-day box office, in a new shopping mall in West Hollywood.

Will the rise of home entertainment mean the fall of movie theaters? Not if exhibitors have anything to say about it. They're fighting back with megascreens, multiplexes, and more.

Friendly sees the cinematic mall-within-a-mall as the logical next step from the freestanding, small multiplex, just as malls are supposedly an evolutionary triumph over the old shopping center. The appeal is aimed at the shopper's mentality: If people browse and sometimes make impulse purchases in stores, why not catch them in a buying fever and offer them the new line in movies?

This concept also offers the exhibitor one defense against the decline in ticket sales, which began in 1979. With sixteen or more screens in a single setting, the exhibitor stands an even better chance of coming up with a popular film than his suburban predecessor did with four or six or eight screens. And there's enough flexibility to take advantage of the blockbuster. "You can't beat this arrangement," explains Friendly. "You can open a very popular film at three or four screens and then slowly cut it back over time, as the popularity wanes." The remaining screens are used for revival programs, foreign films, and special short runs—all, Friendly stresses, presented in pristine, comfortable surroundings.

Now, Drabinsky is hardly the only theater owner to realize that a larger number of smaller theaters means less risk. Owners of old, second-run theaters like the Aero have tried to salvage their large halls by subdividing them, but converting a standing theater can be as frustrating as trying to reroute an existing freeway. Sound filters through the new walls or, worse, bounces off them and renders the dialogue unintelligible. Such makeshift theaters suggest that the only exhibitors who can effectively exploit the multiplex concept are those willing to build new temples to it.

"Conversion wasn't *exactly* a doomed idea," says Bruce Corwin, president of the sixty-eight-screen Metropolitan Theaters Corporation in Los Angeles, "because the large theaters couldn't make it financially any other way. We've done several [conversions], but I'm not necessarily happy with them."

Another, more successful, reincarnation of the older theater is the specialty-film house, which attempts to cut risks by showing more films for shorter runs and pursuing that idiosyncratic, loyal audience of baby boomers who grew up going to the movies and are having trouble kicking the habit. If any segment of the audience believes that going to the movies is a social and cultural experience that cannot be duplicated at home, it is this group, and a growing number of small exhibitors are trying to market specifically to its needs. Chicago's Biograph and Los Angeles's Fox Venice and Nuart were among the first; in Los Angeles the idea has become so popular that the Fox Venice and Nuart are now part of a string of thirty-six such theaters across the country jointly owned by Landmark Theaters Corporation and Movie Inc.

"We're serving a small minority audience that likes the social experience and doesn't care how many times a film has been shown on TV," says Steve Gilula, president of Landmark. "The mass audience isn't as attuned to that, so we're a specialized operation."

For these exhibitors, the battle is in convincing the major distributors to take them and their slow but steady growth seriously. Gilula readily admits that the audience for his programs is "smaller than the audience for cable and home video." But it also represents a "stable marketplace" in a business that has long addressed itself to the youth market—a fickle market that last year poured from $8 billion to $10 billion in quarters into video games. By comparison, 1981 grosses for movie theaters were under $3 billion.

While the traditionalists focus on improving what already exists, the techno-freaks have a completely different approach. They don't expect people to leave their home video centers for a night at the movies unless that night promises them an experience they can't get at home. So this new breed of exhibitors is investing in and refining technical processes that are out of video's league entirely. What they've come up with can't yet replace your basic 70mm-with-Dolby motion picture, but it could soon offer an alternative—and, some say, heighten the "special event" aura of going to the movies.

For now, though, the technologies are simply too cumbersome and expensive for mass consumption. Take Imax, which is shown on screens of up to seventy-five by one hundred feet in custom-built theaters around the world. Until last year, the only Imax productions were documentary or science films (most of the theaters are linked to museums or theme parks). Then producer-director George H. Englund (*The Ugly American*) decided to try a short fictional film called *My Strange Uncle*, starring his wife, Cloris Leachman.

The film was well received in the Imax theaters, but transferring such product to conventional theaters is almost impossible, since most of them don't have a roof high enough to accommodate the huge screen. Associate producer George H. Englund, Jr., estimates that it will be ten years before (a) the technology is sufficiently streamlined to make full-length Imax features feasible, and (b) new, commercial theaters in which to show them can be established and made profitable.

The multiplex theaters are aimed at the shopper's mentality: if people make impulse purchases in stores, why not offer them the new line in movies?

And then there may be more problems: "It isn't clear how long people can sit through this stuff," admits the younger Englund. "A lot of it now is point-of-view stuff that makes people sick. They get queasy and they can't watch it. You give them two hours of that and you'll have them running out of the theater."

Also, Imax is so expensive to produce that a theater would have to offer continual showings, at a slightly higher ticket price. As far as Englund can see, "the only place it could be competitive would be a highly populated or high-traffic area. You have to turn it over a lot, not just show it in the afternoon. Lots of people. Eighteen shows a day."

Even further into the future is a process called Envirovision, a 360-degree, hemispheric projection system requiring a theater with seats that can be positioned at any angle. A film could be shown on a regular screen, with special sequences extended to fill the entire circular space and sound speakers positioned in the round to enhance the effect. But first, the system needs a home: Jerome Armstrong and Alan Kozlowski of Quantum Leap Inc. plan to complete their $850,000 flagship theater in Los Angeles by fall.

Ivan Dryer, president of Laser Images, is another experimental exhibitor based in Los Angeles. He premiered *Crystal Odyssey*, a story with abstract visuals, at the Griffith Park Observatory early this year. Ideally, he'd like to present his work in a $4 million Pyradome, where viewers would lie down and watch an image projected onto a domed ceiling.

Douglas Trumbull, the special effects wizard behind *Close Encounters of the Third Kind* and *Star Trek—The Motion Picture*, has developed a process for photographing and projecting 70mm film at sixty frames per second instead of the standard twenty-four. Showscan's effects are similar to those achieved by 3-D. Trumbull wanted to use it for some sequences in his new film, *Brainstorm*, but theater owners were reluctant to invest in the projection equipment needed for the process. He compromised by using brightly lit 70mm Panavision.

The dark horse in the technology race may actually prove to be 3-D, thanks to systems being developed by the United Artists Theatre Circuit (UATC) and by Eastman Kodak. Although the estimated cost of converting an existing theater to show the new, 70mm product—using two cameras and two projectors—is $48,000, UATC is prepared to spend the money at several of its nine hundred theaters across the country. Tickets for a 3-D feature will run about seven dollars, but the chain believes that the films will be so special that audiences won't mind the extra expense. Meanwhile, Kodak is planning a 3-D movie to be shown at Walt Disney World's Experimental Prototype Community of Tomorrow.

And, lest anyone doubt the lure of the unusual,

it's important to recall the lesson Filmways learned last year about what will and will not draw today's audiences out of their homes and into theaters. Filmways spent millions promoting *Blow Out*, starring the eminently bankable John Travolta. *Blow Out* was supposed to do nothing less than bail out the financially troubled company. But it didn't. What did happen—quietly, simultaneously—was that Filmways' unknown, relatively unpromoted, and critically panned feature called *Comin' at Ya!* started racking grosses respectable enough to attract the attention of business writers, who drew embarrassing comparisons between the company's two features. What did *Comin' at Ya!* have going for it? Just 3-D, that's all.

Not every exhibitor is the proud owner of a state-of-the-art multiplex, and technology will offer only limited salvation. For the surviving single-screen first-run houses, the immediate goal will be to protect their position in the profit equation, which is their best guarantee for the future. NATO chairman A. Alan Friedberg, president of Boston's Sack Theatre chain, says that the service a first-run house provides is more significant than any dollar figure, since it ensures the distributor two crucial things—income from every person who sees the film, unlike the pay and basic cable television systems, and a presold audience for the product when it is recycled to ancillary markets.

"A theater is the only place where the producer, and everyone else who shares in the profits, can be sure that everyone who sees the film pays," says Friedberg. "With cable, you have one person paying $9.95 a month. First, that fee is spread out among several films, and, second, the charge is the same no matter how many nonsubscribers you have in the room. You have twenty people in someone's living room and it's still one payment of $9.95." The smart theater owner, the theory goes, buys the "palace" theory of profitable exhibition, restores his first-run flagship to its former glory, and withstands the video onslaught as successfully as a multiplexer.

"Film companies are interested in maximizing their returns," Friedberg continues. "They want to establish their film. And what would *Raiders* have been without word of mouth from the theaters where it was shown first—or *Arthur*, or *Stripes*? They needed the theatrical run to increase the value of their product. There is a tradition established. First you have the theatrical run, then discs and cassettes, then pay and cable, then network TV."

That is still the order of things, but what of the quickened schedule, thanks to pay television's appetite for movies? Friedberg does not regard himself as an "ostrich." He knows he's in an industry where tradition runs as far back as last season's successes. And he worries that eventually distributors might skip theatrical distribution entirely on certain pictures, if cable offers enough cash for an early shot. "With enough cable subscribers in place," he predicts, "there is the potential that a cable system can offer so much for cable rights that it will be attractive to film companies to just take the money and run."

Given Reagan's desire to free business from government regulation, it's possible that a major studio might acquire a circuit of first-run theaters.

NATO vice-president Joseph Alterman insists that this won't happen, that the distributors "aren't about to throw out their best market." He points triumphantly to Fox's thwarted plan to release *9 to 5* "day and date" (simultaneous release to theaters and the home market). Fox executive Alan J. Hirschfield's idea met with such a negative response from exhibitors—some of whom threatened not to show the film—that the studio retreated to a more acceptable interval between theatrical and home distribution. For those who still foresee the home as the center for all film viewing, exhibitors have a counter-argument. "The analogy is best made to the food industry," suggests Friedberg. "You have readily available at your market instantly prepared, and frequently esoteric, dinners. You have a whole gamut of gadgets to make cooking a fancy meal easy. But, as far as I know, the restaurant business has not been impacted significantly—because people still like to go out."

(His theory will undergo a harsh test in February when Universal offers *The Pirates of Penzance* on a pay-per-view basis for a single showing, probably on the same day the film opens in theaters; some exhibitors are now refusing to show the film. The home video customer will pay from ten to fifteen dollars, of which Universal will receive some sixty percent.)

But even if Friedberg is correct in his restaurant analogy, exhibitors may be facing a bigger problem. A U.S. District Court in New York has before it a case asking that portions of the postwar consent decree be vacated, a move that could change the face of exhibition more radically than the video revolution, and cause a split within the NATO ranks.

The decree required the major studios to divest themselves of the theaters they owned. The same company could not control both distribution and exhibition. As a result, major independent theatrical circuits replaced the studios' circuits, smaller independents carved small niches for themselves between the giants, and competition flourished—supposedly.

In the last few years, however, the boundaries of the decree have been blurred: The Mann theater chain has financed a couple of films, and Loew's theaters have announced that they intend to follow suit. Columbia Pictures owns about thirty-one percent of the Walter Reade theater chain stock, which means, in effect, that it is involved in exhibition. Given the Reagan administration's stated desire to free business from government regulation, it's possible that the restrictions on theater ownership will be relaxed—in which case the majors might be interested in acquiring a circuit composed of those clean, attractive first-run houses.

Paramount lawyer Paul Springer says that he sees "no reason why the courts or government is regulating the motion picture business in any way," and expects the courts to reverse the 1948 decision, but he doubts that the studios will immediately go on a buying spree. Despite Springer's predictions, NATO, which wants the decree upheld, is already trying to shore up its defenses, so that members don't forget their collective obligations, if and when the studios start waving money around.

"The larger circuits are mindful of the potential damage to the small exhibitors," says Friedberg, who points out that exhibitors would have even more trouble surviving if they were forced to compete with studio-owned theaters for product. "And even though an owner's selfish self-interest might dictate his blessing the vacating of the decree, as a matter of conscience and morality NATO is solidly opposed."

As a matter of sound business practice, both sides—the studios and the exhibitors—are hedging their bets, trying to prepare themselves for whatever happens. The studios aren't the only ones spending money on developing the home video market; exhibitors are putting out financial feelers both personally and on behalf of their businesses. Sumner Redstone, president of the 250-screen Northeast Theater Corporation, has admitted investing his own money in Warner Communications stock because of its highly profitable Atari video division. Redstone described the video threat to a *Forbes* reporter as "very, very formidable," and seems to be trying to anticipate the inevitable impact on the theatrical market.

Back in Los Angeles, Bruce Corwin has surveyed the scene and started to get involved in cable television franchising, both personally and as a representative of Metropolitan Theaters. He's formed a subsidiary that will tape concert programs at a Metropolitan theater no longer showing films and sell them to Showtime."The name is really wrong," Corwin observes. "It's really becoming the Metropolitan Entertainment Corporation, and that's how we have to keep thinking."

Uncertain about what is going to happen, all the exhibitors and distributors can agree on is that going to the movies will not be the same in five years. "The only thing that's real," says NATO's Joseph Alterman, "is that there *is* a home entertainment market. The studios are all trying to get the best share they can, but nobody's ready to throw over the theaters and abandon what is still their best market. The economy of it could shift either way. It could be that ancillary markets will always be just that, or it could go the other way. Everyone is couching their bets, watching, and tracking things. It's a very confusing time."

KURT VONNEGUT ON TODAY'S NOVELIST

I am a member of what I believe to be the last recognizable generation of full-time, life-time American novelists. We appear to be standing more or less in a row. It was the Great Depression which made us similarly edgy and watchful. It was World War II which lined us up so nicely, whether we were men or women, whether we were ever in uniform or not. It was an era of romantic anarchy in publishing which gave us money and mentors, willy-nilly, when we were young—while we learned our craft. Words printed on pages were still the principal form of long-distance communication and stored information in America when we were young.

No more.

Nor are there many publishers and editors and agents left who are eager to find some way to get money and other forms of encouragement to young writers who write as clumsily as members of my literary generation did when we started out. The wild and wonderful and expensive guess was made back then that we might acquire some wisdom and learn how to write halfway decently by and by. Writers were needed that much back then.

Television wrecked the short-story branch of the industry, and now accountants and business school graduates dominate book publishing.

It was an amusing and instructive time for writers—for hundreds of them.

Television wrecked the short-story branch of the industry, and now accountants and business school graduates dominate book publishing. They feel that money spent on someone's first novel is good money down a rat hole. They are right. It almost always is.

So, as I say, I think I belong to America's last generation of novelists. Novelists will come one by one from now on, not in seeming families, and will perhaps write only one or two novels, and let it go at that. Many will have inherited or married money.

SUGGESTIONS FOR FURTHER READING

The implications of the information age are too great to be exhaustively covered in an anthology such as this. Good sources are Wilson P. Dizard, Jr., *The Coming Information Age: An Overview of Technology, Economics, and Politics*, New York: Longman, 1982, and Ithiel de Sola Pool, *Technologies of Freedom: On Free Speech in the Electronic Age*, Cambridge, Mass.: Harvard University Press, 1983.

The following may also be of interest:

Douglass Cater, "The Survival of Human Values." *Journal of Communication* 31 (Winter 1981): 190–194. There are several articles in this edition that pertain to the implications of the information age.

Ithiel De Sola Pool, "The Culture of Electronic Print." *Daedalus* III, no. 4 (Fall, 1982): 17–31. Extensive predictions, including the death of copyright.

Marshall McLuhan and Bruce Powers, "Electronic Banking and the Death of Privacy." *Journal of Communications* (Winter 1981): 164–69.

Miles Orvell, "The Screen Revolution." *Technology Review*, February/March 1982, pp. 40–46. Like Richard Blake, Orvell feels that McLuhan's utopian vision of a "global village" was never realized. New technology could help us realize this dream or it could further alienate us.

Those who are interested in the changes taking place in the "old" media could read the following:

Lewis M. Branscomb, "The Electronic Library." *Journal of Communication* 31 (Winter 1981): 143–150. Changes you can expect to see in your library.

Jerry W. Friedham, "Newspapers Today And Tomorrow." *Vital Speeches of the Day*, March 15, 1982, p. 340. The executive vice-president of the American News Publishers Association gives a pep talk to the industry.

Dennis Holder, "The Decade of Specialization." *Washington Journalism Review*, November 1981, pp. 28–32. The author worries about magazine special-

ization, with its possible consequence of narrowing social and intellectual discourse.

Kenneth Robinson, "Public Information and 'Electronic Publishing' Services." ***Journal of Communication,*** **(Autumn 1982): 103–113. We can expect to see a change in AT&T's role as a corporation. The author defends this monopoly's involvement in cable television.**

Michael Schwarz, "Hollywood—Entering an Era of Unparalleled Demand." ***Channels,*** **February/March 1982, p. 26.**

E. Sifton, "What Reading Public?" ***Nation*** **234, May 22, 1982, pp. 627–32. A publishing executive defends the actions of the book publishing industry.**

Index

Notes

Notes

Notes

Notes

Notes

Notes

Notes

Notes

Notes